THE
GUINNESS
BOOK OF
FOOTBALL

INTRODUCTION BY ANDY GRAY

GUINNESS PUBLISHING

Published in Great Britain by Guinness Publishing Ltd, 338 Euston Road, London, NW1 3BD.

'Guinness' is a registered trademark of Guinness Publishing Ltd.

Printed and bound in Great Britain by The Bath Press.

Colour origination by The Litho Origination Group, London.

A catalogue record for this book is available from The British Library

ISBN 0-85112-068-7

Managing Editor
Max Benato

Research Editor
Simon C Gold

Chief Sub-editor
Jenni Moore

Sub-editors
Roderick Easdale
Richard Widdows

Researchers
Jane Bolton
Ben Keith

Proof Readers
Paula Field
Sarah Kovandzich

Design Concept
Peter Jackson

Designer
Keith Jackson

Design
Adam Kelsey
Juliet MacDonald
Helen Weller

Cover Design
Daniel Jackson at Avco

Picture Research
Ellen Root
Laura Jackson

Publishing Director
Ian Castello-Cortes

Contents

Contents

Introduction *by Andy Gray*

So, another season is underway. The World Cup is over and its heroes and villains have returned to club duty around the world – a good proportion of them to England. Seventy-five of the 704 players at the World Cup played for clubs in England – more than in any other country – as good a sign as any of how English football is an increasingly important international stage.

be seeing more of homegrown star Michael Owen as England, and Scotland, attempt to qualify for Euro 2000 – you can find the dates and the background on their opponents in the news features. Meanwhile, European action will be supplied by Arsenal, Aston Villa, Blackburn Rovers, Chelsea, Leeds United, Liverpool and Manchester United, plus Celtic, Rangers, Hearts and

The coming year looks like being a particularly significant one for British football off the pitch, as well as on the pitch. The new Scottish Premier League will crown its first champions, England will continue the preparations for its bid to host the 2006 World Cup, the bulldozers will clear away the old Wembley and Posh Spice and David Beckham will be drawing up their wedding list.

"The 1998-99 title race has already been won – by The Guinness Book of Football"

With Manchester United's Dutch import Jaap Stam – the most expensive defender in the world at £10.75 million – and Chelsea's double act of Frenchman Marcel Desailly and Italian Pierluigi Casiraghi (total value £10 million) among the foreign contingent starring in the Premiership in 1998-99, the trend towards attracting international footballers is set to continue. No doubt we'll

Kilmarnock. Wonder kid Owen is one of more than a thousand players with biographies in the book and his team, Liverpool, one of 122 English, Scottish and European sides profiled – you can even track their form from last season and organise your diary around the English fixtures by turning to the stats pages at the back of the book – a football obsessive's dream.

The Guinness Book of Football has got all the big news stories covered and also includes more than a thousand Guinness facts and records that will truly amaze. It seems to me that the 1998-99 title race has already been won – by The Guinness Book of Football.

I'll prove it yet. Don't go away...

Diary

On the following pages, you will find a blow-by-blow account of what happened in the 1997-98 season, with action from the Premiership and Football League plus international and European matches. Watch the story unfold with the season's winners and losers and then look into the future with the crucial dates for the months ahead, including the European Championship qualifiers and the FA Cup and League Cup finals in 1999.

All the drama at home and away

► Football was in mourning after the death of Princess Diana and matches were rearranged so as not to clash with the funeral. The SFA, however, only agreed to change the timing of Scotland's (4-1 win) World Cup qualifier against Belarus after intense pressure ► England gained a 4-0 win over Moldova and were buoyed by the news that Italy had drawn 0-0 with Georgia ► Two wins in four days for the Republic of Ireland seemed to keep their World Cup hopes alive.

► Having scored two for England against Moldova, Ian Wright, above right, broke Cliff Bastin's goalscoring record in all competitions at Arsenal, after a blistering hat-trick against Bolton ► The European stage beckoned for a number of English clubs. In the UEFA Cup, Arsenal – without an in-form Dennis Bergkamp because of his fear of flying – lost 1-0 in the first round to Greek side PAOK Salonika. Leicester City also failed at the first hurdle against Atletico Madrid. Two clubs that did make it through to the next round of the UEFA Cup were Aston Villa, who beat Girondins Bordeaux, and Liverpool, who beat Celtic ► In the Champions League, Faustino Asprilla grabbed a hat-trick at St James' as Newcastle beat mighty Barcelona 3-2, while Manchester United managed a convincing 3-0 win over Kosice at the group stage.

In the Champions League, Asprilla grabbed a hat-trick as Newcastle beat Barcelona 3-2

Winning at Wembley: England enjoyed a 4-0 win over Moldova in a World Cup qualifier. Man of the Match was France '98 absentee Paul Gascoigne, who got England's third goal of the night.

► Chelsea's successful 1998 Cup Winners Cup campaign was set in motion with a 2-0 win over Slovan Bratislava in the first round, first leg of the tournament ► Bolton Wanderers' inaugural game celebrations at the new Reebok Stadium against Everton were soured when a shot by Bolton striker Nathan Blake appeared to have crossed the line but was not given by the referee. Television replays showed the ball had in fact crossed the line and the repercussions were to be seriously felt at the end of the season ► Mohamed Al Fayed was busy making changes at Fulham. Popular boss Micky Adams was ousted to make way for Kevin Keegan, who in turn employed Ray Wilkins as his deputy. Keegan immediately announced that he had a five-year plan to get the Second Division side into the Premiership ► Sports Minister Tony Banks was booed by England fans at Wembley after newspapers reported that he had voiced doubts about England's ability to win the World Cup.

▶ Proving that there is no stopping the flow of talent from Brazil, 11 would-be Ronaldos, Denilsons and Dungas won the FIFA Under-17 World Championships in Cairo ▶ Manchester United's bad boy Roy Keane was in the headlines again when he put in an impetuous challenge at Elland Road – leaving him with a damaged cruciate ligament and an early end to the 1997-98 season.

Our mistake: When Gary Pallister of Manchester United, along with Nathan Blake of Bolton, was sent off after a brawl, Pallister became the first player to have his red card overturned by the FA when he appealed against the decision.

SEPTEMBER 1998

◯ Hot on the heels of the World Cup, the qualifiers for Euro 2000 start on Saturday, 5 September. England face Sweden away, Scotland, right, are away to Lithuania, the Republic of Ireland play Croatia at home, and Wales host Italy.

◯ Arsenal play their first Champions League fixture on Wednesday, 16 September.

◯ Non-League clubs start their bid for FA Cup glory with the preliminary and first qualifying rounds.

Ian Wright broke Cliff Bastin's goalscoring record at Highbury after scoring his 179th goal against Bolton

The Italian job and more Cup upsets

▶ Manchester United produced one of the most dazzling displays in their European history to overcome Italian giants Juventus 3-2 at Old Trafford in the Champions League, with Teddy Sheringham, Paul Scholes and Ryan Giggs all getting their names on the scoresheet. United also revealed plans to set up a cable TV channel, MUTV, although existing contracts mean the club will be unable to show FA Cup, Premiership, or European games.

▶ There were the usual grumblings about bigger clubs deliberately fielding weakened sides in the Coca-Cola Cup as the third round got under way. A finger was pointed at Manchester United who went out to First Division Ipswich. Arsenal may have fielded a weakened side but still beat Birmingham 4-1 ▶ Everton players defied manager Howard Kendall, who demanded they salute their fans after their 4-1 defeat at Coventry – further indication that the club was in turmoil ▶ In the Premiership, Barnsley put an end to a run of six successive defeats by beating Coventry, but then lost 7-0 at Old Trafford the following week ▶ John Hartson found himself in hot water with both the FA and West Ham after venting his anger on referees ▶ Rangers boss Walter Smith announced he would be stepping down in May.

"I loved giving the Italians a taste of their own medicine," Paul Gascoigne after victory in Rome

Spot the ball: Chelsea suffered a shock 3-2 defeat in the first leg of their Cup Winners Cup tie against Norwegian side Tromso. The second half turned to farce as the pitch became engulfed by a snowstorm.

▶ Back in Europe for the second time in a month, Manchester United looked much less convincing in their 2-1 win over Feyenoord, while Newcastle United lost 1-0 to PSV Eindhoven ▶ In the UEFA Cup, Liverpool were humiliated by French side Strasbourg, losing 3-0 in the away leg, while Aston Villa only managed a goalless draw away to Athletic Bilbao. ▶ Fabrizio Ravenelli left Middlesbrough for French club Marseilles ▶ Scotland booked their place at France '98 (as best second-placed team), with a convincing 2-0 win over Latvia. Everton striker Duncan Ferguson was not present, having announced his retirement from international football at the age of 26 ▶ In Dublin, the Republic of Ireland drew 1-1 with Romania, which kept alive hopes of a place in the World Cup finals via the play-offs ▶ The footballing fraternity sent their best wishes to Sir Bobby Charlton, who celebated his 60th birthday ▶ Referee David Elleray advised United's David Beckham to ignore fans' foul-mouthed taunts about Posh Spice.

▶ England played their last World Cup qualifier against Italy in Rome. Glenn Hoddle played a tactical blinder, and a goalless draw proved sufficient to see England through. "I loved giving them a taste of their own medicine," said Paul Gascoigne. A night of jubilation, however, was marred by the sight of Italian police baton-charging English fans on the terraces. Accusations of poor security and policing followed and the row soured Anglo-Italian relations.

In-ger-lund!: France '98 beckoned as England booked their place in the finals. A battle-scarred Paul Ince was just one of 11 heroes.

OCTOBER 1998

○ Premiership clubs in Europe enter the third round of the League Cup.

○ In the qualifiers for Euro 2000, on Saturday, 10 October, England play Bulgaria, Scotland play Estonia and the Republic of Ireland play Yugoslavia. Four days later, England face Luxembourg, while Scotland and the Republic take on the Faroe Islands and Malta.

○ The Under-17 World Championships take place.

Managerial casualties and club tensions

▶ With a third of the season gone, under-performing managers began to feel the pressure – some more than others. A glum Gerry Francis, right, resigned at Tottenham ▶ Ron Atkinson returned to Hillsborough as manager, although his original departure from the club had not left the fans entirely happy. In Big Ron's first game, Sheffield Wednesday beat high-flying Arsenal 2-0.

▶ Chaos continued at Goodison Park where Everton fans' protests against chairman Peter Johnson became so vehement that he had to have a police escort into the ground before the side's 2-0 defeat against Tottenham ▶ In the UEFA Cup, Aston Villa were left to fly the flag for England as a disappointing Liverpool crashed out to Strasbourg in the second round, second leg ▶ Meanwhile, in the group stage of the European Cup, Manchester United began to look invincible as they enjoyed emphatic wins over Kosice and Feyenoord ▶ Newcastle lost to PSV Eindhoven and Barcelona ▶ Chelsea progressed in the Cup Winners Cup. Playing the return leg against Tromso at Stamford Bridge, the Blues wiped out all memories of the farcical first leg to beat the Norwegian part-timers 7-1.

"Here is the ticket of my dreams – from Heathrow to White Hart Lane," Christian Gross

Wave goodbye: Sheffield Wednesday's David Pleat became the first managerial casualty of the season when he exited Hillsborough to make way for Ron Atkinson.

▶ Former England manager Terry Venables discovered that he wouldn't be going to France '98 as manager of the Australian national side, as he watched the Socceroos fail to qualify after losing to Iran on away goals in the Asia-Oceania play-off ▶ Rumours circulated that Wimbledon were still considering a move to Dublin having failed to find a new home for themselves in south London. The FA said nothing, UEFA said it was unacceptable ▶ Paul Gascoigne was said to be considering a move from Scotland to the English Premiership. "Ten per cent of me wants to go, 90 per cent of me wants to stay," said the Rangers midfielder. ▶ Swiss manager Christian Gross was installed as coach at Tottenham Hotspur. In his first press conference, he pulled out a London Underground ticket and said: "Here is the ticket of my dreams – from Heathrow to White Hart Lane." ▶ Manchester City hero Georgi Kinkladze survived a car crash when his Ferrari hit a lamp-post – and turned out for his club a week later.

When Irish eyes aren't smiling: hopes of a place at France '98 were extinguished for the Republic of Ireland when they lost 3-2 on aggregate to Belgium in their World Cup play-off.

NOVEMBER 1998

○ The architectural plans for the new Wembley stadium are expected to be submitted to the English National Stadium Trust. The architect, Sir Norman Foster, was the man behind Stansted Airport and the new British Museum.

○ In Europe, Arsenal continue their European Cup quest, Chelsea will be trying to hold on to their Cup Winners Cup title and more second and third round action is on the cards in the UEFA Cup for the English teams that have made it so far.

Australia failed to make the World Cup finals, despite not losing a single game in the qualifiers

Christmas is coming...

▶ Christmas came early for Spurs with the news that Jurgen Klinsmann, left, was returning to White Hart Lane. He was followed by the appointment of David Pleat as director of football at the club. The German captain made his debut in a 1-1 draw against north London rivals Arsenal ▶ Over in west London at Stamford Bridge, Ken Bates was in the news once again as he arranged a multi-million pound bond to buy the freehold of the ground from Matthew Harding's estate.

▶ Aston Villa booked their place in the quarter-finals of the UEFA Cup, beating Steaua Bucharest 2-0 in the second leg of the third round ▶ In the European Cup, Newcastle finished third in Group C of the Champions League and crashed out of the tournament in spite of beating Dinamo Kiev 2-0 at St James' ▶ At home, Manchester City staggered from crisis to crisis. Frank Clark was on the verge of resigning. The club had won only two of their last six games and fans were protesting against chairman Francis Lee ▶ The recently installed Spurs coach Christian Gross was considering his future after hearing his Swiss fitness trainer had been refused a work permit and would not be able to join him ▶ At Arsenal, injuries to Tony Adams and an Ian Wright goal drought slowed up their Premiership progress.

In an interview following the World Cup draw, Glenn Hoddle announced he was "not too displeased"

Bingo!: Brazilian striker Ronaldo and FIFA's Sepp Blatter entertained the masses at the World Cup draw in Marseille.

▶ With France '98 only six months away, excitement about the forthcoming draw almost reached fever pitch. Hopes that England would be one of the seeded sides were soon quashed. A general sigh of relief, however, accompanied Tunisia's name being drawn, and an acknowledgment that while Romania and Colombia both boasted a World Cup pedigree, the two countries also had ageing squads. In an interview following the draw, England coach Glenn Hoddle announced he was "not too displeased".

▶ Scotland did not have such good fortune. Craig Brown's team were drawn to play reigning champions Brazil, with Ronaldo among their stars, in the showpiece opening game at the Stade de France. Morocco and Norway were also drawn in their group ▶ Once the drama of the World Cup draw had settled down, attention turned to how many tickets would be available for the games. It was an issue that was to resurface and sour Anglo-French relations on a regular basis over the coming months.

▶ Barnsley defender Dean Jones was charged with misconduct by the FA after failing a random drugs test. He tested positive for amphetamines.
▶ Aston Villa's Stan Collymore was charged with assaulting his former partner. The incident did not seem to affect his goalscoring abilities – he put two past Tottenham on Boxing Day.

Turin cloud: Manchester United's European bubble burst with a 1-0 defeat away against Juventus, but the Reds still finished top of Group B.

DECEMBER 1998

○ Expect the usual disruption to the New Year programme due to seasonal weather conditions and frozen pitches and supporters.

○ The FA Cup enters the second round on Saturday, 5 December – the last phase before the draw that will see Premiership and First Division clubs join the fray.

○ The women's FA Cup enters the third round on Sunday, 6 December.

Scotland's richest woman, Ann Gloag, can afford 11 Ronaldos (£18m each) and the Stade de France (£280m)

New Year cheer – and disappointments

▶ BBC football commentator John Motson, left, sparked controversy when he commented on Radio 5 that he sometimes found it difficult to differentiate between black players. Motty denied he was a racist and that the remark had been taken out of context ▶ The FA stepped up the pressure on FIFA after it was revealed that only 20% of tickets for France '98 would be sent to competing associations – approximately 4,000 seats for each of England's group games.

▶ The first weekend of 1998 was one of hopes, dreams and shocks – there's little in the football fixture list that can beat the drama of the FA Cup third round. The County Ground provided the year's biggest surprise as Vauxhall Conference side Stevenage beat Swindon 2-1. The following day, a classic FA Cup cliffhanger took place at Stamford Bridge as Manchester United took on Cup-holders Chelsea. Down 5-0 at one stage, the Blues fought back with three goals before the final whistle ▶ The draw for the fourth round of the Cup caused further upset when Stevenage drew Newcastle at home and the Magpies appealed to the FA to get the game switched to St James', claiming that the Stevenage ground was unsafe. The FA ruled that the tie should go ahead as planned.

There's little in the football fixture list that can beat the drama of the FA Cup third round

By royal command: Former Manchester United and Chelsea striker Mark Hughes, right, shows off his MBE, alongside one of football's finest, Sir Tom Finney, left.

▶ Paul Gascoigne of Rangers angered Celtic fans when he engaged in another flute-playing incident during the New Year Old Firm derby ▶ More managerial casualties as Bradford's Chris Kamara and Portsmouth's Terry Fenwick were shown the door ▶ On the transfer front, Tomas Brolin made his Premiership comeback, this time at Crystal Palace, while Faustino Asprilla left Newcastle for Parma ▶ Alan Shearer made it back from injury sooner than anticipated, coming on as a sub against Bolton.

▶ Savo Milosevic was told he would never play for Aston Villa again when he had spat on his own supporters after Villa lost 5-0 at Blackburn ▶ Over in Belgium, the draw for the forthcoming Euro 2000 was made ▶ In the League Cup, semi-finalists Liverpool, Middlesbrough, Chelsea and Arsenal were all delighted by the news that the winners of the competition would receive a place in the UEFA Cup the following season after a successful campaign to get the place re-instated.

Hammer blow: West Ham players look on as Paul David of non-League FA Cup hopefuls Emley scores an equaliser. The game ended 2-1 to the Hammers after a late goal from John Hartson.

JANUARY 1999

○ The annual Confederations Cup gets under way.

○ Bid requirements for the World Cup in 2006 are announced by FIFA. England's opposition is expected to include Germany among others.

○ The FA Cup enters its third round stage.

○ The League Cup reaches its quarter-final stage.

○ Two England international friendlies take place.

FEBRUARY 1998

Celebrations and commemorations

▶ The month got off to a bad start when a Sheffield United fan ran onto the pitch at Portsmouth and assaulted the referee's assistant, souring Alan Ball's first game back as manager at Fratton Park ▶ An important date in the Manchester United diary was 7 February, as the club commemorated the 40th anniversary of the Munich air crash. Sir Bobby Charlton, who was with the 'Busby Babes' in Munich, and Nat Lofthouse, led a tribute at Old Trafford.

▶ Tottenham striker Les Ferdinand was brought to book by the FA after he branded the referee in charge of Spurs' replay at Barnsley "an absolute disgrace" for sending off Stephen Clemence. Not only were Spurs knocked out, but Jurgen Klinsmann spent the night in a South Yorkshire hospital after breaking his jaw in the game ▶ Barnsley provided another Cup upset when they put an end to Manchester United's FA Cup hopes with a 3-2 win in the fourth round replay at Oakwell. Other teams to make it safely through to the quarter-finals were Arsenal, West Ham, Coventry, Sheffield United, Leeds United, Wolverhampton Wanderers and Newcastle ▶ The Magpies celebrated their Cup progress by signing Everton skipper Gary Speed, who had been unsettled at the Merseyside club.

Les Ferdinand was brought to book by the FA after he branded a ref "an absolute disgrace"

Boy wonder: Michael Owen made an impressive debut as the youngest player this century to be capped for England, at the age of 18 years and 59 days, in a friendly against Chile.

▶ Blackburn striker Chris Sutton hit the headlines when he withdrew from the England B-squad because he felt he had earned his place in the first team. Glenn Hoddle was not to forget Sutton's choice when it came to later England call-ups ▶ Ruud Gullit was sensationally sacked by Chelsea. A media feeding frenzy followed, as chairman Ken Bates accused Gullit of being too greedy while the Dutchman claimed he was the victim of a club conspiracy. Just hours later, Gianluca Vialli was installed as the new player-manager. In his first match, he steered Chelsea into the Coca-Cola Cup final, beating London rivals Arsenal ▶ More managers received their P45s. Brian Little of Aston Villa and Frank Clark of Manchester City were replaced by John Gregory and Joe Royle, respectively ▶ Mark Goldberg bought a controlling stake in Crystal Palace from outgoing chairman Ron Noades. On announcing the deal, he spoke of his desire to see the return of Terry Venables to Selhurst Park.

Borough buried: after weeks of acrimony on both sides, Newcastle finally saw off Stevenage in the FA Cup fifth round in a replay at St James'. The Magpies won 2-1.

FEBRUARY 1999

○ The FA Cup enters the fifth round on 13 February.

○ The League Cup semi-finals take place.

○ Expect more musical chairs for managers – in February 1998, Manchester City's Frank Clark, right, Aston Villa's Brian Little and Chelsea's Ruud Gullit all got their P45s.

○ An England international is booked in for Saturday, 6 February.

Michael Owen became the youngest England international this century at 18 years and 59 days

MARCH 1998

Tempers flared and football mourned

▶ Newcastle United and England goal supremo Alan Shearer put a dent in his 'Mary Poppins' image when he allegedly punched team-mate Keith Gillespie in a Dublin nightclub ▶ In another extraordinary fracas, Birmingham City manager Trevor Francis briefly resigned when hospitality guests in one of the club's lounge bars insulted and threatened his son. The incident brought to light Francis's fraught relationship with Blues' managing director Karren Brady.

▶ Another alleged bust-up during the first weekend of the month took place when Aston Villa's Stan Collymore accused his former Liverpool team-mate Steve Harkness of making racist comments when the two sides clashed at Villa Park. Harkness denied the claim, the PFA mediated, but the row was never satisfactorily resolved ▶ That same weekend, Manchester United stretched their lead to 11 points at the top of the Premiership and Ladbrokes closed the book on the Championship race ▶ At the bottom of the table, Spurs beat Bolton 1-0 in a relegation six-pointer. The game was overshadowed by a bust-up between Spurs boss Christian Gross and fit-again Jurgen Klinsmann ▶ Arsenal put in a £120 million bid to buy Wembley Stadium, but withdrew the offer a fortnight later.

In the Premiership, Arsenal travelled to Old Trafford and beat Manchester United 1-0. The title race was well and truly back on

Victory for Vialli: Chelsea won their second major trophy in 10 months, beating Middlesbrough 2-0 in the Coca-Cola Cup final at Wembley. Paul Gascoigne made his Boro debut as a substitute.

▶ In the quarter-finals of the FA Cup, Wolves knocked out Leeds with a late goal, Barnsley's Wembley dream came to an end at Newcastle, and Sheffield United and Arsenal both made it through after penalty shoot-outs ▶ Attilio Lombardo was appointed player-manager at Crystal Palace ▶ Gazza ended speculation about his future by signing for Middlesbrough ▶ In Europe, Manchester United crashed out of the European Cup to French club Monaco, and Villa exited on away goals to Atletico Madrid in the quarter-finals of the UEFA Cup ▶ Chelsea remained the only British hope in Europe after winning 5-2 on aggregate in the Cup Winners Cup against Spanish side Real Betis ▶ In the Premiership, Arsenal travelled to Old Trafford and beat Manchester United 1-0, signalling that the title race was well and truly back on ▶ On the other side of Manchester, meanwhile, City's chairman Francis Lee resigned after pressure from board members and fans. On the pitch, City continued their slide into the relegation zone.

▶ Newcastle continued to have one of their worst seasons ever. Out of the FA Cup and heading in the wrong direction in the League, a tabloid expose of directors Freddie Shepherd and Douglas Hall sent shares in the club tumbling and the pair were forced to resign ▶ The final weekend of the month was rocked by the death of a Fulham fan in crowd violence at Gillingham, while three Barnsley players were sent off against Liverpool after the referee was harangued.

A sad day for football: a floral tribute marks the spot where a Fulham fan was killed during a fight outside Gillingham's Priestfield Stadium.

MARCH 1999

◯ More Euro 2000 qualifiers for the home nations. On Saturday, 27 March, England take on Poland at home, Scotland face Bosnia at home and the Republic of Ireland are away to Macedonia. On Wednesday, 31 March, Scotland play host to the Czech Republic.

◯ The League Cup final is on Sunday, 21 March

◯ The quarter-finals of the FA Cup take place on 6 March.

Have I got a goal for you?: Angus Deayton and Frank Bruno battle it out in a celebrity match before the 1998 Coca-Cola Cup final at Wembley.

Trophies, triumphs and relegation tribulations

▶ The future of Wembley was assured when the English National Stadium Trust agreed to buy it from existing owners Wembley PLC for £103 million.

The total costs of redevelopment were estimated to be in the region of £240 million ▶ Arsenal striker and Dutchman Dennis Bergkamp picked up the Professional

Footballers' Association's Player of the Year trophy and Liverpool's Michael Owen was named Young Player of the Year at the annual bash in London.

▶ Chelsea started the month with a surprise setback in their pursuit of the Cup Winners Cup, losing 1-0 away to unfancied Italian side Vicenza in the first leg of the semi-final ▶ London rivals Arsenal showed no such uncertainty when they beat Wolves 1-0 in the FA Cup

semi-final. Their opponents at Wembley, Newcastle, beat Sheffield United 1-0. The scorer was Alan Shearer ▶ Back at Stamford Bridge, for the second leg of the Cup Winners Cup semi-final, Mark Hughes swept Chelsea into the final with a late goal after coming on as a sub.

Chelsea won 3-1 and prepared to meet VfB Stuttgart in the final ▶ In the Premiership title race, Arsene Wenger's increasingly confident Arsenal produced another outstanding performance to go top of the Premiership, beating a shell-shocked Wimbledon 5-0.

England fans spent a day on the phone trying to get hold of newly released World Cup tickets. BT estimated that there were 20 million callers

Stam is the man: Manchester United announced their intention to buy PSV Eindhoven and Dutch defender Jaap Stam for £10.75 million at the end of the 1997-98 season.

▶ The title race was put aside for a few days as national matters came to the fore. Glenn Hoddle made it clear that *all* squad players were expected to report to the England camp, regardless of excuses. It seemed to do the trick – England beat Portugal 3-0 in a pre-World Cup friendly ▶ Media interest fixed on Hoddle's admission that faith healer Eileen Drewery was helping with England's World Cup preparations ▶ England fans spent a day on the phone trying to get hold of newly released World Cup

tickets. BT estimated that 20 million callers attempted to get through to the French ticket line ▶ Back on the pitch, Arsenal edged closer to the Premiership title with a win over Barnsley, who now looked certain for relegation. Manchester United also beat Crystal Palace 3-0, condemning the south London club to the First Division for the 1998-99 season ▶ The month ended in controversy with footage of Alan Shearer apparently attempting to kick Leicester City's Neil Lennon in the face.

Snow good: Arsenal advanced their title bid in a snowswept encounter with Blackburn. Arsenal's win took them to within a point of United, with two games in hand.

APRIL 1999

○ The World Youth Championships (Under-20) take place in Nigeria from 3 April to 24 April.

○ In Europe, the Cup Winners Cup and the European Cup semi-finals take place.

○ The Women's FA Cup semi-finals are on Sunday, 4 April.

○ The FA Cup semi-finals take place on Sunday, 11 April.

○ An England friendly is pencilled in for 28 April.

The world's most expensive defender, Jaap Stam, did not turn professional until 19 years of age

The end of another chapter...

▶ In Stockholm, Dennis Wise, held up the Cup Winners Cup when Chelsea won the trophy for the second time in their history. Nearly 20,000 Blues fans had travelled to the game against VfB Stuttgart to witness dynamo sub Gianfranco Zola score the only goal of the game ▶ Chelsea may have secured their double, but Arsenal were just beginning. On 2 May, they claimed their first Championship title since 1991, against Everton, who were brushed aside 4-0.

▶ Tottenham secured their Premiership status with a 6-2 win over Wimbledon ▶ Manchester City's misery hit rock bottom when they were relegated to the Second Division in spite of beating Stoke 5-2. The Potters also went down, along with Reading ▶ At the top of the First Division, Forest and Boro were promoted ▶ The next weekend, the Premiership season drew to a close. Crystal Palace and Barnsley were already relegated but Everton faced Coventry, and Bolton had to play Chelsea at Stamford Bridge. Everton got a draw – enough to keep them up on goal difference – but Bolton lost 2-0 and found themselves once again dropping to the First Division ▶ Arsenal's Dennis Bergkamp was not fit for the FA Cup final but, along with his PFA award, gained the Football Writers' Association Player of the Year award.

Chelsea may have secured their double, but Arsenal were just beginning. On 2 May, they claimed the Championship title

Saving grace: Sasa Ilic's save from Michael Gray's penalty ensured promotion to the Premiership for Charlton, and an estimated £10 million in extra TV revenue and general business. After extra time, the score had been 4-4.

▶ A Bank Holiday weekend of sunshine awaited those supporters who went to Wembley to see their clubs battle it out in the play-off finals. Charlton Athletic condemned Sunderland to another season in the Nationwide League after a nail-biting penalty shoot-out ▶ Watford had won the Second Division with Bristol City promoted automatically, but high-spending Fulham could only manage fourth play-off place. Kevin Keegan sacked Ray Wilkins and took over the running of the team only to see the Cottagers knocked out by eventual winners Grimsby ▶ In the Third Division, Notts County, Macclesfield and Lincoln had secured automatic promotion with Colchester United beating Torquay in the play-offs ▶ North of the border, Celtic prevented Glasgow rivals Rangers from winning their 10th consecutive title by taking the Championship themselves. The celebrations were soured, however, by the acrimonious departure of Dutch manager Wim Jansen, who had been at Parkhead for only one season.

MAY 1999

○ The UEFA Cup final takes place on 12 May.

○ The Premiership season finishes on Sunday, 16 May.

○ On 22 May, Wembley will play host to the FA Cup final

for the last time before redevelopment gets under way.

○ The European Cup final is on 26 May.

○ The Football League play-offs take place 29-31 May.

Nottingham did the double – Forest were Division 1 Champions and County were Division 3 Champions

Highs and lows

▶ The world woke up on the first day of June in shock at the news that Paul Gascoigne had been dropped by England manager Glenn Hoddle ▶ He wasn't the only big star not to make it to the finals. Romario, Brazil's striking hero of '94 was also out but through injury rather than social exuberance ▶ When Teddy Sheringham was pictured in the tabloids at a Portuguese nightclub two days before leaving for France, a public apology quickly followed.

▶ While the World Cup overshadowed most things in June, there was some action back home with the news that 1966 World Cup hero Geoff Hurst, pictured top, had been knighted ▶ Howard Kendall was shown the door at Everton and was replaced by ex-Rangers boss Walter Smith ▶ Southampton striker Kevin Davies signed for Blackburn for £7.5 million and Chelsea continued their free-spending, securing the services of French defender Marcel Desailly from AC Milan ▶ Terry Venables finally took up his coaching post at Crystal Palace, immediately denying rumours that Diego Maradona would be joining the club ▶ The infamous Vinny Jones was sentenced to 100 hours community service when he was found guilty of assaulting his neighbour.

The newspapers were peppered with stories and speculation as the wait for France '98 became almost intolerable

All change: FIFA's Joao Havelange (centre) bowed out as the organisation's president to make way for Sepp Blatter (left). Both men joined Michel Platini (right) for the Germany v USA game.

▶ The papers were peppered with stories and speculation as the wait for France '98 became almost intolerable. Brazilian Roberto Carlos' thighs filled endless column inches and by 9 June the party in Paris had started to swing. But there was a warning of things to come with news of troubled Aston Villa striker Stan Collymore allegedly attacking his girlfriend, Ulrika Jonsson ▶ The tournament finally got underway when Brazil took on Scotland in front of 80,000 fans at the Stade de France. The game had been preceded by a bizarre opening ceremony which involved the French Olympic trampolining team. It clearly flummoxed the Scots who found themselves a goal down after four minutes. A John Collins penalty squared things up but an unfortunate own goal by Tom Boyd gave Brazil the first three points of the tournament ▶ Sixteen players got their marching orders, including Scotsman Craig Burley, French star Zinedine Zidane and temperamental Dutch striker Patrick Kluivert.

▶ Off the pitch, the carnival atmosphere was spoiled by England fans who fought the local Arab population and French riot police in Marseille, and German neo-Nazis who took on the police in Lens ahead of Germany's game with Yugoslavia. The violence left one policeman in a coma.

Au revoir: while England's World Cup ended on 30 June in extreme disappointment, the people of Marseille must have been more than happy to see the side go out.

JUNE 1999

○ With exactly a year to go to the European Championships in Belgium and Holland, the qualifiers continue with England playing Sweden and Bulgaria (with or without Gazza, right), Scotland playing the Faroe Islands and the Czech Republic and the Republic of Ireland facing Yugoslavia.

○ On 19 June, the Women's World Cup finals kick off in the USA. England won't be there, Sweden are among the favourites.

Denmark's Ebbe Sand scored the fastest ever goal by a substitute – 16 seconds after coming on against Nigeria

What are the Home Nations' chances in Euro 2000? Which European club has unveiled the world's first retractable pitch? Who is the only England manager to have had a hit single? The next 122 pages will answer all these questions and tackle a host of tough topical issues, including hooliganism, racism, referees and player behaviour. If it's news and it's about football, we've got it covered. The hottest topics in football today are debated, the latest facts and figures supplied. From the serious to the funny side, everything you could want to know about the game is in these pages.

THE FINAL COUNTDOWN

The build-up to France '98

On Wednesday, 10 June 1998, the curtain was raised on the biggest and most-hyped World Cup in the competition's 68-year history. The countdown to France '98 received more British media coverage than any other finals, with both England and Scotland's nail-biting route to qualification, the tickets fiasco and Gazza's omission from the final squad.

Having stuttered in their qualification for France '98, finally managing a 0-0 draw with an unimpressive Italy in Rome, England booked their place in the finals. Like the other 31 teams that would be taking part, England embarked on a series of friendlies. Following a disappointing 0-0 draw with Saudi Arabia at Wembley, there was mounting pressure on the side as they met Belgium and Morocco in Casablanca. Neither game offered much cheer, apart from 18-year-old Michael Owen coming on for an injured Ian Wright against Morocco and scoring. The second match, against Belgium, was lost on penalties after a 0-0 draw. After huffing and puffing his way through the games, Gazza found himself left out of Hoddle's final squad, along with Ian Walker, Dion Dublin, Andy Hinchcliffe and Phil Neville.

The countdown to France '98 received more British media coverage than any other finals

Making a massive impression: the World Cup parade on June 9 saw Paris dwarfed by a series of giant figures the height of six-storey buildings marching towards the Place de la Concorde.

○ Scottish preparation for the World Cup was interrupted when reserve goalkeeper Andy Goram withdrew from the squad while on a pre-World Cup tour of the USA, following newspaper allegations about his private life.

○ A record number of teams entered the World Cup – 172 in total. Thirty-two teams qualified for the finals stage with four teams appearing for the first time – Croatia, Jamaica, Japan and South Africa.

The most contentious issue to emerge in the run-up to the World Cup was the paltry ticket allocation given to national associations for their team's matches. Of the 2.5 million tickets available for the tournament, over 35% went to the French and about 25% to sponsors or as part of hospitality packages. Only about 10,000 tickets were made available to England supporters for the group matches and the Tartan Army fared similarly badly. In April, the tournament's organisers opened a telephone hotline for EC citizens to buy the last 110,000 tickets

Blooming spectacular: the opening ceremony for France '98 included a 20-minute spectacular of colour and celebration.

for the first and second round matches but there was more controversy when a third of the 90 operators were assigned to take calls from French citizens on a separate number. Twenty million attempts were made to get through – 15 million of those from Britain. The scarcity of tickets created a huge black market, with prices of up to £1,000 a ticket being quoted. By the time the opening ceremony on 10 June had taken place, the 80,000-strong crowd in the Stade de France and millions around the world were ready for the games to begin.

FRANCE '98 KICKS OFF

The group stage

On 10 June 1998, every football fan's dream came true – more than a month's worth of live, quality football began. It all kicked off at the impressive new Stade de France in Paris, where Brazil – the defending World Cup holders – took on Craig Brown's Scotland. The group stage, played over 17 days, saw a feast of football unfold. In 48 matches, 126 goals were scored and 16 red cards were flourished by referees. France '98 was finally underway.

Within four minutes of the start of the tournament, Brazil made their mark with a goal from Cesar Sampaio. Despite an equalising penalty from Scotland's John Collins, the defending champions managed to steal victory when Tom Boyd produced an unlucky own goal in the second half. The game ended 2-1 to Brazil. That evening, Norway came from behind twice to grab a 2-2 draw against unfancied Morocco, while underdogs Chile also managed a 2-2 draw against Italy the following day, with Chilean striker Marcelo Salas the star man. France, the host nation and a fancied side, cruised to a 3-0 win over South Africa but the first shock of the tournament came on day four. In another goal-packed match, Nigeria beat Spain 3-2, heralding the start of the end for the hotly tipped Spaniards.

In 48 matches, 126 goals were scored and 16 red cards were flourished by referees

Bowing out: newcomers to the World Cup, Japan played some impressive football in the group stage but still failed to win a point against fellow Group H hopefuls Argentina, Jamaica and Croatia.

○ There were four own goals and 13 penalties scored in the group stage of the tournament.

○ Holland's Patrick Kluivert and France's Zinedine Zidane were both sent off during the first round and were suspended for two games.

○ The group stage concluded on June 26, with Brazil, Norway, Italy, Chile, France, Denmark, Nigeria, Paraguay, Holland, Mexico, Germany, Yugoslavia, Romania, England, Argentina and Croatia all going through.

The England World Cup campaign kicked off on day six, with a 2-0 victory over Tunisia – much to the relief of the English fans. The following day Scotland were back in action, this time securing a 1-1 draw against Norway. Hosts France followed up their 3-0 win over South Africa with an even more emphatic 4-0 win over Saudi Arabia but the joy was soured by the sending off of potential star Zinedine Zidane. There were goals aplenty in Groups E and H as Holland and Argentina enjoyed 5-0 wins over South Korea and Jamaica, while in Group F Germany stormed back from a 2-0 deficit against Yugoslavia to draw 2-2. Iran no doubt thanked Allah that they beat the 'Great Satan' (USA) 2-1. On June 22, England kicked off in Toulouse in confident mood but their seeded opponents, Romania, had other ideas and won 2-1 in injury time with a Dan Petrescu goal. While the result was disappointing, Michael Owen's equalising goal after coming on as a substitute provided hope and promise. While the World Cup was just beginning for Owen, it was coming to an end for Scotland, who suffered a 3-0 defeat at the hands of Morocco. But it was Morocco the world sympathised with – they thought they had qualified but Norway pipped them to the post with a shock defeat of Brazil in the last 10 minutes of the game. The taste of defeat in the group stage was too sour for some – Saudi Arabia, Tunisia, the USA and South Korea all sacked their respective coaches. Taking part just isn't enough.

Highs and lows: England's Darren Anderton and team-mate David Beckham (above) experienced joy after both scored against Colombia, while Scotland's Colin Hendry (left) experienced pain as Scotland's World Cup dream came to an end.

German Lothar Matthaus beat his previous joint record of 21 finals games when he played against Yugoslavia

ENGLAND'S COMING HOME

Second round

Football fans around the world hardly had time to catch their breath before the action in the second round got under way in France. The final two matches in the group stage had been played on the evening of June 26. The following day, the 16 countries that had made it through began their bid to make it to the last eight. Seven of the eight seeded countries (Spain missed out) and only one of the four countries making their debut (Croatia) made it to the second round.

Last-gasp qualifiers Norway had no answer to Italy's Christian Vieri and his 18th-minute strike, while the rain failed to dampen the samba mood as Brazil sauntered to a 4-1 victory over Chile with both Ronaldo and Cesar Sampaio scoring twice. The following day, after France could only manage a goalless draw with unfancied Paraguay at full time, France's Laurent Blanc scored the first World Cup golden goal in extra time to send the hosts through. Meanwhile, Nigeria were given a sharp reminder of how good European football can be when Denmark cruised to a 4-1 victory. For the Danes, it was the first time in their history that they had made the quarter-finals. Germany and Holland got through against Mexico and Yugoslavia respectively, while a Davor Suker penalty sent the newly dyed Romanian blonds out.

Owen picked up the ball just inside the Argentinian half, turned and sped towards goal

Golden moment: France's Laurent Blanc secures the host nation's place in the quarter-finals after scoring the first World Cup golden goal on 28 June 1998, against Paraguay.

○ According to *BusinessAge* magazine, David Beckham is Britain's top-earning footballer with £8.1 million a year. If he was to send a second class letter of apology for his sending off to every adult in England over the age of 15, it would cost him £7,791,189, which would still leave him with enough money to pay Tony Blair's salary.

○ There were 23 goals in the second round, one penalty shoot-out and one golden goal – the only one of the tournament.

And so to the last – and most dramatic – game of the final 16, England's clash with Argentina in St Etienne. When Gabriel Batistuta opened the scoring after only six minutes with a penalty, it looked like it might all be over before it had begun. But 18-year-old Michael Owen had other ideas. Four minutes later he was felled by two Argentinian defenders and Alan Shearer gratefully stepped up to equalise from the spot. Six minutes later, Owen picked up the ball just inside the Argentinian half, turned and sped towards goal leaving everyone in his wake and finishing with one of the goals of the tournament. Sadly, joy turned to despair either side of the half time whistle when a superbly executed Argentinian free-kick, put home by Javier Zanetti, squared things up on 45 minutes and David Beckham was sent off in the 47th minute for kicking out. Despite a valiant fight, Hoddle's side were doomed to another glorious exit via a penalty shoot-out. Penalty novices Paul Ince and David Batty saw their shots saved and England were out. The players, not football, were coming home.

Dutch courage: Jaap Stam challenges Yugoslavia's Slavisa Jokanovic in Holland's 2-1 win – secured in the 90th minute by Edgar Davids.

Michael Owen was the only player in the World Cup with a number (20) greater than his age (18)

THE MAN WITH THE MASTER PLAN

Glenn Hoddle

England's 1998 World Cup hopes may have been dashed once again by Argentina but for coach Glenn Hoddle the disappointment had to be set aside as he focused on England's next big challenge – Euro 2000. Early criticism of Hoddle was wiped out by England's performances against Colombia and Argentina. But England's youngest ever coach knows his job is only as safe as the results he secures – and Euro 2000 will provide his next real test.

Glenn Hoddle succeeded Terry Venables as England coach after Euro '96. A tough act to follow, Hoddle may have lacked the media charisma of his predecessor but he began to establish his credentials by ensuring that England qualified for France '98 and won Le Tournoi in 1997.

But then Hoddle has always come across as a focused individual, both as a player for Spurs, Monaco and England and as a coach at Swindon Town and Chelsea. His current job as national coach marks the culmination of his life's work. A complex character, he's often applauded for his convictions at the same time as being criticised for his stubbornness. And as former Chelsea midfielder Nigel Spackman noted in *Glenn Hoddle: The Man and The Manager*: "Glenn will never change… he won't be satisfied until he has achieved completely."

It is Hoddle's ambition to transform the way the game is played by the national side

**Spurring him on to greater glory:
Glenn Hoddle spent 12 years at
Spurs and was a footballing icon
to the White Hart Lane faithful.**

○ Glenn Hoddle was capped for England 53 times and retired from his international playing career at the age of 31.

○ Arsenal coach Arsene Wenger has been a major influence on Hoddle. Their association dates from Hoddle's playing days at Wenger's former French club, Monaco. "He has the qualities to do the England job very well," says Wenger. "He has the determination, desire and intelligence and he should be given time to prove himself. Football needs people like Glenn Hoddle."

Glenn Hoddle's appointment as England coach in 1996 was a departure from the norm. First, at 38, he was the youngest ever appointee. Second, his vision for the future of the English game did not include the traditional flat back four. It's Hoddle's ambition to transform the way the game is played by the national side and youngsters have figured strongly in his plans so far. The inclusion of Michael Owen and Rio Ferdinand in the final 22 for France '98 shows how much faith Hoddle is willing to invest in young players. And with Euro 2000 on the horizon, the backbone of a strong England side is emerging. Yet his ride as national coach has not always been a smooth one. Blackburn striker Chris Sutton became embroiled in a row with Hoddle after he refused to play in the B-team. At times, England's performance in the qualifiers for the World Cup had looked less than convincing. And Hoddle drew criticism in his World Cup finals selection, most notably leaving Paul Gascoigne out of the squad and not playing Owen and Beckham from the start in the early matches. But Hoddle's squad proved themselves beyond doubt against Colombia and Argentina and convinced fans to have faith in the future. Faith plays a major part in Hoddle's plans – the question now is how long England will continue to hold faith with Hoddle.

When you're smiling: Glenn Hoddle and the backroom team celebrate following England's victory over Colombia in the 1998 World Cup.

Born on 27 October 1957, Glenn Hoddle is England's youngest ever national coach

THE ROAD TO THE FINAL

Then there were two...

With 56 games played and just eight remaining, the French finally surrendered to World Cup fever as they prepared for their quarter-final clash with Italy.

Brazil, having casually cast aside Chile in the second round, were raring to go against Denmark, Holland faced Argentina and Germany were going into battle

against Croatia. Only two games now stood between each team and a place in the 1998 World Cup final. Nobody was going out without a fight.

On Friday, 3 July, 77,000 football fans took their seats in the Stade de France for the France v Italy quarter-final. What followed was a game that remained goalless for two hours as each side tried in vain to penetrate their opponents' defence. Italy were lacklustre, while

France once again created opportunities but failed to finish – until the penalty shoot-out. With Demetrio Albertini and Luigi di Biagio missing from the spot, the French went through. Over in Nantes, Brazil were stunned two minutes into their game against Denmark when Martin

Jorgensen scored. But the trophy holders rallied to the cause and within half an hour Bebeto and Rivaldo had turned the deficit into a 2-1 lead. Denmark battled back with a Brian Laudrup equaliser but Rivaldo made sure of Brazil's place in the semi-finals just 10 minutes later.

Two games stood between each team and the final. Nobody was going out without a fight

Auf Wiedersehen: Davor Suker books Croatia's place in the semi-finals with his fourth goal of the tournament and Croatia's third in the quarter-final game against Germany.

○ In the play-off for third place, World Cup newcomers Croatia beat Holland 2-1 at the Parc des Princes, marking a memorable debut.

○ Croatia's Davor Suker won the Golden Boot with six goals. Italy's Christian Vieri and Argentina's Gabriel Batistuta scored five and Mexico's Luis Hernandez, Brazil's Ronaldo and Chile's Marcelo Salas scored four.

○ Dennis Bergkamp won BBC TV's Goal of the Tournament for his strike against Argentina.

The last two semi-final places were settled in dramatic fashion. First, Argentina were put out by Arsenal's Dennis Bergkamp after the Dutchman turned the 1-1 scoreline into a 2-1 win with a wonder goal in the dying seconds. Both sides had seen red as first Dutch defender Arthur Numan and then Ariel Ortega were red-carded. In Lyon, Germany were expecting to book their place in the semis but when Christian Worns was sent off, it took just seconds for the first Croatian goal from Jarni to go in and two more goals in the last 10 minutes of the game sent Germany packing – after one of their worst ever World Cup defeats. Two rest days followed as Brazilian and Dutch fans arrived in Marseille for the first semi-final. But the match was disappointing. Brazil did little in the first half but watch Holland squander a series of chances. Minutes into the second half Ronaldo scored, only to see Holland equalise through a last-gasp Kluivert header. Once again the game went to penalties, once again Brazil were through. Back in the Stade de France for the second semi-final, the air was thick with tension. Nerves got the better of both Croatia and France but, as in Marseille, the second half saw the game burst into life. Davor Suker scored from the kick-off but the French bounced back with Lilian Thuram's first goal for his country. He doubled his tally a minute later, ensuring France's place in the final.

Hot stuff and hot-head: Ronaldo proved instrumental in the win against Holland in the semi-final clash when he burst through to score his fourth goal of the tournament. While France beat Croatia 2-1, they also lost Laurent Blanc, scorer of the first ever golden goal in a World Cup game, for the final.

France '98 final

After 33 days, 171 goals and 64 games of first-class football, the 16th World Cup finals drew to a close at the venue where it all began, the Stade de France. With 32 nations competing, it was the biggest tournament yet and for the French in particular it proved to be the best. For the most part, the football itself did not disappoint – it was fast, fluent and attacking and although the French crowds may have taken time to come round, the Paris scenes on 12 July said it all.

France '98, like all World Cup finals, produced memorable moments both on and off the pitch. On a negative note, hooliganism again reared its ugly head, but it largely failed to mar a generally carnival atmosphere. Fans were treated to some dramatic and exciting football.

For England fans there were highs (Michael Owen's goal against Argentina) and lows (going out yet again after a penalty shoot-out). Mexico's Blanco entertained with his leap over defenders, the ball clamped firmly between his feet, and referee Kim Milton got a roasting for his decision to disallow Sol Campbell's goal against Argentina. Croatia's Slaven Bilic was lambasted for denying France's Laurent Blanc a place in the final, while Croatian striker Davor Suker was applauded for his goals and earned the Golden Boot award.

France '98, like all World Cup finals, produced memorable moments both on and off the pitch

Head over heels: France's number one, Fabien Barthez, clashes with Brazilian number nine Ronaldo. After nearly dropping one save over the line in the first half, the French keeper redeemed himself in the second half with a fine block from Ronaldo.

○ Marcel Desailly is the third player to have been sent off in a World Cup final, after Argentinians Pedro Monzon and Gustavo Dezotti in 1990.

○ Since 1930, the 16 World Cup final matches have averaged 4.0625 goals per game.

○ Eight offsides and 28 fouls were awarded in the 1998 final.

○ 22 red and 257 yellow cards were awarded during France '98.

Shortly before the kick-off for the 16th World Cup final, pandemonium broke out in the press box as the team-sheets were circulated. Ronaldo had been left out of the original starting line-up. In fact, little seemed to go right for the Brazilians as they sought their fifth World Cup trophy. Even though the Brazilian number nine ended up on the pitch, the favourites never really looked like defeating a confident and attacking French side. The South Americans had trouble containing Aime Jacquet's team as France continually caught Brazil on the break. They may not have had an out-and-out striker but in the 27th and 45th minutes, Zinedine Zidane (top left) headed the ball triumphantly into the back of the net. Half-time saw the

We are the champions!: the French squad celebrate winning their first ever World Cup.

introduction of Denilson for Leonardo, but still Brazil failed to up the tempo. Ronaldo looked hopelessly immobile and even Marcel Desailly's dismissal failed to turn the tide. In stoppage time, Emmanuel Petit sealed a well-deserved French victory with a third goal and as the final whistle blew, the Stade de France erupted. Captain Didier Deschamps held the trophy aloft as fans joined in the jubilations, and fireworks lit up the Paris skyline. It proved a fitting conclusion – football had come home to the nation that had dreamed up the World Cup.

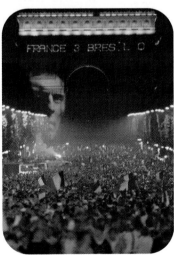

A night to remember: the Champs-Elysees turned into one gigantic street party after the host nation defeated Brazil 3-0 in the final. Overlooking the festivities is French defender Laurent Blanc.

The 16th World Cup final was the first time that the holders (Brazil) played the hosts (France)

THE BOY FROM BRAZIL

Ronaldo

Ronaldo Luiz Nazario da Lima has twice been voted FIFA World Player of the Year – in 1996 and 1997 – before even turning 22 and is considered Brazil's finest since Pele. The Brazilian number nine and Inter Milan number 10 is a football phenomenon and, despite seeing his World Cup dreams evaporate in the final against France, showed glimpses of his breathtaking talent at France '98. The world's highest earning player and goal-scoring maestro has the world at his feet.

Born in Rio de Janeiro on 22 September 1976, Ronaldo's blossoming ball skills were spotted early on as he played in the Rio backstreets. It was Jairzinho, a Seventies' Brazilian football hero, who is credited with discovering and nurturing the 14-year-old's obvious talent. Ronaldo turned professional at Social Ramos in the 1990-91 season, scoring an impressive eight goals in 12 matches. His exceptional goal rate continued at his next club, Sao Cristovao, and when he joined Cruzeiro in 1993, he went on to score 58 goals in 60 games. In 1994 he made his first mark on European football, when he signed to Dutch club PSV Eindhoven and was the Eredivisie's top scorer in his first season. Two seasons later, at Barcelona, he netted 34 goals in 37 games, before joining Italian club Inter in 1997 for a then-record £18 million.

The Inter Milan striker will certainly be hoping that the World Cup in 2002 proves more fruitful

There's that grin again: Ronaldo joins FIFA president Sepp Blatter in Marseille, France, to give him a helping hand in the draw for the 1998 World Cup.

○ Ronaldo finished his first season at Inter Milan as the second highest goalscorer in the Italian Serie A with 25 goals, behind Germany's and Udinese's striker Oliver Bierhoff, who scored 27.

○ As well as being World Player of the Year in 1996 and 1997, Ronaldo has also been a CONMEBOL Under-16 championship medal winner (1991); a Copa America runners-up medal winner (1995); a Cup Winners Cup medal winner with Barcelona (1996); an Olympic bronze medallist (1996); and a UEFA Cup winner with Inter Milan (1998).

"As a lover of football, and if you're passionate about football, you want to see him." Dutchman Ruud Gullit reflected the thoughts of the world as preparations for the 1998 World Cup final fell into confusion with the news that Ronaldo had been crossed off the team sheet for the game against France. Reinstated on a second team sheet, there were rumours about arguments in the dressing room before it was announced that Ronaldo was carrying an ankle injury and that he had been given the all-clear by the team doctor only 45 minutes before the game. What followed was a disappointing performance not only from Ronaldo but from the Brazilian team as a whole. After the match, Brazilian coach Mario Zagallo said: "The truth is that Ronaldo was really not fit to play tonight. For the whole of the first half I was wondering whether to take him off." Sadly, Ronaldo never hit his peak at France '98 and it remains to be seen whether he will join the list of all-time football greats. But the signs are promising – he is fast and fluent and his strike-rate is truly phenomenal. The Inter Milan striker will certainly be hoping that the World Cup in 2002 proves more fruitful than both France '98 and USA '94, when, although he joined the Brazilian squad, the 17-year-old remained on the bench for the tournament.

Built for speed: the world's premier player is extremely fast – on and off the ball. Below, Ronaldo is caught on camera after bursting through the Moroccan defence in Brazil's Group A game against the north Africans in the 1998 World Cup finals.

Ronaldo is the first player to have been voted FIFA World Player of the year twice

DOUBLE AGENTS

Arsenal's 1997-98 double-winning season

It was a dream season for the Gunners and their manager with the Midas touch, Arsene Wenger. "It was the best moment of my sporting life," said the Frenchman after Arsenal won the League and FA Cup double for the second time in their history. Gone are the taunts of "boring, boring Arsenal" – now fans and pundits alike wax lyrical about the club's exciting, attacking style of play. In 1998-99, the European Cup beckons – and then there's always the chance of a treble double…

Opinion on Arsenal's chances of winning silverware seemed mixed at the start of the 1997-98 season. There were grumblings about Arsene Wenger's new spate of continental signings – Christopher Wreh, Luis Boa Morte, Emmanuel Petit, Gilles Grimandi and Marc Overmars among them. And doubts were raised about Wenger's ability to adapt to the rigours and pressures of the English Premiership. "He has no experience of English football," opined Manchester United boss, Alex Ferguson. "He's come from Japan. He should keep his mouth shut." But no one questioned Arsenal's legendary back four and as the season unfolded – albeit a little shaky at times and with a less than desirable disciplinary record – it became apparent that the Gunners were shaping up as the side to take on the cream of Manchester.

On 14 March, the Gunners went to Old Trafford. They won 1-0, trimming United's lead at the top of the table to six points, with three games in hand

Dutch master: Dennis Bergkamp was a £7.5 million signing from Inter Milan. The 1997-98 PFA Player of the Year missed the FA Cup final due to injury.

○ More than 300,000 people turned out to cheer Arsenal as they paraded the 1997-98 Championship trophy and FA Cup on an open-topped bus.

○ The 1971 FA Cup final was goalless after 90 minutes. Steve Heighway scored the first goal in extra time for Liverpool, before Eddie Kelly equalised for the Gunners. Just as it seemed that the game was going to end in a 1-1 draw, a lanky teenager named Charlie George cracked home the winner – securing Arsenal their first double.

Action replay: the 1997-98 side celebrate winning the double, 27 years after the club first achieved the feat. The FA Cup was won after goals from Marc Overmars and Nicolas Anelka, against Newcastle.

Arsenal remained unbeaten in the League until a 3-0 defeat at Derby on 1 November 1997. Ian Wright had long since smashed Cliff Bastin's Highbury record and Dennis Bergkamp had netted the Player of the Month award twice. The only disappointment was an early exit from the UEFA Cup at the hands of PAOK Salonika. Crucially, the week after the derby defeat, Wenger's side beat title rivals Manchester United 3-2 at Highbury. But suddenly, the side began to struggle. Of their next four games, they lost three – against Sheffield Wednesday, Liverpool and Blackburn. But the New Year brought renewed hope. Losing only to Chelsea in the semi-final of the Coca-Cola Cup, Arsenal embarked on a four-month unbeaten run. On 14 March 1998, the Gunners went to Old Trafford in confident and combative mood. They won 1-0, trimming United's lead in the Premiership to six points, with three games in hand. Meanwhile, in the FA Cup, the Gunners had seen off Port Vale, Boro, Palace and West Ham, before beating Wolves in the semis. As Arsenal enjoyed a run of wins, United continued to stumble. Victories over Newcastle, Blackburn and Wimbledon sent shock waves through Old Trafford and in their third from last game, Arsenal secured the title in a 4-0 win over Everton. The double – the second in the club's history – came a fortnight later on 16 May, when Marc Overmars and Nicolas Anelka buried Newcastle 2-0 in the FA Cup final.

Arsenal are the only club to have twice returned to the FA Cup final as holders, and lose – in 1972 and 1980

A MAN FOR ALL SEASONS

Arsene Wenger

If anyone is looking for someone to front an advertising campaign extolling the virtues of a united Europe, they should look no further than Arsene Wenger. By combining continental flair with British steel in an environment inspired by a footballing experience which has stretched from Toulouse to Tokyo, the Arsenal manager has taken the Gunners back to the top of the English game, leading them to the double for the first time in 27 years.

Arsene Wenger was born in Strasbourg on 22 October 1949 and studied economics while playing for French sides Mutzig, Mulhouse and Strasbourg. However, following an undistinguished playing career, he began coaching in 1981, first as Strasbourg's youth team manager, then as assistant manager at Cannes and later with Nancy. But it was with Monaco that he made his name, signing Glenn Hoddle in his first season in 1987 and guiding the club to the French title in 1988. When AC Milan striker George Weah was named FIFA World Player of the Year in 1995 he dedicated his award to Wenger, having played for him at Monaco. "Arsene is the best coach I have ever played for," he said. "I owe all my success to him." In 1995 Wenger left Europe for Japan and repeated the Monaco success at Grampus Eight.

> "Arsene is the best coach I have ever played for. I owe all my success to him," George Weah, FIFA World Player of the Year 1995

Making a point of it: Wenger can command the Arsenal players in any of six languages. He speaks English, French, German, Italian and Spanish, as well as some Japanese.

○ Arsene Wenger won the French League with Strasbourg in 1979 as a player and won again in 1988 as manager of Monaco. He went on to lead the club to the French Cup in 1991 and, at the head of Grampus Eight, picked up the Emperors Cup in 1995 and the Super Cup in 1996. In 1998, he led Arsenal to the Premiership title and the FA Cup.

○ Wenger was French Manager of the Year in 1988, Japanese Manager of the Year in 1995 and English Manager of the Year in 1998.

When Wenger arrived at Arsenal on 28 September 1996, the club was in turmoil – Bruce Rioch had been sacked, caretaker manager Stewart Houston had left to take over at Queen's Park Rangers and youth team manager Pat Rice was temporarily at the helm. Wenger took an ageing squad which had been there and seen it all before, injected some young, foreign blood and gradually moved Arsenal's playing style away from the pragmatic tactics of George Graham's successful reign. He has retained the great British attributes of passion and will to win, which he admires so much, and blended them with the craft and guile more associated with the continent. He was able to convince players to accept radical new training programmes and to change their diet and way of life completely. As well as bringing in nutritionists and a masseuse, he introduced training methods learned from France and Italy. But his success comes from his willingness to learn about his players and the English game for himself. "I have huge respect for the players here, because they want to win and do well. These players have won a lot, yet they are always ready to improve," he says.

Premier performance: the Frenchman is the only non-Scottish manager to have won the English Premier League.

Arsene Wenger is the first foreign manager to win the English League in its 109-year history

EURO-VISION

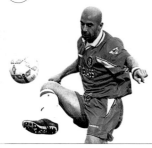

Foreign managers

In 1997-98, for the first time ever, the English League was won by a foreign manager. Arsene Wenger has assured his place in English football history by leading Arsenal not only to the Premiership title, but the double too. And as foreign players increasingly infiltrate British shores, managers are coming with them. While some have found success, others have struggled to adapt to the rigours of one of the most demanding Leagues in the world.

"We always felt Arsene would be a manager to put the club at the top where it belongs," Arsenal's vice-chairman, David Dein, has said. Certainly, Wenger's French revolution at Highbury, in the space of just 20 months, was dramatic. Wenger, an astute tactician, introduced continental flair and class into the Arsenal side in the shape of Patrick Vieira and Emmanuel Petit, with Marc Overmars on the flanks and the explosive combinations of Nicolas Anelka, Christopher Wreh and Dennis Bergkamp up front. At north London rivals Tottenham, Alan Sugar derided the faith put into foreign managers. When Gerry Francis resigned under pressure from the press and fans, Sugar said: "If he put on a mask, called himself Geraldo Francisco and came back here tomorrow, things would turn round immediately."

While some have found success, others have struggled to adapt to the English League

Gross exaggeration?: Rumours of discord with a number of players, particularly Klinsmann, plagued Gross at Spurs.

○ Foreign managers in England and Scotland in the 1997-98 season:

Manager	Nationality	Club	Period
Arsene Wenger	French	Arsenal	full season
Ruud Gullit	Dutch	Chelsea	until Feb 1998
Gianluca Vialli	Italian	Chelsea	from Feb 1998
Attilio Lombardo	Italian	Crystal Palace	13 Mar to 29 Apr 1998
Christian Gross	Swiss	Tottenham Hotspur	from 20 Nov 1997
Jan Sorenson	Danish	Walsall	until 5 May 1998
Jan Molby	Danish	Swansea	until 5 Oct 1997
Danny Bergara	Uruguayan	Doncaster Rovers	29 Oct to 2 Dec 1997
Wim Jansen	Dutch	Celtic	until 18 May 1998

A Wise move?: Dutchman Ruud Gullit departed from Stamford Bridge in February 1998 to make way for Italian Gianluca Vialli. Ironically, it was the former AC Milan player who had brought Vialli to Chelsea from Juventus in the 1996-97 close season.

Arsene Wenger was not the only foreign manager to fill the trophy cabinet of a London club in 1997-98. Chelsea also won a double – the League Cup and Cup Winners Cup – under Gianluca Vialli. The Italian stepped into Dutchman Ruud Gullit's shoes after the latter was sacked. There was much disbelief when Gullit was forced out in February 1998 and the parting was acrimonious. Gullit accused the club of acting dishonourably, while chairman Ken Bates accused the Dutchman of being a 'playboy' manager.

At the opposite end of the Premiership table, two other foreign managers found the going a lot tougher. Relegated Palace appointed Italian Attilio Lombardo as player-manager in April 1998. It was a much derided move – Lombardo could hardly speak a word of English and after one of their many losses declared: "They didn't understand what I said to them." When Gerry Francis resigned from Spurs in November 1997, his place was taken by Christian Gross. The Swissman found the English Premiership an uphill struggle and disputes with his players, particularly Jurgen Klinsmann, did not help. Spurs were saved from the drop but the club suffered one of its worst seasons in recent times. Only time will tell whether Gross can achieve the same kind of success as Wenger.

The first foreign manager in England was Uruguayan Danny Bergara, who managed Rochdale in 1988-89

IN A LEAGUE OF THEIR OWN

The Scottish Premier League

A plan by the top Scottish clubs to form their own breakaway league – much as their English counterparts had done in 1992 – was given the go-ahead by the Scottish Football Association in early 1998 and ratified at an extraordinary meeting in May. So, after 107 years of competing in a league organised by the Scottish Football League, the new Premier League, organised by the Scottish FA, came into being at the beginning of the 1998-99 season.

The plan for the breakaway league was first announced at the end of 1997 to allow clubs time to arrange sponsorship and television deals. The new league will include 10 clubs. At the end of each season, the bottom team will be relegated to the First Division of the Football League, with the champions of that division moving in the opposite direction – as long as they can satisfy certain criteria, including an all-seater stadium with at least a 10,000 capacity and some form of pitch protection. The play-offs between the ninth team in the top flight and the runners-up in Division One has been axed. As a result, the Scottish Football League had to make a one-off payment of £250,000 to 1997-98 Division One runners-up Falkirk, while Motherwell, ninth in the Premier Division, avoided potential relegation.

After 107 years, the top 10 clubs in Scotland will run their own league from 1998-99

Speaking out: Lex Gold, then chairman of Hibs, was the spokesman for the breakaway league before he resigned to concentrate on Hibs' fight to remain in the top division, which was ultimately unsuccessful.

○ Since the old Scottish Premier Division began in 1975, the only time that either Rangers or Celtic did not win it were in 1980, 1984 and 1985 (Aberdeen), and in 1983 (Dundee United).

○ During its 107-year existence, 11 teams won the Scottish League. Apart from the Old Firm clubs, the most successful teams in the League were Aberdeen, Hearts and Hibernian – with four successes each. The only other team to win the League more than once were Dumbarton, who won the first two League Championships, in 1891 and 1892.

With the announcement of a new Scottish Premier League of 10 clubs in May 1998, rumours of a 12 or 14-team set-up were quashed, although a review in the future could alter the numbers. There is a belief by some that the restructuring of the top division in Scotland will enable the national and domestic teams to be more competitive in Europe. How this will be achieved, when the new League involves the same number of games over the same amount of time as the previous league, has been questioned. The new league faced its critics almost from the word go and the swift resignation of the spokesman for the breakaway League, Lex Gold, did little to help settle matters. Gold, who is also chairman of Hibs, gave the reason for his resignation as a need to concentrate on Hibernian's survival in the top flight. Ironically, the new League has gone ahead and Hibs were relegated. There will be many who hope that the new Premier League will provide new excitement and new impetus for the smaller clubs. Rangers have won nine of the last 10 titles but Celtic denied them their 10th consecutive win in 1998. Many will hope that the contest for the first new Premier League title will be even more thrilling.

Heading for a record attempt: Richard Gough returned to Rangers to try to help them win a record 10th successive Championship in 1997-98. They failed, but will be hoping to lift the first-ever Premier League trophy in 1999.

MONEY, MONEY, MONEY...

Transfer fees and wages

During the 1990s, players' wages and transfer fees have sky-rocketed. Liverpool's Robbie Fowler reportedly demanded £50,000 a week to stay at Anfield last season and Jurgen Klinsmann was rumoured to have picked up £1 million for just a few months' work at Spurs. All this is good news for the players of course, and a long way from the days of those like Sir Tom Finney, who reflected last season that: "I started at £12 a week and the top wage was £20."

On 15 December 1995, Jean-Marc Bosman, an FC Liege (Belgium) player, made footballing history when he finally won his five-year battle at the European Court of Justice. The Bosman ruling was a landmark case. It meant that out-of-contract players could become free agents, moving free of charge to a club of their choosing within the EU. It came into effect in the summer of 1996 and revolutionised the European transfer market – the repercussions are increasingly being felt today. In the post-Bosman climate, clubs know that the only way to secure the best talent is to pay through the nose for it. Brian Laudrup's much-publicised move south to Chelsea from Rangers was technically a free transfer, but signing-on fees and wages effectively made the Dane as much as an eight-figure signing.

While the average Premiership player's wage is £200,000 a year, this figure falls to just £25,000 in Division Three

Player power: in 1961, Jimmy Hill took on the Football League in a dispute over pay and conditions. Hill, as chairman of the PFA, argued that players were being treated as 'slaves'. On the 19 January, with a threatened strike on its hands, the League agreed to abolish the maximum wage.

○ In the 1996-97 season, Premiership players were paid £135 million, the average top-flight footballer taking home £6,000 a week.

○ When Sunderland's Alf Common signed for Middlesbrough in 1905 for a record £1,000, it caused a public outcry. The record transfer fee for a British player today is £15 million, paid when Alan Shearer moved to Newcastle United from Blackburn Rovers in July 1996. The world's most expensive player is Brazil's Denilson, signed for £21.5 million by Real Betis from Sao Paulo in 1998.

Football in the 1990s is big business. The Premiership clubs in particular have benefited from TV rights, gate receipts, merchandising, sponsorship and the odd share flotation. Yet this increased revenue has to be balanced against spiralling wage bills. The average Premiership player's wage is £200,000 a year, a figure which falls to £25,000 in Division Three. Not surprisingly, Manchester United had the highest wage bill for the 1996-97 season, at £22.5 million, while Southampton had the lowest in the Premiership. *England's Premier Clubs*, a report from football accountants Deloitte & Touche for the 1996-97 season, revealed details of the modern wage explosion. The report suggested that the trend of escalating player earnings could be a worrying one for the future of the game. With so much of the revenue going straight into the players' pockets, it argued that clubs are in danger of becoming organisations with substantial turnovers yet weak financial foundations. A staggering 68% of Coventry City's turnover, for example, went directly on to the club's wage bill. "The key to football's future financial success is a combination of wage control and income growth," said the report's editor Gary Boon. "Increases in BSkyB income from TV rights and better stadia facilities will see high turnover growth but soaring players' wages will eat into this growth." Another note of warning was that while the higher division clubs are reaping the fruits of football's popularity, the lower ones are at risk of going under. In particular, the arrival of cheap foreign imports has reduced the transfer income for the lower division sides from the Premiership clubs.

Easy come, easy go: Jurgen Klinsmann returned to White Hart Lane in December 1997 for a reputed £1 million. He left just five months later.

The world transfer fee record for a defender is £10.75 million, paid by Manchester United for Holland's Jaap Stam

SMALL FISH IN A BIG POND

Helping the game

The future for lower division clubs

While football's fat cats in the Premiership are getting all the cream, the future for lower division clubs is far from certain. For every successful Manchester United plc or Chelsea Village, there is a struggling Doncaster Rovers or Brighton & Hove Albion. The rise of the super club and the decline of the small club is becoming a worrying trend in the 1990s. The Football Trust remains one of the main sources of funding for clubs in trouble, but it faces an uphill battle.

The problems facing small clubs are legion. The deadline set in the 1990 Taylor Report for all Football League grounds to be all-seater by 1999-2000 is getting close. Financial help for safety improvements and ground redevelopment is available from The Football Trust, but clubs are also expected to raise additional funds. Lower division clubs do not benefit from the vast revenue accrued from selling television rights that has transformed top-flight football over the past few seasons. Twenty clubs in the Premiership share about £200 million, while the 72 Football League clubs divide £25 million between them – the largest slice of the pie going to Division One. And in the post-Bosman climate, smaller clubs do not benefit from a traditional source of income – the cultivation and selling of youth players to the bigger clubs.

As much as 80 per cent of the clubs in the Nationwide Football League are estimated to be operating at a loss

Not the full monty: Doncaster Rovers could not afford to maintain a full squad in the 1997-98 season and ended up conceding 113 goals on the way to being relegated to non-League football.

◯ When Charlton Athletic were promoted to the Premiership in May 1998 via the play-offs, the club was estimated to have increased its coffers by £10 million from TV rights, higher gate receipts and merchandising.

◯ For the 1995-96 season, Wigan Athletic's wage bill represented 223% of the club's annual income.

So what is the future for small clubs? As much as 80 per cent of the clubs in the Football League are estimated to be operating at a loss. Doncaster Rovers replaced Brighton & Hove Albion as the League's most likely club to go under last season. Rovers, who conceded 113 goals and were relegated to the Vauxhall Conference, are indicative of how small clubs are struggling under a sea of debt. Rovers could not even afford to maintain a squad in the 1997-98 season – in March they had only seven full-time professional players on the books – and no permanent coaching staff. Second Division Fulham on the other hand, failed to win promotion but are unlikely to face the difficulties that Brighton or Rovers encountered. The difference is Harrods owner Mohamed Al Fayed, who paid £30 million for the club in May 1997. Fulham, with Fayed's millions, is a club with dreams of a glorious future. Other clubs have a much grimmer time ahead of them.

Dream team: Mohamed Al Fayed (centre right) ploughed millions into Fulham but already his dream management team of Arthur Cox (left), Ray Wilkins (centre left) and Kevin Keegan (right) has faded with the departure of Wilkins.

LEAGUE OF NATIONS

Foreign players

The fact that Arsenal could have played Chelsea during the 1997-98 season with both clubs fielding an entire team of players born outside the British Isles, all playing in their regular positions, highlights the extent of the recent influx of foreign players into the British game. The result has been as exhilarating for fans as it has been exasperating for young local players trying to push their way into the first team and lower division clubs trying to sell their best talent for a good price.

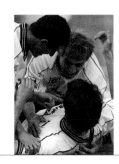

The first overseas player to appear in the Football League was Max Seeburg, a German, who made his debut for Tottenham Hotspur in 1908-09 and went on to play for Leyton Orient, Burnley, Grimsby Town and Reading. He was followed by a steady trickle of players from abroad, most notably Bert Trautmann, another German, who was a former prisoner of war. In 1956, the Manchester City goalkeeper famously broke his neck in the FA Cup Final but played on to help City to a 3-1 win over Birmingham. The first truly international stars did not arrive until 1978 – when World Cup-winning Argentinians Osvaldo Ardiles and Ricky Villa were signed by newly promoted Tottenham. Eight years later, Liverpool became the first team to win the FA Cup final without an Englishman in their side.

There were players from 32 different countries playing in the Premiership in 1997-98

So long: Georgian Georgi Kinkladze experienced the down side of English football when Manchester City were relegated to Division Two at the end of the 1997-98 season. He is now at Ajax.

○ When the squads for France '98 were announced, they showed that 21 English clubs had provided players for the tournament. Twenty clubs in Spain provided players, while 16 clubs in France, Italy and Germany each contributed to various national teams.

○ Seventy-five of France '98's players were signed up to English clubs at the start of the tournament. Seven of Norway's starting line-up for their first game were from English Premiership sides.

The current saturation of foreign talent in Britain can largely be attributed to Australian media baron Rupert Murdoch and Belgian midfielder Marc Bosman. Murdoch has poured millions of pounds into the game in this country by securing TV rights for BSkyB – enabling clubs to pay the sort of wages once only attainable in Italy and Spain. Meanwhile, the Bosman ruling of 1995 now allows for the free transfer of out-of-contract players between clubs within the EEC. Transfer fees may be non-existent, but a player can demand much higher wages. The result of all this is that there were nationals from 32 different countries playing in the Premiership alone in 1997-98, from every continent bar Asia. But although fans might feel the benefit from seeing the likes of Gianfranco Zola and Dennis Bergkamp, lower division clubs are worried about the financial implications. Until now, many of these clubs have been kept afloat by selling young, gifted players to higher division clubs. Now, with clubs looking abroad, there is not the same demand for players from the lower divisions. In the 1995-96 season, Premiership clubs paid foreign clubs £93 million in transfer fees, three times the amount of the previous year, and only £25.2 million to Nationwide League sides. This influx could increase if the Home Office bows to pressure from the FA and the Football League to relax its strict rules

on work permits. But accountant Gerry Boon, head of the Deloitte & Touche football report team, warns: "At least transfers between English clubs keep the money in the domestic game. The £93 million which went overseas left the English game entirely, blowing a massive hole in football's finances."

Latin talent: Italy's Roberto di Matteo was one of eight Chelsea players who went to France '98, while Tottenham Hotspur and Manchester United also fielded eight representatives each.

For France '98, English clubs supplied more players than any other country – 75 in total

DUTY-BOUND

Club versus country

The age-old debate about the conflicting demands of club and country resurfaced yet again in 1997-98. England manager Glenn Hoddle voiced his frustration about players going AWOL in the build-up to France '98, just as some players such as Blackburn's Chris Sutton, pictured right, were voicing their grievances about being left out. But do the demands of the national coach need to be balanced against the club's needs – especially when wage bills are increasingly high?

As a result of the proliferation of tournaments that clubs are now eligible for, the conflict between club and country is becoming more acute. It is a great honour to be capped for your country, but coaches at club level argue that a player's commitment should be primarily with the club. Manchester United, for example, has set its sights firmly on the European Cup in recent seasons and it wants to protect its players from incurring any injuries which might jeopardise its chances. And with England, Scotland, Wales, the Republic of Ireland and Northern Ireland taking part in the qualifiers for Euro 2000, another round of clashes is looming on the horizon. One possible solution is to reduce the Premiership from its current 20 clubs to 18, thus allowing more time between internationals and club matches.

For the international against Portugal, Hoddle made it clear that players who pulled out would jeopardise their chances of making the final 22

Ready for action: David Beckham, Teddy Sheringham, Graeme Le Saux, Alan Shearer and Paul Ince are all England regulars with more than 150 caps between them.

○ While staving off relegation last season, Portsmouth also had to contend with the recurring absence of international players. Paul Hall and Fitzroy Simpson joined Jamaica's Reggae Boyz, while John Aloisi and Craig Foster were unsuccessful in their bid to see Australia qualify.

○ The increasing number of football competitions around the world means that the world's most expensive players such as Ronaldo, who played for Brazil in the Confederations Cup during the 1997-98 season, are increasingly absent from their clubs.

During England's qualification stage for the 1998 World Cup, there were few problems concerning the release of internationals. The England team that triumphed in Rome in October 1997 in a goalless draw against Italy was, apart from the absent injured Alan Shearer, Glenn Hoddle's first-choice side. Problems regarding player availability, however, arose when Hoddle began selecting his squads for friendly warm-up matches, especially the 1-1 draw against Switzerland in March 1998. A significant number of Manchester United players, including the Neville brothers, Nicky Butt, David Beckham, Paul Scholes and Andy Cole, pulled out of the squad citing niggling injuries.

When the same players turned out for the club the following Saturday, a number of newspapers were quick to accuse United of putting club ambition above England glory. For the next international, against Portugal at Wembley in April, Hoddle chose a squad of 34 players and made it clear that withdrawals would not be tolerated. Players who pulled out would jeopardise their chances of making the final 22. Clubs supplying players were informed that only if the player was unfit to travel would they be excused. Hoddle duly got a full squad turning up for duty and England enjoyed a 3-0 victory over Portugal, contrasting with their dismal performance in the previous international.

Come rain or shine: Glenn Hoddle expects every man to do his duty. The England manager issued a warning to players in the run-up to France '98 that if they did not turn up for international duty at Bisham Abbey, they risked losing their place in the squad for the World Cup finals.

The Leeds and West Ham 1997-98 squads both had international representatives from eight different countries

ON YOUR MARKS...

The draw for Euro 2000

Just when you thought you'd watched enough international football to qualify as the new Chelsea chief scout, along come the Euros. With the World Cup barely behind us, it's time to get back down to business with the qualifiers for Euro 2000. With 49 countries from Andorra to Yugoslavia battling it out for a place in the finals, it is the biggest European Championship ever. Even Euro '96 winners Germany must qualify – although being drawn in a group that includes Turkey, Finland, Northern Ireland and Moldova will hardly have them shaking in their boots.

The finals of Euro 2000 will feature 16 teams, the same as Euro '96, including Belgium and Holland — the first joint hosts of a major football tournament. This means that 14 countries must come through the qualifying rounds. In all, there are nine groups of five or six teams with seeded nations Italy, Norway, Germany, Russia, England, Spain, Romania, Yugoslavia and Scotland each heading a separate group. For the home nations, the draw back in January offered little to be happy about. It's the fifth time running that England and Poland have met in the qualifying stages for either the World Cup or the Euro Championships, though Sweden and Bulgaria may prove tougher opponents. The worst luck went to poor Wales – facing four very strong teams including Italy. Neither Irish side has an easy ride, but on paper Scotland have only the Czechs as serious rivals. The top country in each group plus the best overall runner-up will make it through to the finals. The remaining eight runners-up will fight it out in two-legged play-offs to find the remaining four qualifiers.

With 49 countries from Andorra to Yugoslavia, it's the biggest European Championship ever

Low countries lottery: Ghent in Belgium was the venue for the Euro 2000 draw on 18 January 1998. To date, no country from the British Isles has ever reached the final of a European Championship.

◯ A total of nine stadiums will host Euro 2000, four in Holland (Amsterdam, Arnhem, Eindhoven and Rotterdam) and five in Belgium (Antwerp, Bruges, Brussels, Charleroi and Liege). The largest is Ajax's Amsterdam Arena, with its 51,200 all-seater capacity and retractable roof.

◯ The tiny state of Andorra, which lies in the Pyrenees between France and Spain, is competing for the first time.

EURO 2000

GROUP 1
- Italy
- Belarus
- Denmark
- Switzerland
- Wales

GROUP 2
- Norway
- Albania
- Georgia
- Greece
- Latvia
- Slovenia

GROUP 3
- Germany
- Finland
- Moldova
- Northern Ireland
- Turkey

GROUP 4
- Russia
- Andorra
- Armenia
- France
- Iceland
- Ukraine

GROUP 5
- England
- Bulgaria
- Luxembourg
- Poland
- Sweden

GROUP 6
- Spain
- Austria
- Cyprus
- Israel
- San Marino

GROUP 7
- Romania
- Azerbaijan
- Hungary
- Liechtenstein
- Portugal
- Slovakia

GROUP 8
- Yugoslavia
- Croatia
- Macedonia
- Malta
- Rep. of Ireland

GROUP 9
- Scotland
- Bosnia
- Czech Republic
- Estonia
- Faroes
- Lithuania

Germany is the only nation to have won the European Championships more than once – in 1996, 1980 and 1972

GROUPS 1 & 2

GROUP 1

🇮🇹 **Italy**

🏴 **Belarus**

🇩🇰 **Denmark**

🇨🇭 **Switzerland**

🏴󠁧󠁢󠁷󠁬󠁳󠁿 **Wales**

After their dispiriting World Cup qualifying campaign – which included a 7-1 hammering by Holland and a bizarre 6-4 defeat by Turkey – Wales will be hoping for a better showing in their Euro 2000 group. Sadly, the end of the Southall/Rush/Hughes era has left Wales desperately short of quality players, with the obvious exception of Ryan Giggs. Bobby Gould's side may even struggle to avoid the humiliation of finishing above Belarus, who are one of the many former Soviet republics now competing as individual nations in international football.

Group favourites Italy, meanwhile, will be keen to avoid the play-offs, having had to survive a nerve-wracking sudden death encounter with Russia to reach the finals of France '98. With players of the quality of Alessandro Del Piero, Christian Vieri, Paolo Maldini and Chelsea's Roberto Di Matteo in the squad, the azzurri should have no problems in topping this group.

Any side which can leave out Chelsea's Gianfranco Zola, as Italy did for France '98, has a depth of talent which the likes of Wales can sadly only dream about.

Second place looks to be a contest between Denmark and Switzerland. The Danes play neat, attractive football and in Brian Laudrup, the third Chelsea player with an interest in this group, and Manchester United's Peter Schmeichel, they possess two players of genuine world-class ability. They may just prove too strong for Switzerland. The Swiss are not the side they were a few years ago, when they qualified for both Italy '94 and Euro '96 with Blackburn Rovers manager Roy Hodgson at the helm.

Bobby Gould's side may even struggle to avoid the humiliation of finishing above Belarus

The Italian job: Del Piero will hope to make the Euro 2000 finals but Italy's qualifying record is poor – they failed to qualify in 1976, 1984 and 1992.

○ Wales have only once qualified for a European Championships final tournament – in 1976, when they won through to the quarter-finals.

○ Italy and Denmark have both won the European Championships in slightly fortuitous circumstances. Italy won in 1968 after drawing their semi-final with the Soviet Union 0-0 and going through on the toss of a coin. Denmark won in 1992 despite not originally qualifying. They were given a place when Yugoslavia was expelled.

GROUP 2

- 🏴 **Norway**
- 🏴 **Albania**
- 🏴 **Georgia**
- 🏴 **Greece**
- 🏴 **Latvia**
- 🏴 **Slovenia**

Norway were supremely impressive in qualifying for the World Cup – going through the matches unbeaten and conceding only two goals – and can be expected to win a relatively undemanding Group 2 with something to spare. Most of the team are based in England and the likes of Manchester United trio Henning Berg, Ole Gunnar Solskjaer and Ronnie Johnsen, Chelsea's Tore Andre Flo, Liverpool's Oyvind Leonhardsen and Stig Inge Bjornebye, plus Leeds United's Gunnar Halle and Southampton's Egil Ostenstad are likely to be part of Norwegian plans.

Greece will probably prove to be Norway's main rivals. The Greeks were unfortunate not to qualify for France '98. Indeed, if they could have found a way through a massed Danish defence in their last qualifying match, they would have been present at football's biggest ever tournament.

Georgia, too, can live with the best as they showed by holding Italy to a 0-0 draw in 1997 – a result which allowed England to travel to Rome. Georgia will look for inspiration from the former Manchester City winger Georgi Kinkladze, now with Ajax, and will push Greece all the way for a top-two placing.

Of the remaining teams, Latvia are capable of pulling off the occasional surprise result, but are unlikely to be consistent enough to be in contention for qualification. Slovenia and Albania are merely making up the numbers and will engage in their own private battle in which the victor will be delighted to finish one place higher than bottom.

Norway can be expected to win this relatively undemanding group with something to spare

Georgia on his mind: Temur Ketsbaia fights for the ball with Italy's Dino Baggio in a World Cup qualifying match in Tbilisi, in September 1997. Georgia failed to qualify for France '98 but may be inspired for Euro 2000.

○ There were more players based in England in Norway's squad (11) for France '98 than there were in Scotland's squad (eight). The top four teams in the Premiership in 1997-98 provided Norway with a total of six players.

○ In Group 2, only Greece have ever qualified for a European Championship final before, in 1980. They lost to Holland and Czechoslovakia before drawing with eventual winners West Germany.

GROUP 3

- 🇩🇪 **Germany**
- 🇫🇮 **Finland**
- 🇲🇩 **Moldova**
- 🏴 **Northern Ireland**
- 🇹🇷 **Turkey**

Germany may be a side in need of pepping up with some youthful talent, but nonetheless they are clear favourites to win Group 3 in Euro 2000. Germany, and previously West Germany, have qualified for the European Championship finals in every tournament since 1972. As in the qualifying stages for France '98, the Germans are paired with Northern Ireland. The two countries may be at either end of the FIFA rankings, but recent records between the sides mean the Ulstermen should not be overawed at the prospect of meeting the European Champions again. In the recent World Cup qualifying group, the Irish drew 1-1 in Nuremberg before losing 3-1 at home. With players of the calibre of Steve Lomas, Keith Gillespie and Neil Lennon at his disposal, perhaps Lawrie McMenemy can be reasonably optimistic about his team's chances of qualifying for the European Championship finals for the first time.

Turkey and Finland look to be the main challengers to Northern Ireland for the runners-up spot. The Turks had a miserable time at Euro '96, failing to collect a point or score a goal in three matches, and will be hoping to make amends for that disappointment. They will provide particularly stiff opposition in front of their passionate fans in Istanbul.

Meanwhile, the Finns can be tricky customers on their day and, like the Irish, will be keen to qualify for their first finals. Nor should Moldova be underestimated – the former Soviet republic beat Wales in the qualifiers for Euro '96 and, more impressively, defeated Georgia twice.

The Irish should not be overawed at the prospect of meeting the European Champions again

Hat-trick man: after drawing with Germany 1-1 at home, the tables were turned in the second leg of Northern Ireland's World Cup qualifying leg with Germany when Oliver Bierhoff scored a hat-trick in his country's 3-1 win.

○ Northern Ireland and Germany were last drawn in the same qualifying group for the European Championships in 1984. Despite beating the West Germans 1-0 at home and away, Northern Ireland failed to qualify as head of the group on goal difference.

○ Turkey were the only side in Euro '96 not to score a goal.

○ Finland have finished fourth in their group seven times in eight qualifying appearances.

GROUP 4

- **Russia**
- **Andorra**
- **Armenia**
- **France**
- **Iceland**
- **Ukraine**

France will take part in the qualifying games for Euro 2000 after not having to qualify for the recent World Cup as they were hosts. They find themselves in a tricky group, with their opponents including dangerous-looking Russian and Ukrainian teams. Both sides were eliminated from the World Cup qualifiers in the play-offs and will be keen to do better this time around. Russia lost 2-1 on aggregate to Italy, and Ukraine went down 3-1 to Croatia. Russia, with players like former Manchester United and Everton winger Andrei Kanchelskis, plus Igor Kolivanov in their starting line-up, can be fearsome opponents, while Ukraine can be considered virtually a club side as the majority of their players, including their highly rated centre forward Andrei Shevchenko, play for Dynamo Kiev.

All the same France, on recent form, will easily be expected to top Group 4.

Arsenal's young striker Nicolas Anelka could emerge as a key player during the qualifiers, despite not making France's World Cup finals squad, and French boss Aime Jacquet will also raid north London once again to call on the combative Patrick Vieira and Emmanuel Petit in midfield, while Chelsea's central defender Frank Leboeuf should figure, too.

Elsewhere in this group, Iceland, Armenia and Andorra will be involved in their own league-within-a-league to avoid finishing last. Andorra, playing in their first ever international tournament, are clear favourites to collect the wooden spoon and can anticipate some frightful hammerings.

France find themselves in a tricky group, with dangerous-looking Russian and Ukrainian teams

Looking ahead: in the qualifiers for France '98, Russia (in blue) lost 1-0 to Bulgaria in Sofia. Bulgaria qualified automatically, leaving Russia looking forward to Euro 2000.

○ Russia played eight games before the Russian Revolution in 1917. They drew three and lost five, including a 16-0 defeat by Germany and two defeats of 9-0 and 12-0 by Hungary.

○ Armenia have not won a European Championship game in front of a crowd. Their sole victory was in Macedonia, where the game was played behind closed doors as a disciplinary punishment.

ENGLAND'S POLE POSITION

GROUP 5

- England
- Bulgaria
- Luxembourg
- Poland
- Sweden

England have been drawn in a difficult group in the European Championship qualifiers, with Poland, Sweden, Bulgaria and Luxembourg as opponents. Only the winner will automatically qualify for the finals in Belgium and Holland in June 2000 and while Luxembourg should present little problem for England, the remaining three teams in Group 5 pose a real threat to Glenn Hoddle's team, both home and away.

The team to be most wary of are Sweden, despite their failure to qualify for France '98. New manager Tommy Soderberg has promised that the Scandinavians, who were unlucky to lose out to Scotland and Austria in the World Cup qualifying group, will play more exciting, attacking football and there are plenty of players who can turn adventurous play into goals. English fans know all about Newcastle United's Andreas Andersson, former Blackburn Rovers striker Kennet Andersson (no relation) who had a brilliant 1997-98 season at Bologna, and Blackburn Rovers' Martin Dahlin, a classy player who can create as well as score goals. Meanwhile, players such as Jonas Thern, Jesper Blomqvist and former Arsenal man Stefan Schwarz form a creative but combative midfield. Third in the 1994 World Cup in the USA, Sweden will be itching to make up for their subsequent failures to qualify for Euro '96 and France '98.

Bulgaria, too, won't be an easy team for England to get points from, despite the fact that their major playing assets are fast-ageing and that internal wrangling

This is the fifth time that England and Poland have been drawn together since 1989

A new goal: despite the best efforts of Alan Shearer and his team-mates in the Euro '96 finals (against strong sides such as Holland), their European Championship hopes were dashed by Germany in the semi-final. They will be hoping to qualify for Euro 2000 and to go all the way this time.

○ It's 25 years since Poland's draw at Wembley meant that England failed to qualify for the World Cup for the first time in their history. The result wasn't through lack of effort from Alf Ramsey's players, who bombarded the Polish goal, but they were denied victory by poor finishing and the brilliance of the towering goalkeeper Jan Tomaszewski. In fact, it was the Poles who took the lead – through Domarski – after mistakes by Hunter and Shilton. Alan Clarke's 66th-minute equalizing penalty ultimately wasn't enough.

between the team's management and its star players – notably Hristo Stoichkov – has weakened team morale in recent times. Nevertheless, after France '98 they will be a tough proposition in Sofia. The likes of Stoichkov, Lechkov, Ivanov and Kostadinov might be in their thirties but they're not yet finished and young blood, notably Kishishev and Hristov – add zest to Bulgaria's experience.

"It could not be worse" and "England... why again?" were the headlines in the Polish papers when the Euro 2000 draw was announced. Although English fans will never forget the night in 1973 when

the Jan Tomaszewski-inspired Reds put Alf Ramsey's England out of the World Cup, more recent results suggest that the Poles have more to fear from the English than vice versa.

In the nine clashes with the Three Lions since that memorable night, Poland have been defeated six times and the remaining three games have been drawn. This is, amazingly, the fifth time the two countries have been drawn together in a qualifying group for the European Championships or the World Cup since 1989. Nevertheless, Poland are never walkovers, as they proved at Wembley in

the France '98 qualifier when, egged on by an early goal from wonderkid Citko, they could have won a game which they eventually lost.

In terms of minnows, Luxembourg are whales. Although their results in the France '98 qualifiers left a lot to be desired, they took a massive 10 points in the Euro '96 qualifiers, including an historic 1-0 victory over eventual finalists the Czech Republic. Over-complacency should be avoided.

England v Sweden

P15 W6 D5 L4 F27 A19

Last home result:
England 3 Sweden 3
(friendly, Leeds, June 1995)

Last away result:
Sweden 2 England 1
(Euro Championship, Stockholm, June 1992)

England v Luxembourg

P7 W7 D0 L0 F38 A3

Last home result:
England 9 Luxembourg 0
(Euro Championship,
Wembley, December 1982)

Last away result:
Luxembourg 0 England 4
(Euro Championship,
Luxembourg, November 1983)

ENGLAND'S FIXTURES

Saturday 5 September 1998
Sweden (A)

Saturday 10 October 1998
Bulgaria (H)

Wednesday 14 October 1998
Luxembourg (A)

Saturday 27 March 1999
Poland (H)

Saturday 5 June 1999
Sweden (H)

Wednesday 9 June 1999
Bulgaria (A)

Saturday 4 September 1999
Luxembourg (H)

Wednesday 8 September 1999
Poland (A)

England v Bulgaria

P6 W4 D2 L0 F8 A1

Last home result:
England 1 Bulgaria 0
(friendly, Wembley, March 1996)

Last away result:
Bulgaria 0 England 3
(Euro Championship, Sofia, June 1979)

England v Poland

P13 W7 D5 L1 F20 A6

Last home result:
England 2 Poland 1
(World Cup, Wembley, October 1996)

Last away result:
Poland 0 England 2
(World Cup, Katowice, May 1997)

GROUP 6

- **Spain**
- **Austria**
- **Cyprus**
- **Israel**
- **San Marino**

There appears to be a law in international football which stipulates that Spain will always top their qualifying group. There also appears to be another law which states that their form in qualifying need not be replicated in the finals, where, historically, they have a tendency to underperform. The Spanish have a tremendous record in the qualifying stages of both the European Championships and the World Cup, having qualified for all of the last six World Cup tournaments and five of the last six European Championship finals. Spain certainly have the ability to put the rest of Group 6 to the matador's sword, with the young strike force of Raul and Fernando Morientes from Real Madrid's European Cup-winning side, as well as the stylish Fernando Hierro. Other stars Spain can call on include a host of Barcelona players, including goalscoring midfielder Luis Enrique and flying wing back Sergi.

Israel may provide the greatest threat to the Spain. They have a tight defence – only conceding seven goals in their ultimately unsuccessful France '98 campaign – and a superbly creative player in Eyal Berkovic. A lack of fire power though, could be their undoing.

World Cup qualifiers Austria will push Israel hard for second place but unless they can find a worthy successor to veteran striker Toni Polster, they may struggle for goals. Perhaps that will let in the fast-improving Cypriots, who held mighty Russia to a draw in the qualifiers for the last World Cup. San Marino, meanwhile, will be content just to keep their goals-against tally respectable.

The Spanish have a tremendous record in the qualifying stages of the European Championships

Whipping boys: San Marino (in blue), the smallest independent country in Europe, have lost all 18 European Championship qualifying games they have played, scoring three goals and conceding 69 in the process.

○ Israel have only entered the qualifying stages for the European Championships once before – in 1996, and in the World Cup their regional grouping has chopped and changed. They were placed in the European qualifying programme for the World Cup in 1962, 1966, 1982, 1994 and 1998, the Asian qualifying programme in 1958, 1970, 1974 and 1978, and the Oceania qualifiers in 1986 and 1990.

○ Spain are the only side in Group 6 to have ever qualified for the European Championship finals.

GROUP 7

- **Romania**
- **Azerbaijan**
- **Hungary**
- **Liechtenstein**
- **Portugal**
- **Slovakia**

Group 7, at least in theory, looks certain to be a straight fight between Romania and Portugal. Having qualified for France '98, Romania could be considered favourites for automatic qualification. However, their best players are past their peak and this could be a tournament too far for the likes of midfield genius Gheorghe Hagi and the former Tottenham star Gica Popescu.

Portugal, by contrast, are a much younger side and Glenn Hoddle rated them the best team not to make France '98. If the likes of midfielders Figo and Paulo Sousa, along with striker Joao Pinto manage to reproduce the 'sexy football' which Ruud Gullit admired at Euro '96 – and if the side don't try to over-elaborate in front of goal – then the Portuguese should meet expectations.

Looking at the other group members, it's difficult to see a challenger to the big two. Hungary have never qualified for the European Championships, having come third in 1964, been knocked out in the quarter-finals in 1968 and having finished fourth in 1972. Hungarian football is in crisis, as Yugoslavia demonstrated eloquently when they hammered the Magyars 7-1 in Budapest in a World Cup play-off in 1997. Meanwhile, Slovakia are paying the football price for having split from the Czech Republic, and Liechtenstein and Azerbaijan can expect to be on the wrong end of some fearsome thrashings. Their main interest in the group will be to avoid finishing bottom and to record their very first victories in a European Championship match.

Group 7 of Euro 2000 looks certain to be a straight fight between Romania and Portugal

Gheorghe Hagi: a key man for Romania in Euro '96, the gifted playmaker (in yellow) will have to fight off the young pretenders if he is to feature in the side should Romania get to the finals of Euro 2000.

○ Like Israel, Azerbaijan have entered the European Championships once before, in 1996. They lost their first nine matches before drawing 0-0 at home with Poland in their final fixture.

○ Despite joining FIFA and UEFA in 1974, Liechtenstein did not play an international match until 1981. In 1982, they beat China 2-0 in a friendly. China's population is over 100 million, Liechtenstein's around 27,000.

IRISH ENDEAVOUR

GROUP 8

- **Yugoslavia**
- **Croatia**
- **Macedonia**
- **Malta**
- **Rep. of Ireland**

The Irish fell at the final hurdle in their attempt to qualify for France '98 when they were defeated in the play-offs by Belgium, and in the final hurdle for Euro '96 when they were defeated in the play-offs by Holland. The Irish, who have only once qualified for the European Championships, will not be too happy with their draw for Euro 2000. Mick McCarthy's young team are still in a transitional phase and will have to play out of their skins to qualify from a group which includes three countries from the former Yugoslavia – Yugoslavia, Croatia and Macedonia – as well as minnows Malta. Many are complaining that UEFA should have done something to keep the former Yugoslav nations – with Croatia and Serbia so recently at war with one another – apart. McCarthy will be hoping for the Balkan derbies to end in draws so his team might be able to sneak through by picking up the odd three points for a win.

Croatia are particularly tough opponents, having established themselves since they started playing again as a nation (they previously played a handful of games as an Axis state during World War II) as one of Europe's top teams. The likes of Zvonimir Boban, Alen Boksic, Davor Suker, Robert Prosinecki, Robert Jarni, Igor Stimac and Slaven Bilic – all household names in their adopted countries of Italy, Spain and England – are forces to be reckoned with. Croatia, in their characteristic checked shirts, can be a match for any side in the world.

The new Yugoslavia, comprising of Serbia and Montenegro, are also a very classy side, as they proved by thrashing

The Republic of Ireland have only once qualified for the European Championships

Man on a mission: Republic of Ireland manager Mick McCarthy has his work cut out for him if his side are to qualify for the Euro 2000 finals at the top of Group 8.

For their first ever match in a major international tournament, in the 1988 European Championship, Ireland's opponents were from manager Jack Charlton's home country, England. After 20 minutes, the scurrying, tough-tackling Irish scored through Ray Houghton following a defensive mix-up in the England box. From then on it was between the English attackers and goalkeeper Packy Bonner. Bonner, with help from the crossbar, proved to be the more in-form and the most famous victory in Irish football's history was complete.

Hungary 6-1 in Budapest in the World Cup play-offs after coming second in a group which contained an in-form Spain and Euro '96 runners-up the Czech Republic. Like Croatia, most of their classiest players ply their trade in the top leagues in Europe outside their own country. English fans will be familiar with striker Savo Milosevic, while Vladimir Jugovic and Sinisa Mihajlovic have been consistently brilliant in Italy's Serie A and Tenerife anchorman Slavisa Jokanovic, along with Real Madrid striker Predrag Mijatovic, has earned rave reviews in Spain. Before the civil war, Yugoslavia were known as 'the Brazil of Europe' for their stylish and skilful players. They have since split and turned into the Brazils of Europe, and Ireland are unlucky to have them in the same group.

Irish fans will need no introduction to the third and weakest Yugoslav team in the group. Macedonia recorded a historic 3-2 victory over the orange-clad Irish in Skopje in the 1998 World Cup qualifying campaign – which threatened to leapfrog them over Mick McCarthy's men into the play-off place – thanks to two goals from skipper Stojkovski (both from penalties after handballs) and a winner from Barnsley striker Georgi Hristov. Although an earlier 3-0 win in Lansdowne Road was more encouraging, the Irish will want to do better. But they will have to resurrect the defensive solidity which was a feature of Jack Charlton's Irish sides against a slick attack that hit 11 goals against Liechtenstein.

Malta, recently beaten twice by the Faroe Islands, make up the numbers in Group 8, and any less than a six-point return would be a disaster for the Irish.

Rep. of Ireland v Croatia

P1 W0 D1 L0 F2 A2

Last home result:
Rep. of Ireland 2 Croatia 2
(friendly, Dublin, June 1996)

Rep. of Ireland v Yugoslavia

P2 W1 D0 L1 F3 A4

Last home result:
Rep. of Ireland 2 Yugoslavia 0
(friendly, Dublin, April 1988)

Rep. of Ireland v Malta

P5 W5 D0 L0 F16 A0

Last home result:
Rep. of Ireland 2 Malta 0
(World Cup, Dublin, November 1989)
Last away result:
Malta 0 Rep. of Ireland 3
(friendly, Valletta, June 1990)

Rep. of Ireland v Macedonia

P2 W1 D0 L1 F5 A3

Last home result:
Rep. of Ireland 3 Macedonia 0
(World Cup, Dublin, October 1996)
Last away result:
Macedonia 3 Rep. of Ireland 2
(World Cup, Skopje, April 1997)

REPUBLIC OF IRELAND'S FIXTURES

Saturday 5 September 1998
Croatia (H)

Saturday 10 October 1998
Yugoslavia (A)

Wednesday 14 October 1998
Malta (H)

Saturday 27 March 1999
Macedonia (A)

Saturday 5 June 1999
Yugoslavia (H)

Saturday 4 September 1999
Croatia (A)

Wednesday 8 September 1999
Malta (A)

Sunday 10 October 1999
Macedonia (H)

SCOTLAND MEET CZECH MATES

GROUP 9

- ⚔ **Scotland**
- ◣ **Bosnia**
- ▬ **Czech Republic**
- ▬ **Estonia**
- ✚ **Faroes**
- ▬ **Lithuania**

Fate has dealt Scotland what appears to be a kind hand in Group 9 of the Euro 2000 qualifiers, as they seek their third consecutive qualification for the European Championships. Craig Brown's men must fancy their chances of qualifying from a six-team group comprised of the Czech Republic, Lithuania, Bosnia, Estonia and the Faroe Islands. While the Czechs are old foes, and the Tartan Army have crossed swords with Estonia (when they finally bothered to turn up) in the last two World Cup qualifiers, the other three teams have never met Scotland before.

There is little doubt that the Czech Republic are the toughest opponents. Despite not qualifying for France '98, they reached the heady heights of second in the FIFA World Rankings (with only Brazil ahead of them) shortly before the World Cup – and few will forget that it took a golden goal from German Oliver Bierhoff to beat them in the final of Euro '96. New manager Jozev Chovanec is looking to help the team put the disappointments of the World Cup campaign behind them and they will be hungry to reach the finals of the competition they so nearly won in England. English fans will be familiar with their attacking midfielders Patrik Berger and Karel Poborsky, and other players likely to make an impression include a couple of the younger generation – left-footed playmaker Martin Cizek and pacy Marek Zubek.

Scotland have less to fear from their other opponents, though they will do well to come away from their trips to Eastern Europe with full points. During

Scotland are seeking their third consecutive qualification for the European Championships

Tears of a crowd: Czech fans will be hoping their team go one better in Euro 2000 than in 1996 – by qualifying top of Group 9 and going all the way to win the final.

In September 1973, Scotland met Czechoslovakia in a game they needed to win to qualify for the 1974 World Cup finals. One hundred thousand fans packed Hampden Park for a classic match. After an extremely violent opening stage, the fans were silenced after the half-hour by a freak long-range goal from Nehoda. That set up a cavalry charge, with Scotland bombarding the Czech goal – Holton equalized with a thumping header before half-time and then big Joe Jordan, on as a substitute, headed the winner with 15 minutes to go. The final score was 2-1 and qualification.

qualification for the World Cup in France, Estonia managed to hold Craig Brown's team to a 0-0 draw in Monaco (after refusing to fulfil their fixture in Tallinn because of poor floodlights and a revised kick-off time) and, with Derby's Mart Poom in goal and free-scoring Sergei Bragin in midfield, they will be looking to go one better in Tallinn in what might be seen as a grudge match.

Lithuania can also be tricky opponents – Edgardas Jankauskas is the man for the Scottish defence to be wary of, and Tomas Ziukas is an outstanding defender who the Scottish attack will find difficult

to get past. The Republic of Ireland found Lithuania to be far from easy prey during their World Cup qualifying campaign – the Baltic team came away from Lansdowne Road with a creditable goalless draw.

Meanwhile Bosnia, who have finally started playing their home matches in Sarajevo, will have their 20,000 capacity stadium – which was used as a graveyard during the war – full to the rafters hoping for another victory to go alongside their recent defeat of Italy.

Much closer to home for the Scots are the Faroe Islands, although any

neighbourly friendliness from Allan Simonsen's team can be ruled out. The islanders' recent double over Malta, their historic victory over Austria in their first competitive international in 1990, and the fact that they scored three goals in two games against Spain show they are no pushovers, despite the size of their population. At under 50,000, it is roughly the same as an average Ibrox crowd.

SCOTLAND'S FIXTURES

Saturday 5 September 1998
Lithuania (A)

Saturday 10 October 1998
Estonia (H)

Wednesday 14 October 1998
Faroe Islands (H)

Saturday 27 March 1999
Bosnia (H)

Wednesday 31 March 1999
Czech Republic (H)

Saturday 5 June 1999
Faroe Islands (A)

Wednesday 9 June 1999
Czech Republic (A)

Saturday 4 September 1999
Bosnia (A)

Wednesday 8 September 1999
Estonia (A)

Saturday 9 October 1999
Lithuania (H)

Craig Brown: Scotland's highly respected manager was appointed in November 1993, having spent the previous eight years as assistant manager. At the same time, he became technical director. A former Scotland youth international, he won a League championship medal with Dundee as a player. Before entering coaching, he was a head teacher and lecturer.

Scotland v Czechoslovakia
P10 W5 D1 L4 F18 A16
Last home result:
Scotland 3 Czechoslovakia 1
(World Cup, Glasgow, September 1977)
Last away result:
Czechoslovakia 0 Scotland 2
(World Cup, Prague, October 1976)

Scotland v Estonia
P4 W3 D1 L0 F8 A1
Last home result:
Scotland 2 Estonia 0
(World Cup, Kilmarnock, March 1997)
Last away result:
Estonia 0 Scotland 0
(World Cup, Monaco, February 1997)

KICK IT OUT

Racism in football

In spite of the much-lauded campaign 'Kick It Out', events during the 1997-98 season suggested that racism is still alive and kicking in the sport.

In a high-profile incident in February 1998, Aston Villa's Stan Collymore, pictured left, accused his former Anfield team-mate Steve Harkness of making a racist insult on the pitch. The ensuing argument and treatment of the issue by the Professional Footballers' Association failed to satisfactorily resolve the affair.

"Many clubs are taking action to stamp out racism – but more needs to be done," Sports Minister Tony Banks commented during the 1997-98 season. Labour's Football Task Force takes the issue of racism very seriously. Its first report, published in March 1998, noted that racism permeates the game at all levels and takes a variety of forms, both in the non-professional and professional leagues. The report proposed various measures to combat the problem, including making on-pitch racism an automatic red card offence and encouraging local councils to ban racist clubs from using their facilities. Fans from ethnic minorities constitute only 1.1% of Premier League crowds, and the Task Force urged the Football Association to increase the number of black and Asian coaches and referees.

Kick It Out has two aims – to combat racism at football matches and to encourage more fans from ethnic minorities to attend games

Kicking it out: racism in football is nothing new. This famous picture shows Liverpool's John Barnes kicking away a banana as he faces racist abuse from Everton fans in 1988.

○ The first black professional in England was Arthur Wharton, whose goalkeeping skills helped Preston North End win the double in the 1880s. His grave was discovered recently in South Yorkshire and he is now properly commemorated as an early football hero after an active campaign by local fans.

○ The late 1960s and early 1970s saw a big increase in the number of black players. By 1978 there were 50 black professionals.

The 'Let's Kick Racism Out of Football' campaign, set up by the PFA and the Commission for Racial Equality in 1993, was relaunched in October 1997 as an independent body called 'Kick It Out'. It has attracted the vocal support of high-profile footballers and managers such as John Barnes, Tony Adams, Ruud Gullit, Ian Wright and Glenn Hoddle. The campaign has two basic aims – to combat racism on the terraces and on the pitch, and to encourage more fans from ethnic minorities to attend games. "Many clubs are tackling this issue," says Kick It Out's chief co-ordinator, Piara Powar. "But then you get situations like the one at Leicester City last season where Leeds fans chanted

Ruud awakening: the Premiership's first black manager, Dutchman Ruud Gullit, is a keen anti-racist campaigner. In 1987, he dedicated his double award of World and European Player of the Year to the ANC's Nelson Mandela, who was then still imprisoned under South Africa's apartheid regime.

racist abuse at the local Asian community. Things like that set back progress many years." One of the issues that the campaign is currently seeking to address is the lack of Asian professional players, despite the growing popularity of the game with Asian youngsters. Brendon Batson of the PFA believes that "as a result of the Kick It Out campaign, there is a far better atmosphere at football grounds". However, he also agrees with Powar that "proof of our success will be when we see more black, Asian and ethnic supporters attending matches in the knowledge that the game is free of all the damaging aspects of racial intolerance."

PRIDE AND PREJUDICE

Justin Fashanu

There are an ever increasing number of high-profile gay men and women in the arts, media and politics, and laws exist to protect employees against discrimination. Yet in the sporting world, gay athletes remain conspicuous by their absence, with the notable exceptions of tennis stars Billie Jean King and Martina Navratilova – and footballer Justin Fashanu. His tragic suicide in May 1998 has once more put the spotlight on the gay issue.

It's easy to see why gay players prefer to keep their sexual identity a secret. The obstacles facing an openly gay footballer are daunting, as Justin Fashanu found out. Football – a so-called 'man's game' – is fiercely heterosexual, overtly macho and intolerant of sexual difference.

Players are constantly bombarded by lurid tabloid accounts and fickle crowds who are quick to hurl abuse. Yet Fashanu, a physically powerful forward and former B-international, could hardly have realised the extent he had put his career on the line after coming out to the *Sun* in 1990. In a later interview with the *Independent*, he said: "I get respect. I'm not a 5ft 2in effeminate stereotype. People say that football is a macho business, but I think I'm very macho." He also claimed that up to a quarter of all footballers are gay.

In 1990, he admitted he was gay. From that moment on, his life was to change irrevocably

Friends and family remember: John Fashanu, above centre, paid tribute to his brother Justin at his funeral at the London City Cemetery in May 1998. His message, printed on a small card, read simply: "The only thing for sure is that you're free at last."

○ There is a thriving gay football scene in the Sunday League game. Village Manchester FC is Britain's fastest growing gay club. In 1999, the club will represent Manchester in the Gay Olympics.

○ Gay rights activist Peter Tatchell wrote, in an appreciation of Justin Fashanu published in *The Guardian*, that: "Justin and I know of 12 top players who are either gay or bisexual. None has followed his example of openness."

Justin Fashanu, the older brother of former Wimbledon striker John, was born on 19 February 1961 and was destined to have a headline-making life. A Barnardo's boy adopted at the age of five, he began his career at Norwich City and sprung to national prominence in 1980, at the age of 19, with a magnificent volleyed goal against Liverpool. The following year, he signed to Nottingham Forest for £1 million – but the move was a mistake. His prolific scoring rate took a nose-dive and he bore the brunt of Brian Clough's bullying style. After just two seasons, he went to Southampton and then on to Notts County, where he suffered an injury in 1983 that was to keep him out of the game for four years. Fashanu's career began a downward spiral and he rarely stayed long at his many subsequent clubs. Finally, in 1990, he admitted he was gay. From that moment on, his life was to change irrevocably. A rift opened up between him and his brother John, one that was never healed. As his career continued to decline, he was subjected to a series of tabloid allegations, including one that he had had sexual encounters with two Tory MPs. Fashanu's last years were spent coaching in the USA where, at the time of his death, he was facing allegations of assault and sexual assault on a 17-year-old boy. His return home and his subsequent suicide mark the sad demise of a player who had shown such remarkable promise.

Revered and reviled: Justin Fashanu was a man of contradictions. A gay man in a macho world, he never lived up to the early promise he showed at Norwich City, despite a great deal of talent.

Justin Fashanu was Britain's first million pound black player

THE UGLY SIDE

Football hooliganism

With England bidding to host the World Cup in 2006, the Football Association has to convince FIFA that football can 'come home' at least as safely as it did for Euro '96. The FA can justifiably claim that English football hooliganism is diminishing. Since records for football-related arrests began in 1992-93, figures show that arrests per thousand people attending football matches have fallen year on year, from 25.8 to 16.7 for the 1996-97 season, the latest figures available.

England has a reputation for hooliganism being part of its football culture. This culture has been given prominence in books such as John King's *The Football Factory*, Bill Buford's *Among The Thugs* and Dougie and Eddie Brimson's *Capital Punishment*. Although that culture has receded in recent years, with the arrival of all-seater stadiums, inflated ticket prices and the trend for 'family areas', Euro '96 was the first real test. The tournament passed off reasonably peacefully – there were 1,148 football-related arrests, although not all for hooliganism. For example, 173 arrests (15% of the total) were for ticket-touting. The successful policing of the event has encouraged England's prospects in its bid to host an even bigger football tournament – namely the World Cup in 2006.

Home Secretary Jack Straw made appeals to ticketless fans not to travel to France

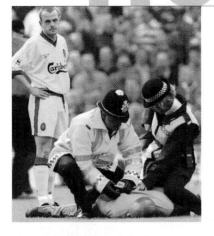

Taking action: a fan is apprehended by police after invading the pitch during Barnsley's game with Liverpool at Oakwell, on 28 March 1998.

○ Shortly before the start of the 1998 World Cup, FIFA had to step in and ask French manufacturing companies to stop the production of souvenir pocket knives.

○ Between 1992-93 and 1996-97, football-related arrests in cup and League games per season fell from 6,327 to 4,400, while attendances increased from 24,535,734 to 26,328,228.

English football hooliganism is unlikely to return to the levels of the Seventies and Eighties, but a number of incidents during the 1997-98 season showed that football violence cannot be considered a thing of the past. On 28 March, Fulham supporter Matthew Fox was beaten to death outside Gillingham's Priestfield stadium following a match. This incident overshadowed another case of hooliganism that day, when Barnsley fans invaded the pitch at Oakwell during the game with Liverpool in an attempt to attack the referee Gary Willard. Another official who was the target for violence was the assistant referee in a match at Portsmouth's Fratton Park ground on 31 January. Edward Martin, the official concerned, was attacked by a Sheffield United fan and ended up in hospital. But the story that hogged the headlines during the 1997-98 season was away from the domestic front. In October 1997, there were clashes in Rome between English fans, who had travelled to England's World Cup qualifier, and the Italian police. It was against this background, as France '98 approached, that Home Secretary Jack Straw made appeals for ticketless fans not to travel to France and, on April 30, police made a pre-emptive strike by means of a series of dawn raids on the homes of suspected troublemakers.

There were five arrests for assaults on police at, or around, football grounds during 1996-97, compared to nine arrests for the same offence in 1995-96. Here, mounted police keep a watchful eye at The Den, Millwall.

In 1996-97, there were 3,577 arrests at League matches, including 1,338 for drink-related offences

NEW LABOUR, NEW ERA?

The Government and football

Football's popularity now extends into the corridors of power. Both the Prime Minister, Tony Blair, and his deputy John Prescott are keen football fans. According to

The Football Trust, Blair is "determined to take an inclusive approach to formulating policy on the national game". In his first year in office, Blair appointed

Chelsea fan Tony Banks as Sports Minister, endorsed England's bid to host the 2006 World Cup and launched the Football Task Force.

Headed up by David Mellor, former Tory minister, Radio 5 Live *606* presenter and Chelsea fan, the Football Task Force was set up in July 1997 to deal with a number of football-related issues. The Task Force has representatives from various footballing bodies such as the

Football Association, Professional Footballers' Association and Football Supporters' Association. Its remit is far-reaching and includes a raft of initiatives from encouraging wider participation by ethnic minorities to improving disabled access to grounds. It also promises to

champion the supporter following concerns about some fans being priced out of the game, and to address the potential conflict between shareholders, players and supporters where clubs are floated on the stock exchange. Some 40 recommendations are expected in all.

In his first year in office, Tony Blair endorsed England's bid to host the 2006 World Cup

Bank on Tony: Tony Banks is a big Chelsea fan, despite representing the constituency of West Ham. However, he upset much of the country when he suggested England were "unlikely" to win the World Cup.

○ Two Barnsley MPs were so incensed by a refereeing decision last season that they tabled a motion in the House of Commons stating: "This House views with incredulity the failure of the referee to award a penalty kick to Barnsley during their FA Cup tie with Manchester United at Old Trafford on February 15th, 1998." Barnsley won the replay 3-2.

○ Alastair Campbell, Tony Blair's chief press secretary, is a keen supporter of Burnley. "I was hooked on Burnley the first time I saw them, aged four," says Campbell. "The further I've moved from the north, the more passionate my desire to see them."

In January 1998, Tony Blair held a champagne reception at Downing Street for some of Britain's top sportsmen and women. Guests of honour were the England football team. The marriage of politics and football has not always been a happy one, but Blair is keen to cement the relationship. An avid supporter of Newcastle United, he has never been one to turn down a football-related photo opportunity. Blair showed off his admirable heading ability to the press in a photocall with the then-manager of the Magpies, Kevin Keegan. More recently, Blair has been actively involved in the World Cup 2006 Campaign, following England's success at hosting Euro '96. Football's first and foremost tournament has not been staged in this country since England won the World Cup in 1966 and England faces some tough competition – Argentina, Germany, Brazil and South Africa are among the other countries making a bid.

But politics and football do not always mix. The Government and Football Supporters' Association, for example, did not see eye-to-eye over whether ticketless fans should travel to France for the 1998 World Cup. Home Secretary Jack Straw backed up a £1 million television advertising campaign telling fans not to go to France in the hope of getting a ticket on the black market. The FSA however, advised fans to ignore Government warnings and dismissed a blanket ban as "unrealistic".

On the ball: both Prime Minister Tony Blair and England manager Glenn Hoddle are well-accustomed to being in the media spotlight and under public scrutiny – and both know a golden photo opportunity when they see one.

Three 'red' teams entered the Premiership in Blair's first year – Middlesbrough, Nottingham Forest and Charlton

David Mellor

"If football calls itself the national game, then it has a responsibility to the nation to live up to that title," says David Mellor. Love him or loathe him, Mellor is an influential figure in British football. The former Tory minister currently hosts Radio 5's popular Saturday football phone-in show *Six-O-Six*, and heads the Government's Football Task Force. A Chelsea stalwart and Fulham supporter, Mellor likes to present himself as a champion of the ordinary fan.

David Mellor was born in 1949 and educated at Swanage Grammar School and Cambridge University. He practised as a lawyer before being elected as a Conservative MP for Putney, London, in 1979. A minister during the Thatcher years, he did stints at the Home Office and Foreign Office and in the National Heritage department. Mellor – and his Chelsea replica shirt – hit the headlines when his affair with a young actress was exposed in the tabloids. He then lost his seat in the 1997 general election and has since concentrated on a media career, most notably as host of 5 Live's *Six-O-Six* show. His high profile certainly gets him noticed. Some see him as a force for positive change, while others are sceptical about his ability to take on football's vested interests as head of the Task Force.

"I'm teased for abandoning Chelsea in favour of Fulham for a few seasons. But I did it for the right reasons. I couldn't stand the National Front"

All aboard: David Mellor and Premiership referee Uriah Rennie launch the Football Task Force's initiative to visit regional grounds around the country to meet and discuss issues with supporters.

○ As a journalist, Mellor writes for the *London Evening Standard* and *Guardian* newspapers, among others.

○ From 1993 to 1997, Mellor was chairman of the Sports Aid Foundation, a charity responsible for raising and distributing more than £2 million per annum to British athletes for training costs.

○ After graduating from Cambridge University, he was called to the bar in 1972 and became a QC in 1987.

Mellor is a busy man. As a broadcaster, he has in the past six years presented more than 350 programmes for BBC national radio. The show he is most commonly identified with is *Six-O-Six*, the football phone-in, which goes out early on a Saturday night and is required listening for fans. Though his style is less abrasive than predecessor Danny Baker, Mellor has proven to be popular. In 1995, he was voted BBC Radio Personality of the Year. But Mellor is not without his critics. Purists have taken him to task over swapping club allegiances – a cardinal sin in many a fan's eyes. Mellor, a Chelsea fan, admits taking his family to west London rival ground Craven Cottage to watch Fulham during the heyday of the hooligan, when racist and abusive chanting was a standard feature of Stamford Bridge terrace life. "I'm sometimes teased for abandoning Chelsea in favour of Fulham for a few seasons," says Mellor. "But I did it for the right reasons. I couldn't stand the

National Front." Racism in football has been one of the key issues which Mellor has sought to address since being appointed chairman of the Football Task Force in 1997. Its first report, published in March 1998, provided a raft of policies to combat the problem. Pro-Mellor supporters argue that he champions the fan. When the Italian police baton-charged

England fans in Rome in October 1997 for example, Mellor was vocal in his condemnation of the Italian authorities. His own son had been caught up in the trouble. Likewise, he attacked the FA over their timing of the launch of the new England kit – a month after Christmas. Whatever your views on Mellor, he appears to be fighting football's corner.

A man with his hands full: Mellor's role at the Football Task Force is to investigate and make recommendations on a wide range of football-related issues such as ticket pricing, racism and hooliganism.

THE BAD BOYS OF FOOTBALL

Player behaviour on the pitch

Roy Keane, Vinnie Jones, David Batty… football has its fair share of so-called 'hard men'. Cantona, right, upset more than just the Crystal Palace fan who was on the receiving end of his kung-fu kick during the 1996-97 season. According to a code of conduct laid down by the Premiership, Football League, Professional Footballers' Association and FA, players on the pitch have a responsibility to behave in a way that preserves the reputation of the game.

Since the majority of football games are now recorded, a player's chances of getting away with an incident are dramatically reduced. A decade ago, ITN cameras witnessed Arsenal's Paul Davis punching Southampton's Glenn Cockerill, breaking his jaw. Davis received a £3,000 fine, plus a nine-match ban. Players can now be hauled before the FA on charges relating to video evidence, as well as the referee's report. "These days, even a match between Rochdale and Hartlepool is covered so any incident is picked up on and analysed," said a PFA spokesman. In September 1997, the PFA launched a campaign under the banner 'Men Behaving Badly' to remind members of their responsibilities. "The reputation of the game is in your hands," it told players. "Make sure you communicate a positive image and encourage sportsmanship."

"The reputation of the game is in your hands," the Professional Footballers' Association

"You've got to be joking ref!": Leeds United players Lucas Radebe, David Wetherall and David Hopkin argue it out with referee Steve Dunn.

FIFA's Fair Play campaign lists a 10-point code of conduct:

1. Play to win.
2. Play fair.
3. Observe the laws of the game.
4. Respect opponents, team-mates, referees, officials and spectators.
5. Accept defeat with dignity.
6. Promote the interests of football.
7. Reject corruption, drugs, racism, violence and other dangers to our sport.
8. Help others to resist corrupting pressures.
9. Denounce those who attempt to discredit our sport.
10. Honour those who defend football's good reputation.

The 1997-98 season witnessed a series of outbursts. Fury spilled over, fists flew and players taunted their own fans as well as the referee. And it was not just spats between opposing players that made the headlines – team-mates also came to blows. At West Ham, dressing-room camaraderie was soon left behind as fellow team-mates John Moncur and Eyal Berkovic squared up to each other on the pitch. Other video nasties included clips of Patrick Vieira clashing with Moncur at the end of a sixth-round FA Cup tie at Highbury. The Frenchman had already been booked 24 times since his Arsenal debut and the ugly off-the-ball incident further consolidated his 'bad boy' reputation. Even England skipper Alan Shearer got involved in an incident with Leicester City's Neil Lennon at the end of the season. 'Shear Folly' screamed the headlines as cameras revealed the Newcastle striker apparently kicking Lennon's head as he lay on the touchline. Shearer avoided a red card but not an FA inquiry. England's number nine was charged with "an alleged breach of the rules" but with the World Cup and FA Cup final looming, the hearing returned a 'not proven' verdict. No sooner had the Shearer incident been forgotten, than Newcastle team-mate David Batty was charged for allegedly pushing the referee. With three sending-offs picked up during the 1997-98 season, he faced at least a five-match ban at the start of 1998-99.

More Magpie misery: Newcastle's Alan Shearer receives a yellow card from referee Paul Durkin during the 1998 FA Cup final against Arsenal.

In a local cup game between Tongham Youth and Hawley in 1969, the ref booked all 22 players, plus a linesman

WHISTLING IN THE DARK?

Referees

Wanted: referees on a part-time basis. Applicants must be quick-thinking, be able to deal with pressure, consent to having their decisions scrutinised by millions, expect abuse – sometimes verbal, sometimes violent – and ridicule. Successful applicants won't get a salary but will receive a £1,000 retainer for the season and £375 per game. Following a season plagued by confrontations between players, managers and referees, would you volunteer?

Following an inaugural meeting between managers and referees in March 1998, there are hopes that confrontations on the pitch can be lessened in the future. One of the major concerns facing the Referees' Association is that the game has become so high profile that the pressure on their members is becoming almost intolerable. During the 1997-98 season, there were a number of highly publicised refereeing decisions tried by TV. In September 1997, Steve Lodge was officiating in a Premiership match between Bolton and Everton when he ruled that a header from Bolton's Gerry Taggart didn't cross the Everton line. The game finished 0-0 but TV replays showed that a goal should have been given. Come May, Bolton were relegated to the First Division on inferior goal difference – to Everton.

All the money involved in the game means that referees are now under much more pressure

Fit for the job: fitness counts when it comes to refereeing, which is why the World Cup officials were put through their paces before the finals. Former FIFA referee Keith Hackett says: "A referee 50 yards away can give the right decision but it won't be accepted, while one 10 yards away can give a decision that is wrong but is accepted by the players."

○ A total of 67 match officials (34 referees and 33 assistant referees) took part in the 1998 World Cup finals.

○ England's representative in the 1998 World Cup was referee Paul Durkin, a 42-year-old housing association manager from Portland, Dorset. As the 'fourth official' at Euro '96, he came on as a 'sub' for injured referee Dermot Gallagher during the tournament.

○ A recent idea debated by the FIFA task Force 2000 was for two referees per match. In Spain, experiments have even been carried out with three referees officiating a match.

In 1997-98, referees were increasingly coming under attack for their decisions. Gerald Ashby's dismissal of Tottenham's Stephen Clemence for diving in the FA Cup tie with Barnsley was criticised by team-mate Les Ferdinand as "the worst decision I have ever seen in all my years in football – and I've played park football". Ferdinand was fined £2,000 for his criticism. "The game is so important now with all the money involved that referees are under much more pressure," says Arthur Smith of the Referees' Association. "An official must come up to the standards set, but mistakes can be made." The Premiership assigns former referees to assess each performance – before the start of the 1997-98 season, one referee was 'relegated' from the Premiership when he failed to meet the points quota. But clubs are keen for referees to go full time and for contentious decisions to be put to a video replay. The FA's director of refereeing, Ken Ridden, concedes that full-time referees "would be fitter, though they shouldn't need encouragement". Television replays have been rejected by FIFA, though Smith says his members are "not averse to modern technology". An issue of more concern to referees today is the increase in violence and threatening behaviour from both players and fans, a fact brought home when a fan attacked linesman Edward Martin at Fratton Park in 1997-98, putting him in hospital.

Red alert: the highly respected Uriah Rennie became the first black referee in the Premiership in 1997-98.

In 1997-98, assistant referee Wendy Toms became the first female match official in the Premiership

A REF FOR ALL SEASONS

David Elleray

David Elleray, spokesman for the Premiership's referees, finished the 1997-98 season mid-table, after issuing 61 yellow cards (and four red ones) in 18 games – an average of 3.39 cards a game. A schoolmaster by profession, Elleray is respected for his knowledge and input into the game. He began his refereeing career 30 years ago, progressing via the local leagues to Football League linesman in 1983 and referee in 1986. In 1992, he made the FIFA referees list.

While it may not be everyone's dream job, refereeing certainly seems to suit David Elleray. He takes a lot of pride in his work and is unafraid of putting forward suggestions on how the game can be improved. At the start of the 1997-98 season, for example, he proposed the notion of a 'sin bin' on Sky TV, similar to the one that operates in rugby league. Players are instantly dismissed from the field for 10 minutes rather than receiving a yellow card – a system that Elleray believes is fairer. The function of the referee, according to Elleray, is to act as a facilitator. "Players and fans enjoy football because, unlike cricket or American football, football is almost non-stop action. The essential attraction and integrity of the game would be lost if we were forever stopping to review incidents."

"Football is almost non-stop action. The attraction and integrity of the game would be lost if we kept stopping to review incidents"

Split-second decision-making: David Elleray waves play on as West Ham's Rio Ferdinand challenges Crystal Palace's Bruce Dyer for the ball.

○ Newcastle midfielder David Batty was charged with misconduct by the FA on 22 May 1998 for pushing David Elleray after being sent off for allegedly punching Blackburn Rover's Garry Flitcroft.

○ David Elleray has appeared at Wembley as a referee, linesman and reserve official and has officiated in over 30 countries. He is 39 years old, single and lives in Harrow, Middlesex.

At heart, David Elleray is a pragmatist rather than a perfectionist. Although he thinks that the 'beautiful game' can be improved upon, he is ambivalent about some of the measures currently being touted. For example, while he agrees that the idea of full-time professional referees seems attractive, he is not convinced that it will improve the quality of decision-making. As regards accusations of inconsistency among refs in the Premiership, Elleray points out

that: "Referees are human beings not robots. However, there should be a general consistency about important decision-making, especially in relation to disciplinary sanctions. That's why all 19 referees on the Premier League list meet regularly." It's all a question of balance. "What's more important," he asks, "open, flowing, non-stop action with human error as part-and-parcel or a quest for the perfect decision every time, regardless of time and delay?"

World stage: Elleray made the FIFA referees list in 1992. He has officiated at Euro '96 and World Cup friendlies, such as the Germany v Brazil game below, but has not yet made it to a finals.

There are 19 Premiership referees including David Elleray, and they meet six or seven times during the season

PLAYING BY THE RULES

Changes in the laws of the game

For decades, the many rules of football remained largely untouched. But in recent years an increasing number of amendments, emanating from FIFA headquarters in Zurich, have affected how the game is now played. The route from an idea to FIFA law is a convoluted process, and many potential changes tried out never make it to fruition. But as Joao Havelange, former FIFA president, says: "The day football becomes perfect, is the day the game dies."

Task Force 2000 is an ad hoc committee that was set up by FIFA in response to some of the criticisms levelled at the standard of play and officiating at Italia '90. New laws such as making tackling from behind a red card offence, and alterations such as the new interpretation of offside and the extension of the back-pass rule, are all the result of Task Force 2000 initiatives. Many other rules and amendments have been considered but not initiated. In the run-up to the 1994 World Cup in the USA, FIFA was said to be considering making the goals higher and even splitting the matches into quarters rather than halves. More recently, in March 1998, it was agreed that the Football Association should conduct experiments in Jersey which would allow a free kick to be advanced by 10 yards.

Since France '98, a tackle from behind now constitutes serious foul play and referees are instructed to take strong action

Golden opportunity: Germany's Oliver Bierhoff scores the first ever 'golden goal' against the Czech Republic during the Euro '96 final at Wembley.

○ The yellow card was introduced in the 1970 World Cup in Mexico.

○ Changes to the rules that have been considered by FIFA include:

- Kick-ins instead of throw-ins – tests were carried out in the second division in Belgium.
- Time-out – the American idea, used in basketball, was tried out in the Women's World Cup in Sweden in 1995.

Two of the most significant rule changes in recent years have been the introduction of the golden goal and the FIFA crackdown on tackling from behind. Since France '98, a tackle from behind now constitutes serious foul play – punishable by a red card – and referees are instructed to take strong action against players who endanger the safety of an opponent. The rule change follows advice given by the FIFA Technical and Sports Medical Committees regarding the alarming number of injuries sustained by players

Too close to call?: tough tackling is an expected part of the game but with the introduction of the red card for all tackles from behind, will players be more cautious and be forced to hold back?

as a result of such tackles. The golden goal, introduced in Euro '96, was also used in France '98 and means that a game that goes into extra time is decided by the first goal scored. The scheme has had its fair share of advocates and detractors. Referee David Will, a member of Task Force 2000, said: "It is somehow artificial for a match to end suddenly. It would be better to play out the full length of extra time but the first goal during this period could count double." But then, would it be as exciting?

UEFA courted controversy at Euro '96 for bending the rules on drafting in new players for an injury-struck Germany

WHEN THE GOING GETS TOUGH...

Player-managers

Being in the managerial hot seat is one thing. But being a manager *and* continuing a playing career is another matter entirely. Yet player-managers are becoming a permanent fixture. Chris Waddle, pictured left, was appointed player-manager at Burnley at the beginning of the 1997-98 season. The Clarets avoided relegation by the narrowest of margins – and Waddle left after just 10 months. Making the transition from player to coach is never easy, combining the two can be heaven – or hell.

"After what has been a difficult season, the club and Chris Waddle have decided to part company," said Burnley chairman Frank Teasdale, in typical football speak. But Waddle was not the only player-manager to find the going tough. Stuart Pearce vacated the Nottingham Forest hot seat after five fraught months as caretaker manager during the 1996-97 season. He may well have been a prime motivator on the pitch but he admitted that he was way out of his depth when it came to the management game. It is a temptation on the club's part to propel fans' favourites into player-management. Yet the marriage can prove to be far from happy. Mark Hateley, an ex-England team-mate of Pearce's and Waddle's, was drafted in to resuscitate Division Three's Hull City. The Tigers finished third from bottom.

Making the transition from player to coach is never easy. It can be heaven – or hell

Who'd be a player-manager?: Crystal Palace's Attilio Lombardo, who could barely speak English, struggled at Selhurst Park.

○ Former England and Chelsea striker Kerry Dixon was appointed player-manager at strife-torn Doncaster Rovers one hour before their first game of the 1996-97 season. The injury-struck Dixon left the club at the start of the following season.

○ 'Hard man' of football Vinnie Jones has managerial aspirations. A player-coach at Queen's Park Rangers, Jones says: "That's part of the reason I came to Rangers. I love the responsibility of working with players."

Player-managers are not restricted to the lower divisions. The Premiership also has its fair share. Chelsea, for example, employed not one but two last season. Out went Ruud Gullit – in came Gianluca Vialli. South of the river, Crystal Palace appointed Attilio Lombardo as player-manager in March 1998. "It was a shock," said the Italian. "After I had agreed, I felt as if I'd been run over by a lorry." The Eagles' experiment proved to be short-lived – Lombardo lasted less than two months.

Of course, being a player-manager presents some intriguing problems. Not least, the dilemma of do you drop yourself or your team-mates? Gullit was criticised for bringing himself on as a sub in important games – then making some defensive howlers. Sammy McIlroy and Danny Wilson have both paid their dues as player-managers at Macclesfield and Barnsley. However, real success only came calling after the two had hung up their boots and concentrated on the coaching.

Rovers non-return: In 1996-97, his first season as player-manager at Tranmere Rovers, John Aldridge scored a total of 20 goals in League and Cup competitions. He called it a day as a player at the end of the 1997-98 season.

In his first season as player-manager at Tranmere Rovers, John Aldridge was the club's highest goalscorer

JUST SAY NO

Drugs and drink

With the transition of footballers from mere players to media darlings, the pressures they face are increasing. In 1997-98, just three players tested positive for drugs. That compares to 12 in 1994-95 (the first season when tests for so-called recreational drugs like cannabis and cocaine were included), seven in 1995-96 and five in 1996-97. The figures may appear to be declining, but they do not take into consideration alcohol, arguably one of the biggest temptations.

As well as illegal drugs, the FA's testing team also tests for alcohol. Using a breathalyser similar to that used by police to test motorists, the team has been checking for alcohol abuse for the last three years. The tests are intended to act as an early warning system. If a player tests positive, it is not a cause for disciplinary action in itself but the club doctor will be informed. Evidence suggests that performance-enhancing drugs have not taken hold of football – the danger comes from 'recreational' drugs, such as cannabis and cocaine, and alcohol, all temptations for today's footballlers who have achieved pop star status. Paul Merson, above right, admitted alcohol and cocaine addiction back in 1994 but has since made a full recovery and was in the England squad for France '98.

Carried out under the auspices of the FA and Sports Council, 600 professional players are tested for illegal substances every season

Tell-tale signs: random drug testing in football is now carried out at all professional clubs on a regular basis and at all levels.

The most famous football player ever to test positive for drugs is Argentinian Diego Maradona. The man with the 'Hand of God' famously tested positive for drugs after Argentina's 2-1 win over Nigeria during USA '94. He had taken an illegal cocktail in a bid to enhance his performance. He was also banned from football for 15 months in March 1991 after testing positive for cocaine while playing for Napoli in Italy.

Carried out under the auspices of the FA and Sports Council, 600 professional players are tested for illegal substances every season. Samples are taken from footballers either at the training ground or after matches and every club receives at least one random visit a season. The FA and the Professional Footballers' Association take the problems of addiction seriously and carry out numerous campaigns to educate younger players in particular,

emphasising the risk not only to their health but to their careers, too. In December 1997, Charlton Athletic's young defender Jamie Stuart was sacked by his club after testing positive for cocaine. Charlton were keen to bring home the message that "drugs won't be tolerated at this club", as a deterrent to young, aspiring players. As long as clubs continue to get tough, there are hopes that all abuse can be eradicated from the game.

Back to work: After his 15-month ban following the 1994 World Cup, Diego Maradona returned to football with Argentina's Boca Junior side on 7 october 1995.

BEERS, CHEERS AND TEARS

The Paul Gascoigne story

There is no doubting that Paul Gascoigne is a football genius, albeit a flawed one. Few players possess his prodigious talent. And, sadly, few players have courted as much controversy. His creative play on the park was always matched by his clowning antics off it and in May 1998, the midfield maestro that enraptured the world at Italia '90 was dropped from the England World Cup squad. His omission sparked a nationwide debate – is this the end of the road for Gazza?

The most talented England player of his generation, Paul Gascoigne's career has spanned more highs and lows than most footballers. At 31, Gazza should have been at his peak, playing on the World Cup stage at France '98 and displaying the sort of ability that marked him out at Italia '90 and Euro '96. Instead, Glenn Hoddle decided that Gazza had not done enough to warrant a place in the final 22. Kebabs, cigarettes and late-night drinking with celebrity mates were not mentioned by the England coach, but probably contributed to the Middlesbrough player's lack of match fitness. It was all a far cry from Gazza's days at Spurs, when he won the hearts of the White Hart Lane crowd with his wayward genius. But even then the joy turned to sorrow when, in the 1991 FA Cup final, a reckless challenge left him with a torn cruciate ligament.

Few players possess Paul Gascoigne's prodigious talent. And, sadly, few players have courted as much controversy

Star pals: Gascoigne's predilection for nights out with celebrity mates, such as Danny Baker, left, and Chris Evans, centre, provided the tabloids with plenty of headlines.

○ Paul Gascoigne signed to Tottenham Hotspur in 1988 at the age of 21 for £2 million.

○ Gascoigne made his Middlesbrough debut as a substitute in the 1998 Coca-Cola Cup final on 29 March.

○ After his omission from the squad for France '98, Gazza admitted being drunk the night before the final squad was announced. He also missed the birth of his son because he was out drinking with his mates.

As tears go by: Gazza bids the fans farewell after receiving a booking in the 1990 World Cup semi-final against Germany. According to England coach Glenn Hoddle, Gazza also broke down when he was told that he was not going to France '98.

From Tottenham, Paul Gascoigne moved to Lazio in 1992. A damaged cruciate ligament had kept him out of the game for 15 months and his career at the Italian club was uneven, though the Romans adored him. The ups and downs continued. In the domestic papers, stories surfaced about niggling injuries, public spats with partner Sheryl, ballooning weight, and boozy nights out with Gateshead mate Jimmy 'Five Bellies'. In the Italian press however, a fully fit Gascoigne still warranted columns of purple prose. Then, in January 1994, Gazza's career took yet another dive when he broke his leg in training. A year later, the midfielder moved yet again, this time to Scottish club Rangers. By now a pattern seemed to be emerging. For every moment of brilliance that Gazza displayed on the pitch, he'd also provide moments off it when he would press the self-destruct button. Drunken brawls and the winding up of Celtic fans with 'flute-playing' were juxtaposed with astounding examples of individual skill, as witnessed in his hat-trick against Aberdeen that won Rangers their eighth consecutive title. And there was *that* sublime goal, scored against Scotland in Euro '96, when the world once again fell and worshipped at his talented feet. On the whole, Euro '96 saw the return to form that Gazza had displayed during Italia '90. Such memories resurfaced again in the build-up to France '98, only this time the unfit Gazza lost his chance to show his undoubted skill in the World Cup arena.

Paul Gascoigne was Rangers' record signing when he was bought for £4.3 million in July 1995

SQUARE DEALS

Coverage of the game on television

Increased revenue from television broadcasting rights has had a major impact on the game – both in terms of filling club coffers and, increasingly, determining when fixtures are played. BSkyB in particular, has transformed the fortunes of English football in recent years with its live coverage of League games. Now, with the dawning of digital TV and the increasing recognition of the money to be made in televising football, the issue of pay-per-view is increasingly under debate.

On 29 May 1998, the chairmen of the Premiership clubs rejected a proposal by BSkyB to introduce experimental pay-per-view coverage of matches in the 1998-99 season. Manchester United supremo Martin Edwards was a keen advocate of the scheme but BSkyB's plans had met with opposition from Peter Leaver, the Premiership's chief executive. Leaver, who had headed the committee in negotiations with Sky, said: "We're determined to act in the best interests of the game and its fans. We want to develop broadcasting arrangements which secure the right future for English football." Although PPV may be off the agenda now, it is too attractive a proposition and money-spinner for the leading clubs to ignore further down the line. If it does come into force, viewers will have to pay per game.

With the dawning of digital TV, the issue of pay-per-view is increasingly under debate

Pulling in the punters: nearly 40,000 pubs and clubs now show live football action on TV screens – most of it courtesy of Sky Sport's satellite coverage.

○ When BSkyB first won the exclusive rights to broadcast live coverage of Premiership games in 1992, the announcement was met with a hail of protest. Now, four-and-a-half million households subscribe.

○ Sky's current deal with the Premiership is worth £670 million over four years.

○ In June 1998, the new Scottish Premier League announced a £45 million four-year deal with Sky for coverage of 30 matches each year from the 1998-99 season. New kick-off times of 6.05pm were agreed.

Much to many people's surprise, World Cup '98 exploded onto our TV screens on two terrestrial channels – ITV and BBC – rather than on satellite. Under the terms of the 1996 Broadcasting Act, the World Cup finals are a sporting 'listed event' and are therefore protected from live coverage by subscription broadcasters. The FA Cup final and Scottish FA Cup final are also included on the list. And terrestrial television has not been entirely squeezed out of the picture when it comes to live coverage of football games. In 1997, ITV – in conjunction with Sky – bought the rights to coverage of the FA Cup until 2001 and it has exclusive rights to show live action from the European Champions League until the year 2000. The BBC meanwhile, negotiates on a season-by-season basis with individual clubs to show live coverage of UEFA Cup fixtures, but it still owns the rights to broadcast the finals of the UEFA Cup, European Super Cup and the Cup Winners Cup. Channel 5 also discovered that live coverage of games is a sure-fire way of winning the ratings war. In 1997-98, Channel 5 followed the European fortunes of Chelsea in the Cup Winners Cup – now it has secured the rights to the home qualifying rounds of Euro 2000. Meanwhile, fans of Italian football can still enjoy their regular fix of Sunday afternoon live coverage, courtesy of Channel 4.

Your match commentators tonight are: ITV's Ian St John, left, and Clive Tyldesley are all smiles now, but can the terrestrial channels keep competing in the digital age?

World Cup '98 was watched by around 37 billion television viewers

FAST FORWARD TO THE FUTURE

The impact of technology on the game

If Sky presenter Andy Gray and his technological wizardry had been around more than 30 years ago, the dispute over Geoff Hurst's goal in the 1966 World Cup final may well have been settled conclusively. The introduction of sophisticated technology such as the miniature goal line camera, right, and Sky's Virtual Replay box of tricks, is altering the face of football. From referees to players, from stadiums to equipment, the scientists are working overtime.

It is not just television coverage that is enjoying technological advances, other elements of the game are also subject to new innovations. The humble football boot has undergone a dazzling range of technological breakthroughs. Adidas reports that there are 50 stages in the design and production process of a boot, from research to distribution. And the work is not just carried out by boffins tucked away in laboratories. Former Liverpool and Middlesbrough striker Craig Johnston played a key role in bringing the Predator, one of the boot names of today, to life. "I have a bit of a boot fetish – I used to clean the boots at Middlesbrough Football Club so I learned a lot about boots early on," he says. The traxion sole, which has blades rather than studs, and the rubber 'fins' and 'jets' are designed to help swerve and power.

hi-tech

The official FIFA World Cup '98 match ball went through a number of tests, including being shot 2,000 times against a steel plate at 50 km/h

Foot technology: the Predator boot went through hundreds of designs, materials and prototypes. The original Predator was introduced during USA '94. The latest version, the Accelerator, was seen on the pitch at France '98.

○ Premiership referees and assistants now use electronic flags which allow the assistant to 'buzz' the referee if he misses a flag signal.

○ During France '98, the official World Cup Web site handled as many as 25 to 50 million visitors per day.

○ Hi-tech scientists have pioneered the first ever robot football teams. In 1997, more than 40 sides took part in a five-a-side RoboCup in Nagoya, Japan, as part of a conference on artificial intelligence.

Watch with Wenger: a number of Premiership
grounds, including Arsenal's Highbury, have
installed 'Jumbotrons' – giant video screens
which show the game as it is played plus
replays, team news and interviews at half-time.

Along with the boot, the ball has been continually updated and reinvented since its first incarnation as an inflated pig's bladder. The Tricolore, the official FIFA World Cup France '98 match ball, boasted "enhanced accuracy and increased energy return" due to a new material, syntactic foam, which is made up of gas-filled, individually-closed micro-balloons "which return energy equally to the ball's 32 panels". Adidas, the designers of the Tricolore, developed the new ball at its Global Technology Centre in Scheinfeld, Germany. It went through a number of stringent tests, ensuring that it met with FIFA requirements, including being shot 2,000 times against a steel plate at 50 kilometres per hour. Meanwhile, in Holland, scientists have produced a retractable pitch – at Vitesse Arnhem's new £47.2m Monnikenhuize stadium. The pitch is electronically rolled up for concerts, so that it remains in pristine condition for the next football fixture.

Dutch side Vitesse Arnhem's retractable pitch is the first of its kind in the world

THEY THINK IT'S ALL OVER...

Sky's state-of-the-art technology

"Stay with me, I'll prove this one yet..." The Snickers ad campaign may have been taking the mickey out of Andy Gray's obsession with disputing dodgy decisions, but Sky's Virtual Replay equipment has serious implications for the way football could be adjudicated in the future. The technology, originally developed in Israel for tracking missiles, turns video frames into 3-D images and gives football commentators the opportunity to consider when a goal is truly a goal.

Two incidents in the 1997-98 season involving disputed goals were analysed by Sky's Virtual Replay system. Although the outcome was hypothetical in the sense that it did not reverse either of the original decisions given by the referee, for the two clubs involved – Bolton Wanderers and Stevenage Borough – the refereeing decisions to disallow and give a goal respectively had real repercussions in the League and FA Cup. In the case of the former, newly promoted Bolton had a goal disallowed by referee Stephen Lodge in an early League game against Everton. The match ended in a draw and Bolton gained just one point. At the end of the season, Bolton were involved in a relegation battle with Everton. Both clubs finished with 40 points but Bolton's inferior goal difference saw them relegated.

Viewers at home can watch a Virtual Replay reconstruction of a real-life incident through the eyes of the referee – or anyone else on the pitch

The virtual truth: Sky's Virtual Replay technology clearly shows that the disallowed goal from Bolton's Gerry Taggart crossed the line and should have counted.

○ Virtual Replay was originally developed in Israel for military purposes – to track and target hi-tech missiles.

○ It takes approximately 20 minutes to convert a real-match incident into a Virtual Replay reconstruction.

○ ORAD, the company that developed Virtual Replay, is currently working on VirtuaLive Soccer – a system that can simulate football highlights over the Internet.

Virtual Replay is an advanced presentation graphic system that converts real-life video action into 3D computer-generated representations. Players are positioned by using real co-ordinates, such as the goal line or penalty box. Once in place, the angle from which you can view the virtual scene can be moved around at will. For viewers at home, this means that they can watch a Virtual Replay reconstruction of an incident in a real-life game through the eyes of the referee, referee's assistant, striker or goalkeeper – indeed, anyone on the pitch. The set of three graphic images, right, were used as evidence that Alan Shearer's goal against Stevenage Borough in the fourth round FA Cup replay did *not* cross the keeper's line. The England striker's header in the 16th minute sent the Magpies on their way to a 2-1 victory and the next round of the Cup after match officials ruled that the ball *had* crossed the line before defender Mark Smith cleared it. After seeing Sky's footage, Borough boss Paul Fairclough said: "It was an amazing goal-line clearance which Mark [Smith] will never get the credit for. Sooner or later, we are going to have to take advantage of modern technology because mistakes or human error are costing clubs millions."

According to Virtual Replay evidence, Geoff Hurst's goal in the 1966 World Cup final didn't go in

FOOTBALL GOES POP

The role of music

It is indicative of how trendy football has become in this country that when Chris Evans asked the group All Saints what football clubs they supported, they quickly answered: "Arsenal", "Arsenal", "Spurs" and "Arsenal", Shaznay being the odd one out. It would be hard to imagine Salt-N-Pepa providing such a quick response if quizzed about their favourite NFL team. What began as a light flirtation between soccer and pop in the Sixties has developed into a number one hit.

Back in the 1960s, Cilla was declaring her love of Liverpool and the Dave Clark Five were pledging their allegiance to Tottenham – the pop and soccer band-wagon was set in motion. But it was the following decade, in the glam era, that footballers began to reciprocate. Stars like Charlie George, Stan Bowles and George Best were seen sporting the same feather-cut hairstyles as David Bowie and the Bay City Rollers. George Best was not just a star player on the pitch, he was a pin-up star off the pitch. But it wasn't until the advent of the 1990 World Cup that football and music became a real hit. While the nation shed tears alongside Paul Gascoigne, Pavarotti crooned Nessun Dorma. At the same time, the first decent pop football song emerged with New Order and the England squad's World In Motion.

The battle for the Premiership title moved to the recording studio with Manchester United's Calypso and Arsenal's Hot Stuff

The spice is right: Victoria Adams and David Beckham ready to seal a deal between the pop and soccer worlds.

The 10 biggest League club hits to 1998 were:

Team	Title	Highest position	Weeks in chart	Year
Manchester United	Come On You Reds	1	15	1994
Liverpool	Anfield Rap	3	6	1988
Liverpool	Pass And Move	4	5	1996
Chelsea	Blue Is The Colour	5	12	1972
Tottenham Hotspur	Ossie's Dream	5	8	1981
Manchester United	Move, Move, Move	6	11	1996
Manchester United	We're Gonna Do It Again	6	6	1995
Leeds United	Leeds United	10	10	1972
Manchester United	Sing Up For The Champions	12	4	1997
Manchester United	Glory Glory Man United	13	5	1983

Hit singles: the battle for the honour to provide France '98 with a song went to former Smith Johnny Marr and Bunnyman Ian McCulloch (featuring the Spice Girls), but Baddiel and Skinner, with The Lightning Seeds, were back in the charts with a revamped Three Lions.

The forthcoming wedding of Posh Spice and David Beckham should keep the tabloids busy for the next year. The couple's engagement was the story of 1997/98 and the press lapped it up, even blaming Beckham's poor performance against Portugal at Wembley on the fact that his fiancé was playing in the arena next door.

Football's starry profile last season was also accompanied by rumours that the Gallagher brothers were going to take up a shirt sponsorship deal with Manchester City and, while on tour in Australia, a disgruntled Noel claiming that he would buy the club on his return to England. Liverpool even managed to form their own group of Spice Boys with Redknapp, McManaman, Fowler and Owen. The Spice Girls returned the favour when Mel C wore a Liverpool shirt on Top of the Pops.

The year of 1998 has also marked the return of the club anthem, after a relatively lean patch. The battle for the Premiership title moved to the recording studio with Manchester United's The United Calypso and Arsenal's remake of Donna Summer's Hot Stuff. The only thing that remains to happen is for a footballer to follow the soap star path of forging out a new career as a pop idol.

Glenn Hoddle is the only England manager to have had a hit single – Diamond Lights also starred Chris Waddle

IT'S SHOWTIME!

The art of goal celebration

Back in the days of baggy shorts and the maximum wage, goal celebrations were a quiet affair – a couple of pats on the back were deemed sufficient. The Nineties changed all that and when, in March 1998, Arsenal striker Christopher Wreh followed his stunning strike against Bolton with an even more stunning double-backwards somersault, he confirmed that goal celebrations had moved into a new era. And that era has cast the football shirt in a new role.

Originality and creativity are key components of the Nineties-style goal celebration – flair and humour are optional, but welcome, extras. It was Middlesbrough's flamboyant striker Fabrizio Ravanelli who can be credited with popularising the shirt celebration.

When he pulled up his shirt to cover his face, he launched a thousand imitations. Variations on a theme included lifting up your shirt to reveal another underneath sporting a subliminal message, tossing your shirt into the crowd, and even taking your shirt off only to find an exact replica hidden underneath. The football shirt phenomenon took off in such a big way that players didn't even wait for the excuse of a goal to take part – Chelsea's Dennis Wise sent a heartfelt message of hope to benched team-mate Gianluca Vialli in the days when Gullit still ruled.

Christopher Wreh's stunning double-backwards somersault confirmed that goal celebrations had moved into a new era

Player protest: Liverpool's Robbie Fowler turned his goal celebration against Norway's SK Brann into a public display of support for the sacked Liverpool dockers.

○ After scoring an impressive equalizer against Coventry in the quarter-final of the 1997-98 FA Cup, Sheffield United's Marcelo Santos Cipriano threw his shirt into the crowd, only to reveal another identical one underneath. Whether the Brazilian star had prepared himself for the possibility of scoring a hat-trick has never been ascertained.

○ Classic goal celebrations of the past include Faustino Asprilla's shirt-on-the-corner flag dance, the Cameroons' Roger Milla and his World Cup shimmy, Brazil's baby-cradling and Aylesbury United's duck walk.

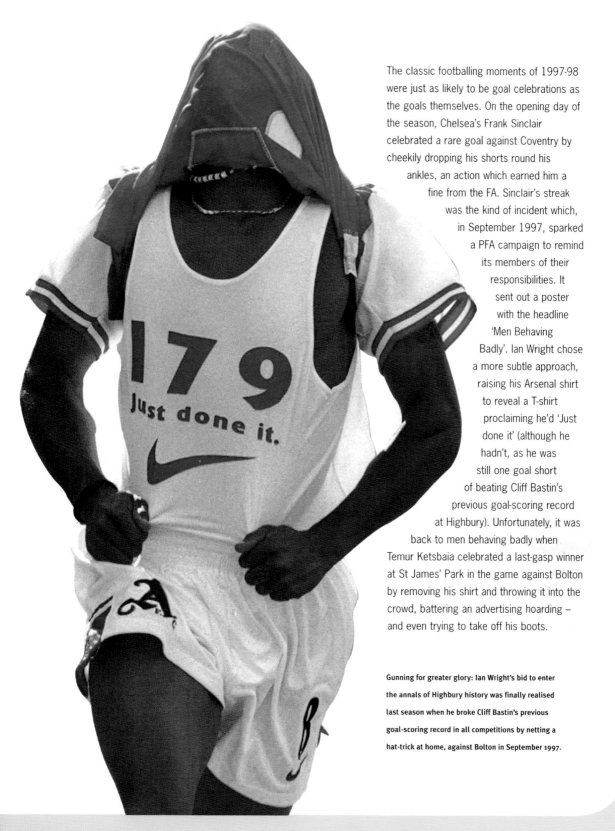

The classic footballing moments of 1997-98 were just as likely to be goal celebrations as the goals themselves. On the opening day of the season, Chelsea's Frank Sinclair celebrated a rare goal against Coventry by cheekily dropping his shorts round his ankles, an action which earned him a fine from the FA. Sinclair's streak was the kind of incident which, in September 1997, sparked a PFA campaign to remind its members of their responsibilities. It sent out a poster with the headline 'Men Behaving Badly'. Ian Wright chose a more subtle approach, raising his Arsenal shirt to reveal a T-shirt proclaiming he'd 'Just done it' (although he hadn't, as he was still one goal short of beating Cliff Bastin's previous goal-scoring record at Highbury). Unfortunately, it was back to men behaving badly when Temur Ketsbaia celebrated a last-gasp winner at St James' Park in the game against Bolton by removing his shirt and throwing it into the crowd, battering an advertising hoarding – and even trying to take off his boots.

Gunning for greater glory: Ian Wright's bid to enter the annals of Highbury history was finally realised last season when he broke Cliff Bastin's previous goal-scoring record in all competitions by netting a hat-trick at home, against Bolton in September 1997.

Ian Wright is Arsenal's all-time leading goalscorer, having netted 185 goals by the end of the 1997-98 season

THE BEAUTIFUL GAME

Football's supermodels

It's not just the pitch but the catwalk that players are gracing nowadays, and it's not just defenders but heads that are turning. The era of the footballer supermodel is truly upon us. West Ham and ex-Queen's Park Rangers striker Trevor Sinclair, right, has turned out for designer Hugo Boss, while Bolton's Dean Holdsworth has strutted his stuff for high street chain Top Man. That's why the model scout is just as likely to be talent-spotting on the pitch as the football scout.

Of course, there's nothing new about good-looking footballers promoting fashion and beauty products. Long before Manchester United's David Beckham landed the contract as the latest Brylcreem Boy, Denis Compton, the Arsenal footballer and England cricket hero of the Forties and Fifties, was also sporting greased-back locks. Fastforwarding to the Sixties, another United favourite, George Best – 'the fifth Beatle' – was lucky enough to have model good looks as well as a collection of model girlfriends. Meanwhile, in the Nineties, the L'Oreal-enhanced and Cerruti-promoting Gallic good looks of Spurs' David Ginola may have been missing from the fields of France '98 but they were no doubt still adorning the bedroom walls of many teenage girls – and their mothers, too.

The model scout is just as likely to be talent-spotting on the pitch as the football scout

The Wright stuff: Arsenal striker Ian Wright models designer gear at the 1997 Premier Menswear fashion show.

○ Before the start of the 1997-98 season, the entire Norwich City team took time off from the training pitch to model the club's new strip, created by top fashion designer Bruce Oldfield.

○ Nottingham and London fashion designer Paul Smith, who designed the official Euro '96 suits for the England team, was also responsible for England's stylish look for France '98.

○ Rangers' top scorer last season, Marco Negri, stripped off his kit to model Calvin Klein underwear at the Cameron House hotel in Scotland.

There's a theory that says footballers are the pop stars of the Nineties. Back in the Seventies and Eighties, players were renowned for their dodgy haircuts and even dodgier sartorial sense. Now even Barry Venison – he of the archetypal footballer's haircut and expensive yet tasteless designer jacket – knows how to look good on TV. The model footballer is perfectly in keeping with the game's current glamorous profile. Footballers can command a fee of around £2,000 for a single modelling appearance. "Because football is so popular and watched by so many people these days, footballers are considered to be celebrities, not just sportsmen," says Brad Parsons, who has represented the likes of Alan Shearer, Jamie Redknapp and Stan Collymore. "This makes them perfect to endorse a product or attract publicity to a catwalk show. On top of that, so many of them are good-looking." In fact, footballers seem to take to the catwalk with ease – perhaps it's down to the fact that they are used to being the focus of everyone's attention. Among those parading on the London catwalk at the 1997 Premier Menswear fashion show, held at Olympia, were Trevor Sinclair, Ian Wright and a host of footballing names, while Anfield team-mates David James, Jamie Redknapp and Phil Babb have all worked as Armani fashion models in the past.

When Jason plays, people watch: Liverpool's Jason McAteer appeared in an ad campaign for Head & Shoulders dandruff shampoo in 1998.

THE MODEL FOOTBALLER

David Ginola

So who saved Tottenham Hotspur from relegation in 1997-98? It certainly wasn't Darren 'Sicknote' Anderton or the man from Italy, Nicola Berti. It wasn't even Jurgen 'Flipper' Klinsmann (so nicknamed in Germany because the ball comes off his shins like a pinball) despite four goals against Wimbledon. No, the hero of White Hart Lane was a man with long flowing locks, sultry eyes and smooth moves, a man as at ease on the catwalk as on the pitch – Frenchman David Ginola.

Without David Ginola, Spurs would have sunk. With David Ginola, your hair could be transformed. Of all the supermodels walking off the pitch and onto the catwalk, David Ginola is the biggest star. His Gallic good looks and cool charisma have seen him strut his stuff at the fashion shows in Paris and get star billing in ad-land. Born in Gassin in France on 25 January 1967, the 5ft 11in hunk weighs 83 kilos, has a golf handicap of 10 and is also married with two children. This latter piece of information may prove unwelcome to the thousands of women around the world who have been wooed by his charms – and yet have never seen a game of soccer in their lives. He was first seen in Britain in the Renault ad, but it was the L'Oreal shampoo advert that made him a heart-throb with the women of America.

The hero of White Hart Lane was a man with long flowing locks, sultry eyes and smooth moves, a man as at ease on the catwalk as on the pitch

Gallic magic: in his first season at White Hart Lane, Ginola wooed the fans on the pitch with his dazzling skills, and off the pitch with his dazzling good looks.

○ Ginola won the French Cup with Paris St-Germain in 1993 and 1995 and the League Cup with the team in 1995. In the 1993-94 season he was voted Player of the Year by the players in the French First Division.

○ Before the World Cup, and despite not making the French squad, David Ginola starred in a number of glossy magazines, including *Hello!* and French *Marie Claire* – in which he expressed the opinion that it was natural for women to be attracted to sweat and bristles.

Hair today, gone tomorrow: Kevin Keegan bought David Ginola for £2.6 million in December 1995. But when Kenny Dalglish took over at the club in 1997, the Frenchman was sold to Spurs for £2.5 million.

April 1998 was a pretty good month for David Ginola. His maverick genius was on full display when Spurs hosted his former team, Newcastle United, at the Lane. Ginola, hailed by one set of fans whenever he got the ball – and roundly booed by the other – created two crucial goals during the game – arguably those that kept Tottenham up.

Off the pitch, Ginola found himself the attention of Newsweek, which had dispatched its Paris correspondent to check him out. News of his prowess on the pitch (and the French national coach's reluctance to acknowledge his skills) and his supermodel status made him the talk of the town.

Despite a telephone call from Spurs manager Christian Gross to French coach Aime Jacquet, recommending Ginola for France's World Cup squad, the French manager failed to be won over. The French could never forgive Ginola for giving the ball away in the last minute of a crucial World Cup qualifier against Bulgaria in Paris in 1993 – Kostadinov scored and Bulgaria rather than France qualified for the USA. After 17 caps with France, Ginola's national career was over. Fortunately for his adoring female fans, viewers were not to be deprived of the gorgeous Ginola during the World Cup. He lent the BBC TV studios an air of 'je ne sais quoi' when he joined Alan Hansen to give his views on the games.

David Ginola was joint leading scorer for Spurs in all competitions in 1997-98 and the club's Player of the Year

OUR SPONSOR TODAY IS...

Sponsorship and advertising

Product endorsement and sponsorship are now standard features of football. Hitching themselves to the wagon of commercialisation, clubs and players are raking it in. Product manufacturers are falling over themselves to sign up the likes of Paul Ince, pictured left with son Thomas and Adidas Predator boots, to endorse their wares. Footballers are used to sell everything from football boots to isotonic drinks, confectionery to breakfast cereal.

Football sponsorship and advertising seem to be a licence to make money. In the latest report by Deloitte & Touche for the 1995-96 season, 6.7% of Manchester United's annual turnover was derived from sponsorship, while Tottenham Hotspur saw their revenue from sponsorship rise 76%, thanks to renegotiated contract extensions with kit and team sponsors. But it's not just the clubs that are benefiting. On top of spiralling wages, big-name players can expect to make a fortune in sponsorship deals and product endorsement. On top of his salary in 1997-98, Alan Shearer had a £500,000 agreement to wear Umbro boots and six-figure deals with Lucozade, McDonald's and Braun. Meanwhile, David Beckham had an £800,000 four-year deal to wear Adidas boots and a £1 million deal to promote Brylcreem.

On top of spiralling wages, big-name players can expect to make a fortune in sponsorship deals

Ronaldo's back: Internazionale's number 10 graces a billboard advertising Pirelli tyres, outside the San Siro stadium in Milan.

- The only major professional club in Europe that does not emblazon sponsorship on its club's shirts is Spanish giant Barcelona.

- Until the 1983-84 season, clubs were not allowed to wear sponsored shirts if the game was being televised.

- Nike's deal with the Brazilian national team is rumoured to be for a 10-year period, with $200 million (£125 million) available for kit and facilities and $20 million (£12.5 million) in cash.

Stop snickering you lot: the recent World Cup provided a feast for advertisers and players alike. Here, some of the England team can be seen in the TV ad for Snickers.

It wasn't just the players and managers who engaged in intensive preparations for France '98 but also the marketing industry that moved up several gears. The World Cup provides the perfect stage for global branding. It is estimated that France '98 cost each global sponsor about £20 million. There were 12 global FIFA sponsors, in addition to eight official and other product and equipment suppliers. Television viewers of World Cup games were typically exposed to seven minutes worth of each advertising hoarding on display –

airtime that corporations such as Nike, Coca-Cola and McDonald's recognise is invaluable in terms of stealing a march on the market competition. The USA giant Nike sponsored six World Cup teams during France '98, including Ronaldo and his Brazilian team-mates. Nike's involvement with the national side even brought speculation that the company influenced team selection – a rumour emphatically denied by the team manager. Nike's campaigns are good examples of how sophisticated global branding has become. The

irreverent style of the TV ads and the Nike symbol are instantly recognisable worldwide. At the beginning of 1998, FIFA announced that Coca-Cola would be extending its sponsorship of the World Cup until 2006. The company will now be one of the official sponsors of the next two World Cups. The agreement marks the first time a sponsor has extended its partnership with FIFA for more than a four-year term. "The global popularity of football makes it a natural fit for Coca-Cola," said a company spokesman.

The first English team to have a sponsor's name on their shirts were Kettering Town, for Kettering Tyres in 1981

SHOP 'TIL YOU DROP

Club merchandise

Gone are the days when club merchandise was restricted to scarves, programmes and a cheap mug with your club name on it. Now clubs have their own catalogues selling everything from replica home and away shirts to embroidery sets (West Ham), inflatable footballs (Manchester City) to pedal bikes (Coventry City), and babygrows to mouse mats (Newcastle United). And the recent World Cup opened up a whole new world of imaginatively branded products.

According to football accountants Deloitte & Touche, in the first six months of the 1996-97 season, the value of merchandising at Manchester United increased by 45% to £18.7 million. And it is calculated by Interbrand that the club's brand name is worth in the region of £127 million. Club merchandising is big business – the Portakabin club shop of the Seventies has now been replaced by the Nineties-style club superstore. But while many appreciate the fun side of investing in a pair of Sunderland socks, there is a serious side to the business.

Manchester United in particular have been criticised for the number of new kits it has produced over the last couple of years. Each new launch means more new stock for the stores and another new must-have design for supporters – at about £40 a throw.

Where better to contemplate the huge range of merchandise than on a Derby County toilet seat

And that's the fifth one this season: Manchester United launch yet another new kit – the club has been severely criticised for introducing so many home and away strips.

○ If everyone in the 30,492 crowd attending Derby's home game against Liverpool in May 1998 had bought a club toilet seat at £19.99, it would have raised £609,535.08.

○ For just £1.99, you could have bought a pack of three World Cup condoms in England team colours. The advice on the packet was to 'shoot safely' – evidently inspired by the 1966 World Cup experience when England's success at Wembley led to a baby boom.

Flicking through a stack of club catalogues reveals the full choice of merchandise now on offer. It ranges from the blindingly obvious (replica shirts) to the downright bizarre (Exeter City garden gnomes). Birmingham City entice female fans with pairs of 'footy lashes' – false eyelashes in club colours – or stylish City garters. Meanwhile, Midlands Premiership rival Aston Villa have gone one better – with a matching garter and suspender belt set in club colours, for £6.50. Talking of matching accessories, Port Vale supporters can get ahead in the perfume stakes with a shampoo, foam bath, body milk and shower gel set – all for a bargain £5.99. Headwear features heavily at relegated Barnsley – the Tykes offer red and white top hats or the occasional sparkly bowler. But for those men looking for a gift for their ladies, how about some Barnsley red lacy underwear with 'I scored' emblazoned on it? Of course, wigs and false hair are a Nineties favourite. When Regi Blinker was at Sheffield Wednesday, the club did a roaring trade in dreadlocked wigs and with the arrival of Ruud Gullit at Chelsea, the supplier seemingly received another call. Then again, how about a £2.99 Lombardo wig from Crystal Palace. Finally, where better to contemplate the huge range of merchandise on offer than on a Derby County toilet seat – yours for just £19.99.

Mega bucks at the Megastore: Chelsea's Megastore, opened in 1997, offers a huge range of merchandise, including this customised Chelsea Vespa scooter – a real snip for true Blues fans at £2,500.

FAIR SHARES?

Football club flotations

The 1990s have seen a flood of football clubs becoming public limited companies. By June 1998 there were 21 listed clubs on the stock exchange. Traditionally, clubs have tended to be owned by local families or industrialists, and directorships were often sought for civic pride. Now football club ownership is increasingly about making money and even the fans can buy a piece of the action. But after several boom years, has the city's soccer bubble burst?

Just like any other company, share flotations are a good way for football clubs to raise extra revenue. Money brought in with the sale of shares can then be ploughed into large capital projects such as new stands and stadia, and can even help to meet the wage bills of star players. With the buying and selling of shares an activity increasingly accessible to ordinary people, fans have been quick to buy their shares on flotation. But they may be a far from safe investment, with a club's share price moving up or down according to achievements both on and off the pitch. When Manchester United exited the European Cup in 1998, the club's share value plummeted. After the Division One play-off final, Charlton's share price rose 23% from 65p to 80p while Sunderland's fell by 19%.

Sunderland's shares rose to 520p after their final League game of 1997-98 – but failure in the play-offs sent the price tumbling

The price is right: since Sunderland floated in December 1996, the club has faced mixed fortunes. The day after losing the 1997-98 play-off final, the club's share price fell by 97.5p to 415p.

○ Premiership performers in 1997-98:

Team	Price at start of season	Price at end of season
Aston Villa	905p	560p
Burden Leisure (Bolton Wanderers)	35p	17p
Chelsea Village	90p	79p
Leeds Sporting	27p	18.5p
Leicester City	92.5p	50p
Manchester United	110.5p	146p
Newcastle United	130p	89.5p
Southampton Leisure	88p	73p
Tottenham Hotspur	91p	70p

During the 1997-98 season, football share prices continued a slump that had begun in early 1997, while the concerns of supporters that the team's performance on the pitch has become less important to the board than the FTSE Index has increased. The city has at times been suspicious of an investment which relies so much on performances in football matches. The smaller the club, the more likely performances on the field will affect the share price, especially as so much financially depends upon being in the Premiership. Sunderland has been one of the best examples of this. In December 1996, shares in the club were floated at 585p. By the beginning of the 1997-98 season they had fallen to 335p following the club's relegation from the Premiership. The shares rose again to 520p after their final League game of 1997-98 – but failure in the play-offs sent the share price tumbling back down. As for Newcastle United, a 1997-98 season plagued by problems in the board room as well as in the dressing room saw the club's share price drop by 31%. Off the pitch, the one overriding issue affecting share prices at all the clubs is pay-per-view. Until pay-per-view in football becomes a reality and the clubs begin to reap the benefits, share prices are unlikely to see much of a rise. But despite the ups and downs of football's performance in the city, some European clubs are beginning to follow England's example – Dutch side Ajax floated in May 1998. As football accountants Deloitte & Touche says: "The honeymoon's over, but there's no divorce."

Shared success: the Ajax squad celebrate winning the League in 1998. Ajax became the only Dutch side to float on the stock market when they launched a share issue in May 1998.

Aston Villa floated in 1997 with a share price of 1100p. In June 1998, the price had dropped to just 492p

ON THE BALL

Women and football

Football is no longer just a man's world. There has been a growth of women's involvement at all levels and in all aspects of the game, at home and abroad – an involvement that stretches from boardroom to touchline, from terrace to pitch. Football – traditionally a male preserve – has become a female one, too.

Figures released in 1998 show that one-in-eight fans attending football matches in the UK are now women, and it is the smaller 'provincial' clubs that have the largest female attendances, not 'glamour' sides such as Manchester United or Chelsea. According to the Football Supporters Association, these female fans are highly committed – almost seven out of 10 are season ticket-holders. As the fan base increases, so too does the number of women players worldwide. But women are not just getting into football as supporters and players. Referee's assistant Wendy Toms, for example, officiates at a senior professional level. While further afield, Sonia Denoncourt has become the first female referee in the Brazilian League – one of 56 international women referees featuring on the 1997 FIFA list.

According to the Football Supporters' Association, female fans are highly committed – about seven out of 10 are season ticket-holders

The Brady punch: Karren Brady was the first woman to become managing director at a professional club. At Birmingham City, she has earned a reputation as a tough negotiator.

○ In December 1921, the FA banned women from playing football in League grounds, stating that "the game is quite unsuitable for females".

○ In 1998, the Arsenal women's team joined their male counterparts by doing their own double.

○ Television coverage of the women's game is still limited but when England played Germany in a World Cup qualifier in March 1998, the match was watched by 120,000 Sky viewers.

The third FIFA Women's World Cup finals are being played in the USA in the summer of 1999 – but England won't be there. The team faced a nightmare qualification group, up against reigning World Champions Norway, reigning European Champions Germany, plus one of the most up-and-coming women's footballing nations in Europe, Holland. England's hopes were dashed in the 89th minute of the game against Norway in May 1998, when their opponents scored a last-gasp winner.

British sides have so far failed to make a real impact on the international scene. The main reason seems to be that while attitudes to women's football are changing and the profile of the game is being raised, players still complain of not being taken seriously or given enough positive encouragement. This is not the case in Scandinavia or the USA, where women's football enjoys almost equal billing with the men's game. But strides are being made in the domestic game in England, with the Arsenal women's team's 1997-98 FA Cup victory being shown live on Sky for the first time.

Girl power: there are more than 700 adult women's teams and 1,000 youth sides in Britain today. In Norway, women's football is hugely popular, with more than 60,000 female players taking to the pitch on a regular basis and in Germany, this figure increases to a staggering 500,000. But as yet, only Italy and Japan have professional women's leagues.

In December 1920, 53,000 fans watched Dick Kerr's Ladies beat local rivals St Helen's 4-0 at Goodison Park

YOU'VE GOT TO HAVE FAITH

Eileen Drewery and the England team

When England coach Glenn Hoddle announced to the world that he was using the faith healing powers of Eileen Drewery, right, to help some of his players overcome injuries, he provoked a storm. There were rumours that his decision to include Drewery in their World Cup campaign had split the England camp. Some players, such as Spurs' Darren Anderton, had responded well to treatment but others, such as Liverpool's Steve McManaman, remained openly sceptical.

Glenn Hoddle's long association with faith healer Eileen Drewery is well documented. As a rising teenage star at Tottenham, Hoddle developed a hamstring injury which the medical staff at White Hart Lane were struggling to cure. At the time, the striker was dating Drewery's daughter, Michelle. According to Hoddle, he chatted to Mrs Drewery about his hamstring problem but declined her offer of help. She decided to pray for Hoddle without his knowledge and, much to his amazement, the Spurs player awoke the following morning to discover that the pain had stopped. After confirmation from a doctor at Tottenham that the hamstring injury had apparently cleared up, the originally sceptical Hoddle was converted. Two decades later, he remains a firm believer.

"Keep your minds open," urged Hoddle following his announcement that Eileen Drewery was an integral part of England's France '98 campaign

A blessing in disguise: two white tigers – considered to be good luck symbols in South Korea – are photographed with a 2002 World Cup ball. South Korea, along with Japan, are hosting the next World Cup finals.

○ Uri Geller fell out with the England coach after he claimed that both Glenn Hoddle and Eileen Drewery had visited him seeking help with preparations for France '98. He also claimed that he had energised the World Cup trophy for England to win, after it was delivered to his house.

○ Glenn Hoddle explains that Eileen Drewery's faith healing powers work by her ability to "trigger the body's natural mechanism for healing". He first visited Drewery 24 years ago, while a player at Spurs.

"Keep your minds open," urged Glenn Hoddle to cynical journalists following his announcement that Eileen Drewery was an integral part of England's backroom team for France '98. The power of mind over matter has always caused controversy. Faith healers such as Drewery and psychics such as Uri Geller provoke a range of responses, from sceptics to believers. But while Geller boasted of his ability to move the ball just before Scotland's Gary McAllister took his penalty kick against England in Euro '96, Drewery has tended to keep out of the media spotlight. The former pub landlady from Essex has worked on a number of England players with success – the most high profile case being Darren Anderton, who has been fighting injury for the past couple of years. Club team-mate Les Ferdinand, who also visited Drewery, retains an open mind about her powers to heal. Others aren't so sure – Ian Wright and Paul Gascoigne both had sessions before France '98 but were ruled out of the final 22. Either way, as long as England was inspired to play well, nobody much cared where the inspiration came from.

Mystic Uri: psychic Uri Geller sent all the England squad a copy of *Uri Geller's Little Book of Mind Power* before this summer's World Cup finals. Each book was rubbed with the 1966 World Cup final ball to inspire the players to victory once more.

Uri Geller is the world's most investigated and celebrated paranormalist

YOUNG GUNS

Developing future talent

A revolution is taking place at the heart of English football. The way that young players are developed is changing dramatically with the implementation of the FA's 'Charter for Quality'. Howard Wilkinson, the FA's technical director, is the driving force behind the charter, which provides the blueprint for a radical overhaul of grass roots youth football. According to Wilkinson, spotting and nurturing the star players of tomorrow is a process that begins today.

"You cannae win anything with kids…" Alan Hansen was to regret his *Match Of The Day* prediction on the first day of the 1995-96 season. The "kids" he was referring to – David Beckham, the Neville brothers, Paul Scholes and Nicky Butt – were the new breed of Manchester United 'Babes'. The club famously went on to win its second double that season, proving that a strong youth policy can reap rich dividends. In 1998, Liverpool's home-grown striker Michael Owen was top scorer for his club and England's youngest ever goalscorer. It is Howard Wilkinson's role at the FA to recognise and capitalise on the potential of young players such as Owen. His long-term objective is to re-establish England as a world force in football and he believes that youth policies play a central role in that aim.

"Coaches abroad rub their hands in glee at the fact we are not making the most of the potential we have in this country," Howard Wilkinson

Heading for success: Liverpool's Michael Owen made his debut against Chile at 18 years and 59 days old, becoming England's youngest international this century. Less than four months later, he became the youngest player ever to score for England, against Morocco.

Howard Wilkinson's recommendations include:

- Clubs to develop football academies and centres of excellence.
- A talent development plan for women's football.
- A national programme for the selection of gifted young players.
- Academies to supercede the FA National Football Centre for coaching, sports medicine and science.
- A national coaching association and network of regional directors.
- A national coach to join England's international youth teams and to eventually become the next England senior coach.

According to Howard Wilkinson: "We are among the top nations in terms of the quantity of people playing the game, but not in terms of quality. Coaches abroad rub their hands in glee at the fact that we are not making the most of the potential we have in this country at the moment." After spending a year consulting with members of the football establishment at all levels and studying youth set-ups in countries such as Italy, Spain, France and Holland, Wilkinson published his Charter for Quality in the summer of 1997. Its wide-reaching proposals will have a major effect on the way that young players will be coached in the future. One of its more radical measures is a recommendation that

Brazilian gold blend: in September 1997, the heirs apparent to Brazil's senior team won the Under-17 World Cup in Cairo. Howard Wilkinson sees Brazil as the model for Britain's youth: "We need to develop Brazil's joie de vivre. It can be taught but we must start at a young age."

children under the age of 10 should not play 11-a-side football. By playing smaller games, Wilkinson believes that youngsters will get more touches of the ball and so develop greater skills. Another of the charter's proposals is that coaching of the most promising young players should be done at academies set up by Premier and Football League clubs. From the age of eight, Wilkinson hopes that the players will be taken under the wing of these academies, where they will have access to the best coaches, as well as the best facilities. "This is the most exciting challenge of my career," said Wilkinson. "This report is all about producing improved English players for England teams."

The youngest FA Cup player, Andrew Awford, was 15 years and 88 days old when he played in a qualifier in 1987

TRAGEDY ON THE TERRACES

Hillsborough update

The tragic events that unfolded at Hillsborough on 15 April 1989 will always weigh heavy in the hearts and minds of football fans. Ninety-six Liverpool supporters lost their lives as a consequence of over-crowding at the Leppings Lane end of the Sheffield Wednesday ground before the kick-off of an FA Cup semi-final between Liverpool and Nottingham Forest. Nine years later, Home Secretary Jack Straw, right, turned down an appeal for a new, full-scale public inquiry.

The Hillsborough Families Support Group (HFSG) has repeatedly petitioned for a fresh public inquiry into what happened on the afternoon of 15 April 1989. The original verdict of accidental death still stands, in spite of protestations from HFSG that serious questions remain unanswered. On 30 June 1997, Home Secretary Jack Straw gave fresh hope to the 'Justice for the 96' campaign when he announced that Lord Justice Stuart-Smith would be reporting on whether a public inquiry should go ahead. "We owe it to everyone, but above all to the families of those who died, to get to the bottom of this matter once and for all," said Straw at the time. On 18 February 1998, the Home Secretary announced to the Commons that Smith's report had found in favour of police evidence and that no new inquiry would be forthcoming.

"We owe it to all the families of those who died to get to the bottom of this matter once and for all," Home Secretary Jack Straw

Another black day: in May 1985, four years before the Hillsborough disaster, 39 fans were killed at the Heysel stadium in Belgium when a wall collapsed at the European Cup final.

○ A benefit concert at Anfield on 10 May 1997, featuring Space, Dodgy, Manic Street Preachers and Lightning Seeds, along with an accompanying live album, raised nearly £500,000 for the Hillsborough Families Support Group.

○ The verdict of 'accidental death' means that no-one can be brought to account for their actions on the day of the disaster.

In the immediate aftermath of Hillsborough, public reaction was largely one of shock and horror, plus confusion about the actual chain of events that led to the tragedy on that fateful afternoon in April 1989. The initial accusation, voiced so famously by the *Sun* newspaper on its front page, had been of drunken, ticketless fans attempting to break into Sheffield Wednesday's ground. This version of events is vehemently denied by the Hillsborough Family Support Group who are still seeking justice – and answers – for the 96 supporters who lost their lives. Jimmy McGovern, the TV writer responsible for *Cracker* and *Prime Suspect* among others, won a BAFTA award for *Hillsborough*, a drama-documentary that was first shown in December 1996. The programme criticised the policing on the day of the tragedy and suggested that there was fresh evidence to justify a new public inquiry. Lord Justice Taylor's original inquiry in 1989 had also concluded that "the main reason for the disaster was failure of police control". However, the verdict of 'accidental death' still stands and there will be no new inquiry. The Hillsborough Families Support Group is bitterly disappointed but plans to carry on the campaign and may consider bringing private prosecutions against members of the South Yorkshire and West Midlands police forces.

Lest we forget: the famous Anfield gates decorated with scarves to commemorate the lives of the 96 Liverpool fans who died at Hillsborough.

Hillsborough was the worst disaster in the history of British football

The Taylor Report

The Hillsborough disaster of 15 April 1989 had far-reaching consequences for British football. First and foremost, it led to Lord Justice Taylor's official inquiry into the tragic events of that fateful afternoon at the Sheffield Wednesday ground. The subsequent Taylor Report caused a revolution in the national game, the repercussions of which are still being felt. The Report's most radical recommendation was that all domestic stadia be converted to all-seaters by 1999-2000.

The Report's main recommendations following Hillsborough included the removal of all perimeter fencing at grounds, improved liaison between the emergency services, and the criminalising of certain behaviour such as throwing missiles. However, it was the all-seater stipulation that had the greatest impact. The Report set a deadline for all English and Scottish Premiership and English First Division clubs to become all-seater by the start of the 1994-95 season. The English Second and Third Divisions and remaining Scottish divisions have until the 1999-2000 season to comply. The Football Trust has played a vital role in assisting smaller clubs, such as Northampton, above, to meet Taylor's recommendations. It has helped to fund much of the building of new stands, as well as safety improvements.

The English Second and Third Divisions and remaining Scottish divisions have until the 1999-2000 season to comply with the Taylor Report

Farewell Baseball Ground, hello Pride Park: Derby County would have had to spend £10 million converting their old ground to an all-seater stadium. Instead, the club decided to move to a new home, aided by a £2.9 million grant from The Football Trust.

○ Despite promotion to the Premiership in 1995-96, Sunderland Football Club retained its terracing in the 1996-97 season when it gained a year's grace in which to move from Roker Park to the Stadium of Light.

○ Since 1990, 14 clubs in England and Scotland have relocated to new stadia.

End of an era: Liverpool fans stood and chanted on the Kop for the last time in April 1994, when the Merseysiders played Norwich City in a League game. Shortly afterwards, the famous stand was demolished to meet the requirements of the Taylor Report.

The modernisation of football grounds following the 1990 Taylor Report has been a long process. Stadium facilities are steadily improving and crowd safety remains high on the agenda. Perimeter fencing has now virtually disappeared from most major football grounds and there has been a systematic improvement in standards of stewarding in the wake of lessons learned from Hillsborough. However, Taylor's recommendations have met with criticism from some quarters. It has been suggested, for example, that the shift from terracing to all-seater stadia has resulted in a loss of atmosphere at games. Also, the cost of Taylor's recommendations has been astronomical. Since 1990, the Football Trust has allocated enough money to clubs to enable upgrade projects totalling more than £477 million to go ahead. Faced with the possibility of spending millions renovating their existing grounds, many clubs such as Derby and Sunderland opted instead to start from scratch, selling their city centre grounds and moving to green-belt sites where land is cheaper. But with the first stage of Taylor's recommendations completed, many of the smaller clubs are finding it hard to meet the 1999-2000 deadline and are looking for help from new sources. Huddersfield Town may have found the solution. The Terriers built their new Alfred McAlpine Stadium in partnership with the local council and rugby club. Other small clubs, however, still face an uncertain future.

Since 1990, the Football Trust has allocated £150 million to clubs to help them upgrade their stadia

GROUNDS FOR IMPROVEMENT

New stadia

With football increasingly being seen as big business, clubs are realising the value of an impressive stadium – such as Sunderland's Stadium of Light, left. At all levels, clubs are using top architects and designers to create innovative, award-winning stadia. In 1995, Huddersfield's McAlpine Stadium won the RIBA Building of the Year Award and in 1998 one of Britain's top architects, Sir Norman Foster, was appointed to design the new Wembley stadium.

On 10 June 1998, millions of football fans across the world focused on one event – the opening ceremony of the 1998 World Cup. When Brazil and Scotland kicked off the tournament, they did so in the Stade de France, the country's new £280 million national stadium with an 80,000 capacity. Opened in January 1998, the stadium has eight levels with four tiers of stands, the lower one retractable. The roof is suspended on 18 steel needles, as if it were floating. Meanwhile, also opened this season, is Dutch club Vitesse Arnhem's 26,600-seat Gelredome, hot on the heels of the impressive Amsterdam Arena. A venue for the 2000 European Championships, the Gelredome cost £47.3 million but it has the added attraction of a retractable pitch – to stop damage to the turf by concert-goers.

The Amsterdam Arena has seating of various colours and patterns, designed by a psychologist to "create a relaxed atmosphere"

New architecture: The Reebok Stadium in Bolton opened in September 1997, at a cost of £35 million and with enough seats to accommodate a crowd of 25,000.

New stadia opened in 1997 and 1998:

Name	Team	Opened	Capacity	Cost
• Stadium of Light	Sunderland	July 1997	42,000	£20 million
• Pride Park	Derby County	July 1997	33,000	£21-22 million
• Britannia Stadium	Stoke City	August 1997	28,000	£14.5 million
• Reebok Stadium	Bolton Wanderers	September 1997	25,000	£35 million
• Madejski Stadium	Reading	September 1998	25,000	£37 million

In September 1998, the latest big money stadium opened in England. Despite relegation to the Second Division at the end of the 1997-98 season, Reading supporters can at least enjoy the new £37 million Madejski Stadium. The complex, like Chelsea Village, is a good example of the way ground improvement is being implemented in the 1990s. As well as a 25,000-seater ground, the complex includes a conference centre, hotel and business park. And as with Sunderland and Mansfield, Reading fans were invited to be part of the new stadium – by buying a brick to carry their personal message on a wall of fame. Sunderland's Stadium Of

Final venue: the World Cup finals began and ended in the Stade de France. Built at a cost of more than £280 million, the space age design holds 80,000 spectators in four tiers of stands, the lowest of which is retractable.

Light, opened in the summer of 1997, has the second highest capacity in the country after Old Trafford, with 42,000 seats. It takes up half of a 40-acre site that will eventually house a leisure facility. Like most new stadiums, Sunderland's ground offers all-round viewing. Gone are the pillars, in comes the cantilevered roof – Manchester United built one of the largest in the world when they extended their North Stand to create an overall capacity of 56,024. But perhaps the most stimulating innovation has come from the new Amsterdam Arena – the seating colours were designed by a psychologist to "create a relaxed atmosphere".

Old Trafford has the largest capacity of any English club ground at 56,024

THE HOME OF FOOTBALL

Wembley's future

After years of public debate, internal wranglings and continued controversy, plans to transform Wembley from a decaying wreck into a "stadium to be proud of" were finally rubber-stamped in April 1998. After the 1999 FA Cup final, the old stadium will be bulldozed – only the famous twin towers of the old Empire building will be left standing – and work will begin on a brand new, state-of-the-art national stadium, costing £240 million and due to be unveiled in 2002.

On 2 April 1998, the English National Stadium Trust (ENST) was given the go-ahead to buy Wembley for £103 million from its owners, Wembley plc. And with £130 million of lottery money, ENST plans to build a high-tech, 80,000-capacity stadium which will host FA and League Cup finals, England matches and maybe even the 2006 World Cup final. Part of the brief for the new design is that the twin towers are retained, but otherwise the architects have been given free rein. ENST's appointed architect will submit details later this year and a decision on the finalised plans is expected to be given the green light soon after. According to sports minister Tony Banks: "The new stadium will help maintain the name of Wembley as the home of world soccer and will reinforce our bid for the 2006 World Cup."

"The new stadium will help maintain the name of Wembley as the home of soccer," Tony Banks

Down Wembley Way: opened in 1923, Wembley stadium is recognised as the home of football, not just in England but in many parts of the world. The twin towers may be built of cold stone, but to serious soccer fans they are living, breathing symbols of the planet's greatest game.

Wembley was first used for football on 28 April 1923 for the 'white horse' FA Cup final between Bolton Wanderers and West Ham United. The official attendance figure for the match was 126,947 (a record for a match in England) but there were actually over 200,000 people inside – many of whom had scaled the fences – and fans soon began to engulf the pitch. There was chaos until PC George Scorey and his white horse Billie appeared, very gently pushing the masses back off the playing area. The game finally went ahead, with Bolton winning 2-0.

The future's bright: this artist's impression shows Wembley as it might look in the future. Architect Sir Norman Foster was appointed to the project in May 1998 and will submit proper drawings in 1999.

When Arsenal tabled a £120 million bid to buy Wembley early in 1998, plans for a new stadium for the country were immediately thrown into doubt. If the 1997-98 Champions had succeeded in their bid to move to Wembley from Highbury (where planning laws have restricted moves to increase capacity from 38,000), then ENST would have had to find another site on which to build a national stadium. In the end Arsenal withdrew, saying it was in the interest of English football.

The lottery money which will partially fund the new stadium was allocated on the premise that the modernisation of Wembley was run by a non-commercial body. So, Wembley plc will continue to operate the stadium until June 1999, but by the time the new building opens three years later it will be in the hands of the non-profit making ENST. Originally built to provide the centrepiece for the British Empire Exhibition of 1924, the new Wembley stadium will usher in a fresh era of English football.

The original Empire stadium was built in just 300 days and cost a mere £750,000

ENGLAND V GERMANY

World Cup 2006 campaign

Matches between England and Germany have become part of football folklore. But there is a battle raging off the field that is every bit as competitive as any penalty shoot-outs or dramatic fixtures between the two nations to date – the fight to host the greatest football tournament of them all, the World Cup.

Forty years after England last hosted the World Cup, the race is on to net the prestigious tournament once again, in 2006. The Football Association has already launched its bid in earnest, despite the fact that the deadline for bids to be in is not until September 1999.

Also fighting for the honour of playing host to the 2006 World Cup is Germany, and a feud between the two nations has broken out following claims by the Germans that the former chairman of the English FA, Sir Bert Millichip, had previously offered unofficial support for Germany's bid, partly in return for Germany supporting England's bid for Euro '96. Neither nation is pulling out and the race is on, with Australia, Egypt, Morocco, South Africa, Peru and Ecuador, Brazil and Argentina all expected to throw their hats into the ring.

Following the success of Euro '96, England's bid to host the 2006 World Cup is a strong one

Home or away?: If England lose their bid for the World Cup in 2006 and Germany are successful, venues such as the 74,000-capacity Olympic stadium in Munich will stage the games.

○ Three of the eight stadia which hosted the 1966 World Cup no longer exist – White City, Roker Park and Ayresome Park.

○ Germany last hosted the World Cup in 1974, eight years after England last hosted the tournament.

○ The provisional timetable for bidding for the 2006 World Cup is:

• January 1999 – list of bid requirements issued by FIFA
• September 1999 – deadline for the submission of bids
• May 2000 – FIFA inspects venues
• June 2000 – winner announced.

Tony Blair, Prime Minister by the time England officially unveiled its bid, has become the chief advocate for England's World Cup 2006 campaign. He has refused to be bullied by German notables such as Franz Beckenbauer and Germany manager Berti Vogts, who have been calling for England to back down. Even German captain Jurgen Klinsmann has chipped in, saying: "Germany helped England a lot to get Euro '96. It would be a fair move for the English to withdraw."

Following the success of Euro '96, England's bid to host the 2006 World Cup is a strong one. There were 1,279,371 spectators at Euro '96 compared with just 429,000 at the previous Championship in Sweden and 810,000 when it was hosted in Germany in 1988. The cumulative TV audience was 6.68 billion in 192 countries, a 65% increase on 1992, and the overall profit made was about £69 million. However, there were some 16 teams in the 1996 finals, compared to eight in previous years. But the fervour and exhilarating atmosphere of the tournament was undeniable and makes claims that it was the best European Championship ever hard to dispute. It is certainly hoped that when FIFA's six representatives from Asia, Africa, North and Central America, South America, Oceania and Europe vote, they will bear all this in mind. Also in England's favour is that former FIFA President Joao Havelange has backed England's bid, even if he has also given the nod to South Africa and Germany, and that Wembley, the national stadium, is about to be completely rebuilt.

Jules Rimet still gleaming: in 1966, England beat off a bid from West Germany to host the World Cup. The country was brought virtually to a standstill as World Cup fever spread and England went on to win the Jules Rimet trophy. The Football Association will be hoping for similar success in 2006.

England are bidding to be only the third country, after Mexico and France, to host two World Cup finals

DECADE OF DOMINANCE

Manchester United Football Club plc

Manchester United may have lost the 1997-98 Premiership title to Arsenal, but it did not stop the Reds from finishing the season top of accountants Deloitte & Touche's latest table of profitability. In 1995-96, the club was the most successful in Europe in terms of finance. Manchester United Football Club plc has the game's money-men rubbing their hands in glee and to them, the club's success on the pitch is of far less interest than their financial performance.

Manchester United's future – financial or otherwise – looked far from bright at the beginning of Alex Ferguson's reign in 1986. The club finished the Eighties in shaky form but went on to win the 1990 FA Cup. It marked a turning in the Reds' fortunes – on and off the pitch – and in the following year, United floated on the stock market. As the club's share price soared, so did its performance in the League and cups. In 1991, United won the European Cup Winners Cup and the Premiership trophy ended up at Old Trafford in 1993, 1994, 1996 and 1997.

In 1996, United became the first club to win the League and Cup double twice – having first secured it in 1994. These successes on the pitch were mirrored by the club's share prices on the stock market but, likewise, a poor 1997-98 season saw the share price drop.

The club has over 2,000 merchandising lines... selling everything from replica shirts to credit cards and insurance policies

Touchline tension: Manchester United's performance on the pitch has repercussions off it – share prices can take a tumble if the manager does not get the results expected.

○ The club is preparing to launch its own pay-per-view channel. The venture should be a real money-spinner, especially if United secure the broadcasting rights to their matches after Sky's deal ends in 2001.

○ Following United's shock exit from the European Cup in the 1997-98 season, £7.8 million was wiped off the club's shares.

○ During the 1996-97 season, Manchester United made £6.2 million from TV revenue alone.

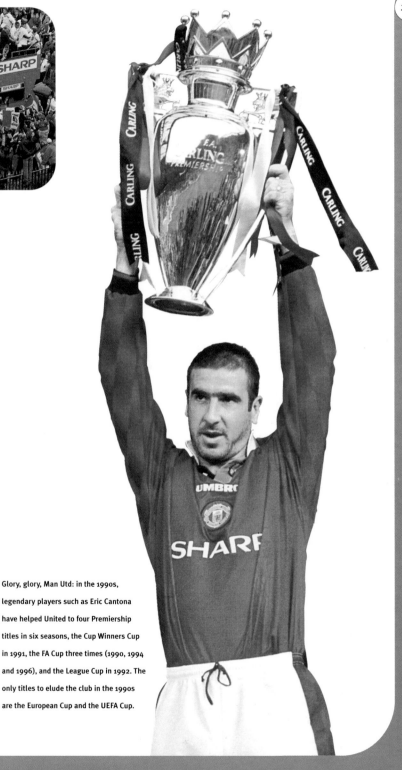

Manchester United have more followers worldwide than any other club, thanks to its success on the pitch and some extremely clever marketing. From Malaysia to Malta, South Africa to South Australia, the Reds have captured the hearts – and wallets – of millions. The club has over 2,000 merchandising lines to satisfy the consumer hunger of its widespread supporters, selling everything from replica shirts to credit cards and insurance policies. The Reds were the first club to produce an official magazine in 1994, *Manchester United Magazine* – the biggest-selling football monthly in the country. It is no wonder that United finished the 1996/97 tax year with an £87.9 million turnover, and a pre-tax profit of £27.5 million. The club also holds the record for the biggest domestic wage bill – a staggering £22.5 million – which makes it all the more gruelling for Ferguson that his well-paid stars have had limited success in Europe. Most notably, they have failed to win the trophy he covets above all others – the European Cup. After further failure in the Champions League in 1997-98, it is an ambition that still eludes him.

Glory, glory, Man Utd: in the 1990s, legendary players such as Eric Cantona have helped United to four Premiership titles in six seasons, the Cup Winners Cup in 1991, the FA Cup three times (1990, 1994 and 1996), and the League Cup in 1992. The only titles to elude the club in the 1990s are the European Cup and the UEFA Cup.

Manchester United have won the FA Cup a record nine times, including three times in the 1990s

Alex Ferguson

Alex Ferguson is the most successful manager in the history of British football. During his time in charge at St Mirren, Aberdeen and Manchester United, he has landed no fewer than 20 trophies, including four Premiership titles at Old Trafford in the past six seasons. But in view of the disappointments of the 1997-98 season, the United boss – currently the Premiership's longest-serving manager – may be feeling the pressure.

The Reds' manager lives, breathes and sleeps football. Visit 'The Cliff', Manchester United's training ground, at 7am on any weekday morning and there will be just one car in the car park – Ferguson's gleaming BMW. "My all-consuming passion is football," he admits. "Always has been, always will be. I'm not a golfer and I don't go down the pub to relax – I haven't been in a pub since I was a young man. My whole objective is to work hard and make certain I have a job for life at United." And following an almost unimaginable trophy-less season, it's certain that the 56-year-old Scotsman will be working round the clock to ensure success in 1998-99. Unless that success comes about relatively swiftly, he is likely to find himself at the mercy of the press and fans alike.

"My objective is to work hard and make certain I have a job for life at Manchester United"

Remember you're a womble: Ferguson reveals his two signings for the new season from Wimbledon – a nippy little winger (above left) and a classy central midfield playmaker (above right).

○ Alex Ferguson's honours as manager:

- Scottish First Division title 1977 (St Mirren)
- Scottish Premier title 1985, 1984, 1980 (Aberdeen)
- Scottish Cup 1986, 1984, 1983, 1982 (Aberdeen)
- Scottish League Cup 1986 (Aberdeen)
- Premiership title 1997, 1996, 1994, 1993
- FA Cup 1996, 1994, 1990
- League Cup 1992
- Cup Winners Cup 1991 (Manchester United), 1983 (Aberdeen)

Millennium man: after more than a decade at Manchester United, including a disappointing 1997-98 season, Ferguson is intent on remaining at Old Trafford well into the next century. "Everyone keeps asking me when I'm going to retire. I just say to them, 'What the hell am I going to do if I do that?'."

Alex Ferguson was born in the working-class Glasgow district of Govan on 31 December 1941. The son of a shipyard worker, he puts the secret of his success down to his Govan roots. He proved an adept, though hardly gifted footballer, turning out for Queens Park, St Johnstone, Dunfermline, Stranraer and Falkirk, as well as his beloved Rangers. But it is as a manager rather than as a player that Ferguson has made his mark. He has an uncanny ability to motivate the whole club. At Aberdeen he turned an average Scottish team into one of the best in Europe. At United, he has rebuilt a crumbling, languishing giant into a golden empire.

Ferguson's reputation is fearsome. "When the players believe they have cracked it, it's my job to bring them crashing back to reality," he says. "All I have to say is that it's tea-cup time… and the players are ducking for cover – though the last cup I threw was at Gordon Strachan – and I missed."

Alex Ferguson is the only English Premiership manager to win the double twice – in 1994 and 1996

USA '98

Major League Soccer

In 1998, the USA qualified for the World Cup finals for the third time in succession. Four years before, it had hosted the finals amid a good deal of fanfare and razzmatazz. But, despite attempts within the country to bring soccer to the fore, the game is still playing second fiddle to basketball, baseball, American football and even ice hockey. The most popular clubs draw crowds of over 20,000, but for others the numbers drop to about 4,000.

Major League Soccer, America's professional soccer league, was set up in 1996 with 10 clubs as members. The previous attempt at a soccer league, the NASL, had ended in 1984 after marketing and planning flaws meant it never took off. Today's MLS has a unique ownership and operating system whereby operator investors buy not only into a team, but into the League as well. Player contracts are owned by the League, and the League buys and sells players and assigns them to teams. The operator investor pays the operating costs, except salaries, and runs the team. In 1998, two new clubs were added to the MLS, one in Chicago and the other in South Florida. The League hopes to expand again in the year 2000 and by 2003 to have reached its optimum of 16 teams.

The MLS has begun to gather support, with the average attendance of 16,000 in the first two seasons exceeding the 10-12,000 projection

Political interest: in a sign that football is becoming more important in the US, the national team meet President Bill Clinton. In 1994, it had been left to the vice-president to present the World Cup trophy to Brazil.

○ Teams in the MLS can spend a maximum $1.5 million (£940,000) on wages. Sunil Gulati, who supervises MLS transactions, boasted that he stocked all 10 teams in the inaugural season for "slightly more than half as much as it cost Newcastle to sign Alan Shearer".

○ MLS players featured in five teams in the 1998 World Cup, excluding the USA – Mexico, Colombia, Chile, Nigeria and Jamaica.

○ The US soccer season runs from March to October.

When FIFA awarded the United States the 1994 World Cup, it imposed one condition – that a professional soccer league must be instituted in a nation that had already rejected the game. FIFA had been hugely encouraged by the fact that football matches at the 1984 Olympic games in Los Angeles had averaged crowds of over 40,000 and a sell-out crowd of 100,000 had watched the final. FIFA was also aware of the billions of dollars flowing through major American professional sport. The first game of Major League Soccer was played on 6 April 1996. Plans to increase the size of the goals were rejected but, despite this, the MLS proudly proclaimed that its goal average of 3.3 per game in the first two seasons was one of the highest of any professional league in the world. The league is slowly gathering support, with the average attendance of 16,000 in the first two seasons exceeding the 10-12,000 projection. During the 1996 and 1997 seasons, TV ratings on the ESPN channel were comparable to that of the network's college basketball and National Hockey League broadcasts, leading to new deals with ESPN and ABC for the 1998 season. MLS teams are limited to five foreigners in their roster of 20 players in order to ensure grassroots development and Project-40 is a scheme that has been set up to nurture home talent and to fund training with MLS teams.

A new beginning: the USA was awarded the 1994 World Cup finals by FIFA on the condition that the country went about launching a successful national league.

CONTINENTAL DRIFT

South American football

Last season, as ever, the main South American stars were playing their football for club sides outside of the continent. Despite providing some of the greatest players and most successful national sides, South America is a place where a television rather than a ticket provides the best view of the continent's football talent. Economic reasons provide some of the impetus for departure, but other problems continue to dog the domestic game.

River Plate may have won Argentina's title race by a point from Boca Juniors in an exciting finish in 1998, but the final weeks of the competition were marred by accusations of bribery among some clubs. Even worse were the scenes of violence which accompanied certain games, including San Lorenzo's final match with Huracan, which had to be suspended less than a third of the way through because of crowd trouble. In Colombia, celebrations in Cali, following America's title win – their first in five years – ended in four deaths and 82 injuries, as the celebrations descended into a mixture of drunkenness and traffic accidents. In Brazil, the domestic season was marred less by violence than by match-fixing scandals and in-fighting between clubs, leading to the abandonment of a number of games.

South America is a place where a television rather than a ticket provides the best view of the continent's football talent

Latin passion: religion and football go hand-in-hand in South America as the two most important things in life. Many of the world's greatest players such as Pele and Maradona, plus today's Ronaldo, started their footballing lives playing on the streets of South America.

○ The South American Soccer Confederation (CONMEBOL) has 10 members: Argentina, Bolivia, Brazil, Chile, Colombia, Ecuador, Paraguay, Peru, Uruguay and Venezuela.

○ In 1998, River Plate won the Argentinian title; Vasco da Gama won in Brazil; Colo Colo won in Chile; Bolivar won in Bolivia; Alicanza Lima won in Peru; Olimpia won in Paraguay; America won in Colombia; Betar Jerusalem won in Venezuela; Barcelona won in Ecuador; and Penarol topped the Uruguayan league.

Copa loada the action: Mexico's America take on Argentina's River Plate in the Copa Libertadores, the South American version of the European Cup. Open to the League champions and runners-up in each country, the competition was won in 1998 by Brazilian club Cruzeiro.

Confusion was never far away in 1998 and South America's bewildering array of tournaments became even more complicated with speculation that the Super Cup – restricted to former winners of the Libertadores Cup, the South American title – may not be contested again, with clubs from Argentina and Brazil expressing a preference for the new, more lucrative, Mercosur Cup. Despite all the chaos, South American countries were once again well-represented at the World Cup, highlighting the gap between international and domestic football on the continent. But there were encouraging signs in Brazil with Sports Minister Pele working to put clubs on a more professional footing. And new players continue to emerge. Edmundo was Player of the Season in Brazil with a record 29 Championship goals although, like so many South Americans, he now plays his club football abroad. And in Chile, the Player of the Year was Marcelo Salas. But, again, he has left Argentina's River Plate for Italian club Lazio.

The South American Championship is the longest-running tournament in international football

EASTERN PROMISE

Football in Asia

There are two main viewpoints as to why FIFA decided to hold the 2002 World Cup in Japan and South Korea. One is that it is a reward for the strides Asian football has made in the 1990s and reflects the growth in popularity of football in that region. Another is that although football is attracting more players and crowds in Asia, it could do better and the World Cup should boost football's profile in the face of cricket and baseball, which are other big sports in the region.

When the first World Cup of the 21st century was awarded to Asia, there was no hint that the economies in the south-east corner of Asia were going to be facing bankruptcy or collapse in the period leading up to the tournament. There is now concern as to whether Japan and South Korea, both finalists in France '98, can host the tournament. The South Korean government has expressed fears that it will not be able to fund the building of a stadium big enough to host the latter stages of the tournament, following its economic collapse in 1997, and the Japanese are worried as to whether sufficient funds will be available to make the huge outlay needed to put on such an event. However, Japan is in a better position than its co-hosts in that it has enough decent-sized football grounds already.

There was amazing interest in the World Cup, with more than 65,000 applications for France '98 despite France being over 12 hours away

If you're happy and you know it: South Korea's Pohang Steelers celebrate victory in Hong Kong over China's Dalian club in the 17th Asian Club Championship in April 1998. After a controversial penalty shoot-out, Dalian officials boycotted the medal ceremony.

○ Japan qualified for their first World Cup finals in 1998, thus avoiding being the only hosts not to have qualified for a World Cup outside of their host year.

○ South Korea are the most successful Asian qualifiers for the World Cup finals, having qualified five times.

○ The co-hosts of the next World Cup, Japan and South Korea, were both ranked in FIFA's top 20 immediately prior to France '98.

Towering achievement: room lights in tower blocks in downtown Seoul are used to celebrate South Korea's role as co-hosts of the 2002 World Cup.

Despite economic difficulties in the region, the Asian Football Confederation is in good shape with 43 national associations now affiliated. Four members were at the 1998 World Cup – Saudi Arabia, South Korea, Japan and Iran, with South Korea qualifying for its fourth World Cup in a row. Within those associations, Japan probably has the strongest and best-funded league, having attracted players like Gary Lineker in the past to heighten the J-League status. Average crowds are about 19,000 and football is valiantly competing with the other great sporting pastimes of the Japanese – golf and baseball. There was also amazing interest in the World Cup, with the Association receiving more than 65,000 applications for 1998 World Cup tickets despite the fact that France is over 12 hours away by plane. Overall, Asian football is on the up. The number of people taking up the game across the continent is soaring, and even in China it is drawing big crowds. Fans can now enjoy European football on television with English football especially popular. Sponsorship and TV coverage is pumping money into the game and, despite worries about the financial security of both countries, Japan and South Korea are determined to host the 2002 World Cup.

2002 will be the first time the World Cup finals have ever been held in Asia

Football in Africa

African football has made great progress in the 1990s. Cameroon got to the quarter-finals of the 1990 World Cup, Liberian striker George Weah of AC Milan was World Footballer of the Year in 1995, Nigeria won the Olympic title in 1996 and the allocation for African finalists in the World Cup finals was increased to five for 1998. With African players flocking to European clubs, the quality of the game is fast improving.

Despite predictions that an African country would win the World Cup by the year 2000 – made in the 1950s by England manager Walter Winterbottom and later repeated by Pele – and hopes that South Africa might host the 2006 tournament, the grass-roots game in Africa is still beset by financial difficulties and political upheaval. Countries like Liberia are forced to rely on players such as Weah to pay their own way when playing for their country, while many national associations are hampered by in-fighting and government interference.

Nigeria have been banned from the last two African Nations Cups for political reasons and the 1996 Olympics was won in the face of in-fighting between Nigerian officials. The Super Eagles probably could have achieved more on the pitch, were it not for the problems off it.

Nigeria's World Cup squad in 1998 included players from clubs in 10 different countries – with none from Nigerian clubs

Developing talent: football is a passionate game across the countries of Africa and increasingly, the continent is producing world-class players in demand from clubs in Europe.

○ The first African nation in a World Cup finals was Egypt in 1934. The next time Africa took part in a finals was in 1970, when Morocco competed. In 1998, a record five African nations – Cameroon, Morocco, Nigeria, South Africa and Tunisia – took part in the World Cup finals in France.

○ The youngest player at France '98 was Cameroon's Samuel Eto'o, who was just 17 years and 92 days old when the tournament began.

With Nigeria banned from the 1998 African Nations Cup, South Africa were many people's favourites to retain the title. However, it was not South Africa but Egypt, another emerging African nation, that took the Cup in February. With African players in demand by many club sides in Europe, South Africa took only seven players from their domestic league to the World Cup, the rest of the team being made up from players based abroad – including Leeds' Lucas Radebe, Bolton's Mark Fish and Fulham's Andre Arendse. Nigeria's World Cup squad was even more extreme, with players from clubs in 10 different countries – but none from Nigerian clubs. With so many players now playing in Europe, African national teams are becoming more professional – only financial and political problems stand in their way.

Continental champions: Egypt's captain, Hassan Hossam, holds up the African Nations Cup after beating holders South Africa 2-0 in Ouagadougou, Burkina Faso, in February 1998.

Five African nations played in the 1998 World Cup finals – the most in the competition's history

SO NEAR, YET SO FAR

Australian football

The tremendous potential for football in Australia has long been acknowledged. In November 1997, when the Socceroos took to the pitch at the Melbourne Cricket Ground to face Iran in the play-off for France '98, the game finally took precedence. On a weekend when Australia was hosting a cricket Test against New Zealand and an international golf tournament, the national sporting focus had come to rest on a single game of soccer.

The raising of Australia's football profile began in April 1995 with the appointment of David Hill, head of the Australian Broadcasting Corporation, to the post of chairman of the game's governing body, Soccer Australia. Under his leadership, the organisation moved to restructure the National Soccer League by trying to force the clubs to shift the focus from their 'ethnic' European supporter bases and open them up to new fans. Some Sydney and Melbourne clubs were expelled from the League, with replacement clubs sought from Brisbane, Canberra, Newcastle and Perth, to make the game truly national. While this restructuring was taking place, with inevitable contests and court cases between clubs and the national body, Soccer Australia moved to boost the fortunes of the national side – the Socceroos.

Venables began to mould Australia into a team which could play fluent, attacking football

Downhearted: the Socceroos missed out on a place in the 1998 World Cup finals, despite not losing a game.

○ Australia's second leg of the play-off against Iran attracted a crowd of 85,022.

○ English clubs are much-favoured by Australian players, including Mark Bosnich of Aston Villa, pictured top right, Stan Lazaridis of West Ham and Harry Kewell of Leeds.

○ Australia failed to qualify for France '98, despite not losing a game. They won all six games prior to drawing both legs of the play-off with Iran.

In June 1998, the Socceroos said goodbye to manager Terry Venables with an ignominious 7-0 defeat at the hands of Croatia. Just over 18 months before, in November 1996, the former England manager had been appointed head coach of the Australian national side in a blaze of publicity. Venables overcame the problems of distance and time zones and began to mould a team which could play fluent, attacking football. He proceeded to take the Socceroos into the World Cup play-off with Iran. After a slightly lucky 1-1 draw in Iran, the Socceroos hosted the return leg at Melbourne on 29 November 1997. Throughout the game, they

were all over their opposition and with 20 minutes to play were cruising at 2-0. But spectacularly, in the space of just four minutes, Iran scored twice to go through to the World Cup finals on away goals. For the first 70 minutes of the game, and for the first time in Australia's history, football had been the success story of Australian sport. The Socceroos later reached the final of the Confederations Cup before losing to Brazil but now the focus of the sport has begun to swing towards the Sydney Olympics and the huge under-23 football tournament that it will host. There is even talk of a bid to host the 2010 World Cup finals.

Adios El Tel: originally criticised for being a part-time coach – dubbed El Telepathy by one Australian writer – Terry Venables won admiration for getting Australia into the World Cup play-off, but failed to get the team through.

1997-98 winners

There were plenty of winners in 1998, but the one that topped them all was Dennis Bergkamp. Winner of a Championship medal, he was also the Professional Footballers' Association Player of the Year, the Football Writers' Association Player of the Year, third in FIFA's World Footballer of the Year poll and the man behind the Goal of the Season (his strike against Leicester City). The only award to elude him was an FA Cup medal after he missed the final.

Two of England's finest footballers were knighted in 1998 – former Preston North End winger Tom Finney, who received his award in the New Year's Honours List, and 1966 World Cup hero Geoff Hurst, honoured in the Queen's Birthday List. Finney, the Football Writers' Player of the Year in 1954 and 1957, and Hurst, became the fifth and sixth 'footballing knights' respectively, after Stanley Matthews, Alf Ramsey, Matt Busby and Bobby Charlton. Chelsea's Mark Hughes was also honoured, receiving an MBE. In 1985, Hughes had been voted PFA Young Player of the Year. In 1998, that award went to Liverpool's Michael Owen. Only once in the last eight years has the award not been won by a Manchester United or Liverpool player. Even then the odd man out, Newcastle United's Andy Cole, now plays at Old Trafford.

Two of England's finest footballers were knighted in 1998 – Tom Finney and Geoff Hurst

Medal winners: Sir Tom Finney (left) and Chelsea's Mark Hughes received a knighthood and an MBE respectively, in the 1998 New Year's Honours List.

◯ Winning teams in the 1997-98 season included:

- Arsenal – FA Cup winners and League Champions
- Chelsea – League Cup and Cup Winners Cup winners
- Nottingham Forest – Division One Champions
- Watford – Division Two Champions
- Notts County – Division Three Champions
- Celtic – Scottish Premier and Scottish League Cup winners
- Hearts – Scottish FA Cup winners

Inter Milan striker Ronaldo, described by many as the new Pele, was voted FIFA World Footballer of the Year and European Footballer of the Year in 1998. But despite all his brilliance, Ronaldo was not able to score against Scotland in the World Cup – Scotland's success in qualifying for the finals was recognised north of the border with the Bell's October 1997 Player of the Month award going to "the Scotland squad". Scotland's Player of the Year was Celtic's Craig Burley, while the PFA Player of the Year award was picked up by team-mate Jackie McNamara. Scotland's Manager of the Year was Jim Jefferies, who guided Hearts to their first trophy in 25 years, when they won the Scottish FA Cup.

In most years, a Ferguson is an award winner, and so it was in 1998, only instead of Manchester United manager Alex picking up an award, the Ferguson in question was Ipswich's Alan – Groundsman of the Year in Division One. The Premiership Groundsman of the Year was Arsenal's Steve Braddock. Finally, England's Manager of the Year award was always destined to be Arsene Wenger's after the Frenchman led the Arsenal side to only the second double in their history. Even Wimbledon's Joe Kinnear is a fan of Wenger's: "He's a smashing bloke, thoughtful, articulate and pleasant."

Teen sensation: Liverpool's Michael Owen secured the PFA Young Player of the Year trophy. In 1998, he also won his first international cap, scored his first England goal and played for England in France '98.

Andy Gray is the only man to have won the PFA Player and Young Player of the Year awards in one year – 1977

EUROPEAN GLORY

Chelsea 1997-98

1997-98 was the most successful season in Chelsea's history, with the team winning two trophies in one season for the first time – the Coca-Cola Cup and the European Cup Winners Cup. The side also finished a creditable fourth in the Premiership. However, 1997-98 will also be remembered as one of the more controversial seasons in the club's history with the surprise sacking of Dutch manager Ruud Gullit in February, and his replacement by Italian player Gianluca Vialli.

Expectations were high in August 1997 – Chelsea had won the FA Cup the previous May, bringing silverware to Stamford Bridge for the first time in 26 years. There was a belief that this was just the beginning, and with Gullit signing Graeme Le Saux, Norwegian Tore Andre Flo and Uruguayan Gustavo Poyet, more was expected. The Charity Shield was lost on penalties to Manchester United but soon the Premiership was under way. Chelsea's season in the Premiership proved to be one of ups and downs. By Christmas they were just off the pace following thumping victories over Barnsley (6-0), Derby (4-0), Spurs (6-1) and Sheffield Wednesday (4-1). But as the new year was ushered in Chelsea began to tumble down the table, before four victories in the last six games resulted in a fourth place finish.

Chelsea's pursuit of cups both at home and abroad began with a 4-0 aggregate win in Europe

Lucky Luca: within three months and a day of becoming Chelsea's manager, Gianluca Vialli had brought home two major trophies to the club.

○ Chelsea's defence of the FA Cup in 1997-98 lasted just one game during which, at one stage, they were 5-0 down to Manchester United. They finally clawed back three goals but it was still not enough to keep them in the competition.

○ In 1980, Graham Rix missed for Arsenal in the penalty shoot-out of the Cup Winners Cup final, sending the team to a 5-4 defeat. Eighteen years later, as assistant manager at Chelsea, he was to make the decisive substitution decision for Chelsea in the Cup Winners Cup final, bringing on Gianfranco Zola and ensuring victory.

Chelsea's pursuit of cups both at home and abroad began with a 4-0 aggregate win over Slovakia's Slovan Bratislava in the first round of the Cup Winners Cup. Chelsea powered their way through the next round, after a slight hesitation in the snowstorm of Tromso, Norway, and by January had booked their place in the Coca-Cola Cup semi-finals following wins over Blackburn, Southampton and Ipswich. They lost the first leg 2-1 against Arsenal and then, on 12 February 1998, the club announced that manager Ruud Gullit had been sacked. With three crucial games due to take place in as many weeks, speculation about the sudden departure was rife. Gullit claimed he was the victim of a conspiracy, while chairman Ken Bates accused the Dutchman of being a "playboy". Gianluca Vialli took

Super sub: just 22 seconds after coming on to the pitch in Stockholm, Chelsea's Italian striker Gianfranco Zola ran on to Dennis Wise's through ball and beat the keeper to score the only goal of the Cup Winners Cup final against Stuttgart.

over as player-manager and guided the team to the Coca-Cola Cup final in his first game – an emotional 3-1 victory over Arsenal. He followed this with a 5-2 aggregate win over Spain's Real Betis in Europe, but could not secure a win against Manchester United in the Premiership. Come March and extra-time goals from Frank Sinclair and Roberto Di Matteo gave Chelsea a 2-0 victory in the Coca-Cola Cup final and their first trophy of the season. A late goal from substitute Mark Hughes in the second leg of the Cup Winners Cup semi-final against Italy's Vicenza sent Chelsea through to the final. Then, in a fairly dour Cup Winners Cup final, the one moment of inspiration came in the 71st minute when substitute Gianfranco Zola scored the only goal of the match – ensuring club history was made.

Chelsea are the only British club to have won the Cup Winners Cup twice – in 1971 and 1998

The following pages include all the teams in the Premiership and Divisions One, Two and Three of the English League at the start of the 1998-99 season, including Halifax, promoted from the Vauxhall Conference. They are followed by the 10 teams in Scotland's new Premier League and 20 European teams that enjoyed success in 1997-98 and will be competing in Europe in 1998-99 against Arsenal, Aston Villa, Blackburn Rovers, Chelsea, Leeds United, Liverpool and Manchester United. The teams are arranged alphabetically within each group and the next two pages will explain how the information on each team page has been organised and what has been included.

Team information

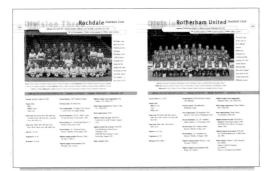

Each Premiership team includes an action shot taken during the 1997-98 season, while Division One teams have squad pictures taken at the start of the season. Player biographies appear for Premiership, Division One and Scottish Premier clubs and include all players who played in the first team in the 1997-98 season and were still with the club at the end of the season. Transfers include all those that took place between the 1997 close season and deadline day, 1998. All Division Two and Three teams include a picture of the squad taken at the start of the 1997-98 season. They do not include player biographies. The European teams include action shots from 1997-98 and the latest team information. All club information is as up-to-date as possible for the 1998-99 season. In the rare cases where new information was unavailable, the previous season's information is included.

Web site: Where the club has an official Web site, the address is included.

Ground history: Any grounds the club have used since their formation.

Previous name: Any names the club was called before the current name was adopted.

First League game: The first game after entry into the Football League, including date, division, opposition, venue and score.

Highest League scorer (aggregate): The player who has scored the most League goals for the club over more than one season.

Ground: The club's current stadium, including capacity for the 1998-99 season.

Most League appearances: The player who has played the most League games for the club and the years in which he played.

Stands: The names of the stands at the stadium at the start of the 1998-99 season.

Most capped player: The player who has won the most caps while at the club. The figure does not refer to caps the player may have won while at other clubs.

Home strip and **Away strip:** The colours for the 1998-99 season.

Highest transfer fee paid: The record amount paid by the club for a player.

Sponsor: The company that is sponsoring the team in 1998-99. Where the sponsor had not been decided at the time of going to press, 'unknown' has been entered.

Highest transfer fee received: The record amount paid to the club for a player.

Major trophies: League Championship and major Cup successes. The most recent victory comes first – (old) refers to the old divisions before the Premiership started in 1992-93.

Programme: The cost of the officially endorsed matchday magazine.

Nottingham Forest *Football Club*

186

→ **Address** | Nottingham Forest FC, City Ground, Nottingham NG2 5FJ

Tel: 0115 982 4444 | **Tickets:** 0115 982 4445 | **Clubline:** 0891 121174

In 1998-99 Forest will be hoping to repeat their success of the 1977-78 season, when they won the League in the first season after promotion. They also became the first side to do the League and League Cup 'double' in the same year.

→ **Web site:** http://www.nottinghamforest.co.uk   → **Chief executive:** Phil Soar   → **Manager:** Dave Bassett   → **Year formed:** 1865

Ground: City Ground (30,567)

Stands: Main
Trent End
Executive
Bridgford

Home strip: Red shirts with black and white trim, white shorts with black and red trim, red socks with black trim

Away strip: White shirts with black and red trim, black shorts, white socks

Sponsor: Pinnacle

Programme: £1.60

Nickname: Forest

Ground history: 1865 Forest Recreation Ground
1879 The Meadows
1880 Trent Bridge Cricket Ground
1882 Parkside, Lenton
1885 Gregory Ground, Lenton
1890 Town Ground
1898 City Ground

Previous name: None

First League game: 3 September 1892, Division 1, drew 2-2 (a) v Everton

Record attendance: 49,946 v Manchester United, 28 October 1967

Record victory: 14-0 v Clapton, FA Cup 1st round, 17 January 1891

Record defeat: 1-9 v Blackburn Rovers, Division 2, 10 April 1937

Highest League scorer (season): Wally Ardron, 36, 1950-51

Highest League scorer (aggregate): Grenville Morris, 199, 1898-1913

Most League appearances: Bob McKinley, 614, 1951-1970

Most capped player: Stuart Pearce, 76, England, 1985-1997

Highest transfer fee paid: £3.5m to Celtic for Pierre van Hooijdonk, March 1997

Highest transfer fee received: £8.5m from Liverpool for Stan Collymore, June 1995

Major trophies: Division 1 (old) Champions (1) 1977-78
Division 2 (old) Champions (2) 1921-22, 1906-07
Division 3 (South) Champions (1) 1950-51
FA Cup Winners (2) 1959, 1898
League Cup Winners (4) 1978, 1979, 1989, 1990
European Cup Winners (2) 1980, 1979

Nickname: The colloquial name the club is often referred to by its supporters.

Record attendance: For a match held at the club's current stadium and involving the home team.

Highest League scorer (season): The player who has scored the most League goals for the club in one season.

Record defeat: The most goals conceded in a League or major Cup game, excluding any preliminary rounds.

Record victory: The most goals scored in a League or major Cup game, excluding any preliminary rounds.

Arsenal Football Club

Arsenal Football Club
Arsenal Football Club
Arsenal Football Club
Arsenal Football Club
Arsenal Football Club
Arsenal Football Club
Arsenal Football Club
Arsenal Football Club
Arsenal Football Club
Arsenal Football Club
Arsenal Football Club

→ **Address** | Arsenal FC, Arsenal Stadium, Avenell Road, Highbury, London N5 1BU

Tel: 0171 704 4000 | **Tickets:** 0171 704 4040 | **Clubline:** 0891 202021

Player of the Year Dennis Bergkamp has such a violent fear of flying that he will probably miss most of the 1998-99 European Cup away legs. He missed the UEFA Cup game in Greece against PAOK Salonika last season, when Arsenal lost 1-0.

→ **Web site:** http://www.arsenal.co.uk   → **Chairman:** Peter Hill-Wood   → **Manager:** Arsene Wenger   → **Year formed:** 1886

Ground: Highbury (38,548)

Stands: East
 West
 Clock End
 North Bank

Home strip: Red shirts with white trim, white shorts with red trim, white socks with red trim

Away strip: Yellow shirts with navy blue trim, navy blue shorts, navy blue socks with yellow trim

Sponsor: JVC

Programme: £2

Nickname: Gunners

Ground history: 1886 Plumstead Common
 1887 Sportsman Ground
 1888 Manor Ground

 1890 Invicta Ground
 1893 Manor Ground
 1913 Highbury

Previous names: Dial Square
 Royal Arsenal
 Woolwich Arsenal

First League game: 2 September 1893, Division 2, drew 2-2 (h) v Newcastle United

Record attendance: 73,295 v Sunderland, Division 1, 9 March 1935

Record victory: 12-0 v Loughborough Town, Division 2, 12 March 1900

Record defeat: 0-8 v Loughborough Town, Division 2, 12 December 1896

Highest League scorer (season): Ted Drake, 42, 1934-35

Highest League scorer (aggregate): Cliff Bastin, 150, 1930-1947

Most League appearances: David O'Leary, 558, 1975-1993

Most capped player: Kenny Sansom, 77, England, 1980-1988

Highest transfer fee paid: £7.5m to Inter Milan (Italy) for Dennis Bergkamp, June 1995

Highest transfer fee received: £5m from West Ham United for John Hartson, February 1997

Major trophies: Premiership Champions **(1)** 1997-98
 Division 1 (old) Champions **(10)** 1990-91, 1988-89, 1970-71, 1952-53, 1947-48, 1937-38, 1934-35, 1933-34, 1932-33, 1930-31
 FA Cup Winners **(7)** 1998, 1993, 1979, 1971, 1950, 1936, 1930
 League Cup Winners **(2)** 1993, 1987
 Cup Winners Cup Winners **(1)** 1994

Tony Adams – An inspirational captain who signed in November 1980 as a schoolboy, he overcame adversity in spectacular style in 1997-98.

Nicolas Anelka – A February 1997 signing from Paris St-Germain, he is a lightning fast striker who reaped a good number of goals.

Steve Bould – A tribunal-set £390,000 signing from Stoke City in June 1988, he has been a huge asset to the club, although injury prevented an extended run in the side in 1997-98.

Jason Crowe – He appeared briefly as a substitute twice – against Crystal Palace in the FA Cup and Birmingham City in the Coca-Cola Cup.

Lee Dixon – An experienced attacking right back who signed for £350,000 from Stoke City in January 1988, he had an excellent Championship-winning season.

Remi Garde – A free signing from French side Racing Strasbourg in August 1996, he is a right-sided midfielder who filled in for Lee Dixon during the first half of the season.

Gilles Grimandi – A June 1997 signing from AS Monaco, he is a defensive player who scored his only goal of the season in the 1-0 win against Crystal Palace in February.

Stephen Hughes – A talented young midfielder who, again, was mainly used from the bench, but looks to have an excellent future.

Martin Keown – In his second spell at Arsenal after re-signing from Everton for £2 million in February 1993, he is a commanding England international centre half who shared defensive responsibilities with Steve Bould during the 1997-98 season.

Gavin McGowan – A versatile defender, he made his only appearance from the bench in

Arsenal's 1-0 victory over Crystal Palace in February 1998.

Alex Manninger – The first Austrian goalkeeper in the Premiership, he deputised for David Seaman without conceding a goal in the six League games he played in early 1998.

Scott Marshall – A 6ft 1in central defender, he started his only Premiership game in the 2-0 victory over Coventry back in August 1997.

Alberto Mendez – A June 1997 signing from German side FC Feucht, he qualifies to play for either Germany or Spain and made his Premiership debut in the 0-2 away defeat by Sheffield Wednesday in November 1997.

Luis Boa Morte – The young Portuguese forward was mainly used as a substitute after signing from Sporting Lisbon in June 1997 for £1.75 million.

Ray Parlour – The right-sided midfielder, who turned professional in March 1991, had a wonderful season and will undoubtedly be a driving force in Arsenal's pursuit of the 1998-99 European Cup.

Emmanuel Petit – 'Manu' was signed from AS Monaco for £3.5 million in June 1997 and the blond midfield playmaker turned in some Championship-winning performances in the middle of the park, working closely with Patrick Vieira.

David Platt – An experienced midfielder who was used mainly from the bench during 1997-98, his finest moment came with the headed winner against Manchester United in November 1997.

Isaiah Rankin – His only appearance came as a substitute against north London rivals Spurs in December.

David Seaman – England's number one goalkeeper, he signed for £1.3

million from Crystal Palace in May 1990 and despite six League games out with a broken finger, was once again indispensable.

Matthew Upson – Signed from Luton for £2 million in May 1997, four Premiership starts was all the young defender could manage due to the excellent form of Nigel Winterburn.

Patrick Vieira – A £4 million signing from AC Milan in August 1996, he was one of the Gunners' finest players during the 1997-98 season.

Paolo Vernazza – A midfielder who made just one Premiership start – in the 1-0 home win over Crystal Palace in February 1998.

Nigel Winterburn – Arsenal's most consistent player during the 1997-98 Championship-winning season, the left back signed in May 1987 from Wimbledon for £350,000. His energy and commitment seem to defy his 34 years.

Christopher Wreh – Cousin of AC Milan's George Weah, the striker signed from AS Monaco for £300,000 in August 1997 and scored some important goals.

Transferred in:
• Marc Overmars (Ajax, £7m)
• Christopher Wreh
  (Monaco, £300,000)
• Alex Manninger
  (Casino Graz, £500,000)
• Emmanuel Petit (Monaco, £3.5m)
• Gilles Grimandi
  (Monaco, undisclosed)
• Luis Boa Morte
  (Sporting Lisbon, £1.75m)
• Alberto Mendez
  (FC Feucht, £250,000)

Transferred out:
• Paul Shaw (Millwall, £250,000)
• Ian Selley (Fulham, £500,000)
• Glenn Helder
  (NAC Breda, undisclosed)
• Vince Bartram (Gillingham, free)
• Paul Merson (Middlesbrough, £5m)

Marc Overmars – A sublimely talented left-sided midfielder who signed from Dutch giants Ajax for £7 million in June 1997, he was instrumental in helping Arsenal to Championship success.

Dennis Bergkamp – Player of the Year in 1997-98, he was a £7.5 million signing from Inter Milan in the summer of 1995 and his vision, skill and goalscoring have made him one of the best players in the Premiership.

Ian Wright – Arsenal's record leading goalscorer in all competitions, Wright came from Crystal Palace in 1991 for £2.5 million. He missed the end of the season due to injury, but still managed to score 11 goals.

Aston Villa Football Club

Aston Villa Football Club
Aston Villa Football Club
Aston Villa Football Club
Aston Villa Football Club
Aston Villa Football Club
Aston Villa Football Club
Aston Villa Football Club
Aston Villa Football Club
Aston Villa Football Club
Aston Villa Football
Aston Villa
Aston Villa Club

→ **Address** | Aston Villa FC, Villa Park, Trinity Road, Birmingham B6 6HE

Tel: 0121 327 2299 | **Tickets:** 0121 327 5353 | **Clubline:** 0891 121148

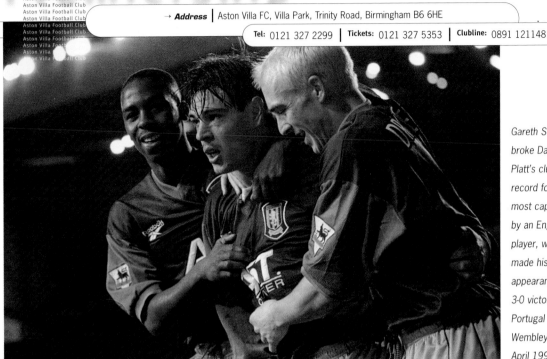

Gareth Southgate broke David Platt's club record for the most caps won by an England player, when he made his 23rd appearance in the 3-0 victory over Portugal at Wembley in April 1998.

→ **Web site:** http://www.astonvilla-fc.co.uk   → **Chairman:** Doug Ellis   → **Manager:** John Gregory   → **Year formed:** 1874

Ground: Villa Park (39,372)

Stands: North
Holte End
Doug Ellis
Trinity Road

Home strip: Claret shirts with sky blue and white trim, white shorts with claret and sky blue trim, sky blue socks with claret and white trim

Away strip: Turquoise shirts with black and white trim, black shorts with turquoise and white trim, turquoise socks with black and white trim

Sponsor: LDV Vans

Programme: £1.80

Nickname: Villains

Ground history: 1874 Aston Park
1876 Perry Barr
1897 Villa Park

Previous name: None

First League game: 8 September 1888, Football League, drew 1-1 (a) v Wolverhampton Wanderers

Record attendance: 76,588 v Derby County, FA Cup 6th round, 2 March 1946

Record victory: 13-0 v Wednesbury Old Athletic, FA Cup 1st round, 30 October 1886

Record defeat: 1-8 v Blackburn Rovers, FA Cup 3rd round, 16 February 1889

Highest League scorer (season): Tom 'Pongo' Waring, 49, 1930-31

Highest League scorer (aggregate): Harry Hampton, 215, 1904-1920
Billy Walker, 215, 1919-1934

Most League appearances: Charlie Aitken, 561, 1961-1976

Most capped player: Paul McGrath, 51, Republic of Ireland, 1989-1996

Highest transfer fee paid: £7m to Liverpool for Stan Collymore, May 1997

Highest transfer fee received: £5.5m from Bari (Italy) for David Platt, July 1991

Major trophies: Division 1 (old) Champions (7) 1980-81, 1909-10, 1899-1900, 1898-99, 1896-97, 1895-96, 1893-94
Division 2 (old) Champions (2) 1959-60, 1937-38
Division 3 (old) Champions (1) 1971-72
FA Cup Winners (7) 1957, 1920, 1913, 1905, 1897, 1895, 1887
League Cup Winners (5) 1996, 1994, 1977, 1975, 1961
European Cup Winners (1) 1982

Gareth Barry – A versatile performer, the captain of Aston Villa's youth team was impressive in the last two games of the season, against Sheffield Wednesday and Arsenal.

Mark Bosnich – The colourful Australian goalkeeper had a quiet but effective season in 1997-98, a vast improvement on the previous season when he was in and out of the side through injury.

Darren Byfield – A 21-year-old striker with bags of promise, Byfield was restricted to eight first team appearances in 1997-98, mostly as substitute. His only start came just after Christmas against Leeds in a game where he showed enough promise to suggest he'll be getting more chances.

Gary Charles – An accomplished defender who made a successful return from a serious knee injury which ruled him out of the entire 1996-97 season, Charles contested the right wing-back berth with Fernando Nelson, making 25 appearances and impressing with his ability to go forward.

Mark Draper – A playmaker who again proved himself to be a key figure for Villa, Draper often controls games with his accurate passing and is capable of building moves from a deep position. However, it looks likely that the midfielder will remain on the fringes of the England squad, having failed to improve on his 1996 call-up for the World Cup qualifier in Moldova.

Ugo Ehiogu – An imposing and impressive centre back, Ehiogu can count himself unlucky not to have earned at least an England B-cap after yet another consistent season. He hardly missed a game as he continued his strong defensive partnership with Gareth Southgate and Steve Staunton, and his only black mark was a last-day sending-off for two bookable offences.

Simon Grayson – The utility man, signed by former Villa manager Brian Little for £1.35 million in June 1997, looked worth every penny as he performed well in a variety of positions. The former Leicester player made appearances across the midfield, at right wing back, and as part of a three-man central defence, chipping in with vital FA Cup goals against Portsmouth and West Brom.

Lee Hendrie – A 20-year-old roving midfielder who was finally allowed the chance to show his undoubted talent midway through the 1997-98 season, Hendrie progressed through the youth system and came to prominence after John Gregory had succeeded Little as manager. He gave Villa some attacking spark from midfield and earned an England B-cap against Russia in April 1998.

Julian Joachim – A nippy forward who enjoyed a good latter half of the season, Joachim eventually displaced unsettled striker Savo Milosevic and an out-of-form Stan Collymore. His pace troubled defenders, he chipped in with some important goals, and at 23, there's still time for him to fulfil the outstanding promise he showed as a teenager.

Fernando Nelson – The Portuguese international was scarcely out of the Villa side when Little was in charge, but found himself out of favour once Gregory took over in March 1998. Capable of playing at full back or in midfield, Nelson is technically gifted, but occasionally a touch lightweight for the rigours of the Premiership.

Michael Oakes – Unable to dislodge Bosnich at Villa Park, Oakes would be first-choice goalkeeper at many Premiership sides. He made just nine appearances in the 1997-98 season, compared to 23 in the previous one, in what must have been a frustrating season spent mainly on the bench.

Riccardo Scimeca – A classy defender and England Under-21 captain, Scimeca had his most productive season ever at Villa, making 29 appearances despite tough competition for the centre-back places. Injury against Atletico Madrid in March spoilt the final weeks of the 1997-98 season.

Steve Staunton – A highly rated Republic of Ireland international defender, Staunton was one of Aston Villa's most committed performers in spite of the almost constant speculation about his future. His long-range shooting and crossing ability proved an attacking bonus.

Ian Taylor – Local lad Taylor probably had his best season yet in Villa colours since joining the club in 1994. He tirelessly worked the pitch, getting from box to box to help out in defence and provide support in attack when required, and contributed several important goals.

Richard Walker – A young reserve striker, Walker made just one first-team appearance – and that was for a single minute after coming on as substitute against Leeds in December 1997.

Alan Wright – The diminutive left back played well last season and is also effective as a wing back, where he is able to go forward and use his creative skills to support the attack.

Gareth Southgate – A cultured central defender and skipper, Southgate's cool head and leadership qualities were vital to the Villa cause in a season that also saw him consolidate his defensive role in the England side.

Stan Collymore – The striker was once Britain's most expensive footballer but despite flashes of his undoubted talent, he failed to sparkle in 1997-98. A goal return of eight was a major disappointment for Villa.

Transferred in:
- Simon Grayson
  (Leicester, £1.35m)
- David Curtolo
  (Vasterhas, £300,000)

Transferred out:
- Gareth Farrelly
  (Everton, £700,000)
- Phil King (Swindon, free)
- Andy Townsend
  (Middlesbrough, £500,000)
- Scott Murray
  (Bristol City, £150,000)
- Sasa Curcic (Crystal Palace, £1m)

Dwight Yorke – The Trinidad & Tobago international was top scorer for Villa for the third successive season. A pacy striker and an occasional midfielder, Yorke is a prized asset at Villa Park.

Blackburn Rovers *Football Club*

→ Address | Blackburn Rovers FC, Ewood Park, Blackburn, Lancashire BB2 4JF

Tel: 01254 698888 | **Tickets:** 01254 671666 | **Clubline:** 0891 121014

Roy Hodgson's arrival at Ewood marked a change of fortune for Rovers in 1997-98. The team finished sixth (seven places higher than in 1996-97) in the League and earned a place in Europe.

→ Web site: http://www.rovers.co.uk **→ Chairman:** Robert Coar **→ Manager:** Roy Hodgson **→ Year formed:** 1875

Ground: Ewood Park (31,367)

Stands: Walker Steel
Jack Walker
Blackburn End
Darwen End

Home strip: White and blue halved shirts, white shorts, white socks

Away strip: Yellow shirts, navy blue shorts, yellow socks

Sponsor: CIS

Programme: £2

Nickname: Rovers

Ground history: 1876 Oozehead Ground
1877 Pleasington Cricket Ground
1879 Alexandra Meadows
1881 Leamington Ground
1890 Ewood Park

Previous name: None

First League game: 15 September 1888, Football League, drew 5-5 (h) v Accrington

Record attendance: 62,522 v Bolton Wanderers, FA Cup 6th round, 2 March 1929

Record victory: 11-0 v Rossendale, FA Cup 1st round, 13 October 1884

Record defeat: 0-8 v Arsenal, Division 1, 25 February 1933

Highest League scorer (season): Ted Harper, 44, 1925-26

Highest League scorer (aggregate): Simon Garner, 168, 1978-1992

Most League appearances: Derek Fazackerley, 596, 1970-1986

Most capped player: Bob Crompton, 41, England, 1902-1914

Highest transfer fee paid: £7.5m to Southampton for Kevin Davies, June 1998

Highest transfer fee received: £15m from Newcastle United for Alan Shearer, July 1996

Major trophies: Premiership Champions **(1)** 1994-95
Division 1 (old) Champions **(2)** 1913-14, 1911-12
Division 2 (old) Champions **(1)** 1938-39
Division 3 (old) Champions **(1)** 1974-75
FA Cup Winners **(6)** 1928, 1891, 1890, 1886, 1885, 1884

Anders Andersson – A 24-year-old Swedish international midfielder signed from Malmo in July 1997, Andersson found first team opportunities limited in his first season at Ewood Park.

James Beattie – A young striker with a prolific scoring record at junior level, Beattie made his debut in the 1996-97 season due to an injury crisis at Blackburn and made five more appearances in 1997-98.

Marlon Broomes – A highly rated central defender starting to stake a claim for a first team place, Broomes has already been capped by England at several levels and has trained with the full England squad.

Gary Croft – A stylish left back and strong tackler, Croft was signed from Grimsby in March 1996 for £1 million, and was given more chances to establish himself in the side in 1997-98 thanks to Graeme Le Saux's departure to Chelsea.

Martin Dahlin – A 1994 World Cup hero with Sweden, Dahlin signed for £2 million in July 1997 from Italian Serie A club AS Roma, but struggled to break up the Kevin Gallacher and Chris Sutton strike partnership, scoring just six goals in 1997-98.

Callum Davidson – The unlucky left back was signed from St Johnstone for £1.75 million but spent three months injured before finally making his debut in the 4-1 drubbing by Arsenal – and pulling his hamstring.

Damien Duff – A left winger with pace, skill and an eye for goal, Duff signed from Republic of Ireland side Lourdes Celtic in March 1996, and is considered to be one of the Premiership's brightest prospects.

Alan Fettis – A Northern Ireland international keeper, Fettis made 10 first team appearances in 1997-98 to replace an injured Tim Flowers, but then lost his place to John Filan.

John Filan – A Sydney-born goalkeeper signed from Coventry as cover for Flowers when Shay Given left for Newcastle, Filan is a confident keeper who clears his lines well.

Garry Flitcroft – A strong-running midfielder signed from Manchester City in a £3 million deal in March 1996, Flitcroft formed part of a highly competitive midfield with Tim Sherwood and Billy McKinlay.

Tim Flowers – A shoulder injury sidelined Rovers' first choice goalkeeper in February, but he returned to keep a crucial clean sheet in the final game to help the club secure a UEFA Cup spot for the 1998-99 season.

Kevin Gallacher – Quick, clever and a good finisher, Scotland's World Cup striker finally put serious injuries behind him in the 1997-98 season to form a profitable partnership up front with Chris Sutton to generate an impressive 41 goals.

Stephane Henchoz – A Swiss defender who had played previously under manager Roy Hodgson both at club and international level, the solid and composed Henchoz established an effective defensive partnership with Colin Hendry.

Jeff Kenna – A Republic of Ireland international, full-back Kenna signed from Southampton in March 1995 and notched up the most appearances of any Blackburn player last season.

Billy McKinlay – A Scottish international signed from Dundee in October 1995 for £1.75 million, McKinlay became a first team regular in 1997-98 and is an ideal midfield partner for Tim Sherwood.

Per Pedersen – The first signing following Alan Shearer's departure, Pedersen failed to make much impact. He played just twice last season and spent time on loan to Borussia Moenchengladbach.

Tore Pedersen – A £500,000 signing in September 1997, Pedersen has over 40 caps for Norway but didn't figure in the side after Christmas.

Stuart Ripley – A lively winger who sadly pulled his hamstring just minutes into a substitute appearance for England in September 1997, Ripley returned to the Rovers flank six weeks later in impressive form.

Patrick Valery – A former French Under-21 defender, Valery started the season but lost his place and never made the impact that was expected.

Jason Wilcox – A left winger who progressed through the ranks to make his debut in 1990, Wilcox is a superb crosser of the ball and gives the team good balance, though he was twice sent off in the 1997-98 season.

Transferred in:
• Anders Andersson
  (Malmo, £500,000)
• Martin Dahlin (AS Roma, £2m)
• Stephane Henchoz (Hamburg, £2m)
• Patrick Valery (Bastia, free)
• Tore Pedersen
  (St Pauli, £500,000)
• Callum Davidson
  (St Johnstone, £1.75m)

Transferred out:
• Graeme Le Saux (Chelsea, £5m)
• Henning Berg
  (Manchester United, £5m)
• Lars Bohinen (Derby £1.45m)
• Ian Pearce (West Ham, £2m)
• Paul Warhurst
  (Crystal Palace, £1.55m)
• Nicky Marker
  (Sheffield United, £400,000)
• Chris Coleman (Fulham, £2.1m)
• Georgios Donis (AEK Athens, free)
• Matt Holmes (Charlton, £250,000)
• Graham Fenton (Leicester, £1.1m)
• Niklas Gudmundsson
  (Malmo, £300,000)
• Steve Hitchen (Macclesfield, free)

Chris Sutton – The joint leading scorer in the Premiership was in superb form, scoring 21 goals in all competitions. He also made the headlines when he refused to play for the England B-team.

Tim Sherwood – A battling midfielder, Sherwood began at Watford before moving to Norwich, then Rovers. Mooted as a possible England player, he had to settle for another consistent season at Ewood Park.

Colin Hendry – The heart of the Blackburn side, Hendry is one of the most respected defenders in the League. The Scotland central defender again produced a series of outstanding performances in 1997-98.

Charlton Athletic *Football Club*

Charlton Athletic Football Club
Charlton Athletic Football Club
Charlton Athletic Football Club
Charlton Athletic Football Club
Charlton Athletic Football Club
Charlton Athletic Football Club
Charlton Athletic Football Club
Charlton Athletic Football Club
Charlton Athletic Football Club
Charlton Athletic Football Club
Charlton Athletic Football Club

→ **Address** | Charlton Athletic FC, The Valley, Floyd Road, Charlton, London SE7 8BL

Tel: 0181 333 4000 | **Tickets:** 0181 333 4010 | **Clubline:** 0891 121146

Alan Curbishley's squad enjoyed a fabulous second half to the 1997-98 season, with a club record run of eight League wins which put them into a play-off position – and eventually secured them promotion to the Premiership.

→ **Web site:** http://www.charlton-athletic.co.uk → **Chairman:** Martin Simons → **Manager:** Alan Curbishley → **Year formed:** 1905

Ground: The Valley (16,000)

Stands: North
South
East
West

Home strip: Red shirts with white trim, white shorts with red trim, red socks with white trim

Away strip: Ecru shirts with black trim, black shorts with ecru trim, ecru socks with black trim

Sponsor: Mesh Computers

Programme: £1.80

Nickname: Addicks

Ground history: 1906 Siemen's Meadow
1907 Woolwich Common
1909 Pound Park
1913 Horn Lane
1920 The Valley
1923 The Mount
1924 The Valley
1985 Selhurst Park
1991 Upton Park
1992 The Valley

Previous name: None

First League game: 27 August 1921, Division 3 (South), won 1-0 (h) v Exeter City

Record attendance: 75,031 v Aston Villa, FA Cup 5th round, 12 February 1938

Record victory: 8-1 v Middlesbrough, Division 1, 12 September 1953

Record defeat: 1-11 v Aston Villa, Division 2, 14 November 1959

Highest League position: Division 1 (old), runners-up, 1936-37

Highest League scorer (season): Ralph Allen, 32, Division 3 (South), 1934-35

Highest League scorer (aggregate): Stuart Leary, 153, 1953-1962

Most League appearances: Sam Bartram 583, 1934-1956

Most capped player: John Hewie, 19, Scotland, 1956-1960

Highest transfer fee paid: £700,000 to Grimsby Town for Clive Mendonca, June 1997

Highest transfer fee received: £2.8m from Leeds United for Lee Bowyer, July 1996

Major trophies: Division 3 (South) Champions **(2)** 1934-35, 1928-29
FA Cup winners **(1)** 1947

Bradley Allen – A £400,000 signing from Queen's Park Rangers in March 1996, his first two seasons at The Valley were blighted by injury.

Stuart Balmer – A right-footed central defender, he came from Celtic in 1990 for £120,000. A good distributor, he has captained the side.

Anthony Barness – 'Barney' has made the most of his appearances at left back during his second spell at Charlton after periods at Chelsea, Middlesbrough and Southend.

Mark Bowen – Brought in primarily as cover in September 1997 after a short spell in Japan's J-League, this experienced Welsh international provided solid cover at left back in 1997-98.

Mark Bright – A surprise free transfer from Swiss side SC Sion in April 1997, he was hit by a hernia problem in the autumn. An experienced target man and proven scorer, his overall contribution was crucial on his return.

Steve Brown – A tall, strong, right-sided defender who can also play in midfield and occasionally stands in as keeper, Brown lost his place in the first team at the end of February.

Phil Chapple – A threat at set pieces and corners due to his height, he came from Cambridge for £100,000 in 1993. His solid performances were important in Charlton's 1997-98 promotion-winning run.

Paul Emblen – A £7,500 signing from non-League Tonbridge Angels in May 1997, he failed to break through into the senior side in 1997-98.

Sasa Ilic – A Yugoslavian goalkeeper born in Australia, he signed from non-League Stamcroft in August 1997 and made his debut away at Stoke City in February 1998. He will now forever be remembered as the man who made the £10 million save in the play-off final against Sunderland.

Keith Jones – A slight-built but tough-tackling midfielder, he was signed from Southend for £150,000 in September 1994. He was a hard-working figure in Charlton's 1997-98 promotion-winning season.

Steve Jones – Signed for £400,000 in February 1997 from West Ham, Jones played only two games before sustaining a serious knee injury. The 1997-98 season proved equally frustrating, but his goals were vital.

Mark Kinsella – Charlton's crucial midfield general came for £200,000 from Colchester in 1996. A great passer, he made his full international debut for the Republic of Ireland against the Czechs in February 1998 and was ever-present for Charlton.

Paul Konchesky – The youngest player ever to appear for Charlton in a competitive match, he was 16 years and 93 days old when he appeared against Oxford United in August 1997. Despite his promise, he has yet to secure a first-team spot.

Kevin Lisbie – A quick forward capped at Under-18 level by England, he made his debut in the Coca-Cola Cup against Burnley in September 1996 – but remained Curbishley's favourite sub for most of 1997-98.

Danny Mills – Born in Norwich, this England Under-21 full back signed in March 1998 for £250,000 from his home town club. He showed his style by scoring his first League goal soon after joining Charlton.

Paul Mortimer – A skilful, left-sided midfielder who returned to The Valley in 1994 after spells with Aston Villa and Crystal Palace, he has not really met expectations.

Kevin Nicholls – A combative midfield player who made his full debut as early as 1996, the former England Under-18 captain was put out of action in December 1997 following a knee operation.

Scott Parker – A trainee who turned professional in October 1997, the 17-year-old midfielder made his debut as a substitute in 1997-98.

Andy Petterson – The much-loaned Australian broke into the side after injury to Mike Salmon on New Year's Day 1996, keeping his place with good performances before losing out to Ilic in March 1998.

John Robinson – Born in Zimbabwe, he is now a full Welsh international winger. Signed from Brighton for £75,000 in September 1992, he was an automatic choice in 1997-98.

Richard Rufus – He was made captain of the England Under-21 team at the start of the 1996-97 season and has continued to mature as a defender – scoring his first goal in the play-offs.

Mike Salmon – A £100,000 signing from Wrexham in July 1989, he is a solid reserve goalkeeper who made nine League appearances in 1997-98.

Jamie Stuart – Though he signed professional forms in January 1995, the talented left back spent most of the 1997-98 season in the reserves.

Eddie Youds – Signed from Bradford City on transfer deadline day in March 1998 for £550,000, he is an experienced 28-year-old defender.

Transferred in:
- Clive Mendonca (Grimsby, £700,000)
- Matt Holmes (Blackburn, £250,000)
- Mark Bright (FC Sion, free)
- Mark Bowen (Shimizu-S-Pulse, free)
- Sasa Ilic (Stamcroft, free)
- Danny Mills (Norwich, £250,000)
- Eddie Youds (Bradford, £550,000)

Transferred out:
- Brendan O'Connell (Wigan, £120,000)
- Paul Linger (Orient, free)
- Carl Leaburn (Wimbledon, £300,000)

Clive Mendonca – A record £700,000 signing from Grimsby in June 1997, it was his striking goal tally that took Charlton to the play-offs in 1997-98 and his hat-trick in the play-off final that helped ensure promotion.

Shaun Newton – Comfortable anywhere down the right side, Newton is powerfully built and very fast. He has England Under-21 caps to his credit – but needs to work on his crossing.

Matt Holmes – A left-sided midfielder signed from Blackburn for £250,000 in the summer of 1997, Holmes was injured just five days before the start of the 1997-98 season and then broke his leg in February 1998.

Chelsea Football Club

Chelsea Football Club
Chelsea Football Club
Chelsea Football Club
Chelsea Football Club
Chelsea Football Club
Chelsea Football Club
Chelsea Football Club
Chelsea Football Club
Chelsea Football Club
Chelsea Football Club
Chelsea Football Club

→ **Address** | Chelsea FC, Stamford Bridge, London SW6 1HS

Tel: 0171 385 5545 | **Tickets:** 0171 386 7799 | **Clubline:** 0891 121159

Chelsea have twice won the Cup Winners Cup in their history – in 1971 and 1998. Coincidentally, they happen to be the same years that London rivals Arsenal won both of their FA Cup and Championship doubles.

→ **Web site:** http://www.chelseafc.co.uk   → **Chairman:** Ken Bates   → **Player-manager:** Gianluca Vialli   → **Year formed:** 1905

Ground: Stamford Bridge (34,700)

Stands: East
  West
  Shed End
  Matthew Harding

Home strip: Blue shirts with white and yellow trim, blue shorts with white and yellow trim, white socks

Away strip: White shirts with blue trim, white shorts, white socks with blue trim

Sponsor: Autoglass

Programme: £2.50

Nickname: Blues

Ground history: 1905 Stamford Bridge

Previous name: None

First League game: 2 September 1905, Division 2, lost 0-1 (a) v Stockport County

Record attendance: 82,905 v Arsenal, Division 1, 12 October 1935

Record victory: 13-0 v Jeunesse Hautcharage (Luxembourg), Cup Winners Cup 1st round, 2nd leg, 29 September 1971

Record defeat: 1-8 v Wolverhampton Wanderers, Division 1, 26 September 1953

Highest League scorer (season): Jimmy Greaves, 41, 1960-61

Highest League scorer (aggregate): Bobby Tambling, 164, 1958-1969

Most League appearances: Ron Harris, 655, 1962-1980

Most capped player: Ray Wilkins, 24, England, 1973-1979

Highest transfer fee paid: £5.4m to Lazio (Italy) for Pierluigi Casiraghi, July 1998

Highest transfer fee received: £2.5m from Celtic for Craig Burley, July 1997

Major trophies: Division 1 (old) Champions **(1)** 1954-55
Division 2 (old) Champions **(2)** 1988-89, 1983-84
FA Cup Winners **(2)** 1997, 1970
League Cup Winners **(2)** 1998, 1965
Cup Winners Cup Winners **(2)** 1998, 1971

Celestine Babayaro – Chelsea beat off interest from Inter Milan and Juventus to sign the Nigerian left back from Anderlecht – but a broken leg and the form of Graeme Le Saux and Danny Granville limited his first team appearances in 1997-98.

Steve Clarke – Signed from St Mirren for £422,000 in 1987, Clarke rounded off another solid season with his first goal for six years in the 4-1 home win over Liverpool.

Nick Crittenden – A right wing back signed from the juniors, Crittenden made his first team debut against Southampton in the Coca-Cola Cup.

Ed De Goey – The Dutch international goalkeeper was bought from Feyenoord for £2.25 million in June 1997. At 6ft 6in, he's Chelsea's tallest ever player and was a revelation in the Cup Winners Cup.

Roberto Di Matteo – The Italian midfielder arrived from Lazio in July 1996 and confirmed his reputation as a big game player with a fine goal in the 1998 Coca-Cola Cup final.

Michael Duberry – A strong centre back with plenty of pace, Duberry missed a couple of months in 1997-98 with an ankle injury, but returned to cement his place in the side.

Tore Andre Flo – Tall, strong and surprisingly skilful, the Norwegian striker signed from SK Brann Bergen for £300,000 in July 1997 and more than proved his worth with 15 goals.

Danny Granville – An exciting prospect at left back, picked up for just £300,000 from Cambridge in March 1997, Granville deputised magnificently for Le Saux in the Cup Winners Cup final.

Steven Hampshire – A young professional who can play either as an attacking midfielder or striker, Hampshire made his debut in the Coca-Cola Cup against Blackburn.

Jon Harley – A tough, skilful midfielder who graduated from the Lilleshall School of Excellence, Harley managed to chalk up just three appearances, in April 1998.

Kevin Hitchcock – The third choice keeper has been with the club since 1988, but played just twice all season.

Mark Hughes – The ever-popular Welsh striker, who signed from Manchester United for £1.5 million, contributed his usual quota of goals, including a priceless strike against Vicenza in the Cup Winners Cup semi-final second leg.

Paul Hughes – A former England schoolboy who came through the Chelsea ranks, Hughes found his opportunities limited in 1997-98.

Dmitri Kharine – The Russian international goalkeeper was sidelined for 18 months with a ruptured cruciate ligament but returned in February 1998 as Chelsea's first choice shot-stopper.

Bernard Lambourde – A Frenchman who can play in defence or midfield, Lambourde remained something of a fringe player after being sent off in his fourth game against Liverpool.

Graeme Le Saux – In his second spell at the club, having returned from Blackburn, the England left back's pace, creativity and positional sense boosted Chelsea's defensive balance.

David Lee – After recovering from a broken leg, the former Chelsea trainee was called upon just once in his 10th professional season.

Andy Myers – A left-sided defender, Myers found himself down the pecking order for a first team place, but still notched up 17 appearances.

Eddie Newton – A composed, hardworking midfielder, Newton returned to the side for the successful run-in and played in both Cup finals.

Mark Nicholls – A goal-poaching striker, Nicholls was largely restricted to substitute appearances last season but two goals against Coventry gave a glimpse of his talent.

Dan Petrescu – Arguably Chelsea's best player in the 1998 Cup Winners Cup final, this Romanian international right wing back played as a right-sided midfielder in 1997-98.

Gustavo Poyet – Signed from Real Zaragoza, the midfielder suffered a cruciate ligament injury early in the season but returned in April and by the end of 1997-98 had scored five goals from 16 starts.

Frank Sinclair – A popular player with the fans, the Jamaican international defender scored the crucial opener in the Coca-Cola Cup final.

Gianluca Vialli – An incredible season for the former Italian international striker started on the bench and ended in glory as a trophy-winning manager and the club's leading scorer with 19 goals in 34 games.

Dennis Wise – A £1.6 million signing from Wimbledon in 1990, the Blues captain is a combative and creative midfielder who has now played more than 300 games for the club.

Transferred in:
- Graeme Le Saux (Blackburn, £5m)
- Bernard Lambourde (Bordeaux, £1.5m)
- Ed De Goey (Feyenoord, £2.25m)
- Tore Andre Flo (SK Brann Bergen, £300,000)
- Gustavo Poyet (Real Zaragoza, free)
- Celestine Babayaro (Anderlecht, £2.25m)

Transferred out:
- Frode Grodas (Spurs, free)
- Craig Burley (Celtic, £2.5m)
- Scott Minto (Benfica, free)
- Jimmy Aggrey (Fulham, free)
- Erland Johnsen (Rosenborg, free)
- Paul Parker (released)

Jody Morris – A gifted 19-year-old midfielder, Morris progressed through the junior ranks and showed great composure when called upon to play in the Cup Winners Cup semi-final.

Gianfranco Zola – Signed for £4.5 million from Parma in 1996, the Italian striker walked away with the 1997 Footballer of the Year award, and scored the goal which brought the 1998 Cup Winners Cup to Chelsea.

Frank Leboeuf – The Frenchman consolidated his status as a favourite at the Bridge in 1997-98 with his thoughtful defending, ability going forward and his impressive form in the Coca-Cola Cup final.

Coventry City *Football Club*

Coventry City Football Club
Coventry City Football Club
Coventry City Football Club
Coventry City Football Club
Coventry City Football Club
Coventry City Football Club
Coventry City Football Club
Coventry City Football Club
Coventry City Football Club
Coventry City Football Club
Coventry City Football Club

→ **Address** | Coventry City FC, Highfield Road Stadium, King Richard Street, Coventry CV2 4FW

Tel: 01203 234000 | **Tickets:** 01203 234020 | **Clubline:** 0891 121166

Coventry City Player of the Year Dion Dublin scored 23 goals during the 1997-98 season. A virtual reject from Old Trafford, he was only two goals short of Andy Cole's total of 25 goals in all competitions.

→ **Web site:** http://www.ccfc.co.uk → **Chairman:** Barry Richardson → **Manager:** Gordon Strachan → **Year formed:** 1883

Ground: Highfield Road (23,662)

Stands: Main
East
West
M & B

Home strip: Sky blue shirts with navy blue trim, sky blue shorts with navy blue trim, sky blue socks with navy blue trim

Away strip: Purple and yellow striped shirts, purple shorts with yellow trim, purple socks with yellow trim

Sponsor: Subaru

Programme: £2

Nickname: Sky Blues

Ground history: 1883 Binley Road
1887 Stoke Road
1899 Highfield Road

Previous name: Singers

First League game: 30 August 1919, Division 2, lost 0-5 (h) v Tottenham Hotspur

Record attendance: 51,455 v Wolverhampton Wanderers, Division 2, 29 April 1967

Record victory: 9-0 v Bristol City, Division 3 (South), 28 April 1934

Record defeat: 2-10 v Norwich City, Division 3 (South), 15 March 1930

Highest League position: Division 1 (old), 6th place, 1969-70

Highest League scorer (season): Clarrie Bourton, 49, 1931-32

Highest League scorer (aggregate): Clarrie Bourton, 171, 1931-1937

Most League appearances: Steve Ogrizovic, 502, 1992-1998

Most capped player: Peter Ndlovu, 26, Zimbabwe, 1992-1997

Highest transfer fee paid: £3.25m to Grasshoppers Zurich (Switzerland) for Viorel Moldovan, January 1998

Highest transfer fee received: £3.75m from Liverpool for Phil Babb, September 1994

Major trophies: Division 2 (old) Champions (1) 1966-67
Division 3 (old) Champions (1) 1963-64
Division 3 (South) Champions (1) 1935-36
FA Cup Winners (1) 1987

George Boateng – Born in Ghana but captain of the Holland Under-21 side, Boateng was signed for a bargain £250,000 from Feyenoord and gave the City midfield a much-needed edge after making his League debut against Liverpool in December 1997.

Willie Boland – A youth and Under-21 player for the Republic of Ireland, the former trainee was almost a permanent midfield sub for Gordon Strachan during 1997-98.

Gary Breen – The rangy Republic of Ireland defender found the going tough after signing from Birmingham in 1997 for £2.5 million, but he became a key member of the side during their fine run after New Year.

David Burrows – Formerly with West Bromwich Albion, Liverpool and West Ham, this experienced left back signed from Everton for £1.1 million in 1995. First choice at number 3 in 1997-98, he operated mainly in midfield.

Andrew Ducros – The diminutive forward made only a handful of appearances in 1997-98.

Marcus Hall – A Coventry-born trainee, this speedy England Under-21 wing back began to show signs of throwing off his "inconsistent" tag and made a valuable contribution to City's left side in 1997-98.

Simon Haworth – Signed from Cardiff City in 1997, the 6ft 4in striker broke through as a replacement for Dion Dublin in October, but remained a sub for most of the season.

Magnus Hedman – Lined up as a replacement for the evergreen Steve Ogrizovic, the Swedish keeper signed for £600,000 from AIK Stockholm and enjoyed a spell between City's posts in the midwinter period.

Martin Johansen – He followed twin brother Michael into the Premiership (Michael went to Bolton), the boys

having won Danish championship medals in their teens, but failed to establish a regular place in the team.

Viorel Moldovan – Coventry shelled out a club record £3.25 million to Grasshoppers Zurich for the potential of this hugely successful Romanian striker at New Year, but playing him at number 9, with Dublin reverting to defence, was only temporary and he failed to excite in 1997-98.

Roland Nilsson – Sweden's Player of the Year in 1996, this vastly experienced right back returned to England from Helsingborg for £200,000 and was an automatic choice at number 2 all season. With Sheffield Wednesday until 1994, he has over 90 caps for his country.

Steve Ogrizovic – 'Oggy' still proved to be top-class at the age of 40, even though Magnus Hedman kept goal during Coventry's midwinter purple patch. Formerly at Liverpool and signed from Shrewsbury in 1982, Ogrizovic was Player of the Year in 1996-97 – his 17th season with the club – and in 1997-98 earned a Merit Award from the PFA.

John Salako – Injuries continued to dog the talented England winger who was signed from Crystal Palace for £1.5 million. He didn't play after November in 1997 and was eventually loaned to Bolton.

Richard Shaw – Already an experienced centre back when he signed from Palace in 1995, he has always been an automatic selection for Coventry. However, he was briefly displaced by Dublin in February and March, with Moldovan up front.

Sam Shilton – Son of ex-England keeper Peter, the left-sided midfielder made just two starts in 1997-98.

Trond Egil Soltvedt – Signed by Strachan after helping unfancied Rosenborg to the last eight of the European Cup, the Norwegian player

is a purposeful attacking midfielder who settled well into English football, latterly dovetailing neatly with Boateng.

Gavin Strachan – The manager's promising son was involved in over half the season's games for Coventry and also got a call-up to the Scotland Under-21 squad.

Paul Telfer – First choice in the right-side midfield berth since his arrival from Luton in 1995, Telfer's hard work and crosses were a major factor in securing City's mid-table position.

Noel Whelan – The strapping young forward was signed from Leeds in 1995 and soon developed a good understanding with Dublin. Injury kept him out until December 1997, but he then combined well with leading scorers Dublin and Huckerby to help forge City's great run between Boxing Day and mid-April, when they lost only one of their 16 matches.

Paul Williams – Signed from Derby in 1995, he developed as a ball-playing centre back with City before being outclassed by Breen. He was very much 'the third man' in 1997-98.

Transferred in:
- Roland Nilsson (Helsingborg, £200,000)
- Magnus Hedman (AIK Stockholm, £600,000)
- Kyle Lightbourne (Walsall, £500,000)
- Martin Johansen (FC Copenhagen, £500,000)
- Trond Egil Soltvedt (Rosenborg, £500,000)
- George Boateng (Feyenoord, £250,000)
- Viorel Moldovan (Grasshoppers Zurich, £3.25 million)

Transferred out:
- Kevin Richardson (Southampton, free)
- Kyle Lightbourne (Stoke, £425,000)

Darren Huckerby – Signed from Newcastle for £1 million in 1996, he made a big impact on his arrival and was a star attraction in 1997-98, his dribbling and shooting skills thrilling millions of TV viewers.

Dion Dublin – A £2 million buy from Manchester United in 1994, he's led the scoring list for the last three seasons, despite often playing in defence. Mostly up front in 1997-98, his form earned him an England cap.

Gary McAllister – Coventry's 33-year-old club captain and key midfielder, who came from Leeds for £3 million, saw his season – and World Cup prospects with Scotland – end in December with a cruciate ligament.

Derby County *Football Club*

→ **Address** | Derby County FC, Pride Park Stadium, Derby DE24 8XL

Tel: 01332 667503 | **Tickets:** 01332 667519 | **Clubline:** 0891 121187

The first-ever League game at the brand new, state-of-the-art Pride Park, against Wimbledon on 13 August 1997, ended after an hour, when the floodlights failed and the stadium was plunged into darkness.

→ **Web site:** http://www.dcfc.co.uk → **Chairman:** Lionel Pickering → **Manager:** Jim Smith → **Year formed:** 1884

Ground: Pride Park (33,000)

Stands: East
North
Toyota West
Mansfield Bitter

Home strip: White shirts with black trim, black shorts with white trim, black socks with white trim

Away strip: Gold shirts with blue and white trim, blue shorts with white trim, gold socks with blue and white trim

Sponsor: Unknown

Programme: £2

Nickname: Rams

Ground history: 1884 Racecourse Ground
1895 Baseball Ground
1997 Pride Park

Previous name: Derbyshire County

First League game: 8 September 1888, Football League, won 6-3 (a) v Bolton Wanderers

Record attendance: 30,492 v Liverpool, Premiership, 10 May 1998

Record victory: 12-0 v Finn Harps, UEFA Cup 1st round, 1st leg, 15 September 1976

Record defeat: 2-11 v Everton, FA Cup 1st round, 1 January 1890

Highest League scorer (season): Jack Bowers, 37, 1930-31
Ray Straw, 37, 1956-57

Highest League scorer (aggregate): Steve Bloomer, 293, 1892-1906, 1910-1914

Most League appearances: Kevin Hector, 486, 1966-1978, 1980-1982

Most capped player: Peter Shilton, 34, England, 1987-1992

Highest transfer fee paid: £2.7m to Rosario Central (Argentina) for Horacio Angel Carbonari, May 1998

Highest transfer fee received: £2.9m from Liverpool for Dean Saunders, July 1991

Major trophies: Division 1 (old) Champions **(2)** 1974-75, 1971-72
Division 2 (old) Champions **(4)** 1986-87, 1968-69, 1914-15, 1911-12
Division 3 (North) Champions **(1)** 1956-57
FA Cup Winners **(1)** 1946

Francesco Baiano – The Italian striker, who was bought for a bargain £1.5 million from Fiorentina, fitted slickly into Derby's forward line and netted 13 goals in 36 games in 1997-98, including Premiership braces against Sheffield Wednesday, Leicester and Bolton.

Lars Bohinen – A Norwegian international who provides a creative force from midfield, Bohinen joined the Rams from Blackburn in March 1998 and featured in nine games for County, scoring once.

Deon Burton – An exciting forward who became a hero in Jamaica after his scoring feats for the national team, he has yet to establish himself at club level. He rarely played a full 90 minutes in 1997-98 and only hit three goals – although at 21 he has time on his side.

Lee Carsley – The solid and steady midfield anchorman played a key role in Derby's climb to the top half of the table in 1997-98 and attracted interest from Everton and Spurs.

Christian Dailly – A Scottish international, he has completed a successful transition from striker to centre back since his early days with Dundee United. Still only 24, he is likely to mature into an accomplished defender for club and country.

Rory Delap – A youngster with a great deal of promise who was signed for £800,000 in February 1998 from Carlisle, he played 13 games at right wing back and was called up to the Republic of Ireland squad.

Steve Elliott – A promising midfielder, just 19, he made his first-team debut in the Coca-Cola Cup against Southend.

Russell Hoult – Derby's regular goalkeeper in 1996-97 lost his place the following season to impressive Estonian arrival Mart Poom and was unable to regain his number one status again, making only three appearances.

Jonathan Hunt – Signed from Division One outfit Birmingham City for £500,000 before the start of 1997-98, he struggled to make an impact. The right-sided midfielder played 23 games, mainly as a substitute.

Robert Kozluk – Another young prospect, Kozluk was used sporadically throughout the 1997-98 season when needed, making 12 appearances and turning in some consistent performances.

Jacob Laursen – The Danish defender was a reliable and assured figure at the heart of the Derby back four in 1997-98.

Mart Poom – The Estonian keeper quickly displaced Hoult as first choice between the sticks after arriving at the tail-end of the 1996-97 season. He is an extremely dedicated figure who happily puts himself through extra training.

Darryl Powell – The former Portsmouth man and Jamaican international, who can play at the back or in midfield, he was unable to command a regular place in the team in 1997-98.

Gary Rowett – A popular figure among fans at Pride Park, Rowett followed where he left off in 1996-97, performing well either at right back or in the centre of defence. He was a bargain buy from Everton at £300,000, back in July 1995.

Mauricio Solis – The Costa Rican has failed to make the same kind of impact enjoyed by his compatriot, Paulo Wanchope.

Igor Stimac – An influential centre back, he missed two months between October and December, as well as the final month of the 1997-98 season. The Croatian's calming play at the back was sorely missed during those periods.

Dean Sturridge – The speedy striker settled into life at Pride Park quickly once he'd decided to stay with the club. The perfect foil for Wanchope, he hit 10 goals despite a cartilage operation at the start of the season and a minor car crash.

Robin van der Laan – Derby's club captain had a miserable time in 1997-98, missing six months of the season with an ankle injury. The Dutch midfielder was absent between October 1997 and April 1998.

Ron Willems – A young Dutch striker, he made only 12 appearances and found it difficult to break into the team regularly in 1997-98. He played whenever any of the first-choice forwards were unavailable and didn't feature after the game at Manchester United in February 1998.

Transferred in:
- Deon Burton (Portsmouth, £1.5m)
- Francesco Baiano (Fiorentina, £1.5m)
- Jonathan Hunt (Birmingham, £500,000)
- Stefano Eranio (AC Milan, free)
- Richard Knight (Burton Albion, nominal)
- Lars Bohinen (Blackburn, £1.45m)
- Rory Delap (Carlisle, £800,000)

Transferred out:
- Ashley Ward (Barnsley, £1.3m)
- Matt Carbon (WBA, £800,000)
- Paul Trollope (Fulham, £600,000)
- Nick Wright (Carlisle, £350,000)
- Sean Flynn (WBA, £250,000)
- Christophe Remy (Oxford, free)
- Martin Taylor (Wycombe, free)
- Paul McGrath (Sheffield United, free)
- Marco Gabbiadini (released)

Stefano Eranio – Snapped up by manager Jim Smith on a free transfer from AC Milan, the midfielder was brilliant on occasions, although he was sent off twice. His appearances were sadly restricted due to injury.

Paulo Wanchope – The long-legged Costa Rican continued to build on the promise he showed at the end of the 1996-97 season, firing 17 goals (10 before Christmas) and signing off with the winner against Liverpool.

Chris Powell – The left back was yet again a model of consistency for Derby, playing in 43 games and scoring two goals in 1997-98. Having joined from Southend in 1996, he is one of the club's best recent signings.

Everton *Football Club*

→ **Address** | Everton FC, Goodison Park, Liverpool L4 4EL

Tel: 0151 330 2200 | **Tickets:** 0151 330 2300 | **Clubline:** 0891 121199

Goalkeeper Neville Southall left Goodison Park for Stoke City in 1998, after a club record 750 appearances, with a record 578 of them in the League.

→ **Web site:** http://www.evertonfc.com → **Chairman:** Peter Johnson → **Manager:** Howard Kendall (to June 1998) → **Year formed:** 1878

Ground: Goodison Park (40,185)

Stands: Park
Bullens Road
Goodison Road
Gwladys Street

Home strip: Royal blue shirts with white, black and yellow trim, white shorts with blue and yellow trim, white socks with blue and yellow trim

Away strip: Black and yellow striped shirts, black shorts, yellow socks with black trim

Sponsor: one 2 one

Programme: £1.80

Nickname: Toffees

Ground history: 1878 Stanley Park
1882 Priory Road
1884 Anfield Road
1892 Goodison Park

Previous name: St Domingo

First League game: 8 September 1888, Football League, won 2-1 (h) v Accrington

Record attendance: 78,299 v Liverpool, Division 1, 18 September 1948

Record victory: 11-2 v Derby County, FA Cup 1st round, 18 January 1890

Record defeat: 4-10 v Tottenham Hotspur, Division 1, 11 October 1958

Highest League scorer (season): Dixie Dean, 60, 1927-28

Highest League scorer (aggregate): Dixie Dean, 349, 1925-1937

Most League appearances: Neville Southall, 578, 1981-1998

Most capped player: Neville Southall, 92, Wales, 1981-1997

Highest transfer fee paid: £5.75m to Middlesbrough for Nick Barmby, November 1996

Highest transfer fee received: £8m from Fiorentina (Italy) for Andrei Kanchelskis, February 1997

Major trophies: Division 1 (old) Champions (**9**) 1986-87, 1984-85, 1969-70, 1962-63, 1938-39, 1931-32, 1927-28, 1914-15, 1890-91
Division 2 (old) Champions (**1**) 1930-31
FA Cup Winners (**5**) 1995, 1984, 1966, 1933, 1906
Cup Winners Cup Winners (**1**) 1985

Graham Allen – The defender made only one start in the 1997-98 season – in the club's 3-1 win over Chelsea in January.

Michael Ball – A talented young local defender, he scored his first Premiership goal in the 2-2 draw against Arsenal in September 1997, before establishing himself as a first-team regular after Christmas.

Slaven Bilic – A £4.25 million signing and Britain's most expensive defender when he signed from West Ham in May 1997, the Croatian international defender had another inconsistent season.

Michael Branch – A young striker who was beset by injury in 1997-98, he managed only one Premiership start – against Derby in September.

Richard Dunne – A Dubliner who came from Home Farm in October 1996, he made his 1997-98 debut in the 3-2 win over Bolton midseason.

Gareth Farrelly – Signed from Aston Villa in July 1997, the Republic of Ireland international established himself in November after injury – and scored the goal against Coventry that kept Everton in the Premiership.

Paul Gerrard – Signed from Oldham in July 1996 for £1 million, he was understudy to Neville Southall in goal and was then kept out by the arrival of Myhre from December 1997.

Tony Grant – A young midfielder who has struggled with injuries, he had an extended first-team run in the New Year.

Don Hutchison – A tough-tackling midfielder who signed from Sheffield United in a £1 million deal in February 1998, he added much-needed bite to the side in the relegation battle.

Francis Jeffers – A young trainee, he came on as a substitute in the defeat by Manchester United in December.

Gavin McCann – The young midfield player featured in a handful of games during 1997-98, following his season debut in the 1-0 defeat by Newcastle in September 1997.

Mickael Madar – An aggressive striker signed on a free transfer from Spain's Deportivo La Coruna in December 1997, he scored on his debut in the 3-1 win at Crystal Palace in January 1998 – but found more goals difficult to come by.

Thomas Myhre – Not yet 25, the Norwegian goalkeeper signed from Viking Stavanger for £500,000 in November 1997. He kept clean sheets in his first three games – and his place for the season.

John O'Kane – Signed from Manchester United in January 1998, he became a permanent feature in the fight for Premiership survival.

John Oster – Howard Kendall beat a posse of bosses to sign the 19-year-old Welsh international striker for £1.5 million from Grimsby in July 1997, but he spent as much time on the bench as on the pitch in his first season – and scored only twice.

Terry Phelan – An experienced, attacking left back signed in January 1997 for £850,000 from Chelsea, the Republic of Ireland star was forced out in November with injury.

Craig Short – One of Everton's most consistent players and an automatic choice in defence throughout 1997-98, he was signed in July 1995 from Derby County in a deal worth £2.4 million plus Gary Rowett.

Tony Thomas – An attacking right back signed from neighbours Tranmere Rovers in August 1997 for £400,000 plus appearances, his outings for the club he supported as a boy were restricted by injury.

Carl Tiler – The much-travelled defender was an automatic choice

after being signed in November 1997, following a short spell at Sheffield United. His coolness under pressure was a valuable asset.

Mitch Ward – At home in defence or midfield, he came to Goodison from Sheffield United in November as part of the Tiler deal, but failed to establish a regular first-team place.

Dave Watson – Everton's longest-serving player, he was signed for £900,000 from Norwich back in 1986. The man who captained the club to the FA Cup win over Manchester United in 1995, he was still a key factor in Everton's fight in 1997-98, at the age of 36.

Danny Williamson – Signed from West Ham, he was a regular at number four until Christmas 1997, when he was hit by injury.

Transferred in:
- Slaven Bilic (West Ham, £4.25m)
- Gareth Farrelly (Aston Villa, £700,000)
- John Oster (Grimsby, £1.5m)
- Tony Thomas (Tranmere, £400,000)
- Carl Tiler (Sheffield United, deal)
- Mitch Ward (Sheffield United, deal)
- Thomas Myhre (Viking Stavanger, £500,000)
- Mickael Madar (La Coruna, free)
- Don Hutchison (Sheffield United, £1m)
- John O'Kane (Manchester United, £250,000)

Transferred out:
- Earl Barrett (Sheffield Wednesday, free)
- Andy Hinchcliffe (Sheffield Wednesday, £2.75m)
- David Unsworth (West Ham, deal)
- Gary Speed (Newcastle, £5.5m)
- Neville Southall (Stoke, free)
- Graham Stuart (Sheffield United, deal)
- Claus Thomsen (AB Copenhagen, £500,000)
- Jon O'Connor (Sheffield United, £150,000)

Nick Barmby – Everton's record buy had trouble winning over the fans, but his contribution during 1997-98's relegation struggle was crucial and he scored some vital goals in a tough season for Everton.

Danny Cadamarteri – Just after turning 18, he endeared himself to the Goodison faithful in October 1997 by scoring against Liverpool – his fifth goal in six starts – but then spent much of the season on the bench.

Duncan Ferguson – Committed and controversial, the £4.4 million buy from Rangers in 1994 is skilful on the ground as well as strong in the air. But, as in previous years, injury and suspension kerbed his up-front role.

Leeds United *Football Club*

Leeds United Football Club
Leeds United Football Club
Leeds United Football Club
Leeds United Football Club
Leeds United Football Club
Leeds United Football Club
Leeds United Football Club
Leeds United Football Club
Leeds United Football Club
Leeds United Football Club
Leeds United Football Club
Leeds United Football Club

→ **Address** | Leeds United FC, Elland Road, Leeds LS11 0ES

Tel: 0113 226 6000 | **Tickets:** 0113 226 1000 | **Clubline:** 0891 121180

The 1997-98 Leeds team had a strong international line-up with players having made their mark in the national squads of England, the Republic of Ireland, Norway, Austria, Scotland, Australia, South Africa and Portugal.

→ **Web site:** http://www.lufc.co.uk   → **Chairman:** Peter Ridsdale   → **Manager:** George Graham   → **Year formed:** 1904

Ground: Elland Road (40,204)

Stands: Revie North
South
East
West

Home strip: White shirts with yellow and blue trim, white shorts with yellow and blue trim, white socks with yellow and blue trim

Away strip: Yellow and blue halved shirts, blue shorts with light blue and yellow trim, blue socks with yellow, light blue and white trim

Sponsor: Packard Bell

Programme: £2

Nickname: United or Whites

Ground history: 1904 Elland Road

Previous name: Leeds City

First League game: 28 August 1920, Division 2, lost 0-2 (a) v Port Vale

Record attendance: 57,892 v Sunderland, FA Cup 5th round replay, 15 March 1967

Record victory: 10-0 v Lyn Oslo (Norway), European Cup 1st round, 1st leg, 17 September 1969

Record defeat: 1-8 v Stoke City, Division 1, 27 August 1934

Highest League scorer (season): John Charles, 42, 1953-54

Highest League scorer (aggregate): Peter Lorimer, 168, 1965-1979, 1983-1986

Most League appearances: Jack Charlton, 629, 1952-1973

Most capped player: Billy Bremner, 54, Scotland, 1965-1975

Highest transfer fee paid: £4.5m to Manchester United for Lee Sharpe, August 1996

Highest transfer fee received: £3.5m from Everton for Gary Speed, June 1996

Major trophies: Division 1 (old) Champions **(3)** 1991-92, 1973-74, 1968-69
Division 2 (old) Champions **(3)** 1989-90, 1963-64, 1923-24
FA Cup Winners **(1)** 1972
League Cup Winners **(1)** 1968

Mark Beeney – Signed from Brighton & Hove Albion for £350,000 in April 1993, Beeney made his debut in the final game of that season. He played 27 games in goal the next season, but since then has been second choice keeper.

Lee Bowyer – A young midfielder who came from Charlton for £2.6 million in July 1996 in a record deal for a teenager. He has captained the England Under-21 side, and has been part of the full England squad.

Alf-Inge Haaland – A Norwegian international who signed from Nottingham Forest in June 1997 for £1.6 million, he found himself a regular spot in midfield.

Gunnar Halle – George Graham's first signing, from Oldham in December 1996 for £400,000, the Norwegian international has played for Leeds in a variety of positions in defence and midfield.

Ian Harte – A young Republic of Ireland international, Harte plays at centre back for his country, though his versatility has seen him play most of his games for Leeds at left back or left wing back, and even up front. He has scored impressive goals for both club and country and is the nephew of Gary Kelly.

Martin Hiden – Signed from Austrian side Rapid Vienna in February 1998, he prefers to play centre back but will play at left or right back, and has represented Austria.

David Hopkin – A £3.25 million signing from Crystal Palace in July 1997, the club captain is a goalscoring midfielder, for club and Scotland. His most famous goal was a last gasp winner in the play-off final in his last game for Palace.

Gary Kelly – From League of Ireland side Home Farm in September 1991, he is a converted winger who normally plays at right back but has

also played in midfield for his club and the Republic of Ireland.

Mark Jackson – A Yorkshire-born product of the youth system, Jackson has represented England at Under-21 level and can play in midfield or defence. He was given a sub's outing on the last day of the season.

Harry Kewell – Signed from the New South Wales Soccer Academy in December 1995, Kewell began as a left back but normally plays in attack or midfield. He has also played for his native Australia.

Derek Lilley – A physical forward who signed from Scottish club Greenock Morton for in excess of £500,000 in March 1997.

Stephen McPhail – A Dubliner from the same Home Park Club as Gary Kelly, the Republic of Ireland Under-18 international is noted for the quality of his left foot which has brought comparisons with Liam Brady. It is hoped that he might develop into the playmaker Leeds lack, but in 1997-98 only made starts from the bench.

Lee Matthews – A 6ft 2in England Under-18 striker, he made his debut in January 1998 as a substitute.

Alan Maybury – A young defender who came from Irish Boy's Club St Kevin's in August 1995 and led Leeds to the FA Youth Cup, the Republic of Ireland Under-18 international made his full debut in the 1997-98 season, playing many times at right back.

Robert Molenaar – A no-nonsense central defender, he is popular with the fans who dubbed him 'the Terminator'. He has been in and out of the team since signing in January 1997 from Dutch club FC Volendam for £900,000.

Lucas Radebe – A skilful defender who signed from South African side Kaizer Chiefs in September 1994 for £250,000, he is comfortable on the

ball, which sometimes sees him playing in midfield. He is a good man-marker, and South Africa's captain.

Bruno Ribeiro – A goal-scoring midfielder who signed from Portuguese club Vitoria Clube de Setubol for £500,000 in June 1997, he has Under-21 caps for Portugal.

David Robertson – The thrice-capped Scottish left back signed from Rangers for £500,000 in May 1997. Quick on the attack, his first season for Leeds was disrupted by injury.

Rod Wallace – A pacy forward who sometimes plays midfield or on the wing, he signed from Southampton in June 1991 for £1.6 million. His finishing is sometimes erratic but can also be impressive.

David Wetherall – A Sheffield University chemistry graduate who was signed from Sheffield Wednesday in July 1991 in a £250,000 deal that also included Jon Newsome, he is strong in the air and often the target at set pieces. He and Wallace were the only members of the 1997-98 side who played in the Championship season of 1991-92.

Transferred in:
- Alf-Inge Haaland
  (Nottingham Forest, £1.6m)
- Jimmy Floyd Hasslebaink
  (Boavista, £2m)
- Martin Hiden (Rapid Vienna, £1.3m)
- David Hopkin
  (Crystal Palace, £3.25m)
- Bruno Ribeiro (Vitoria, £500,000)
- David Robertson
  (Rangers, £500,000)

Transferred out:
- Tomas Brolin (released)
- Brian Deane (Sheffield United, £1m)
- Tony Dorigo (Torino, free)
- Pierre Laurant (Bastia, £400,000)
- Richard Jobson
  (Manchester City, free)
- Carlton Palmer (Southampton, £1m)
- Ian Rush (Newcastle, free)
- Tony Yeboah (PSV Hamburg, £1m)

Lee Sharpe – First capped by England in 1991, the talented winger has not seen his career develop as he would have hoped. A cruciate ligament injury meant he missed the entire 1997-98 campaign.

Jimmy Floyd Hasslebaink – A £2 million snip from Portuguese side Boavista in June 1997 after a 27-goal season, he was almost as prolific for Leeds in 1997-98, the rangy striker being named Player of the Year.

Nigel Martyn – The England international arrived in July 1996 for £2.25 million from Crystal Palace in a record deal for a goalkeeper. He was an instant success and was Player of the Year in his first season at Leeds.

Leicester City *Football Club*

→ **Address** | Leicester City FC, City Stadium, Filbert Street, Leicester LE2 7FL

Tel: 0116 291 5000 | **Tickets:** 0116 291 5296 | **Clubline:** 0891 211185

In the 1997-98 season, Leicester beat Coventry City at Highfield Road for the first time in 21 years. But they lost again to West Ham at Upton Park, where they have failed to win since England's World Cup-winning year of 1966.

→ **Web site:** http://www.lcfc.co.uk   → **Football committee chairman:** Phillip Smith   → **Manager:** Martin O'Neill   → **Year formed:** 1884

Ground: City Stadium (21,500)

Stands: Carling
Shanks and McEwan
North
East

Home strip: Blue shirts with white trim, white shorts with blue trim, blue socks with white trim

Away strip: White shirts, blue shorts, white socks

Sponsor: Walkers Crisps

Programme: £2

Nickname: Filberts or Foxes

Ground history: 1884 Victoria Park
1887 Belgrave Road
1888 Victoria Park
1891 Filbert Street

Previous name: Leicester Fosse

First League game: 1 September 1894, Division 2, lost 3-4 (a) v Grimsby Town

Record attendance: 47,298 v Tottenham Hotspur, FA Cup 5th round, 18 February 1928

Record victory: 10-0 v Portsmouth, Division 1, 20 October 1928

Record defeat: 0-12 v Nottingham Forest, Division 1, 21 April 1909

Highest League position: Division 1 (old), runners-up, 1928-29

Highest League scorer (season): Arthur Rowley, 44, 1956-57

Highest League scorer (aggregate): Arthur Chandler, 273, 1923-1935

Most League appearances: Adam Black, 528, 1920-1935

Most capped player: John O'Neill, 39, Northern Ireland, 1980-1986

Highest transfer fee paid: £1.6m to Oxford United for Matt Elliott, January 1997

Highest transfer fee received: £3.25m from Aston Villa for Mark Draper, July 1995

Major trophies: Division 2 (old) Champions **(6)** 1979-80, 1970-71, 1956-57, 1953-54, 1936-37, 1924-25
League Cup Winners **(1)** 1997

Pegguy Arphexad – Signed on a free transfer from French side Racing Club de Lens early in the 1997-98 season, he went on to make a handful of appearances.

Stuart Campbell – A young right-sided midfielder, his initial first-team outings were at Old Trafford and Anfield.

Tony Cottee – After two spells with West Ham, during which he scored 117 goals, he arrived at Filbert Street in August 1997 from Malaysia and went on to score two goals against his former club on the last day of the season.

Graham Fenton – A young forward who was a £1.1 million purchase from Blackburn in August 1997, Fenton scored three goals in a first season in which he appeared mainly as a substitute.

Steve Guppy – A tricky winger with good crossing ability, he began his career under Martin O'Neill at Wycombe Wanderers. Kevin Keegan signed him for Newcastle and then he moved on to Port Vale who sold him to Leicester for £850,000 in February 1997, where he became ever-present.

Muzzy Izzet – A strong-running midfielder who was signed from Chelsea for £650,000 in March 1996, he might have played for Turkey, but rejected the spell of national service which would have been part of the package. He only missed one game of the 1997-98 season and was voted Player of the Year.

Pontus Kaamark – A right back for Sweden who more frequently plays on the left for Leicester, he was signed from Swedish side IFK Gothenberg for £840,000 in November 1995. Previous seasons have seen him unlucky with injuries, but in 1997-98 he was ever-present on the pitch.

Kasey Keller – The American keeper was signed from Millwall for £900,000 in August 1996. Man of the Match in the Coca-Cola Cup semi-final in 1996-97, the US international continued his good form for Leicester in 1997-98.

Sam McMahon – A former Young Player of the Year at Filbert Street, the 22-year-old right-footed midfielder is a product of the youth system. He made just one substitute appearance in 1997-98.

Ian Marshall – An unconventional centre forward who signed from Ipswich for £875,000, his goal rate in 1997-98 was one every three games.

Garry Parker – The Foxes' first-choice penalty taker, he is an experienced midfield playmaker who signed for £550,000 from Aston Villa in February 1995. It was his free kick which led to the winning goal in the 1997 Coca-Cola Cup final.

Spencer Prior – Bought by his former boss Martin O'Neill for £600,000 from Norwich City in August 1996, he has a strong aerial presence and enjoys getting forward as part of a five-man defence.

Robbie Savage – A creative midfielder who signed from Crewe in July 1997 for £400,000, he loves to get forward. Savage scored twice in 1997-98.

Robert Ullathorne – A tough-tackling, left wing back who was signed from Spanish side Osasuna in a deal worth £600,000 in February 1997, Ullathorne's first season was plagued by an ankle injury. Aside from Emile Heskey, he was the only other Leicester player to earn a red card in 1997-98.

Steve Walsh – Club captain, he is a left-sided central defender whose season was once again plagued by injuries and suspension. He was

signed for £100,000 from Wigan in June 1986 and lifted the Coca-Cola Cup in 1997.

Julian Watts – The central defender came from Sheffield Wednesday for £210,000 in March 1996, but has struggled for a first-team place since the arrival of Matt Elliott. He made only three substitute appearances in 1997-98.

Stuart Wilson – A promising young forward and product of City's youth system, he has still to carve out a regular first-team spot, having made only substitute appearances in 1997-98.

Theo Zagorakis – Greece's national captain signed for £750,000 in February 1998 from PAOK Salonika. He is an anchorman who quickly slotted in between defence and midfield, scoring one goal in his 13 appearances for Leicester.

Transferred in:
- Pegguy Arphexad
  (Racing Club de Lens, free)
- Tony Cottee (Selangor, £500,000)
- Robbie Savage (Crewe, £400,000)
- Theo Zagorakis
  (PAOK Salonika, £750,000)
- Graham Fenton (Blackburn, £1.1m)

Transferred out:
- Steve Claridge (Wolves, £350,000)
- Mark Robins
  (Club Deportivo Ourense, free)
- Mike Whitlow (Bolton, £700,000)
- Jamie Lawrence (Bradford, £50,000)

Emile Heskey – The club's top scorer in 1997-98, the tough England Under-21 centre forward is nicknamed 'Bruno', after boxer Frank. His strength and pace make him a strong prospect for the future.

Neil Lennon – A Northern Ireland international, he came from Crewe for £750,000 in February 1996. A confident midfielder, he handled the incident involving Shearer towards the end of the season with maturity.

Matt Elliott – A wholehearted defender who came from Oxford United for £1.6 million in January 1997, he deservedly won his first cap for Scotland in 1997 and was ever-present for Leicester in 1997-98.

Liverpool *Football Club*

Liverpool Football Club
Liverpool Football Club
Liverpool Football Club
Liverpool Football Club
Liverpool Football Club
Liverpool Football Club
Liverpool Football Club
Liverpool Football Club
Liverpool Football Club
Liverpool Football Club
Liverpool Football Club

→ **Address** | Liverpool FC, Anfield Road, Liverpool L4 0TH

Tel: 0151 263 2361 | **Tickets:** 0151 260 8680 | **Clubline:** 0891 121184

All 11 players that made up Liverpool's team for their first-ever competitive match in September 1893 were Scottish. In 1997-98, the only player born in Scotland was Dominic Matteo – a member of the England squad.

→ **Chairman:** David Moores   → **Manager:** Roy Evans   → **Year formed:** 1892

Ground: Anfield (41,197)

Stands: Main
Anfield Road
Centenary
Spion Kop

Home strip: Red shirts with white trim, red shorts, red socks

Away strip: Yellow shirts with red and black trim, yellow shorts with red and black trim, yellow socks with red and black trim

Sponsor: Carlsberg

Programme: £2

Nickname: Reds or Pool

Ground history: 1892 Anfield

Previous name: None

First League game: 2 September 1893, Division 2, won 2-0 (a) v Middlesbrough Ironopolis

Record attendance: 61,905 v Wolverhampton Wanderers, FA Cup 4th round, 2 February 1952

Record victory: 11-0 v Stromsgodset Drammen (Norway), European Cup Winners Cup 1st round, 1st leg, 17 September 1974

Record defeat: 1-9 v Birmingham City, Division 2, 11 December 1954

Highest League scorer (season): Roger Hunt, 41, 1961-62

Highest League scorer (aggregate): Roger Hunt, 245, 1959-1969

Most capped player: Ian Rush, 67, Wales, 1980-1996

Most League appearances: Ian Callaghan, 640, 1960-1978

Highest transfer fee paid: £8.5m to Nottingham Forest for Stan Collymore, June 1995

Highest transfer fee received: £7m from Aston Villa for Stan Collymore, May 1997

Major trophies: Division 1 (old) Champions **(18)** 1989-90, 1987-88, 1985-86, 1983-84, 1982-83, 1981-82, 1979-80, 1978-79, 1976-77, 1975-76, 1972-73, 1965-66, 1963-64, 1946-47, 1922-23, 1921-22, 1905-06, 1900-01
Division 2 (old) Champions **(4)** 1961-62, 1904-05, 1895-96, 1893-94
FA Cup Winners **(5)** 1992, 1989, 1986, 1974, 1965
League Cup Winners **(5)** 1995, 1984, 1983, 1982, 1981
European Cup Winners **(4)** 1984, 1981, 1978, 1977
UEFA Cup Winners **(2)** 1976, 1973

Phil Babb – A Republic of Ireland international, he signed from Coventry in September 1994 for £3.6 million. A composed central defender, he did not enjoy a consistent run in the side in 1997-98.

Patrik Berger – A Czech Republic international who signed from Borussia Dortmund in August 1996 for £3.25 million, he is a goalscoring midfield player who has failed to maintain a lengthy run in the first team.

Stig Bjornebye – A Norwegian international defender who signed from Rosenborg in December 1992 for £600,000, he is a tough-tackling, left wing back and an accurate crosser of the ball.

Jamie Carragher – A young midfielder who marked his debut with a goal against Aston Villa in January 1997, he came into the side more during the 1997-98 season. His power and strength have earned him England Under-21 recognition.

Robbie Fowler – An awesome goal-poacher who can score anywhere in or around the box, he is a full England international, although a cruciate ligament injury ruined the chance to show his skills in the World Cup.

Brad Friedel – After problems with his application for a work permit, Friedel finally signed for £1 million from Major League Soccer team Columbus Crew in December 1997. The American international keeper kept David James out of the side in the latter stages of the 1997-98 campaign.

Steve Harkness – A versatile defender who suffered a broken leg in April 1996, he came back to fitness and had a very consistent 1997-98 season at left back.

David James – A 6ft 5in goalkeeper who signed from Watford for £1 million in June 1992, he has been accused of being erratic and lost his place towards the end of the season.

Rob Jones – After missing most of the 1996-97 season through injury, the attacking right back returned to the side after Jason McAteer broke his leg in January 1998. He signed from Crewe Alexandra for £300,000 in October 1991.

Bjorn Tore Kvarme – Another capture from Norway's Rosenborg, this time on a free transfer, he is a cultured right back who missed part of the 1997-98 season due to injury, after which his form seemed to diminish.

Oyvind Leonhardsen – A £4 million signing from Wimbledon in June 1997, he is a Norwegian international who had a consistent, if unspectacular, 1997-98 season.

Jason McAteer – A Liverpool supporter who signed from Bolton Wanderers for £4.5 million in September 1995, the midfielder was soon converted to an attacking right wing back. The Republic of Ireland international broke his leg against Blackburn in January 1998, but was back to full fitness by April.

Dominic Matteo – A talented central defender who broke into the side in the 1996-97 season, he has not looked back, earning a call-up to the England squad for the game against Chile in February 1998.

Danny Murphy – Signed from Crewe for £1.5 million in July 1997, he is a young, talented midfield creator who can play just behind the front two and really came to the fore from mid-season onwards, playing in a makeshift forward role.

Jamie Redknapp – Son of West Ham boss Harry, he signed from Bournemouth for £500,000 in January 1991. He is a talented midfielder whose passing ability, coupled with his creative visionary skills, has produced some spectacular goals. However, his international and domestic careers have been dogged by injury.

Karlheinze Riedle – An experienced German international striker and European Cup winner, he signed for £1 million from European champions Borussia Dortmund, although he was not the instant hit Liverpool expected.

Neil Ruddock – A tough, no-nonsense central defender who signed from Tottenham in July 1993 for £2.5 million, 'Razor' Ruddock spent the final part of the season on loan to Queen's Park Rangers.

Michael Thomas – Signed for £1.5 million from Arsenal in December 1991, Thomas fell out of favour at Anfield with the signing of Ince and had a spell on loan to Middlesbrough during the 1997-98 season.

David Thompson – A young attacking midfielder who hit his debut Anfield goal against Crystal Palace in April 1998.

Mark Wright – An experienced central defender with 45 England caps, he signed in July 1991 from Derby for £2.2 million. He hardly featured during 1997-98 due to a back injury.

Transferred in:
- Danny Murphy (Crewe, £1.5m)
- Brad Friedel (Columbus Crew, £1m)
- Hauker Ingi Gudnasson (Keflavik, £150,000)
- Paul Ince (Inter Milan, £4.2m)
- Oyvind Leonhardsen (Wimbledon, £4m)
- Karlheinze Riedle (Borussia Dortmund, £1m)

Transferred out:
- John Barnes (Newcastle, free)
- Paul Dalglish (Newcastle, free)
- Mark Kennedy (Wimbledon, £1.75m)
- Lee Jones (Tranmere, £100,000)

Michael Owen – A mercurial young striker who has stunning pace and scoring ability, he is the youngest England international this century, debuting against Chile in February 1998, aged 18 years and 59 days.

Paul Ince – 'The Guvnor' signed from Inter Milan for £4.2 million in July 1997 and supplies the much-needed steel to a flair-filled midfield. His grit and determination are vital to both Liverpool and England.

Steve McManaman – A gifted midfielder whose dribbling skills, coupled with his tireless running, have earmarked him as one of the best players in the Premiership and an England international.

Manchester United *Football Club*

Manchester United Football Club
Manchester United Football Club
Manchester United Football Club
Manchester United Football Club
Manchester United Football Club
Manchester United Footb
Manchester United Footb
Manchester United Football Club
Manchester United Football Club
Manchester United Football Club
Manchester United Football Club

→ **Address** | Manchester United FC, Old Trafford, Manchester M16 0RA

Tel: 0161 872 1661 | **Tickets:** 0161 872 0199 | **Clubline:** 0891 121161

It's estimated that there are about 20 million Manchester United fans living in China. That's enough to fill Old Trafford just over 354.5 times.

→ **Web site:** http://www.sky.co.uk/sports/manu   → **Chairman:** Martin Edwards   → **Manager:** Alex Ferguson   → **Year formed:** 1878

Ground: Old Trafford (56,024)

Stands: North
South
East
West

Home strip: Red shirts with black and white trim, white shorts with red trim, black socks with white trim

Away strip: White shirts with black trim, white shorts with black trim, white socks with black trim

Sponsor: Sharp

Programme: £1.80

Nickname: Red Devils

Ground history: 1880 North Road
1893 Bank Street
1910 Old Trafford (Maine Road 1941-1949)

Previous name: Newton Heath

First League game: 3 September 1892, Division 1, lost 3-4 (a) v Blackburn Rovers

Record attendance: 70,504 v Aston Villa, Division 1, 27 December 1920

Record victory: 10-1 v Wolverhampton Wanderers, Division 1, 15 October 1892

Record defeat: 0-7 v Blackburn Rovers, Division 1, 10 April 1926
0-7 v Aston Villa, Division 1, 27 December 1930
0-7 v Wolverhampton Wanderers, Division 2, 26 December 1931

Highest League scorer (season): Dennis Viollet, 32, 1959-60

Highest League scorer (aggregate): Bobby Charlton, 198, 1956-1973

Most League appearances: Bobby Charlton, 606, 1956-1973

Most capped player: Bobby Charlton, 106, England, 1958-1970

Highest transfer fee paid: £10.75m to PSV Eindhoven (Holland) for Jaap Stam, May 1998

Highest transfer fee received: £7m from Inter Milan (Italy) for Paul Ince, June 1995

Major trophies: Premiership Champions **(4)** 1996-97, 1995-96, 1993-94, 1992-93
Division 1 (old) Champions **(7)** 1966-67, 1964-65, 1956-57, 1955-56, 1951-52, 1910-11, 1907-08
Division 2 (old) Champions **(2)** 1974-75, 1935-36
FA Cup Winners **(9)** 1996, 1994, 1990, 1985, 1983, 1977, 1963, 1948, 1909
League Cup Winners **(1)** 1992
European Cup Winners **(1)** 1967-68
Cup Winners Cup Winners **(1)** 1990-91

Henning Berg – An experienced, versatile defender with over 45 caps for Norway, Berg was signed for £5 million from Blackburn in the summer of 1997. Most of his games have been as a central defender.

Wes Brown – A product of United's youth system, the tall sweeper made his debut in May 1998 against Leeds.

Nicky Butt – A Manchester lad, this committed midfielder made the grade from trainee to first-team regular. Already a full England international, he's equally at home defending in midfield or in an attacking role.

Michael Clegg – A stocky full back who signed professional forms in the summer of 1995, Clegg was part of the side that went out of Europe in the 1-1 draw with Monaco in March.

Andy Cole – In January 1995, Cole became a record £7 million signing from Newcastle. In 1997-98, he continued his form as the club's leading scorer and matured enough to push for an England place.

Jordi Cruyff – A post Euro '96 signing from Barcelona for £1 million, the young Dutch international forward spent another frustrating season unable to establish a regular place.

John Curtis – An England-Under-21 international, Curtis is yet another product of United's successful youth policy. He made his Premiership debut in defence in the club's 7-0 win over Barnsley in October 1997.

Denis Irwin – A vastly experienced Republic of Ireland full back signed from Oldham in June 1990, the 32-year-old is also a free-kick specialist and the club's most reliable penalty taker.

Ronny Johnsen – Signed for over £1 million from Besiktas in July 1996, the Norwegian international is a skilful, imposing player who settled at centre back in the 1997-98 season.

Roy Keane – A strong-running, hard-tackling midfield general, he came from Nottingham Forest in 1993. The Republic of Ireland star saw his season end in September 1997 with a cruciate ligament injury.

Brian McClair – The team's longest-serving player, McClair has played in over 300 League games for United and scored close to 100 goals. In the 1997-98 season he served mainly as an experienced, hard-working sub.

David May – A former Blackburn central defender who broke into Glenn Hoddle's England squad in March 1997, May was largely out of action for the 1997-98 season.

Philip Mulryne – A midfielder who was a member of the 1995 FA Youth Cup winning team and is a regular reserve and A-team player, he is also a full Northern Ireland international.

Gary Neville – Neville has proved to be an outstanding full back at both club and national level. He made his debut for United in 1994 and at 23 is an England regular.

Phil Neville – At 21, Gary's younger brother has followed his meteoric rise from trainee to full England honours in under five years. In 1997-98 he often had to play in midfield – a role less familiar than a part in the back four.

Erik Nevland – A free signing from Norwegian club Viking Stavanger in May 1997, the young striker made his debut in October 1997.

Gary Pallister – The second longest-serving first-team player at the club, 33-year-old Pallister arrived from Middlesbrough in 1989 and is an accomplished England player. Injury limited his appearances in the second half of the 1997-98 season.

Kevin Pilkington – A young keeper noted for his long goal kicks, he has represented England at schoolboy level. The 24-year-old turned pro in

the summer of 1992 and made his first-team debut in November 1994.

Peter Schmeichel – Signed from Denmark's Brondby for £550,000 in August 1991, the theatrical 34-year-old keeper is among the world's best.

Paul Scholes – A hard-working forward who scores as well as provides goals, Scholes broke into the England set-up during Le Tournoi in 1997. He struggled in the 1997-98 season with a knee problem but came back to score in the World Cup.

Ole Gunnar Solskjaer – Norway's talented striker settled easily into the Premiership after arriving in July 1996 for £1.5 million, but he made the starting line-up on far fewer occasions in 1997-98.

Ben Thornley – Another youngster who has had limited chances in the first team, Thornley suffers from comparison with Giggs and Beckham. His League debut was as a substitute at West Ham in February 1994.

Michael Twiss – A Salford lad who made one FA Cup sub appearance.

Raimond van der Gouw – Signed for United in July 1996 from Dutch side Vitesse Arnhem, Van der Gouw provided cover for Schmeichel in 1997-98, including against Monaco.

Ronnie Wallwork – Manchester-born Wallwork made his debut as a sub for Gary Pallister in October 1997. In December, he went on loan to Carlisle United and ended the season on loan to Stockport County.

Transferred in:
• Teddy Sheringham (Spurs, £3.5m)
• Henning Berg (Blackburn, £5m)
• Jonathon Greening
  (York, undisclosed)
• Jaap Stam (PSV, £10.75m)

Transferred out:
• Neil Mustoe (Wigan, free)
• John O'Kane (Everton, £250,000)

David Beckham – An intelligent playmaker as well as a spectacular goalscorer, Beckham often made the headlines in 1997-98 as much because of his engagement to Posh Spice as for his football.

Teddy Sheringham – Subject of a high-profile move from Spurs in the summer of 1997 for £3.5 million, Sheringham provides a link between midfield and attack for United and England. He scores for both, too.

Ryan Giggs – A skilful dribbler, Giggs is one of the most exciting players in the League. The youngest ever Welsh international, his talent to set up and score goals was sorely missed by United in the spring fixtures of 1998.

Middlesbrough *Football Club*

Middlesbrough Football Club
Middlesbrough Football Club
Middlesbrough Football Club
Middlesbrough Football Club
Middlesbrough Football Club
Middlesbrough Football Club
Middlesbrough Football
Middlesbrough Football Club
Middlesbrough Football Club
Middlesbrough Football Club
Middlesbrough Football Club

→ **Address** | Middlesbrough FC, Cellnet Riverside Stadium, Middlesbrough TS3 6RS

Tel: 01642 877700 | **Tickets:** 01642 877745 | **Clubline:** 0891 424200

The 1997-98 season set two new post-war records for promotion-winning Middlesbrough – a total of 36 players were used in the squad and 20 different goalscorers, who notched up 77 goals in the League.

→ **Chairman:** Steve Gibson   → **Manager:** Bryan Robson   → **Year formed:** 1876

Ground: Cellnet Riverside Stadium (35,000)

Stands: North
South
East
West

Home strip: Red shirts with white trim, white shorts with red trim, red socks with white and navy blue trim

Away strip: Sky blue and white striped shirts with navy blue trim, navy blue shorts with white and sky blue trim, navy blue socks with white and sky blue trim

Sponsor: Cellnet

Programme: £2

Nickname: Boro

Ground history: 1876 Archery Ground, Albert Park
1879 Breckon Hill
1882 Linthorpe Road Ground
1903 Ayresome Park
1995 Cellnet Riverside Stadium

Previous names: None

First League game: 2 September 1899, Division 2, lost 0-3 (a) v Lincoln City

Record attendance: 30,228 v Oxford United, Division 1, 3 May 1998

Record victory: 9-0 v Brighton & Hove Albion, Division 2, 23 August 1958

Record defeat: 0-9 v Blackburn Rovers, Division 2, 6 November 1954

Highest League scorer (season): George Camsell, 59, 1926-27

Highest League scorer (aggregate): George Camsell, 326, 1925-1939

Most League appearances: Tim Williamson, 563, 1902-1923

Most capped player: Wilf Mannion, 26, England 1946-1951

Highest transfer fee paid: £7m for Fabrizio Ravanelli from Juventus (Italy), August 1996

Highest transfer fee received: £12m from Atletico Madrid (Spain) for Juninho, July 1997

Major trophies: Division 1 Champions **(1)** 1994-95
Division 2 (old) Champions **(3)** 1973-74, 1928-29, 1926-27

Alun Armstrong – A £1.6 million striker signed from Stockport County in February 1998, he scored on his debut against Sunderland.

Steve Baker – A Republic of Ireland Under-21 international at age 17, he can play in all positions in the back four. Baker, now 19, signed a new contract in December 1997.

Marlon Beresford – A £400,000 signing from Burnley in March 1998, the keeper debuted the same month.

Clayton Blackmore – The Welsh international, who came to Boro on a free transfer in July 1994, suffered an ankle injury in the first – and his last – game of the 1997-98 season.

Marco Branca – A £1 million Italian striker from Inter Milan, he scored after four minutes on his debut in the Coca-Cola Cup semi-final against Liverpool – to take Boro into the final.

Andy Campbell – A quick, young striker and England Under-18 international, he was the first 16-year-old to play in the Premiership when he debuted for the club in April 1996.

Andy Dibble – A Welsh goalkeeper who signed in January 1998, Dibble made his debut against Nottingham Forest.

Gianluca Festa – A £2.7 million signing from Inter Milan in January 1997, Festa is an attacking full back or central defender who signed a new five-year contract in March 1998.

Curtis Fleming – A strong-tackling left back, Fleming is a Republic of Ireland international who was signed for £50,000 in August 1991 from Irish club St Patrick's. He has played nearly 200 games for the club.

Paul Gascoigne – A sublimely talented midfielder who signed from Glasgow Rangers in March 1998 for £3.45 million, his first game for Boro was the 1998 Coca-Cola Cup Final.

Craig Harrison – A talented young left back who came up through the ranks and made his debut in the Coca-Cola Cup at Barnet in 1997-98.

Craig Hignett – Signed from Crewe during the 1992-93 season for £500,000, he is an attacking midfielder who scored his 100th career goal in January 1998.

Vladimir Kinder – The Slovakian international signed for £1.3 million from Slovan Bratislava in January 1997 and is a pacy left back.

Craig Liddle – A defender-cum-midfielder who came from non-League Blyth Spartans having been released by Aston Villa as a youngster, he went on loan to Darlington in 1997-98.

Neil Maddison – A £300,000 signing from Southampton in October 1997, he played in all positions bar goalkeeper for the Saints and proved just as versatile for Boro.

Alan Moore – A Republic of Ireland international midfielder, he missed most of the 1997-98 season due to a double calf operation in November.

Fabio Moreira – A versatile Brazilian defender, cousin and brother-in-law of ex-Boro player Emerson, he signed from Portugal's Desportivo de Chaves in 1996, but didn't make his first appearance until late 1997.

Robbie Mustoe – A hardworking midfielder who signed from Oxford for £375,000 in July 1990, he is Boro's longest-serving player.

Anthony Ormerod – An exciting, 19-year-old midfielder, Ormerod has represented England at Under-18 level.

Nigel Pearson – Boro's captain and centre back, who signed from Sheffield Wednesday in July 1994 in a £750,000 deal, made his 100th appearance for Boro in 1997-98.

Hamilton Ricard – A tall, strong, quick Colombian striker who signed for £2 million in February 1998 from Colombia's Deportivo Cali.

Ben Roberts – An England Under-21 goalkeeper, he missed most of the 1997-98 season with a back injury.

Mark Schwarzer – A tall, Australian goalkeeper signed from Bradford in February 1997 for £1.25 million, he was Boro's first choice in 1997-98.

Phil Stamp – An attacking, young midfielder, Stamp was denied a regular first-team place in 1997-98 due to extensive injuries.

Robbie Stockdale – A trainee right back, Stockdale made his debut in the FA Cup third round replay against Queen's Park Rangers.

Mark Summerbell – A young, combative midfielder, he signed a new contract in 1998 as Boro headed back to the Premiership.

Steve Vickers – A central defender who signed from Tranmere Rovers for £700,000 in December 1993.

Transferred in:
- Paul Merson (Arsenal, £5m)
- Andy Townsend (Aston Villa, £500,000)
- Neil Maddison (Southampton, £300,000)
- Andy Dibble (free)
- Marco Branca (Inter Milan, £1m)
- Alun Armstrong (Stockport, £1.6m)
- Hamilton Ricard (Deportivo Cali, £2m)
- Marlon Beresford (Burnley, £400,000)
- Paul Gascoigne (Rangers, £3.45m)

Transferred out:
- Juninho (Atletico Madrid, £12m)
- Fabrizio Ravanelli (Olympique Marseille, £5.25m)
- Alan White (Luton Town, £60,000)
- Gary Walsh (Bradford, £250,000)
- Derek Whyte (Aberdeen, £200,000)
- Chris Freestone (Northampton, £75,000)
- Emerson (Tenerife, £4.2m)

Andy Townsend – A £500,000 capture from Aston Villa in August 1997, he is a hard-running, creative midfield general. A Republic of Ireland regular, his influence in the middle was vital to Boro's promotion.

Paul Merson – A £5 million signing from Arsenal in July 1997, he was in outstanding form in 1997-98, helping Boro back into the top flight and earning a recall to the England squad. He was the club's Player of the Year.

Mikkel Beck – A fast, powerful Danish international striker, he was signed on a free transfer from German second division side Fortuna Cologne after playing for his country in Euro '96.

Newcastle United *Football Club*

→ **Address** | Newcastle United FC, St James' Park, Newcastle-upon-Tyne NE1 4ST

Tel: 0191 201 8400 | **Tickets:** 0191 261 1571 | **Clubline:** 0891 121190

The last time Newcastle won a major piece of silverware was 43 years ago, in 1955. None of today's team had been born, manager Kenny Dalglish was just four years old, and the first experimental colour television broadcasts were carried out by the BBC.

→ **Web site:** http://www.newcastle-utd.co.uk → **Chairman:** Sir John Hall → **Manager:** Kenny Dalglish → **Year formed:** 1882

Ground: St James' Park (36,610)

Stands: East
Milburn
Exhibition
Sir John Hall

Home strip: Black and white striped shirts, black shorts with white trim, black socks with white trim

Away strip: Blue shirts with gold trim, blue shorts with gold trim, blue socks with gold trim

Sponsor: Newcastle Brown Ale

Programme: £1.80

Nickname: Magpies

Ground history: 1881 Stanley Street
1886 St James' Park

Previous names: Stanley
Newcastle East End

First League game: 2 September 1893, Division 2, drew 2-2 (a) v Royal Arsenal

Record attendance: 68,386 v Chelsea, Division 1, 3 September 1930

Record victory: 13-0 v Newport County, Division 2, 5 October 1946

Record defeat: 0-9 v Burton Wanderers, Division 2, 15 April 1895

Highest League scorer (season): Hughie Gallacher, 36, 1926-27

Highest League scorer (aggregate): Jackie Milburn, 178, 1946-1957

Most League appearances: Jim Lawrence, 432, 1904-1922

Most capped player: Alf McMichael, 40, Northern Ireland, 1950-1960

Highest transfer fee paid: £15m to Blackburn Rovers for Alan Shearer, July 1996

Highest transfer fee received: £7m from Manchester United for Andy Cole, January 1995

Major trophies: Division 1 (old) Champions **(4)** 1926-27, 1908-09, 1906-07, 1904-05
Division 1 Champions **(1)** 1992-93
Division 2 (old) Champions **(1)** 1964-65
FA Cup Winners **(6)** 1955, 1952, 1951, 1932, 1924, 1910

Philippe Albert – A tall, strong, Belgian international signed from Anderlecht for £2.65 million in August 1994, Albert is one of the most adventurous centre backs in the Premiership, with a real eye for goal.

Andreas Andersson – The Swedish striker was signed from AC Milan for £3 million in January 1998. Fast, direct and strong in the air, he found the goal touch elusive in the run-in.

John Barnes – After arriving on a free transfer from Liverpool in August 1997, he found a new lease of life. But while he turned out to be a shrewd purchase by his old friend Kenny Dalglish, the 34-year-old found the going tougher at the end of the season in the battle against the drop.

Warren Barton – A versatile defender who can also play in midfield, he was signed from Wimbledon in July 1995 for £4 million.

David Batty – A ball-winning midfield general with a 'never-say-die' attitude, he was signed from Blackburn for £3.75 million in March 1996. His improved passing skills have made him a regular for England and United.

Nikolaos Dabizas – Signed from Olympiakos in March 1998 for £2 million, the 24-year-old international defender/midfielder impressed Kenny Dalglish in the 1997-98 Champions League. In May he became the first Greek to appear in an FA Cup final.

Keith Gillespie – He came to St James' Park as part of the £7 million deal that took Andy Cole to Old Trafford. The Northern Ireland winger has an assured first touch, pace and crossing ability, making him an automatic choice.

Andrew Griffin – Signed from Stoke in January 1998 for £1.5 million, he's an attacking left back.

Des Hamilton – A young, strong-running defender who signed from

Bradford City for £2 million in March 1997, he's been capped at Under-21 level by England but has yet to claim a regular spot for United.

Shaka Hislop – Although the 6ft 4in keeper shared duties with Shay Given last season, his performances earned him a call-up to the England B-squad in February 1998.

Steve Howey – Injury derailed this experienced defender's England career in 1996, but he fought his way back into the Newcastle side in August 1997.

Aaron Hughes – The locally groomed 20-year-old defender's debut was a baptism of fire against Barcelona in the Nou Camp. Already a Northern Ireland international, he has a bright future.

Temuri Ketsbaia – A Georgian international signed from Greek side AEK Athens on a free transfer in the summer of 1997, his quick soccer brain and scoring ability made him a hit with Magpie fans.

Darren Peacock – A ball-playing central defender who signed from Queen's Park Rangers for £2.7 million in March 1994, the 30-year-old began to feel the pinch from young rivals towards the end of the season.

Stuart Pearce – A free transfer from Forest in July 1997, the ex-England captain remains a tough-tackling, committed player with a powerful shot. He played centre back as well as left back in 1997-98.

Alessandro Pistone – A young left-sided defender signed from Inter Milan for £4.3 million in July 1997, he can run at defenders and is a good crosser of the ball.

Ian Rush – One of the most prolific scorers in the history of the British game with Liverpool, he came on a free transfer in August 1997 after a brief spell at Leeds. The 'Indian

summer' theory didn't work, however, and he was used sparingly.

Alan Shearer – The world's most expensive player when he signed from Blackburn for £15 million in July 1996, an early-season injury to the England captain scuppered Newcastle in the League and Europe.

Gary Speed – A left-sided playmaker and goalscorer, the experienced Welsh player signed in a high-profile transfer from Everton in February 1998 for £5.5 million.

Pavel Srnicek – Signed from Czech side Banik Ostrava for £350,000 in February 1991, he remained third choice keeper in 1997-98.

Jon Dahl Tomasson – The young Dane signed from Dutch side Heerenveen in May 1997 for £2.2 million but has yet to fulfil his potential at the club.

Transferred in:
- John Barnes (Liverpool, free)
- Ian Rush (Leeds, free)
- Ralf Keidel
  (Schweinfurt, undisclosed)
- Carlos Robledo
  (Sydney Olympic, undisclosed)
- Paul Dalglish (Liverpool, free)
- Andreas Andersson
  (AC Milan, £3m)
- Andrew Griffin (Stoke, £1.5m)
- Gary Speed (Everton, £5.5m)
- Nikolaos Dabizas
  (Olympiakos, £2m)
- James Coppinge
  (Darlington, £250,000)
- Paul Robinson
  (Darlington, £250,000)
- Alessandro Pistone
  (Inter Milan, £4.3m)

Transferred out:
- Peter Beardsley
  (Bolton, £500,000)
- John Beresford
  (Southampton, £1.5m)
- Paul Brayson (Reading, £100,000)
- James Crawford
  (Reading, £50,000)
- Robbie Elliott (Bolton, £2.5m)

Robert Lee – A £700,000 purchase from Charlton in September 1992, he's a hardworking midfielder with a good scoring record. Though not a front-line England player, he's often a member of the squad.

Shay Given – Signed as a 21-year-old from Blackburn in July 1997, the Republic of Ireland international's shot-stopping, agility and confidence gave him the edge over Hislop in the battle for the keeper's jersey.

Steve Watson – A strong, skilful right-sided utility player with the pace and ability to turn defence into attack, Watson is one of the most consistent players at St James' Park.

Nottingham Forest *Football Club*

Nottingham Forest Football Club
Nottingham Forest Football Club
Nottingham Forest Football Club
Nottingham Forest Football Club
Nottingham Forest Football Club
Nottingham Forest Footb

→ **Address** | Nottingham Forest FC, City Ground, Nottingham NG2 5FJ

Tel: 0115 982 4444 | **Tickets:** 0115 982 4445 | **Clubline:** 0891 121174

In 1998-99, Forest will be hoping to repeat their success of the 1977-78 season, when they won the League in the first season after promotion. They also became the first side to do the League and League Cup 'double' in the same year.

→ **Web site:** http://www.nottinghamforest.co.uk → **Chief executive:** Phil Soar → **Manager:** Dave Bassett → **Year formed:** 1865

Ground: City Ground (30,567)

Stands: Main
Trent End
Executive
Bridgford

Home strip: Red shirts with black and white trim, white shorts with black and red trim, red socks with black trim

Away strip: White shirts with black and red trim, black shorts, white socks

Sponsor: Pinnacle

Programme: £1.60

Nickname: Forest

Ground history: 1865 Forest Recreation Ground
1879 The Meadows
1880 Trent Bridge Cricket Ground
1882 Parkside, Lenton
1885 Gregory Ground, Lenton
1890 Town Ground
1899 City Ground

Previous name: None

First League game: 3 September 1892, Division 1, drew 2-2 (a) v Everton

Record attendance: 49,946 v Manchester United, 28 October 1967

Record victory: 14-0 v Clapton, FA Cup 1st round, 17 January 1891

Record defeat: 1-9 v Blackburn Rovers, Division 2, 10 April 1937

Highest League scorer (season): Wally Ardron, 36, 1950-51

Highest League scorer (aggregate): Grenville Morris, 199, 1898-1913

Most League appearances: Bob McKinley, 614, 1951-1970

Most capped player: Stuart Pearce, 76, England, 1985-1997

Highest transfer fee paid: £3.5m to Celtic for Pierre van Hooijdonk, March 1997

Highest transfer fee received: £8.5m from Liverpool for Stan Collymore, June 1995

Major trophies: Division 1 (old) Champions **(1)** 1977-78
Division 2 (old) Champions **(2)** 1921-22, 1906-07
Division 3 (South) Champions **(1)** 1950-51
FA Cup Winners **(2)** 1959, 1898
League Cup Winners **(4)** 1978, 1979, 1989, 1990
European Cup Winners **(2)** 1980, 1979

Chris Allen – A regular in the reserves, he made his 1997-98 debut by scoring in the 8-0 drubbing of Doncaster Rovers in the Coca-Cola Cup in August 1997.

Craig Armstrong – A young, left-sided utility player who signed professional forms in June 1992, he has struggled to make an impact and was used largely as a substitute in 1997-98.

Chris Bart-Williams – A midfielder picked up from Sheffield Wednesday for £2.5 million in 1995, he played much of the 1997-98 season on the left, scoring the Championship-winning goal against Reading.

Dave Beasant – The first goalkeeper to captain an FA Cup-winning side, when he led Wimbledon to the title in 1988, he was originally brought on loan from Southampton in a move which was made permanent in November 1997. The former England international gave a string of consistent performances behind a solid defence.

Thierry Bonalair – A Parisian signed from Swiss side Neuchatel Xamax in June 1997, he can operate at wing back or in midfield. Bonalair finished the season at right back after Des Lyttle's injury.

Colin Cooper – The team captain missed two months with a leg wound but returned to renew a solid central defensive partnership with Steve Chettle that dates back to Cooper's arrival from Millwall in 1993.

Scot Gemmill – The son of Forest hero and former assistant manager Archie, Scot cemented his own reputation with consistent displays which impressed Scotland manager Craig Brown, leading to a place in the World Cup squad.

Steve Guinan – A young forward who signed straight from school in 1992, he only featured in a handful of games during 1997-98.

Marlon Harewood – The promising young defender, born in August 1979, was given a first team debut in the final League game of the season against West Brom.

Jon Olav Hjelde – A £600,000 signing from Rosenborg in August 1997, Forest manager Dave Bassett rejected a £3 million offer from Bologna for him just a month later. But the Norwegian struggled to break the Cooper/Chettle partnership.

Andy Johnson – A versatile player who can play in defence, midfield or attack, Johnson arrived from Norwich in the summer of 1997 and after early injury problems established himself in the centre of the Forest midfield with his good passing ability and pace.

Des Lyttle – A right back who joined Forest from Swansea in 1993, strong and determined with a good tackle, he was ever-present in 1997-98 until an injury against Sunderland in March meant he missed the glorious end of season.

Ian Moore – Born in Birkenhead, Moore joined Forest from Tranmere Rovers for £1 million in March 1997 but had an unsettled 1997-98, making just three starts – although he scored a crucial equalizer against Stoke in February.

Marco Pascolo – A back-up goalkeeper bought from Cagliari in July 1997 for £750,000, he was restricted to just two games after Dave Beasant arrived.

Alan Rogers – A young defender who followed Ian Moore to Forest from Tranmere Rovers in a £2 million deal (with rather more success), Rogers made the left-back position his own in the 1997-98 season and racked up 43 League appearances.

Steve Stone – The injury-prone former England player recovered from a hernia operation to return to the side in October 1997, but suffered a hamstring tear just three months later, in January 1998. When he did play, he was back to his effervescent best on the right of midfield.

Geoff Thomas – Another former England midfielder who joined Forest from Wolves, he found his chances mostly limited to substitute appearances after a back injury struck in September.

Ian Woan – Once tipped as a future England international, he was only a peripheral figure in the Forest squad, starting just three games all season after an operation on his right knee. The consistency of the other midfielders got the nod over Woan's more mercurial skills.

Transferred in:
- Dave Beasant (Southampton, free)
- Thierry Bonalair (Neuchatel, free)
- Marco Pascolo
  (Cagliari, £750,000)
- Geoff Thomas (Wolves, free)
- Alan Rogers (Tranmere, £2m)
- Jon Olav Hjelde
  (Rosenborg, £600,000)
- Glyn Hodges (Hull City, free)
- Christian Edwards
  (Swansea, £175,000)

Transferred out:
- Nicola Jerkan (Rapid Vienna, free)
- Dean Saunders
  (Sheffield United, free)
- Steve Howe (Swindon, £30,000)
- Vance Warner
  (Rotherham, undisclosed)
- Daniel George (Doncaster, free)
- Alf-Inge Haaland (Leeds, £1.6m)
- Bryan Roy (Hertha Berlin, £1.5m)
- Jason Lee (Watford, £200,000)
- Steve Blatherwick
  (Burnley, £150,000)
- Justin Walker
  (Scunthorpe, undisclosed)
- Gareth Bough (Corby Town, free)
- David Phillips (Huddersfield, free)
- Paul Smith (Lincoln, £20,000)
- Andy Porteus
  (Manchester City, free)

Pierre Van Hooijdonk – In his first full season at the club, Van Hooijdonk was Forest's star player, scoring 34 goals in 47 appearances and justifying every penny of the £3.5 million Forest paid to Celtic.

Kevin Campbell – In his third season at the club, this powerful striker silenced his critics with 23 League goals in an awesome partnership with Van Hooijdonk that netted 57 goals in all competitions.

Steve Chettle – A local lad who joined the club as an apprentice, he turned professional in 1986. Partnered with Colin Cooper, he was again a rock at the heart of Forest's defence as he neared 500 career games.

Sheffield Wednesday *Football Club*

Sheffield Wednesday Football Club
Sheffield Wednesday Football Club
Sheffield Wednesday Football Club
Sheffield Wednesday Football Club
Sheffield Wednesday Foot
Sheffield Wednesday Foo
Sheffield Wednesday Football Club
Sheffield Wednesday Football Club
Sheffield Wednesday Football Club
Sheffield Wednesday Football Club

→ **Address** | Sheffield Wednesday FC, Hillsborough, Sheffield S6 1SW

Tel: 0114 221 2121 | **Tickets:** 0114 221 2400 | **Clubline:** 0891 121186

Sheffield Wednesday, who played five games on Wednesdays during the 1997-98 season, are so-called because the founders of the Wednesday Cricket Club in 1820 were local craftsmen whose weekly half-day was Wednesday.

→ **Web site:** http://www.swfc.co.uk → **Chairman:** David Richards → **Manager:** Ron Atkinson (to May 1998) → **Year formed:** 1867

Ground: Hillsborough (39,500)

Stands: North
South
West
Kop

Home strip: Blue and white striped shirts with black trim, black shorts with blue and white trim, black socks with blue and white trim

Away strip: Gold, navy blue and white shirts, navy blue shorts with white trim, gold socks with navy blue and white trim

Sponsor: Sanderson

Programme: £2

Nickname: Owls

Ground history: 1867 Dronfield
1887 Olive Grove
1899 Owlerton/Hillsborough

Previous name: The Wednesday

First League game: 3 September 1892, Division 1, won 1-0 (a) v Notts County

Record attendance: 72,841 v Manchester City, FA Cup 5th round, 17 February 1934

Record victory: 12-0 v Halliwell, FA Cup 1st round, 17 January 1891

Record defeat: 0-10 v Aston Villa, Division 1, 5 October 1912

Highest League scorer (season): Derek Dooley, 46, 1951-52

Highest League scorer (aggregate): Andrew Wilson, 197, 1900-1920

Most League appearances: Andrew Wilson, 502, 1900-1920

Most capped player: Nigel Worthington, 50, Northern Ireland, 1984-1996

Highest transfer fee paid: £4.5m to Celtic for Paolo Di Canio, August 1997

Highest transfer fee received: £2.75m from Blackburn Rovers for Paul Warhurst, August 1993

Major trophies: Division 1 (old) Champions **(4)** 1929-30, 1928-29, 1903-04, 1902-03 Division 2 (old) Champions **(5)** 1958-59, 1955-56, 1951-52, 1925-26, 1899-1900 FA Cup Winners **(3)** 1935, 1907, 1896 League Cup Winners **(1)** 1991

Manuel Agogo – An Under-18 regular who made one appearance as a substitute in the 1997-98 season.

Niclas Alexandersson – A right-sided attacking midfielder who signed rom IFK Gothenburg for £750,000 in December 1997, Alexandersson is a full international for Sweden who Wednesday have tied to a three-and-a-half year contract.

Peter Atherton – A versatile defender who was signed from Coventry in July 1994 for £800,000, he scored his first goal of the season in the 3-2 win over Southampton in November.

Earl Barrett – Signed from Everton in February 1998 on a free transfer after injury to Ian Nolan, he has full England honours and made his debut in the 3-0 defeat by Derby County soon after signing.

Lee Briscoe – A product of the Owls' youth policy, he is a left-sided defensive midfielder who had limited first team chances during the 1997-98 season.

Benito Carbone – The winger signed from 1998 UEFA Cup winners Inter Milan in October 1996 for £3 million. He has the talent to take on the best the Premiership has to offer and scored some outstanding individual goals in the 1997-98 season.

Matt Clarke – A young keeper who deputised for the injured Kevin Pressman in the 0-0 draw with Coventry in September 1997 and played a further two games. He signed for £325,000 from Rotherham in July 1996.

Andy Hinchcliffe – A surprise £2.75 million signing from Everton in January 1998, the left back is a dead-ball specialist. He made his scoring debut in the 3-3 draw at home to Liverpool on St Valentine's Day, 1998.

Ritchie Humphreys – A young forward who has progressed through the youth ranks but has had limited chances in the first team due to the good form of Di Canio and Carbone.

Graham Hyde – A tenacious midfielder who signed professional forms in July 1989, he has yet to find a regular place in the side.

Jim Magilton – A strong midfield player who signed from Southampton in September 1997 for £1.6 million, he had a good run in the side after signing, but was reduced to coming on from the bench during the last half of the season.

Jon Newsome – A £1.6 million signing from Norwich City in March 1996, is in his second spell at Hillsborough, having broken through the youth ranks before signing for Leeds. He was one of Wednesday's most consistent players during the 1997-98 season.

Steve Nicol – An experienced defender who signed for a nominal fee in November 1995 from Notts County, he only appeared a handful of times in the first team in 1997-98.

Ian Nolan – A pacy full back who signed from Tranmere Rovers for £1.5 million in August 1994, he was ever-present until February 1998 when injury forced him to be replaced by new signing Earl Barrett.

Scott Oakes – A skilful winger signed from Luton Town in August 1996 for £425,000, he only made a handful of substitute appearances during the 1997-98 season.

Mark Pembridge – A Wales international midfield player who signed from Derby County in July 1995 for £900,000, he was a very consistent performer in a mediocre season for the Owls.

Kevin Pressman – Virtually ever-present during the 1997-98 season, he is a product of the youth system and has played nearly 300 games for the club in goal. He even scored one

of the penalties in the 5-3 shoot-out victory over Watford in the third round of the FA Cup in January 1998.

Petter Rudi – The Norwegian signed from Molde in October 1997 and is a midfielder who links up well with the front men.

Goce Sedloski – An international defender for Macedonia who signed from Croatian side Hadjuk Split for £750,000 in February 1998, he made his debut away at Bolton in March 1998.

Dejan Stefanovic – Signed from Red Star Belgrade in December 1995 for £2 million, the strong defender has had an inconsistent season and was forced to fight for his place.

Emerson Thome – A free transfer from Portugal's Benfica in March 1998, the Brazilian defender made his debut away at Barnsley in April.

Guy Whittingham – An ex-army corporal who signed from Aston Villa in December 1994 for £700,000, he is a strong attacking player who scored three goals in as many games against Manchester United, Bolton and Arsenal in November 1997.

Transferred in:
- Stuart Jones (Weston-Super-Mare, £100,000)
- Earl Barrett (Everton, free)
- Emerson Thome (Benfica, free)
- Goce Sedloski (Hadjuk Split, £750,000)
- Andy Hinchcliffe (Everton, £2.75m)
- Niclas Alexandersson (IFK Gothenburg, £750,000)
- Jim Magilton (Southampton, £1.6m)
- Petter Rudi (Molde, £800,000)
- Paolo Di Canio (Celtic, £4.5m)
- Francesco Sanetti (Genoa, free)

Transferred out:
- David Hirst (Southampton, £2m)
- Maik Taylor (Fulham, £700,000)
- Patrick Blondeau (Girondins de Bordeaux, £800,000)
- Wayne Collins (Fulham, £450,000)

Des Walker – A £2.75 million signing from Sampdoria, he is a classy central defender who started his career with Forest. He had another consistently good season at the heart of the Owls' defence.

Paolo Di Canio – A record £4.5 million buy from Celtic in August 1997, the charismatic striker's rate in 1997-98 averaged more than a goal every three games and earned him the club's Player of the Year award.

Andy Booth – A £2.6 million signing from Huddersfield in July 1996, he found it hard to keep his place during the 1997-98 season due to the outstanding form of Paolo Di Canio and Benito Carbone.

Southampton *Football Club*

→ **Address** | Southampton FC, The Dell, Milton Road, Southampton SO15 2XH

Tel: 01703 220505 | **Tickets:** 01703 228575 | **Clubline:** 0898 121178

Ten years ago, during the 1988-89 season, Southampton became the first British club in history to include three brothers – Danny, Rodney and Raymond Wallace.

→ **Web site:** http://www.soton.ac.uk/~saints → **Chairman:** Rupert Lowe → **Manager:** David Jones → **Year formed:** 1885

Ground: The Dell (15,252)

Stands: East
West
Archers Road
Milton Road

Home strip: Red and white striped shirts with black trim, black shorts with red trim, white socks with red and black trim

Away strip: Yellow shirts with blue trim, yellow shorts with blue trim, yellow socks with blue trim

Sponsor: Sanderson

Programme: £1.80

Nickname: Saints

Ground history: 1885 Antelope Ground
1897 County Cricket Ground
1898 The Dell

Previous name: Southampton St Mary's

First League game: 28 August 1920, Division 3, drew 1-1 (a) v Gillingham

Record attendance: 31,044 v Manchester United, Division 1, 8 October 1969

Record victory: 9-3 v Wolverhampton Wanderers, Division 2, 18 September 1965

Record defeat: 0-8 v Tottenham Hotspur, Division 2, 28 March 1936
0-8 v Everton, Division 1, 20 December 1971

Highest League position: Division 1 (old), runners-up, 1983-84

Highest League scorer (season): Derek Reeves, 39, 1959-60

Highest League scorer (aggregate): Mike Channon, 182, 1966-77, 1979-82

Most League appearances: Terry Paine, 713, 1956-1974

Most capped player: Peter Shilton, 49, England, 1983-1987

Highest transfer fee paid: £2m to Sheffield Wednesday for David Hirst, October 1997

Highest transfer fee received: £3.4m from Blackburn Rovers for Alan Shearer, August 1992

Major trophies: Division 3 (old) Champions **(1)** 1959-60
Division 3 (South) Champions **(1)** 1921-22
FA Cup winners **(1)** 1976

Steve Basham – A local YTS trainee who signed professional forms in June 1996, his games in 1997-98 were restricted to substitute appearances.

Francis Benali – A restaurant-owning left back, he made his debut at Derby back in October 1988. Tough-tackling and committed as ever, he has now played over 300 games for the club.

John Beresford – A £1.5 million signing from Newcastle United in February 1998, he's an experienced left-sided midfielder who was the Magpies' leading scorer in the 1997-98 Champions League. He featured regularly after his arrival at The Dell, effectively replacing young winger Matt Oakley.

Jason Dodd – A versatile defender signed from non-League Bath City for £50,000 in March 1989, he made the right-back position his own.

Richard Dryden – A £150,000 signing from Bristol City just before the 1996-97 season (during which time he made 35 appearances), his role in 1997-98 was restricted by the form of Monkou and Lundekvam.

Kevin Gibbens – A local lad who signed from trainee, he made his first start in the 4-2 win at West Ham in April 1998.

David Hirst – A record £2 million capture from Sheffield Wednesday in October 1997, Hirst is a strong forward with pace, skill and a well of experience. It was no coincidence that Saints' season was transformed with his arrival and that of Richardson and Palmer.

David Hughes – A hard-working, attacking midfielder who came from non-League Weymouth in July 1991, the Welsh Under-21 player has been consistently unlucky with injuries and has had a spell on loan in Sweden. Most of his appearances in 1997-98 were as a substitute.

Stig Johansen – The Norwegain striker signed from Norway's Bodo-Glimt for £600,000 in August 1997, he found himself struggling for a place following the arrivals of Hirst and Davies.

Paul Jones – The 6ft 2in keeper for Wales was signed from Stockport County in July 1997 for an undisclosed fee. An excellent shot-stopper, he replaced Dave Beasant and was voted Player of the Year.

Claus Lundekvam – A tall central defender signed by Graeme Souness from Norwegian club SK Brann for £400,000 in September 1996, he missed the first five games of 1997-98 due to a dislocated shoulder. After his return, he missed just one game.

Ken Monkou – The Surinam-born 6ft 3in centre back was signed from Chelsea for £750,000 in August 1992. A former Feyenoord player, he formed a formidable – and very tall – partnership with Lundekvam in the middle part of 1997-98.

Matt Oakley – A young winger who had an inconsistent season and lost his place to John Beresford in February. However, he remains a good prospect for the future – and worth his England Under-21 call-up.

Carlton Palmer – A £1 million signing from Leeds United in September 1997, Palmer is a tall player who can play in both defence and midfield. Not always thought worthy of his 18 England caps, his arrival transformed Saints – his debut was a seminal 3-0 win over West Ham on 4 October.

Kevin Richardson – An extremely experienced midfield playmaker who signed from Coventry for £150,000 in September 1997. He has made over 500 career League appearances and has proved an outstanding replacement for Jim Magilton.

Duncan Spedding – A defender who signed professional forms back in

July 1994, he played a handful of games early in the 1997-98 season on the left side of midfield – a role later filled by Oakley and Beresford.

Lee Todd – An attacking left back who followed manager David Jones to The Dell in the summer of 1997 as part of the deal which secured Paul Jones, he played the first part of the season before the experienced Benali was then preferred at number 3.

Phil Warner – Southampton-born, the young full back made his debut on the last day of the 1997-98 season.

Andy Williams – A former winger for the Welsh Under-18 squad, he played in the first game of 1997-98 and twice more in the League – but was then relegated to a sub's role.

Transferred in:
- Kevin Davies (Chesterfield, £750,000)
- Paul Jones (Stockport, undisclosed)
- Lee Todd (Stockport, deal)
- Stig Johansen (Bodo-Glimt, £600,000)
- Kevin Richardson (Coventry, £150,000)
- Carlton Palmer (Leeds, £1m)
- David Hirst (Sheffield Wednesday, £2m)
- John Beresford (Newcastle, £1.5m)
- Cosimo Sarli (Torino, free)

Transferred out:
- Jim Magilton (Sheffield Wednesday, £1.6m)
- Christer Warren (Bournemouth, £50,000)
- Michael Evans (West Bromwich Albion, £500,000)
- Neil Maddison (Middlesbrough, £300,000)
- Dave Beasant (Nottingham Forest, free)
- Simon Charlton (Birmingham, £200,000)
- Matthew Robinson (Portsmouth, £50,000)
- Robbie Slater (Wolves, £50,000)
- Alan Neilson (Fulham, £225,000)
- Maik Taylor (Fulham, £700,000)

Matt Le Tissier – A technically gifted footballer with the ability to score spectacular goals, his customary burden of responsibility was lifted in 1997-98 by the performances of Ostenstad, Davies and Hirst.

Egil Ostenstad – A powerfully built £800,000 capture from Norwegian side Viking Stavanger in 1996, the forward forged a strong partnership with Hirst in the second half of the 1997-98 season.

Kevin Davies – Signed from Chesterfield in May 1997 (after their great FA Cup run) for £750,000, his contribution to Saints' fine mid-season run was vital. He can play on the right as well as up front.

Tottenham Hotspur *Football Club*

→ **Address** | Tottenham Hotspur FC, 748 High Road, Tottenham, London N17 0AP

Tel: 0181 365 5000 | **Tickets:** 0181 365 5050 | **Clubline:** 0891 335555

Three Tottenham players reached milestones in the last away game of 1997-98. Calderwood played his 150th League match for Spurs and Campbell made his 200th senior appearance for the club, while Anderton played in his 250th senior game.

→ **Web site:** http://www.spurs.co.uk → **Chairman:** Alan Sugar → **Manager:** Christian Gross → **Year formed:** 1882

Ground: White Hart Lane (36,200)

Stands: East
  West
  South
  North

Home strip: White shirts with navy blue trim, navy blue shorts with white trim, white socks

Away strip: Navy blue shirts with white trim, white shorts, blue socks with white tops

Sponsor: Hewlett Packard

Programme: £2

Nickname: Spurs

Ground history: 1883 Tottenham Marshes
  1888 Northumberland Park
  1899 White Hart Lane

Previous name: Hotspur

First League game: 1 September 1908, Division 2, won 3-0 (h) v Wolverhampton Wanderers

Record attendance: 75,038 v Sunderland, FA Cup 6th round, 5 March 1938

Record victory: 13-2 v Crewe Alexandra, FA Cup 4th round replay, 3 February 1960

Record defeat: 0-7 v Liverpool, Division 1, 2 September 1978

Highest League scorer (season): Jimmy Greaves, 37, Division 1, 1962-63

Highest League scorer (aggregate): Jimmy Greaves, 220, 1961-1970

Most League appearances: Steve Perryman, 655, 1969-1986

Most capped player: Pat Jennings, 74, Northern Ireland, 1965-1977

Highest transfer fee paid: £6m to Newcastle United for Les Ferdinand, July 1997

Highest transfer fee received: £5.5m from Lazio (Italy) for Paul Gascoigne, May 1992

Major trophies: Division 1 (old) Champions **(2)** 1960-61, 1950-51
FA Cup Winners **(8)** 1991, 1982, 1981, 1967, 1962, 1961, 1921, 1901
League Cup Winners **(2)** 1973, 1971
Cup Winners Cup Winners **(1)** 1963
UEFA Cup Winners **(2)** 1984, 1972

Darren Anderton – A £2 million signing from Portsmouth in June 1992, the England player has been nicknamed 'Sicknote' due to his ongoing injury crisis, but he came back at the end of the season.

Chris Armstrong – Another injury-prone striker, he cost a then-club record £4.5 million from Crystal Palace in June 1995. His return in February helped Spurs' survival.

Espen Baardsen – A young, US-born Norwegian international keeper, he deputised well for Ian Walker for two months at the start of 1998.

Nicola Berti – A free transfer from Inter Milan at New Year, this talented midfielder solidified the midfield and scored vital goals.

Garry Brady – A right-sided midfielder, the Scottish youth was used as a substitute by Gross.

Colin Calderwood – A World Cup defender for Scotland, he signed in July 1993 from Swindon for £1.25 million. In the middle of 1997-98, Gross moved Calderwood into a midfield role.

Stephen Carr – Almost ever-present in 1997-98, the former trainee earned a call-up into the Republic of Ireland squad following some fine displays as an attacking right back.

Stephen Clemence – Son of Spurs, Liverpool and England legend Ray, he's a skilful midfield player who had an excellent first full season in the Premiership during tough times.

Jose Dominguez – A diminutive Portuguese winger signed from Sporting Lisbon in August 1997 for £1.2 million, he was in and out of the team under Gerry Francis and then sidelined after Christian Gross's appointment in November 1997.

Justin Edinburgh – A loan spell from Southend was made permanent in July 1990 but after nearly 300 games for Spurs he lost his left-back berth to Clive Wilson in November 1997.

Neale Fenn – A young striker who made a handful of appearances during 1997-98, he ended the season on loan to Norwich City.

Les Ferdinand – A record, if reluctant, £6 million signing from Newcastle in July 1997, the England international missed much of the season through injury and experienced a goal drought from August 1997 to April 1998.

Ruel Fox – A tricky winger who signed from Newcastle in October 1995 for £4.2 million. On his day, he can turn matches as well as defenders, but his form remained erratic in 1997-98.

David Howells – An experienced and influential midfield campaigner who played well over 300 games for the club, he was blighted in 1997-98 with injuries and disagreements with new manager Christian Gross and left the club at the end of the season.

Steffen Iversen – A young forward signed from Norway's Rosenborg for £2.6 million in December 1996, his promising season was wrecked by an injury sustained in August 1997.

Jurgen Klinsmann – Footballer of the Year with Spurs in 1994-95, he returned to White Hart Lane from Italian club Sampdoria in December 1997. A World Cup winner in 1990, he remains one of the game's finest finishers – highlighted by the four-goal blitz at Wimbledon in May that secured Spurs' Premiership survival.

Gary Mabbutt – Spurs' club captain and longest-serving player, he's a model professional who played nearly 600 times for the club after joining from Bristol Rovers in 1982. The 36-year-old made his final appearance for Spurs on the last day of the 1997-98 season.

Paul Mahorn – The local forward made three appearances from the bench in 1997-98.

Allan Nielsen – A Danish international midfielder signed from Brondby for £1.65 million in August 1996, he had a season of mixed fortunes.

Moussa Saib – A £2.6 million buy from Spanish side Valencia in February 1998, the Algerian national team captain is a powerful midfield playmaker who made a good impression despite injuries.

John Scales – The centre back signed from Liverpool in 1996 for £2.6 million, but struggled to secure a regular first-team place in 1997-98.

Andy Sinton – The former England left-winger, signed from Sheffield Wednesday in January 1996 for £1.5 million, held his midfield place only for the middle part of the season.

Ian Walker – England's reserve keeper missed two months of the season with injury but came back for the 3-1 win at Crystal Palace in March – and helped ensure survival.

Clive Wilson – Signed from Queen's Park Rangers in June 1995, the 36-year-old right back enjoyed an extended run in the side with the arrival of Christian Gross.

Transferred in:
• Jose Dominguez
  (Sporting Lisbon, £1.2m)
• Jurgen Klinsmann (Sampdoria, free)
• Nicola Berti (Inter Milan, free)
• Frode Grodas (Chelsea, free)
• Moussa Saib (Valencia, £2.6m)

Transferred out:
• Leon Townley (released)
• Kevin Maher (released)
• Stuart Nethercott (Millwall, free)
• Jamie Clapham (Ipswich, £300,000)
• Dean Austin (released)
• Ronny Rosenthal (Watford, free)

Sol Campbell – Despite Tottenham's poor season, Campbell's club form was good enough to earn a call-up to Glenn Hoddle's England side. A Londoner, he's the product of the FA School of Excellence.

Ramon Vega – A defender for his native Switzerland, Vega joined Spurs from Italy's Cagliari in January 1997 for £3.7 million. He is tall and powerful and can be dangerous at set pieces.

David Ginola – A £2.5 million signing from Newcastle in July 1997, the French maestro had an outstanding season from midfield and was the club's Player of the Year. However, he failed to make the France squad.

West Ham United *Football Club*

West Ham United Football Club
West Ham United Football Club
West Ham United Football Club
West Ham United Football Club
West Ham United Football Club
West Ham United Football Club
West Ham United Football Club
West Ham United Football Club
West Ham United Football Club
West Ham United Football Club
West Ham United Football Club

→ **Address** | West Ham United FC, Boleyn Ground, Green Street, Upton Park, London E13 9AZ

Tel: 0181 548 2748 | **Tickets:** 0181 548 2758 | **Clubline:** 0891 121165

In 1998, ex-Hammers and 1966 World Cup final hat-trick hero Geoff Hurst received a knighthood. The other goalscorer in that final, Martin Peters, was also a West Ham player, as was the captain, Bobby Moore.

→ **Web site:** http://www.westhamunited.co.uk → **Chairman of football:** Terence Brown → **Manager:** Harry Redknapp → **Year formed:** 1895

Ground: Boleyn Ground (26,014)

Stands: Bobby Moore
Centenary
East
West

Home strip: Claret shirts with blue trim, white shorts with claret stripe, claret socks

Away strip: Pale blue shirts with blue trim, dark blue shorts with pale blue stripe, dark blue socks

Sponsor: Unknown

Programme: £2

Nickname: Hammers

Ground history: 1895 Memorial Recreation Ground, Canning Town
1904 Boleyn Ground

Previous name: Thames Ironworks

First League game: 30 August 1919, Division 2, drew 1-1 (h) v Lincoln City

Record attendance: 43,322 v Tottenham Hotspur, Division 1, 17 October 1970

Record victory: 10-0 v Bury, League Cup 2nd round, 25 October 1983

Record defeat: 2-8 v Blackburn Rovers, Division 1, 26 December 1963

Highest League position: Division 1 (old), 3rd place, 1985-86

Highest League scorer (season): Vic Watson, 50, 1929-30

Highest League scorer (aggregate): Vic Watson, 298, 1920-1935

Most League appearances: Billy Bonds, 663, 1967-1988

Most capped player: Bobby Moore, 108, England, 1958-1974

Highest transfer fee paid: £3.5m to Arsenal for John Hartson, February 1997

Highest transfer fee received: £4.5m from Everton for Slaven Bilic, June 1997

Major trophies: Division 2 (old) Champions **(2)** 1980-81, 1957-58
FA Cup Winners **(3)** 1980, 1975, 1964
European Cup Winners Cup **(1)** 1965

Samassi Abou – The French forward was signed in October 1997 from Cannes. Although he struggled to become a regular choice, he sparkled on several occasions and became a favourite of the fans.

Tim Breacker – A League Cup winner with Luton, the veteran right back now has well over 250 appearances for West Ham under his belt. He lost his place in February 1998 when West Ham restructured their defence.

Craig Forrest – The Canadian keeper was signed from Ipswich, where he had played for 13 seasons, in the 1997 close season. He made 20 appearances for the Hammers before being dropped in favour of Bernard Lama, who arrived on loan.

Lee Hodges – A young striker who was signed from Plymouth, he made five appearances as a substitute.

Andrew Impey – A pacy winger recruited from London neighbours QPR, Impey switched effectively from a traditional wide role to that of right wing back.

Paul Kitson – Hartson's regular striking partner at the end of the 1996-97 season, he found his progress hampered by injury. He did not play between September and February and managed only 17 appearances, hitting five goals.

Frank Lampard – The attacking midfielder, and son of the assistant manager, established himself in the first team in 1997-98 and won England B-team honours. He played 42 games for the Hammers and scored seven times, including a Coca-Cola Cup hat-trick against Walsall.

Stan Lazaridis – The Australian winger showed his true qualities after coming back from a broken leg sustained early in his West Ham career. He only scored twice in 1997-98 but his stunning 35-yard strike against Newcastle in February

will live a long time in the memory of West Ham fans.

Steve Lomas – A tenacious midfielder, the Northern Ireland international won plenty of admirers for his work-rate and inspirational performances in 1997-98. He scored the winner against former club Manchester City in the FA Cup 4th round.

Scott Mean – Another disappointing season for a young midfielder once tipped for big things after following England's Jamie Redknapp into the Premiership from Bournemouth. He made just three appearances late in the season, all as substitute.

Ludek Miklosko – The giant Czech goalkeeper played 15 times at the start of the 1997-98 campaign but was then injured.

John Moncur – A neat and tidy midfielder, he had to work hard to keep his place in the side in 1997-98. He played 24 times but the arrival of Berkovic and the emergence of Lampard meant he was often squeezed out of contention.

Emmanuel Omoyinmi – A late arrival from Dundee United in March 1998, 'Manny' was limited to just five appearances, but the striker did enjoy a moment of glory, scoring twice in the 3-3 draw with Crystal Palace in May.

Ian Pearce – The rugged central defender, signed from Blackburn Rovers in September 1997, filled the void created by Richard Hall's long-term absence. A regular, he was consistently solid throughout the 1997-98 season.

Steve Potts – The former England youth international joined West Ham as an apprentice and made his debut back in 1985. The defender has played over 400 times for the club, including over 30 appearances in 1997-98.

Trevor Sinclair – An exciting crowd-pleaser, he re-ignited his career when he moved from QPR in January 1998. He hit five goals in his first seven games for the club and featured either in a wide role or as a central striker.

David Unsworth – A strong centre back who was capped once by England, he slotted in comfortably as the left-sided defender in West Ham's back three. Signed from Everton in August 1997, he made 41 appearances – and was dismissed against Crystal Palace in the penultimate game of the season.

Transferred in:
- Eyal Berkovic (Maccabi Haifa, £1.7m)
- Andrew Impey (QPR, £1.2m)
- Craig Forrest (Ipswich, £400,000)
- David Unsworth (Everton, deal)
- Ian Pearce (Blackburn, £2m)
- Samassi Abou (Cannes, £300,000)
- Trevor Sinclair (QPR, £2.3m)
- Stephen Bywater (Rochdale, £300,000)
- Mohamed Berthe (Gaz Ajaccio, free)
- Javier Margas (Universidad, £500,000)
- Emmanuel Omoyinmi (Dundee United, March)

Transferred out:
- Slaven Bilic (Everton, £4.5m)
- Danny Williamson (Everton, deal)
- Marc Rieper (Celtic, £1.3m)
- Michael Hughes (Wimbledon, £1.6m)
- Iain Dowie (QPR, deal)
- Keith Rowland (QPR, deal)
- Steven Blaney (Brentford, free)
- Ian Bishop (Manchester City, free)

Eyal Berkovic – The Israeli midfield playmaker created several goals and scored nine himself. Brilliant throughout the season, he courted controversy, clashing with rival fans and even a team-mate once.

John Hartson – Powerful in the air and skilful on the deck, the Welsh international fired 24 goals. But his season was marred by suspensions – he was sent off twice and sat out the last four games of the season.

Rio Ferdinand – The classy centre back established himself in the side in 1997-98 and made it to the World Cup (along with cousin Les) as part of the England squad, despite being dropped from an earlier squad.

196

Premiership
Wimbledon Football Club
Wimbledon Football Club
Wimbledon Football Club
Wimbledon Football Club
Wimbledon Football Club
Wimbledon Football Club
Wimbledon Football Club
Wimbledon Football Club
Wimbledon Football Club
Wimbledon Football Club
Wimbledon Football Club
Wimbledon Football Club

Wimbledon *Football Club*

→ **Address** | Wimbledon FC, Selhurst Park Stadium, London SE25 6PY

Tel: 0181 771 2233 | **Tickets:** 0181 771 8841 | **Clubline:** 0891 121175

Speculation surrounding Wimbledon's relocation to Dublin was eventually dismissed early in 1998, following UEFA disapproval.

→ **Web site:** http://www.wimbledon-fc.co.uk → **Chairman:** Stanley Reed → **Manager:** Joe Kinnear → **Year formed:** 1889

Ground: Selhurst Park (26,309)

Stands: Main
Whitehorse Lane
Holmesdale Road
Arthur Wait

Home strip: Blue shirts with gold trim, blue shorts with gold trim, blue socks with gold trim

Away strip: Red shirts with black trim, red shorts with black trim, red socks with black trim

Sponsor: Elonex

Programme: £2

Nickname: Dons or Crazy Gang

Ground history: 1889 Wimbledon Common
1912 Plough Lane
1991 Selhurst Park

Previous name: Wimbledon Old Centrals

First League game: 20 August 1977, Division 4, drew 3-3 (h) v Halifax Town

Record attendance: 30,115 v Manchester United, Premiership, 9 May 1993

Record victory: 7-2 v Windsor & Eton, FA Cup 1st round, 22 November 1980

Record defeat: 0-8 v Everton, League Cup 2nd round, 29 August 1978

Highest League position: Premiership, 6th place, 1993-94

Highest League scorer (season): Alan Cork, 29, 1983-84

Highest League scorer (aggregate): Alan Cork, 145, 1977-1992

Most League appearances: Alan Cork, 430, 1977-1992

Most capped player: Kenny Cunningham, 26, Republic of Ireland, 1994-1998

Highest transfer fee paid: £2m to Liverpool for Mark Kennedy, March 1998
£2m to Crystal Palace for Andy Roberts, March 1998

Highest transfer fee received: £4m from Newcastle United for Warren Barton, June 1995

Major trophies: Division 4 Champions **(1)** 1982-83
FA Cup Winners **(1)** 1988

Neal Ardley – One of several Wimbledon first-teamers to progress through the youth ranks, Ardley's favoured position is wide, on the right of midfield.

Dean Blackwell – A former Don trainee, Blackwell's central defensive partnership with Chris Perry again made the club a tough side to score against in 1997-98.

Stewart Castledine – In demand as a model, Castledine is less sought after in the first team. He again found opportunities hard to come by in 1997-98 and has now made fewer than 30 League appearances in seven seasons.

Andy Clarke – Signed from Barnet in 1991, this fast forward has struggled to get a run in the team and has earned the tag of 'supersub'. Of his 21 games in 1997-98, 19 were made from the bench.

Carl Cort – A bright prospect, he's a tall striker who had a great start to the 1997-98 season, scoring six goals by November, before suffering a barren patch.

Kenny Cunningham – Signed from Millwall in November 1994, Cunningham was a near ever-present full back in 1997-98. He fits well into a tight defence and creates chances with his accurate crossing.

Robbie Earle – Toe and calf injuries, plus Jamaica's World Cup qualifiers, disrupted the season for this popular midfielder. Earle joined the Dons from Port Vale in July 1991 and is rapidly approaching 300 games for the club.

Efan Ekoku – A tall, strong and quick striker who cost £900,000 when he signed from Norwich, Ekoku's ankle injury made 1997-98 a poor season.

Jason Euell – A broken arm stopped the exciting young striker in his tracks in October, but he returned to finish the season as leading scorer despite an apparent loss of confidence in front of goal.

Peter Fear – A versatile player who was used sparingly in 1997-98, Fear's best performance coincided with his team's worst performance of the season – a 6-2 defeat to Tottenham in which he scored both goals for Wimbledon.

Damian Francis – The promising young attacking midfielder was given two games in 1997-98, both as a substitute – in the 5-0 defeat by Arsenal and the 6-2 drubbing by London rivals Tottenham.

Paul Heald – A popular goalkeeper who arrived at Selhurst Park in July 1995, Heald found himself second choice to Neil Sullivan in 1997-98, and played just twice.

Michael Hughes – A £1.6 million arrival from West Ham in September, the Northern Ireland international winger immediately found a place in the fans' hearts with his exciting play and won their Player of the Year award.

Duncan Jupp – A right back who has played for Scotland Under-21s, Jupp's appearances were limited in the 1997-98 season by Kenny Cunningham's fine form.

Mark Kennedy – An exceptionally gifted winger signed from Liverpool on transfer deadline day for £2 million, Kennedy has made just four appearances so far, but great things are expected of him.

Alan Kimble – A reliable left back signed from Cambridge in July 1993, Kimble has yet to let the team down. He was involved in a battle for a first team place in 1997-98, but still put in some solid performances.

Carl Leaburn – A £300,000 buy from Charlton Athletic, Leaburn is good in the air and controls the ball well. He endeared himself to fans with a brace in the 3-0 win over Crystal Palace in February 1998.

Brian McAllister – The Scotland international defender, who came up through the ranks, struggled to break into the back four in 1997-98 and was restricted to a handful of games.

Chris Perry – One of the League's most under-rated defenders, Perry was again the key to Wimbledon's miserly defence. Though only 5ft 8in tall, he is good in the air and his well-timed tackles have led many to tip him as a future England player.

Alan Reeves – The tough central defender made just one substitute appearance in 1997-98.

Andy Roberts – Proving to be an excellent signing from rivals Palace, Robert rarely gives the ball away in his role in the centre of midfield.

Ben Thatcher – An attacking defender who operated at left back for much of the season, Thatcher was sent off twice in 1997-98, including a second-minute dismissal in a 2-1 loss to West Ham.

Transferred in:
- Mark Kennedy (Liverpool, £2m)
- Michael Hughes (West Ham, £1.6m)
- Andy Roberts (Crystal Palace, £2m)
- Ceri Hughes (Luton, £400,000)
- Carl Leaburn (Charlton, £300,000)
- Staale Solbakken (Lillestrom, £250,000)

Transferred out:
- Oyvind Leonhardsen (Liverpool, £3.5m)
- Dean Holdsworth (Bolton, £3.5m)
- Vinny Jones (QPR, £500,000)
- Staale Solbakken (Molde, £300,000)
- Scott Fitzgerald (Millwall, £50,000)
- Aidan Newhouse (Fulham, free)
- Grant Payne (Woking, free)
- Stuart Searle (Woking, free)

Marcus Gayle – The striker struggled in 1997-98 to build upon his excellent season in 1996-97, suffering from injury and scoring just four times as the manager rotated his forwards looking for an effective partnership.

Ceri Hughes – Signed from Luton Town in the summer of 1997 as a replacement for Oyvind Leonhardsen, the Welsh international midfielder spent much of the season finding his Premiership feet.

Neil Sullivan – The Scottish international, born in England, has been the Dons' regular keeper for the last two seasons. A good shot-stopper who is confident dealing with crosses, he rarely makes mistakes.

Barnsley *Football Club*

→ **Address** | Barnsley FC, Oakwell Ground, Barnsley, South Yorkshire S71 1ET

Tel: 01226 211211 | **Tickets:** 01226 211211 | **Clubline:** 0891 121152

Love was in the air during Barnsley's Premiership season – De Zeeuw, Ward, Sheridan, Leese and Bosancic all became fathers, Eaden and Appleby were expectant, and Barnard was preparing to wed.

Top row • P Smith • S McClare • S Hulson • C Morgan • P Wilkinson • T Bullock • L Leese • D Watson • S Davis • M Hume • P Bagshaw • D Sheridan • M Tarmey **Middle row** • E Winstanley • D Jones • R Prendergast • L Beckett • J Perry • C Rose • A Gregory • D Shenton • A De Zeeuw • E Tinkler • L Ten Heuvel • A Moses • N Thompson • N Rimmington • M Shotton **Bottom row** • P Shirtliff • C Marcelle • A Liddell • N Eaden • M Bullock • N Redfearn • D Wilson • M Appleby • J Hendrie • J Bosancic • A Krizan • G Hristov • C Walker

→ **Web site:** http://www.yorkshire-web.co.uk/bfc   → **Chairman:** John Dennis   → **Manager:** Danny Wilson   → **Year formed:** 1887

Ground: Oakwell (18,806)

Stands: ORA
East
West
Spion Kop

Home strip: Red shirts with white trim, white shorts with red trim, red socks with white trim

Away strip: Royal blue and black striped shirts, black shorts with royal blue trim, black socks with royal blue trim

Sponsor: ORA

Programme: £1.80

Nickname: Tykes, Reds or Colliers

Ground history: 1887 Oakwell Ground

Previous name: Barnsley St Peter's

First League game: 1 September 1898, Division 2, lost 0-1 (a) v Lincoln City

Record attendance: 40,255 v Stoke City, FA Cup 5th round, 15 February 1936

Record victory: 9-0 v Loughborough Town, Division 2, 28 January 1899
9-0 v Accrington Stanley, Division 3 (North), 3 February 1934

Record defeat: 0-9 v Notts County, Division 2, 19 November 1934

Highest League position: Premiership, 19th place, 1997-98

Highest League scorer (season): Cecil McCormack, 33, 1950-51

Highest League scorer (aggregate): Ernie Hine, 122, 1921-1926, 1934-1938

Most League appearances: Barry Murphy, 509, 1962-1978

Most capped player: Gerry Taggart, 35, Northern Ireland, 1990-1995

Highest transfer fee paid: £1.5m for Georgi Hristov from Partizan Belgrade (Yugoslavia), July 1997

Highest transfer fee received: £1.5m from Nottingham Forest for Carl Tiler, May 1991

Major trophies: FA Cup Winners **(1)** 1912 Division 3 (North) Champions **(3)** 1954-55, 1938-39, 1933-34

Mattie Appleby – A central defender signed from Darlington for £200,000 in July 1996, he lost favour with the manager in October 1997.

Darren Barnard – An August 1997 signing from Bristol City for £750,000, he's a left wing back who can score both from open play and free kicks. He was first choice at number 3 all season and earned his first cap for Wales in March 1998.

Jovo Bosancic – The former Croatia Under-21 midfielder joined the Reds in July 1996 from sunny Madeira. He struggled to hold a regular first-team place in 1997-98.

Martin Bullock – Signed from non-League Eastwood Town for £15,000 in September 1993, this attacking midfielder's season saw him increasingly moving out of the super-sub role and finding a more permanent place in the team.

Arjan de Zeeuw – A tall, strong central defender signed from Dutch side Telstar for £250,000 in November 1995, he was Oakwell's Player of the Year in his first season and remained impressive during the promotion campaign. In 1997-98, he missed crucial games between February and March through injury.

Nicky Eaden – A local lad and a regular since 1993, he was ever-present in the promotion-winning side of 1996-97 and the experienced right wing back missed only a handful of games last season.

Jan-Aage Fjortoft – The tall Norwegian forward signed in January 1998 from Sheffield United for £800,000. A scorer of some spectacular goals, he alternated in the first team with Hristov.

Georgi Hristov – The Macedonia international striker was a record club signing in June 1997 from Partizan Belgrade, with whom he won three consecutive Yugoslav League titles.

A proven scorer, he had a patchy season in the unfamiliar environment of a fight against relegation, spending much of 1998 on the bench.

Scott Jones – A young, left-sided defender, he came into the side in February 1998 and made headlines with two of the three goals that beat Manchester United in the FA Cup.

Ales Krizan – The experienced Slovenian defender was signed from his home country's Maribor Branik in July 1997 and established himself in September. However, he then lost his place between December and March through injury.

Lars Leese – Signed from Bayer Leverkusen for £250,000 in June 1997, the German keeper remained understudy to David Watson throughout the season.

Andy Liddell – A former Under-21 forward for Scotland, almost half the 25-year-old's appearances in the 1997-98 season were as a substitute.

Clint Marcelle – Signed from Portuguese side Felgueiras in 1996, the Trinidad midfielder scored the second goal against Bradford in the promotion-clinching game of 1997 – but in 1997-98 spent more time on the bench than on the pitch.

Peter Markstedt – A £400,000 capture from Swedish side Vasteras in November 1997, the tall, strong central defender was drafted in to shore up the leaky defence, and his debut was in a 1-0 win at Liverpool.

Chris Morgan – The Barnsley-born central defender worked his way up from YTS status.

Adie Moses – A local product, the England Under-21 international has turned into an impressively versatile player, at home in almost any defensive position. He missed only a handful of games in 1997-98.

Neil Redfearn – The inspirational 32-year-old Barnsley captain arrived from Oldham for £150,000 in September 1991. The midfielder was top scorer in the promotion season and again in 1997-98.

Darren Sheridan – Rescued by Barnsley from non-League football in July 1993, he became a midfield regular in 1994. Despite making fewer appearances in 1997-98, he remained a favourite with the fans.

Peter Shirtliff – The centre back graduated from player to first-team coach in 1997-98.

Laurens Ten Heuvel – A striker who signed from Dutch side FC Den Bosch in March 1996, injury led to him making just a couple of substitute appearances in 1997-98.

Neil Thompson – An experienced left back signed from Ipswich in June 1996, he was edged out of the left wing back role by Darren Barnard.

David Watson – A Barnsley boy who joined the club as an associated schoolboy, he became first choice keeper in 1994 and held off the challenge from Leese in 1997-98 – despite conceding six goals or more three times in the League.

Transferred in:
- Darren Barnard
  (Bristol City, £700,000)
- Jan Aage Fjortoft
  (Sheffield United, £800,000)
- Georgi Hristov
  (Partizan Belgrade, £1.5m)
- Ales Krizan
  (Maribor Branik, £310,000)
- Lars Leese
  (Bayer Leverkusen, £250,000)
- Peter Markstedt
  (Vasteras, £400,000)
- Eric Tinkler (Cagliari, £650,000)
- Ashley Ward (Derby, £1.3m)

Transferred out:
- Paul Wilkinson (Millwall, undisclosed)
- Steven Davis (Oxford, undisclosed)

Eric Tinkler – A combative midfielder signed from Italian club Cagliari in June 1997, he is a South African international. He held his place until late January before an end of season only peppered with full appearances.

John Hendrie – The experienced Scot was signed from Middlesbrough in October 1996 for £250,000 and was Barnsley's Player of the Year in his first season. His second season was hampered by injury.

Ashley Ward – The strong, predatory forward was signed from Derby County in September 1997 for £1.3 million. He was then first choice at number 10 and was voted Player of the Year by the club's supporters.

Birmingham City *Football Club*

Birmingham City Football Club
Birmingham City Football Club
Birmingham City Football Club
Birmingham City Football Club
Birmingham City Football Club
Birmingham City Football
Birmingham City Football

→ **Address** | Birmingham City FC, St Andrew's, Small Heath, Birmingham B9 4NH

Tel: 0121 772 0101 | **Tickets:** 0121 772 0101 | **Clubline:** 0891 121188

Pipped at the play-off post by Sheffield United on goal difference in 1997-98, Birmingham City improved on their 1996-97 position of 10th place by finishing seventh.

Top row • M O'Connor • D Wassall • P Furlong • J Bass • M Johnson • M Grainger • N Forster

Middle row • A Lowe • C Holland • S Robinson • T Hey • K Poole • I Bennett • P Ndlovu • P Tait • P Devlin • N McDiarmid

Bottom row • M Mills • K Francis • B Hughes • S Bruce • T Francis • G Ablett • J Bowen • B Horne • F Barlow

→ **Web site:** http://www.bcfc.com   → **Chairman:** David Gold   → **Manager:** Trevor Francis   → **Year formed:** 1875

Ground: St Andrew's (25,812)

Stands: Main
Railway End
Brew XI Kop
Tilton Road

Home strip: Blue and white shirts, white shorts, blue socks

Away strip: Black and white shirts, black shorts with white trim, white socks with black trim

Sponsor: Auto Windscreens

Programme: £1.70

Nickname: Blues

Ground history: 1875 Arthur Street
1877 Muntz Street, Small Heath
1906 St Andrew's

Previous names: Small Heath Alliance
Birmingham

First League game: 3 September 1892, Division 2, won 5-1 (h) v Burslem Port Vale

Record attendance: 67,341 v Everton, FA Cup 5th round, 11 February 1939

Record victory: 12-0 v Walsall Town Swifts, Division 2, 17 December 1892
12-0 v Doncaster Rovers, Division 2, 11 April 1903

Record defeat: 1-9 v Blackburn Rovers, Division 1, 5 January 1895
1-9 v Sheffield Wednesday, Division 1, 13 December 1930

Highest League position: Division 1 (old), 6th place, 1955-56

Highest League scorer (season): Joe Bradford, 29, 1927-28

Highest League scorer (aggregate): Joe Bradford, 249, 1920-1935

Most League appearances: Frank Womack, 491, 1908-1928

Most capped player: Malcolm Page, 28, Wales 1971-1979

Highest transfer fee paid: £1.5m to Chelsea for Paul Furlong, July 1996
£1.5m to Port Vale for Jon McCarthy, September 1997

Highest transfer fee received: £2.5m from Coventry City for Gary Breen, January 1997

Major trophies: Division 2 (old) Champions (5) 1994-95, 1954-55, 1947-48, 1920-21, 1892-93
League Cup Winners (1) 1963

Gary Ablett – A highly experienced central defender who signed from Everton in June 1996 for £390,000, Ablett has also played for Liverpool and holds two League championship medals and two FA Cup medals.

Dele Adebola – A tall, fast, powerful striker, Adebola was signed from Crewe Alexandra in February 1998 for £1 million. Less than two weeks later, he returned to his former club in Blues' colours and scored in their 2-0 victory.

Jonathan Bass – The former trainee signed professional forms in 1994. A versatile defender, the 22-year-old has flourished under Trevor Francis.

Ian Bennett – A highly rated keeper, Bennett signed from Peterborough United for £325,000 in December 1993. He holds the club record of nine consecutive clean sheets, which he earned in 1994.

Simon Charlton – A reliable left back who signed from Southampton in December 1997 for £200,000, Charlton made his debut in the Blues' 2-1 win at home against Manchester City. He likes going forward and is a fine crosser of the ball.

Howard Forinton – The 23-year-old forward was signed from non-League Yeovil Town for £70,000 in July 1997 but has yet to make a regular place in the first team.

Nicky Forster – Shortly after signing from Brentford in early February 1997, Forster injured his knee ligaments. The England Under-21 was unable to return to action until October 1997.

Gerry Gill – A right back signed from Yeovil Town for £30,000 in the 1997 close season, Gill made a late League debut in April 1998.

Martin Grainger – A free-kick specialist, Grainger signed from Brentford for £400,000 in March

1996 and has proved himself to be a tough-tackling defender. Previous clubs include Colchester United, who he helped secure the Vauxhall Conference title in 1992.

Tony Hey – A Berlin-born midfielder, Hey signed from second division Bundesliga side Fortuna Cologne for £300,000 in July 1997. His transfer was instigated by former England international Tony Woodcock, who is an agent in Germany. Unfortunately, the player was quickly hit by injury.

Chris Holland – An attacking midfielder who signed permanently for £600,000 from Newcastle United in October 1996 after a short spell on loan, Holland can provide creativity in the middle of the pitch, though he struggled to hold down a first team place in the 1997-98 season.

Bryan Hughes – A member of the Wrexham team that knocked the Blues out of the FA Cup in 1996, midfielder Hughes joined the club in March 1997 for £700,000 and has performed well in his wide role.

Michael Johnson – Nicknamed 'Magic' after the American basketball player, Johnson was a £225,000 purchase from Notts County in September 1995. This fast, yet solid, defender began as a County trainee.

Jon McCarthy – Trevor Francis equalled the club transfer record when he signed the Northern Ireland international from Port Vale for £1.5 million in September 1997. Skilled and enthusiastic, he had a nervous start before becoming a regular.

Chris Marsden – A combative midfielder snapped up for £500,000 from Stockport in October 1997, the 29-year-old scored the only goal of the game in his debut against rivals Wolves. Marsden, who spent an injury-plagued 10 months at Molineux earlier in his career and was given a free transfer to Notts County, had his career revived at Stockport.

Martin O'Connor – The former Walsall midfielder was originally targeted for Birmingham City by previous manager Barry Fry during the 1995-96 season. However, O'Connor ended up spending a brief spell with Fry at Peterborough instead before finally arriving at St Andrew's in November 1996 for £400,000.

Kevin Poole – A free transfer from Leicester City in August 1997, the Blues' 35-year-old reserve keeper is an experienced goal-stopper, having also played for Aston Villa and Middlesbrough during his career.

Darren Purse – A centre back who can also play at full back, Purse signed from Oxford United in February 1998 for £700,000.

Steve Robinson – A promising young Nottingham-born winger who progressed through the ranks at St Andrew's and turned professional in June 1993, Robinson lost his place for a chunk of the season but enjoyed a regular slot from March 1997.

Darren Wassall – Signed from Derby County for £100,000 in May 1997, the centre back spent much of the following season out of action after two Achilles tendon operations.

Transferred in:
- Jon McCarthy (Port Vale, £1.5m)
- Chris Marsden (Stockport County, £500,000)
- Simon Charlton (Southampton, £200,000)
- Dele Adebola (Crewe Alexandra, £1m)
- Darren Purse (Oxford United, £700,000)

Transferred out:
- Jason Bowen (Reading, £200,000)
- Andy Legg (Reading £100,000)
- Kevin Francis (Oxford, £100,000)
- Paul Devlin (Sheffield United, £250,000 deal)
- Barry Horne (Huddersfield, free)
- Ricky Otto (released)
- Steve Sutton (released)

Steve Bruce – A free transfer from Manchester United in July 1996, the 37-year-old central defender has won a host of honours at club level and is a former England B-international.

Paul Furlong – Furlong, a record signing in July 1996 at £1.5 million from Chelsea, notched up a hat-trick double in January 1998 against Stoke and Stockport, and is generous in creating chances for colleagues.

Peter Ndlovu – The Zimbabwe-born international striker was signed from Coventry City in July 1997 for a modest £200,000. He has proven scoring ability and quickly became a favourite with Blues fans.

Bolton Wanderers *Football Club*

Bolton Wanderers Football Club
Bolton Wanderers Football Club
Bolton Wanderers Football Club
Bolton Wanderers Football Club
Bolton Wanderers Football Club
Bolton Wanderers Football

→ **Address** | Bolton Wanderers FC, Reebok Stadium, Burnden Way, Lostock, Bolton BL6 6JW

Tel: 01204 673673 | **Tickets:** 01204 673601 | **Clubline:** 0891 121164

Bolton's sponsors came into being in 1895 when local man Joe Foster invented the spiked running shoe. The company was renamed Reebok in the 1950s and became a household name.

Top row • P Frandsen • S Taylor • J Phillips • C Fairclough • G Strong • M Doherty • N Blake • H Aljofree • S Whittaker • N Spooner • J Sheridan • A Todd • S Coleman **Middle row** • E Simpson • C Dyson • B Small • N Cox • G Taggart • J Pollock • G Ward • M Glennon • K Branagan • R Elliott • L Potter • S Sellars • M Johansen • D Crombie • S Carroll **Bottom row** • A Thompson • A Gunnlaugsson • C Todd • G Bergsson • P Brown • J McGinlay • S McAnespie

→ **Web site:** http://www.boltonwfc.co.uk   → **Chairman:** Gordon Hargreaves   → **Manager:** Colin Todd   → **Year formed:** 1874

Ground: Reebok Stadium (25,000)

Stands: Main
Family
Nat Lofthouse
South

Home strip: White shirts with navy blue and red trim, navy blue shorts with white and red trim, navy blue socks with white and red trim

Away: Navy blue shirts with white and red trim, navy blue shorts with white and red trim, navy blue socks with white and red trim

Sponsor: Reebok

Programme: £2

Nickname: Trotters

Ground history: 1874 Smithfield Park
Recreation Ground
1879 Cockle's Field
1881 Pikes Lane
1895 Burnden Park
1997 Reebok Stadium

Previous name: Christ Church

First League game: 8 September 1888, Football League, lost 3-6 (h) v Derby County

Record attendance: 25,000 v Arsenal, Premiership, 31 March 1998

Record victory: 13-0 v Sheffield United, FA Cup 2nd round, 1 February 1890

Record defeat: 1-9 v Preston North End, FA Cup 2nd round, 10 December 1887

Highest League position: Division 1 (old), 3rd place, 1924-25, 1920-21, 1891-92

Highest League scorer (season): Joe Smith, 38, 1920-21

Highest League scorer (aggregate): Nat Lofthouse, 256, 1946-1960

Most League appearances: Eddie Hopkinson, 519, 1956-1969

Most capped player: Nat Lofthouse, 33, England, 1950-1958

Highest transfer fee paid: £3.5m to Wimbledon for Dean Holdsworth, October 1997

Highest transfer fee received: £4.5m from Liverpool for Jason McAteer, September 1995

Major trophies: Division 1 Champions **(1)** 1996-97
Division 2 (old) Champions **(2)** 1977-78, 1908-09
Division 3 (old) Champions **(1)** 1972-73
FA Cup Winners **(4)** 1958, 1929, 1926, 1923

Hasney Aljofree – The Manchester-born England youth cap made his debut in the heartlifting win over Blackburn in April. He was the seventh player to wear the number 3 shirt for Bolton during 1997-98.

Peter Beardsley – The gifted and much-capped 36-year-old England forward, signed for £500,000 from Newcastle in August 1997, made 17 appearances (scoring twice) before joining Kevin Keegan's new regime at Fulham on loan in January 1998.

Gudni Bergsson – Signed from Spurs for £115,000 in 1995 (his debut was as a sub in the League Cup final), the tall, experienced Icelandic player has proved a bargain buy. He is equally at home at right back or in central defence.

Keith Branagan – Signed from Gillingham on a free transfer in 1992, he was a member of three Bolton promotion-winning sides. The imposing Republic of Ireland international keeper remained first choice in 1997-98.

Neil Cox – A £1.2 million buy from Middlesbrough in May 1997, the experienced right back settled in the number 2 shirt from New Year until the end of the season.

Chris Fairclough – A classy central defender, he was kept out until December by an injury sustained in the last game of the 1996-97 season. He joined Bolton from Leeds for £450,000 in the summer of 1995.

Per Frandsen – Signed for £350,000 from FC Copenhagen in 1996, the tall Danish midfielder played a vital role in taking Bolton into the Premiership – and nearly kept them there in 1997-98 with a fine solo run and shot in the final game at Chelsea. He was voted the players' Player of the Year.

Arnar Gunnlaugsson – Signed from IA Akranes of Iceland for £100,000 in

July 1997, the international midfielder has also played in Holland, Germany and France. Colin Todd used him as a sub for much of the season.

Dean Holdsworth – Bolton signed this experienced striker from Wimbledon for a club record £3.5 million in October 1997 in an attempt to bolster the chances of Premiership survival. But the 28-year-old carried niggling injuries and disappointed.

Michael Johansen – Like his twin brother Martin at Coventry, former FC Copenhagen star Michael has struggled to secure first-team football in England since becoming Bolton's fourth £1 million signing in 1996. Over half his appearances in midfield in 1997-98 were as a sub.

Steve McAnespie – A Scottish Under-18 full back signed from Kilmarnock for £900,000 in 1995, he's yet to secure a first-team place.

Jimmy Phillips – Bolton paid Middlesbrough £300,000 in 1993 to sign the full back and utility player for his second spell at Bolton. In 1997-98, his form was patchy and appearances limited.

Scott Sellars – Signed from Newcastle for £750,000 in 1996, he became a permanent and influential presence in the side's midfield – but a serious injury ended his 1997-98 season in early February.

John Sheridan – The experienced Republic of Ireland midfielder moved from Sheffield Wednesday to Bolton for £180,000 in December 1996 after a month on loan. He reappeared in March following the injury to Scott Sellars and the departure of Jamie Pollock.

Greg Strong – Formerly with Wigan, this tall central defender acted as cover during 1997-98.

Gerry Taggart – A rugged centre half signed from Barnsley for £1.5 million

in 1995, he lost his place through injury in October 1997, reappearing only at the end of the campaign.

Alan Thompson – A forceful left-sided midfielder with a fierce shot and impressive scoring record, he joined Bolton from Newcastle for £250,000 in 1993 and has been an automatic choice ever since.

Andy Todd – Hampered by injuries since signing from Middlesbrough for £250,000 in 1995, the manager's son has played at full back, centre back and midfield. In 1997-98, he figured mainly in central defence on his way to being voted the supporters' Player of the Year.

Gavin Ward – The much-travelled keeper, signed from Bradford City for £280,000 in 1996, provided cover for Keith Branagan in 1997-98, notably during the dark days of December.

Mike Whitlow – The 29-year-old left back was signed from Leicester City for £700,000 after the injury to Robbie Elliott in September 1997 and was the regular number 3 for Bolton until January.

Transferred in:
- Mike Whitlow
 (Leicester, £700,000)
- Dean Holdsworth
 (Wimbledon, £3.5m)
- Peter Beardsley
 (Newcastle, £500,000)
- Robbie Elliott (Newcastle, £2.5m)
- Mark Fish (Lazio, £2.5m)
- Arnar Gunnlaugsson
 (IA Akranes, £100,000)

Transferred out:
- John McGinlay
 (Bradford, £650,000)
- Bryan Small (Bury, free)
- Jamie Pollock
 (Manchester City, £1m)

Robbie Elliott – A £2.5 million signing from Newcastle in July 1997, this talented and versatile defender suffered a double fracture against Everton in September and missed the rest of Bolton's torrid season.

Nathan Blake – Leading marksman last season with 15 goals, the Welsh international had increased scoring responsibilities with the departure of the prolific John McGinlay. He was signed from Sheffield United in December 1996 for £1.35 million.

Mark Fish – A member of the South Africa squad for France '98, Fish was signed from Italian side Lazio for £2.5 million in August 1997. Originally a striker, he settled into Bolton's back line for much of the 1997-98 season.

Bradford City *Football Club*

Bradford City Football Club
Bradford City Football Club
Bradford City Football Club
Bradford City Football Club
Bradford City Football Club
Bradford City Football Club
Bradford City Football Club
Bradford City Football Club
Bradford City Football Club

→ **Address** | Bradford City AFC, Valley Parade, Bradford, West Yorkshire BD8 7DY

Tel: 01274 773355 | **Tickets:** 01274 770022 | **Clubline:** 0891 888640

During the 1997-98 season, Bradford used 32 players for their 46 games. Fifty years ago, in the 1948-49 season, the club used a total of 40 different players in 42 Division 3 (North) games.

Top row • N Mohan • J Dreyer • R Steiner • E Youds • D Sepp **Second row •** O B Sundgot • R Liburd • J Lawrence • A O'Brien • L Davies • G Kulcsar • Edinho • W Jacobs • R Blake • S Murray • P Beagrie **Third row •** D Donaldson • I McLean • N Pepper • C Midgley • M Prudhoe • D Moore • J Gould • G Watson • A Kiwomya • C Wilder • C Ramage **Bottom row •** C Hutchings • S Redmond • M Hunter • R Hassell • C Kamara • G Richmond • P Jewell • M Ellis • S Smith

→ **Chairman:** Geoffrey Richmond   → **Manager:** Paul Jewell   → **Year formed:** 1903

Ground: Valley Parade (18,018)

Stands: Allied Colloids
Diamond Seal Kop
Sunwin
Symphony Group

Home strip: Claret and amber striped shirts, black shorts with claret and amber trim, black socks with claret and amber trim

Away strip: Blue shirts with claret and amber trim, black shorts with claret and amber trim, black socks with blue, claret and amber trim

Sponsor: JCT 600

Programme: £1.80

Nickname: Bantams

Ground history: 1903 Valley Parade

Previous name: None

First League game: 1 September 1903, Division 2, lost 0-2 (a) v Grimsby Town

Record attendance: 39,146 v Burnley, FA Cup 4th round, 11 March 1911

Record victory: 11-1 v Rotherham United, Division 3 (North), 25 August 1928

Record defeat: 1-9 v Colchester United, Division 4, 30 December 1961

Highest League position: Division 1 (old), 5th place, 1910-11

Highest League scorer (season): David Layne, 34, 1961-62

Highest League scorer (aggregate): Bobby Campbell, 121, 1979-1983, 1983-1986

Most League appearances: Cecil Podd, 502, 1970-1984

Most capped player: Harry Hampton, 9, Northern Ireland, 1911-1914

Highest transfer fee paid: £650,000 to Bolton Wanderers for John McGinlay, November 1997

Highest transfer fee received: £2m from Newcastle United for Des Hamilton, March 1997

Major trophies: Division 2 (old) Champions **(1)** 1907-08
Division 3 (old) Champions **(1)** 1984-85
Division 3 (North) Champions **(1)** 1928-29
FA Cup Winners **(1)** 1911

Robbie Blake – A young striker who signed from Darlington for £300,000 in March 1997, Blake is a strong-running forward who had a favourable strike rate during the 1997-98 season.

Peter Beagrie – An experienced midfielder who signed from Manchester City in July 1997 for £50,000, he spent the second half of the season on loan to former club Everton, helping them retain Premiership status.

Paul Bolland – A trainee, he made his debut as a substitute against Stockport County in January 1998.

Mark Bower – A young central defender, he made his League debut as a substitute in the 3-2 victory over Norwich City in April 1998, when he played out of position at left-back.

Lawrence Davies – A first-year professional released by Leeds United, the Welsh striker was signed at the end of the 1996-97 season and made his debut as a substitute in the 3-1 defeat by Tranmere in March 1998.

John Dreyer – A tribunal-set £25,000 signing from Stoke City in November 1996, he is a defender who played in a third of the games of 1997-98.

Gareth Grant – A hat-trick hero of Bradford's Northern Intermediate League Cup Final victory against Leeds United, he was given his first-team debut as a substitute in the penultimate home game of the 1997-98 season against Queen's Park Rangers.

Jamie Lawrence – A skilful winger with good pace, he transferred to the Bantams from Leicester City for £50,000 in June 1997. He was one of Bradford's most consistent players during the 1997-98 season.

Darren Moore – A 1997 close season signing from Doncaster

Rovers for £310,000, Moore is a 6ft 3in central defender who started his League career at Torquay United.

Shaun Murray – An attacking midfielder who was a £210,000 signing from Scarborough in the summer of 1994, Murray played in the majority of games during the 1997-98 campaign.

Andrew O'Brien – A talented young defender who has represented England at Under-18 level, O'Brien made his first-team debut when bradfor played Queen's Park Rangers in October 1996.

Nigel Pepper – A £105,000 capture from York City in February 1997, he is a tough-tackling midfielder with an eye for goal.

Mark Prudhoe – An experienced goalkeeper, Prudhoe was signed from Stoke City in 1997 for a tribunal-set £70,000, although due to Gary Walsh's good form his appearances have only just reached double figures.

Craig Ramage – A talented midfielder who signed from Watford on a free transfer in the summer of 1997, he is capable of scoring goals but failed to meet expectations in his first season at the club.

Dennis Sepp – A free transfer from Dutch second division side HSC 21 in 1997, injury prevented Sepp from commanding a regular place in the team, although he played frequently from the bench.

Robert Steiner – Signed for £500,000 in July 1997 from Swedish side IFK Norrkoping, Steiner is a forward for Sweden with good aerial presence. He was a regular in the Bradford City squad during 1997-98 and weighed in with his fair share of goals.

Daniel Verity – A young defender who signed professional forms at

the end of March 1998, Verity appeared for the first team only from the bench.

Gary Walsh – An experienced keeper who was Peter Schmeichel's understudy at Old Trafford, he was signed from Middlesbrough for £500,000 in October 1997. He appeared regularly for the team in his first season and earned the club's Player of the Year award.

Edinho – A Brazilian striker who signed from Portuguese side VSC Guimaraes for £250,000 in February 1997, he is a key player in the squad and has established himself as City's penalty-taker.

Transferred in:
- Peter Beagrie
  (Manchester City, £50,000)
- Jamie Lawrence
  (Leicester, £50,000)
- John McGinlay (Bolton, £650,000)
- Darren Moore
  (Doncaster, £310,000)
- Mark Prudhoe (Stoke, £70,000)
- Craig Ramage (Watford, free)
- Dennis Sepp (HSC 21, free)
- Robert Steiner
  (IFK Norrkoping, £500,000)
- Gary Walsh
  (Middlesbrough, £500,000)
- Robert Zabica
  (Spearwood, £150,000)

Transferred out:
- David Brightwell
  (Northampton Town, free)
- Jonathan Gould (Celtic, free)
- Andy Kiwomya (Halifax, free)
- George Kulcsar
  (Queen's Park Rangers, £260,000)
- Richard Liburd (Carlisle, free)
- Craig Midgley (Hartlepool, £10,000)
- Nicky Mohan (Wycombe, £100,000)
- Marco Sas (FC Basle, free)
- Ole Bjorn Sundgot (Molde FK, free)
- Chris Wilder
  (Sheffield United, £150,000)
- Eddie Youds
  (Charlton Athletic, £550,000)
- Robert Zabica (Spearwood, free)

John McGinlay – Signed for £650,000 in November 1997 after proving a revelation in Bolton's 1996-97 Division One Championship-winning season, the end of the 1997-98 season saw him battling with injury.

Wayne Jacobs – A strong, left-sided defender who has taken over as club captain, he signed on a free transfer from Rotherham United in 1994. A new contract commits him to Bradford until the turn of the century.

Bristol City *Football Club*

→ **Address** | Bristol City FC, Ashton Gate, Bristol BS3 2EJ

Tel: 0117 963 0630 | **Tickets:** 0117 966 6666 | **Clubline:** 0891 121176

If you add each of the digits in the club's main switchboard telephone number together they make 36, which equals the club's record number of League goals scored in a season – by Don Clark in 1946-47.

Top row • L Carey • M Hale • G Goodridge • P Tisdale • S Phillips • K Welch • S Naylor • J Brennan • M Bell • J Bent • A Locke

Middle row • T Fawthrop • Dr Dasgupta • R Edwards • B Tinnion • S Goater • S Taylor • M Hewlett • S Paterson • M Shail • C Cramb • D Hobbs • P Amos

• M Gibson **Bottom row** • M Vanes • K Langan • T Doherty • D Plummer • T Connor • J Ward • B Footman • S Dyche • D Barclay • M Bokoto • G Owers

→ **Web site:** http://www.bcfc.co.uk   → **Chairman:** Scott Davidson   → **Manager:** John Ward   → **Year formed:** 1894

Ground: Ashton Gate (21,479)

Stands: Carling Atyeo
Evening Post Dolman
Database Computers Wedlock
Brunel Ford Williams

Home strip: Red shirts with white trim, white shorts with red trim, red socks with white trim

Away strip: Yellow shirts with green trim, green shorts with yellow and red trim, green socks with red trim

Sponsor: Sanderson Computer Recruitment

Programme: £2

Nickname: Robins

Ground history: 1894 St John's Lane
1904 Ashton Gate

Previous name: Bristol South End

First League game: 7 September 1901, Division 2, won 2-0 (a) v Blackpool

Record attendance: 43,335 v Preston North End, FA Cup 5th round, 16 February 1935

Record victory: 11-0 v Chichester City, FA Cup 1st round, 5 November 1960

Record defeat: 0-9 v Coventry City, Division 3 (South), 28 April 1934

Highest League position: Division 1 (old), runners-up, 1906-07

Highest League scorer (season): Don Clark, 36, 1946-47

Highest League scorer (aggregate): John Atyeo, 314, 1951-1966

Most League appearances: John Atyeo, 597, 1951-1966

Most capped player: Billy Wedlock, 26, England, 1907-1914

Highest transfer fee paid: £500,000 to Arsenal for Andy Cole, July 1992

Highest transfer fee received: £1.75m from Newcastle United for Andy Cole, March 1993

Major trophies: Division 2 (old) Champions **(1)** 1905-06
Division 3 (South) Champions **(3)** 1954-55, 1926-27, 1922-23

Dominic Barclay – A bright local forward who came through the ranks, he has not consolidated his place since his senior debut in 1993-94.

Mickey Bell – Formerly with Northampton, Wycombe's Player of the Year 1996-97 was snapped up by City in July 1997. A stylish defender who provides options on the left, he missed only two League games and scored an invaluable nine goals.

Jim Brennan – Born in Toronto, he was signed from Canadian club Sora Lazio in 1994. He made his senior debut in 1996-97 and started five times the following season, acting as cover for Bell and Tinnion.

Louis Carey – A local lad who came through the Ashton Gate ranks, he established himself as an 18-year-old in the first-team midfield and in 1997-98 he was a key figure in City's run up the Division 2 table from October.

Tommy Doherty – The Bristol-born YTS trainee broke into the League side in September 1997 and was given a run in the first team by manager John Ward. An England Under-18 player, he's one of City's most exciting prospects.

Sean Dyche – Bought by City in July 1997 after impressive performances in Chesterfield's 1996-97 FA Cup run, the attack-minded defender was confined by a back injury to just 11 excellent games in the autumn.

Rob Edwards – A utility player, the former trainee was signed from Carlisle for £135,000 in 1991. Now a full international for Wales, he was an automatic choice during the 1997-98 season.

Gregory Goodridge – A Barbados international with over 30 caps, he started in England with Torquay but came to City via Queen's Park Rangers in 1996. After a patchy first season, he hit form from September 1997, scoring some vital goals.

Matt Hewlett – A Bristol-born England youth player, he made his debut back in 1993 but didn't become a regular in midfield until two years later. He missed a couple of chunks of the 1997-98 season due to injury and John Ward's tactical changes.

Adam Locke – Previously with Southend, Locke was released as a midfielder by Colchester in 1997 and has become a valuable player at right back for City, missing only a handful of games in the promotion-winning season.

Kevin Langan – A Channel Islander who worked his way up through City's School of Excellence, the 19-year-old made several substitute appearances in 1997-98.

Scott Murray – Born in Aberdeen, he was bought from Aston Villa in December 1997. A striker converted to right midfield, he spent most of the campaign as a well-used substitute.

Stuart Naylor – The 6ft 4in keeper joined City in the summer of 1996 after 10 years at West Bromwich Albion. He lost his place to Welch at the end of that season and for nearly all of 1997-98.

Gary Owers – A versatile midfielder and an FA Cup finalist in 1992, the Geordie signed from Sunderland for £300,000 in December 1994. City's only ever-present in 1996-97, he missed the middle part of the following season with a nasty foot injury.

Scott Paterson – A Scot who failed to make the senior Liverpool side in two seasons at Anfield, he was signed on a free transfer in 1994. He made only one start in 1997-98.

Dwayne Plummer – Captain of City's youth team, he debuted in 1995-96 but made only one appearance, off the bench, in 1997-98.

Mark Shail – The tall Swede cost £45,000 from Yeovil Town in 1993 but a series of frustrating injuries prevented him claiming a regular first-team slot in 1997-98.

Paul Tisdale – Manager John Ward's first signing in July 1997, this Malta-born midfielder was mainly used as a substitute in 1997-98, making only three starts.

Steve Torpey – A Londoner bought from Swansea in August 1997, the 6ft 3in striker has not only aerial power but skill with both feet. After injuring his cheekbone on his debut, he had a good run between September and November.

Keith Welch – Signed from Rochdale for £200,000 in 1991, he won back the keeper's jersey from Stuart Naylor in April 1997 and retained it until injured two games from the end of the 1997-98 season with a fractured pelvis.

Shaun Taylor – A vastly experienced defender, he arrived in 1996, and wore the number 5 shirt throughout the 1997-98 season. Hugely popular, he was voted the fans' Player of the Year for the second time running.

Brian Tinnion – Forever famous at Ashton Gate as the man whose goal knocked Liverpool out of the 1994 FA Cup, he signed from Bradford City the previous year for £180,000. He had one of his best seasons in 1997-98.

Transferred in:
- Mickey Bell (Wycombe, £150,000)
- Sean Dyche (Chesterfield, £325,000)
- Adam Locke (Colchester, free)
- Colin Cramb (Doncaster, £150,000)
- Steve Torpey (Swansea, £400,000)
- Scott Murray (Aston Villa, £150,000)
- Paul Tisdale (Southampton, free)

Transferred out:
- Darren Barnard (Barnsley, £700,000)
- Paul Allen (Millwall, free)
- Junior Bent (Blackpool, free)
- Martin Kuhl (Leyton Orient, free)
- Kevin Nugent (Cardiff, free)
- David Seal (Northampton, £90,000)
- Paul Agostino (Munich 1860, free)
- Shaun Goater (Manchester City, £450,000)

Colin Cramb – Doncaster's leading scorer in 1996-97 with 23 goals, the Scottish striker was signed on a tribunal-fixed fee in July and played a key role in helping City go from Division 2 to Division 1.

Bury *Football Club*

Bury Football Club
Bury Football Club
Bury Football Club
Bury Football Club
Bury Football Club
Bury Football Club

→ Address | Bury FC, Gigg Lane, Bury BL9 9HR

Tel: 0161 764 4881 | **Tickets:** 0161 705 2144 | **Clubline:** 0930 190003

Three of Bury's first-team squad at the end of the 1997-98 season were signed from non-League clubs – Chris Lucketti, Tony Rigby and Player of the Year Nick Daws. They came from Halifax, Barrow and Altrincham respectively.

Top row • A Randall • P Butler • B Linighan • C Lucketti • R Jepson
Middle row • A Woodward • A Gray • T Battersby • D Kiely • L Bracey • I Hughes • G Armstrong • D Johnson
Bottom row • N Daws • R Matthews • D Pugh • S Ternent • S Ellis • L Johnrose • D West • T Rigby

→ Chairman: Terry Robinson   **→ Manager:** Neil Warnock   **→ Year formed:** 1885

Ground: Gigg Lane (11,841)

Stands: Main
South
Manchester Road End
Cemetery End

Home strip: White shirts, blue shorts, blue socks

Away strip: Red shirts, black shorts, black socks

Sponsor: Birthdays

Programme: £1.80

Nickname: Shakers

Ground history: 1885 Gigg Lane

Previous name: None

First League game: 1 September 1894, Division 2, won 4-2 (h) v Manchester City

Record attendance: 35,000 v Bolton Wanderers, FA Cup 3rd round, 9 January 1960

Record victory: 12-1 v Stockton, FA Cup 1st round replay, 2 February 1897

Record defeat: 0-10 v West Ham United, League Cup 2nd round, 2nd leg, 25 October 1983

Highest League position: Division 1 (old), 4th place, 1925-26

Highest League scorer (season): Craig Madden, 35, 1981-82

Highest League scorer (aggregate): Craig Madden, 129, 1978-1986

Most League appearances: Norman Bullock, 506, 1920-1935

Most capped player: Bill Gorman, 10, Republic of Ireland, 1936-1938

Highest transfer fee paid: £200,000 to Ipswich Town for Chris Swailes, November 1997

Highest transfer fee received: £375,000 from Southampton for David Lee, October 1991

Major trophies: Division 2 Champions **(1)** 1996-97
Division 2 (old) Champions **(1)** 1894-95
Division 3 (old) Champions **(1)** 1960-61
FA Cup Winners **(2)** 1903, 1900

Gordon Armstrong – A 1996 close season signing from Sunderland, he missed much of Bury's Championship season with a recurring hamstring injury, but was the club's regular left wing back during 1997-98.

Paul Butler – A powerful centre half, he was a £130,000 signing from Rochdale in July 1996 and slotted in well alongside Chris Lucketti in the back four. The pair were automatic selections in 1997-98.

Tony Ellis – An experienced striker signed from Blackpool in December 1997 for £70,000, he figured heavily after joining and his goals proved precious in the quest for First Division survival.

Nigel Jemson – A £100,000 signing from Oxford United in February 1998, the much-travelled striker has spent time at Preston North End, Nottingham Forest, Sheffield Wednesday and Notts County, plus several other clubs on loan. His experience helped Bury through the dark days of the season.

Lennie Johnrose – The club's midfield general came from Hartlepool in 1993 for £20,000. He scored in the final game of the 1996-97 season to ensure the Second Division trophy came to Gigg Lane but his 1997-98 campaign was not as consistent as the last.

Chris Lucketti – A highly rated central defender who came from Halifax Town in October 1993 for £50,000, Lucketti is such a consistent performer that he was voted Player of the Year for the third successive time in 1997. He took over the captaincy from the injured David Pugh during the 1997-98 campaign.

Rob Matthews – A hard-working, tricky winger who signed from York City in January 1996 in a £100,000 deal, he only had a handful of first-team starts in 1997-98 due to a knee injury sustained in March 1997 at Preston and the long-term effects of the resulting operation.

Mark Patterson – Now in his second spell at Gigg Lane, he signed in December 1997 for £125,000 from Sheffield United, having first gone to Bolton. His strong tackling and ball-winning commitment in midfield made a valuable contribution to a tough season for Bury.

Jason Peake – A versatile 26-year-old midfielder, he signed from Brighton & Hove Albion in October 1997. Despite considerable experience at Halifax and Rochdale before Brighton, he featured in only a handful of games during the 1997-98 season.

David Pugh – A left-sided player who came to Gigg Lane from Chester City in August 1994, Pugh soon became club skipper. He has been extremely unfortunate with a series of injuries, though he was able to return as a substitute for the Championship-clinching game of 1996-97 against Millwall. However, yet more problems sidelined him for the 1997-98 season and he played just once.

Adrian Randall – A £100,000 signing from York City in December 1996, he is a skilful midfield player who shows composure when going forward, although he was used mainly as a substitute during the 1997-98 campaign.

Tony Rigby – A skilful and exciting midfield player who came to Bury in January 1993 from non-League side Barrow, Rigby is a valuable member of the squad.

Bryan Small – A 5ft 9in left back, Small signed from Bolton Wanderers after impressing during a loan spell in March 1998. The Shakers were immediately strengthened and were unbeaten in his first seven games – but his appearances were less frequent in 1997-98.

Chris Swailes – The club's record signing, Swailes came from Ipswich Town in November 1997 for £200,000, with David Johnson moving in the other direction to Portman Road. He's a 6ft 2in centre back renowned for his defensive qualities – yet he scored on his debut for Bury away at Oxford United soon after signing.

Peter Swan – A free transfer from Burnley in August 1997, he's a versatile squad player who can play both in defence and in a more attacking midfield role. Almost a third of his appearances in 1997-98 were as a substitute.

Dean West – An energetic and attacking wing back with an eye for goal, he was sidelined for most of the 1997-98 campaign due to a hernia operation early in the season.

Andy Woodward – A free signing from Crewe Alexandra in March 1995, he is a strong central defender who was used mainly as a squad member in 1997-98, with over a third of his League appearances coming as a substitute.

Transferred in:
- Tony Ellis (Blackpool, £70,000)
- Jason Peake (Brighton, free)
- Mark Patterson (Sheffield United, £125,000)
- Bryan Small (Bolton, free)
- Chris Swailes (Ipswich, £200,000)
- Peter Swan (Burnley, free)
- Nigel Jemson (Oxford, £100,000)

Transferred out:
- Andy Gray (Millwall, free)
- Ian Hughes (Blackpool, £200,000)
- Ronnie Jepson (Oldham, £30,000)
- David Johnson (Ipswich, deal)

Dean Kiely – A keeper who has represented England at both schoolboy and youth levels, Kiely didn't miss a game in the 1997-98 season. He was signed from York City in August 1996 for £125,000.

Tony Battersby – He joined Bury on a permanent basis in May 1997 after impressing during a loan spell from Notts County. A powerful striker and a good passer, he played half the games in 1997-98.

Nick Daws – A bargain £10,000 signing from Altrincham in August 1992, he's a battling midfield player. His efforts were rewarded at the end of the 1997-98 season with the club's Player of the Year award.

Crewe Alexandra Football Club
Crewe Alexandra Football Club
Crewe Alexandra Football Club
Crewe Alexandra Football Club
Crewe Alexandra Football Club
Crewe Alexandra Football Club
Crewe Alexandra Football
Crewe Alexandra Football Club
Crewe Alexandra Football Club

210

Crewe Alexandra *Football Club*

→ **Address** | Crewe Alexandra FC, Gresty Road, Crewe CW2 6EB

Tel: 01270 213014 | **Tickets:** 01270 252610 | **Clubline:** 0891 333333

Dario Gradi is the longest-serving manager in the Football League. By the end of the 1997-98 season he had been Crewe manager for a total of 820 games, including 678 League matches, 130 cup ties and 12 play-off games.

Top row • J Moralee • P Charnock • S Pope • P Anthrobus • D Adebola • C Lightfoot • A Westwood • F Tierney

Middle row • T McPhillips • J Fleet • S Holland • R Norris • L Unsworth • N Cutler • J Kearton • M Rivers • P Smith • N Baker • D Gradi

Bottom row • K Street • K Lunt • D Wright • S Smith • S McAuley • S Johnson • C Little • J Collins • S Garvey

→ **Chairman:** John Bowler   → **Manager:** Dario Gradi   → **Year formed:** 1877

Ground: Gresty Road (6,000)

Stands: Mornflake Oats Family
LC Charles
Ringways
Old

Home strip: Red shirts with white trim, white shorts with red trim, red socks with white trim

Away strip: White shirts with navy and gold trim, white shorts with navy and gold trim, white socks with navy and gold trim

Sponsor: LC Charles

Programme: £2

Nickname: Railwaymen

Ground history: 1877 Gresty Road

Previous name: None

First League game: 3 September 1892, Division 2, lost 1-7 (a) v Burton Swifts

Record attendance: 20,000 v Tottenham Hotspur, FA Cup 4th round, 30 January 1960

Record victory: 8-0 v Rotherham United, Division 3 (North), 1 October 1932

Record defeat: 2-13 v Tottenham Hotspur, FA Cup 4th round replay, 3 February 1960

Highest League position: Division 1, 11th place, 1997-98

Highest League scorer (season): Terry Harkin, 35, 1964-65

Highest League scorer (aggregate): Bert Swindells, 126, 1928-1939

Most League appearances: Tommy Lowry, 436, 1966-1978

Most capped player: Bill Lewis, 9, Wales, 1890-1894

Highest transfer fee paid: £500,000 to Shrewsbury Town for Dave Walton, November 1997

Highest transfer fee received: £1.5m from Liverpool for Danny Murphy, July 1997

Major trophies: None

Steve Anthrobus – This tall striker started his career with Wimbledon before moving to Shrewsbury Town. Crewe signed him for £75,000 in March 1997 and he was a first choice for much of 1997-98.

Ademola Bankole – The 6ft 3in Nigerian keeper was kept in the reserves by Kearton's consistency.

James Collins – A young midfield player who came up through Crewe's productive YTS ranks, he's still jostling for a place in the team after completing his second year as a full-time player.

Mark Foran – The 6ft 2in central defender acted as cover after signing from Peterborough for £25,000 during the 1997-98 season.

Steve Garvey – A wide player who has had his fair share of injury, he made his way through the youth system and signed professional forms in October 1991. He has played in over 130 games for the club, but failed to gain a regular place in 1997-98.

Seth Johnson – A promising former YTS player who made his debut in March 1997 and has been a valued automatic choice ever since. Still only 19, he's a talented midfielder who can also play in defence.

Jason Kearton – A popular Australian keeper, he spent eight seasons as an understudy to Neville Southall at Everton before moving to Crewe. He made his debut away at Chesterfield in October 1996 and played regularly in the 1997-98 season.

Chris Lightfoot – A versatile player at home anywhere in the back four or midfield, Lightfoot signed from Wigan in March 1996 for £50,000. In 1997-98 he was used by Dario Gradi mainly as a utility substitute.

Colin Little – Bought from non-League Hyde United for £50,000 in

1996, he scored two vital goals in the 1996-97 play-offs against Luton – and emerged as top scorer in 1997-98 after the departure of fellow striker Dele Adebola for Birmingham.

Kenny Lunt – A graduate of the FA School of Excellence at Lilleshall, he's a midfielder who has been capped for England at schoolboy and youth levels. He made his full Crewe debut in August 1997 against Swindon Town and found a regular spot for the rest of the season.

John Pemberton – An experienced full back, previously with Rochdale, Crystal Palace, Sheffield United and Leeds – as well as several seasons at Gresty Road – the 33-year-old is now player-coach at Crewe, though his first-team appearances are rare.

Steve Pope – Another YTS graduate, his debut was in the Coca-Cola Cup against Sheffield Wednesday in August 1997. Hit by injury, he did not enjoy a regular place in the side.

Mark Rivers – A local lad, Rivers graduated through the ranks to the first team, marking his debut in 1995 with two goals. He was injured in 1996-97, but returned to the Crewe attack in 1997-98.

Peter Smith – Yet another graduate of the FA School at Lilleshall, and capped by England at schoolboy and youth levels (despite being born in North Wales), he largely appeared as a substitute in 1997-98.

Kevin Street – Crewe-born and bred, this hardworking midfielder has come up through the YTS ranks with the youth and reserve teams. Though he made plenty of appearances in 1997-98, most were as a substitute.

Francis Tierney – Another YTS graduate who plays up front but made few appearances in 1997-98.

Lee Unsworth – A defender who played for non-League sides Atherton

LR and Ashton United before joining Crewe during the 1994-95 season, Unsworth has become an established and valued member of the squad, able to play in a number of positions.

Dave Walton – A strong, competitive central defender, he was the club's record signing when he arrived from Shrewsbury Town in November 1997. The record fee of £500,000 rose with appearances and increased as he claimed a regular place.

Ashley Westwood – A £40,000 signing from Manchester United in 1995, he's a strong central defender with good pace. After more than 20 outings in 1997-98, he lost his first-team place in January.

Gareth Whalley – The Manchester-born midfield player had assessment spells with Liverpool and Spurs before joining Crewe's YTS scheme, and played in the Football League side against the Italians in 1995. He claimed a regular place from January 1998.

David Wright – A strong defender who recently graduated from Crewe's famous YTS scheme, he has yet to find a first-team place.

Jermaine Wright – A versatile midfield player who is also comfortable on the right wing, he signed from Wolves for £25,000 in the winter and played a handful of games in 1998.

Transferred in:
- Paul Holsgrove (Reading, free)
- Dave Walton (Shrewsbury, £500,000)
- Marcus Bignot (Kidderminster, £150,000)
- Mark Foran (Peterborough, £25,000)
- Jermaine Wright (Wolves, £25,000)

Transferred out:
- Danny Murphy (Liverpool, £1.5m)
- Paul Holsgrove (Stoke, free)
- Dele Adebola (Birmingham, £1m)
- Jamie Moralee (released)

Marcus Bignot – A pacy player signed from non-League Kidderminster Harriers for £150,000 in the summer of 1997, he made the right-back slot his own during the 1997-98 season.

Phil Charnock – A hard-working midfielder who came to Gresty Road first on loan and then in a permanent move before the 1996-97 season, Charnock was an automatic choice in 1997-98.

Shaun Smith – Signed from non-League Emley in 1992, his common berth is at left back. Scorer of the Wembley goal that beat Brentford to gain promotion in 1997, Smith is also the team's regular penalty taker.

Crystal Palace *Football Club*

Crystal Palace Football Club
Crystal Palace Football Club
Crystal Palace Football Club
Crystal Palace Football Club
Crystal Palace Football Club
Crystal Palace Football C
Crystal Palace Football C
Crystal Palace Football Club
Crystal Palace Football Club
Crystal Palace Football Club

→ **Address** | Crystal Palace FC, Selhurst Park, London SE25 6PU

Tel: 0181 768 6000 | **Tickets:** 0181 771 8841 | **Clubline:** 0891 400333

Terry Venables is the 29th Palace manager and the fifth to return to Palace for a second spell – after Steve Coppell, Malcolm Allison, Arthur Rowe and Tom Bromilow.

Top row • S Kember • S Burton • A Linighan • D Tuttle • C Nash • G Ormshaw • K Miller • H Hreidarsson • N Emblen • G Ndah • G Sadley

Middle row • R Wilkins • D Boxall • J Fullarton • K Muscat • N Shipperley • C Veart • P Warhurst • G Davies • R Lewington

Bottom row • D Freedman • D Gordon • M Edworthy • A Roberts • S Coppell • A Lombardo • S Rodger • B Dyer • L McKenzie

→ **Web site:** http://www.cpfc.co.uk   → **Chairman:** Mark Goldberg   → **Manager:** Terry Venables   → **Year formed:** 1905

Ground: Selhurst Park (26,309)

Stands: Main
Whitehorse Lane
Holmesdale Road
Arthur Wait

Home strip: Red shirts with blue trim, red shorts with blue trim, red and blue striped socks

Away strip: White shirts with blue and red trim, white shorts with blue trim, white socks with blue and red stripes

Sponsor: TDK

Programme: £2

Nickname: Eagles

Ground history: 1905 Sydenham Hill
1915 Herne Hill
1918 The Nest
1924 Selhurst Park

Previous name: None

First League game: 28 August 1920, Division 3, lost 1-2 (a) v Merthyr Tydfil

Record attendance: 51,482 v Burnley, Division 2, 11 May 1979

Record victory: 9-0 v Barrow, Division 4, 10 October 1959

Record defeat: 0-9 v Burnley, FA Cup 2nd round replay, 10 February 1909
0-9 v Liverpool, Division 1, 12 September 1989

Highest League position: Division 1 (old), 3rd place, 1990-91

Highest League scorer (season): Peter Simpson, 46, 1930-31

Highest League scorer (aggregate): Peter Simpson, 153, 1930-1936

Most League appearances: Jim Cannon, 571, 1973-1988

Most capped player: Eric Young, 19, Wales, 1989-1992

Highest transfer fee paid: £2.75m to Strasbourg for Valerien Ismael, January 1998

Highest transfer fee received: £4.5m from Tottenham Hotspur for Chris Armstrong, June 1995

Major trophies: Division 1 Champions **(1)** 1993-94
Division 2 (old) Champions **(1)** 1978-79
Division 3 (old) Champions **(1)** 1920-21

Marcus Bent – A young striker who came from Brentford in January 1998 for £300,000, Bent is carving out a niche as a central target man.

Danny Boxall – A promising young defender before being hit by injury, 20-year-old Boxall spent part of the season on loan at Oldham.

Tomas Brolin – After falling out with Leeds United, the seasoned Swedish international striker signed for Palace in January 1998. In March, he was surprisingly appointed player-assistant to player-manager Attilio Lombardo.

Sagi Burton – A defender who signed from trainee in 1995, Burton made his Premiership debut in December 1997 and made three first-team appearances in the 1997-98 season.

Sasa Curcic – A £1 million signing on transfer deadline day, the Yugoslav international midfielder described his move as a "gift from the Gods" after a miserable time at Aston Villa.

Bruce Dyer – At just 18 years old, Dyer was signed from Watford in March 1994 for £1.1 million. An England Under-21 international, he scored a hat-trick in the FA Cup against Leicester in January 1998.

Marc Edworthy – A regular right wing back, Edworthy was signed from Plymouth in May 1995 for £350,000.

Jamie Fullarton – A creative midfielder, Fullarton signed from French club Bastia in the summer of 1997, and made his full Premiership debut against Chelsea in September.

Rory Ginty – The 21-year-old Galway-born winger was signed from trainee in 1994 and is a reserves regular.

Herman Hreidarsson – A tall central defender, Hreidarsson joined Palace from Icelandic side IVB in July 1997.

Valerien Ismael – A French Under-21 international, Ismael signed in January

1998 for £2.75 million from French first division side Strasbourg.

Matt Jansen – A young striker who signed from Carlisle for £1 million in February 1998, Jansen was injured soon after arriving, but played in the latter part of the season.

Andy Linighan – An experienced central defender and former England B-team player, 35-year-old Linighan signed from Arsenal in January 1997 for £150,000. After a shaky start, he settled easily into the squad.

Leon McKenzie – A young centre forward who was injured for much of the 1997-98 season, he is the nephew of former boxing world champion Duke and the son of British boxing champion Clinton.

Kevin Miller – The 6ft 1in keeper signed from Watford in June 1997 for £1.25 million. He began his career at Newquay, turned pro at Exeter and moved to Birmingham before Watford.

Michele Padovano – A November 1997 signing from Italian side Juventus, Padovano was injured after just five games – and then had to wait months before a first-team return.

Robert Quinn – A Republic of Ireland Under-21 international, the young defender only appeared once for Palace in the 1997-98 season.

Simon Rodger – Palace's longest-serving professional, midfielder Rodger came from Bognor Regis Town in July 1990 for a mere £1,000.

Neil Shipperley – A 6ft 1in centre forward, Shipperley was a £1 million buy from Southampton in October 1996. A former England Under-21 international, Shipperley's father, David, was also a League footballer.

Jamie Smith – The 23-year-old right back came from Wolves in October 1997 in an exchange deal involving Kevin Muscat and Dougie Freedman.

David Tuttle – A no-nonsense central defender, he came to Selhurst Park from Sheffield United in a swap deal with Gareth Taylor in March 1996. His defensive skills helped Palace to the Premiership – at the expense of his old club – in the play-off final of 1997 but he started the 1997-98 season with an early injury.

Transferred in:
- Kevin Miller (Watford, £1.25m)
- Herman Hreidarsson (IVB, £500,000)
- Jamie Fullarton (Bastia, free)
- Paul Warhurst (Blackburn, £1.55m)
- Attilio Lombardo (Juventus, £1.6m)
- Neil Emblen (Wolves, £2m)
- Itzhik Zohar (Royal Antwerp, £1.2m)
- Jamie Smith (Wolves, deal)
- Michele Padovano (Juventus, £1.7m)
- Marcus Bent (Brentford, £300,000)
- Valerien Ismael (Strasbourg, £2.75m)
- Tomas Brolin (non-contract)
- Matt Jansen (Carlisle, £1m)
- Sasa Curcic (Aston Villa, £1m)

Transferred out:
- Tom Evans (Scunthorpe, free)
- Andy Cyrus (Exeter City, free)
- Ray Houghton (Reading, free)
- Chris Day (Watford, £225,000)
- David Hopkin (Leeds, £3.25m)
- Tony Scully (Manchester City, £150,000)
- Dean Wordsworth (Stevenage, free)
- Jason Harris (Leyton Orient, £25,000)
- Dougie Freedman (Wolves, deal)
- Kevin Muscat (Wolves, deal)
- Ivano Bonetti (Genoa, free)
- George Ndah (Swindon, £350,000)
- Gareth Davies (Reading, £175,000)
- Carl Veart (Millwall, £125,000)
- Itzhik Zohar (Maccabi Haifa, released)
- Neil Emblen (Wolves, £900,000)
- Andy Roberts (Wimbledon, £2m)

Paul Warhurst – Equally at home in the centre of defence or leading the attack, Warhurst joined for £1.55 million in July 1997 from Blackburn. He has also played for Manchester City, Oldham and Sheffield Wednesday.

Dean Gordon – A left wing back, Gordon has only ever played for Palace, graduating from trainee status in July 1991. The 25-year-old is a former England Under-21 international, winning 13 caps.

Attilio Lombardo – An Italian international midfielder, Lombardo signed from Juventus for £1.6 million in August 1997. He was briefly made player-manager in March 1998 – in spite of the fact he spoke little English.

Grimsby Town *Football Club*

Grimsby Town Football Club
Grimsby Town Football Club
Grimsby Town Football Club
Grimsby Town Football Club
Grimsby Town Football Club
Grimsby Town Football C
Grimsby Town Football C

→ **Address** | Grimsby Town FC, Blundell Park, Cleethorpes, North East Lincolnshire DN35 7PY

Tel: 01472 697111 | **Tickets:** 01472 697111 | **Clubline:** 0891 555855

Years ending in nine are always significant to Grimsby. They were named Grimsby Town in 1879, moved to Blundell Park in 1899, were promoted in 1929 and 1979, and reached the FA Cup semi-final in 1939.

Top row • P Groves • N Woods • G Rodger • A Davidson • M Lever • P Handyside • S Livingstone
Middle row • M Bielby • J Lester • K Jobling • A Fickling • K Black • J Brown • J Neil • L Stephenson • B Chapman • G Delahunt
Bottom row • T Gallimore • N Southall • J McDermott • D Wrack • A Buckley • J Cockerill • D Clare • T Widdrington • M Bloomer

→ **Chairman:** William Carr   → **Manager:** Alan Buckley   → **Year Formed** 1878

Ground: Blundell Park (8,870)

Stands: John Smith's Family
Pontoon
Main
Osmond

Home strip: Black and white striped shirts, black shorts with white trim, black socks with white trim

Away strip: Blue shirts, white shorts, blue socks

Sponsor: Dixon Motors

Programme: £1.50

Nickname: Mariners

Ground history: 1880 Clee Park
1889 Abbey Park
1899 Blundell Park

Previous name: Grimsby Pelham

First League game: 3 September 1892, Division 2, won 2-1 (h) v Northwich Victoria

Record attendance: 31,657 v Wolverhampton Wanderers, FA Cup 5th round, 20 February 1937

Record victory: 9-2 v Darwen, Division 2, 15 April 1899

Record defeat: 1-9 v Arsenal, Division 1, 28 January 1931

Highest League position: Division 1 (old), 5th place, 1934-35

Highest League scorer (season): Pat Glover, 42, 1933-34

Highest League scorer (aggregate): Pat Glover, 180, 1930-1939

Most League appearances: Keith Jobling, 448, 1953-1969

Most capped player: Pat Glover, 7, Wales, 1931-1939

Highest transfer fee received: £2m from Everton for John Oster, July 1997

Highest transfer fee paid: £300,000 to Southampton for Tommy Widdrington, July 1996
£300,000 to West Bromwich Albion for Kevin Donovan, July 1997

Major trophies: Division 2 (old) Champions **(2)** 1933-34, 1900-01
Division 3 (old) Champions **(1)** 1979-80
Division 3 (North) Champions **(2)** 1955-56, 1925-26
Division 4 Champions **(1)** 1971-72

Kingsley Black – A former Luton and Northern Ireland international winger who joined the club for £25,000 in July 1996 from Nottingham Forest, Black started the season as a first team regular, but spent the latter part on the bench.

Wayne Burnett – The former Plymouth midfielder joined the club from Huddersfield in January 1998 after initially arriving on loan. His skilful displays, which helped the side into Division One, plus his winning goal in the Auto Windscreens Shield final against Bournemouth made his £100,000 fee look like a bargain.

Danny Butterfield – The young defender played 10 games after turning professional in August 1997.

Daryl Clare – The Jersey-born midfielder made his Mariners debut aged 17, but didn't establish himself in the first team until November 1997. A promising attacker, Clare made most of his appearances last season as a sub, yet still managed to impress.

Jim Dobbin – The veteran midfielder returned to Grimsby on a free transfer from Scarborough in March 1998. His only appearance came in the League game against Burnley.

Tony Gallimore – The former Stoke left back, who joined the club in March 1996 in a £125,000 move from Carlisle, had a consistent season and looked particularly strong going forward.

Paul Groves – A goalscoring midfielder, Groves returned to the club for a second spell in July 1997. An ever-present in his favourite attacking midfield role, he scored an impressive 12 goals during the 1997-98 promotion-winning season.

Peter Handyside – A Scottish Under-21 defender, Handyside missed only five games in the 1997-98 season and was impressive in the play-offs.

However, Handyside's physical style of play earned him 11 bookings.

Kevin Jobling – A left-sided utility player, Jobling has notched up nearly 300 League games for Grimsby since signing in 1988. The 30-year-old featured heavily as a sub in 1997-98.

Mark Lever – Another product of the Mariners' youth system, Lever is a strong defender and a real club man. He passed the 350-game mark for the Mariners in 1997-98 after 10 years at Blundell Park.

Steve Livingstone – A former Coventry player, Livingstone is a physical striker who sometimes plays at centre back. His strike rate since his move to Grimsby in October 1993 however has not been prolific, with just 39 goals in 200 appearances.

John McDermott – McDermott has played the majority of his Grimsby career as an attacking right back. He is currently the club's longest-serving player, having joined from school in 1987, and is a crowd favourite.

Lee Nogan – A former Welsh international striker who was a £170,000 signing from Reading in July 1997, Nogan was a replacement for Mariners' hero Clive Mendonca.

Jason Pearcey – The 27-year-old goalkeeper was signed from Mansfield Town in 1994 and was Grimsby's number one choice during the 1996-97 season. However, he made only five appearances in 1997-98 following the arrival of Aidan Davison at the club.

Graham Rodger – Rodger is a tough central defender and a former FA Cup winner with Coventry City. He joined Grimsby from Luton Town for £135,000 in January 1992 and has been a consistent performer for the Mariners and an occasional club captain.

David Smith – The diminutive winger rejoined Mariners boss Alan Buckley in January 1998 after a £200,000 move from West Bromwich Albion. The former Coventry and Birmingham player scored on his Grimsby debut against Brentford and netted again in the play-off semi-final draw with Fulham.

Tommy Widdrington – The Geordie midfielder, who signed from Southampton for £300,000 in July 1996, was sidelined from January onwards with a serious back injury.

Darren Wrack – Wrack was born near Blundell Park yet started his career at Derby. An attacking midfielder, he moved to Grimsby in 1996 for £100,000, yet failed to make his mark in the first team. At 22, he is still young enough to make it in the professional game.

Transferred in:
- Aidan Davison (Bradford City, free)
- Paul Groves (WBA, £250,000)
- Lee Nogan (Reading, £170,000)
- Kevin Donovan (WBA, £300,000)
- David Smith (WBA, £200,000)
- Wayne Burnett (Huddersfield, £100,000)

Transferred out:
- Gary Childs (Wisbech Town, free)
- Craig Shakespeare (Scunthorpe, free)
- Clive Mendonca (Charlton, £600,000)
- John Oster (Everton, £1.5m)
- Joby Gowshall (Lincoln City, free)
- Neil James (Scunthorpe, free)
- Paul Harsley (Scunthorpe, free)
- Andy Quy (Stevenage, free)
- Jim Neil (Scunthorpe, free)
- Nicky Southall (Gillingham, free)

Jack Lester – An ex-England schoolboy and talented forward, Lester missed only a handful of games in the 1997-98 season and scored nine goals, including a superb hat-trick against Oldham in the Coca-Cola Cup.

Kevin Donovan – A pacy right-sided midfielder, Donovan had his best ever goalscoring season with 21 goals, including the all-important Wembley winner against Northampton in the play-off final.

Aidan Davison – The Northern Ireland keeper was signed on a free from Bradford in July 1997. A dependable shot-stopper, Davison missed only five games all season and played a major part in his side's promotion.

Huddersfield Town *Football Club*

Huddersfield Town Football Club
Huddersfield Town Football Club
Huddersfield Town Football Club
Huddersfield Town Football Club
Huddersfield Town Footb
Huddersfield Town Footb
Huddersfield Town Footb

→ **Address** | Huddersfield Town AFC, Alfred McAlpine Stadium, Huddersfield HD1 6PX

Tel: 01484 484100 | **Tickets:** 01484 484123 | **Clubline:** 0891 121635

Huddersfield nicknamed their 1997-98 season the 'Great Escape'. In order to achieve their escape from relegation to the Second Division, they used a club record number of players in the first team – 37 in all.

Top row • R Edwards • T Heary • J Illingworth • W Burnett • M Browning • C Hurst • S Murphy • I Lawson • R Ryan • T Cowan

Middle row • G Murphy • D Facey • K Gray • S Baldry • D O'Connor • S Collins • S Francis • J Dyson • D Edmondson • P Dalton • J Dickens

Bottom row • M Stewart • L Makel • A Morrison • T Yorath • P Jackson • T Dolan • S Jenkins • A Payton • D Beresford

→ **Web site:** http://www.huddersfield-town.co.uk/htfc → **Chairman:** Malcolm Asquith → **Manager:** Peter Jackson → **Year formed:** 1908

Ground: Alfred McAlpine Stadium (19,600)

Stands: Gardner Merchant
Laurence Batley
John Smith's
Panasonic

Home strip: Cobalt blue and white striped shirts with blue trim, white shorts, white socks with cobalt blue trim

Away strip: Ecru and jade shirts, ecru and jade shorts, ecru and jade hooped socks

Sponsor: Panasonic

Programme: £1.80

Nickname: Terriers

Ground history: 1908 Leeds Road
1994 Alfred McAlpine Stadium

Previous names: None

First League game: 3 September 1910, Division 2, won 1-0 (a) v Bradford Park Avenue

Record attendance: 18,775 v Birmingham City, Division 2, 6 May 1995

Record victory: 10-1 v Blackpool, Division 1, 13 December 1930

Record defeat: 1-10 v Manchester City, Division 2, 7 November 1987

Highest League scorer (season): Sammy Taylor, 35, 1919-20
George Brown, 35, 1925-26

Highest League scorer (aggregate): Jimmy Glazzard, 142, 1946-1956

Most League appearances: Billy Smith, 521, 1913-1934

Most capped player: Jimmy Nicholson, 31, Northern Ireland, 1965-1971

Highest transfer fee paid: £1.2m to Bristol Rovers for Marcus Stewart, July 1996

Highest transfer fee received: £2.7m from Sheffield Wednesday for Andy Booth, July 1996

Major trophies: Division 1 (old) Champions **(3)** 1925-26, 1924-25, 1923-24
Division 2 (old) Champions **(1)** 1969-70
Division 4 Champions **(1)** 1979-80
FA Cup Winners **(1)** 1922

Wayne Allison – A local striker who returned to the club from Swindon in November 1997 for £800,000, he ended the season with six goals and the usual quota of assists.

Paul Barnes – A free-scoring striker who topped Burnley's scoring charts in 1996-97, he joined Town in a swap deal involving Andy Payton in January 1998 and should prove a useful buy.

David Beresford – A winger who arrived at the club on deadline day in 1997, his appearances in 1997-98 were severely curtailed by double hernia operations.

Marcus Browning – A substitute for Bristol Rovers when they played Town in the 1995 Second Division play-off final, the midfielder missed most of 1997-98 with injury.

Sam Collins – A central defender who came through the youth set-up to make his debut alongside brother Simon in 1995-96, he suffered injuries early in the year, but regained his place in March 1998.

Paul Dalton – Back in favour, he has flourished in a free role under Peter Jackson and Terry Yorath, finishing the 1997-98 season with 13 goals from 26 starts.

Darren Edmondson – He signed in March 1997 from Carlisle and began the season well before a hamstring injury restricted his performances.

Rob Edwards – A skilful midfielder who came via Crewe's footballing academy and scored the winner on his 1996 debut, he found himself in the first team in 1997-98.

Delroy Facey – A bustling striker given his debut as a 16-year-old, he suffered a long-term injury and appeared just three times in 1997-98.

Steve Francis – A popular goalkeeper signed from Reading in 1993, he started the season but fell victim to a virus and could only watch as on-loan Stephen Harper impressed.

Kevin Gray – A central defender who captained Mansfield at 19, he joined the Terriers in 1994 and put in another series of assured performances in defence in 1997-98.

Thomas Heary – A Dublin-born midfielder or defender who signed from trainee in 1996, his first-team outings were restricted in 1997-98.

Sean Hessey – A central defender previously with Liverpool, he signed on a free from Leeds in March 1998 and made his debut as an 86th-minute substitute against Reading.

Barry Horne – A former Welsh skipper who had an unhappy time with Birmingham before becoming Peter Jackson's first signing in October 1997. His experience proved invaluable in midfield.

Chris Hurst – A central midfielder signed from non-League Emley in August 1997, he made just four appearances during 1997-98.

Steve Jenkins – A Welsh international who began as a winger, after signing from Swansea, he appears regularly as an attacking right back for Town.

Ian Lawson – A home-grown centre forward, he is seen as the next Andy Booth. But, of his 19 appearances in 1997-98, only three were starts and he failed to get on the scoresheet.

Andy Morrison – A Scot who became the club's most expensive defender when he signed from Blackpool for £500,000 in the summer of 1996, he has been dogged by knee injuries.

Martin Nielsen – A utility player signed from FC Copenhagen in March 1998, he was used just three times.

Derek O'Connor – A young goalkeeper from Dublin, he came through the club's youth ranks and made his debut in August 1997 against Bradford City.

David Phillips – A very experienced Welsh international who played at the highest level for Nottingham Forest, Manchester City, Norwich and Coventry before joining Town on a free transfer and slotting effortlessly into the defence.

Lee Richardson – A central midfielder who is strong and skilful on the ball with a powerful shot, his 1997-98 season was dogged by injury and suspension.

Alex Smith – A left back who can play in midfield, he was signed from Swindon midway through 1997-98 and only given a handful of games.

Marcus Stewart – Many were surprised when a top flight club didn't come in for this former England schoolboy when he left Bristol Rovers in July 1996, but Huddersfield stepped in and reaped the rewards of his 16 goals in 1997-98.

Transferred in:
- Wayne Allison (Swindon, £800,000)
- Grant Johnson
  (Dundee United, £90,000)
- Lee Richardson (Oldham, £65,000)
- Chris Hurst (Emley, £30,000)
- Paul Barnes (Burnley, deal)
- David Phillips (Forest, free)
- Barry Horne (Birmingham, free)
- Alex Dyer (Barnet, free)
- Damien Brennan (Belvedere, free)
- Martin Nielsen
  (FC Copenhagen, free)
- Alex Smith (Swindon, free)
- Sean Hessey (Leeds, free)

Transferred out:
- Lee Sinnott (Oldham, £100,000)
- Ryan Gonsalves (Halifax, free)
- Steve Sanders (Doncaster, free)
- Wayne Burnett
  (Grimsby, £100,000)
- Andy Payton (Burnley, deal)
- Gary Crosby (free)
- Lee Makel (Hearts, £75,000)
- Alex Dyer (Notts County, free)

Grant Johnson - A central midfielder who arrived from Dundee United in November 1997, Johnson slotted straight into the first team and produced a series of stirring performances.

Jon Dyson – A central defender or right back who signed on a part-time basis in 1990 when still a university student, he enjoyed an outstanding 1997-98 until injury and suspension disrupted the second half.

Simon Baldry – A right wing stalwart born in Huddersfield and brought up through the youth ranks, Baldry's substitute appearances outweighed his first-team starts during the 1997-98 season.

Ipswich Town *Football Club*

Ipswich Town Football Club
Ipswich Town Football Club
Ipswich Town Football Club
Ipswich Town Football Club
Ipswich Town Football Club
Ipswich Town Football Club
Ipswich Town Football Club

→ **Address** | Ipswich Town FC, Portman Road, Ipswich, Suffolk IP1 2DA

Tel: 01473 400500 | **Tickets:** 01473 400555 | **Clubline:** 0839 664488

Ipswich enjoyed the best League run in their history towards the end of 1997-98, winning 12 and drawing four of their 16 games, between defeats at home to Birmingham on Boxing Day and away to Nottingham Forest on 5 April.

Top row • L Bell • N Gregory • M Venus • D Williams • K Ellis • S Niven • M Burgess

Middle row • B Klug • J Kennedy • T Mowbray • J Cundy • J Scowcroft • C Forrest • R Wright • D Sonner • A Tanner • R Naylor • C Swailes • W Brown • D Roberts

Bottom row • S Milton • M Stockwell • M Taricco • P Mason • A Mathie • G Williams • G Burley • K Gaughan • C Keeble • D Theobald • K Dyer • G Uhlenbeek • B Petta

→ **Web site:** http://www.itfc.co.uk → **Chairman:** David Sheepshanks → **Manager:** George Burley → **Year formed:** 1878

Ground: Portman Road (22,600)

Stands: North
Pioneer
Cobbold
Churchman's

Home strip: Blue shirts with white trim, white shorts with blue trim, blue socks with white trim

Away strip: Orange shirts with navy blue trim, navy blue shorts with orange trim, navy blue socks with orange trim

Sponsor: Greene King

Programme: £1.80

Nickname: Blues or Town

Ground history: 1878 Portman Road

Previous name: Ipswich

First League game: 27 August 1938, Division 3 (South), won 4-2 (h) v Southend United

Record attendance: 38,110 v Leeds United, FA Cup 6th round, 8 March 1975

Record victory: 7-0 v Street, FA Cup 1st round, 26 November 1938
7-0 v Portsmouth, Division 2, 7 November 1964
7-0 v Southampton, Division 1, 2 February 1974
7-0 v West Bromwich Albion, Division 1, 6 November 1976
7-0 v Skeid Oslo (Norway), UEFA Cup 1st round, 3 October 1979

Record defeat: 1-10 v Fulham, Division 1, 26 December 1963

Highest League scorer (season): Ted Phillips, 41, 1956-57

Highest League scorer (aggregate): Ray Crawford, 203, 1958-1963, 1966-1969

Most League appearances: Mick Mills, 591, 1966-1982

Most capped player: Allan Hunter, 47, Northern Ireland, 1971-1979

Highest transfer fee paid: £1m to Tottenham Hotspur for Steve Sedgley, June 1994

Highest transfer fee received: £1.9m from Tottenham Hotspur for Jason Dozzell, August 1993

Major trophies: Division 1 (old) Champions **(1)** 1961-62
Division 2 (old) Champions **(3)** 1991-92, 1967-68, 1960-61
Division 3 (South) Champions **(2)** 1956-57, 1953-54
FA Cup Winners **(1)** 1978
UEFA Cup Winners **(1)** 1981

Wayne Brown – A young defender who has progressed through the ranks at Portman Road and made his debut in the 1-1 draw with Middlesbrough in January 1998.

Jamie Clapham – A £300,000 purchase from Tottenham Hotspur in March 1998, the 22-year-old full back is not afraid to join the attack.

Matt Holland – A versatile and dynamic midfielder signed from Bournemouth in July 1997 for £800,000, he was a consistent force during the 1997-98 campaign and was voted Player of the Year.

David Johnson – A former Manchester United apprentice, the Jamaica-born striker came from Bury in November 1997 in a deal that saw defender Chris Swailes move to Gigg Lane. Valued at about £800,000, he was called up to the England Under-21 squad in December 1997. The same month, Johnson's goals bankrolled Ipswich's amazing rise up the table – and doubled his value.

Chris Keeble – A versatile young midfielder, his only appearance this season came in the last minute at Port Vale. He's the son of former Newcastle and West Ham star Vic.

John Kennedy – A promising right back who signed professional forms after graduating through the youth system. Like Keeble, his debut came as a second-half substitute during the 3-1 win at Port Vale in December.

Paul Mason – A left-sided midfielder signed from Aberdeen for £400,000 in June 1993, Paul is renowned for his spectacular goals and was the club's top League scorer in the 1996-97 season. However, injury kept him out for all but one game of 1997-98.

Alex Mathie – A £500,000 signing from Newcastle in February 1995, he was voted Player of the Month exactly three years later. A proven scorer with good pace, he struck up a fine partnership with Johnson in the second half of the 1997-98 season.

Simon Milton – The 35-year-old midfielder was signed from Bury in July 1987 for just £5,500. He enjoyed a profitable testimonial season in 1997-98 but talented youngsters kept him largely in the reserve team.

Tony Mowbray – Signed from Celtic in October 1995 for £250,000, the former Middlesbrough stalwart was a mainstay of the back four in 1997-98, despite turning 35 in November.

Richard Naylor – A young striker who goes by the nickname of 'Bambam', he managed to rack up a couple of goals in his role as super-sub.

Bobby Petta – Capped by the Netherlands at both Under-18 and Under-21 level, he was a free signing from Dutch club Feyenoord in June 1996. The tricky 24-year-old winger turned in some match-turning performances during 1997-98.

Jamie Scowcroft – Born in Bury St Edmunds and one of the few local products, he's a talented striker who worked his way up through the ranks at Portman Road and has won England Under-21 caps.

Danny Sonner – A Northern Ireland international, he's a right-sided central midfield player who came on a free transfer from German side Preussen Cologne in June 1996. He was recommended to Ipswich by former England star Tony Woodcock.

Mick Stockwell – A tireless midfielder or defender who joined Ipswich as an apprentice in 1981 and has played over 400 games for the club, the 33-year-old was as committed as ever during the 1997-98 campaign. He was Player of the Year in 1992-93.

Adam Tanner – After testing positive for cocaine and being suspended by the FA for three months, this versatile player reappeared for the final game of 1996-97, but failed to retain a regular first-team place in 1997-98.

Mauricio Taricco – A tough-tackling defender who signed from Argentinian side Argentinos Juniors for £175,000 in September 1994, he received over 75% of the poll in the supporters' Player of the Year awards for 1996-97. His father was also a footballer and played for Juventus.

Gus Uhlenbeek – A Surinam-born winger who signed from Dutch club SV Tops in the summer of 1995, he only featured in a handful of games this season.

Mark Venus – After nearly 300 League appearances for Wolves, Venus joined Ipswich in the summer of 1997 in the deal that took Steve Sedgley in the opposite direction. Like Sedgley, Venus can play in midfield or defence.

Richard Wright – One of the best young goalkeepers in the country, he represents England at Under-21 level and is widely tipped as a long-term successor to David Seaman. Ipswich-born and 6ft 2in tall, he's strong, agile and very quick off his line.

Transferred in:
- Jamie Clapham
  (Tottenham, £300,000)
- David Johnson (Bury, deal)
- David Kerslake (Tottenham, free)
- Matt Holland
  (Bournemouth, £800,000)
- Mark Venus (Wolves, deal)

Transferred out:
- David Kerslake (released)
- Neil Gregory
  (Colchester, £50,000)
- Chris Swailes (Bury, deal)
- Kevin Gaughan (released)
- Kevin Ellis (released)
- Craig Forrest
  (West Ham, £400,000)
- Steve Sedgley (Wolves, deal)

Jason Cundy – A strong, experienced central defender who was signed from Tottenham in October 1996 for £200,000. He's also played for Chelsea and has worn the captain's armband for Town.

Kieron Dyer – Born in Ipswich, Dyer is a talented midfielder whose mature displays in 1997-98 brought regular caps for England at Under-21 and B-level – and the attentions of almost every wealthy Premiership club.

Geraint Williams – A former Welsh international, he was Ipswich's record buy in 1992 when he came from Derby for £650,000. Though club skipper, the midfielder played out the 1997-98 season in the reserves.

Norwich City *Football Club*

→ **Address** | Norwich City FC, Carrow Road, Norwich NR1 1JE

Tel: 01603 760760 | **Tickets:** 01603 761661 | **Clubline:** 0891 121144

Ninety years ago, Norwich moved to The Nest, their new ground built on the side of a cliff. A 50ft-high wall was put up at The Nest to stop the ball flying over – but it also acted as a brake on players running towards it.

Top row • D Hilton • J Polston • K O'Neill • R Newman • K Scott • D Broughton • I Roberts • M Jackson • J Green • A Coote

Middle row • S Foley • L Marshall • D Mills • G Tipple • C Wilson • A Marshall • R Green • B Gunn • K Davis • D Kenton • D Sutch • K Simpson • T Sheppard

Bottom row • J Shore • A Forbes • S Carey • N Adams • R Fleck • J Faulkner • M Walker • C Fleming • M Milligan • D Eadie • V Segura • C Bellamy

→ **Web site:** http://www.ecn.co.uk/ncfc → **Chairman:** Barry Lockwood → **Caretaker manager:** John Faulkner → **Year formed:** 1902

Ground: Carrow Road (21,994)

Stands: Norwich and Peterborough
 Barclay
 South
 Geoffrey Watling City

Home strip: Yellow shirts with green trim, yellow shorts, yellow socks with green trim

Away strip: All green

Sponsor: Colman's

Programme: £2

Nickname: Canaries

Ground history: 1902 Newmarket Road
 1908 The Nest
 1935 Carrow Road

Previous name: None

First League game: 28 August 1920, Division 3, drew 1-1 (a) v Plymouth Argyle

Record attendance: 43,984 v Leicester City, FA Cup 6th round, 30 March 1963

Record victory: 10-2 v Coventry City, Division 3 (South), 15 March 1930

Record defeat: 0-7 v Walsall, Division 3 (South), 13 September 1930
 0-7 v Sheffield Wednesday, Division 2, 19 November 1938

Highest League position: Premiership, 3rd place, 1992-93

Highest League scorer (season): Ralph Hunt, 31, 1955-56

Highest League scorer (aggregate): Johnny Gavin, 122, 1945-1954, 1955-1958

Most League appearances: Ron Ashman, 592, 1947-1964

Most capped player: Mark Bowen, 35, Wales, 1988-1996

Highest transfer fee paid: £1m to Leeds United for Jon Newsome, June 1994

Highest transfer fee received: £5m from Blackburn Rovers for Chris Sutton, July 1994

Major trophies: Division 2 (old) Champions **(2)** 1985-86, 1971-72
 Division 3 (South) Champions **(1)** 1933-34
 League Cup Winners **(2)** 1985, 1962

Neil Adams – A £250,000 capture from Oldham in February 1994, he's a talented winger who returned in March 1998 after breaking his foot in December – and helped City clear of the relegation danger zone.

Craig Bellamy – A graduate of Norwich's youth policy, Bellamy was the club's leading scorer in the 1997-98 season, despite playing mainly from midfield. His season was capped by a full international debut for Wales against Jamaica in March.

Drewe Broughton – Although he's a pacy young centre forward whose performances in 1996-97 earned him a professional contract, he failed to claim a first-team place in the 1997-98 season.

Shaun Carey – A Republic of Ireland Under-21 midfielder who graduated to the senior squad from trainee status, he featured only sporadically during the 1997-98 campaign.

Adrian Coote – A strong centre forward seen by some as a young Chris Sutton, he made his debut in September 1997. Though born in Norfolk, he made the full Northern Ireland squad this season.

Darren Eadie – Despite a season disrupted by injury, Eadie remains a classy forward with good close control and has been rewarded with call-ups to Glenn Hoddle's squads.

Adrian Forbes – A quick right winger, Forbes was one of the most consistent players during the 1997-98 campaign, scoring a handful of goals.

Erik Fuglestad – A November 1997 signing from Norwegian club Viking Stavanger under the Bosman Ruling, Fuglestad is a left-sided defender who made his debut against Middlesbrough soon after signing.

Peter Grant – A £150,000 signing in August 1997 from Celtic, where he

spent 15 seasons, he's a combative midfielder and has proved to be one of the more consistent Norwich players.

Matt Jackson – Norwich City's club captain, Jackson is a classy defender signed from Everton in December 1996 for £450,000. His aerial presence, pace and intelligence have made him a firm fans' favourite and in 1997-98 he was the club's Player of the Year.

Darren Kenton – A versatile right-sided defender who made his full debut against Manchester City in February 1998, Darren is rated an excellent prospect for the future.

Chris Llewellyn – A young, attacking midfield player, Llewellyn has been rewarded with a call-up to the B-squad for Wales. A good first touch and mature vision are complemented by an eye for goal.

Lee Marshall – Signed from non-League Enfield for an initial £15,000, this promising defender recovered from breaking his ankle in November 1997 to feature in the latter stages of the 1997-98 season.

Mike Milligan – An £850,000 signing from Oldham in June 1994, he's a tireless midfielder who never gives less than 100%.

Rob Newman – A 34-year-old central defender signed from Bristol City in July 1991 for £600,000, Newman joined Wigan on loan in March 1998 for the rest of the season.

Keith O'Neill – Now a full Republic of Ireland international, O'Neill signed from Dublin's Home Farm and made his debut for the Canaries as an 18-year-old in September 1994. Injury restricted him to a handful of starts up front in 1997-98.

John Polston – An experienced central defender, Polston signed from Spurs in July 1990 for £300,000.

Despite his pedigree and value to the squad, he was not able to hold down a regular place last season.

Iwan Roberts – Long admired by Mike Walker, Roberts was an £850,000 capture from Wolves in July 1997. However, the Welsh forward failed to produce the goals in his first season.

Kevin Scott – Signed from Spurs in February 1997 for £250,000, the tall, experienced central defender featured in nearly half of Norwich's matches in 1997-98.

Victor Segura – A free transfer from Spanish second division side Lleida in July 1997, Segura is a left-sided defender who was named Man of the Match after his debut performance against Wolves in August 1997.

Karl Simpson – A graduate of Norwich's youth policy, Simpson is an attacking right-sided midfielder whose appearances have been restricted by the consistency of Neil Adams.

Andy Marshall – A highly rated goalkeeper who has cemented his place at number one this season, the England Under-21 international is regarded as one of the best keepers outside the Premiership.

Craig Fleming – A June 1997 signing from Oldham for £600,000, Fleming is a mature defender who is strong in the tackle. Despite his experience, injuries caused him to miss more than half the Canaries' games.

Transferred in:
- Craig Fleming (Oldham, £600,000)
- Victor Segura (Lleida, free)
- Erik Fuglestad (Viking Stavanger, free)
- Peter Grant (Celtic, £150,000)
- Iwan Roberts (Wolves, £850,000)

Transferred out:
- Robert Fleck (Reading, £60,000)
- Bryan Gunn (Hibernian, £10,000)
- Damian Hilton (Brighton, free)
- Danny Mills (Charlton, £250,000)
- Carl Bradshaw (released)

Daryl Sutch – A versatile defender who made his debut in October 1990 at Watford, he was one of Norwich's most consistent players during an often difficult season that saw him notch up 200 appearances in total.

Oxford United *Football Club*

→ **Address** | Oxford United FC, Manor Ground, Headington, Oxford OX3 7RS

Tel: 01865 761503 | **Tickets:** 01865 761503 | **Clubline:** 0891 440055

For about £58, you can eat and sleep Oxford United with a duvet cover and pillow case (£26.99), an alarm clock (£11.99), a bedside lamp (£11.99), a mug (£4.99) and a fridge magnet (£1.99).

Top row • K Nash • M Crosby • J Clinkard • Dr G Sacks • P Rhoades-Brown • M Evans **Second row** • L Robinson • M Angel • A Rose • J Cook • M Harrison • P Powell • N Banger • C Remy • M Gray **Third row** • P Whitehead • B Ford • D Smith • J Beauchamp • S Marsh • M Aldridge • N Jemson • S Weatherstone • N Emsden • E Jackson **Bottom row** • P Gilchrist • B Wilsterman • P Whelan • S Massey • D Smith • M Ford • M Stevens • M Murphy • D Purse

→ **Web site:** http://www.oufc.co.uk → **Managing director:** Keith Cox → **Manager:** Malcolm Shotton → **Year formed:** 1893

Ground: Manor Ground (9,572)

Stands: Beech Road Stand
Osler Road Stand
London Road Terrace
Cuckoo Lane Terrace

Home strip: Yellow shirts, navy shorts, navy socks

Away strip: All white

Sponsor: Unipart

Programme: £1.70

Nickname: U's

Ground history: 1893 Headington Quarry
1894 Wootten's Field
1898 Sandy Lane
1902 Britannia Field
1909 Sandy Lane
1910 Quarry Recreation Ground
1914 Sandy Lane
1922 The Paddock, Manor Road
1925 Manor Ground

Previous names: Headington
Headington United

First League game: 18 August 1962, Division 4, lost 2-3 (a) v Barrow

Record attendance: 22,730 v Preston North End, FA Cup 6th round, 29 February 1964

Record victory: 9-1 v Dorchester Town, FA Cup 1st round, 11 November 1995

Record defeat: 0-6 v Liverpool, Division 1, 22 March 1986

Highest League position: Division 1 (old), 18th place, 1985-86

Highest League scorer (season): John Aldridge, 30, 1984-85

Highest League scorer (aggregate): Graham Atkinson, 73, 1962-1973

Most League appearances: John Shuker, 480, 1962-1977

Most capped player: Jim Magilton, 18, 1990-1994

Highest transfer fee paid: £285,000 to Gillingham for Colin Greenall, February 1988

Highest transfer fee received: £1.6m from Leicester City for Matt Elliott, January 1997

Major trophies: Division 3 (old) Champions **(2)** 1983-84, 1967-68
Division 2 (old) Champions **(1)** 1984-85
League Cup Winners **(1)** 1986

Mark Angel – Signed on a free transfer from Sunderland in 1995, he is a tricky winger capable of playing on either flank and made 27 appearances in 1997-98, scoring once.

Nicky Banger – Released from Oldham during the summer of 1997, the quick and busy forward, formerly with Southampton, featured in 33 games for Oxford in 1997-98 and scored four goals.

James Cook – 1997-98 was a patchy season for the midfielder. He made 21 appearances, mostly after coming off the bench and when he did start a game, he was often withdrawn.

Steve Davis – Davis was snapped up from York City after leaving Barnsley, where he helped The Tykes achieve promotion to the Premiership in 1996-97. In 1997-98, the defender made 15 appearances at the heart of the Oxford back four and was able to score twice.

Mike Ford – A club stalwart, in 1997-98 he was yet again a consistent figure at full back for the team he has now served loyally for 10 years, following his move from Cardiff in 1988 for £150,000.

Kevin Francis – A towering forward who proved to be an awesome threat in the air after signing from Birmingham City in February 1998, Francis contributed seven goals in just 15 games in a United shirt.

Martin Gray – Gray continued to fulfil a valuable role in 1997-98, his second full season as an Oxford United player following his move from Sunderland in April 1996. A midfield man very much in the David Batty mould, Gray worked tirelessly to win the ball and distributed it neatly and sensibly.

Elliot Jackson – The young goalkeeper, rated as a good shot-stopper, is also capable of dealing with crosses but made just six appearances early on in 1997-98.

Simon Marsh – A young full back and former trainee who has often found his path to the first team blocked by more established members of the squad, the 21-year-old made more of an impact in 1997-98, with 16 appearances.

Stuart Massey – The former Crystal Palace man is a willing and hard worker in the Oxford midfield but only made 19 appearances in 1997-98, compared to 36 the previous season.

Matt Murphy – The striker was again in and out of the team in a 1997-98 season which included a month on loan to Scunthorpe. He made 35 appearances for Oxford, although most were made after coming off the bench, and scored three times.

Paul Powell – A promising young defender, Powell featured regularly throughout the 1997-98 season, making 23 appearances and scoring once.

Christophe Remy – Once of French club Auxerre, right back Remy was awarded a two-year contract by United after moving from Derby. He made 21 appearances for Oxford in 1997-98, but found his season hampered by injury.

David Smith – 'Smudger' came from Norwich in July 1994 and provides the link between defence and midfield, although he can also play as sweeper when needed. He made 51 appearances and even managed to add to his United goal tally in 1997-98 – he has now scored twice in 182 games for the club.

Mark Stevens – A young striker, his first-team experience in 1997-98 was limited to just two minutes on the pitch – against Nottingham Forest in August 1997.

Simon Weatherstone – The teenage striker is considered a bright prospect, having signed pro forms in 1997 while still in the YTS scheme. He made 11 late appearances as a substitute in 1997-98 and scored against eventual Champions Nottingham Forest in January 1998.

Phil Whelan – The giant defender should have been a major influence for Oxford in 1997-98 after arriving from Middlesbrough, but his injury problems resurfaced and he only made nine appearances.

Phil Whitehead – A strong goalkeeper, he continued to rule the roost as the club's number one, despite the presence of Jackson as back-up.

Brian Wilsterman – A Dutch defender who joined Oxford in February 1997 after a 12-year career spent in Holland and Belgium, he showed signs of adapting to the English game last season, making 25 appearances.

Phil Gilchrist – The centre back produced some outstanding displays in United's defence in 1997-98, putting his noted speed and strength to good use. He rarely missed a game and scored two goals.

Les Robinson – A defender who has been at the club since 1990, Robinson was again a consistent member of the United back four, playing 53 times and even notching up two goals.

Transferred in:
• Kevin Francis
  (Birmingham City, £100,000)
• Steve Davis (Barnsley, £75,000)
• Nicky Banger (Oldham, free)
• Christophe Remy (Derby, free)

Transferred out:
• Darren Purse
  (Birmingham, £700,000)
• Bobby Ford
  (Sheffield United, £400,000)
• Paul Moody (Fulham, £200,000)
• Nigel Jemson (Bury, £100,000)
• Todd Lumsden
  (Barry Town, non-contract)

Joey Beauchamp – The nippy winger is in his second spell at the Manor Ground after brief stints at West Ham and Swindon Town. He has a lethal shot, as evidenced by 19 goals in 51 games in 1997-98.

Portsmouth *Football Club*

→ **Address** | Portsmouth FC, Fratton Park, Frogmore Road, Portsmouth PO4 8RA

Tel: 01705 731204 | **Tickets:** 01705 618777 | **Clubline:** 0891 121182

During his 20 years at Portsmouth, keeper Alan Knight has played 662 League games for the club and holds the League record for the most appearances for one club by a goalkeeper.

Top row • G Rees • H Thorp • R Perrett • A Thomson • M Thompson • S Bundy **Middle row •** G Neave • K Waldon • I McDonald • J Durnin • J Hawley • P Harries • J Aloisi • A Knight • A Flahavan • M Svensson • M Allen • A Williams • D Hinshelwood • M Hinshelwood • J Trigg • S North **Bottom row •** C Foster • R Enes • D Hillier • A McLoughlin • S Igoe • D Waterman • A Awford • A Ball • A Whitbread • R Pethick • R Simpson • L Russell • N Jukes • J Carter • M Vlachos

→ **Web site:** http://www.pompey.co.uk → **Chairman:** Jim Gregory → **Manager:** Alan Ball → **Year formed:** 1898

Ground: Fratton Park (19,179)

Stands: North
South
KJC
Milton End

Home strip: Blue shirts with red and white trim, white shorts, red socks with white trim

Away strip: Yellow shirts with blue trim, blue shorts, blue socks with yellow trim

Sponsor: KJC

Programme: £2

Nickname: Pompey

Ground history: 1898 Fratton Park

Previous name: None

First League game: 28 August 1920, Division 3, won 3-0 (h) v Swansea Town

Record attendance: 51,385 v Derby County, FA Cup 6th round, 26 February 1949

Record victory: 9-1 v Notts County, Division 2, 9 April 1927

Record defeat: 0-10 v Leicester City, Division 1, 20 October 1928

Highest League scorer (season): Guy Whittingham, 42, 1992-93

Highest League scorer (aggregate): Peter Harris, 193, 1946-1960

Most League appearances: Jimmy Dickinson, 764, 1944-1965

Most capped player: Jimmy Dickinson, 48, England, 1944-1965

Highest transfer fee paid: £650,000 to Celtic for Gerry Creaney, January 1994

Highest transfer fee received: £2m from Tottenham Hotspur for Darren Anderton, May 1992

Major trophies: Division 1 (old) Champions **(2)** 1949-50, 1948-49
Division 3 (old) Champions **(2)** 1982-83, 1961-62
Division 3 (South) Champions **(1)** 1923-24
FA Cup Winners **(1)** 1939

Martin Allen – Nicknamed 'Mad Dog' for his battling qualities in midfield, he missed much of the 1996-97 season after a knee operation and made only a few first-team starts in 1997-98.

Andy Awford – A stylish central defender, he made his Pompey debut as a 16-year-old in April 1989 and has won Schoolboy, Under-18, Under-19 and Under-21 caps for England. He has been plagued by injury but made a solid return to the side in November 1997.

Jimmy Carter – A winger who arrived on a free transfer from Arsenal in July 1995, he has also played for Liverpool and Millwall. He made about a dozen appearances in 1997-98, starting many from the bench.

Aaron Cook – A second-year trainee, Cook has yet to break into the first team on a regular basis.

John Durnin – A striker turned midfielder, he came from Oxford United for £200,000 five years ago. The 1997-98 season saw him notch up some 30 appearances, although many were from the bench.

Robbie Enes – An Australian international, Enes signed from Sydney United for £175,000 in October 1997, after problems with a work permit were solved by taking out Portuguese nationality.

Aaron Flahavan – A former apprentice, he shared goalkeeping duties with Alan Knight in 1997-98.

Craig Foster – A £320,000 signing from Australia's Club Marconi, the midfielder is a regular Australian international who arrived in September 1997 and vied for a regular spot.

Paul Hall – A forward with good pace, the Jamaican player signed from Torquay in March 1993.

Sammy Igoe – A diminutive 5ft 6in, Igoe graduated through the ranks at Portsmouth, having joined the club's School of Excellence at Basingstoke at the age of 11. He was another midfield player forced to jostle for a regular place in the team in 1997-98.

Alan Knight – He joined Pompey as an apprentice in 1977 and made his League debut more than 20 years ago, in April 1978. In 1997-98, he continued to be one of Portsmouth's most called-upon players.

Alan McLoughlin – A former Manchester United apprentice, he came from Southampton in March 1992. The attacking midfielder has scored some important goals for both Pompey and the Republic of Ireland.

Russell Perrett – A tall, strong central defender who was released by Pompey in 1991, only to return in September 1995 for £5,000. His place in the team was taken by Awford from late 1997.

Robbie Pethick – A £30,000 capture from non-League Weymouth in October 1993, he is an attacking right-sided wing back who rarely missed a game in 1997-98.

Matthew Robinson – A left-sided defender who came from Southampton for £50,000 in February 1998, he has a good first touch and immediately secured himself a first-team place.

Lee Russell – A versatile defender who can turn to midfield, he was desperately unlucky with injuries in 1997-98, restricting his appearances to the early part of the season.

Fitzroy Simpson – A hard-working midfielder who came from Manchester City as part of a deal that saw Kit Symons go the other way in August 1995, his 1997-98 season was made complete by joining the Jamaica World Cup squad in training.

Mathias Svensson – A strong-running Swedish international striker who was signed from Sweden's Elfsborg in November 1996 for £75,000, the former car salesman is a favourite with the fans.

Andy Thomson – A £75,000 purchase from Swindon in January 1996, he is a 6ft 3in central defender who was a regular in the side for most of the 1997-98 campaign.

Hamilton Thorp – A 6ft 3in striker signed from Australian side West Adelaide Sharks for £75,000 in July 1997, his role was largely restricted to that of substitute.

Andy Turner – A left-winger signed by Terry Venables in September 1996 for £250,000 after making 28 appearances for Spurs, the Under-21 Republic of Ireland international was hit by injury in 1997-98.

Michalis Vlachos – A tough Greek international defender who signed on a free transfer from AEK Athens during the 1997-98 season, he has had valuable Champions League experience and is a fine addition to the often frail Pompey rearguard.

David Waterman – A young central defender who had limited first-team opportunities in 1997-98.

Transferred in:
- Matthew Robinson (Southampton, £50,000)
- Michalis Vlachos (AEK Athens, free)
- John Aloisi (Cremonese, £300,000)
- Craig Foster (Club Marconi, £320,000)
- Robert Enes (Sydney, £175,000)
- Hamilton Thorp (West Adelaide Sharks, £75,000)

Transferred out:
- Andy Cook (Millwall, £50,000)
- Gavin Reece (released)
- Adam Williams (released)
- Ashkan Karimzadeh (released)
- Mark Thompson (released)
- Lee Bradbury (Manchester City, £3m)
- Deon Burton (Derby, £1.5m)

Adrian Whitbread – The tough defender and club captain made a loan deal permanent when he signed for Portsmouth in October 1996 from West Ham and turned out almost without fail in the 1997-98 season.

David Hillier – A ball-winning midfielder, Hillier thrived at Arsenal under George Graham but moved to Pompey in November 1996 after losing favour with Bruce Rioch. He is a key player at Fratton Park.

John Aloisi – An Australian international, this striker signed from Italian side Cremonese for £300,000 in August 1997. Aloisi was the club 's leading striker in his first season at Portsmouth.

Port Vale Football Club
Port Vale Football Club
Port Vale Football Club
Port Vale Football Club
Port Vale Football Club
Port Vale Football Club
Port Vale Football Club
Port Vale Football Club
Port Vale Football Club
Port Vale Football Club
Port Vale Football Club

226

Port Vale *Football Club*

→ **Address** | Port Vale FC, Vale Park, Burslem, Stoke-on-Trent ST6 1AW

Tel: 01782 814134 | **Tickets:** 01782 814134 | **Clubline:** 0891 121636

Port Vale are the only club in the English League named after a place that doesn't exist. Their name comes from the venue of the club's inaugural meeting, which was at Port Vale House in Burslem.

Top row • J Jansson • A Tankard • S Armstrong • N Aspin • S Williams • L Mills • G Griffiths • J Holwyn • J O'Reilly • R Koordes • L Burns • S Talbot • D Glover

Middle row • S Nicholls • M Grew • M Foyle • W Corden • M Boswell • P Musselwhite • A van Heusden • A Hill • R Eyre • R Carter • J Cooper

Bottom row • M Carragher • I Bogie • T Naylor • J Rudge • A Porter • B Dearden • T McShane • J McCarthy • D Stokes

→ **Web site:** http://www.port-vale.co.uk   → **Chairman:** William Bell   → **Manager:** John Rudge   → **Year formed:** 1876

Ground: Vale Park (22,356)

Stands: Lorne Street
Sentinel (Bycars)
Mizuno (Railway Paddock)
Caudwell (Hamil Street)

Home strip: White shirts with black trim, black shorts, black socks with white trim

Away strip: Yellow shirts with black trim, yellow shorts with black trim, yellow socks

Sponsors: Tunstall Assurance

Programme: £1.50

Nickname: Valiants

Ground history: 1876 Limekin Lane, Longport
1881 Westport
1884 Moorland Road, Burslem
1886 Athletic Ground, Cobridge
1913 Recreation Ground, Hanley
1950 Vale Park

Previous name: Burslem Port Vale

First League game: 3 September 1892, Division 2, lost 1-5 (a) v Small Heath

Record attendance: 49,749 v Aston Villa, FA Cup 5th round, 20 February 1960

Record victory: 9-1 v Chesterfield, Division 2, 24 September 1932

Record defeat: 0-10 v Sheffield United, Division 2, 10 December 1892
0-10 v Notts County, Division 2, 26 February 1895

Highest League position: Division 1, 8th place, 1996-97

Highest League scorer (season): Wilf Kirkham, 38, Division 2, 1926-27

Highest League scorer (aggregate): Wilf Kirkham, 164, 1923-1929, 1931-1933

Most League appearances: Roy Sproson, 761, 1950-1972

Most capped player: Sammy Morgan, 7, Northern Ireland, 1972-1973

Highest transfer fee paid: £500,000 to Lincoln City for Gareth Ainsworth, September 1997

Highest transfer fee received: £1.5m from Birmingham City for Jon McCarthy, September 1997

Major trophies: Division 3 (North) Champions **(2)** 1953-54, 1929-30
Division 4 Champions **(1)** 1958-59

Gareth Ainsworth – A right-winger who was bought in September 1997 for a record £500,000 from Lincoln City, Ainsworth was one of the club's most consistent players in terms of appearances during 1997-98.

Ian Bogie – A ball-playing midfielder who began his career in the same Newcastle United youth side as Paul Gascoigne, Bogie signed from Leyton Orient for £50,000 in March 1995. His creativity in the middle often leads to goalscoring opportunities.

Liam Burns – A Northern Ireland Under-18 central defender who signed professional forms in July 1997, he made his first-team debut as a substitute against Sunderland in January 1998 in an unaccustomed left wing-back role.

Matthew Carragher – Signed on a free transfer from Wigan in the summer of 1997, he made over 100 appearances at Springfield Park and earned the distinction of being the club's longest-serving player. Still only 22, he is a young, tough-tackling right back who quickly settled in at Port Vale.

Richard Eyre – A right-winger who signed from trainee status in July 1995, he gained his first taste of senior action in December 1997 in the very last minute of the game against Ipswich.

Martin Foyle – An experienced forward who joined Vale from Oxford United in June 1991 for a then club record fee of £375,000, Foyle found himself third choice behind Mills and Naylor in 1997-98, despite being a regular goalscorer.

Dean Glover – A strong centre half who signed from Middlesbrough for £200,000 in early 1989, he continued to jostle for first-team play in 1997-98. The 34-year-old enjoyed a benefit match in May 1998 and in the past has helped the club gain promotion and the Autoglass trophy.

Gareth Griffiths – A 6ft 4in centre back who came from non-League Rhyl for £1,000 in February 1993, he has been incredibly unlucky with injuries – first suffering a double hernia, then a cruciate ligament injury. He made few appearances in 1997-98 and enjoyed a loan spell at Shrewsbury Town mid-season.

Andy Hill – A solid-tackling right back who was signed from Manchester City in August 1995 for £150,000, he began his career at Manchester United but was unable to break into the first team. He was a Port Vale team regular for most of 1997-98, despite a hamstring injury.

Jan Jansson – A former Swedish international who made a loan deal permanent when he signed for £150,000 from Swedish club SK Norkopping in the summer of 1997, he is a skilful midfielder who made the number 11 spot his at the end of the 1997-98 season.

Rogier Koordes – In direct competition with Wayne Corden for the left-wing role, the Dutchman was brought to the club for £70,000 last season and appeared in around a quarter of the games in 1997-98.

Lee Mills – A powerful striker who signed from Derby County as part of a loan deal in February 1995, he was the club's leading scorer during the 1997-98 season. That was one better than the season before when he was pipped by Tony Naylor.

Paul Musselwhite – Edged out of the number one spot for much of the 1996-97 season, he returned as the club's first choice keeper in 1997-98. Musselwhite has been at the club six years, following his move from Scunthorpe in July 1992 for £17,500.

Andy Porter – A former YTS trainee, Porter is Port Vale's longest-serving player, having joined 13 years ago, in August 1985. In that time, the fiery

midfielder has notched up around 400 appearances and scored some 26 goals for the club.

Mark Snijders – A 6ft 2in defender who signed from Dutch first division club AZ Alkmaar on a free transfer in September 1997, he quickly earned himself a regular spot.

Dean Stokes – He made his debut at left back in a 1-1 draw at home to Burnley in December 1993 after signing for £5,000 from non-League Halesowen Town in January of that year. He continued his sporadic form in 1997-98.

Stewart Talbot – A strong-running midfielder who moved from non-League Moor Green in August 1994, he was virtually ever-present during 1997-98.

Allen Tankard – Vale's regular left back, he was signed from Wigan Athletic for £87,500 in July 1993 and made his debut in a 2-1 defeat away at Burnley on 14 August 1993. He continues to find a regular place in the team.

Arjan van Heusden – A £4,500 purchase from Dutch side Noordwijk in August 1994, he is a tall keeper who was kept on the bench by Musselwhite for much of the 1997-98 season and ended it on loan to Barnet.

Wayne Corden – A right-footed left-winger who is a former Vale trainee, he stepped into Steve Guppy's boots after the latter's move to Leicester last season. His current contract ties him to the club until 2000.

Tony Naylor – A prolific scorer after signing from Crewe for £150,000 in July 1994, he likes to run at defenders and can turn sharply. After two seasons as highest goalscorer he just lost out in 1997-98 to Mills.

Transferred in:
- Jan Jansson
  (SK Norkopping, £150,000)
- Matt Carragher (Wigan, free)
- Gareth Ainsworth
  (Lincoln, £500,000)
- Mark Snijders (AZ Alkmaar, free)

Transferred out:
- Jon McCarthy (Birmingham, £1.5m)
- Justin O'Reilly (Southport, £5,000)

Neil Aspin – Club captain and fearless defender, Aspin came from Leeds, where he made 244 appearances. Signed for £140,000 in July 1989, he has become the rock at the heart of the defence.

Queens Park Rangers *Football Club*

Queens Park Rangers Football Club
Queens Park Rangers Football Club
Queens Park Rangers Football Club
Queens Park Rangers Football Club
Queens Park Rangers Football Club
Queens Park Rangers Foo
Queens Park Rangers Fo
Queens Park Rangers Football Club
Queens Park Rangers Football Club
Queens Park Rangers Football Club

→ **Address** | Queens Park Rangers FC, Loftus Road Stadium, South Africa Road, London W12 7PA

Tel: 0181 743 0262 | **Tickets:** 0171 740 0503 | **Clubline:** 0891 121162

In 1967, QPR won a unique double – the Third Division Championship and the League Cup in the first year it was played at Wembley. Rodney Marsh scored 11 goals en route to Cup glory.

Top row • T Challis • L Charles • N Quashie • C Plummer • K Ready • M Mahoney-Johnson • S Morrow • S Slade • P Murray • K Gallen • P Bruce

Middle row • B Oteng • S Burtenshaw • M Browse • C Hamilton • M Sheron • M Perry • P Hart • R Hurst • T Roberts • L Harper • S Yates • S Barker • B Morris

• W Neill • G Micklewhite **Bottom row** • J Hollins • M Rose • D Maddix • M Brazier • M Graham • S Houston • G Peacock • R Brevett • T Sinclair • J Spencer • B Rioch

→ **Web site:** http://www.qpr.co.uk → **Chairman:** Chris Wright → **Manager:** Ray Harford → **Year Formed:** 1886

Ground: Loftus Road (19,148)

Stands: South Africa Road
Ellerslie Road
Loft
Paddock

Home strip: Blue and white hooped shirts, blue shorts, white socks

Away strip: Red and black hooped shirts, black shorts, red socks

Sponsor: Ericsson

Programme: £1.80

Nicknames: Rangers, R's or Superhoops

Ground history: 1886 Welfords Field
1888 London Scottish Ground
1889 Home Park
1889 Kensal Rise Green
1889 Brondesbury Park
1889 Gun Club
1889 Barn Elms

1892 Kilburn Cricket Ground
1897 National Athletic Ground
1901 St Quintins Avenue
1902 National Athletic Ground
1904 Royal Agricultural Society
1907 Park Royal
1917 Loftus Road (1931, 1962 White City)

Previous name: St Jude's

First League game: 28 August 1920, Division 3, lost 1-2 (h) v Watford

Record attendance: 35,353 v Leeds United, Division 1, 27 April 1974

Record victory: 9-2 v Tranmere Rovers, Division 3, 3 December 1960

Record defeat: 1-8 v Mansfield Town, Division 3, 15 March 1965
1-8 v Manchester United, Division 1, 19 March 1969

Highest League position: Division 1 (old), runners-up, 1975-76

Highest League scorer (season): George Goddard, 37, 1929-30

Highest League scorer (aggregate): George Goddard, 172, 1926-1934

Most League appearances: Tony Ingham, 519, 1950-1963

Most capped player: Alan McDonald, 52, Northern Ireland, 1981-1997

Highest transfer fee paid: £2.35m to Chelsea for John Spencer, November 1996
£2.35m to Stoke City for Mike Sheron, July 1997

Highest transfer fee received: £6m from Newcastle United for Les Ferdinand, June 1995

Major trophies: Division 2 (old) Champions **(1)** 1982-83
Division 3 (old) Champions **(1)** 1966-67
Division 3 (South) Champions **(1)** 1947-48

Simon Barker – The veteran player was once again the driving force behind Rangers' midfield in what was his 10th year at Loftus Road, following his move from Blackburn Rovers in August 1988.

Ian Barraclough – A defender signed from Notts County during 1997-98, Barraclough stepped into the left-back place vacated by Rufus Brevett's move to Fulham.

Paul Bruce – A former trainee and member of the England Under-19 squad, Bruce made a handful of appearances in 1997-98, usually in an attacking role.

Iain Dowie – An experienced striker who has captained Northern Ireland, Dowie was part of the transfer deal which took Trevor Sinclair to Upton Park during the 1997-98 season. Unfortunately, a chest infection brought an early end to his season.

Kevin Gallen – A talented young striker, he made an encouraging return to the side in 1997-98 after injury wiped out almost all of his playing time in 1996-97. He looked close to a return to his potent best at the end of the season.

Lee Harper – A young goalkeeper who moved from Arsenal for £125,000 (rising to £250,000) for regular first-team football, he became the club's number one choice. He was named by the players as Player of the Year in 1997-98 after some great performances.

Antti Heinola – A Finland international who arrived at Loftus Road mid-season in 1997-98, Heinola struggled to assert himself and claim a starting role in the side.

Vinny Jones – The infamous midfield hardman became QPR's player-coach when he arrived from Wimbledon in March 1998. His wholehearted displays went some way to saving Rangers from the drop.

George Kulscar – The Australian was Ray Harford's first signing as Rangers boss, arriving from Bradford City for £250,000. He operates a holding role in midfield, where he can demonstrate his ball-winning skills.

Steve Morrow – A Northern Ireland international who can fill a number of roles across the defence and in midfield, Morrow was used mainly as a centre back in 1997-98.

Paul Murray – A young midfielder with bags of promise, Murray was snapped up from Carlisle United in 1996 and turned in some composed, impressive performances before breaking his leg against Norwich City in February 1998.

Gavin Peacock – The former Newcastle and Chelsea man can play as an attacking midfielder or, when needed, as an out-and-out striker. He performed to great effect in 1997-98, hitting 10 goals.

Mark Perry – A young right back who made sporadic appearances, especially early on in the 1997-98 campaign, he was eventually superceded by more experienced defenders.

Karl Ready – The club captain, who has been at QPR since his trainee days, was a great success in 1997-98 as a steady and consistent member of the back four. Being voted Player of the Year by the supporters was just reward for his efforts.

Matthew Rose – A central defender of some promise, Rose came in May 1997 from a club noted for their defenders – Arsenal. He showed up well in the early months of the season before a knee operation in December 1997 hampered his progress.

Keith Rowland – He moved to Rangers with Iain Dowie from West Ham and slotted comfortably into a full-back role, although the Northern Ireland international faced tough competition for a first-team place.

Tony Scully – An exciting left winger who has the ability to go past players and send accurate crosses over the top, Scully has represented the Republic of Ireland at every level bar the full team. He joined QPR from Manchester City in March 1998.

Steve Slade – 1997-98 was another disappointing season for the former England Under-21 international striker. He had hoped to re-start his career with Rangers after leaving Spurs, but was used mostly as a substitute in 1997-98.

Steve Yates – A dependable defender, he continued to turn in some consistent displays in 1997-98 despite some heavy competition for places in the Rangers back four.

Transferred in:
- Michael Sheron (Stoke, £2.35m)
- Matthew Rose (Arsenal, £500,000)
- Lee Harper (Arsenal, £125,000)
- Antti Heinola (Heracles, £100,000)
- Iain Dowie (West Ham, deal)
- Keith Rowland (West Ham, deal)
- Vinny Jones (Wimbledon, £500,000)
- Tony Scully (Manchester City, £155,000)
- Ian Barraclough (Notts County, £50,000)

Transferred out:
- Trevor Sinclair (West Ham, £2.3m)
- Andy Impey (West Ham, £1.2m)
- Rufus Brevett (Fulham, £375,000)
- Jurgen Sommer (Columbus, £175,000)
- Matthew Brazier (Fulham, £65,000)
- Daniele Dichio (Sampdoria, free)
- Alan McDonald (Swindon, free)

Mike Sheron – A reliable forward, formerly of Manchester City, Stoke and Norwich, Sheron was top scorer for Rangers in 1997-98 with 11 goals but still has yet to play to his full potential.

Nigel Quashie – A young central midfielder very much in the mould of playmaker, he possesses a good touch, great vision and likes to get forward. His performances in 1997-98 earned him an England B cap.

Danny Maddix – A defender who can play at right back or at centre back, Maddix has been at Rangers for 10 years and had hoped to be part of Jamaica's World Cup squad, but didn't make the final cut.

Sheffield United *Football Club*

→ **Address** | Sheffield United FC, Bramall Lane, Sheffield S2 4SU

Tel: 0114 221 5757 | **Tickets:** 0114 221 1889 | **Clubline:** 0891 888650

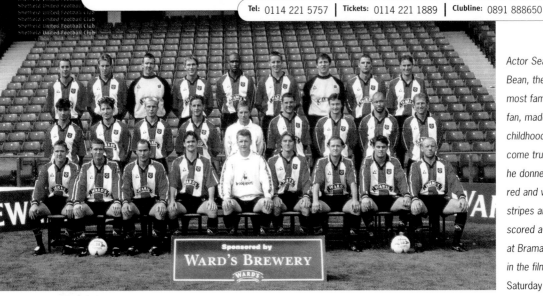

Actor Sean Bean, the Blades' most famous fan, made his childhood dream come true when he donned the red and white stripes and scored a penalty at Bramall Lane – in the film When Saturday Comes.

Top row • D Hutchison • C Tiler • A Kelly • G Taylor • B Deane • J A Fjortoft • S Tracey • M Vonk • A Scott

Middle row • V Borbokis • C Short • R Nilsen • D Holdsworth • W Donachie • D White • P Katchuro • P McGrath • N Marker

Bottom row • N Henry • M Beard • D Whitehouse • A Walker • N Spackman • W Quinn • J Ebbrell • M Ward • M Patterson

→ **Web site:** http://www.sufc.co.uk → **Acting Football Chairman:** Kevin McCabe → **Manager:** Steve Thompson (to June 1998) → **Year formed:** 1889

Ground: Bramall Lane (30,300)

Stands: Laver
John Street
Kop
Bramall Lane

Home strip: Red and white striped shirts, black shorts, black socks

Away strip: All white

Sponsor: Ward's Brewery

Programme: £1.50

Nickname: Blades

Ground history: 1889 Bramall Lane

Previous name: None

First League game: 3 September 1892, Division 2, won 4-2 (h) v Lincoln City

Record attendance: 68,257 v Leeds United, FA Cup 5th round, 15 February 1936

Record victory: 11-2 v Cardiff City, Division 1, 1 January 1929

Record defeat: 0-13 v Bolton Wanderers, FA Cup 2nd round, 1 February 1890

Highest League scorer (season): Jimmy Dunne, 41, 1930-31

Highest League scorer (aggregate): Harry Johnson, 205, 1919-1930

Most League appearances: Joe Shaw, 629, 1948-1966

Most capped player: Billy Gillespie, 25, Northern Ireland, 1911-1932

Highest transfer fee paid: £1.2m to West Ham United for Don Hutchison, January 1996

Highest transfer fee received: £2.7m from Leeds United for Brian Deane, July 1993

Major trophies: Division 1 (old) Champions **(1)** 1897-98
Division 2 (old) Champions **(1)** 1952-53
Division 4 (old) Champions **(1)** 1981-82
FA Cup Winners **(4)** 1925, 1915, 1902, 1899

Mark Beard – Popular in the dressing room because of his lively character, the right back made only a couple of substitute appearances in 1997-98.

Jon Cullen – A young midfielder who found the net 12 times for Hartlepool, he signed for United for £250,000 in January 1998.

Traianos Dellas – An imposing centre back, the Greek Under-21 captain was signed for £300,000 in August 1997 but spent much of the time injured.

Shaun Derry – Another young, gifted player, Derry arrived from Notts County in January 1998 for £700,000 and made eight starts either in defence or in a midfield role.

Paul Devlin – A busy forward with a decent scoring record from his days at Notts County and Birmingham, Devlin was signed from the latter in March 1998 but made just four appearances, with a single goal.

Bobby Ford – An industrious midfielder, he played nearly 30 games for United following his £400,000 transfer from Oxford United in November 1997.

Ian Hamilton – A midfielder renowned for his vision, passing and control, he signed from West Brom in March 1998 and immediately won a place in the side.

Nick Henry – The former Oldham Athletic midfielder should have played a huge part in United's plans in 1997-98, but injury robbed the team of his ball-winning qualities.

David Holdsworth – A highly rated centre back, he is a mainstay of the Blades' defence.

Marcelo – The Brazilian forward proved a shrewd signing when United picked him up from Spanish outfit Deportivo Alaves in October 1997. He went on to score seven goals in just 17 games.

Nicky Marker – The veteran midfielder played over 55 games in 1997-98.

Lee Morris – The youngster made eight substitute appearances.

Roger Nilsen – The Norwegian continued to look a class act on the left side of the United defence and proved his worth occasionally in a more central role.

Wayne Quinn – A fantastic first senior season from the young left wing back who had graduated to the first team after two seasons in the reserves. He has also won England Under-21 and B-team call-ups.

Lee Sandford – An experienced defender who, like Nilsen, plays on the left side, he can move inside when needed.

Dean Saunders – An experienced striker, formerly of Liverpool and Villa, he joined on a free transfer in November 1997. The Welsh international fired 12 goals in 29 games to finish joint leading scorer.

Graham Stuart – A versatile, attacking player, he moved to Bramall Lane in November 1997. Capable of playing in midfield or as a striker, he hit five goals in 33 games.

Gareth Taylor – A tall striker whose main strength is in the air, he finished the season with 10 goals.

Simon Tracey – The goalkeeper has had nine seasons with United but was second choice to Kelly in 1997-98.

Michael Vonk – The Dutchman's season was a virtual non-starter thanks to a cruciate knee ligament operation he underwent last year. He made just three appearances in 1997-98.

David White – Injury limited the winger to a single substitute's appearance last season.

Dane Whitehouse – The pacy left winger made 23 appearances, scoring six times, before being injured in November 1997.

Chris Wilder – A competent right back who played for United between 1986 and 1989, he rejoined from Bradford at the end of last season and played a handful of games.

Curtis Woodhouse – The defender made just 10 appearances, filling in at left back in 1997-98.

Transferred in:
- Brian Deane (Leeds, £1.5m)
- Vassilis Borbokis (AEK Athens, £900,000)
- Nicky Marker (Blackburn, £400,000)
- Paul McGrath (Derby, free)
- Traianos Dellas (Aris Salonika, £300,000)
- Matt George (Aston Villa, free)
- Marcelo (Deportivo Alaves, £400,000)
- Bobby Ford (Oxford, £400,000)
- Graham Stuart (Everton, deal)
- Dean Saunders (Nottingham Forest, free)
- Shaun Derry (Notts County, £700,000)
- Jon Cullen (Hartlepool, £250,000)
- John O'Connor (Everton, deal)
- Ian Hamilton (West Brom, undisclosed)
- Paul Devlin (Birmingham, £200,000)

Transferred out:
- John Reed (Blackpool, free)
- Matt Hocking (Hull, undisclosed)
- Andy Scott (Brentford, £75,000)
- Carl Tiler (Everton, deal)
- Mitch Ward (Everton, deal)
- Charlie Hartfield (Swansea, non-contract)
- Mark Patterson (Bury, £125,000)
- Brian Deane (Benfica, £1m)
- Jan Aage Fjortoft (Barnsley, £800,000)
- Don Hutchison (Everton, £1m)
- Steve Hawes (Doncaster, non-contract)
- Richard Tracey (Rotherham, free)

Alan Kelly – The Republic of Ireland international eventually won his battle for the number 1 jersey from Simon Tracey and became a hero with his saves in the FA Cup quarter-final penalty shoot-out against Coventry.

Petr Katchouro – The Belarus international had a disappointing time, coming off the back of winning the supporters' Player of the Year award in 1996-97. The striker made only sporadic appearances in 1997-98.

Vassilis Borbokis – The Greek international was one of United's best performers of the 1997-98 season. Borbokis was an eye-catching figure, raiding down United's right flank in the wing-back role.

Stockport County *Football Club*

Stockport County Football Club
Stockport County Football Club
Stockport County Football Club
Stockport County Football Club
Stockport County Football Club
Stockport County Football Club
Stockport County Football Club
Stockport County Football Club
Stockport County Football Club

→ **Address** | Edgeley Park, Hardcastle Road, Edgeley, Stockport SK3 9DD

Tel: 0161 286 8888 | **Tickets:** 0161 286 8888 | **Clubline:** 0891 121638

In 1997-98, the Hatters finished in their highest ever League position – eighth in Division One, with Brett Angell and Sean Connelly both making 51 appearances for the club in all competitions.

Top row • M Bound • B Angell • I Gray • N Edwards • C Woodthorpe • L Jones **Second row** • G Lewis • S Carden • J Gannon • A Mutch • D Kilduff • G Ansell

Third row • J P King • K Charana • T Bennett • S Connelly • D Searle • N De Costa • L Cavaco • L Shearer • K Cooper

Bottom row • A Armstrong • M Nash • M Flynn • G Megson • C Marsden • K Durkan • T Dinning

→ **Web site:** http://www.stockportmbc.gov.uk./county → **Chairman:** Brendan Elwood → **Manager:** Gary Megson → **Year formed:** 1883

Ground: Edgeley Park (11,541)

Stands: Hardcastle Road
Cheadle End
Vernon Building Society
Halway End Terrace

Home strip: Blue and white striped shirts, blue shorts, blue socks

Away strip: Sunshine yellow with green trim, green shorts, green socks

Sponsor: Frederic Robinson

Programme: £1.80

Nickname: Hatters or County

Ground history: 1883 Heaton Norris Recreation Ground
1884 Heaton Norris Wanderers Cricket Ground
1885 Chorlton's Farm, Chorlton's Lane

1886 Heaton Norris Cricket Ground
1887 Wilkes' Field, Belmont Street
1899 Nursey Inn, Green Lane
1902 Edgeley Park

Previous name: Heaton Norris Rovers

First League game: 1 September 1900, Division 2, drew 2-2 (a) v Leicester Fosse

Record attendance: 27,883 v Liverpool, FA Cup 5th round, 11 February 1950

Record victory: 13-0 v Halifax Town, Division 3 (North), 6 January 1934

Record defeat: 1-8 v Chesterfield, Division 2, 19 April 1902

Highest League position: Division 1, 8th place, 1997-98

Highest League scorer (season): Alf Lythgoe, 46, 1933-34

Highest League scorer (aggregate): Jack Connor, 132, 1951-1956

Most League appearances: Andy Thorpe, 489, 1978-1986, 1988-1992

Most capped player: Martin Nash, 6, Canada, 1996-1998

Highest transfer fee paid: £250,000 to Tranmere Rovers for Paul Cook, October 1997

Highest transfer fee received: £1.6m from Middlesbrough for Alun Armstrong, February 1998

Major trophies: Division 3 (North) Champions **(2)** 1936-37, 1921-22
Division 4 Champions **(1)** 1966-67

Brett Angell – A popular goalscorer who began his career at Stockport and went on to Southend, Everton and Sunderland before returning to County for a second spell in 1996, he was leading scorer in 1996-97 and again topped the goal charts in 1997-98.

Tom Bennett – A Scotland-born midfielder, he has enjoyed an upturn in career fortunes since moving to County from Wolves in 1995. He enjoyed another fruitful season as the team's primary playmaker.

Chris Byrne – A gifted young midfielder, he was nearly lost to professional football when he was released by Crewe at 18. But after brief spells with Macclesfield and Sunderland he was signed by County in November 1997 for £200,000. He hit seven League goals in 1997-98.

Luis Cavaco – A talented Portuguese winger, Cavaco only made it onto the pitch as a sub in 1998, after suffering an horrific double leg fracture in April 1997.

Sean Connelly – The right back made nearly 50 appearances in what was his sixth year at Stockport since arriving from non-League Hallam in 1992. The fans' choice as Player of the Year in 1997-98.

Paul Cook – A cultured midfielder who was signed in October 1997, he scored against former club Wolves on his debut. He possesses a sweet left foot and can score goals from distance.

Kevin Cooper – A left-sided midfielder with attacking flair, Cooper joined from Derby in the summer of 1997 and became a favourite with County supporters, scoring some match-winning goals.

Tony Dinning – The centre half joined Stockport on a free transfer from Newcastle in 1994. He featured in almost 30 games during the 1997-98 season and impressed with his vision and control.

Keiron Durkan – He started the season in possession of the number seven shirt but lost his place and returned to the reserves, where he was a regular goalscorer from midfield.

Mike Flynn – Stockport's club captain enjoyed another good season at Edgeley Park and continued to be one of the most popular players at the club, again performing well at centre back.

Stephen Grant – A centre forward who was once with Sunderland, he was picked up from Irish club Shamrock Rovers and signed after impressing in trials. He made promising strides when taking over from Middlesbrough-bound Alun Armstrong, scoring three times in nine games.

Ian Gray – Recruited from Rochdale for an initial fee of £200,000, Gray is a goalkeeper who is very highly regarded at Stockport, although he played understudy to Nixon in the 1997-98 season.

Martin McIntosh – The tall central defender signed from Hamilton in August 1997 and developed into a brilliant acquisition, playing over 40 games at the heart of the County back four.

Andy Mutch – A veteran striker who made his name by forming a devastating partnership with Steve Bull at Wolves, he spent 1997-98 mainly in the reserves.

Damon Searle – A left back with Welsh caps at Schoolboy, Youth and Under-21 level, Searle regained his favourite role after the departure of Lee Todd to Southampton just before the start of the 1997-98 season.

Simon Travis – An England Under-18 international who was picked up for £10,000 from Welsh side Hollywell Town, Travis is a quick full back who featured in a handful of games in 1997-98, mostly as substitute.

Aaron Wilbraham – A striker who graduated from the youth team to start the last six League games of 1997-98, he scored once in the 4-1 defeat at Manchester City on April 4.

Colin Woodthorpe – An experienced defender formerly with Norwich and Aberdeen, he competed with Searle for the left-back spot in 1997-98, losing his place in November, but regaining it by February.

Jim Gannon – He fulfils a sterling role deep in midfield, acting as a ball-winner with neat distribution. He joined County in 1990 and has agreed a new deal which will take him to 10 years' service.

Eric Nixon – A goalkeeper who joined County for £96,000 from Tranmere in August 1997, he is famous for creating a record in 1986-87 by playing in all four divisions in the same season.

Transferred in:
- Paul Cook (Tranmere, £250,000)
- Colin Woodthorpe (Aberdeen, £200,000)
- Ian Gray (Rochdale, £200,000)
- Ken Charlery (Barnet, £80,000)
- Vas Kalogeracos (Perth Glory, £60,000)
- Martin McIntosh (Hamilton Academicals, undisclosed)
- Simon Travis (Hollywell, £10,000)
- Stephen Grant (Shamrock Rovers, undisclosed)
- Eric Nixon (Tranmere, £96,000)

Transferred out:
- Alun Armstrong (Middlesbrough, £1.6m)
- Paul Jones (Southampton, £900,000)
- Lee Todd (Southampton, deal)
- Chris Marsden (Birmingham, £500,000)
- Neil Edwards (Rochdale, £25,000)
- Jonathan Cross (Witton Albion, free)
- Richard Landon (Macclesfield, free)
- Adie Mike (Doncaster, free)
- Danny Yongo (Witton Albion, free)
- Gordon Cowans (Burnley, non-contract)
- John Jeffers (Hednesford, free)
- Sean Mannion (Stella Maris, free)

Sunderland *Football Club*

Sunderland Football Club
Sunderland Football Club
Sunderland Football Club
Sunderland Football Club
Sunderland Football Club
Sunderland Football Club
Sunderland Football Club
Sunderland Football Club
Sunderland Football Club
Sunderland Football Club
Sunderland Football Club

→ *Address* | Sunderland AFC, Stadium of Light, Sunderland SR5 1SU

Tel: 0191 551 5000 | Tickets: 0191 551 5151 | Clubline: 0898 121140

Kevin Phillips was voted Nationwide Division One Player of the Year in 1998 after scoring a post-war club record 35 goals in all competitions, in Sunderland's unsuccessful bid for a swift return to the top flight.

Top row • K Phillips • S Aiston • M Bridges • P Heckingbottom • C Makin • J Eriksson • T Coton • E Zoetebier • L Perez • J Craddock • R Ord

• A Melville • L Clark • M Gray • N Quinn • B Saxton **Bottom row** • J Mullin • S Agnew • C Russell • M Smith • K Heiselberg • A Rae • P Bracewell • P Reid

• K Ball • M Scott • C Byrne • A Johnston • D Williams • G Hall • D Holloway

→ **Web site:** www.sunderland-afc.com → **Chairman:** Bob Murray → **Manager:** Peter Reid → **Year formed:** 1879

Ground: Stadium of Light (42,000)

Stands: Vaux Breweries
Metro FM
McEwans
West

Home strip: Red and white striped shirts, black shorts, black socks

Away strip: Navy blue shirts with red and white hoops, navy blue shorts with red and white trim, navy blue socks with red and white trim

Sponsor: Lambton's Smooth Ale

Programme: £1.70

Nickname: Rokerites

Ground history: 1879 Blue House Field
1882 Groves Field
·1883 Horatio Street

1884 Abbs Field
1886 Newcastle Road
1898 Roker Park
1997 Stadium of Light

Previous name: Sunderland and District Teachers

First League game: 13 September 1890, Football League, lost 2-3 (h) v Burnley

Record attendance: 41,214 v Stoke City, Division 1, 25 April 1998

Record victory: 11-1 v Fairfield, FA Cup 1st round, 2 February 1895

Record defeat: 0-8 v West Ham United, Division 1, 19 October 1968
0-8 v Watford, Division 1, 25 September 1982

Highest League scorer (season): Dave Halliday, 43, 1928-29

Highest League scorer (aggregate): Charlie Buchan, 209, 1911-1925

Most League appearances: Jim Montgomery, 537, 1962-1977

Most capped player: Charlie Hurley, 38, Republic of Ireland, 1957-1968

Highest transfer fee paid: £2.5m to Newcastle United for Lee Clark, June 1997

Highest transfer fee received: £1.5m from Crystal Palace for Marco Gabbiadini, September 1991

Major trophies: Division 1 (old) Champions **(6)** 1935-36, 1912-13, 1901-02, 1894-95, 1892-93, 1891-92
Division 1 Champions **(1)** 1995-96
Division 2 (old) Champions **(1)** 1975-76
Division 3 (old) Champions **(1)** 1987-88
FA Cup Winners **(2)** 1973, 1937

Kevin Ball – The club captain was signed from Portsmouth in 1990 for £350,000. Originally a central defender, he is now regarded as a midfield hard man capable of shackling opponents' dangermen and weighing in with the occasional goal.

Michael Bridges – A locally produced England Under-21 international, he made a sensational impact on the first team in 1996 but injuries and the form of Kevin Phillips and Niall Quinn restricted his appearances in 1997-98.

Jody Craddock – Signed from Cambridge United for £400,000 on the day Sunderland opened the Stadium of Light, he is powerful in the air and strong in the tackle and deputised successfully for the injured Andy Melville in 1997-98.

Daniele Dichio – Restricted mainly to substitute appearances since Reid rescued the striker in January 1998 from his Italian nightmare with Sampdoria, Dichio has gained more attention for his DJ-ing skills (under the name Mello-D) than his performances on the pitch.

Darren Holloway – A young, local defender who has come through the youth ranks, he is equally at home at right back or in central defence. He capped a fine debut season at first-team level with England Under-21 and B-team appearances.

Allan Johnston – He earned the nickname 'Magic' following a brilliant hat-trick against Rangers while playing for Hearts in 1996. After a brief spell in France for Rennes, he signed for Sunderland in April 1997 for £550,000 and mesmerised the opposition in his first full season at the club.

Chris Makin – The former England Under-21 defender signed from Marseilles in 1996 for £500,000. An uncompromising defender, he can play in both full back positions.

Andy Melville – The Welsh international stalwart found his route back to the first team blocked by the impressive form of Craddock and Darren Williams. He had a successful loan spell at Bradford in 1998.

Lionel Perez – The maverick French goalkeeper was bought from Bordeaux for £200,000 in August 1996, where he spent three seasons. He has established a cult status on Wearside due to his instinctive reflex saves and peroxide blonde crop, although he is occasionally vulnerable under the high ball.

Kevin Phillips – Arguably the best buy by any club in 1997-98 as Peter Reid paid Watford an initial £350,000 for the striker with additional payments agreed for a certain number of appearances and if Sunderland achieved promotion. He went on to become England's leading goalscorer with 35 goals. With electric pace, a bright future should lie ahead for the man who used to clean Shearer's boots as an apprentice at Southampton.

Niall Quinn – He has played over 60 times for the Republic of Ireland and is the country's third highest goalscorer of all time. Signed from Manchester City for £1.3 million in August 1996, he has brushed aside injury troubles to form a highly effective partnership with Phillips.

Alex Rae – The goalscoring midfielder was signed from Millwall for £1 million in June 1996, which was then a joint Sunderland transfer record. The Scotland B-international has been unlucky not to tie down a regular first team spot. Sunderland's best attacking displays have come when his aggression and accurate passing have combined with Lee Clark's deft touches in the centre of midfield.

Martin Scott – After being tipped by some for an England call-up in 1996,

the former Bristol City defender has been the victim of a string of injuries.

Martin Smith – When fit, he is a free-scoring crowd pleaser, but the Sunderland-born midfielder has been ravaged by injury over the last two seasons, and has been unable to recapture consistently the form that made him an England Under-21 international.

Nicky Summerbee – He arrived in 1997 in a swap deal that saw Roker hero Craig Russell move to Manchester City. A tricky operator on the right wing, he capped his season with a tremendous goal in Sunderland's heartbreaking play-off final defeat at Wembley.

Darren Williams – The Middlesbrough-born player was signed from York City for £50,000 in 1996 as a midfielder, but has adapted well to take up a central defensive role.

Richard Ord – The former skipper offers experienced cover in defence. The fans' chant of "who needs Cantona when we've got Dicky Ord?" is a reflection of his calm nature and his precise distribution skills.

Lee Clark – Signed from Newcastle United for £2.5 million on the day he made the full England squad in 1997, Clark has cast aside local prejudices and established himself as the fulcrum of the midfield.

Transferred in:
- Lee Clark (Newcastle, £2.5m)
- Nicky Summerbee (Manchester City, deal)
- Luke Weaver (Leyton Orient, £250,000)
- Chris Makin (Marseille, £500,000)
- Kevin Phillips (Watford, £350,000)
- Daniele Dichio (Sampdoria, £750,000)
- Jody Craddock (Cambridge, £400,000)

Transferred out:
- Craig Russell (Manchester City, deal)
- Gareth Hall (Swindon Town, free)
- Chris Byrne (Stockport, £100,000)

Michael Gray – Subject of the popular northeast play *How To Marry A Footballer*, the skilful, hard-working left wing back is a favourite with fans and has a scintillating partnership on the left with Johnston.

Swindon Town *Football Club*

→ **Address** | Swindon Town FC, County Ground, County Road, Swindon, Wiltshire SN1 2ED

Tel: 01793 430430 | **Tickets:** 01793 529000 | **Clubline:** 0891 121640

Main Sponsors of Swindon Town F.C.
Nationwide

Five former Swindon managers have World Cup pedigree – Lou Macari and Ossie Ardiles (players, 1978), Glenn Hoddle and John Gorman (coaches, 1998), and Steve McMahon (player, 1986).

Top row • W Allison • M Seagraves • F Digby • S Mildenhall • F Talia • S Finney • K Watson **Second row** • A McDonald • M Walters • C Taylor • G Elkins • M Robinson • S Leitch • I Culverhouse • F Darras • A Finlayson **Third row** • L Collins • P Holcroft • P King • D Bullock • W O'Sullivan • T Gooden • S Cowe

Bottom row • J Drysdale • J Trigg • R MacLaren • S McMahon • M Walsh • L O'Neill • A Smith

→ **Web site:** http://www.swindon-fc.demon.co.uk → **Chairman:** Rikki Hunt → **Manager:** Steve McMahon → **Year formed:** 1879

Ground: County Ground (15,700)

Stands: South
Arkell's
Rover Family
Stratton Bank

Home strip: Red shirts with green and white trim, red shorts, red socks with green and white trim

Away strip: Black and blue striped shirts, blue shorts, black socks with blue trim

Sponsor: Nationwide

Programme: £2

Nickname: Robins

Ground history: 1879 Bradfords Field
Globe Field
The Croft
1895 County Ground

Previous names: Swindon Spartans

First League game: 28 August 1920, Division 3, won 9-1 (h) v Luton Town

Record attendance: 31,668 v Arsenal, FA Cup 3rd round, 15 January 1972

Record victory: 10-1 v Farnham United Breweries, FA Cup 1st round, 28 November 1925

Record defeat: 1-10 v Manchester City, FA Cup 4th round replay, 29 January 1930

Highest League position: Premiership, 22nd place, 1993-94

Highest League scorer (season): Harry Morris, 47, 1926-27

Highest League scorer (aggregate): Harry Morris, 215, 1926-1933

Most League appearances: John Trollope, 770, 1960-1980

Most capped player: Rod Thomas, 30, Wales, 1967-1973

Highest transfer fee paid: £800,000 to West Ham United for Joey Beauchamp, August 1994

Highest transfer fee received: £1.75m from Manchester City for Kevin Horlock, January 1997

Major trophies: Division 2 Champions **(1)** 1995-96
Division 4 Champions **(1)** 1985-86
League Cup Winners **(1)** 1969

Brian Borrows – A former Coventry favourite, Borrows signed an 18-month deal in November 1997. Able to play anywhere at the back, he's particularly useful as a sweeper.

Darren Bullock – Signed for £400,000 from Huddersfield in February 1997, Bullock is a tough-tackling midfielder who started the season on the bench, but forced his way into the 1997-98 starting line-up.

Lee Collins – A ball-winning midfielder, Collins missed most of the 1996-97 season through injury but returned in 1997-98 to try and establish himself as a regular in the first team.

Steve Cowe – A lively, energetic striker bought from Aston Villa where he came through the youth ranks, Cowe struggled to find a place in the first team in 1997-98.

Philippe Cuervo – A gifted French midfielder who impressed on trial and was signed on a free transfer in the summer of 1997, Cuervo carried his form into the start of the season, but struggled with a hip problem.

Ian Culverhouse – The former Norwich star signed for £250,000 in December 1994, but made only 12 appearances in 1997-98 after initially losing his place due to injury.

Sol Davis – A promising left wing back who managed two goals in just six games, Davis offered hope at the end of the season with his stylish play.

Steve Finney – A striker who had a great start to his Swindon career, Finney returned from a loan spell at Cambridge in November 1997 to score three goals in three games as a replacement for the departed Wayne Allison.

Ty Gooden – A disappointing previous season was put behind him as Gooden returned to the first team as an ever-present playing either as left wing back or as an attacking midfielder.

Christopher Hay – A speedy young striker picked up from Celtic, Hay started superbly with 13 goals in just 20 games before Christmas.

Steve Howe – An attacking midfielder, Howe signed from Forest in January 1997 after first team opportunities dried up at the City Ground.

David Kerslake – A defender who is most effective as a right wing back, Kerslake was welcomed back to Swindon for his third spell after signing on a free from Ipswich.

Scott Leitch – A strong Scottish midfielder, Leitch took over as the Robins captain when Mark Seagraves was sidelined due to injury.

Paul McAreavey – A young striker who came through the youth ranks, McAreavey made his debut as a sub in the 5-0 defeat at Norwich in April.

Steve McMahon – The Swindon manager restricted his playing time to just seven minutes last season, coming on as a substitute against Huddersfield in August 1997.

Steve Mildenhall – A promising young keeper, Mildenhall impressed in his four appearances in 1997-98 keeping three clean sheets.

George Ndah – A lightning-fast striker signed from Palace for £500,000 in November 1997, Ndah scored a cracker on his debut against Boro, but has yet to fulfil his potential.

Iffy Onuora – A striker signed in March 1998, Onuora made the perfect start when he headed the winning goal at QPR, but suffered a fractured cheekbone four games later in a clash with the referee.

Michael Pattimore – A young defender who has captained Wales Under-18s, Pattimore made his League debut in March 1997, but was unhappy with just two substitute appearances in 1997-98.

Mark Robinson – A club record £600,000 signing in July 1994, Robinson can play at full back, centre back or as a sweeper but missed three months with injury in 1997-98.

Mark Seagraves – A former Liverpool apprentice, defender Seagraves was club captain before a serious injury ended his campaign in September.

Frank Talia – An agile keeper who signed from Blackburn in November 1995, Talia played just three games in 1997-98 due to a knee injury, but has signed a new three-year deal.

Craig Taylor – The younger brother of former Town favourite Shawn, Craig missed the season's start with injury, but had a dream debut – scoring a cracker against Port Vale in October.

Kevin Watson – A product of Tottenham's junior ranks, Watson arrived at Swindon on a free transfer in July 1996 and put in some good displays at the heart of the midfield in the 1997-98 season.

Transferred in:
- Chris Hay (Celtic, £330,000)
- Craig Taylor (Dorchester, £25,000)
- Philippe Cuervo (St Etienne, free)
- Phil King (Aston Villa, free)
- Alan McDonald (QPR, free)
- Brian Borrows (Coventry, free)
- George Ndah (Crystal Palace, £500,000)
- Steve Howe (Nottingham Forest, £30,000)
- David Kerslake (Ipswich, free)
- Iffy Onuora (Gillingham, £100,000)

Transferred out:
- Wayne O'Sullivan (Cardiff, £75,000)
- Peter Thorne (Stoke, £350,000)
- Wayne Allison (Huddersfield, £800,000)
- Frederic Darras (Red Star Paris, free)
- Alex Smith (Huddersfield, free)
- Jason Drysdale (released)

Fraser Digby – The club's longest-serving player was his usual confident, reliable self between the posts in 1997-98, though he did suffer the indignity of a red card for a handball at QPR, which was later revoked.

Mark Walters – A former England star snapped up after Southampton released him in July 1996, Walters' pace and trickery make him a popular player, but a knee injury forced him out for several months in 1997-98.

Alan McDonald – A veteran Northern Ireland international signed from his only previous club, QPR, in the summer of 1997, McDonald brought experience and commitment to the centre of Swindon's defence.

Tranmere Rovers *Football Club*

→ **Address** | Tranmere Rovers FC, Prenton Park, Prenton Road West, Birkenhead, Wirral L42 9PN

Tel: 0151 608 4194 | **Tickets:** 0151 609 0137 | **Clubline:** 0891 121646

John Aldridge is the highest post-war goalscorer. By the end of the 1997-98 season, he had scored 473 career goals, having surpassed Jimmy Greaves' previous record in his first full season as Tranmere's player-manager.

Top row • A Morgan • K McIntyre • D Challinor • G Branch • G Jones • M Pereira • L O'Brien • K Irons • J Morrissey

Middle row • W Rimmer • D Philpotts • L Parry • A Parkinson • S Simonsen • C Hill • E Nixon • A Mahon • D Coyne • M Howard • S Mungall • R Mathais

• K Sheedy **Bottom row** • A Thompson • S Connolly • R Williams • G Stevens • J McGreal • J Aldridge • L Jones • P Cook • D Kelly • A Thorn

→ **Web site:** http://www.merseyworld.com/rovers → **Chairman:** Frank Corfe → **Manager:** John Aldridge → **Year formed:** 1885

Ground: Prenton Park (16,700)

Stands: Kop
Main
Cowshed
Borough Road

Home strip: White shirts with blue trim, blue shorts with white trim, white socks with blue trim

Away strip: Green shirts with orange and white trim, white shorts with orange and green trim, green socks with orange and white trim

Sponsor: Metropolitan Borough of Wirral

Programme: £1.60

Nickname: Rovers

Ground history: 1885 Steele's Field
1887 Ravenshaw Field
1912 Prenton Park

Previous names: Belmont

First League game: 27 August 1921, Division 3 (North), won 4-1 (h) v Crewe Alexandra

Record attendance: 24,424 v Stoke City, FA Cup 4th round, 5 February 1972

Record victory: 13-4 v Oldham Athletic, Division 3 (North), 26 December 1935

Record defeat: 1-9 v Tottenham Hotspur, FA Cup 3rd round replay, 14 January 1953

Highest League position: Division 1, 4th place, 1992-93

Highest League scorer (season): Robert 'Bunny' Bell, 34, 1933-34

Highest League scorer (aggregate): Ian Muir, 142, 1985-1995

Most League appearances: Harold Bell, 595, 1946-1960

Most capped player: John Aldridge, 30, Republic of Ireland, 1991-1997

Highest transfer fee paid: £450,000 to Aston Villa for Shaun Teale, August 1995

Highest transfer fee received: £2m from Nottingham Forest for Alan Rogers, July 1997

Major trophies: Division 3 (North) Champions (1) 1937-38

John Aldridge – The player-manager restricted his appearances to just 14 in 1997-98 (seven as a sub) but still showed why he's Britain's top post-war scorer, with five goals, including two on the last day of the season, his retirement game.

Graham Branch – A quick forward, he started 1997-98 in the first team but was relegated to the bench before going on loan to Wigan. He returned in January and flitted around the fringes of the side.

Dave Challinor – A former England Under-21 defender who bagged a place in the *Guinness Book of Records* with a throw-in of over 46 metres, he played consistently for 37 games in 1997-98 and scored his first goal for the club against Portsmouth in April.

Danny Coyne – A 5ft 11in goalkeeper who came through the youth system and started 1997-98 as first choice, Coyne suffered a persistent groin injury which ended his season early.

Stephen Frail – A £75,000 January 1998 signing from Hearts, where he played a minor part in the Scottish club's successful season, Frail played a handful of games at full back, but injury cut short his progress.

Clinton Hill – A 19-year-old local defender who turned professional in July 1997, he was given his debut against League leaders Nottingham Forest in October, and clocked up 18 games by the end of the season.

Kenny Irons – A strong player who reads the game well and prefers to operate just behind the front two, Kenny started 1997-98 on the bench, but quickly established himself in the team's engine room, playing 49 games.

Gary Jones – A 6ft 3in striker who can also play at centre back or in midfield, he finally found a way past Aldridge into the first team

and finished the 1997-98 season in sparkling form, netting six times in the last 10 games.

David Kelly – An experienced striker signed from Sunderland in August 1997, he fitted seamlessly into the attack and finished his first season at the club as top scorer with 14 goals.

Kevin McIntyre – A product of the Tranmere youth system, McIntyre is a promising defender who was given his first two games at the club as a substitute in 1997-98. Both appearances came against soon-to-be promoted sides – Nottingham Forest and Charlton Athletic.

Alan Mahon – An attacking midfielder with flair and vision, his 22 appearances in 1997-98 started and finished on the substitute's bench, but big things are expected from this highly rated youngster.

Mick Mellon – A lively midfielder who works hard, Mellon was signed at the end of October 1997 and went on to play 36 times but struggled to reproduce the goalscoring form that made him so popular at Blackpool.

John Morrissey – The longest-serving player at the club after signing from Wolves for a paltry £8,000 back in October 1985, Morrissey is a skilful winger with a good cross who was in and out of the team for most of 1997-98.

Liam O'Brien – A former Manchester United and Newcastle man who signed for £250,000 in January 1994, he plays the ball well in the centre of the park and is capable of spectacular goals. He put in another season of dependable performances as the team's primary playmaker in 1997-98.

Andy Parkinson – A striker who was signed from Liverpool just before his 18th birthday in May 1997, Parkinson was mostly used as a substitute during the 1997-98 season but

scored a memorable winner in the FA Cup fourth round to give Tranmere a well-earned victory over Sunderland.

Steve Simonsen – A former England youth keeper, he took over between the posts for the visit to Bradford in November 1997 and never looked back, securing the number one shirt with a series of fine displays, including seven consecutive clean sheets at the turn of the year.

Gary Stevens – A veteran right back with 46 England caps, he joined Rovers in 1994 from Glasgow Rangers (for £350,000) and was a virtual ever-present in 1997-98 until an ankle operation in January sidelined him for the rest of the season.

Andy Thompson – A highly competitive player brought in for free from Wolves during the summer of 1997, he immediately claimed the left-back spot and made over 50 appearances in 1997-98.

Alan Morgan – 1997-98 was a breakthrough of sorts for this versatile former trainee. Handed a League debut in 1996 after four years without a game, he added a further 23 appearances in defence and midfield.

John McGreal – Another fine season from a composed, central defender who is often compared to his hero, Alan Hansen. Made club captain by John Aldridge, he continues to impress Premiership scouts.

Transferred in:
- David Kelly
  (Sunderland, £350,000)
- Lee Jones (Liverpool, £100,000)
- Ryan Williams
  (Mansfield, £70,000)
- Andy Thompson (Wolves, free)
- Dirk Hebel (Bursaspor, free)
- Stephen Frail (Hearts, £75,000)
- Mauro Pereira (Casa Pia, free)
- Mick Mellon (Blackpool, £285,000)

Transferred out:
- Alan Rogers (Forest, £2m)
- Tony Thomas (Everton, £400,000)
- Pat Nevin (Kilmarnock, £60,000)
- Gary Scott (Rotherham, free)
- Eric Nixon (Stockport, £100,000)
- Paul Cook (Stockport, £250,000)
- Ricky Lampkin (Northwich, free)

Lee Jones – Signed from Liverpool for £100,000 in June 1997 after a loan spell in which he scored five from eight games, he started 1997-98 in similar vein. But having reached 10 by early December, the goals dried up.

Watford *Football Club*

Watford Football Club
Watford Football Club
Watford Football Club
Watford Football Club
Watford Football Club
Watford Football Club
Watford Football Club
Watford Football Club
Watford Football Club
Watford Football Club
Watford Football Club

→ **Address** | Watford FC, Vicarage Road Stadium, Watford, Hertfordshire WD1 8ER

Tel: 01923 496000 | **Tickets:** 01923 496010 | **Clubline:** 0891 104104

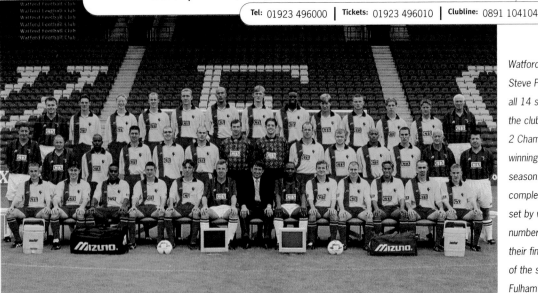

Watford player Steve Palmer wore all 14 shirts during the club's Division 2 Championship-winning 1997-98 season. He completed the set by wearing the number 9 shirt in their final game of the season at Fulham on 2 May.

Top row • K Wheeler • D Grieves • N Lowndes • R Page • K Millen • J Lee • D Ward • G Noel-Williams • L Melvang • C Pluck • D Perpetuini • D Ludden • R Clare

Middle row • J Gilligan • G Johnson • V Cave • S Talboys • D Thomas • T Mooney • A Chamberlain • C Day • S Palmer • P Kennedy • M Hyde • M Rooney • T Walley

• P Edwards **Bottom row** • C Johnson • R Johnson • W Andrews • P Robinson • C Easton • K Jackett • G Taylor • L Blissett • S Slater • N Gibbs • R Flash • D Bazeley • A Johnson

→ **Web site:** http://www.watfordfc.com → **Chairman:** Sir Elton John → **Manager:** Graham Taylor → **Year formed:** 1891

Ground: Vicarage Road (22,000)

Stands: Main
Sir Stanley Rous
Vicarage Road End
Rookery

Home strip: Yellow and red shirts with black trim, red shorts, red socks with yellow and black trim

Away strip: Light blue and dark blue striped shirts with dark blue trim, dark blue shorts, dark blue socks with red trim

Sponsor: CTX

Programme: £2

Nickname: Hornets

Ground history: 1891 Cassio Road
1922 Vicarage Road

Previous name: West Herts

First League game: 28 August 1920, Division 3, won 2-1 (a) v Queen's Park Rangers

Record attendance: 34,099 v Manchester United, FA Cup 4th round replay, 3 February 1969

Record victory: 10-1 v Lowestoft, FA Cup 1st round, 27 November 1926

Record defeat: 0-10 v Wolverhampton Wanderers, FA Cup 1st round replay, 13 January 1912

Highest League position: Division 1 (old), runners-up, 1982-83

Highest League scorer (season): Cliff Holton, 42, 1959-60

Highest League scorer (aggregate): Luther Blissett, 148, 1976-1983, 1984-1988, 1991-1992

Most League appearances: Luther Blissett, 415, 1976-1983, 1984-1988, 1991-1992

Most capped player: John Barnes, 31, England, 1983-1987
Kenny Jackett, 31, Wales, 1983-1988

Highest transfer fee paid: £550,000 to AC Milan for Luther Blissett, August 1984

Highest transfer fee received: £2.3m from Chelsea for Paul Furlong, May 1994

Major trophies: Division 2 Champions **(1)** 1997-98
Division 3 (old) Champions **(1)** 1968-69
Division 4 (old) Champions **(1)** 1977-78

Wayne Andrews – A prolific scorer in youth and reserve games, he became a regular squad member in 1997-98 but failed to make a start in the League.

Damon Bazeley – A winger converted to full back, the former trainee was ousted from the number 2 spot by the revival of Nigel Gibbs but ended the 1997-98 season with a useful run up front alongside Jason Lee.

Alec Chamberlain – Signed from Sunderland in July 1996 for just £40,000, he came into his own in 1997-98 following Kevin Miller's move to Palace and was ever-present in the League campaign, earning the Player of the Year title.

Chris Day – Signed in the close season from Palace as part of the deal that saw Kevin Miller go, the reserve keeper played only once in 1997-98.

Clint Easton – A former trainee who filled in well in midfield for injured seniors during 1996-97, he again covered in 1997-98 from the bench.

Nigel Gibbs – Watford's longest-serving player made his debut as an 18-year-old back in 1983 – against Sparta Prague in the UEFA Cup. Given a free transfer in 1996, he signed a new contract and again became the automatic choice at right back – a position he held for most of the Championship season as he renewed his association with Watford manager Graham Taylor.

Alon Hazan – A current Israeli international with 63 caps, this utility player spent over 13 seasons with four Israeli clubs before being bought by Watford in January 1998 on the recommendation of Ronny Rosenthal. He finally broke into the first team in April 1998.

Micah Hyde – Graham Taylor took the 22-year-old Cambridge captain

on tour to Finland in the close season and was impressed enough to buy him on a fee-plus-appearances basis. The fees were gladly paid as his visionary midfield play became a key factor in Watford's success.

Jason Lee – Graham Taylor's first signing on his return to Watford was the tall striker known as much for his bizarre hairstyles as his play. He proved a good buy for Watford, making the number 9 shirt his own in 1997-98 and creating as well as scoring goals.

Nathan Lowndes – Arriving as a former trainee from Leeds in 1995, Lowndes has yet to fulfil his early promise.

Keith Millen – Signed in March 1994 from Brentford in an exchange deal, the 6ft 2in centre back missed only a handful of games in 1997-98.

Tommy Mooney – A Vicarage Road favourite since arriving from Southend in 1994, he was converted from forward to defender by Graham Taylor and missed only three League games in the 1997-98 campaign.

Robert Page – Watford's young club captain is a Welsh international defender who has been a first-team regular since 1994 – and again was almost ever-present in 1997-98.

Steve Palmer – Nicknamed 'The Professor' at Ipswich because of his Cambridge University degree, the tall midfielder arrived in 1995. He proved a good investment and played in every position in 1997-98.

Colin Pluck – A strong, young challenger to Page and Millen at centre back, the former trainee made his League debut in September 1997.

Paul Robinson – An aggressive left-sided player, Robinson continued the progress he made in 1996-97 and became a regular squad member.

Ronny Rosenthal – Arriving at Liverpool via Standard Liege, the Israeli striker moved on to several seasons at Spurs before Watford secured him on a free transfer at the start of the 1997-98 season.

Stuart Slater – Formerly with West Ham, Celtic (who paid a record £1.5 million for him), Ipswich and Leicester, the stocky midfielder came on a free transfer in 1996. However, he failed to hold a regular place after October 1997 because of a series of injuries.

Tommy Smith – The YTS player is a promising forward and made his League debut in the 1997-98 season at Vicarage Road, against Oldham.

David Thomas – Under-21 Welsh international 'Dai' was signed from Swansea in the close season as a partner for Jason Lee, but failed to deliver.

Transferred in:
- Jason Lee (Nottingham Forest, £200,000)
- David Thomas (Swansea, £100,000)
- Micah Hyde (Cambridge, £100,000)
- Chris Day (Crystal Palace, £225,000)
- Peter Kennedy (Notts County, £130,000)
- Ronny Rosenthal (Tottenham, free)
- Alon Hazan (Ironi Ashdod, £200,000)

Transferred out:
- Kevin Miller (Crystal Palace, £1.3m)
- Kevin Phillips (Sunderland, £350,000)
- David Connolly (Feyenoord, free)
- Steve Talboys (Borehamwood, free)

Richard Johnson – A busy midfielder, he came over from Newcastle Astrals in Australia and made his first-team debut in 1991. Noted for his long-range strikes, he remained a regular throughout the 1997-98 season.

Gifton Noel-Williams – The youngest player ever to score in the League for Watford (in November 1996, aged 16), this tall, quick striker with a bright future became a permanent member of the squad in 1997-98.

Peter Kennedy – After seriously reconsidering his future in the game, he had a fine season following his move from Notts County in July 1997, racking up 13 goals from his position at left wing back.

West Bromwich Albion *Football Club*

West Bromwich Albion Football Club
West Bromwich Albion Football Club
West Bromwich Albion F...
West Bromwich Albion F...
West Bromwich Albion Football Club
West Bromwich Albion Football Club
West Bromwich Albion F...ball Club
West Bromwich Albion Football Club

→ **Address** | West Bromwich Albion FC, The Hawthorns, Halfords Lane, West Bromwich B71 4LF

Tel: 0121 525 8888 | **Tickets:** 0121 525 8888 | **Clubline:** 0891 121193

The Hawthorns is the last remaining League stadium to have been built in the 19th century. At 551 feet above sea level, it is also the highest Football League ground in the UK.

Top row • S Nicholson • D Bennett • L Hughes • P Raven • C Adamson • G Germaine • P Crichton • S Murphy • G Potter • T Dobson • M Rodosthenous

Middle row • J Trewick • C Regis • D Craven • A McDermott • C Tranter • P Mardon • N Spink • A Miller • K Kilbane • T James • D Bowman • D Gilbert • P Mitchell

• R O'Kelly **Bottom row** • S Coldicott • D Burgess • R Sneekes • A Hunt • P Holmes • R Harford • D Smith • I Hamilton • P Peschisolido • P Butler • B Taylor

→ **Web site:** http://www.wba.co.uk → **Chairman:** Anthony Hale → **Manager:** Denis Smith → **Year formed:** 1878

Ground: The Hawthorns (25,326)

Stands: Family
Apollo 2000
Brew 11
Travel West Midlands Community

Home strip: Blue and white striped shirts with white trim, white shorts, blue and white hooped socks

Away strip: Red and blue shirts, blue shorts, red and blue socks

Sponsor: West Bromwich Building Society

Programme: £1.50

Nickname: Baggies

Ground history: 1878 Cooper's Hill
1879 Dartmouth Park
1881 Bunn's Field
1882 Four Acres
1885 Stoney Lane
1900 The Hawthorns

Previous name: West Bromwich Strollers

First League game: 8 September 1888, Football League, won 2-0 (a) v Stoke

Record attendance: 64,815 v Arsenal, FA Cup 6th round, 6 March 1937

Record victory: 12-0 v Darwen, Division 1, 4 April 1892

Record defeat: 3-10 v Stoke City, Division 1, 4 February 1937

Highest League scorer (season): William Richardson, 39, 1935-36

Highest League scorer (aggregate): Tony Brown, 218, 1961-1981

Most League appearances: Tony Brown, 574, 1961-1981

Most capped player: Stuart Williams, 33, Wales, 1954-1962

Highest transfer fee paid: £1.25m to Preston North End for Kevin Kilbane, May 1997

Highest transfer fee received: £1.5m from Manchester United for Bryan Robson, October 1981

Major trophies: Division 1 (old) Champions **(1)** 1919-20
Division 2 (old) Champions **(2)** 1910-11, 1901-02
FA Cup Winners **(5)** 1968, 1954, 1931, 1892, 1888

Chris Adamson – A former YTS player, the reserve goalkeeper had to be patient with second-string football for most of 1997-98 but played three times in April, excelling against Huddersfield.

Jason van Blerk – The Australian player joined West Brom from Manchester City for £250,000 in March 1998 and immediately filled the left-back role.

Daryl Burgess – An adaptable defender who graduated from apprentice at the club, he overcame a troublesome leg injury late in 1997 and featured in 30 matches. He can play at right back, centre back or as sweeper.

Peter Butler – A much-travelled player, mostly with lower league experience, Butler was the club's midfield anchorman in 1997-98 and made nearly 40 appearances during the season.

Matt Carbon – An England Under-21 international snapped up from Derby County for £800,000 in February 1998, Carbon is Albion's most expensive defender. Quick and mobile, he impressed in his 16 appearances.

Stacy Coldicott – A local youngster, Coldicott was one of several players competing for a midfield berth in 1997-98. Keen and competitive, he featured 24 times, mostly as a substitute.

Paul Crichton – A vastly experienced keeper, formerly with Grimsby, he was replaced by Alan Miller and loaned out to Aston Villa in October 1997, returning to Albion towards the end of the season.

Tony Dobson – A defender with top-flight experience, having played for Coventry City and Blackburn Rovers, he made 15 appearances during 1997-98 but was unable to find a regular spot.

Micky Evans – West Brom fans had high hopes of Evans when he joined from Southampton in October 1997, but before he could make his debut the striker suffered a double fracture of the cheekbone when training with the Republic of Ireland and featured mainly as a substitute after that.

Sean Flynn – A tigerish midfielder, his non-stop running and willingness to have a crack at goal have been on display since he came from Derby in August 1997.

David Gilbert – On his day he can be a fine attacking midfielder, as he showed in his spell with Grimsby Town before signing for West Brom in August 1995, but he suffered a miserable time in 1997-98, making just four short appearances as substitute.

Paul Holmes – He began the 1997-98 season contesting the right-back berth with Andrew McDermott and came through to win the battle, making 35 appearances.

Lee Hughes – The striker recruited from non-League Kidderminster has been a Baggies' fan since boyhood. He began 1997-98 on the bench but forced his way into the starting line-up, finishing as joint leading scorer on 14 goals.

Kevin Kilbane – The young Republic of Ireland winger became the club's record signing in May 1997 at £1.25 million.

Andrew McDermott – The young Australian full back joined from Queen's Park Rangers in March 1997. His passing ability won him a place in the team early in the season, before Holmes replaced him.

Paul Mardon – Capped once by Wales, this highly rated central defender was excellent until November 1997 – when he fell victim to an injury which saw him out of action for the rest of the season.

Shaun Murphy – The Australian defender with Under-21 and Olympic Games experience was sidelined for the early part of the 1997-98 season after a hernia operation.

Graham Potter – He can play on the left side of defence or in midfield but only played five times in 1997-98 and was loaned to Northampton Town for a short spell in October 1997.

Brian Quailey – The young striker made five brief appearances as a substitute in 1997-98.

James Quinn – The Northern Ireland forward was considered a snip at £350,000 when he joined from Blackpool in February 1998, and is a favourite with fans.

Paul Raven – The long-serving Albion centre back played 12 games at the start of 1997-98 before injury forced him out of action in October.

Transferred in:
- Kevin Kilbane (Preston, £1.25m)
- Sean Flynn (Derby, £250,000)
- Micky Evans (Southampton, £500,000)
- Matt Carbon (Derby, £800,000)
- James Quinn (Blackpool, £350,000)
- Jason van Blerk (Manchester City, £250,000)

Transferred out:
- Paul Peschisolido (Fulham, £1.1m)
- Kevin Donovan (Grimsby, £300,000)
- Paul Groves (Grimsby, £250,000)
- Dave Smith (Grimsby, £100,000)
- Gareth Hamner (Shrewsbury, £10,000)
- Craig Herbert (Shrewsbury, free)
- Lee Knight (Hednesford, free)
- Roger Joseph (Leyton Orient, free)
- Nigel Spink (Millwall, free)
- Paul Agnew (Swansea, free)
- Michael Rodosthenous (Cambridge, free)
- Dean Craven (Shrewsbury, free)

Alan Miller – The former Arsenal, Middlesbrough and England Under-21 keeper arrived in March 1997. Big and commanding, Miller also has superb reflexes and played well throughout the 1997-98 season.

Andy Hunt – The former Newcastle United striker netted 14 times in 1997-98 despite often playing as the lone front man. He seemed destined to leave the club at one stage, but remained at The Hawthorns.

Richard Sneekes – The Dutchman was again the most creative player in West Brom's ranks in 1997-98, bringing other players into the game and triggering many fine moves with his vision.

Wolverhampton Wanderers *Football Club*

Wolverhampton Wanderers Football Club
Wolverhampton Wanderers Football Club
Wolverhampton Wanderers
Wolverhampton Wanderers
Wolverhampton Wanderers Football Club
Wolverhampton Wanderers Football Club
Wolverhampton Wanderers Football Club

→ Address | Wolverhampton Wanderers FC, Molineux Stadium, Waterloo Road, Wolverhampton WV1 4QR

Tel: 01902 655000 | **Tickets:** 01902 653653 | **Clubline:** 0891 121103

Wolves have played in FA Cup finals at five venues – the Oval (1889), Fallowfield, Manchester (1893), Crystal Palace (1896, 1908), Stamford Bridge (1921) and Wembley (1939, 1949, 1960).

Top row • M Jones • D Ferguson • C Robinson • S Osborn • G Crowe • J Wright • M Gilkes

Middle row • C Lee • D Goodman • N Emblen • S Sedgley • D Richards • J Bray • M Stowell • A Williams • D Foley • R Leadbetter • J Smith • M McGhee

Bottom row • M Hickman • D Hancock • R Keane • S Froggatt • M Atkins • S Bull • K Curle • S Corica • C Westwood • T Daley • B Holmes • T Davies

→ Web site: http://www.wolves.co.uk **→ Chairman:** Jonathan Hayward **→ Manager:** Mark McGhee **→ Year formed:** 1877

Ground: Molineux Stadium (28,500)

Stands: Jack Harris
John Ireland
Stan Cullis
Billy Wright

Home strip: Black and gold shirts with white trim, black shorts with gold trim, black and gold hooped socks

Away strip: White shirts with teal and gold trim, teal shorts with white and gold trim, teal socks with white and gold trim

Sponsor: Goodyear

Programme: £1.50

Nickname: Wolves

Ground history: 1877 Windmill Field
1879 John Harper's Field
1881 Dudley Road
1889 Molineux

Previous name: St Luke's

First League game: 8 September 1888, drew 1-1 (h) v Aston Villa

Record attendance: 61,315 v Liverpool, FA Cup 5th round, 11 February 1939

Record victory: 14-0 v Crosswells Brewery, FA Cup 2nd round, 13 November 1886

Record defeat: 1-10 v Newton Heath, Division 1, 15 October 1892

Highest League scorer (season): Dennis Westcott, 38, 1946-47

Highest League scorer (aggregate): Steve Bull, 247, 1986-1998

Most League appearances: Derek Parkin, 501, 1967-1982

Most capped player: Billy Wright, 105, England, 1946-1959

Highest transfer fee paid: £1.8m to Bradford City for Dean Richards, May 1995

Highest transfer fee received: £2m from Crystal Palace for Neil Emblen, August 1997

Major trophies: Division 1 (old) Champions **(3)** 1958-59, 1957-58, 1953-54
Division 2 (old) Champions **(2)** 1976-77, 1931-32
Division 3 (old) Champions **(1)** 1988-89
Division 3 (North) Champions **(1)** 1923-24
Division 4 Champions **(1)** 1987-88
FA Cup Winners **(4)** 1960, 1949, 1908, 1893
League Cup Winners **(2)** 1980, 1974

Mark Atkins – A Championship-winning midfielder with Blackburn, he signed for £1 million in September 1995. He can also play in defence and was his reliable self in 1997-98.

Steve Claridge – A journeyman striker who usually becomes a popular figure with fans for his whole-hearted commitment and workrate, he signed from Leicester in March 1998 but didn't have long to prove himself.

Steve Corica – A right-sided midfielder signed in February 1996, his second season was wrecked by a knee injury – after just four minutes of action.

Glenn Crowe – A physical young Irish striker who joined the club as a trainee, he made his debut as a substitute against Bradford in February 1998.

Neil Emblen – A yo-yo season saw the defender-midfielder sold to Crystal Palace for a record £2 million in the summer of 1997, only to return to Molineux for a cut-price £900,000 on deadline day.

Dominic Foley – The young Irishman made one start and six substitute appearances for Wolves before ending the season on loan to Watford.

Dougie Freedman – A live-wire striker signed from Crystal Palace in October 1997, Freedman started in style, including scoring a hat-trick against Norwich. But his form fell away and he ended the season on the bench.

Steve Froggatt – A left-winger who was tipped for great things with Aston Villa, he now plays as a wing back or in midfield and had an outstanding 1997-98 season despite injury.

Michael Gilkes – A pacy winger who signed in March 1997 for £150,000, he failed to break into the first team.

Don Goodman – A tough striker signed from Sunderland for £1.2 million in December 1994, he reached double figures in goals in 1997-98, including the strike which took the club to the FA Cup semi-finals.

Robbie Keane – A nippy, competitive striker who is one of the most exciting prospects in the Nationwide League and already a Republic of Ireland international, he finished as the club's top scorer in 1997-98.

Dariusz Kubicki – A tough-tackling, attacking full back, he played 16 games early in 1997-98 before being loaned out to Tranmere Rovers.

Kevin Muscat – A defender for Australia, he signed in October 1997 after a year at Crystal Palace. Strong in the tackle and good going forward, Muscat can operate on either flank.

Lee Naylor – A young left back who turned professional in July 1997, he produced a number of promising performances in his first full season.

Simon Osborn – A hard-working midfielder who causes problems for the opposition with his probing passes, he missed the start of 1997-98 but returned to become an important member of the squad.

Mixu Paatelainen – A big, powerful Finnish striker, he arrived from Bolton in the summer of 1997 and never really got a run in the side, although he still grabbed some vital goals.

Dean Richards – A highly rated central defender who missed the first half of 1997-98 with a serious knee injury, he returned on Boxing Day to shore up the defence with Curle.

Carl Robinson – After debuting in the last game of 1996-97, a break midway through the 1997-98 season appeared to restore his energy and he came back strongly in the midfield.

Steve Sedgley – A versatile player, he signed from Ipswich after spells at Coventry and Spurs and slotted effortlessly into the role of sweeper.

Hans Segers – A Dutch goalie sadly best-known for his trial over a betting scandal, he became an FA Cup hero with his penalty save against Leeds.

Paul Simpson – A left-winger with an excellent cross, he showed he is equally able to operate as a central striker after signing from Derby.

Robbie Slater – At his most effective down the right flank, Slater arrived on deadline day from Southampton.

Mike Stowell – An experienced goalkeeper, he missed out on FA Cup glory when gastric flu gave Hans Segers the chance to step in.

Chris Westwood – A Dudley-born young defender, he has progressed through the junior ranks and played six times up to Christmas 1997.

Adrian Williams – A tall, commanding central defender who has suffered his fair share of injuries in the past, he was again struck with hamstring and cruciate ligament problems this term.

Transferred in:
- Steve Sedgley (Ipswich, deal)
- Isidro Diaz (Wigan, contract)
- Paul Simpson (Derby, £75,000)
- Jason Roberts (Hayes, £250,000)
- Kevin Muscat (Palace, deal)
- Dougie Freedman (Palace, deal)
- Neil Emblen (Palace, £900,000)
- Robbie Slater (Southampton, £50,000)
- Steve Claridge (Leicester, £350,000)

Transferred out:
- Neil Emblen (Palace, £2m)
- Iwan Roberts (Norwich, £850,000)
- Mark Venus (Ipswich, deal)
- Brian Law (Millwall, free)
- Dennis Pearce (Notts County, free)
- Andy Thompson (Tranmere, free)
- Geoff Thomas (Forest, free)
- Jamie Smith (Palace, deal)
- Robert Sawyers (Barnet, free)
- Isidro Diaz (Wigan, free)
- Jermaine Wright (Crewe, £25,000)

Steve Bull – The highest scoring West Midlands-based player ever, thanks to well over 200 League goals, he struggled with injury in 1997-98, but still netted nine goals with his trademark hustling, all-action style.

Keith Curle – The team captain and inspiration at the centre of defence, Curle missed few games and was again vital to the 1997-98 League and Cup campaigns with his tough tackling, pace and good organisation.

Darren Ferguson – A hard-working midfielder destined to sit in the shadow of his more illustrious father, Alex, he was forced out by injury in early February but reappeared on the last day of the 1997-98 season.

Blackpool Football Club
Blackpool Football Club
Blackpool Football Club
Blackpool Football Club
Blackpool Football Club
Blackpool Football Club

246

Division Two

Blackpool *Football Club*

→ **Address** | Blackpool FC, Bloomfield Road Ground, Blackpool FY1 6JJ

Tel: 01253 405331 | **Tickets:** 01253 404331 | **Clubline:** 0891 121648

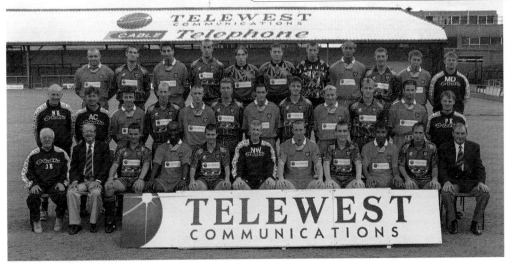

Vicki Oyston is the only female chairman of a professional football club in the country, having taken over from her husband in the 1996 close season.

Top row • G Brabin • J Quinn • C Malkin • T Butler • H Heighton • S Banks • P Barnes • C Carlisle • P Clarkson • J Cross • M Davies

Middle row • M Hennigan • A Crawford • P Carden • D Bradshaw • B Ormerod • A Rogan • K Russell • B Dixon • J Reed • J Lydiate • T Ellis • P Kelly

Bottom row • J Burke • F O'Donoghue • P Haddow • M Bryan • M Bonner • N Worthington • D Linighan • M Mellon • A Preece • L Philpott • J Chapman

→ **Web site:** http://www.cyberscape.co.uk/users/bfc → **Chairman:** Vicki Oyston → **Manager:** Nigel Worthington → **Year formed:** 1887

Ground: Bloomfield Road (11,295)

Stands: Telewest
North
East
West

Home strip: Tangerine shirts with navy blue trim, tangerine shorts with navy blue trim, tangerine socks with navy blue trim

Away strip: Navy blue shirts with tangerine trim, navy blue shorts with tangerine trim, navy blue socks with tangerine trim

Sponsor: Telewest Communications

Programme: £1.70

Nickname: Seasiders

Ground history: 1887 Raikes Hall Gardens
1897 Athletic Ground
1899 Raikes Hall Gardens
1899 Bloomfield Road

Previous name: None

First League game: 5 September 1896, Division 2, lost 1-3 (a) v Lincoln City

Record attendance: 38,098 v Wolverhampton Wanderers, Division 1, 17 September 1955

Record victory: 7-0 v Reading, Division 2, 7 November 1928
7-0 v Preston North End, Division 1, 1 May 1948
7-0 v Sunderland, Division 1, 5 October 1957

Record defeat: 1-10 v Small Heath, Division 2, 2 March 1901
1-10 v Huddersfield Town, Division 1, 13 December 1930

Highest League position: Division 1 (old), runners-up, 1955-56

Highest League scorer (season): Jimmy Hampson, 45, 1929-30

Highest League scorer (aggregate): Jimmy Hampson, 246, 1927-1938

Most League appearances: Jimmy Armfield, 568, 1952-1971

Most capped player: Jimmy Armfield, 43, England, 1952-1971

Highest transfer fee paid: £275,000 to Millwall for Chris Malkin, October 1996

Highest transfer fee received: £750,000 from Queen's Park Rangers for Trevor Sinclair, August 1993

Major trophies: Division 2 (old) Champions **(1)** 1929-30
FA Cup Winners **(1)** 1953

Bournemouth *Football Club*

Bournemouth Football Club
Bournemouth Football Club
Bournemouth Football Club
Bournemouth Football Club
Bournemouth Football Club
Bournemouth Football Club
Bournemouth Football Club
Bournemouth Football Club
Bournemouth Football Club
Bournemouth Football Club

→ **Address** | AFC Bournemouth, Dean Court Ground, Bournemouth, Dorset BH7 7AF

Tel: 01202 395381 | **Tickets:** 01202 395381 | **Clubline:** 0891 121163

Ted MacDougall scored 42 League goals in the 1970-71 season and a record nine in a single FA Cup match. In 1997-98, ninth placed Bournemouth scored 57 League goals and six FA Cup goals.

Top row • E Howe • A Griffin • O Coll • D Wells • J Glass • S Fletcher • R Murray • F Rolling

Middle row • S O'Driscoll • J Harrington • R Beardsmore • L Cotterell • J Williams • J Vincent • J O'Neill • N Young • S Hardwick

Bottom row • J Hayter • M Dean • J Jenkins • S Robinson • M Machin • I Cox • J Bailey • M Rawlinson • D Town

→ **Chairman:** Trevor Watkins   → **Manager:** Mel Machin   → **Year formed:** 1899

Ground: Dean Court (10,500)

Stands: Redknapp
 Bolton
 Newsham
 Norris

Home strip: Red and black shirts with white trim, black shorts, black socks

Away strip: Navy blue and yellow shirts, navy blue shorts, navy blue and yellow socks

Sponsor: Seward Rover

Programme: £1.60

Nickname: Cherries

Ground history: 1899 Castlemain Road
 1910 Dean Court

Previous names: Boscombe
 Bournemouth & Boscombe Athletic

First League game: 25 August 1923, Division 3 (South), lost 1-3 (a) v Swindon Town

Record attendance: 28,799 v Manchester United, FA Cup 6th round, 2 March 1957

Record victory: 11-0 v Margate, FA Cup 1st round, 20 November 1971

Record defeat: 0-9 v Lincoln City, Division 3, 18 December 1982

Highest League position: Division 2 (old), 12th place, 1987-88

Highest League scorer (season): Ted MacDougall, 42, 1970-71

Highest League scorer (aggregate): Ron Eyre, 202, 1924-1933

Most League appearances: Sean O'Driscoll, 423, 1984-1995

Most capped player: Gerry Peyton, 7, Republic of Ireland, 1986-1991

Highest transfer fee paid: £210,000 to Gillingham for Gavin Peacock, August 1989

Highest transfer fee received: £800,000 from Everton for Joe Parkinson, March 1994

Major trophies: Division 3 (old) Champions (1) 1986-87

Bristol Rovers *Football Club*

→ **Address** | Bristol Rovers FC, Memorial Ground, Filton Avenue, Horfield, Bristol BS7 0AQ

Tel: 0117 977 2000 | **Tickets:** 0117 909 8848 | **Clubline:** 0891 664422

If all of the 9,275 seats at the Memorial Ground were sold at the top ticket price of £18, it would net £166,950, enough to buy 982,205 programmes, with 88p left over for the bus fare home.

Top row • P Beadle • A Collett • A Tillson • S Higgs

Second row • J French • M Hayfield • J Perry • B Gayle • S Foster • J Alsop

Third row • J Trollope • P Kite • L Zabek • B Hayles • D Pritchard • T White • M Lockwood • G Power • L Martin • J Skinner

Bottom row • R Dolling • S Parmenter • J Law • P Bater • I Holloway • T Ramasut • J Cureton • G Penrice • F Bennett • R Kendall

→ **Chairman:** Denis Dunford   → **Manager:** Ian Holloway   → **Year formed:** 1883

Ground: Memorial Ground (9,275)

Stands: Centenary
West

Home strip: Blue and white quartered shirts, white shorts, blue socks

Away strip: Yellow shirts, black shorts, black socks

Sponsor: Cowlin Construction

Programme: £1.80

Nickname: Pirates

Ground history: 1883 Purdown
1897 Eastville
1986 Twerton Park
1996 Memorial Ground

Previous names: Black Arabs
Eastville Rovers
Bristol Eastville Rovers

First League game: 28 August 1920, Division 3, lost 0-2 (a) v Millwall

Record attendance: 8,078 v Bristol City, Division 2, 16 March 1997

Record victory: 7-0 v Brighton & Hove Albion, Division 3 (South), 29 November 1952
7-0 v Swansea City, Division 2, 2 October 1954
7-0 v Shrewsbury Town, Division 3, 21 March 1964

Record defeat: 0-12 v Luton Town, Division 3 (South), 13 April 1936

Highest League position: Division 2 (old), 6th place, 1958-59, 1955-56

Highest League scorer (season): Geoff Bradford, 33, 1952-53

Highest League scorer (aggregate): Geoff Bradford, 242, 1949-1964

Most League appearances: Stuart Taylor, 546, 1966-1980

Most capped player: Neil Slatter, 10, Wales, 1983-1989

Highest transfer fee paid: £370,000 to Queens Park Rangers for Andy Tillson, November 1992

Highest transfer fee received: £1.4m from Huddersfield Town for Marcus Stewart, July 1996

Major trophies: Division 3 (old) Champions **(1)** 1989-90
Division 3 (South) Champions **(1)** 1952-53

Burnley *Football Club*

→ **Address** | Burnley FC, Turf Moor, Burnley BB10 4BX

Tel: 01282 700000 | **Tickets:** 01282 700010 | **Clubline:** 0891 121153

The 1997-98 season ended in disappointment for former player-manager Chris Waddle, when the club just avoided relegation. New manager Stan Ternent, from Division One's Bury, took over in May 1998.

Top row • G Little • I Helliwell • V Overson • M Winstanley • M Beresford • C Woods • C Mawson • S Blatherwick • M Gentile • I Duerden • P Eastwood

Middle row • N Gleghorn • G Harrison • J Hoyland • A Cooke • R Huxford • C Carr-Lawton • P Smith • M Ford • D Matthew

Bottom row • M Williams • P Barnes • C Brass • C Vinnicombe • G Cowans • C Waddle • G Roeder • D Eyers • J Heffernan • P Weller • G West

→ **Web site:** http://www.clarets.co.uk   → **Chairman:** Frank Teasdale   → **Manager:** Stan Ternent   → **Year formed:** 1882

Ground: Turf Moor (22,546)

Stands: Endsleigh
Bob Lord
East
James Hargreaves

Home strip: Claret and blue shirts, claret shorts, blue socks

Away strip: Yellow and navy blue shirts, yellow shorts, yellow socks

Sponsor: P3 Computers

Programme: £1.70

Nickname: Clarets

Ground history: 1882 Turf Moor

Previous name: Burnley Rovers

First League game: 8 September 1888, Football League, lost 2-5 (a) v Preston North End

Record attendance: 54,775 v Huddersfield Town, FA Cup 6th round, 23 February 1924

Record victory: 9-0 v Darwen, Division 1, 9 January 1892
9-0 v Crystal Palace, FA Cup 2nd round replay, 10 February 1909
9-0 v New Brighton, FA Cup 4th round, 26 January 1957
9-0 v Penrith, FA Cup 1st round, 17 January 1984

Record defeat: 0-10 v Aston Villa, Division 1, 29 August 1925
0-10 v Sheffield United, Division 1, 19 January 1929

Highest League scorer (season): George Beel, 35, 1927-28

Highest League scorer (aggregate): George Beel, 178, 1923-1932

Most League appearances: Jerry Dawson, 522, 1907-1928

Most capped player: Jimmy McIlroy, 51, Northern Ireland, 1951-1962

Highest transfer fee paid: £350,000 to Birmingham City for Paul Barnes, September 1995

Highest transfer fee received: £750,000 from Luton Town for Steve Davis, August 1995

Major trophies: Division 1 (old) Champions (2) 1959-60, 1920-21
Division 2 (old) Champions (2) 1972-73, 1897-98
Division 3 (old) Champions (1) 1981-82
Division 4 (old) Champions (1) 1991-92
FA Cup Winners (1) 1914

Chesterfield Football Club
Chesterfield Football Club
Chesterfield Football Club
Chesterfield Football Club
Chesterfield Football Club
Chesterfield Football Club
Chesterfield Football Club

250

Chesterfield *Football Club*

→ **Address** | Chesterfield FC, Recreation Ground, Chesterfield, Derbyshire S40 4SX

Tel: 01246 209765 | **Tickets:** 01246 209765 | **Clubline:** 0891 555818

Kevin Davies became the club's record transfer when he signed for Southampton in May 1997 for £750,000. After just one season at the club, his value increased 10-fold and he went to Blackburn for £7.5 million.

Top row • J Lomas • T Lormor • A Leaning • B Mercer • D Carr • J Hewitt

Middle row • A Shaw • I Dunn • M Williams • S Wilkinson • I Breckin • A Morris • S Gaughan • C Beaumont • R Willis • L Rogers • D Rushbury

Bottom row • M Jules • T Curtis • C Perkins • K Randall • J Duncan • J Howard • P Holland • M Ebdon

→ **Chairman:** Norton Lea → **Manager:** John Duncan → **Year formed:** 1866

Ground: Recreation Ground (8,667)

Stands: Cross Street Terrace
Saltergate
Centre
Wing

Home strip: Royal blue shirts with red and white trim, royal blue shorts with red and white trim, royal blue socks with red and white trim

Away strip: Red shirts with blue and white trim, red shorts with blue and white trim, red socks with blue and white trim

Sponsor: Kenning (home)
GK Group (away)

Programme: £1.60

Nickname: Blues or Spireites

Ground history: 1866 Spital
1884 Recreation Ground

Previous name: Chesterfield Town

First League game: 2 September 1899, Division 2, lost 1-5 (a) v Sheffield Wednesday

Record attendance: 30,968 v Newcastle United, Division 2, 7 April 1939

Record victory: 10-0 v Glossop North End, Division 2, 17 January 1903

Record defeat: 0-10 v Gillingham, Division 3, 5 September 1987

Highest League position: Division 2 (old), 4th place, 1946-47

Highest League scorer (season): Jimmy Cookson, 44, 1925-26

Highest League scorer (aggregate): Ernie Moss, 161, 1969-1976, 1979-1981, 1984-1986

Most League appearances: Dave Blakey, 613, 1948-1967

Most capped player: Walter McMillen, 4, Northern Ireland, 1936-1939

Highest transfer fee paid: £150,000 to Carlisle United for Phil Bonnyman, March 1980

Highest transfer fee received: £750,000 from Southampton for Kevin Davies, May 1997

Major trophies: Division 3 (North) Champions **(2)** 1935-36, 1930-31
Division 4 Champions **(2)** 1984-85, 1969-70

Colchester United *Football Club*

Colchester Football Club
Colchester Football Club
Colchester Football Club
Colchester Football Club
Colchester Football Club
Colchester Football Club
Colchester Football Club
Colchester Football Club
Colchester Football Club
Colchester Football Club
Colchester Football Club

→ **Address** | Colchester United FC, Layer Road, Colchester, Essex CO2 7JJ

Tel: 01206 508800 | **Tickets:** 01206 508800 | **Clubline:** 0891 737300

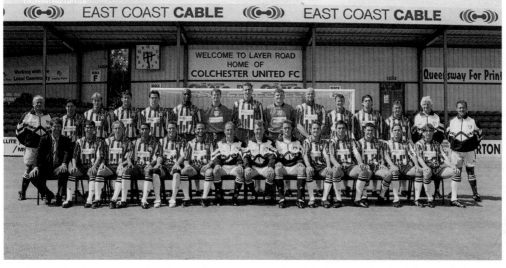

Top row • P Dyer • S Betts • T Adcock • R Wilkins • A Skelton • S Forbes • G Caldwell • M Sale • C Emberson • P Cawley • D Gregory • P Abrahams
• I Hathaway • B Owen • G Harrop **Bottom row** • S Evans • J Dunne • G Armitage • D Rainford • T Lock • R Bates • M Cook
• S Wignall • S Whitton • K Duguid • D Greene • N Haydon • P Buckle • S Stamps

In 1998-99, Colchester will be looking to better their best ever League position of 5th in the old Division 3, after a David Gregory goal in the play-off final against Torquay ensured Second Division football for the U's.

→ **Chairman:** Peter Heard   → **Manager:** Steve Wignall   → **Year formed:** 1937

Ground: Layer Road (7,619)

Stands: Barside Terrace
Layer Road
East Coast Cable
East Anglian Daily Times

Home strip: Blue and white striped shirts, blue shorts with white trim, white socks with blue trim

Away strip: Yellow shirts with navy trim, navy shorts with yellow trim, yellow socks with navy trim

Sponsor: Guardian Direct (home)
Ashby's (away)

Programme: £1.80

Nickname: U's

Ground history: 1937 Layer Road

Previous name: Colchester Town

First League game: 19 August 1950, Division 3 (South), drew 0-0 (a) v Gillingham

Record attendance: 19,072 v Reading, FA Cup 1st round, 27 November 1948

Record victory: 9-1 v Bradford City, Division 4, 30 December 1961

Record defeat: 0-8 v Leyton Orient, Division 4, 15 October 1989

Highest League position: Division 3 (old), 5th place, 1958-59, 1979-80

Highest League scorer (season): Bobby Hunt, 38, 1961-62

Highest League scorer (aggregate): Martyn King, 130, 1956-1964

Most League appearances: Micky Cook, 613, 1969-1984

Most capped player: None

Highest transfer fee paid: £50,000 to Ipswich Town for Neil Gregory, March 1998

Highest transfer fee received: £150,000 from Charlton Athletic for Mark Kinsella, September 1996

Major trophies: None

Division Two

Fulham *Football Club*

Fulham Football Club
Fulham Football Club
Fulham Football Club
Fulham Football Club
Fulham Football Club
Fulham Football Club

→ **Address** | Fulham FC, Craven Cottage, Stevenage Road, London SW6 6HH

Tel: 0171 384 4700 | **Tickets:** 0171 384 4700 | **Clubline:** 0891 440044

During the 1997-98 season, Fulham used 37 different players in the 56 League and Cup matches that they played, using 48 different combinations of the squad.

Top row • D Freeman • C Coleman • M Lawrence • I McGuckin • J Aggrey • P Moody • R Scott • T Thorpe • S Morgan

Middle row • J Marshall • A Smith • I Selley • R Carpenter • A Arnott • A Arendse • M Walton • M Conroy • S Stewart • M Blake • C Smith • J Nolan

Bottom row • R McAree • P Brooker • P Trollope • M Thomas • R Wilkins • P Bracewell • F Sibley • P Peschisolido • R Herrera • N Smith • S Hayward

→ **Website:** http://www.fulhamfc.co.uk   → **Chairman:** Mohamed Al Fayed   → **Manager:** Kevin Keegan   → **Year formed:** 1879

Ground: Craven Cottage (19,250)

Stands: Stevenage Road
Riverside
Hammersmith End
Putney End

Home strip: White shirts with black trim, black shorts, white socks

Away strip: Yellow shirts with black trim, black shorts, yellow socks

Sponsor: Demon Internet

Programme: £2

Nickname: Cottagers

Ground history: 1879 Star Road
Eel Brook Common
Lillie Road
Putney Lower Common
Ranelagh House

Barn Elms
Purser's Cross
Eel Brook Common
Half Moon
Captain James Field
1896 Craven Cottage

Previous name: Fulham St Andrews

First League game: 3 September 1907, Division 2, lost 0-1 (h) v Hull City

Record attendance: 49,335 v Millwall, Division 2, 8 October 1938

Record victory: 10-1 v Ipswich Town, Division 1, 26 December 1963

Record defeat: 0-10 v Liverpool, League Cup 2nd round, 1st leg, 23 September 1986

Highest League position: Division 1 (old), 10th place, 1959-60

Highest League scorer (season): Frank Newton, 43, 1931-32

Highest League scorer (aggregate): Gordon Davies, 159, 1978-1984, 1986-1991

Most League appearances: Johnny Haynes, 594, 1952-1970

Most capped player: Johnny Haynes, 56, England, 1952-1970

Highest transfer fee paid: £2.1m to Blackburn Rovers for Chris Coleman, December 1997

Highest transfer fee received: £333,333 from Liverpool for Richard Money, May 1980

Major trophies: Division 2 (old) Champions **(1)** 1948-49
Division 3 (South) Champions **(1)** 1931-32

Gillingham Football Club

Gillingham Football Club
Gillingham Football Club
Gillingham Football Club
Gillingham Football Club
Gillingham Football Club
Gillingham Football Club
Gillingham Football Club
Gillingham Football Club
Gillingham Football Club
Gillingham Football Club

→ **Address** | Gillingham FC, Priestfield Stadium, Redfern Avenue, Gillingham, Kent ME7 4DD

Tel: 01634 851854 | **Tickets:** 01634 851854 | **Clubline:** 0891 332211

The goalkeeper in Gillingham's record FA Cup win of 10-1, against Gorleston in November 1957, was the unfortunate 16-year-old Dennis Evans, who was making his debut.

Top row • W Jones • P Smith • S Tydeman • L Fortune West • R Edge • I Chapman • K Bremner **Second row** • T Pulis • N Masters • S Ratcliffe • G Butters • R Green • J Stannard • S Butler • G Thomas • A Pennock • M Bryant • L Parsons **Third row** • L Piper • M O'Connor • D Bailey • A Hessenthaler • P Scally • M Galloway • A Akinbiyi • J Pinnock • S Norman **Bottom row** • B Sinclair • D Bovis • P Hobbs • J Corbett • R Radbourne • T Osborne

→ **Chairman:** Paul Scally → **Manager:** Tony Pulis → **Year formed:** 1893

Ground: Priestfield Stadium (10,600)

Stands: New
Main
Rainham End
Gillingham End

Home strip: Blue shirts with red and white trim, blue shorts with red and white trim, white socks

Away strip: Red shirts with blue and white trim, red shorts with blue and white trim, red socks

Sponsor: Unknown

Programme: £1.60

Nickname: Gills

Ground history: 1893 Priestfield Stadium

Previous name: New Brompton

First League game: 28 August 1920, Division 3, drew 1-1 (h) v Southampton

Record attendance: 23,002 v Queen's Park Rangers, FA Cup 3rd round, 10 January 1948

Record victory: 10-0 v Chesterfield, Division 3, 5 September 1987

Record defeat: 2-9 v Nottingham Forest, Division 3 (South), 18 November 1950

Highest League position: Division 3 (old), 4th place, 1978-79

Highest League scorer (season): Brian Yeo, 31, 1973-74
Ernie Morgan, 31, 1954-55

Highest League scorer (aggregate): Brian Yeo, 136, 1963-1975

Most League appearances: John Simpson, 571, 1957-1972

Most capped player: Tony Cascarino, 3, Republic of Ireland, 1981-1987

Highest transfer fee paid: £250,000 to Norwich City for Ade Akinbiyi, January 1997

Highest transfer fee received: £1.2m from Bristol City for Ade Akinbiyi, May 1998

Major trophies: Division 4 Champions **(1)** 1963-64

Lincoln City *Football Club*

Lincoln City Football Club
Lincoln City Football Club
Lincoln City Football Club
Lincoln City Football Club
Lincoln City Football Club
Lincoln City Football Club
Lincoln City Football Club
Lincoln City Football Club
Lincoln City Football Club
Lincoln City Football Club
Lincoln City Football Club
Lincoln City Football Club

→ **Address** | Lincoln City FC, Sincil Bank Stadium, Lincoln LN5 8LD

Tel: 01522 880011 | **Tickets:** 01522 880011 | **Clubline:** 0930 555900

Ten years ago, in August 1988, Rick Ranshaw spent just two minutes on the pitch after replacing the injured Bobby Cumming – and then never played in the League again.

Top row • S Holmes • J Robertson • B Richardson • J Vaughan • M Hone • C Alcide

Middle row • S Bimson • P Miller • J Gowshall • J Whitney • C Stones • G Austin • D Chandler • L Thorpe • K Oakes

Bottom row • J Barnett • T Fleming • G Ainsworth • J Beck • S Westley • S Brown • J Martin • P Stant

→ **Web site:** http://isfa.com/server/web/Lincoln   → **Chairman:** John Reames   → **Caretaker manager:** Shane Westley   → **Year formed:** 1884

Ground: Sincil Bank (10,918)

Stands: South Park
Stacey West
Linpave
St Andrews
EGT Family

Home strip: Red and white striped shirts, black shorts with red trim, red socks with black trim

Away strip: Royal blue shirts with red and white trim, royal blue shorts with red and white trim, royal blue socks with red and white trim

Sponsor: Lincolnshire Echo

Programme: £1.70

Nickname: Red Imps

Ground history: 1883 John O'Gaunt's Ground
1894 Sincil Bank

Previous name: None

First League game: 3 September 1892, Division 2, lost 2-4 (a) v Sheffield United

Record attendance: 23,196 v Derby County, League Cup 4th round, 15 November 1967

Record victory: 11-1 v Crewe Alexandra, Division 3 (North), 29 September 1951

Record defeat: 3-11 v Manchester City, Division 2, 23 March 1895

Highest League position: Division 2 (old), 5th place, 1901-02

Highest League scorer (season): Allan Hall, 42, 1931-32

Highest League scorer (aggregate): Andy Graver, 143, 1950-1961

Most League appearances: Tony Emery, 402, 1946-1959

Most capped player: David 'Harry' Pugh, 3, Wales, 1900-1901
George Moulson, 3, Republic of Ireland, 1947-1948

Highest transfer fee paid: £75,000 to Carlisle United for Dean Walling, September 1997

Highest transfer fee received: £500,000 from Port Vale for Gareth Ainsworth, September 1997

Major trophies: Division 3 (North) Champions (**3**) 1951-52, 1947-48, 1931-32
Division 4 Champions (**1**) 1975-76

Luton Town Football Club
Luton Town Football Club
Luton Town Football Club
Luton Town Football Club
Luton Town Football Club
Luton Town Football Club
Luton Town Football Club

Luton Town *Football Club*

→ **Address** | Luton Town FC, Kenilworth Road Stadium, 1 Maple Road, Luton, Bedfordshire LU4 8AW

Tel: 01582 411622 | **Tickets:** 01582 416976 | **Clubline:** 0891 121123

Luton's Joe Payne entered the record books on 13 April 1936 when he scored 10 goals in the 12-0 win over Bristol Rovers. His record for the most goals in a League game remains unbeaten.

Top row • R Kean • S Evers • S Douglas • S Augustine • A Barr • P McLaren • S Davies • G Doherty • M Spring • I Jones • A Fotiadis • R Harvey • D Marshall

Second row • B Bird • C Newbery • C Goodyear • P Lowe • W Turner • P Showler • D Oldfield • M Thomas • N Abbey • I Feuer • K Davis • M Johnson • C Willmott • G Alexander

• J Moore • T Peake • K Leather • L Shannon **Third row** • L George • T Thorpe • S Davis • N Terry • D Kohler • L Lawrence • C Bassett • C Green • G Waddock • J James • T Sweeney

Bottom row • J Cox • R Lawes • S Fraser • D Howe • J Ayres • D Tate • N Webb • E Boyce • M Jerry • M McIndoe • A Scarlett • D McKoy

→ **Chairman:** David Kohler   → **Manager:** Lennie Lawrence   → **Year formed:** 1885

Ground: Kenilworth Road (9,975)

Stands: Main
New
Kenilworth Road
Oak Road
Executive Box

Home strip: White shirts with blue trim, blue shorts, blue and white socks

Away strip: Yellow shirts with blue trim, blue shorts, yellow socks with blue and red trim

Sponsor: Universal Salvage Auctions

Programme: £1.60

Nickname: Hatters

Ground history: 1885 Dallow Lane
1897 Dunstable Road
1905 Kenilworth Road

Previous name: Luton Wanderers
Luton Excelsior

First League game: 4 September 1897, Division 2, drew 1-1 (a) v Leicester Fosse

Record attendance: 30,069 v Blackpool, FA Cup 6th round replay, 4 March 1959

Record victory: 12-0 v Bristol Rovers, Division 3 (South), 13 April 1936

Record defeat: 0-9 v Small Heath, Division 2, 12 November 1898

Highest League position: Division 1 (old), 7th place, 1986-87

Highest League scorer (season): Joe Payne, 55, Division 3 (South), 1936-37

Highest League scorer (aggregate): Gordon Turner, 243, 1949-1964

Most League appearances: Bob Morton, 495, 1948-1964

Most capped player: Mal Donaghy, 58, Northern Ireland, 1980-1988

Highest transfer fee paid: £850,000 to OB Odense (Denmark) for Lars Elstrup, August 1989

Highest transfer fee received: £2.5m from Arsenal for John Hartson, January 1995

Major trophies: Division 2 (old) Champions **(1)** 1981-82
Division 3 (South) Champions **(1)** 1936-37
Division 4 Champions **(1)** 1967-68
League Cup Winners **(1)** 1988

Macclesfield Town *Football Club*

Macclesfield Town Football Club
Macclesfield Town Football Club
Macclesfield Town Football Club
Macclesfield Town Football Club
Macclesfield Town Football Club
Macclesfield Town Football Club
Macclesfield Town Football Club
Macclesfield Town Football Club

→ **Address** | Macclesfield Town FC, Moss Rose Ground, London Road, Macclesfield SK11 7SP

Tel: 01625 264686 | **Tickets:** 01625 264686 | **Clubline:** 0930 555835

Macclesfield Town have been promoted two seasons running – from the Vauxhall Conference to Division Two. They won the Conference in 1996-97 with the smallest playing squad in the League's history.

Top row • P Everson • D Gardner • S Whittaker • R Landon • S Payne • E Sodje • S Hitchen • A Mason • M Gardiner • P Davenport

Middle row • S Wade • D Ohandjianian • C Rose • S Wood • G Clyde • R Price • N Peel • N Sorvel • A Levendis • E Campbell

Bottom row • D Tinson • N Mitchell • S McIlroy • N Howarth • G Prescott • P Power • J Askey

→ **Web site:** http://www.mtfc.co.uk → **Chairman:** Alan Cash → **Manager:** Sammy McIlroy → **Year formed:** 1875

Ground: Moss Rose (6,685)

Stands: London Road Terrace
Silkmen Terrace
Estate Road
Star Lane End

Home strip: Blue shirts with white trim, white shorts with blue trim, blue socks with white trim

Away strip: White shirts with blue trim, blue shorts with white trim, white socks with blue trim

Sponsor: Bodycote

Programme: £1.50

Nickname: Silkmen

Ground history: 1891 Moss Rose

Previous name: Macclesfield

First League game: 9 August 1997, Division 3, won 2-1 (h) v Torquay United

Record attendance: 9,003 v Winsford United, Cheshire Senior Cup 2nd round, 14 February 1948

Record victory: 9-0 v Hartford St John's, FA Cup 1st Round, 8 November 1884

Record defeat: 7-0 v Walsall, FA Cup 2nd round, 6 December 1997

Highest League position: Division 3, runners-up, 1997-98

Highest League scorer (season): Steve Wood, 14, 1997-98

Highest League scorer (aggregate): Steve Wood, 14, 1997-98

Most League appearances: Ryan Price, 46, 1997-98

Most capped player: None

Highest transfer fee paid: £30,000 to Stevenage Borough for Efetobore Sodje, August 1997

Highest transfer fee received: £50,000 from Sheffield United for Mike Lake, 1988

Major trophies: None

Manchester City *Football Club*

Manchester City Football Club
Manchester City Football Club
Manchester City Football Club
Manchester City Football Club
Manchester City Football Club
Manchester City Football Club
Manchester City Football Club
Manchester City Football Club

→ **Address** | Manchester City FC, Maine Road, Moss Side, Manchester M14 7WN

Tel: 0161 224 5000 | **Tickets:** 0161 226 2224 | **Clubline:** 0891 121191

Despite an average crowd of over 30,000, and a 5-2 victory over Stoke in the final game of the 1997-98 season, Manchester City were relegated, subjecting them to their first season out of the top two divisions in their history.

Top row • I Brightwell • A Kernaghan • K Horlock • U Rosler • N Summerbee • L Crooks • J Foster • L Bradbury • T Vaughan • P Beesley **Middle row** • R Bailey • R Evans • R Money • E McGoldrick • N Heaney • G Brennan • M Margetson • T Wright • G Wiekens • R Ingram • C Greenacre • G Smith • A Stepney • I Miller
Bottom row • P Edwards • N Clough • G Creaney • P Dickov • S Thomas • G Kinkladze • F Clark • A Hill • K Symons • S Hiley • R Edghill • M Brown • M Phillips • A Hartford

→ **Web site:** http://www.mcfc.co.uk → **Chairman:** David Bernstein → **Manager:** Joe Royle → **Year formed:** 1880

Ground: Maine Road (33,148)

Stands: Main
Kippax
Platt Lane
North

Home strip: Sky blue-shirts with navy blue and white trim, white shorts with navy trim, navy blue socks with red and white trim

Away strip: Yellow and navy blue striped shirts, navy blue shorts with yellow trim, navy socks with yellow trim

Sponsor: Brother

Programme: £1.80

Nickname: Citizens

Ground history: 1880 Clowes Street
1881 Kirkmanshulme Cricket Ground
1882 Queens Road
1884 Pink Bank Lane

1887 Hyde Road
1923 Maine Road

Previous names: West Gorton St Mark's
Gorton FC
Ardwick

First League game: 3 September 1892, Division 2, won 7-0 (h) v Bootle

Record attendance: 84,569 v Stoke City, FA Cup 6th round, 3 March 1934

Record victory: 10-1 v Huddersfield Town, Division 2, 7 November 1987
10-1 v Swindon Town, FA Cup 4th round, 29 January 1930

Record defeat: 1-9 v Everton, Division 1, 3 September 1906

Highest League scorer (season): Tommy Johnson, 38, 1928-29

Highest League scorer (aggregate): Tommy Johnson, 158, 1919-1930
Eric Brook, 158, 1928-1939

Most League appearances: Alan Oakes, 565, 1959-1976

Most capped player: Colin Bell, 48, England, 1966-1979

Highest transfer fee paid: £3m to Portsmouth for Lee Bradbury, July 1997

Highest transfer fee received: £5m from Ajax for Georgi Kinkladze, June 1998

Major trophies: Division 1 (old) Champions **(2)** 1967-68, 1936-37
Division 2 (old) Champions **(6)** 1965-66, 1946-47, 1927-28, 1909-10, 1902-03, 1898-99
FA Cup Winners **(4)** 1969, 1956, 1934, 1904
League Cup Winners **(2)** 1976, 1970
Cup Winners Cup Winners **(1)** 1970

Millwall *Football Club*

→ **Address** | Millwall FC, The Den, Zampa Road, London SE16 3LN

Tel: 0171 232 1222 | **Tickets:** 0171 231 9999 | **Clubline:** 0891 400300

Millwall remained unbeaten at home for two years and nine months between April 1964 and January 1967, winning or drawing 59 League games in all.

Top row • S Aris • D Savage • A McLeary • B Law • T Witter • D Webber • K Stevens • S Fitzgerald • P Sturgess • D Hockton

Middle row • G Chapman • K Brown • R Newman • G Robertson • T Carter • J Connor • D Nurse • D Canoville • L McRobert • B Bowry • G Docherty

Bottom row • M Bircham • L Neill • J Dair • P Hartley • K O'Callaghan • B Bonds • P Holland • M Doyle • B Markey • G Lavin • P Allen

Chairman: Theo Paphitis → **Manager:** Keith Stevens → **Year formed:** 1885

Ground: The Den (20,146)

Stands: North
South
East
West

Home strip: Blue shirts with silver trim, silver shorts, blue socks with silver trim

Away strip: White shirts with black trim, black shorts, white socks with black trim

Sponsor: Live TV

Programme: £1.70

Nickname: Lions

Ground history: 1885 Glengall Road
1886 Manchester Road
1890 East Ferry Road
1901 North Greenwich
1910 The Den, Cold Blow Lane
1993 The Den, Zampa Road

Previous names: Millwall Rovers
Millwall Athletic

First League game: 28 August 1920, Division 3, won 2-0 (h) v Bristol Rovers

Record attendance: 20,093 v Arsenal, FA Cup 3rd round, 10 January 1994

Record victory: 9-1 v Torquay United, Division 3 (South), 29 August 1927
9-1 v Coventry City, Division 3 (South), 19 November 1927

Record defeat: 1-9 v Aston Villa, FA Cup 4th round, 28 January 1946

Highest League position: Division 1, 7th place, 1992-93

Highest League scorer (season): Richard Parker, 37, 1926-27

Highest League scorer (aggregate): Teddy Sheringham, 93, 1984-1991

Most League appearances: Barry Kitchener, 523, 1967-1982

Most capped player: Eamonn Dunphy, 22, Republic of Ireland, 1966-1971

Highest transfer fee paid: £800,000 to Derby County for Paul Goddard, December 1989

Highest transfer fee received: £2.3m from Crystal Palace for Andy Roberts, July 1995

Major trophies: Division 2 (old) Champions **(1)** 1987-88
Division 3 (South) Champions **(2)** 1937-38, 1927-28
Division 4 Champions **(1)** 1961-62

Northampton Town Football Club

→ **Address** | Northampton Town FC, Sixfields Stadium, Upton Way, Northampton NN5 5QA

Tel: 01604 757773 | **Tickets:** 01604 588338 | **Clubline:** 0839 664477

Ninety years ago, Northampton's most capped player, Edwin Lloyd-Davies, joined the club. By the time he left in 1914, he had entered the club's record books as the oldest player, at 42 years of age.

Top row • D Casey • C DeVito • J Hunt • C Lee • T Godden • L Colkin • J White • I Clarkson • G Thompson
Middle row • C Heggs • D Peer • D Brightwell • B Turley • I Sampson • A Woodman • D Martin • D Rennie • J Gayle
Bottom row • I Atkins • A Gibb • R Hunter • M Warner • R Warburton • P Conway • S Parrish • J Frain • K Wilson

→ **Web site:** http://web.ukonline.co.uk/ntfc → **Chairman:** Barry Ward → **Manager:** Ian Atkins → **Year formed:** 1897

Ground: Sixfields Stadium (7,653)

Stands: Dave Bowen
Alwyn Hargreaves
West
South

Home strip: Claret and white shirts with yellow trim, white shorts with claret and yellow trim, white socks with claret and yellow trim

Away strip: Orange shirts with black and white trim, black shorts with orange trim, black socks with white trim

Sponsor: Nationwide

Programme: £1.50

Nickname: Cobblers

Ground history: 1897 County Ground
1994 Sixfields

Previous names: None

First League game: 28 August 1920, Division 3, lost 0-2 (a) v Grimsby Town

Record attendance: 7,461 v Barnet, Division 3, 15 October 1994

Record victory: 10-0 v Walsall, Division 3 (South), 5 November 1927

Record defeat: 0-10 v Bournemouth and Boscombe Athletic, Division 3 (South), 3 September 1939

Highest League position: Division 1 (old), 21st place, 1965-66

Highest League scorer (season): Cliff Holton, 36, 1961-62

Highest League scorer (aggregate): Jack English, 135, 1947-60

Most League appearances: Tommy Fowler, 521, 1946-1961

Most capped player: Edwin Lloyd-Davies, 12, Wales, 1908-1914

Highest transfer fee paid: £90,000 to Bristol City for David Seal, September 1997

Highest transfer fee received: £265,000 from Watford for Richard Hill, July 1987

Major trophies: Division 3 (old) Champions **(1)** 1962-63
Division 4 (old) Champions **(1)** 1986-87

Notts County *Football Club*

Notts County Football Club
Notts County Football Club
Notts County Football Club
Notts County Football Club
Notts County Football Club
Notts County Football Club
Notts County Football Club
Notts County Football Club
Notts County Football Club
Notts County Football Club
Notts County Football Club

→ **Address** | Notts County FC, Meadow Lane, Nottingham NG2 3HJ

Tel: 0115 952 9000 | **Tickets:** 0115 955 7210 | **Clubline:** 0891 888684

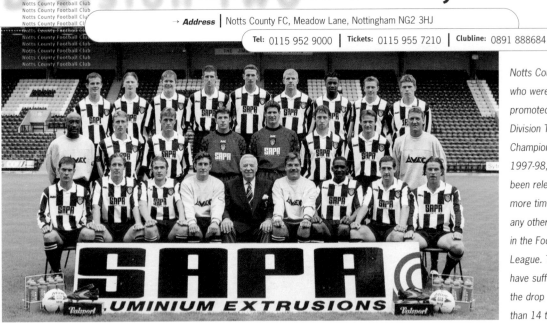

Notts County, who were promoted as Division Three Champions in 1997-98, have been relegated more times than any other club in the Football League. They have suffered the drop no less than 14 times.

Top row • B Marshall • P Mitchell • C Dudley • G Jones • I Barraclough • P Robinson • D Pearce • M Robson • S Finnan

Middle row • R Cleary • S Cunnington • I Hendon • D Ward • M Pollitt • S Derry • I Richardson • A Young

Bottom row • D Randall • G Strodder • M Redmile • M Smith • D Parvis • S Allardyce • D White • G Hogg • S Farrell

→ **Chairman:** Derek Pavis   → **Manager:** Sam Allardyce   → **Year formed:** 1862

Ground: Meadow Lane (20,300)

Stands: Kop
Family
Derek Pavis
Jimmy Sirrel

Home strip: Black and white striped shirts, black shorts, black socks with white trim

Away strip: Yellow shirts with black trim, yellow shorts with black trim, yellow socks with black trim

Sponsor: SAPA

Programme: £1.50

Nickname: Magpies

Ground history: 1862 The Park
1864 The Meadows
1877 Beeston Cricket Ground
1880 Castle Ground
1883 Trent Bridge Cricket Ground
1910 Meadow Lane

Previous name: Notts

First League game: 15 September 1888, Football League, lost 1-2 (a) v Everton

Record attendance: 47,310 v York City, FA Cup 6th round, 12 March 1955

Record victory: 15-0 v Rotherham Town, FA Cup 1st round, 24 October 1885

Record defeat: 1-9 v Blackburn Rovers, Division 1, 16 November 1889
1-9 v Aston Villa, Division 1, 29 September 1888
1-9 v Portsmouth, Division 2, 9 April 1927

Highest League position: Division 1 (old), 3rd place, 1900-01, 1890-91

Highest League scorer (season): Tommy Keetley, 39, 1930-31

Highest League scorer (aggregate): Les Bradd, 125, 1967-1978

Most League appearances: Albert Iremonger, 564, 1904-1926

Most capped player: Kevin Wilson, 15, Northern Ireland, 1990-1994

Highest transfer fee paid: £650,000 to Sheffield United for Tony Agana, November 1991

Highest transfer fee received: £2.5m from Derby County for Craig Short, September 1992

Major trophies: Division 2 (old) Champions **(3)** 1922-23, 1913-14, 1896-97
Division 3 Champions **(1)** 1997-98
Division 3 (South) Champions **(2)** 1949-50, 1930-31
Division 4 Champions **(1)** 1970-71
FA Cup Winners **(1)** 1894

Oldham Athletic *Football Club*

Oldham Athletic Football Club
Oldham Athletic Football Club
Oldham Athletic Football Club
Oldham Athletic Football Club
Oldham Athletic Football Club
Oldham Athletic Football Club
Oldham Athletic Football Club
Oldham Athletic Football Club
Oldham Athletic Football Club
Oldham Athletic Football Club
Oldham Athletic Football Club

→ **Address** | Oldham Athletic AFC, Boundary Park, Oldham OL1 2PA

Tel: 0161 624 4972 | **Tickets:** 0161 624 4972 | **Clubline:** 0891 121142

In June 1967, when Oldham played St Paul's of Salisbury in Rhodesia, a local witch doctor spread voodoo powers along the home team's goal line to prevent the Latics scoring. Oldham ran out 6-0 winners.

Top row • S Redmond • R Graham • D Hodgson • S Garnet • I Ormondroyd • L Sinnott • S McCarthy • B Hart • C Serrant

Middle row • B Urmson • T Orlygsson • M Allott • M Rush • I Ironside • G Kelly • A Holt • L Richardson • D McNiven • A Moreno

Bottom row • A Richie • S McNiven • S Barlow • L Duxbury • N Warnock • P Reid • P Rickers • A Hughes • R Reid

→ **Web site:** http://www.u-net.com/latics   → **Chairman:** Ian Stott   → **Manager:** Andy Ritchie   → **Year formed:** 1895

Ground: Boundary Park (13,700)

Stands: Seton
Ellen Group
George Hill
Lookers

Home strip: Blue shirts with white trim, blue shorts with white trim, blue socks with white trim

Away strip: White shirts with claret trim, claret shorts, claret socks

Sponsor: Slumberland

Programme: £1.50

Nickname: Latics

Ground history: 1895 Sheepfoot Lane
1905 Boundary Park

Previous name: Pine Villa

First League game: 9 September 1907, Division 2, won 3-1 (a) v Stoke

Record attendance: 47,671 v Sheffield Wednesday, FA Cup 4th round, 25 January 1930

Record victory: 11-0 v Southport, Division 4, 26 December 1962

Record defeat: 4-13 v Tranmere Rovers, Division 3 (North), 26 December 1935

Highest League position: Division 1 (old), runners-up, 1914-15

Highest League scorer (season): Tom Davis, 33, 1936-37

Highest League scorer (aggregate): Roger Palmer, 141, 1980-1994

Most League appearances: Ian Wood, 525, 1966-1980

Most capped player: Gunnar Halle, 37, Norway, 1991-1996

Highest transfer fee paid: £750,000 to Aston Villa for Ian Olney, June 1992

Highest transfer fee received: £1.7m from Aston Villa for Earl Barrett, February 1992

Major trophies: Division 2 (old) Champions **(1)** 1990-91
Division 3 (old) Champions **(1)** 1973-74
Division 3 (North) Champions **(1)** 1952-53

Preston North End *Football Club*

Preston North End Football Club
Preston North End Football Club
Preston North End Football Club
Preston North End Football Club
Preston North End Football Club
Preston North End Football Club
Preston North End Football
Preston North End Football
Preston North End Football Club
Preston North End Football Club
Preston North End Football Club
Preston North End Football Club

→ **Address** | Preston North End FC, Deepdale, Preston PR1 6RU

Tel: 01772 902020 | **Tickets:** 01772 902000 | **Clubline:** 0891 660220

Preston's most illustrious player was Tom Finney, who received a knighthood in 1998. A one-club man known as the 'Preston plumber', he played 473 games in all competitions for the club and scored 187 League goals.

Top row • S Davey • P Sparrow • D Reeves • J Squires • D Lucas • T Moilanen • C Murdock • S Gregan • R Kidd • J Darby

Middle row • M Rathbone • L Cartwright • K Nogan • P Morgan • M Jackson • G Parkinson • J Macken • L Ashcroft • M Appleton • D Barrick • B Hickson

Bottom row • P McKenna • G Atkinson • N McDonald • D Moyes • B Gray • G Peters • D Shaw • S Harrison • K O'Hanlon • M Rankine • M Holt

→ **Web site:** http://www.prestonnorthend.co.uk → **Chairman:** Bryan Gray → **Manager:** David Moyes → **Year formed:** 1881

Ground: Deepdale (21,000)

Stands: Tom Finney
North
Pavilion
Town End

Home strip: White shirts with silver and blue trim, white shorts with silver and blue trim, white socks with silver and blue trim

Away strip: Royal blue shirt with navy blue and green trim, royal blue shorts, royal blue socks with green trim

Sponsor: BAXI

Programme: £1.80

Nickname: Lilywhites or North End

Ground history: 1881 Deepdale

Previous name: None

First League game: 8 September 1888, Football League, won 5-2 (h) v Burnley

Record attendance: 42,684 v Arsenal, Division 1, 23 April 1938

Record victory: 26-0 v Hyde, FA Cup 1st round, 15 October 1887

Record defeat: 0-7 v Blackpool, Division 1, 1 May 1948

Highest League scorer (season): Ted Harper, 37, 1932-33

Highest League scorer (aggregate): Tom Finney, 187, 1946-1960

Most League appearances: Alan Kelly, 447, 1961-1975

Most capped player: Tom Finney, 76, England, 1946-1958

Highest transfer fee paid: £500,000 to Manchester United for Michael Appleton, August 1997

Highest transfer fee received: £1.2m from West Bromwich Albion for Kevin Kilbane, June 1997

Major trophies: Division 1 (old) Champions **(2)** 1889-90, 1888-89
Division 2 (old) Champions **(3)** 1950-51, 1912-13, 1903-04
Division 3 Champions **(1)** 1995-96
Division 3 (old) Champions **(1)** 1970-71
FA Cup Winners **(2)** 1938, 1889

Reading Football Club
Reading Football Club
Reading Football Club
Reading Football Club
Reading Football Club
Reading Football Club

Reading *Football Club*

→ **Address** | Reading FC, Madejski Stadium, Junction 11, M4, Reading, Berkshire RG2 0FL

Tel: 0118 968 1000 | **Tickets:** 0118 975 2853 | **Clubline:** 0891 121000

Reading will play the 1998-99 season in the brand new, purpose-built, 25,000 all-seater Madejski Stadium located five miles from Elm Park – in Division 2.

Top row • R Grant • S Swales • A Bernal • P Parkinson • M Thorp • B Hunter • L Hodges • T Morley • D Wdowczyk • A Pardew

Middle row • P Turner • K McPherson • C Asaba • S Lovell • S Bibbo • S Mautone • N Hammond • M Meaker • L Primus • D Caskey • K Dillon

Bottom row • A Harris • R Houghton • M Booty • B Glasgow • B Smith • T Bullivant • N Roach • A Freeman • J Lambert • M Williams • S Kean

→ **Web site:** http://www.readingfc.co.uk → **Chairman:** John Madejski → **Manager:** Tommy Burns → **Year formed:** 1871

Ground: Madejski Stadium (25,000)

Stands: Norfolk Road
 Suffolk Road
 Tilehurst Road
 Wantage Road

Home strip: Royal blue and white hooped shirts, white shorts with royal blue and white trim, royal blue and white hooped socks

Away strip: Burgundy and amber shirts, burgundy and amber shorts, burgundy and amber socks

Sponsor: Auto Trader

Programme: £1.80

Nickname: Royals

Ground history: 1871 Reading Recreation Ground and Reading Cricket Ground
 1882 Coley Park
 1889 Caversham Cricket Ground
 1896 Elm Park
 1998 Madejski Stadium

Previous names: Hornets
 Earley

First League game: 28 August 1920, Division 3, won 1-0 (a) v Newport County

Record attendance: 33,042 v Brentford, FA Cup 5th round, 19 February 1927

Record victory: 10-2 v Crystal Palace, Division 3 (South), 4 September 1946

Record defeat: 0-18 v Preston North End, FA Cup 1st round, 1894

Highest League position: Division 1, runners-up, 1994-95

Highest League scorer (season): Ronnie Blackman, 39, 1951-52

Highest League scorer (aggregate): Ronnie Blackman, 158, 1947-1954

Most League appearances: Martin Hicks, 500, 1978-1991

Most capped player: Jimmy Quinn, 17, Northern Ireland, 1993-1995

Highest transfer fee paid: £800,000 for Carl Asaba from Brentford, August 1997

Highest transfer fee received: £1.58m from Newcastle United for Shaka Hislop, August 1995

Major trophies: Division 2 Champions **(1)** 1993-94
 Division 3 (old) Champions **(1)** 1985-86
 Division 3 (South) Champions **(1)** 1925-26
 Division 4 Champions **(1)** 1978-79

Stoke City *Football Club*

→ **Address** | Stoke City FC, Britannia Stadium, Stanley Matthews Way, Stoke-on-Trent ST4 4EG

Tel: 01782 592222 | **Tickets:** 01782 592200 | **Clubline:** 0891 121040

Club president Sir Stanley Matthews holds the record for the longest League career – 32 years and 10 months. He is also England's oldest goalscorer, scoring against Northern Ireland aged 41 years and 248 days.

Top row • S Sturridge • R Wallace • P Thorne • J Whittle • C Muggleton • S Tweed • Z Angola • P Stewart • M McNally **Middle row** • A Grimes • M Birch
• G Stokoe • R Burgess • G McMahon • M Devlin • P Morgan • S Fraser • K Nyamah • M Macari • P Macari • D Talbot • S Woods • I Liversedge
Bottom row • R Heath • D Schreuder • G Kavanagh • A Pickering • L Sigurdsson • M Pejic • C Bates • A Griffin • K Keen • N Mackenzie • R Forsyth • D Crowe

→ **Vice-chairman:** Keith Humphreys   → **Manager:** Brian Little   → **Year formed:** 1863

Ground: Britannia Stadium (28,000)

Stands: North
McEwan
Sentinel
Signal Radio

Home strip: Red and white striped shirts, white shorts, red and white hooped socks

Away strip: White shirts with royal blue trim, royal blue shorts with white trim, royal blue socks with white trim

Sponsor: Britannia

Programme: £1.80

Nickname: Potters

Ground history: 1863 Sweeting's Field
1878 Victoria Ground
1997 Britannia Stadium

Previous names: Stoke Ramblers
Stoke
Stoke-upon-Trent

First League game: 8 September 1888, Football League, lost 0-2 (h) v West Bromwich Albion

Record attendance: 26,664 v Manchester City, Division 1, 3 May 1998

Record victory: 10-3 v West Bromwich Albion, Division 1, 4 February 1937

Record defeat: 0-10 v Preston North End, Division 1, 14 September 1889

Highest League position: Division 1 (old), 4th place, 1935-36

Highest League scorer (season): Freddie Steele, 33, 1936-37

Highest League scorer (aggregate): Freddie Steele, 142, 1934-1949

Most League appearances: Eric Skeels, 506, 1958-1976

Most capped player: Gordon Banks, 36, England, 1967-1972

Highest transfer fee paid: £580,000 for Paul Peschisolido from Birmingham City, July 1994

Highest transfer fee received: £2.35m for Mike Sheron from Queen's Park Rangers, January 1998

Major trophies: Division 2 (old) Champions **(3)** 1992-93, 1962-63, 1932-33
Division 3 (North) Champions **(1)** 1926-27
League Cup Winners **(1)** 1972

Walsall Football Club

→ **Address** | Walsall FC, Bescot Stadium, Bescot Crescent, Walsall WS1 4SA

Tel: 01922 622791 | **Tickets:** 01922 622791 | **Clubline:** 0891 555800

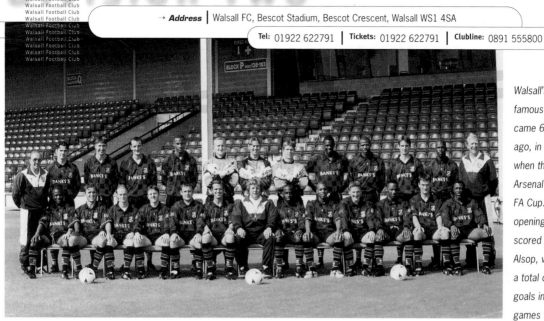

Walsall's most famous victory came 65 years ago, in 1933, when they beat Arsenal 2-0 in the FA Cup. The opening goal was scored by Gilbert Alsop, who scored a total of 169 goals in 222 games for Walsall.

Top row • T Bradley • D Rogers • I Roper • M Perry • C Platt • M Smith • D Nesbitt • J Walker • M Ricketts • J Williams • S Ryder • M Blake • E McManus

Bottom row • J Keister • W Evans • D Keates • G Porter • J Hodge • A Viveash • J Sorensen • R Boli • L Donowa

• W Thomas • A Watson • D Mountfield • D Beckford

→ **Web site:** http://www.saddlers.co.uk → **Acting chairman:** Mike Lloyd → **Manager:** Ray Grayden → **Year formed:** 1888

Ground: Bescot Stadium (9,000)

Stands: H L Fellows
Gilbert Alsop
Banks's
William Sharp

Home strip: Red shirts with black trim, red shorts with black trim, red socks with black trim

Away strip: Green shirts with black and white trim, black shorts with white trim, green socks with white trim

Sponsor: Banks's

Programme: £1.50

Nickname: Saddlers

Ground history: 1888 The Chuckery
1893 Wood Green Oval
1893 West Bromwich Road
1896 Hillary Street
1900 West Bromwich Road
1901 Hillary Street/Fellows Park
1990 Bescot Stadium

Previous name: Walsall Town Swifts

First League game: 3 September 1892, Division 2, lost 1-2 (h) v Darwen

Record attendance: 8,619 v Leeds United, FA Cup 3rd round, 7 January 1995

Record victory: 10-0 v Darwen, Division 2, 4 March 1899

Record defeat: 0-12 v Small Heath, Division 2, 17 December 1892
0-12 v Darwen, Division 2, 26 December 1896

Highest League position: Division 2 (old), 6th place, 1898-99

Highest League scorer (season): Gilbert Alsop, 39, 1933-34, 1934-35

Highest League scorer (aggregate): Tony Richards, 182, 1954-1963

Most League appearances: Colin Harrison, 473, 1964-1982

Most capped player: Mick Kearns, 15, Republic of Ireland, 1973-1978

Highest transfer fee paid: £175,000 to Birmingham City for Alan Buckley, June 1979

Highest transfer fee received: £600,000 from West Ham United for David Kelly, July 1988

Major trophies: Division 4 (old) Champions **(1)** 1959-60

Wigan Athletic *Football Club*

→ **Address** | Wigan Athletic FC, Springfield Park, Wigan WN6 7BA

Tel: 01942 244433 | **Tickets:** 01942 244433 | **Clubline:** 0891 121655

Wigan Athletic have spent their entire 66-year existence at Springfield Park. However, they are now gearing up for an August 1999 move to Robin Park. The new JJB Stadium will seat 25,000 people, 3.4 times more than Springfield.

Top row • T Black • D Lowe • C Bishop • I Kilford • P McGibbon • N Fitzhenry • G Johnson • B O'Connell

Middle row • S Farnworth • S Morgan • G Jones • L Butler • A Saville • R Carroll • P Rogers • S Green • J Benson

Bottom row • P Warne • D Lee • K Sharp • J Deehan • C Greenall • R Martinez • G Lancashire

→ **Chairman:** David Whelan   → **Manager:** John Deehan   → **Year formed:** 1932

Ground: Springfield Park (7,290)

Stands: Phoenix
St Andrew's
Springfield End
Shevington End

Home strip: Blue shirts with white trim, blue shorts with white and green trim, blue socks with white trim

Away strip: White shirts with green trim, white shorts with green trim, white socks with blue trim

Sponsor: JJB Sports

Programme: £1.50

Nickname: Latics

Ground history: 1932 Springfield Park

Previous name: None

First League game: 19 August 1978, Division 4, drew 0-0 (a) v Hereford United

Record attendance: 27,526 v Hereford United, FA Cup 2nd round, 12 December 1953

Record victory: 7-1 v Scarborough, Division 3, 11 March 1997

Record defeat: 1-6 v Bristol Rovers, Division 3, 3 March 1990

Highest League position: Division 3 (old), 4th place, 1985-86, 1986-87

Highest League scorer (season): Graeme Jones, 31, 1996-97

Highest League scorer (aggregate): Peter Houghton, 62, 1978-1984

Most League appearances: Kevin Langley, 317, 1981-1986, 1990-1994

Most capped player: Roy Carroll, 1, Northern Ireland, 1997
Pat McGibbon, 1, Northern Ireland, 1997

Highest transfer fee paid: £350,000 to Hull City for Roy Carroll, April 1997

Highest transfer fee received: £329,000 from Coventry City for Peter Atherton, August 1991

Major trophies: Division 3 Champions **(1)** 1996-97

Wrexham Football Club
Wrexham Football Club
Wrexham Football Club
Wrexham Football Club
Wrexham Football Club
Wrexham Football Club
Wrexham Football Club

Division Two

Wrexham Football Club

→ **Address** | Wrexham FC, Racecourse Ground, Mold Road, Wrexham LL11 2AH

Tel: 01978 262129 | **Tickets:** 01978 262129 | **Clubline:** 0891 121642

See the World. **Differently.**

MINERA ROOF TRUS
TEL WREXHAM (0978

Despite the fact that Wrexham celebrated their centenary in 1973 and are celebrating 125 years of existence in 1998, it has recently come to light that the club was actually formed in 1872, not 1873.

Top row • T Humes • K Connolly • L Edwards • A Marriott • M Cartwright • D Walsh • B Jones • M McGregor **Second row** • S Weaver • C Sear • G Shone • S Watkin • D Ridler • B Carey • D Spink • S Williams • D Brammer • K Russell • B Prandle • M Pejic **Third row** • S Hughes • W Phillips • G Owen • N Roberts • C Skinner • J Jones • B Flynn • K Reeves • P Hardy • P Ward • P Roberts • J Cross • D Hall **Bottom row** • D Brace • M Chalk • N Wainwright • A Griffiths • S Thomas • R Morris

→ **Chairman:** Pryce Griffiths   → **Manager:** Brian Flynn   → **Year formed:** 1872

Ground: Racecourse Ground (11,600)

Stands: Yale
Marstons
The Kop

Home strip: Red shirts with white trim, white shorts with red trim, white socks with red trim

Away strip: Gold shirts with navy blue trim, navy blue shorts with gold trim, navy blue socks with gold trim

Sponsor: Wrexham Lager (home strip)
Carlsberg (away strip)

Programme: £1.70

Nickname: Robins

Ground history: 1872 Acton Park
1872 Racecourse Ground

Previous name: None

First League game: 27 August 1921, Division 3 (North), lost 0-2 (h) v Hartlepools United

Record attendance: 34,445 v Manchester United, FA Cup 4th round, 26 January 1957

Record victory: 10-1 v Hartlepool United, Division 4, 3 March 1962

Record defeat: 0-9 v Brentford, Division 3, 15 October 1963

Highest League position: Division 2 (old), 15th place, 1978-79

Highest League scorer (season): Tom Bamford, 44, 1933-34

Highest League scorer (aggregate): Tom Bamford, 175, 1928-1934

Most League appearances: Arfon Griffiths, 592, 1959-1979

Most capped player: Dai Davies, 28, Wales, 1977-1981

Highest transfer fee paid: £210,000 to Liverpool for Joey Jones, October 1978

Highest transfer fee received: £700,000 from Birmingham City for Bryan Hughes, March 1997

Major trophies: Division 3 (old) Champions **(1)** 1977-78

Wycombe Wanderers *Football Club*

→ **Address** | Wycombe Wanderers FC, Adams Park, Hillbottom Road, High Wycombe, Bucks HP12 4HJ

Tel: 01494 472100 | **Tickets:** 01494 441118 | **Clubline:** 0891 446855

The club's most successful manager was Martin O'Neill, now Leicester City's manager. He won more than 50% of matches for the club, taking them from the Vauxhall Conference to Division 2 in just over five years.

Top row • G Wraight • M Harkin • K Ryan • K Scott • A Beeton • S Brown • A Patton

Middle row • A Cole • J Kavanagh • P McCarthy • M Taylor • B Parkin • M Forsyth • J Cornforth • D Jones

Bottom row • J Cousins • M Simpson • M Stallard • R Hill • J Gregory • N Smillie • P Read • S McGavin • D Carroll

→ **Web site:** http://www.wycombewanderers.co.uk → **Chairman:** Ivor Beeks → **Manager:** Neil Smillie → **Year formed:** 1884

Ground: Adams Park (10,000)

Stands: Amersham and Wycombe College
Servispak
Valley Terrace
Roger Vere

Home strip: Navy and sky blue quartered shirts, navy shorts with sky blue trim, navy socks with sky blue trim

Away strip: Yellow and navy blue quartered shirts, yellow shorts, yellow socks

Sponsor: Verco

Programme: £1.80

Nickname: Chairboys

Ground history: 1884 The Rye
1895 Loakes Park
1991 Adams Park

Previous name: None

First League game: 14 August 1993, Division 3, drew 2-2 (a) v Carlisle United

Record attendance: 9,007 v West Ham United, FA Cup 3rd round, 7 January 1995

Record victory: 5-0 v Burnley, Division 2, 15 April 1997
5-0 v Hitchen Town, FA Cup 2nd round, 3 December 1994

Record defeat: 0-5 v Walsall, Auto Windscreens Shield 1st round, 7 November 1995

Highest League position: Division 2, 6th place, 1994-95

Highest League scorer (season): Miguel Desouza, 18, 1995-96

Highest League scorer (aggregate): Miguel Desouza, 29, 1995-1997

Most League appearances: Dave Carroll, 206, 1993-1998

Most capped player: None

Highest transfer fee paid: £150,000 to Coventry City for John Williams, August 1995

Highest transfer fee received: £375,000 from Swindon Town for Keith Scott, November 1993

Major trophies: None

York City *Football Club*

→ **Address** | York City FC, Bootham Crescent, York YO3 7AQ

Tel: 01904 624447 | **Tickets:** 01904 624447 | **Clubline:** 0891 121643

Sixty years ago, in March 1938, York registered a record attendance of 28,123 against Huddersfield Town at Bootham Crescent. Today, the same ground can take 8,975 fans, less than one third of the record number.

Top row • M Tinkler • M Reed • J Sharples • T Barras • A Warrington • M Samways • N Tolson • S Tutill • A Pouton • N Campbell
Middle row • D Bell • S Bushell • R Cresswell • D Rush • A Little • A McMillan • J Greening • W Hall • J Miller
Bottom row • G Himsworth • G Bull • P Atkinson • R Rowe • G Murty • S Jordan • P Stephenson

→ **Chairman:** Douglas Craig → **Manager:** Alan Little → **Year formed:** 1922

Ground: Bootham Crescent (8,975)

Stands: Main
Popular
David Longhurst
Grosvenor Road

Home strip: Red shirts with blue and white trim, red shorts with blue and white trim, red socks with blue hoops

Away strip: Blue and black striped shirts, black shorts, blue socks

Sponsor: Portakabin

Programme: £1.75

Nickname: Minstermen

Ground history: 1922 Fulfordgate
1932 Bootham Crescent

Previous name: None

First League game: 31 August 1929, Division 3 (North), won 2-0 (a) v Wigan Borough

Record attendance: 28,123 v Huddersfield Town, FA Cup 6th round, 5 March 1938

Record victory: 9-1 v Southport, Division 3 (North), 2 February 1957

Record defeat: 0-12 v Chester, Division 3 (North), 1 February 1936

Highest League position: Division 2 (old), 15th place, 1974-75

Highest League scorer (season): Bill Fenton, 31, 1951-52
Arthur Bottom, 31, 1954-55, 1955-56

Highest League scorer (aggregate): Norman Wilkinson, 125, 1954-1966

Most League appearances: Barry Jackson, 481, 1958-1970

Most capped player: Peter Scott, 7, Northern Ireland, 1976-1978

Highest transfer fee paid: £140,000 to Burnley for Adrian Randall, December 1995

Highest transfer fee received: £450,000 from Port Vale for Jon McCarthy, July 1995

Major trophies: Division 4 Champions **(1)** 1983-84

Barnet Football Club
Barnet Football Club
Barnet Football Club
Barnet Football Club
Barnet Football Club
Barnet Football Club

270

Barnet *Football Club*

→ **Address** | Barnet FC, Underhill Stadium, Barnet Lane, Barnet, Herts EN5 2BE

Tel: 0181 441 6932 | **Tickets:** 0181 449 6325 | **Clubline:** 0891 121544

Barnet have the smallest ground capacity of any team in the Football League. The Underhill Stadium holds just 4,057 people. Until 1926, the club was still holding its meetings in the Red Lion pub on Barnet Hill.

Top row • G Anderson • U Onwere • S Serle • R Sawyers • M Basham • J Doolan • L Howarth • L Harrison • G Heald • M Brady • P Wilson • D Samuels • T Mustafa

Bottom row • T McMenemy • S Devine • K Charlery • S McGliesh • K Adams • P Simpson • S Stockley • W Goodhind • B Manuel • M Harle • J Ford

→ **Chairman:** Tony Kleanthous → **Manager:** John Still → **Year formed:** 1888

Ground: Underhill Stadium (4,057)

Stands: Main
South
North Terrace
East Terrace

Home strip: Amber and black shirts, black shorts, white socks

Away strip: Blue shirts, blue shorts, blue socks

Sponsor: Loaded

Programme: £1.50

Nickname: Bees

Ground history: 1888 Queens Road
1901 Totteridge Lane
1907 Underhill Stadium

Previous name: Barnet Alston

First League game: 17 August 1991, Division 4, lost 4-7 (h) v Crewe Alexandra

Record attendance: 11,026 v Wycombe Wanderers, FA Amateur Cup 4th round, 1951-52

Record victory: 6-0 v Lincoln City, Division 4, 4 September 1991

Record defeat: 0-6 v Port Vale, Division 2, 21 August 1993

Highest League position: Division 2, 24th place, 1993-94

Highest League scorer (season): Gary Bull, 20, 1991-92

Highest League scorer (aggregate): Sean Devine, 46, 1991-1998

Most League appearances: Paul Wilson, 216, 1991-1998

Most capped player: None

Highest transfer fee paid: £130,000 to Peterborough United for Greg Heald, August 1997

Highest transfer fee received: £800,000 from Crystal Palace for Dougie Freedman, September 1995

Major trophies: None

Brentford *Football Club*

→ **Address** | Brentford FC, Griffin Park, Braemar Road, Brentford, Middlesex TW8 0NT

Tel: 0181 847 2511 | **Tickets:** 0181 847 2511 | **Clubline:** 0891 121108

During their first season in Division Four in 1962-63, Brentford became the first club to play against all 91 teams then comprising the Football League.

Top row • M Bent • D McGhee • R Goddard • R Taylor • J Bates • C Hutchings • G Hurdle

Middle row • J Omigie • G Duffy • L Harvey • T Fernandes • K Dearden • G Benstead • S Myall • K Dennis

Bottom row • R Denys • S Spencer • I Anderson • C Oatway • S Canham • S Wormall • K Rapley • P Barrowcliff

→ **Web site:** http://www.redweb.co.uk/brentford   → **Chairman:** Tony Swaisland   → **Manager:** Micky Adams   → **Year formed:** 1889

Ground: Griffin Park (12,763)

Stands: Brook Road
New Road
Braemar Road
Ealing Road Terrace

Home strip: Red and white striped shirts, black shorts, black socks with red trim

Away strip: Blue and yellow shirts, blue shorts with yellow trim, yellow socks with blue trim

Sponsor: GMB

Programme: £1.50

Nickname: Bees

Ground history: 1889 Clifden House Ground
1892 Benns Field
1895 Shotters Field
1898 Cross Roads
1900 Boston Park
1904 Griffin Park

Previous name: None

First League game: 28 August 1920, Division 3 (South), lost 0-3 (a) v Exeter City

Record attendance: 38,678 v Leicester City, FA Cup 6th round, 26 February 1949

Record victory: 9-0 v Wrexham, Division 3, 15 October 1963

Record defeat: 0-7 v Swansea Town, Division 3 (South), 8 November 1924
0-7 v Walsall, Division 3 (South), 19 January 1957

Highest League position: Division 1 (old), 5th place, 1935-36

Highest League scorer (season): Jack Holliday, 38, 1932-33

Highest League scorer (aggregate): Jim Towers, 153, 1954-1961

Most League appearances: Ken Coote, 514, 1949-1964

Most capped player: John Buttigieg, 14, Malta, 1988-1990

Highest transfer fee paid: £275,000 to Chelsea for Joe Allon, November 1992

Highest transfer fee received: £800,000 from Reading for Carl Asaba, August 1997

Major trophies: Division 2 (old) Champions **(1)** 1934-35
Division 3 (old) Champions **(1)** 1991-92
Division 3 (South) Champions **(1)** 1932-33
Division 4 Champions **(1)** 1962-63

Brighton & Hove Albion *Football Club*

Brighton & Hove Albion Football Club
Brighton & Hove Albion Football Club
Brighton & Hove Albion Football Club
Brighton & Hove Albion Football Club
Brighton & Hove Albion Football Club
Brighton & Hove Albion Football Club
Brighton & Hove Albion Football Club
Brighton & Hove Albion Football Club
Brighton & Hove Albion Football Club
Brighton & Hove Albion Football Club
Brighton & Hove Albion Football Club

→ **Address** | Brighton & Hove Albion FC, 118 Queens Road, Brighton BN1 3XG

Tel: 01273 778855 | **Tickets:** 01273 778855 | **Clubline:** 0891 800609

For the second season in succession, Brighton have avoided the drop into non-League football by one position – at the expense of Hereford United in 1996-97 and Doncaster Rovers in 1997-98.

Top row • J Jackson • R Reinelt • R McNally • P Smith • M Morris • J Humphrey • S Tuck • M Stuart

Middle row • K Mayo • C Maskell • J Rowlands • M Ormerod • S Storer • R Johnson • N Rust • D Allan • D Mundee • P Armstrong

Bottom row • J Riddell • G Hobson • I Baird • P McDonald • S Gritt • J Minton • E Saul • J Westcott • J Wood

→ **Web site:** http://www.seagulls.co.uk   → **Chairman:** Dick Knight   → **Manager:** Brian Horton   → **Year formed:** 1901

Ground: Priestfield Stadium (10,422)

Stands: Redfern Avenue
Gillingham End
Rainham End
Gordon Road

Home strip: Blue and white shirts, blue shorts with red and white trim, white socks with blue and red trim

Away strip: Red shirts with blue and white trim, red shorts with blue and white trim, red socks with blue and white trim

Sponsor: Sandtex

Programme: £1.50

Nickname: Seagulls

Ground history: 1901 County Ground
1902 Goldstone Ground
1997 Priestfield Stadium

Previous name: None

First League game: 28 August 1920, Division 3, lost 0-2 (a) v Southend United

Record attendance: 9,890 v Lincoln City, Division 3, 2 May 1998

Record victory: 10-1 v Wisbech Town, FA Cup 1st round, 13 November 1965

Record defeat: 0-9 v Middlesbrough, Division 2, 23 August 1958

Highest League position: Division 1 (old), 13th place, 1981-82

Highest League scorer (season): Peter Ward, 32, 1976-77

Highest League scorer (aggregate): Tommy Cook, 114, 1921-1929

Most League appearances: Tug Wilson, 509, 1922-1936

Most capped player: Steve Penney, 17, Northern Ireland, 1983-1991

Highest transfer fee paid: £500,000 to Manchester United for Andy Ritchie, October 1980

Highest transfer fee received: £900,000 from Liverpool for Mark Lawrenson, August 1981

Major trophies: Division 3 (South) Champions **(1)** 1957-58
Division 4 Champions **(1)** 1964-65

Cambridge United *Football Club*

→ **Address** | Cambridge United FC, Abbey Stadium, Newmarket Road, Cambridge CB5 8LN

Tel: 01223 566500 | **Tickets:** 01223 566500 | **Clubline:** 0891 555885

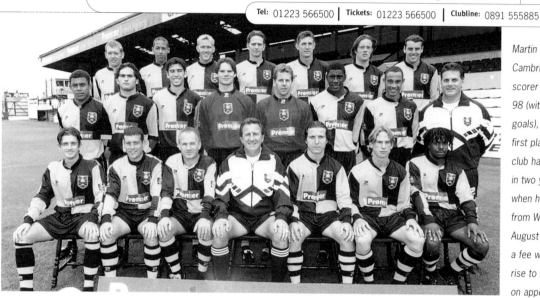

Martin Butler, Cambridge's top scorer in 1997-98 (with 13 goals), was the first player the club had paid for in two years when he signed from Walsall in August 1997 for a fee which could rise to £22,500 on appearances.

Top row • P Wilson • M Joseph • J Campbell • C Foster • J Taylor • I Ashbee • P Wanless
Middle row • M Kyd • A Hayes • B Chenery • S Marshall • S Barrett • T Benjamin • J Barnwell • K Steggles
Bottom row • D Williamson • J Rees • D Preece • R McFarland • B Beall • A Wilde • M Joseph

→ **Web site:** http://www.cambridgeunited.com → **Chairman:** Reg Smart → **Manager:** Roy McFarland → **Year formed:** 1919

Ground: Abbey Stadium (9,667)

Stands: Main
Habbin
North Terrace
South Terrace

Home strip: Amber shirts with black trim, black shorts, black socks

Away strip: Light blue and dark blue shirts, dark blue shorts, dark blue socks

Sponsor: Premier

Programme: £1.50

Nickname: U's

Ground history: 1919 Abbey Stadium

Previous name: Abbey United

First League game: 15 August 1970, Division 4, drew 1-1 (h) v Lincoln City

Record attendance: 14,000 v Chelsea, friendly, 1 May 1970

Record victory: 7-2 v Cardiff City, Division 2, 7 May 1994

Record defeat: 0-6 v Aldershot, Division 3, 13 April 1974
0-6 v Darlington, Division 4, 28 September 1974
0-6 v Chelsea, Division 2, 15 January 1983

Highest League position: Division 2 (old), 8th place, 1979-80

Highest League scorer (season): David Crown, 24, 1985-86

Highest League scorer (aggregate): Alan Biley, 74, 1975-1980

Most League appearances: Steve Spriggs, 416, 1975-1987

Most capped player: Tom Finney, 7, Northern Ireland, 1979-1980

Highest transfer fee paid: £190,000 to Luton Town for Steve Claridge, November 1992

Highest transfer fee received: £1m from Manchester United for Dion Dublin, August 1992

Major trophies: Division 3 (old) Champions (1) 1990-91

Cardiff City *Football Club*

Cardiff City Football Club
Cardiff City Football Club
Cardiff City Football Club
Cardiff City Football Club
Cardiff City Football Club
Cardiff City Football Club
Cardiff City Football Club
Cardiff City Football Club
Cardiff City Football Club
Cardiff City Football Club

→ **Address** | Cardiff City FC, Ninian Park, Cardiff CF1 8SX

Tel: 01222 398636 | **Tickets:** 01222 398636 | **Clubline:** 0891 121171

Cardiff City are the only team in 117 years of the FA Cup to have taken the prestigious trophy out of England, when they defeated Arsenal 1-0 in April 1927.

Top row • J Eckhard • S Young • J Fowler • M Harris • L Jarman • K Nugent • K Lloyd • L Phillips

Middle row • J Cross • J Rollo • J Rendall • J Hallworth • T Elliott • S White • C Dale

Bottom row • C Beech • G Stoker • S Partridge • D Penney • A Carss • W O'Sullivan • C Middleton

→ **Web site:** http://www.styrotech.co.uk/ccafc → **Chairman:** Samesh Kumar → **Manager:** Frank Burrows → **Year formed:** 1899

Ground: Ninian Park (14,980)

Stands: Canton
Popular Bank
Grange End Terrace
Grandstand

Home strip: Blue shirts with white sleeves, white shorts, white socks with blue trim

Away strip: Yellow shirts, blue shorts, yellow socks

Sponsor: CMB

Programme: £1.60

Nickname: Bluebirds

Ground history: 1899 Riverside
Sophia Gardens
Old Park
Fir Gardens
1910 Ninian Park

Previous name: Riverside
Riverside Albion

First League game: 28 August 1920, Division 2, won 5-2 (a) v Stockport County

Record attendance: 57,893 v Arsenal, Division 1, 22 April 1953

Record victory: 9-2 v Thames United, Division 3 (South), 6 February 1932

Record defeat: 2-11 v Sheffield United, Division 1, 1 January 1926

Highest League position: Division 1 (old), runners-up, 1923-24

Highest League scorer (season): Stan Richards, 30, 1946-47

Highest League scorer (aggregate): Len Davies, 127, 1920-1931

Most League appearances: Phil Dwyer, 471, 1972-1985

Most capped player: Alf Sherwood, 39, Wales, 1946-1956

Highest transfer fee paid: £180,000 to San Jose Earthquakes (USA) for Godfrey Ingram, September 1982

Highest transfer fee received: £500,000 from Coventry City for Simon Haworth, May 1997

Major trophies: Division 3 Champions **(1)** 1992-93
Division 3 (South) Champions **(1)** 1946-47
FA Cup Winners **(1)** 1927

Carlisle United *Football Club*

→ **Address** | Carlisle United AFC, Brunton Park, Carlisle CA1 1LL

Tel: 01228 526237 | **Tickets:** 01228 526237 | **Clubline:** 0891 230011

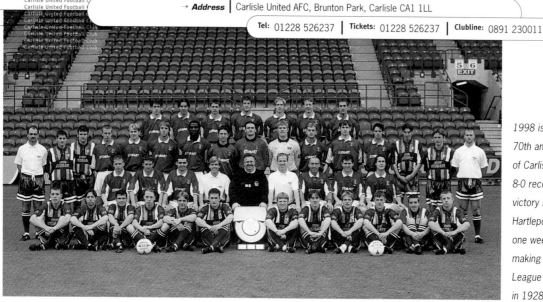

1998 is the 70th anniversary of Carlisle's 8-0 record victory against Hartlepool – just one week after making their League debut, in 1928.

Top row • J Hampton • L Taylor • P Boertien • R Milligan • K Sandwith • J Thorpe • T Harrison

Second row • P Devlin • J Benson • K Swanson • B Barr • T Hooper • R Bowman • S Pounewatchy • M Swann • T Caig • G Dixon • W Varty • R Delap • M Jansen

• E Harrison • L Bell • N Dalton **Third row** • G McAlindon • A Couzens • O Archdeacon • D Wilkes • M Knighton • J Halpin • W Aspinall • I Stevens • R Prokas

Bottom row • S Miller • L Burton • B Stevens • J Hewe • A Douglas • C Barton • M Jones • C Thompson • J Heath • A Hodgson • M Irving • G Skelton

→ **Chairman:** Michael Knighton   → **First team coaches:** David Wilkes and John Halpin   → **Year formed:** 1904

Ground: Brunton Park (16,300)

Stands: Petteril End
East
West
Warwick Road End

Home strip: Blue shirts with white and red trim, white shorts with blue and red trim, white socks with blue and red trim

Away strip: Gold shirts with green, red and white stripes, gold shorts with green and red trim, gold socks with green trim

Sponsor: Eddie Stobart

Programme: £1.50

Nickname: Cumbrians or Blues

Ground history: 1904 Milholme Bank
1905 Devonshire Park
1909 Brunton Park

Previous name: Shaddongate United

First League game: 25 August 1928, Division 3 (North), won 3-2 (a) v Accrington Stanley

Record attendance: 27,500 v Birmingham City, FA Cup 3rd round, 5 January 1957
27,500 v Middlesbrough, FA Cup 5th round, 7 February 1970

Record victory: 8-0 v Hartlepool United, Division 3 (North), 1 September 1928
8-0 v Scunthorpe United, Division 3 (North), 25 December 1952

Record defeat: 1-11 v Hull City, Division 3 (North), 14 January 1939

Highest League position: Division 1 (old), 22nd place, 1974-75

Highest League scorer (season): Jimmy McConnell, 42, 1928-29

Highest League scorer (aggregate): Jimmy McConnell, 126, 1928-1932

Most League appearances: Alan Ross, 466, 1963-1979

Most capped player: Eric Welsh, 4, Northern Ireland, 1966-1967

Highest transfer fee paid: £121,000 to Notts County for David Reeves, December 1993

Highest transfer fee received: £1m from Crystal Palace for Matt Jansen, January 1998

Major trophies: Division 3 Champions **(1)** 1994-95
Division 3 (old) Champions **(1)** 1964-65

Chester City Football Club
Chester City Football Club
Chester City Football Club
Chester City Football Club
Chester City Football Club
Chester City Football Club
Chester City Football Club
Chester City Football Club
Chester City Football Club
Chester City Football Club
Chester City Football Club
Chester City Football Club

276

Chester City *Football Club*

→ **Address** | Chester City FC, The Deva Stadium, Bumpers Lane, Chester CH1 4LT

Tel: 01244 371376 | **Tickets:** 01244 371376 | **Clubline:** 0891 121633

The fathers of top Premiership strikers Chris Sutton and Michael Owen have both played for Chester. Mike Sutton played between 1967 and 1969 and Terry Owen played between 1972 and 1977.

Top row • C Warrington • P Clench • M Woods • N Richardson • S Whelan • A Milner • J Jones • G Bennet • C Priest

Middle row • S Walker • J Murphy • J Alsford • R Sinclair • D Flitcroft • W Brown • S Reid • R Thomas • D Fogg

Bottom row • R Dobson • R McDonald • N Fisher • G Shelton • I Jenkins • K Ratcliffe • S Rimmer • R Davidson • M Giles

→ **Chairman:** Mark Guterman   → **Manager:** Kevin Ratcliffe   → **Year formed:** 1885

Ground: Deva Stadium (6,000)

Stands: North
South
East
West

Home strip: Blue and white striped shirts, white shorts with blue trim, blue socks with white trim

Away strip: White shirts with claret trim, claret shorts with white trim, claret socks with white trim

Sponsor: Saunders Honda

Programme: £1.50

Nickname: Blues or City

Ground history: 1885 Faulkner Street
1898 The Old Showground
1901 Whipcord Lane
1906 Sealand Road
1990 Moss Rose, Macclesfield
1992 Deva Stadium

Previous name: Chester

First League game: 2 September 1931, Division 3 (North), drew 1-1 (a) v Wrexham

Record attendance: 5,638 v Preston North End, Division 3, 2 April 1994

Record victory: 12-0 v York City, Division 3 (North), 1 February 1936

Record defeat: 2-11 v Oldham Athletic, Division 3 (North), 19 January 1952

Highest League position: Division 3 (old), 5th place, 1977-78

Highest League scorer (season): Dick Yates, 36, 1946-47

Highest League scorer (aggregate): Stuart Rimmer, 135, 1984-1988, 1991-1998

Most League appearances: Ray Gill, 406, 1951-1962

Most capped player: William Lewis, 13, Wales, 1891-1899

Highest transfer fee paid: £94,000 to Barnsley for Stuart Rimmer, August 1991

Highest transfer fee received: £300,000 from Liverpool for Ian Rush, April 1980

Major trophies: None

Darlington *Football Club*

→ **Address** | Darlington FC, Feethams Ground, Darlington DL1 5JB

Tel: 01325 465097 | **Tickets:** 01325 465097 | **Clubline:** 0891 101555

Since the end of the Second World War, Darlington have had 28 managers. On average, this works out to be a tenure of one year, 11 months per manager.

Top row • C Shutt • D Roberts • S Shaw • R Hope • J de Vos • L Turnbull • K Lowe • M Oliver • B Atkinson

Middle row • P Darke • P Robinson • L Brydon • L Papaconstantinou • A Crosby • D Preece • P Brumwell • G Naylor • M Barnard • A Thompson

Bottom row • W Guimmarra • M Riley • G Bannister • D Hodgson • Captain J Wood • S Gibson • I Leckie • N Tarrant

→ **Web site:** http://www.darlingtonfc.force9.co.uk → **Chairman:** Bernard Lowery → **Manager:** David Hodgson → **Year formed:** 1883

Ground: Feethams (7,750)

Stands: West
East
North Terrace
South Terrace

Home strip: White shirts with black and red trim, black shorts, white socks

Away strip: Red shirts with black trim, red shorts, red socks

Sponsor: Darlington Building Society

Programme: £1.50

Nickname: Quakers

Ground history: 1883 Feethams

Previous name: None

First League game: 27 August 1921, Division 3 (North), won 2-0 (h) v Halifax Town

Record attendance: 21,023 v Bolton Wanderers, League Cup 3rd round, 14 November 1960

Record victory: 9-2 v Lincoln City, Division 3 (North), 7 January 1928

Record defeat: 0-10 v Doncaster Rovers, Division 4, 25 January 1964

Highest League position: Division 2 (old), 15th place, 1925-26

Highest League scorer (season): David Brown, 39, 1924-25

Highest League scorer (aggregate): Alan Walsh, 90, 1978-1984

Most League appearances: Ron Greener, 442, 1955-1968

Most capped player: Jason de Vos, 3, Canada, 1997-98

Highest transfer fee paid: £95,000 to Motherwell for Nick Cusack, January 1992

Highest transfer fee received: £300,000 from Preston North End for Sean Gregan, November 1996

Major trophies: Division 3 (North) Champions (1) 1924-25
Division 4 Champions (1) 1990-91

Exeter City *Football Club*

Exeter City Football Club
Exeter City Football Club
Exeter City Football Club
Exeter City Football Club
Exeter City Football Club
Exeter City Football Club

→ **Address** | Exeter City FC, St James Park, Exeter EX4 6PX

Tel: 01392 254073 | **Tickets:** 01392 254073 | **Clubline:** 0891 121634

Of the 20 players on Exeter's books at the start of the 1997-98 season, none of them were born in February, March or June. Three players each were born in May, August and October.

Top row • S Flack • J Gardner • S Gayle • A Bayes • M Hare • L Braithwaite • J Williams

Middle row • M Chapman • P Fox • C Curran • L Baddeley • B McConnell • M Devlin • C Fry • J Minett • B Clark • M Radford • N Blake

Bottom row • P Birch • S Ghazghazi • J Richardson • I Doble • D Rowbotham • N Medlin • A Cyrus

→ **Chairman:** Ivor Doble   → **Player-manager:** Peter Fox   → **Year formed:** 1904

Ground: St James Park (10,570)

Stands: Main Grandstand
Cowshed
Big Bank End
St James Road

Home strip: Red and white striped shirts, white shorts, red socks with white trim

Away strip: All yellow

Sponsor: Exeter Friendly Society

Programme: £1.70

Nickname: Grecians

Ground history: 1904 St James Park

Previous name: None

First League game: 28 August 1920, Division 3 (old), won 3-0 (h) v Brentford

Record attendance: 20,984 v Sunderland, FA Cup 6th round replay, 4 March 1931

Record victory: 9-1 v Aberdare, FA Cup 1st round, 26 November 1927

Record defeat: 0-9 v Notts County, Division 3 (South), 16 October 1948
0-9 v Northampton Town, Division 3 (South), 12 April 1958

Highest League position: Division 3 (old), 8th place, 1976-77

Highest League scorer (season): Fred Whitlow, 33, 1932-33

Highest League scorer (aggregate): Tony Kellow, 129, 1976-1978, 1980-1983, 1985-1988

Most League appearances: Arnold Mitchell, 495, 1952-1966

Most capped player: Dermot Curtis, 1, Republic of Ireland, 1963

Highest transfer fee paid: £65,000 to Blackpool for Tony Kellow, March 1980

Highest transfer fee received: £500,000 from Glasgow Rangers for Chris Vinnicombe, November 1989
£500,000 from Manchester City for Martin Phillips, November 1995

Major trophies: Division 4 Champions **(1)** 1989-90

Halifax Town *Football Club*

→ **Address** | Halifax Town FC, Shay Stadium, Halifax HX1 2YS

Tel: 01422 345543 | **Tickets:** 01422 345543 | **Clubline:** 0891 227328

Halifax's Conference-winning season saw them remain unbeaten at home – they won 17 and drew four of their 21 games, a record achieved by no other club in the English or Scottish Leagues in 1997-98.

Top row • M Midwood • P Stoneman • L Martin • B Kilcline • A Woods • C Boardman • G Horsfield

Middle row • N Horner • J Murphy • D Lyons • M Rosser • J Brown • A Thackeray • M Bradshaw

Bottom row • A Russell-Cox • P Hand • D Place • W Griffiths • K Hulme • G Mulhall • J Patterson • G Brook • K O'Regan • T Gildert

→ **Chairman:** John Stockwell → **Manager:** George Mulhall → **Year formed:** 1911

Ground: Shay Stadium (7,449)

Stands: Main
Skircoat Road
New North Terrace

Home strip: Blue shirts with white trim, blue shorts with white trim, white socks

Away strip: Green shirts with yellow and white trim, yellow shorts, green socks

Sponsor: Nationwide

Programme: £2

Nickname: Shaymen

Ground history: 1911 Sandhall Lane
1919 Exley
1921 Shay Stadium

Previous name: None

First League game: 27 August 1921, Division 3 (North), lost 0-2 (a) v Darlington

Record attendance: 36,885 v Tottenham Hotspur, FA Cup 5th round, 14 February 1953

Record victory: 7-0 v Bishop Auckland, FA Cup 2nd round replay, 10 January 1967

Record defeat: 0-13 v Stockport County, Division 3 (North), 6 January 1934

Highest League position: Division 3 (old), 3rd place, 1970-71

Highest League scorer (season): Albert Valentine, 34, 1934-35

Highest League scorer (aggregate): Ernest Dixon, 129, 1922-1930

Most League appearances: John Pickering, 367, 1965-1974

Most capped player: None

Highest transfer fee paid: £50,000 to Hereford United for Ian Juryeff, September 1990

Highest transfer fee received: £250,000 from Watford for Wayne Allison, July 1989

Major trophies: None

Hartlepool United *Football Club*

Hartlepool United Football Club
Hartlepool United Football Club
Hartlepool United Football Club
Hartlepool United Football Club
Hartlepool United Football Club
Hartlepool United Football Club
Hartlepool United Football Club
Hartlepool United Football Club

→ **Address** | Hartlepool United FC, Victoria Park, Clarence Road, Hartlepool, Cleveland TS24 8BZ

Tel: 01429 272584 | **Tickets:** 01429 272584 | **Clubline:** None

Hartlepool reached their highest ever position in the League 30 years ago – 22nd in Division 3 (old) – in the 1968-69 season. However, their 39 points from 10 wins and 19 draws also heralded the drop back to Division 4.

Top row • C Beech • M Nash • J Allon • G Lee • D Ingram • J Cullen • I Gallagher • P Baker • D Knowles

Middle row • G Hinchley • J-O Pederson • T Miller • S Hutt • S Howard • W Dobson • M Hollund • G Davies • G Downey • R Lucas • T Miller • B Horner

Bottom row • I Clark • M Barron • S Halliday • B Honour • R Bradley • M Tait • C McDonald • S Irvine • P Walton

→ **Chairman:** Ken Hodcroft → **Manager:** Mick Tait → **Year formed:** 1908

Ground: Victoria Park (7,229)

Stands: Cyril Knowles
Town End
Millhouse
Rink End

Home strip: Royal blue and white shirts, royal blue shorts, royal blue socks

Away strip: Grey and navy blue shirts, navy blue shorts, grey socks

Sponsor: Cameron's

Programme: £1.50

Nickname: Pool

Ground history: 1908 Victoria Park

Previous names: Hartlepools United
Hartlepool

First League game: 27 August 1921,
Division 3 (North), won 2-0 (a) v Wrexham

Record attendance: 17,426 v Manchester
United, FA Cup 3rd round, 5 January 1957

Record victory: 10-1 v Barrow, Division 4,
4 April 1959

Record defeat: 1-10 v Wrexham, Division 4,
3 March 1962

Highest League position: Division 3 (old),
22nd place, 1968-69

Highest League scorer (season): William
Robinson, 28, 1927-28
Joe Allon, 28, 1990-91

Highest League scorer (aggregate): Ken
Johnson, 98, 1949-1964

Most League appearances: Wattie Moore,
447, 1948-1964

Most capped player: Ambrose Fogarty, 1,
Republic of Ireland, 1964

Highest transfer fee paid: £60,000 to
Barnsley for Andy Saville, March 1992

Highest transfer fee received: £300,000
from Chelsea for Joe Allon, August 1991

Major trophies: None

Hull City Football Club
Hull City Football Club
Hull City Football Club
Hull City Football Club
Hull City Football Club
Hull City Football Club
Hull City Football Club
Hull City Football Club
Hull City Football Club
Hull City Football Club

Hull City *Football Club*

→ **Address** | Hull City FC, Boothferry Park, Boothferry Road, Hull, East Yorkshire HU4 6EU

Tel: 01482 351119 | **Tickets:** 01482 506666 | **Clubline:** None

Hull City are the only club in the English League with a name that has no letters you can colour in – either in lower or upper case.

Top row • G Gordon • I Wright • R Dewhurst • A Brown • S Thomson • T Brien • M Greaves • R Peacock • P Fewings

Middle row • M McGum • B Kirkwood • S Sharman • S Trevitt • G Rioch • S Wilson • A Doncel • J Marks • D Darby • J Radcliffe • R Arnold

Bottom row • P Dickinson • N Mann • S Maxfield • A Lowthorpe • M Hateley • M Quigley • P Wharton • C Baxter • W Joyce

→ **Chairman:** David Lloyd   → **Manager:** Mark Hateley   → **Year formed:** 1904

Ground: Boothferry Park (13,594)

Stands: West
South
Kempton Road
North Terrace

Home strip: Amber and black striped shirts, black shorts, black socks with amber trim

Away strip: All white

Sponsor: University of Hull

Programme: £1.50

Nickname: Tigers

Ground history: 1904 Boulevard Ground
1905 Anlaby Road
1946 Boothferry Park

Previous name: None

First League game: 2 September 1905, Division 2, won 4-1 (h) v Barnsley

Record attendance: 55,019 v Manchester United, FA Cup 6th round, 26 February 1949

Record victory: 11-1 v Carlisle United, Division 3 (North), 14 January 1939

Record defeat: 0-8 v Wolverhampton Wanderers, Division 2, 4 November 1911

Highest League position: Division 2 (old), 3rd place, 1909-10

Highest League scorer (season): Bill McNaughton, 41, 1932-33

Highest League scorer (aggregate): Chris Chilton, 195, 1960-1971

Most League appearances: Andy Davidson, 520, 1952-1967

Most capped player: Terry Neill, 15, Northern Ireland, 1970-1973

Highest transfer fee paid: £200,000 to Leeds United for Peter Swan, March 1989

Highest transfer fee received: £750,000 from Middlesbrough for Andy Payton, November 1991

Major trophies: Division 3 (old) Champions
(1) 1965-66
Division 3 (North) Champions **(2)** 1948-49, 1932-33

Leyton Orient *Football Club*

Leyton Orient Football Club
Leyton Orient Football Club
Leyton Orient Football Club
Leyton Orient Football Club
Leyton Orient Football Club
Leyton Orient Football Club
Leyton Orient Football Club
Leyton Orient Football Club
Leyton Orient Football Club
Leyton Orient Football Club
Leyton Orient Football Club

→ **Address** | Leyton Orient FC, Leyton Stadium, Brisbane Road, Leyton, London E10 5NE

Tel: 0181 926 1111 | **Tickets:** 0181 926 1111 | **Clubline:** 0891 121150

Snooker maestro Barry Hearn, chairman of Leyton Orient, took over the cash-strapped east London club in 1995.

Top row • R Joseph • S Howes • J Channing • M Warren • D Morrison • D Brown • D Hanson

Middle row • S Clark • C West • S Hicks • P Hyde • L Weaver • L Shearer • D Smith • T Richards

Bottom row • S Winston • S McGleish • A Inglethorpe • D Naylor • M Ling • C Griffiths • J Baker

→ **Web site:** http://www.matchroom.com/orient → **Chairman:** Barry Hearn → **Manager:** Tommy Taylor → **Year formed:** 1881

Ground: Brisbane Road (13,842)

Stands: South
North Terrace
East
West

Home strip: Red shirts with white centre panel, white shorts with red trim, black socks

Away strip: Yellow shirts with white centre panel, white shorts with yellow trim, black socks

Sponsor: Marchpole

Programme: £1.50

Nickname: O's

Ground history: 1884 Glyn Road
1896 Whittles Athletic Ground
1900 Millfields Road
1930 Lea Bridge Road
1937 Brisbane Road

Previous names: Glyn Cricket Club
Eagle
Orient
Clapton Orient

First League game: 2 September 1905, Division 2, lost 1-2 (a) v Leicester Fosse

Record attendance: 34,345 v West Ham United, FA Cup 4th round, 25 January 1964

Record victory: 9-2 v Chester, League Cup 3rd round, 15 October 1962

Record defeat: 0-8 v Aston Villa, FA Cup 4th round, 30 January 1929

Highest League position: Division 1 (old), 22nd place, 1962-63

Highest League scorer (season): Tom Johnston, 35, 1957-58

Highest League scorer (aggregate): Tom Johnston, 121, 1956-1958, 1959-1961

Most League appearances: Peter Allen, 432, 1965-1978

Most capped player: John Chiedozie, 8, Nigeria, 1977-1981

Highest transfer fee paid: £175,000 to Wigan Athletic for Paul Beesley, October 1989

Highest transfer fee received: £600,000 from Notts County for John Chiedozie, August 1981

Major trophies: Division 3 (old) Champions **(1)** 1969-70
Division 3 (South) Champions **(1)** 1955-56

Mansfield Town *Football Club*

Mansfield Town Football Club
Mansfield Town Football Club
Mansfield Town Football Club
Mansfield Town Football Club
Mansfield Town Football Club
Mansfield Town Football Club
Mansfield Town Football
Mansfield Town Football Club

→ **Address** | Mansfield Town FC, Field Mill Ground, Quarry Lane, Mansfield, Nottinghamshire NG18 5DA

Tel: 01623 623567 | **Tickets:** 01623 623567 | **Clubline:** 0891 121311

Seats from the club's old West Stand were sold to fans at the end of 1997-98 for £10 each. If all of the 2,132 seats were sold, it would raise £21,320, enough to pay for just under a quarter of record signing Lee Peacock.

Top row • M Sisson • M Peters • J Doolan • S Hadley • D Clarke • I Christie

Middle row • B Shaw • B Sedgemore • S Whitehall • D Roberts • S Eustace • S Watkiss • I Bowling • J Schofield • L Holbrook • I Hollett

Bottom row • T Ford • S Harper • L Williams • S Parkin • J Walker • D Kerr • B Statham

→ **Chairman:** Keith Haslam → **Manager:** Steve Parkin → **Year formed:** 1897

Ground: Field Mill (5,289)

Stands: West
North
Quarry Lane
Bishop Street

Home strip: Amber shirts with royal blue trim, amber shorts with royal blue trim, amber socks with royal blue trim

Away strip: Blue shirts with white trim, white shorts, blue socks

Sponsor: Unknown

Programme: £1.50

Nickname: Stags

Ground history: 1897 Westfield Lane
1899 Ratcliffe Gate
1901 Newgate Lane
1912 Ratcliffe Gate
1919 Field Mill

Previous names: Mansfield Wesleyans
Mansfield Wesley

First League game: 29 August 1931, Division 3 (South), won 3-2 (h) v Swindon Town

Record attendance: 24,467 v Nottingham Forest, FA Cup 3rd round, 10 January 1953

Record victory: 9-2 v Rotherham United, Division 3 (North), 27 December 1932
9-2 v Hounslow Town, FA Cup 1st round replay, 5 November 1962

Record defeat: 1-8 v Walsall, Division 3 (North), 19 January 1933

Highest League position: Division 2 (old), 21st place, 1977-78

Highest League scorer (season): Ted Harston, 55, 1936-37

Highest League scorer (aggregate): Harry Johnson, 104, 1931-1936

Most League appearances: Rod Arnold, 440, 1970-1983

Most capped player: John McCelland, 6, Northern Ireland, 1979-1980

Highest transfer fee paid: £90,000 to Carlisle United for Lee Peacock, November 1997

Highest transfer fee received: £655,000 from Swindon Town for Colin Calderwood, July 1985

Major trophies: Division 3 (old) Champions **(1)** 1976-77
Division 4 Champions **(1)** 1974-75

Peterborough United *Football Club*

Peterborough Football Club
Peterborough Football Club
Peterborough Football Club
Peterborough Football Club
Peterborough Football Club
Peterborough Football Club
Peterborough Football Club
Peterborough Football Club
Peterborough Football Club

→ **Address** | Peterborough United FC, London Road Ground, London Road, Peterborough PE2 8AL

Tel: 01733 563947 | **Tickets:** 01733 563947 | **Clubline:** 0891 121654

Peterborough United got their nickname in 1934 when, at a public meeting to discuss the formation of the club, those present were promised a "posh team, worthy of the city".

Top row • S Davies • A Koogi • G Heald • M Foran • M Tyler • B Griemink • J Quinn • A Neal • D Farrell • C McMenamin

Middle row • G Ogbourne • N Lewis • A Boothroyd • M Carruthers • M Bodley • A Edwards • M De Souza • D Linton • Z Rowe • A Drury • N Inman

Bottom row • C Turner • G Grazioli • D Payne • S Castle • B Fry • P Boizot • P Neal • W Bullimore • C Cleaver • S Houghton • R Johnson

→ **Chairman:** Peter Boizot → **Manager:** Barry Fry → **Year formed:** 1934

Ground: London Road (15,675)

Stands: Main
Freemans Family
London Road End
Moy's End

Home strip: Royal blue shirts with white trim, white shorts with blue trim, blue socks with white trim

Away strip: Red shirts, red shorts, red socks

Sponsor: Thomas Cook

Programme: £1.50

Nickname: The Posh

Ground history: 1934 London Road

Previous name: None

First League game: 20 August 1960, Division 4, won 3-0 (h) v Wrexham

Record attendance: 30,096 v Swansea, FA Cup 5th round, 20 February 1963

Record victory: 8-1 v Oldham Athletic, Division 4, 26 November 1969

Record defeat: 1-8 v Northampton, FA Cup 2nd round replay, 23 December 1946

Highest League position: Division 1, 10th place, 1992-93

Highest League scorer (season): Terry Bly, 52, 1960-61

Highest League scorer (aggregate): Jim Hall, 122, 1967-1971

Most League appearances: Tommy Robson, 482, 1968-1981

Most capped player: Tony Millington, 8, Wales, 1966-1969

Highest transfer fee paid: £350,000 to Walsall for Martin O'Connor, July 1996

Highest transfer fee received: £650,000 from Birmingham City for Martin O'Connor, November 1996

Major trophies: None

Plymouth Argyle *Football Club*

→ Address | Plymouth Argyle FC, Home Park, Plymouth, Devon PL2 3DQ

Tel: 01752 562561 | **Tickets:** 01752 562561 | **Clubline:** 0839 442270

Thirty years ago, Plymouth were the victims of the only League goal ever scored by a referee. The ball was deflected off the inside of Ivan Robinson's foot in the 1-0 Division Three defeat by Barrow.

Top row • G Clayton • J Ashton • P Wotton • S Perkins • M Heathcote • T James • S Collins • J Beswetherick • K Summerfield

Middle row • N Medhurst • G Anthony • J Rowbottom • M Patterson • C Billy • J Sheffield • J Dungey • M Saunders • R Mauge • R Bushby • C Leadbitter • K Blackwell

Bottom row • K Francis • C Corrazin • E Jean • N Illman • M Jones • D McCauley • A Littlejohn • P Williams • M Barlow • A Sargent

→ Chairman: Dan McCauley **→ Manager:** Mick Jones **→ Year formed:** 1886

Ground: Home Park (19,630)

Stands: Lyndhurst
Devonport End
Grandstand
Mayflower

Home strip: Green shirts with black and white trim, green shorts, green and black hooped socks

Away strip: Green and black striped shirts, black shorts, green and black socks

Sponsor: Rotolok

Programme: £1.50

Nickname: Pilgrims

Ground history: 1901 Home Park

Previous name: None

First League game: 28 August 1920, Division 3, drew 1-1 (h) v Norwich City

Record attendance: 43,596 v Aston Villa, Division 2, 10 October 1936

Record victory: 8-1 v Millwall, Division 2, 16 January 1932
8-1 v Hartlepool United, Division 2, 7 May 1994

Record defeat: 0-9 v Stoke City, Division 2, 17 December 1960

Highest League position: Division 2 (old), 4th place, 1931-32, 1952-53

Highest League scorer (season): Jack Cock, 32, 1925-26

Highest League scorer (aggregate): Sammy Black, 180, 1924-1938

Most League appearances: Kevin Hodges, 530, 1978-1992

Most capped player: Moses Russell, 20, Wales, 1912-1928

Highest transfer fee paid: £300,000 to Port Vale for Peter Swan, July 1994

Highest transfer fee received: £750,000 from Southampton for Mickey Evans, March 1997

Major trophies: Division 3 (old) Champions **(1)** 1958-59
Division 3 (South) Champions **(2)** 1951-52, 1929-30

Rochdale *Football Club*

Rochdale Football Club
Rochdale Football Club
Rochdale Football Club
Rochdale Football Club
Rochdale Football Club
Rochdale Football Club
Rochdale Football Club
Rochdale Football Club
Rochdale Football Club
Rochdale Football Club
Rochdale Football Club

→ **Address** | Rochdale AFC, Spotland Stadium, Willbutts Lane, Rochdale, Lancashire OL11 5DS

Tel: 01706 644648 | **Tickets:** 01706 644648 | **Clubline:** 0891 555858

Rochdale came third out of 93 football grounds, including Wembley, in the 1998 Colman's Football Food Guide for the quality and value-for-money of food and drink sold in the stadium – a pie costs £1.20.

Top row • N Irwin • I Bryson • R Painter • A Farrell • M Stuart • A Russell • G Robson • N Taylor **Second row •** K Hicks • J Robson • J Pender • M Leonard • S Bywater • I Gray • K Hill • D Bayliss • D Bywater • J Hinnigan **Third row •** D Gray • C Taylor • A Fensome • A Barlow • M Bailey • G Barrow • A Gouck • S Whitehall • M Carter • J Wilkinson • S Wilson **Bottom row •** P Edghill • D Stevens • P Loft • S Litster • A Brannelly • D Lambert • G Hicks • R Thompson • M Wilkinson

→ **Web site:** http://www.rochdale-football-club.co.uk → **Chairman:** David Kilpatrick → **Manager:** Graham Barrow → **Year formed:** 1907

Ground: Spotland Stadium (9,228)

Stands: Main
WMG
Willbutts Lane
Sandy Lane

Home strip: Royal blue shirts with white trim, royal blue shorts with white trim, royal blue socks with white trim

Away strip: Yellow shirts with black trim, black shorts, black socks with yellow trim

Sponsor: Carcraft

Programme: £1.60

Nickname: The Dale

Ground history: 1907 Spotland Stadium

Previous name: Rochdale Town

First League game: 27 August 1921, Division 2, won 6-3 (h) v Accrington Stanley

Record attendance: 24,231 v Notts County, FA Cup 2nd round, 10 December 1949

Record victory: 8-1 v Chesterfield, Division 3 (North), 18 December 1926

Record defeat: 1-9 v Tranmere Rovers, Division 3 (North), 25 December 1931

Highest League position: Division 3 (old), 9th place, 1969-70

Highest League scorer (season): Bert Whitehurst, 44, 1926-27

Highest League scorer (aggregate): Reg Jenkins, 119, 1964-1973

Most League appearances: Graham Smith, 317, 1966-1974

Most capped player: None

Highest transfer fee paid: £80,000 to Scunthorpe for Andy Flounders, August 1991

Highest transfer fee received: £300,000 from Wimbledon for Alan Reeves, September 1994
£300,000 from Stockport County for Ian Gray, August 1997

Major trophies: None

Rotherham United *Football Club*

→ **Address** | Rotherham United FC, Millmoor Ground, Rotherham S60 1HR

Tel: 01709 512434 | **Tickets:** 01709 512434 | **Clubline:** 0891 121637

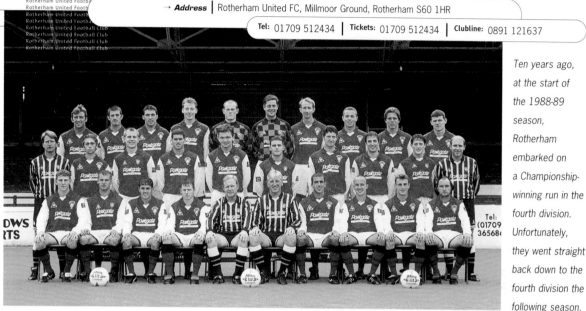

Ten years ago, at the start of the 1988-89 season, Rotherham embarked on a Championship-winning run in the fourth division. Unfortunately, they went straight back down to the fourth division the following season.

Top row • S Thompson • A Hayward • M Monington • G Bos • P Pettinger • B Mimms • A Knill • R Pell • A Brownrigg • L Glover

Middle row • B Russell • D Hudson • D Bass • M Druce • N Richardson • J Taylor • S Heath • R McKenzie • B Shuttleworth • I Bailey

Bottom row • G Scott • T Berry • P Hurst • P Dillon • J Breckin • R Moore • A Roscoe • S Goodwin • M Clark • D Garner

→ **Web site:** http://www.rotherhamufc.u.net.com → **Chairman:** Kenneth Booth → **Manager:** Ronnie Moore → **Year formed:** 1870

Ground: Millmoor (11,533)

Stands: Main
Millmoor Lane
Tivoli
Railway End

Home strip: Red shirts with white sleeves, white shorts with red trim, red socks with black trim

Away strip: White shirts, black shorts, black socks

Sponsor: one 2 one

Programme: £1.50

Nickname: Merry Millers

Ground history: 1870 Red House Ground
1907 Millmoor

Previous names: Thornhill United
Rotherham County

First League game: 30 September 1919, Division 2, won 2-0 (h) v Nottingham Forest

Record attendance: 25,170 v Sheffield United, Division 2, 13 December 1952

Record victory: 8-0 v Oldham Athletic, Division 3 (North), 26 May 1947

Record defeat: 1-11 v Bradford City, Division 3 (North), 25 August 1928

Highest League position: Division 2 (old), 3rd place, 1954-55

Highest League scorer (season): Wally Ardron, 38, 1946-47

Highest League scorer (aggregate): Gladstone Guest, 130, 1946-1956

Most League appearances: Danny Williams, 459, 1946-1962

Most capped player: Shaun Goater, 18, Bermuda, 1989-1996

Highest transfer fee paid: £150,000 to Millwall for Tony Towner, August 1980
£150,000 to Port Vale for Lee Glover, August 1996

Highest transfer fee received: £325,000 from Sheffield Wednesday for Matt Clarke, July 1996

Major trophies: Division 3 (old) Champions
(1) 1980-81
Division 3 (North) Champions
(1) 1950-51
Division 4 Champions **(1)** 1988-89

Scarborough *Football Club*

Division Three
Scarborough Football Club
Scarborough Football Club
Scarborough Football Club
Scarborough Football Club
Scarborough Football Club
Scarborough Football Club
Scarborough Football Club
Scarborough Football Club
Scarborough Football Club
Scarborough Football Club
Scarborough Football Club

→ **Address** | Scarborough FC, The McCain Stadium, Seamer Road, Scarborough YO12 4HF

Tel: 01723 375094 | **Tickets:** 01723 375094 | **Clubline:** 0891 121650

1998 marks the club's centenary at Seamer Road. Originally called the Athletic Ground, the name was changed to the McCain Stadium with Scarborough's promotion to the Football League in 1987.

Top row • C Tate • S Boyes • J Kay • J Murray • M Russell • T Bennett • S Brodie

Middle row • S Bochenski • C Van Der Velden • P Atkin • J Rockett • K Martin • G Bennett • G Williams • M McElhatton • J Mitchell

Bottom row • M Lee • C Sutherland • L Robinson • M Wadsworth • J Russell • R McHale • E Bazeyla • G Carr • B Worrall

→ **Web site:** http://www.yorkshirecoast.co.uk/scarbrofc → **Chairman:** John Russell → **Manager:** Mick Wadsworth → **Year formed:** 1879

Ground: The McCain Stadium (6,400)

Stands: McCain
Seamer Road
Edgehill Road
John Smith's

Home strip: White shirts with red and green trim, white shorts with red and green trim, white socks with red and green trim

Away strip: Lime shirts with black trim, lime shorts with black trim, lime socks with black trim

Sponsor: Arnott Insurance

Programme: £1.50

Nickname: Boro or Seadogs

Ground history: 1879 North Marine Cricket Ground
1887 Recreation Ground
1898 Athletic Ground/McCain Stadium

Previous name: None

First League game: 15 August 1987, Division 4, drew 2-2 (h) v Wolverhampton Wanderers

Record attendance: 11,162 v Luton Town, FA Cup 3rd round, 8 January 1938

Record victory: 6-0 v Rhyl Athletic, FA Cup 1st round, 29 November 1930

Record defeat: 1-7 v Wigan Athletic, Division 3, 11 March 1997

Highest League position: Division 4, 5th place, 1988-89

Highest League scorer (season): Darren Foreman, 27, 1992-93

Highest League scorer (aggregate): Darren Foreman, 35, 1991-1995

Most League appearances: Ian Ironside, 183, 1988-1991, 1992, 1994-1997

Most capped player: Martin Russell, 3, Republic of Ireland, 1989-1992

Highest transfer fee paid: £102,000 to Leicester City for Martin Russell, March 1989

Highest transfer fee received: £240,000 from Notts County for Chris Short, September 1990

Major trophies: None

Scunthorpe United *Football Club*

→ Address | Scunthorpe United FC, Glanford Park, Doncaster Road, Scunthorpe DN15 8TD

Tel: 01724 848077 | **Tickets:** 01724 848077 | **Clubline:** 0891 121652

The smallest away crowd at Glanford Park in the 1997-98 season was made up of 69 Shrewsbury Town fans. The biggest away crowd was 1,900 Grimsby Town fans.

Top row • D D'Auria • C Shakespeare • S McAuley • J Eyre • S Housham • P Harsley

Middle row • N Adkins • M Gavin • R Wilcox • M Sertori • T Clark • D Stamp • C Hope • M Walsh • P Wilson

Bottom row • J Forrester • A Calvo-Garcia • M Lillis • D Rowing • K Wagstaff • B Laws • L Marshall • J Walker

→ Web site: http://freespace.virgin.net/su.fc/scunthorpe-utd   **→ Chairman:** Keith Wagstaff   **→ Player-manager:** Brian Laws   **→ Year formed:** 1899

Ground: Glanford Park (9,210)

Stands: Caparo Merchant Bar
Evening Telegraph
GMB
British Steel

Home kit: Claret and sky blue shirts, white shorts, white socks with claret and sky blue trim

Away kit: Navy blue and yellow shirts, navy blue shorts with yellow trim, yellow socks with navy blue trim

Sponsor: Motek

Programme: £1.70

Nickname: The Iron

Ground history: 1899 Old Showground
1988 Glanford Park

Previous name: Scunthorpe
& Lindsay United

First League game: 19 August 1950, Division 3 (North), drew 0-0 (h) v Shrewsbury Town

Record attendance: 8,775 v Rotherham United, Division 4, 1 May 1989

Record victory: 9-0 v Boston United, FA Cup 1st round, 21 November 1953

Record defeat: 0-8 v Carlisle United, Division 3 (North), 25 December 1952

Highest League position: Division 2 (old), 4th place, 1961-62

Highest League scorer (season): Barrie Thomas, 31, 1961-62

Highest League scorer (aggregate): Steve Cammack, 110, 1979-1981, 1981-1986

Most League appearances: Jack Brownsword, 597, 1950-1965

Most capped player: None

Highest transfer fee paid: £80,000 to York City for Ian Helliwell, August 1991

Highest transfer fee received: £400,000 from Aston Villa for Neil Cox, February 1991

Major trophies: Division 3 (North) Champions (1) 1957-58

Shrewsbury Town Football Club

→ **Address** | Shrewsbury Town FC, Gay Meadow, Shrewsbury SY2 6AB

Tel: 01743 360111 | **Tickets:** 01743 360111 | **Clubline:** 0891 121194

Three generations of one family have served the club by fishing balls out of the River Severn during home games. On average, two to three balls fly over the Riverside terrace per match.

Top row • J Cope • R Scott • M Dempsey • P Wilding • N Ward • M Taylor • K Seabury • S Wray • L Taylor

Middle row • M Kearney • M Musgrove • A Briscoe • E Nwadike • B Gall • P Edwards • M Williams • N Blaney • R Preece • C Walker

Bottom row • M Naylor • I Reed • D Currie • D Walton • J King • P Evans • M Brown • A Berkley • G Hamner

→ **Web site:** http://www.shrewsburytown.co.uk → **Chairman:** Roland Wycherley → **Manager:** Jake King → **Year formed:** 1886

Ground: Gay Meadow (8,000)

Stands: Wakeman
Centre
Family
Station

Home kit: Blue shirts, white shorts, blue socks with white trim

Away kit: Yellow shirts, blue shorts, yellow socks with blue trim

Sponsor: Ternhill

Programme: £1.50

Nickname: Town

Ground history: 1886 Old Shrewsbury Racecourse
1889 Amblers Field
1893 Sutton Lane
1895 Copthorne
1910 Gay Meadow

Previous name: None

First League game: 19 August 1950, Division 3 (North), drew 0-0 (a) v Scunthorpe United

Record attendance: 18,917 v Walsall, Division 3, 29 April 1961

Record victory: 11-2 v Marine, FA Cup 1st round, 11 November 1995

Record defeat: 1-8 v Norwich City, Division 3 (South), 13 September 1952
1-8 v Coventry City, Division 3, 22 October 1963

Highest League position: 8th place, Division 2 (old), 1984-85, 1983-84

Highest League scorer in a season: Arthur Rowley, 38, 1958-59

Highest League scorer (aggregate): Arthur Rowley, 152, 1958-1965

Most League appearances: Colin Griffin, 406, 1975-1989

Most capped player: Jimmy McLaughlin, 5, Northern Ireland, 1960-1962, 1964-1967
Bernard McNally, 5, Northern Ireland, 1978-1987

Highest transfer fee paid: £100,000 to Aldershot for John Dungworth, November 1979
£100,000 to Southampton for Mark Blake, August 1990

Highest transfer fee received: £700,000 from Crewe Alexandra for Dave Walton, October 1997

Major trophies: Division 3 (old) Champions **(1)** 1978-79
Division 3 Champions **(1)** 1993-94

Southend United *Football Club*

Southend United Football Club
Southend United Football Club
Southend United Football Club
Southend United Football Club
Southend United Footbal
Southend United Football
Southend United Football Club
Southend United Football Club
Southend United Football Club
Southend United Football Club

→ **Address** | Southend United FC, Roots Hall, Victoria Avenue, Southend-on-Sea SS2 6NQ

Tel: 01702 304050 | **Tickets:** 01702 304090 | **Clubline:** 0839 664443

Southend always go back to their Roots Hall. They were first there between 1906 and 1914 and moved back to the site in 1955. They have now played well over 1,000 games at the ground.

Top row • M Jones • P Taylor • C Perkins • S Royce • A Rammell • T Henriksen • J Boere • N Jones • J Nielsen
Middle row • S Barham • J Gowens • A Clarke • P Williams • A Harris • M Stimson • P Leggatt • P Johnson
Bottom row • L Roget • P Byrne • P Trevivian • A Martin • M Marsh • A Thomson • P Gridelet

→ **Chairman:** Victor Jobson → **Manager:** Alvin Martin → **Year formed:** 1906

Ground: Roots Hall (12,306)

Stands: East
West
Frank Walton
Universal Cycles

Home strip: Blue shirts with black, white and grey trim, white shorts with black, blue and grey trim, blue socks with white trim

Away strip: Yellow and red shirts, red shorts, yellow socks with red trim

Sponsor: Progressive Printing

Programme: £1.60

Nickname: Shrimpers or Blues

Ground history: 1906 Roots Hall
1919 Kursaal
1934 Southend Greyhound Stadium
1955 Roots Hall

Previous name: None

First League game: 28 August 1920, Division 3, won 2-0 (a) v Brighton & Hove Albion

Record attendance: 31,090 v Liverpool, FA Cup 3rd round, 10 January 1979

Record victory: 10-1 v Golders Green, FA Cup 1st round, 24 November 1934
10-1 v Brentwood, FA Cup 2nd round, 7 December 1968

Record defeat: 1-9 v Brighton & Hove Albion, Division 3, 27 November 1965

Highest League position: Division 1, 13th place, 1994-95

Highest League scorer (season): Jim Shankly, 31, 1928-29
Sammy McCrory, 31, 1957-58

Highest League scorer (aggregate): Roy Hollis, 122, 1953-1960

Most League appearances: Sandy Anderson, 451, 1950-1963

Most capped player: George McKenzie, 9, Republic of Ireland, 1937-1939

Highest transfer fee paid: £750,000 to Crystal Palace for Stan Collymore, November 1992

Highest transfer fee received: £3.57m from Nottingham Forest for Stan Collymore, June 1993

Major trophies: Division 4 Champions **(1)** 1980-81

Swansea City Football Club
Swansea City Football Club
Swansea City Football Club
Swansea City Football Club
Swansea City Football Club
Swansea City Football Club
Swansea City Football Cl

Swansea City *Football Club*

→ **Address** | Swansea City FC, Vetch Field, Swansea SA1 3SU

Tel: 01792 474114 | **Tickets:** 01792 462584 | **Clubline:** 0891 121639

Swansea's first away League game of the 1997-98 season ended in a 4-7 defeat by Hull. Seventy years ago, in the 1927-28 season, the Swans also lost by the same score, this time against Manchester City.

Top row • J Harris • C Edwards • J Jones • R Freestone • L Jones • A Newhouse • J Price

Middle row • P Morgan • J Moreira • J Coates • M Clode • K Ampadu • S Watkin • R Appleby • T Bird • K O'Leary • N Cusack • A Curtis • R Walton

Bottom row • R Casey • S Jones • D Lacey • D O'Gorman • K Walker • A Cork • G Jones • L Jenkins • L Brown • R King

→ **Web site:** http://www.swansfc.co.uk → **Chairman:** Steve Hamer → **Manager:** John Hollins → **Year formed:** 1912

Ground: Vetch Field (12,000)

Stands: Jewson Family
East
Centre
King

Home strip: White shirts with black and maroon trim, white shorts with black and maroon trim, white socks with black and maroon trim

Away strip: Maroon shirts with white and black trim, maroon shorts with white and black trim, maroon socks with white and black trim

Sponsor: Unknown

Programme: £1.70

Nickname: Swans

Ground history: 1912 Vetch Field

Previous name: Swansea Town

First League game: 28 August 1920, Division 3, won 2-0 (a) v Portsmouth

Record attendance: 32,796 v Arsenal, FA Cup 4th round, 17 February 1968

Record victory: 12-0 v Sliema Wanderers (Malta), Cup Winners Cup 1st round, 1st leg, 15 September 1982

Record defeat: 0-8 v Liverpool, FA Cup 3rd round replay, 9 January 1990
0-8 v Monaco, Cup Winners Cup 1st round, 2nd leg, 1 October 1991

Highest League position: Division 1 (old), 6th place, 1981-82

Highest League scorer (season): Cyril Pearce, 35, 1931-32

Highest League scorer (aggregate): Ivor Allchurch, 166, 1949-1958, 1965-1968

Most League appearances: Wilfred Milne, 585, 1920-1937

Most capped player: Ivor Allchurch, 42, Wales, 1949-1968

Highest transfer fee paid: £340,000 to Liverpool for Colin Irwin, August 1981

Highest transfer fee received: £375,000 from Crystal Palace for Chris Coleman, June 1991
£375,000 from Nottingham Forest for Des Lyttle, July 1993

Major trophies: Division 3 (South) Champions **(2)** 1948-49, 1924-25

Torquay United *Football Club*

→ **Address** | Torquay United FC, Plainmoor, Torquay TQ1 3PS

Tel: 01803 328666 | **Tickets:** 01803 328666 | **Clubline:** None

Striker Rodney Jack's St Vincent & the Grenadines beat Puerto Rico twice in the 1998 World Cup qualifiers, but lost twice to Jamaica, Mexico and Honduras, scoring six and conceding 30 goals in the process.

Top row • L Barrow • J Gittens • A Watson • A McFarlane • J Robinson • W Thomas • P Mitchell
Middle row • I Pearce • D Davey • C Oatway • A Gurney • M Gregg • P Gibbs • W Hockley • P Lloyd • P Distin
Bottom row • L Hapgood • R Jack • K Hodges • M Benney • S McCall • T Bedeau • M Preston

→ **Chairman:** Mervyn Benney   → **Manager:** Wes Saunders   → **Year formed:** 1899

Ground: Plainmoor (6,003)

Stands: Family
Away End
Popular Side
Main Grandstand

Home strip: Yellow and navy blue striped shirts, navy blue shorts with yellow trim, yellow socks with navy blue trim

Away strip: White shirts with navy blue and yellow trim, white shorts with navy blue trim, white socks with navy blue trim

Sponsor: Westward Developments

Programme: £1.70

Nickname: Gulls

Ground history: 1899 Teignmouth Road
1901 Torquay Recreation Grounds
1905 Cricketfield Road
1907 Torquay Cricket Ground
1910 Plainmoor

Previous names: Torquay Town

First League game: 27 August 1927, Division 3 (South), drew 1-1 (h) v Exeter City

Record attendance: 21,908 v Huddersfield Town, FA Cup 4th round, 29 January 1955

Record victory: 9-0 v Swindon Town, Division 3 (South), 8 March 1952

Record defeat: 2-10 v Fulham, Division 3 (South), 7 September 1931
2-10 v Luton Town, Division 3 (South), 2 September 1933

Highest League position: Division 3 (old), 4th place, 1967-68

Highest League scorer (season): Sammy Collins, 40, 1955-56

Highest League scorer (aggregate): Sammy Collins, 204, 1948-1958

Most League appearances: Dennis Lewis, 443, 1947-1959

Most capped player: Rodney Jack, St Vincent & the Grenadines, 1995-1998

Highest transfer fee paid: £60,000 to Dundee for Wes Saunders, July 1990

Highest transfer fee received: £185,000 from Manchester United for Lee Sharpe, June 1988

Major trophies: None

Aberdeen *Football Club*

→ **Address** | Aberdeen FC, Pittodrie Stadium, Aberdeen AB24 5QH

Tel: 01224 650400 | **Tickets:** 01244 632328 | **Clubline:** 0891 121551

Aberdeen's most successful manager was Alex Ferguson, who, between 1978 and 1986, led the club to four Scottish Cups, three League titles, the League Cup, the Super Cup and the Cup Winners Cup.

Top row • B Bett • L Barclay • M Hart • D Young • M Craig • D Young • J Inglis • B O'Neil • R Esson • T Kombouare • M Newell

• J Buchan • M Kpedekpo • D Wyness • R Duncan • K Williamson • D Buchan • C Clark **Middle row** • D Wylie • S Hogg • P McGuire • M Newlands • G Smith

• D Shearer • T Tzvetanov • D Windass • M Watt • D Stillie • N Walker • P Bernard • S Glass • R Anderson • D Rowson • I Good • K Milne • T Scott • J Sharp

Bottom row • J Kelman • D Jarvie • I Kiriakov • B Dodds • R Aitken • J Leighton • T Craig • E Jess • J Miller • N Cooper • K Burkinshaw

→ **Web site:** http://www.afc.co.uk → **Chairman:** Stewart Milne → **Manager:** Alex Miller → **Year formed:** 1903

Ground: Pittodrie Stadium (22,199)

Stands: Main
  Richard Donald
  South
  Merkland

Home strip: All red with white trim

Away strip: White shirts, black shorts with red trim, black socks

Sponsor: Atlantic Telecom

Programme: £1.50

Nickname: Dons

Ground history: 1903 Pittodrie

Previous name: None

Record attendance: 45,061 v Hearts, Scottish Cup 4th round, 13 March 1954

Record victory: 13-0 v Peterhead, Scottish Cup 3rd round, 9 February 1923

Record defeat: 0-8 v Celtic, Division 1, 30 January 1965

Highest League scorer (season): Benny Yorston, 38, 1929-30

Highest League scorer (aggregate): Joe Harper, 199, 1969-1973, 1976-1986

Most League appearances: Willie Miller, 556, 1973-1990

Most capped player: Alex McLeish, 77, Scotland, 1980-1993

Highest transfer fee paid: £1m to Oldham Athletic for Paul Bernard, October 1995

Highest transfer fee received: £1.75m from Coventry City for Eoin Jess, March 1996

Major trophies: Premier Division Champions **(3)** 1984-85, 1983-84, 1979-80
Division 1 Champions **(1)** 1954-55
Scottish Cup Winners **(7)** 1990, 1986, 1984, 1983, 1982, 1970, 1947
Scottish League Cup Winners **(6)** 1995-96, 1989-90, 1985-86, 1976-77, 1955-56, 1945-46
Cup Winners Cup Winners **(1)** 1983

Russell Anderson – A regular Under-21 international for Scotland, Anderson is a product of Aberdeen's youth policy and made his club debut at 18. He took over from captain Stewart McKimmie at right back halfway through the 1996-97 season and was an automatic selection in 1997-98.

Paul Bernard – The club's record signing in 1995 at £1 million, Bernard came back strongly early last season after struggling with injuries in the previous campaign. A former Scottish Under-21 international, he's a firm favourite with the fans.

Jamie Buchan – Son of Aberdeen, Manchester United and England centre back Martin Buchan, Jamie has become a Pittodrie favourite in his own right, though he had to wait until April 1998 to get a regular place in the team at number two. A versatile player, he's capable of playing anywhere in the back four or in midfield.

Michael Craig – As in 1996-97, this speedy winger found it difficult to break into the first team last season. The nephew of former assistant Dons boss Tommy Craig, the Scotland Under-21 player signed at 17 from Celtic in 1995.

Ricky Gillies – Signed from St Mirren in August 1997 for £400,000, this talented midfielder was tipped for international stardom but failed to break out of his regular position on the bench in 1997-98 in what was a difficult campaign.

Stephen Glass – Rated one of the best left-sided midfield players in Scotland, Glass continued to build on his place in the side during the 1997-98 season.

John Inglis – Known in the Aberdeen dressing-room as Zeus, this powerful centre back was signed from St Johnstone back in 1993. He had

a trial with Fulham early in the 1996-97 season but then regained his place in the Aberdeen squad in September 1998 and again in December after losing it to Toni Kornbouare.

Ilian Kiriakov – Resembling Gordon Strachan in the way he plays, this Bulgarian international midfielder was signed from Anorthosis Famagusta, Cyprus, for £400,000. He missed the first part of the season but returned to first team duty in November 1997.

Joe Miller – The diminutive midfielder is now at Aberdeen for the second time, having had several seasons with Celtic. A wise old head at 30, the former Scottish Under-21 player also has an eye for goal and a lethal shot. Normally a first team regular, he lost favour with the Miller regime midway through the 1997-98 season.

Mike Newell – Signed in 1997 from Birmingham City for £100,000 after an unhappy spell there under Trevor Francis, Newell immediately became a first team regular at Pittodrie. Now 33, the target man won a League Championship medal with Blackburn Rovers in 1995.

Brian O'Neil – He began his career as a midfielder at Celtic but was unhappy at Parkhead after a series of injuries. Since moving to Aberdeen in the summer of 1997 for £750,000, he has settled in well at the heart of the defence. A good reader of the game, he is also an excellent passer and has the ability to turn defence quickly into attack.

David Rowson – Almost an ever-present in the 1996-97 season, it was thought Rowson's place would be in danger with all the summer signings of 1997, but he responded by filling in with his customary commitment at the back and in midfield. Indeed, this utility player wore 11 different numbers during the 1997-98 season.

Gary Smith – A stylish defender who returned to Pittodrie for £200,000 in the summer of 1997 after a year in France with Rennes, Smith looked comfortable both at centre back and left back and was a real star turn for the Dons during the 1997-98 season.

Derek Stillie – Signed from Notts County, Stillie – a former Under-21 international – kept the goalkeeper's jersey he earned at the end of the 1996-97 season at the start of 1997-98, but then lost his place to Scotland international Jim Leighton for the remainder of the campaign.

Tzanko Tzvetanov – A Bulgarian international who played for his country during the European Championships in 1996, this pacy full back was signed from Waldorf Mannheim for £650,000 in August 1996. Renowned for his surging runs, Tzvetanov lost his place before Christmas and struggled to regain his place under manager Alex Miller.

Derek Whyte – A Scottish international who was formerly with Celtic and Middlesbrough, Whyte moved to Pittodrie for £100,000 in December 1997. A towering defender, he settled in well at centre back and endeared himself to the club's fans with his all-out style of play.

Dean Windass – Signed from Hull City for £700,000 in November 1995, this fiery midfield player has a real eye for goal and struck up a prolific partnership with Billy Dodds in the 1997-98 season.

Darren Young – A steely young midfielder who broke into the first team in 1996-97, Young failed to retain his place during the 1997-98 season and found himself cast in the role of sub.

Derek Young – Younger brother of Darren, he was likewise used as a sub during the 1997-98 season.

Billy Dodds – An £880,000 buy from St Johnstone in 1994, this livewire, hard-working striker was again a major factor in Aberdeen's fortunes after beginning the season on the substitute's bench.

Eoin Jess – Returning to Aberdeen for £650,000 after a spell at Coventry City, the Scottish international has also enjoyed a return to form in a new, deeper role, playing just in front of the defence.

Jim Leighton – The veteran keeper became an automatic choice from August 1997, having returned to Pittodrie from Hibs after a nine-year absence. Club Player of the Year, he kept goal for Scotland in France '98.

Celtic *Football Club*

Celtic Football Club
Celtic Football Club
Celtic Football Club
Celtic Football Club
Celtic Football Club
Celtic Football Club
Celtic Football Club
Celtic Football Club
Celtic Football Club
Celtic Football Club
Celtic Football Club
Celtic Football Club

→ **Address** | Celtic FC, Celtic Park, Glasgow G40 3RE

Tel: 0141 556 2611 | **Tickets:** 0141 551 8653 | **Clubline:** 0891 196721

Celtic were the first British club to win the European Cup. Led by Billy McNeill, Jock Stein's men outclassed Inter Milan in Lisbon to win 2-1 in 1967 – the year when Celtic won all competitions open to them.

Top row • P Grant • C Hay • T Johnston • G Marshall • S Kerr • S Donnelly • D Hannah • H Larsson

Middle row • B Scott • S Gray • A Stubbs • E Annoni • M Mackay • M Wieghorst • C Burley • T Boyd • M MacLeod

Bottom row • D Jackson • B McLaughlin • J P McBride • J McNamara • W Jansen • T McKinlay • A Thom • S Mahe • P O'Donnell

→ **Web site:** http://www.celticfc.co.uk   → **Managing director:** Fergus McCann   ▸ **Manager:** Tommy Svensson   → **Year formed:** 1888

Ground: Celtic Park (60,000)

Stands: Main
North
East
West

Home strip: Green and white hooped shirts, white shorts, green and white socks

Away strip: All black with yellow trim

Sponsor: Umbro

Programme: £1.50

Nickname: Bhoys

Ground history: 1888 Old Celtic Park
1892 Celtic Park

Previous name: None

Record attendance: 92,000 v Rangers, Division 1, 1 January 1938

Record victory: 11-0 v Dundee, Division 1, 26 October 1895

Record defeat: 0-8 v Motherwell, Division 1, 30 April 1937

Highest League scorer (season): Jimmy McGrory, 50, 1935-36

Highest League scorer (aggregate): Jimmy McGrory, 398, 1923-1937

Most League appearances: Alex McNair, 548, 1904-1925

Most capped player: Packie Bonner, 80, Republic of Ireland, 1981-1997

Highest transfer fee paid: £5.5m to Bolton Wanderers for Alan Stubbs, May 1996

Highest transfer fee received: £3m from Nottingham Forest for Pierre van Hooijdonk, February 1998

Major trophies: Premier Division Champions **(7)** 1998, 1988, 1986, 1982, 1981, 1979, 1977
Division 1 Champions **(29)** 1974, 1973, 1972, 1971, 1970, 1969, 1968, 1967, 1966, 1954, 1938, 1936, 1926, 1922, 1919, 1917, 1916, 1915, 1914, 1910, 1909, 1908, 1907, 1906, 1905, 1898, 1896, 1894, 1893
Scottish Cup Winners **(30)** 1995, 1989, 1988, 1985, 1980, 1977, 1975, 1974, 1972, 1971, 1969, 1967, 1965, 1954, 1951, 1937, 1933, 1931, 1927, 1925, 1923, 1914, 1912, 1911, 1908, 1907, 1904, 1900, 1899, 1892
Scottish League Cup Winners **(10)** 1997-98, 1982-83, 1974-75, 1969-70, 1968-69, 1967-68, 1966-67, 1965-66, 1957-58, 1956-57
European Cup Winners **(1)** 1967

Enrico Annoni – Signed from AS Roma for £300,000 in March 1997, Annoni is a big crowd favourite and a hard man to beat. The tough Italian defender made only 15 starts last season due to injury but finished strongly towards the end.

Regi Blinker – A former team-mate of Henrik Larsson at Dutch club Feyenoord, the Surinam-born player started 19 times in the 1997-98 season after his swap deal from Sheffield Wednesday involving Paolo di Canio. A strangely old-fashioned winger, Blinker proved successful on Celtic's left flank.

Harald Brattbakk – In his 18 appearances in 1997-98, he struggled to maintain the prolific goalscoring form that had inspired Celtic to buy him from Norwegian club Rosenborg in December 1997 (28 goals in 26 games). But it was his goal as a substitute against St Johnstone on the last day of the season that clinched Celtic's first League championship for 10 years.

Jonathan Gould – Signed from Bradford City for a nominal fee in August 1997, the London-born keeper soon became a permanent fixture in the side after replacing Gordon Marshall for a friendly against Roma early on in the 1997-98 season. Gould capped a great season at Parkhead by replacing Andy Goram in the Scottish World Cup finals squad.

David Hannah – Signed from Dundee United in December 1996 for £550,000, this no-nonsense player can operate in a midfield or defensive capacity and scored once in 15 games during the 1997-98 season.

Darren Jackson – After arriving from Hibernian for more than £1 million – he was Wim Jansen's first signing – this strong-running forward missed most of the 1997-98 season due to brain surgery in September

1997. However, he bounced back to help the club win the League – and booked his passage to France '98 with Scotland.

Tommy Johnson – Having played three straight games after his £2.4 million move from Aston Villa in April 1997, Tommy Burns' last signing before leaving the club found himself out of favour with Dutch coach Wim Jansen and played only six games in the 1997-98 season.

Paul Lambert – Signed from German club Borussia Dortmund in November 1997, Lambert was considered to be the buy of the season. The former European Cup winner added class and stability to Celtic's midfield and formed a fine working partnership with Craig Burley.

Henrik Larsson – The Swedish international striker settled in well at Parkhead following his move from Feyenoord in July 1997 and missed only one game during the season. A skilful player who is not afraid to try the outrageous – a fact that endears him to Celtic supporters – Larsson was the club's top scorer in 1997-98 with 19 goals.

Malky Mackay – As in previous seasons following his free transfer from Scottish club Queen's Park in August 1994, the defender failed to claim a regular first-team slot during the 1997-98 season.

Tosh McKinlay – Bought from Hearts for £350,000 in November 1994, the defender has obviously enjoyed playing for the club of his boyhood heroes. However, the Scotland international missed much of the 1997-98 season through injury and spent many games on the bench.

Jackie McNamara – A right back when he first arrived from Dunfermline for a bargain £650,000 in October 1995, McNamara was switched to the right side of midfield

by Wim Jansen rather than his more usual full-back position. He relished his new role and won a trip to France with the Scotland World Cup squad. For Celtic, he scored a rare but outstanding goal against Kilmarnock that many of his team-mates would consider to be the goal of the 1997-98 season.

Stephane Mahe – Signed from Rennes in August 1997, Mahe settled comfortably into the left-back position and enjoyed pushing into midfield, where he linked up well with Paul Lambert.

Phil O'Donnell – A skilful midfielder, he was signed from Motherwell for £1.75 million in September 1994. He played 21 games in the 1997-98 season and although 11 of them were as a sub he figured strongly in the dramatic run-in.

Marc Rieper – The great Dane and former West Ham United player made a rather shaky start following his move to Celtic in September 1997. But he soon became a commanding figure in the remainder of the season, forming a strong partnership with Alan Stubbs at the back and making his impact felt in the Coca-Cola Cup final as the opening scorer.

Alan Stubbs – A club record signing of £5.5 million from Bolton Wanderers in May 1996, Stubbs struggled with both injuries and form early on in 1997-98 but went on to notch up 40 appearances, forming a strong partnership at the heart of the defence with team-mate Marc Rieper.

Morten Wieghorst – Signed from Dundee for £600,000 in December 1995, the Danish international midfielder had probably his best ever season for Celtic in 1997-98, scoring eight goals for his club. The Man of the Match in the 1998 Coca-Cola Cup final travelled to France '98 as part of the Denmark squad.

Simon Donnelly – The diminutive Glaswegian scored 15 goals in the 1997-98 season, though he went off the boil towards the end. He plays mostly in midfield but can also act as a striker for Celtic and for Scotland.

Tom Boyd – Signed in a swap deal for Chelsea striker Tony Cascarino back in February 1992, the defender has been a solid performer ever since. Now club captain, he travelled to the World Cup with Scotland.

Craig Burley – Playing brilliantly at times in Celtic's midfield following his transfer from Chelsea in July 1997, Burley capped a great club season by keeping Scotland alive in France '98, with his goal against Norway.

Dundee *Football Club*

Dundee Football Club
Dundee Football Club
Dundee Football Club
Dundee Football Club
Dundee Football Club
Dundee Football Club
Dundee Football Club
Dundee Football Club
Dundee Football Club
Dundee Football Club

→ **Address** | Dundee FC, Dens Park Stadium, Sandeman Street, Dundee DD3 7JY

Tel: 01382 826104 | **Tickets:** 01382 889966 | **Clubline:** None

In 1946-47, Dundee won the old Division 2 title with a goal record of 113 scored and 30 conceded in just 26 games. In 1997-98, they won the First Division by scoring 52 goals and conceding 24 in 36 games.

Top row • E Annand • R Raeside • B Thomson • B Irvine • J McGlashan • L Maddison • J O'Driscoll **Second row** • C Tully • D Adamczuk • P Briadfoot • G Rae • M Slater • I Anderson
• P Clark • D Magee • G Bogie **Third row** • H Hay • J Crosbie • S Milne • L Wilkie • H Robertson • G McGlynn • D Rogers • J Langfield • G Shaw • G Bain • J Elliot • S McDermott
• J Cashley • R Farningham **Bottom row** • K Cameron • M Dickie • B Smith • T Robertson • J Grady • J McCormack • J McInally • M Melling • K McGhee • L Mair • W Dryden

→ **Web site:** http://www.dundeefc.co.uk → **Chairman:** Jim Marr → **Manager:** Jocky Scott → **Year formed:** 1893

Ground: Dens Park Stadium (14,177)

Stands: Main
East Terrace
South Enclosure
Provost Road

Home strip: Dark blue and white shirts, white shorts with dark blue trim, dark blue socks with white trim

Away strip: White shirts with navy blue trim, navy blue shorts, white socks with navy blue trim

Sponsor: Unknown

Programme: £1

Nickname: Dark Blues or The Dee

Ground history: 1893 Carolina Port
1898 Dens Park

Previous name: None

Record attendance: 43,024 v Rangers, Scottish Cup 2nd round, 7 February 1953

Record victory: 10-0 v Alloa Athletic, Division 2, 9 March 1947
10-0 v Dunfermline Athletic, Division 2, 22 March 1947

Record defeat: 0-11 v Celtic, Division 1, 26 October 1895

Highest League scorer (season): Alan Gilzean, 52, 1963-64

Highest League scorer (aggregate): Alan Gilzean, 111, 1960-1964

Most League appearances: Doug Cowie, 341, 1946-1961

Most capped player: Alex Hamilton, 24, Scotland, 1962-1965

Highest transfer fee paid: £200,000 to Manchester United for Jim Leighton, February 1992

Highest transfer fee received: £600,000 from Celtic for Morten Wieghorst, December 1995

Major trophies: First Division Champions **(3)** 1997-98, 1991-92, 1978-79
Division 1 Champions **(1)** 1961-62
Division 2 Champions **(1)** 1946-47
Scottish Cup Winners **(1)** 1910
League Cup Winners **(3)** 1973-74, 1952-53, 1951-52

Dariusz Adamczuk – Signed from Polish club Pogon Stettin in January 1996 for a second spell at Dens Park, the attacking left back and former Polish international impressed in 1997-98, making 38 League and Cup appearances.

Graham Bayne – The 18-year-old rookie forward was brought up through the youth system. He made only one appearance in 1997-98 but may get more opportunities in 1998-99.

Robert Douglas – Dundee's number one keeper is tipped for future full Scotland caps and played for the B-team against Wales in the run up to the World Cup finals. He was signed from Livingston by John McCormack in August 1997 in a swap deal worth £100,000 and including Kevin Magee. He was almost ever-present in 1997-98.

John Elliot – Another Dundee youngster with promise, the teenage striker featured in 22 League and Cup games in 1997-98, netting twice.

Ray Farningham – The veteran player-coach, in his second spell at the club after returning in June 1994, featured three times in 1997-98. Now 37, he is unlikely to feature in the Premier campaign.

James Grady – A real snip at just £25,000, from Clydebank in June 1997, former boss John McCormack interrupted a family get-together and dashed to Glasgow to sign the little 27-year-old. His crucial 14 goals from 40 appearances in 1997-98 showed why.

Brian Grant – The experienced defender has previously played for Stirling Albion, Aberdeen and Hibs, before moving to Dens Park for £50,000 in March 1998. The 34-year-old went on to make six appearances before the end of the season.

Brian Irvine – The inspirational centre half signed from Aberdeen on a free transfer in June 1997. The former Scotland star was rock solid in 40 games in the 1997-98 season and has shown tremendous courage since being diagnosed as having MS in 1995.

Russell Kelly – The young midfielder was signed from Chelsea in February 1997 after failing to make an impression at Stamford Bridge. He featured 18 times for Dundee during the 1997-98 season and scored two goals.

Steve McCormick – The giant striker has enjoyed a prolific scoring record, particularly in his two years with Stirling Albion. He arrived at Dens midway through the 1997-98 season for a nominal fee and went on to make 14 appearances, scoring four goals.

John McGlashan – The steady midfielder signed from Rotherham United in June 1997. More hard-working than polished, the 31-year-old scored his first goal after Jocky Scott's appointment as manager in February 1998. He made 10 appearances in total during the promotion-winning season and scored two goals.

Jim McInally – This vastly experienced and versatile midfielder has played for Celtic, Nottingham Forest, Coventry City, Dundee United, Raith Rovers – and Scotland. Now 34, he is as fit as ever and made 37 appearances and scored once in 1997-98, following his move to the club in June 1997.

Lee Maddison – A free transfer signing from Northampton Town in July 1997, the well-travelled full back made 29 appearances and scored one goal in his first season at Dens Park.

Darren Magee – Since arriving from Milngavie Wanderers, the midfielder

has quietly, but effectively, made his mark under John McCormack and Jocky Scott. The 21-year-old played 19 games in the club's promotion-winning season and should be more than able to cope with top-flight football in 1998-99.

Stephen Milne – Only 17 and a product of the club's youth policy, Milne made three appearances in the 1997-98 season.

Gavin Rae – The 20-year-old made just three appearances during the 1997-98 season but at only 20, the defender has time on his side and has shown he has potential.

Robert Raeside – The South Africa-born centre half is mainly a squad player and scored one goal in just 11 games in 1997-98.

Darren Rogers – The Liverpudlian defender arrived at Dens Park from Chester City in August 1997. A real personality, he is a no-nonsense left-footer rather than a stylish player. Aged 22, he played 40 games and scored one goal in the promotion-winning season.

Barry Smith – Captain at just 24 years of age and a real star for Dundee during the 1997-98 season as sweeper, the former Celtic player was signed by former manager Jim Duffy for £100,000 in December 1995. A model of consistency, he was a virtual ever-present and scored one goal from his 40 appearances.

Billy Thomson – The veteran back-up keeper, who has played for Partick Thistle, St Mirren, Dundee United, Motherwell, Rangers and Scotland, is now 40 years old and the Dens' goalkeeping coach. He made just one appearance as a player in the 1997-98 season.

Craig Tully – The 22-year-old defender, who signed for Dundee in April 1994, managed 21 appearances in 1997-98.

Jerry O'Driscoll – A promising striker, he suffered from injury in 1997-98 and managed just 19 appearances and two goals. He is yet another Dundee player brought up through the youth ranks.

Iain Anderson – The Scotland Under-21 star is a hot tip to dazzle in the new Premier League. Already valued at £1 million, the winger featured 37 times in the First Division title-winning campaign and scored six goals.

Eddie Annand – A striker brought to Dens from Clyde by sacked boss John McCormack in a £90,000 deal at the start of the 1997 season, he scored 14 goals from 39 games in 1997-98.

Dundee United Football Club

Dundee United Football Club
Dundee United Football Club
Dundee United Football Club
Dundee United Football Club
Dundee United Football Club
Dundee United Football Club
Dundee United Football Club
Dundee United Football Club
Dundee United Football Club
Dundee United Football Club

→ **Address** | Dundee United FC, Tannadice Park, Tannadice Street, Dundee DD3 7JW

Tel: 01382 833166 | **Tickets:** 01382 833166 | **Clubline:** 0891 881909

David Narey, who holds the record for the most League appearances for the club, was also capped 35 times by Scotland and made 76 appearances for Dundee United in European games.

Top row • M Perry • S Pressley • S Dykstra • A Maxwell • N Duffy • K Olofsson

Middle row • D Rankine • G Liveston • R McKinnon • L Zetterlund • D Sinclair • S McKimmie • E Pedersen • G Wallace • I Campbell

Bottom row • R Winters • G McSwegan • D Bowman • T McLean • M Malpas • J Dolan • A McLaren

→ **Chairman:** Jim McLean   → **Manager:** Tommy McLean   → **Year formed:** 1909

Ground: Tannadice Park (14,209)

Stands: East
West
Fair Play
George Fox

Home strip: Tangerine shirts, black shorts, tangerine socks

Away strip: White shirts, white shorts, white socks

Sponsor: Telewest

Programme: £1.50

Nickname: Terrors

Ground history: 1909 Tannadice Park

Previous name: Dundee Hibernian

Record attendance: 28,000 v Barcelona, Fairs Cup 2nd round, 16 November 1966

Record victory: 14-0 v Nithsdale Wanderers, Scottish Cup 1st round, 17 January 1931

Record defeat: 1-12 v Motherwell, Division 2, 23 January 1954

Highest League scorer (season): John Coyle, 41, 1955-56

Highest League scorer (aggregate): Peter McKay, 158, 1947-1954

Most League appearances: David Narey, 612, 1973-1994

Most capped player: Maurice Malpas, 55, Scotland, 1984-1993

Highest transfer fee paid: £750,000 to Coventry City for Steven Pressley, July 1995

Highest transfer fee received: £4m from Rangers for Duncan Ferguson, July 1993

Major trophies: Premier Division Champions (**1**) 1982-83
Division 2 Champions (**2**) 1928-29, 1924-25
Scottish Cup Winners (**1**) 1994
Scottish League Cup Winners (**2**) 1980-81, 1979-80

Julian Alsford – The strong central defender joined the club from Chester just before the 1997-98 transfer deadline in a combined £200,000 deal with team-mate Iain Jenkins.

Mikael Andersson – The Swedish winger, initially on loan, signed in November 1997. After his debut against Aberdeen, he only featured in two more games during the season.

Paul Black – The 20-year-old midfielder, who came through the Dundee United youth ranks four years ago, only played for the Terrors once in the 1997-98 season, coming on as a substitute in the 8-0 UEFA Cup win over CE Principat in October.

Davie Bowman – The long-serving midfielder and Scotland international celebrated his 12th year with the club in 1997-98. Previously with Hearts and Coventry, Bowman featured in over half of the games.

Jim Dolan – A hardworking midfielder and good team player, Dolan joined the club in January 1997 after nine years with Motherwell. But his goalscoring record is hardly prolific – in more than 200 League appearances he has only scored five times.

Neil Duffy – The 31-year-old midfielder has flitted in and out of the Terrors first team. Of his 10 appearances last season, eight came as a substitute and none came in the last two months of the season.

Craig Easton – A Terrors youth team graduate, Easton broke into the first team in January 1997. A Scotland Under-21 international midfielder, he made more than 30 appearances in the 1997-98 season and managed to score twice.

Iain Jenkins – Jenkins joined the club from Chester in March 1998 along with fellow Englishman Julian Alsford. He showed great composure on the

ball in his seven appearances for the club before the end of the season.

Siggi Jonsson – The former Arsenal and Sheffield Wednesday midfielder signed in December 1997 in a £75,000 move from Swedish side Orebro. An Icelandic international, Jonsson had time to show glimpses of his class.

Stewart McKimmie – The Aberdeen-born defender played 14 seasons for his hometown club but left Pittodrie in March 1997 to wind his career down with the Terrors. His only appearances last season came right at the start of the campaign and at 35 he could now be ready to hang up his boots.

Ray McKinnon – A strong all-round midfielder, McKinnon is in his second spell at United. He started his career at Tannadice in 1987 and returned in November 1995.

Andy McLaren – A strong attacking force and former Rangers youth player, McLaren's six goals last season came mainly from his appearances as a substitute.

Gary McSwegan – A £375,000 signing in October 1995, McSwegan started the season on fire, netting three hat-tricks in his first four games. But the goals started to dry up and he found himself warming the bench for the latter part of the 1997-98 season.

Erik Pedersen – A former Norwegian international, Pedersen has rarely missed a game since joining the club in October 1996, bravely playing through a painful pelvic injury towards the end of the 1997-98 season.

Maurice Malpas – Malpas celebrates 20 years of professional football at Tannadice Park this year. A club legend, he's now played more than 600 games for the Terrors and at 36 he still oozes class in the heart of the Dundee United defence.

Goran Marklund – The young Swede arrived at the club in the summer of 1997 in a £100,000 move from Vasulund. Despite showing great promise in pre-season, Marklund only made the first team on four occasions. However, he is still considered a player for the future.

Mark Perry – The 27-year-old joined the club in 1989 and can operate either in midfield or defence. A tall, consistent player, he is highly rated and tipped for international honours.

Steven Pressley – 'Elvis' had yet another superb season at the back for the Terrors and has been a virtual ever-present in the side since his move from Coventry in August 1995.

Davie Sinclair – The 28-year-old defender arrived from Millwall in February 1997 but failed to find a regular place in the starting line-up. Loaned out to Livingston for a month, he returned to Tannadice before the season's end to make three more substitute appearances.

Magnus Skoldmark – The Swedish defender and former team-mate of Lars Zetterlund had been plying his trade in China before his move to Scotland early in 1997-98.

Steven Thompson – The 19-year-old forward is set for a bright future after impressing in his first professional season. Despite only three starts for the Terrors, he netted two goals.

Paul Walker – The diminutive midfielder is yet another Tannadice youth team graduate. At 21, he has time on his side to make it in the game after failing to shine in his only two first-team outings in 1997-98.

Robbie Winters – Since joining Dundee United in 1993, Winters has become a firm favourite with the fans. A skilful, attacking player who scored 17 goals last season, the 23-year-old is tipped for the big time.

Lars Zetterlund – The veteran Swede had a strong campaign in his first full season at the club. A talented ball-playing defender, he played in the Gothenburg side that beat United in the 1987 UEFA Cup final.

Kjell Olofsson – The club's top scorer in 1997-98 with 23 goals, Olofsson has become a firm favourite with the Tannadice faithful with some spectacular strikes and his general unselfish play.

Sieb Dykstra – The Dutch keeper joined in December 1996 in a £100,000 move from QPR. An ever-present in 1997-98, Dykstra is well regarded in Scotland after a previous spell with Motherwell.

Dunfermline Athletic Football Club

→ **Address** | Dunfermline Athletic FC, East End Park, Halbeath Road, Dunfermline, Fife KY12 7RB

Tel: 01383 724295 | **Tickets:** 01383 724295 | **Clubline:** 0930 555060

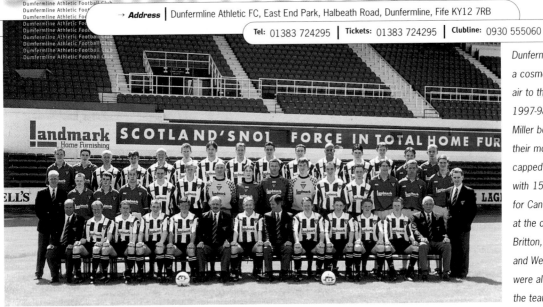

Dunfermline had a cosmopolitan air to them in 1997-98. Colin Miller became their most capped player with 15 games for Canada while at the club, and Britton, Ireland and Welsh were all on the teamsheet.

Top row • J Gallagher • K Donnelly • H French • J Fraser • R Sharp • G Shaw • C Ireland • I den Bieman • A Tod • S Welsh • D Barnett • G Louden • C Martin • S Boyle • A Reid **Middle row** • G Robertson • C McGroarty • A Hoxley • D Currie • M McCulloch • A Smith • I Westwater • M Parkin • Z Lemajic • D Hay • D Bingham • C Nish • D Hay • C Templeton • J Nelson **Bottom row** • P Yeates • G Shields • M Millar • S Petrie • C Miller • D Campbell • C Robertson • B Paton • H Curran • A Moore • D Fleming • S Young • D McParland

→ **Chairman:** Roy Woodrow   → **Manager:** Bert Paton   → **Year formed:** 1885

Ground: East End Park (12,500)

Stands: South
West
North
East

Home strip: Black and white striped shirts with white trim, black shorts, black socks with white trim

Away strip: Blue shirts with white trim, white shorts with blue trim, white socks with blue trim

Sponsor: Landmark

Programme: £1.50

Nickname: Pars

Ground history: 1885 East End Park

Previous name: None

Record attendance: 27,816 v Celtic, Division 1, 30 April 1968

Record victory: 11-2 v Stenhousemuir, Division 2, 27 September 1930

Record defeat: 1-11 v Hibernian, Scottish Cup 3rd round replay, 26 October 1889

Highest League scorer (season): Bobby Skinner, 53, 1925-26

Highest League scorer (aggregate): Charlie Dickson, 154, 1955-1964

Most League appearances: Norrie McCathie, 497, 1981-1996

Most capped player: Colin Miller, 15, Canada, 1995-1998

Highest transfer fee paid: £540,000 to Girondins de Bordeaux (France) for Istvan Kozma, August 1989

Highest transfer fee received: £650,000 from Celtic for Jackie McNamara, October 1995

Major trophies: First Division Champions **(2)** 1995-96, 1988-89
Second Division Champions **(1)** 1985-86
Division 2 Champions **(1)** 1925-26
Scottish Cup Winners **(2)** 1968, 1961

David Bingham – A local lad, Bingham was bought to the club in September 1995 from Forfar Athletic, where he had been top scorer for two seasons. Injuries and loss of form combined to produce a slow start at Dunfermline, but the midfielder-forward began to make a bigger contribution in the 1997-98 season.

Ivo den Bieman – The club's popular Dutchman has been used in a variety of defensive positions since joining the club from Dundee in August 1993 but he is probably most effective operating wide on the right. His unconventional style, long throw-ins and – when they work – superb crosses all combine to make him a firm favourite with Pars fans, though the player spent much of 1997-98 as a substitute.

John Fraser – A promising product of Dunfermline's youth policy, Fraser made his debut for the club at the end of the 1996-97 season but struggled to break into the first team in 1997-98 following a series of injuries. When he did appear, he put in some fine midfield performances.

Hamish French – The 34-year-old was signed from Dundee United for £150,000 in October 1991 and is now Dunfermline's second longest-serving player. A regular in the 1997-98 season, French became the club's current leading goalscorer with 59 career goals in more than 250 appearances, even though he now plays most of his football in midfield.

Richard Huxford – Signed from Burnley just before the transfer deadline in March 1998, this skilful but combative midfielder performed well in the closing stages of the season. Born in Scunthorpe, Huxford has a wealth of experience with English clubs, including Barnet, Millwall, Birmingham City, Bradford City and Burnley.

Craig Ireland – A centre half signed at 20 years of age from Aberdeen for £70,000 in February 1996, Ireland lost form early on in the 1997-98 season but returned in March and looked an entirely different prospect, topping off his fine performances with a goal against Motherwell.

Scott McCulloch – Originally a member of the Rangers youth squad, McCulloch recovered from a serious car accident at Hamilton Academical before joining the Pars in December 1997. A towering and tough-tackling defender, he made his debut against Dundee United and proved during the season that he's always willing to push forward and make driving runs at the opposition.

Paul McDonald – An old-style winger who went straight into the first team against Hibernian in January 1998 following his move from Brighton & Hove Albion, McDonald made only a handful of appearances and was unable to secure a regular place.

Marc Millar – A midfield stalwart signed from Brechin City in October 1994, Millar experienced a frustrating 1997-98 season following a series of injuries that restricted his number of appearances.

Stewart Petrie – Top scorer at Forfar Athletic before his £70,000 move to Dunfermline in August 1993, Petrie plays either through the middle or wide on the left from where he can fire in telling crosses – a role which seemed to suit the club's style in the 1997-98 season.

Raymond Sharp – A straightforward, tough-tackling defender, Sharp was signed by the club for the second time in November 1996 after two years at Preston North End. He is a former Scotland Under-21 international and although he's made nearly 200 appearances for Dunfermline, he struggled in vain

to regain his place in the team during the 1997-98 season.

George Shaw – A target buy for Pars manager Bert Paton for some time, Shaw became a Dunfermline player in a swap deal that took Derek Fleming to Dundee in September 1997. Lack of match fitness and injuries, however, restricted his appearances in the 1997-98 season.

Greg Shields – Bert Paton paid a substantial amount for this young Rangers defender in June 1997. The pacy full back was automatic choice in the number two shirt throughout the 1997-98 season and didn't miss a game in any of the League or Cup fixtures.

Andrew Tod – A versatile player who has played up front and in midfield as well as his current position in the heart of defence, Tod missed only one game in the 1997-98 season and only two games in nearly 200 League and Cup games for the club since signing from Keity Hearts in 1993. He has a keen eye for goal, is good at set pieces, and scored six times last season.

Steve Welsh – A fitness fanatic, Welsh was signed by Bert Paton following a second spell at Peterborough and bolstered the defence in the latter stages of the 1996-97 season. In the following season however, he failed to regain his place after early injuries. Formerly in the army, he has also played for Cambridge United and Partick Thistle.

Ian Westwater – A former Scotland youth international who played in the Premier League for Hearts at 16, Westwater moved to Dunfermline in March 1985 for £4,000. The skilful shot-stopper returned to East End Park in 1994 after a spell at Falkirk and a series of inspired performances kept him firmly between the posts in 1997-98.

Andy Smith – The striker broke his leg in his first match after signing from Airdrie in July 1995 but has been a real power ever since, first in midfield and, in 1997-98, up front, netting 26 goals in total.

Gerry Britton – Signed from Dundee in July 1996, Britton was an instant hit with the fans and was top scorer for the 1996-97 season. But injury kept the former Celtic and Partick player out until late in the 1997-98 season.

Craig Robertson – The club's longest-serving player took over as captain in 1996 but missed the first half of last season through injury. A great reader of the game, he can make effective runs into the opposition's penalty area.

Heart of Midlothian *Football Club*

Heart of Midlothian Football Club
Heart of Midlothian Football Club
Heart of Midlothian Football Club
Heart of Midlothian Football Club
Heart of Midlothian Football Club
Heart of Midlothian Footb...
Heart of Midlothian Footb...
Heart of Midlothian Football Club
Heart of Midlothian Football Club
Heart of Midlothian Football Club
Heart of Midlothian Football Club

→ **Address** | Heart of Midlothian FC, Tynecastle Stadium, Gorgie Road, Edinburgh EH11 2NL

Tel: 0131 200 7200 | **Tickets:** 0131 200 7201 | **Clubline:** 0131 200 7255

In 1997-98, Hearts record compared to the previous season included: six more wins, one less draw, five less defeats, 37 more goals and 17 more points.

Top row • S Fulton • D McPherson • R McKenzie • G Rousset • M Hogarth • D Weir • P Ritchie

Middle row • C Cameron • D Murie • S Callachan • T Flogel • N Pointon • S Adam • G Murray • J Hamilton • A McManus • J Goss • G Naysmith

Bottom row • S Salvatori • N McCann • B Logan • P Hegarty • B Brown • G Locke • J Jefferies • P Houston • A Rae • J Robertson • S Frail

→ **Web site:** http://www.heartsfc.co.uk → **Chairman:** Leslie Deans → **Manager:** Jim Jefferies → **Year formed:** 1874

Ground: Tynecastle Stadium (17,960)

Stands: Main
Roseburn
Wheatfield
Gorgie Road

Home strip: Maroon shirts with white trim, white shorts, maroon socks with white trim

Away strip: White shirts with maroon trim, white shorts with maroon trim, white socks with maroon trim

Sponsor: Strongbow

Programme: £1.50

Nickname: Hearts

Ground history: 1874 The Meadows
1878 Powderhall
1881 Old Tynecastle
1886 Tynecastle Stadium

Previous name: None

Record attendance: 53,396 v Rangers, Scottish Cup 3rd round, 13 February 1932

Record victory: 15-0 v King's Park (Stirling), Scottish Cup 2nd round, 3 February 1937

Record defeat: 1-8 v Vale of Leven, Scottish Cup 3rd round, 21 October 1888

Highest League scorer (season): Barney Battles, 44, 1930-31

Highest League scorer (aggregate): John Robertson, 214, 1982-1998

Most League appearances: Gary Mackay, 515, 1980-1997

Most capped player: Bobby Walker, 29, Scotland, 1900-1913

Highest transfer fee paid: £750,000 to Newcastle United for John Robertson, December 1988

Highest transfer fee received: £2m from Rangers for Alan McLaren, September 1994

Major trophies: First Division Champions **(1)** 1979-80
Division 1 Champions **(4)** 1959-60, 1957-58, 1896-97, 1894-95
Scottish Cup Winners **(6)** 1998, 1956, 1906, 1901, 1896, 1891
Scottish League Cup Winners **(4)** 1962-63, 1959-60, 1958-59, 1954-55

Stephane Adam – The French striker joined the club from Metz at the end of the 1996-97 season. A prolific scorer, he netted 12 goals in his first season with Hearts, including the vital second in the Scottish Cup final against Rangers in May 1998.

Stuart Callaghan – A tidy midfielder, Callaghan has been at the club for four years, yet has not made the same impression on the first team that he did at youth level.

Colin Cameron – A versatile player capable of fitting in anywhere in an attacking position, Cameron was a first-team regular in 1997-98 and scored the penalty against Rangers in the Scottish Cup final.

Thomas Flogel – The Austrian international joined Hearts in July 1997 but, at 37, was used sparingly as a forward during the season, although he still scored seven goals.

Steve Fulton – A product of Celtic's youth system, Fulton joined Hearts in 1995. A Scotland Under-21 international midfielder, he had a terrific 1997-98 season and missed just one game.

Jim Hamilton – The Aberdeen-born youngster joined Hearts in December 1996 and is a proven goalscorer. A Scotland Under-21 international, he netted 15 goals in his first full season at Tynecastle, impressing the fans with some hardworking displays.

Derek Holmes – The 19-year-old midfielder spent three months on loan to Cowdenbeath but was recalled to the Hearts squad for the final League game of the season, in which he scored with his first touch after coming on as an 80th-minute substitute.

Gary Locke – A fan as well as a player, Locke is a tough tackler as well as a skilled ball player. But having battled back after a cruciate ligament injury four years ago, he still struggled with his fitness during the 1997-98 season.

Neil McCann – The Greenock-born winger joined from Dundee in a £200,000 deal, after originally agreeing a move to Austria. An exciting youngster, McCann has great pace and skill on the ball and is another Under-21 international. He started the 1997-98 season on fire and was widely tipped for a place in Scotland's 1998 World Cup squad but failed to make the grade.

Roddy McKenzie – A capable replacement for keeper Gilles Rousset when called upon, McKenzie is another Under-21 international who started his career with Hearts before moving to Stenhousemuir. He returned to Tynecastle in 1996 and played five games in 1997-98.

Allan McManus – A Hearts youth product, the 23-year-old full back is good in the air and solid on the ground. A bit-part player since his first team bow back in December 1995, he featured only once in the Hearts side after Christmas 1997.

Lee Makel – The former Newcastle and Blackburn midfielder joined Hearts from Huddersfield Town for £75,000 in March 1998 and made six appearances before the season's end, three as a substitute.

David Murie – The young defender started his Hearts career on Boxing Day 1996 but has since struggled to make the starting line-up. It is hoped that he will get more of a chance in the 1998-99 campaign after featuring only twice last season.

Grant Murray – The young midfielder had few chances to shine in 1997-98 but did get an extended run in the first team after Christmas.

Gary Naysmith – The 19-year-old defender featured heavily in the first team squad after the New Year and scored two memorable goals in the process. A pacy full back, Naysmith is definitely one for the future.

Neil Pointon – The former Manchester City and Everton defender joined Hearts from Oldham Athletic in October 1995 and has since been used as a full back and in midfield. An excellent crosser of the ball, his career north of the border has been somewhat hindered by injuries and he only featured in two games after the New Year was ushered in in 1998.

Jose Quitongo – The little winger has been a revelation for Hearts since his £80,000 move from Hamilton Academical in January 1998. Used mainly as a substitute, the former Benfica man scored five times in his 18 appearances in the 1997-98 season and soon became a firm favourite with the fans.

Paul Ritchie – Yet another product of Hearts youth side, he made the jump to the first team at the same time as full back Allan McManus. The Scotland Under-21 international is a powerful defender, good in the air, and comfortable on the ground. He was a virtual ever-present in the 1997-98 season and was voted Man of the Match in the Scottish Cup final victory over Rangers.

Kevin Thomas – The former Scotland Under-21 striker played in only two games for Hearts in the 1997-98 season, both in August at the start of the campaign. In April 1998, he moved to Stirling Albion on loan.

David Weir – The big defender capped an excellent season for Hearts with a call-up to the Scotland squad for the 1998 World Cup finals. Weir joined the club from Falkirk in July 1996 and made an immediate impact on the side. He was constantly watched by scouts last season, when he missed just one game, and could be set for a move into the big time in Scotland or England.

Gilles Rousset – An outstanding performer since joining the club in 1995, the French keeper has become a huge favourite with the fans. He enjoyed another consistent season in 1997-98.

Dave McPherson – The 34-year-old defender is nearing the end of a successful career. A crowd favourite, his 1997-98 season didn't start until January but his return showed the fans what they had been missing.

Stefano Salvatori – The Italian utility player, who signed for Hearts on a free in July 1996, was one of the club's most consistent performers in the 1997-98 season, filling in in defence and midfield.

Kilmarnock Football Club
Kilmarnock Football Club
Kilmarnock Football Club
Kilmarnock Football Club
Kilmarnock Football Club
Kilmarnock Football Club
Kilmarnock Football Club

306

Kilmarnock *Football Club*

→ **Address** | Kilmarnock FC, Rugby Park, Rugby Road, Kilmarnock KA1 2DP

Tel: 01563 525184 | **Tickets:** 01563 525184 | **Clubline:** 0891 633249

In 1997-98, for the first time in their nine seasons in the Scottish Premier Division, Kimarnock won more games than they lost and finished with their highest placing in the Scottish League in 29 years.

Top row • R Lennox • A Kerr • M Roberts • K Doig • K McGowne • C Meldrum • D Anderson • C McKie • M Graham • G Tallon • G Hay **Middle row** • P Finnigan • G McCutcheon • D Bagan • S Hamilton • M Baker • N Whitworth • D Lekovic • J McIntyre • W Findlay • A Mitchell • A Burke • R Vincent • J Dillon **Bottom row** • H Allan • M Reilly • G MacPherson • G McCabe • R Williamson • J Clark • R Montgomerie • P Wright • G Hollas

→ **Web site:** http://www.kilmarnockfc.co.uk → **Chairman:** Bill Costley → **Manager:** Bobby Williamson → **Year formed:** 1869

Ground: Rugby Park (18,128)

Stands: East
West
Moffat
Chadwick

Home strip: Blue and white striped shirts, white shorts, red socks

Away strip: Gold shirts with navy trim, navy shorts, navy socks

Sponsor: Sports Division

Programme: £1.50

Nickname: The Killie

Ground history: 1869 Rugby Park (Dundonald Road)
1873 The Grange
1873 Holm Quarry
1876 The Grange
1876 Holm Quarry
1879 Rugby Park

Previous name: None

Record attendance: 35,995 v Rangers, Scottish FA Cup quarter-final, 10 March 1962

Record victory: 11-1 v Paisley Academical, Scottish FA Cup 1st round, 18 January 1930

Record defeat: 1-9 v Celtic, Division 1, 13 August 1938

Highest League scorer (season): Harry 'Peerie' Cunningham, 34, 1927-28 Andy Kerr, 34, 1960-61

Highest League scorer (aggregate): Willie Culley, 148, 1912-1923

Most League appearances: Alan Robertson, 481, 1972-1988

Most capped player: John Nibloe, 11, Scotland, 1924-1932

Highest transfer fee paid: £340,000 to St Johnstone for Paul Wright, March 1995

Highest transfer fee received: £420,000 from Reading for Jim McIntyre, March 1998

Major trophies: Division 1 Champions **(1)** 1964-65
Division 2 Champions **(2)** 1898-99, 1897-98
Scottish Cup Winners **(3)** 1997, 1929, 1920

David Bagan – The 21-year-old attacking midfielder continued where he'd left off from the 1996-97 season with some good displays early in the 1997-98 campaign. He is rated an outstanding prospect for the future.

Martin Baker – Having joined Kilmarnock from St Mirren for £175,000 in the close season, the talented left back is a tough tackler and has earned himself eight yellow cards and one red card since he's been at the club.

Alex Burke – 'Wee Burkey' has burst into the Kilmarnock side and the Scotland Under-21 team over the past two seasons. The 1996-97 Young Player of the Year had another good campaign last season, scoring three goals. Still only 20, he should have a great career ahead of him.

Kevin Doig – The defender was a regular reserve team player in 1997-98 but only made one first team appearance.

Steven Hamilton – The 23-year-old defender was called up for six first-team games in 1997-98 but was unfortunate to finish on the losing side on four of those occasions.

John Henry – Killie paid Clydebank £175,000 for Henry in August 1994, where he had a reputation as a midfield goalscorer. Though the goals seem to have dried up after his move to Rugby Park, he still showed glimpses of quality in the 1997-98 season.

Gary Holt – A powerful midfielder, Holt has impressed Killie fans with his versatility down the left flank and registered two goals in the 1997-98 season.

Dylan Kerr – The defender celebrated another strong season at Rugby Park by agreeing a new two-year deal with the club in May 1998. The season started late for the former Sheffield Wednesday, Leeds and Reading player but he went on to give a number of dependable performances at the back.

Jim Lauchlan – Considered to be a future Scotland international, the big defender established himself in the Killie side during the 1997-98 season and is now a firm favourite of the Rugby Park faithful.

Gary McCutcheon – The 19-year-old youngster had just one minute of first-team action at Rugby Park in 1997-98 and spent the last five months of the season on loan to Stenhousemuir. The promising striker returned to the club in May 1998.

Kevin McGowne – McGowne, who joined the club from St Johnstone early in the 1996-97 campaign, enjoyed another consistent season in the Kilmarnock defence. A tough competitor, he received nine yellow cards and one red as he helped his side to a European place in 1998-99.

Gus MacPherson – Since his move to Killie from Rangers in 1991, this strong utility player has been a real favourite at Rugby Park. A seasoned campaigner in the Kilmarnock defence, MacPherson made 33 appearances in 1997-98 and only blotted his copybook with two sendings off.

Gordon Marshall – An experienced goalkeeper who was signed from Celtic in January 1998 after the swift exit of Yugoslav Dragoje Lekovic to Spanish side Sporting Gijon, Marshall did enough in his 13 games before the end of the 1997-98 season to convince the fans of his quality.

Colin Meldrum – A Scotland Under-21 international and an outstanding prospect in goal, Meldrum proved an able deputy to Lekovic over the past two seasons and was expected to keep his place after the Yugoslav's departure. However, the signing of Gordon Marshall kept him out of the side for all but three games after November.

Ally Mitchell – He has been a regular first-team player since his move to the club from East Fife in July 1991. Used predominantly as a winger or midfielder, he has now made more than 250 appearances for Killie. The 29-year-old featured in 39 games in 1997-98 but finished the campaign on the bench.

Martin O'Neill – The former Scotland Under-21 international signed from Clyde in a player exchange deal in August 1997. Although a talented midfield playmaker, he went on to make only four substitute appearances all season.

Mark Reilly – A solid defender, Reilly started his career with Motherwell before joining Killie in the 1991 close season. Originally a full back, he has spent most of his career at Rugby Park playing as a midfielder. An ever-present in the squad in the 1997-98 season, he earned a call-up to the Scotland B-team after some great performances.

Mark Roberts – A talented midfielder, Roberts made his Killie debut aged just 16, at the end of the 1991-92 season. He scored nine goals from 19 starts during the 1997-98 season and is seen as an important part of the club's future.

Robert Vincent – The young midfielder made just two substitute appearances early in the 1997-98 season before spending a month on loan to Albion Rovers in March 1998.

Paul Wright – Killie's top scorer in 1997-98 was rewarded with a Scotland B call-up towards the end of the season, adding to his Youth and Under-21 caps. A lethal striker, he passed the 100 League goal mark halfway through the 1997-98 campaign.

Ray Montgomerie – The long-serving Kilmarnock skipper and defender recently passed the 350-game mark for the club, where his never-say-die attitude is greatly appreciated by the fans.

Pat Nevin – Signed from Tranmere at the start of the 1997-98 season, the former Scotland international was particularly brilliant towards the end of the season and showed his class for Killie by scoring five goals.

Jerome Vareille – The big French striker netted seven goals in 1997-98. He finished the season on the bench but was still linked with a move to Premiership-bound Nottingham Forest.

Motherwell *Football Club*

Motherwell Football Club
Motherwell Football Club
Motherwell Football Club
Motherwell Football Club
Motherwell Football Club
Motherwell Football Club

Address | Motherwell FC, Fir Park, Fir Park Street, Motherwell, Lanarkshire ML1 2QN

Tel: 01698 333333 | **Tickets:** 01698 333030 | **Clubline:** 0891 121553

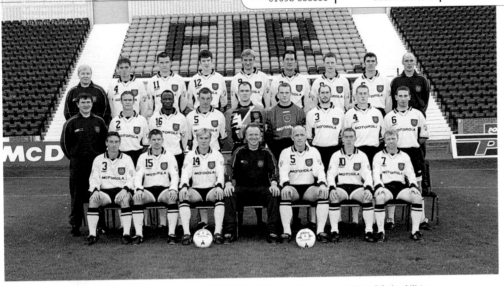

The only player to have appeared in every game for Well in the 1997-98 season was goalkeeper Stevie Woods, who conceded 72 goals in 43 games – an average of 1.67 goals per game.

Top row • J Porteous • S Valakari • L McCulloch • K Christie • G Denham • W Falconer • S Craigan • O Coyle • A Watson

Middle row • J Griffin • S McMillan • E Shivute • J Philliben • S Woods • G Gow • S McSkimming • J Hendry • I Ross

Bottom row • D Arnott • E May • T Coyne • A McLeish • B Martin • B Davies • M Weir

→ **Chairman:** Bill Dickie   → **Manager:** Harri Kampman   → **Year formed:** 1886

Ground: Fir Park (13,800)

Stands: Davie Cooper
  Main
  South
  East

Home strip: Amber shirts with claret trim, white shorts, amber socks

Away strip: White shirts with claret trim, white shorts with claret trim, white socks with claret trim

Sponsor: Motorola

Programme: £1.50

Nickname: Well

Ground history: 1886 Roman Road
  1889 Dalziel Park
  1895 Fir Park

Previous name: None

Record attendance: 35,632 v Rangers, Scottish Cup 4th round replay, 12 March 1952

Record victory: 12-1 v Dundee United, Division 2, 23 January 1954

Record defeat: 0-8 v Aberdeen, Premier Division, 26 March 1979

Highest League scorer (season): Willie McFadyen, 52, 1931-32

Highest League scorer (aggregate): Hugh Ferguson, 283, 1916-1925

Most League appearances: Bobby Ferrier, 613, 1919-1941

Most capped player: Tommy Coyne, 13, Republic of Ireland, 1993-1997

Highest transfer fee paid: £500,000 to PSV Eindhoven (Holland) for Mitchell van der Gaag, March 1995

Highest transfer fee received: £1.75m from Celtic for Phil O'Donnell, September 1994

Major trophies: First Division Champions **(2)** 1984-85, 1981-82
Division 1 Champions **(1)** 1931-1932
Division 2 Champions **(2)** 1968-69, 1953-54
Scottish Cup Winners **(2)** 1952, 1991
League Cup Winners **(1)** 1950-51

Dougie Arnott – Signed in 1986, Arnott is the longest-serving player at Fir Park and the only remaining member of the 1991 Scottish Cup-winning team. Now 36, the striker's appearances were limited to four starts, six substitutions and one goal in the 1997-98 season.

Kevin Christie – Just 22, Christie has shown his potential since signing from East Fife in March 1997. The versatile youngster mainly featured in defence, but was also used as midfield cover.

Owen Coyle – A former Bolton and Dundee United striker, Coyle's goals have been a major factor in Motherwell's continuing status in the top flight. Now 32, he finished as the club's joint top scorer in the 1997-98 season with 16 goals.

Steven Craigan – A promising defender for the future, 21-year-old Craigan was used sparingly by Motherwell last season. He made just seven first team starts at left back and centre half.

Billy Davies – Signed from Dunfermline in 1994, the 34-year-old played for Rangers at the height of his career. A creative midfielder, his lack of first-team action in 1997-98 was attributed to a fallout with former boss Alex McLeish.

Greig Denham – One of Motherwell's brightest young stars, Alex McLeish likened Denham's central defensive talents to his own as a youngster. Solid on the ground and dependable in the air, the 21-year-old formed a sound partnership with Brian Martin as he racked up 21 appearances in the 1997-98 season.

Willie Falconer – A versatile player, Falconer was pressed into action all over the park during the 1997-98 season. Signed in 1996 from Celtic, he is most comfortable as an attacking midfielder and scored four times.

Eric Garcin – Frenchman Garcin quickly won praise for his ball-playing style when he arrived on a one-year deal from Toulouse in November 1997. He slotted into the Well defence and also proved he can pack a good shot – particularly from free kicks – and managed one goal in his 13 appearances.

John Hendry – The £200,000 signing from Tottenham has suffered a miserable three years at Fir Park. The 28-year-old striker hit just one goal in 10 starts in 1997-98 as his form continued to desert him.

Stefan Lindqvist – One of new manager Harri Kampman's first signings, Lindqvist arrived from Gothenburg on a short-term deal in March 1998. The vastly experienced Swede played in midfield five times and scored once.

Lee McCulloch – A Scotland Under-21 regular, McCulloch's raw talent saw him break into the first team in the 1997-98 season aged just 17. A tall striker, Lee made just seven starts but was on the bench a further 21 times. He scored twice and is sure to develop.

Steve McMillan – Another member of the Scotland Under-21 side, his impressive qualities as a left back and midfielder have seen him catch the eye of many bigger clubs and have made him a favourite with the fans. The 22-year-old made 39 starts in 1997-98 and scored once.

Shaun McSkimming – Signed for £350,000 from Kilmarnock, McSkimming has never really lived up to his potential in three seasons at the club. Used mainly on the left side of midfield, he suffered an injury-plagued 1997-98 season and made just 14 starts, scoring only once.

Brian Martin – One of the mainstays of the Motherwell side in the 1990s, Martin has won international

recognition for his fine form at Fir Park. Signed from St Mirren in 1991, he made 39 appearances in 1997-98. The 35-year-old defender played his last game for the club against Aberdeen on the final day of the season.

Eddie May – A play-anywhere type who favours a right wing-back role, May arrived at Fir Park in a swap deal that took Steve Kirk to Falkirk in 1995. He has still to win over many of the club's fans.

John Philliben – An unsung hero, Philliben is a solid if unspectacular stopper who has operated for his 12 years at the club as cover for the first-choice central defenders.

Eliphas Shivute – A lively and unpredictable player from Namibia, Shivute's form has faded after an explosive start to his career in Scotland. Signed on a free under the Bosman ruling, the lightning-fast winger scored on only his second start in September 1997 against Rangers at Ibrox. But he made just a further 10 starts during the season, although he was impressive in the African Nations Cup.

Scott Thomson – The young keeper was given his debut against Aberdeen on the last day of the season, letting in two, including a penalty.

Simo Valakari – A quietly effective but doggedly determined midfielder, the 25-year-old was signed from Finn PA in his native Finland in February 1997. He made 24 appearances during the 1997-98 season, playing just in front of the defence.

Stevie Woods – A much-criticised goalkeeper who was nevertheless an ever-present in the Motherwell side last season, he signed from Preston in 1994 and spent two seasons as understudy to Scott Howie before claiming the number one shirt in 1997.

Mickey Weir – A winger who spent most of his career with boyhood idols Hibs, he has struggled to find consistency since his move in March 1997. He made 18 starts in 1997-98 and scored in the win over Celtic.

Ian Ross – A young defender who can also operate in midfield, Ross leapt to instant fame with the winner against Celtic on his debut in 1996. However, the 23-year-old remains on the fringes of the first team.

Tommy Coyne – A Republic of Ireland international, Coyne enjoyed success at Celtic and Tranmere before joining Well in 1993. Top scorer in every season at the club, he notched up another 16 goals in 1997-98.

Rangers *Football Club*

Rangers Football Club
Rangers Football Club
Rangers Football Club
Rangers Football Club
Rangers Football Club
Rangers Football Club
Rangers Football Club
Rangers Football Club
Rangers Football Club
Rangers Football Club
Rangers Football Club

→ **Address** | Rangers FC, Ibrox Stadium, Edmiston Drive, Glasgow G51 2XD

Tel: 0141 427 8500 | **Tickets:** 0141 427 8877 | **Clubline:** 0990 991997

Dutchman Dick Advocaat is only the 10th manager in Rangers' 125-year history. He arrived at the club in 1998, following a spell as coach at Dutch club PSV Eindhoven.

Top row • C Moore • E B Andersen • L Amoruso • G Petric • A Niemi • A Goram • T Snelders • J Bjorklund • J Johanson • J Albertz • S Porrini

Middle row • B Ferguson • S Wright • T Vidmar • S Wilson • A McLaren • G Durie • P Gascoigne • I Ferguson • P Van Vossen • J Thern • A Cleland • G Bollan

Front row • G Gattuso • M Negri • S McCall • A McCoist • B Laudrup • I Durrant • S Rozental • D McInnes • C Miller • S Stensaas

→ **Web site:** http://www.rangers.co.uk   → **Chairman:** David Murray   → **Manager:** Dick Advocaat   → **Year formed:** 1873

Ground: Ibrox Stadium (50,411)

Stands: Main, Govan, Broomloan Road, Copland Road

Home strip: Blue shirts with dark blue, red, white and black trim, white shorts with dark blue and red trim, black shorts with red trim

Away strip: Red shirts with blue and white trim, blue shorts with white trim, blue socks with red and white trim

Sponsor: McEwan's

Programme: £1.50

Nickname: Gers

Ground history: 1873 Fleshers' Haugh
   1875 Burnbank
   1876 Kinning Park
   1887 Ibrox
   1899 Ibrox Park

Previous name: None

Record attendance: 118,567 v Celtic, Division 1, 2 January 1939

Record victory: 14-2 v Blairgowrie, Scottish Cup 1st round, 20 January 1934

Record defeat: 2-10 v Airdrieonians, 1886

Highest League scorer (season): Sam English, 44, 1931-32

Highest League scorer (aggregate): Ally McCoist, 249, 1982-1998

Most League appearances: John Greig, 496, 1962-1978

Most capped player: Ally McCoist, 58, Scotland, 1986-1998

Highest transfer fee paid: £4.3m to Lazio (Italy) for Paul Gascoigne, July 1995

Highest transfer fee received: £5.58m from Marseille (France) for Trevor Steven, August 1991

Major trophies: Premier Division Champions **(12)** 1997, 1996, 1995, 1994, 1993, 1992, 1991, 1990, 1989, 1987, 1978, 1976
Division 1 Champions **(35)** 1975, 1964, 1963, 1961, 1959, 1957, 1956, 1953, 1950, 1949, 1947, 1939, 1937, 1935, 1934, 1933, 1931, 1930, 1929, 1928, 1927, 1925, 1924, 1923, 1921, 1920, 1918, 1913, 1912, 1911, 1902, 1901, 1900, 1899, 1891
Scottish Cup Winners **(27)** 1996, 1993, 1992, 1981, 1979, 1978, 1976, 1973, 1966, 1964, 1963, 1962, 1960, 1953, 1950, 1949, 1948, 1936, 1935, 1934, 1932, 1930, 1928, 1903, 1898, 1897, 1894
Scottish League Cup Winners **(20)** 1996-97, 1993-94, 1992-93, 1990-91, 1988-89, 1987-88, 1986-87, 1984-85, 1983-84, 1981-82, 1978-79, 1977-78, 1975-76, 1970-71, 1964-65, 1963-64, 1961-62, 1960-61, 1948-49, 1946-47
Cup Winners Cup Winners **(1)** 1972

Jorg Albertz – An attacking left-sided midfielder, Albertz scored 14 goals in the 1997-98 season. Known as 'the Hammer' because of a thunderous left foot, he came from German club Hamburg for £4 million in July 1996.

Lorenzo Amoruso – Injured in a friendly game after his May 1997 move from Fiorentina for £4 million, Amoruso came back for six games at the end of a frustrating season.

Joachim Bjorklund – Signed from Vicenza for £1.7 million in July 1996, the Swedish international defender made the number six jersey his own at Ibrox in 1997-98.

Alex Cleland – The Scottish international right back, along with Gary Bollan, was bought from Dundee United in January 1995 for a joint fee of £750,000. He is effective going forward and quick at getting back.

Gordon Durie – The hardworking target man, who was bought from Spurs for £1 million in December 1993, contributed 10 goals in 1997-98 and his performances helped secure a team place for France '98, – the only Rangers representative.

Ian Durrant – The local lad has been with Rangers for most of his playing career apart from five games on loan to Everton. A midfielder, he suffered from injuries in the 1997-98 season and is now used sparingly – eight of his 11 games were as a substitute.

Barry Ferguson – A midfielder and a product of Ibrox Youth, the 20-year-old has been held back by the size and quality of the squad but still played 11 games in 1997-98.

Ian Ferguson – An £850,000 buy from St Mirren in February 1988, the tenacious Scottish international midfielder has suffered from injury and was a fringe player in 1997-98.

Gennaro Gattuso – Signed on a free from Italian club Perugia in 1997, this

skilful and hardworking midfielder played 34 games last season and bagged eight goals.

Richard Gough – One of the great modern servants of the club and a rock at the heart of the Rangers defence, Gough returned to captain the side from September 1997 after a spell with Kansas City Wizards.

Jonatan Johansson – Signed from FC Flora of Estonia in August 1997 for £500,000, the 23-year-old striker started only two games in 1997-98.

Brian Laudrup – Rangers' leading scorer in 1996-97 scored only four goals last season but the Danish international's contribution in a free role behind the strikers was telling – even after his move to Chelsea was agreed.

Stuart McCall – Signed from Everton for £1.2 million in 1991, the Scottish midfielder was a committed Rangers player for seven seasons but injury curbed his contribution in 1997-98.

Derek McInnes – An attacking midfielder bought from Greenock Morton in November 1995 for £250,000, McInnes played only once in 1997-98.

Charlie Miller – Another youth product, Miller made his debut in the first team in 1992 but failed to secure a first team place in the Rangers midfield last season.

Craig Moore – Secured on a free from the Australian Institute of Sport in 1993, this left-sided defender drifted in and out of the side.

Antti Niemi – A Finnish international, Niemi was signed from Copenhagen in June 1997 for £1.5 million and under-studied Andy Goram before playing several matches in the closing stages of the season.

Gordan Petric – Signed from Dundee United in July 1995 for £1.5 million,

this Yugoslavian international central defender struggled for a place during the 1997-98 season and found himself up against the likes of Richard Gough.

Sergio Porrini – A stylish centre half signed from Juventus in June 1997 for £3.2 million, Porrini played 35 games in the 1997-98 season and chipped in with four goals.

Sebastian Rozental – Plagued by injury since his £3.8 million transfer from Universidad Catolica in January 1997, the Chilean international striker played only four games in 1997-98, three of them coming as substitute.

Theo Snelders – With FC Twente in Holland before moving to Aberdeen for eight years, Snelders was bought for £200,000 in March 1996 as cover for the keeper. He played nine games last season when first choice Goram was injured but was later replaced by Niemi.

Stale Stensaas – Another summer signing, this time from Rosenborg of Norway at a cost of £1.75 million, Stensaas started the 1997-98 season well but lost his regular place at left back in the first team in the New Year.

Jonas Thern – Sweden's international midfielder, signed from Roma in July 1997 on a free, battled it out for a regular first-team place during the 1997-98 season but still started in 23 games.

Tony Vidmar – Signed on a free transfer from Dutch club NAC Breda, Vidmar played only sporadically in the Rangers defence during the 1997-98 season.

Peter van Vossen – The Dutch international striker, who arrived at the club as part of a swap deal in 1996, came on as a substitute in just three games during the 1997-98 season.

Ally McCoist – McCoist has scored more than 300 goals for Rangers since his debut in 1983 and showed no signs of stopping in 1997-98, registering on the scoresheet a further 15 times.

Marco Negri – Signed from Perugia for £3.7 million in 1997, the Italian international striker amassed 36 goals in 38 matches in his first season – including five in one match – despite drying up after Christmas.

Andy Goram – Signed from Hibernian for £1 million in June 1991, Goram was first-choice keeper for Rangers throughout their golden era in the 1990s and also for his country – until he gave up his place at France '98.

St Johnstone *Football Club*

→ **Address** | St Johnstone FC, McDiarmid Park, Crieff Road, Perth PH1 2SJ

Tel: 01738 626961 | **Tickets:** 01738 626961 | **Clubline:** 0891 121559

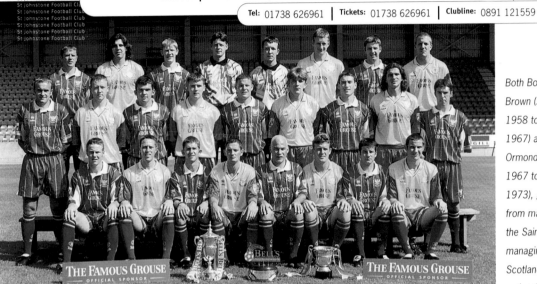

Both Bobby Brown (June 1958 to February 1967) and Willie Ormond (March 1967 to January 1973), graduated from managing the Saints to managing Scotland's national squad.

Top row • J O'Neil • N Dasovic • S Tosh • A Main • S Robertson • I Ferguson • A Whiteford • R Grant

Middle row • A Preston • G Brown • C Davidson • D Griffin • K OHalloran • J Weir • J McQuillan • A Serkerlioglu • C King

Bottom row • K McAnespie • P Scott • E Donaldson • G Bowman • G O'Boyle • L Jenkinson • G Farquahar • S McCluskey

→ **Chairman:** Geoff Brown   → **Manager:** Paul Sturrock   → **Year formed:** 1884

Ground: McDiarmid Park (10,700)

Stands: Ormond
 Main
 East
 North

Home strip: Royal blue shirts, white shorts with royal blue trim, royal blue socks with white trim

Away strip: White shirts, white shorts with yellow and blue trim, white socks with blue trim

Sponsor: Scottish Hydro-Electric

Programme: £1.50

Nickname: Saints

Ground history: 1885 St Johnstone Recreation Grounds
 1924 Muirton Park
 1989 McDiarmid Park

Previous name: None

Record attendance: 10,504 v Rangers, Premier Division, 20 October 1990

Record victory: 9-0 v Albion Rovers, League Cup 1st round, 9 March 1946

Record defeat: 1-10 v Third Lanark, Scottish Cup 1st round, 24 January 1903

Highest League scorer (season): Jimmy Benson, 33, 1931-32

Highest League scorer (aggregate): John Brogan, 114, 1977-1983

Most League appearances: Drew Rutherford, 298, 1977-1985

Most capped player: George O'Boyle, 12, Northern Ireland, 1994-1998

Highest transfer fee paid: £380,000 to Dundee for Billy Dodds, July 1994

Highest transfer fee received: £1.75 million from Blackburn Rovers for Callum Davidson, February 1998

Major trophies: Division 1 Champions (3) 1996-97, 1989-1990, 1982-83 Division 2 Champions (3) 1962-63, 1959-60, 1923-24

Gary Bollan – A £100,000 signing from Rangers during the 1997-98 season, he is a 24-year-old veteran of the Rangers reserves and got his chance when Callum Davidson moved south to Blackburn Rovers.

Paddy Connolly – After two years of speculation, Connolly finally joined the club for £300,000 from Airdrieonians towards the end of last year, but played in only four games during the 1997-98 season for the Saints.

Nick Dasovic – A solid midfielder who is not afraid to have a shot on goal, this Canadian international joined the club from FC Trelleborgs of Sweden in 1996, having previously played in Canada, Croatia and France.

Danny Griffin – A versatile Northern Ireland international equally at home in the heart of defence or midfield, Griffin's season was cut short after undergoing a double hernia operation. Later returning to fitness, Griffin came back into the side towards the end of the 1997-98 season.

Leigh Jenkinson – A former Coventry City winger who joined St Johnstone in December 1995 for an undisclosed fee (thought to be six figures), Jenkinson was drafted in as a supplier of ammunition for the strikers. He played in 28 games in 1997-98 and contributed three goals himself.

Paul Kane – An experienced midfield playmaker who joined the club under the Bosman ruling after a spell with Norwegian club Viking Stavanger, Kane played a key role in St Johnstone's midfield in 1997-98.

Alan Kernaghan – A central defender who took a substantial pay cut to come to McDiarmid Park, Kernaghan arrived from Manchester City initially on a three-month loan. But the Northern Ireland international, who signed in May 1998, become a key figure in the side, playing 31 games last season.

Kieran McAnespie – A product of St Johnstone's youth policy, the promising 19-year-old Scotland Under-21 player made three impressive appearances for the club last year, two of them as a sub.

Stuart McCluskey – Along with Danny Griffin, Scotland Under-21 regular McCluskey is also a product of the St Johnstone youth policy. McCluskey played just once for the first team in 1997-98, but instantly made an impact, coming off the bench to score against Motherwell in the League.

John McQuillan – Now established as a regular after a rather shaky start at McDiarmid Park, McQuillan signed from Dundee for £85,000 after beginning his playing career with Stranraer. An attacking full back who seems to go from strength to strength, he played 39 games in all competitions for St Johnstone during the 1997-98 season.

Alan Main – Bought from Dundee United in 1995 for £150,000, St Johnstone's first choice goalkeeper established himself in the side in the 1996-97 season and set a club record eight consecutive clean sheets. He proved himself again in 1997-98 with a string of fine shot-stopping displays.

Keith O'Halloran – The former Republic of Ireland international defender arrived from Middlesbrough in March 1998 as a late boost to the Premier's new boys but struggled to maintain a regular place during the 1997-98 season.

John O'Neil – Signed from Dundee United in the summer of 1994 for £100,000, O'Neil was initially playing on the wing, though in recent seasons he has been something of a utility man, scoring five goals in the 1997-98 season.

Alan Preston – A left back who joined the Saints as part of the swap deal that took Alan Moore to Dunfermline in March 1994, Preston was an automatic choice in the 1997-98 season, with 40 first-team appearances.

Stephen Robertson – Main's highly rated goalkeeping understudy won a Scottish Under-21 call-up in 1997-98, but due to the fine form of St Johnstone's senior keeper only managed to play twice for the club's first team.

Philip Scott – A local lad who joined St Johnstone from Scone Thistle in 1991, Scott is now the club's longest-serving player, in spite of his tender 23 years. He struggled with injury in the 1997-98 season and must have been disappointed with his solitary goal in 26 games, compared to the 12 he scored in the 1996-97 season.

Jim Weir – Since signing from Hearts as part of a swap deal in 1994, Weir has become club captain and has led by example from the centre of defence. Unfortunately, he ruptured an Achilles tendon in the penultimate game of the 1997-98 season against Motherwell and could be out of the side until Christmas 1998.

Andy Whiteford – Another fine product of the youth system at St Johnstone, Whiteford started his playing career as a striker but now plays at either full back or centre half. He made his League debut in the dramatic last game of the 1997-98 season against Celtic at Parkhead.

Davide Xausa – A Canadian international striker who turned down a contract at Portuguese club Sporting Lisbon in order to pursue his studies, Xausa played only once in the first team in the 1997-98 season but still showed enough promise to earn himself a one-year contract with St Johnstone.

Gerry McMahon – The former Tottenham Hotspur player and Northern Ireland international winger-cum-striker arrived from Stoke City in 1997-98 for £85,000, made 10 appearances and scored one goal.

Roddy Grant – He first joined the club in 1990 and returned in 1995 after spells with Dunfermline and Partick Thistle. The striker makes up in skill what he lacks in pace and scored three goals in 1997-98.

George O'Boyle – Another Northern Ireland international striker, O'Boyle joined the club from Dunfermline for £200,000 in 1994 and finished top scorer in the 1997-98 season – with 10 goals.

Ajax Football Club
Ajax Football Club
Ajax Football Club
Ajax Football Club
Ajax Football Club
Ajax Football Club
Ajax Football Club
Ajax Football Club
Ajax Football Club
Ajax Football Club
Ajax Football Club

314

Ajax *Football Club*

→ **Address** | AFC Ajax, Arena Boulevard 29, 1100 AM Amsterdam Zuidoost, Netherlands

Tel: 00 31 20 3111444 | **Fax:** 00 31 20 3111480

When Ajax beat Torino in the 1992 UEFA Cup final they became only the second side to have won all three senior European club competitions. Juventus had pioneered the hat-trick in 1985.

Ajax's Finnish star Jari Litmanen enjoys his penalty against Feyenoord in October – early days in the club's surge towards their 27th League title. Second highest scorer after Shota Arveladze, he scored a hat-trick in Ajax's 5-0 defeat of PSV in the Dutch Cup final.

→ **Web site:** http://www.ajax.nl   → **Ground:** Amsterdam Arena (51,324)   → **Manager:** Morten Olsen   → **Year formed:** 1900

In only their second season at the futuristic Amsterdam Arena, Ajax romped to an impressive League and Cup double in 1997-98. It was a dream start for coach Morten Olsen (whose record of 102 caps for Denmark was broken by Peter Schmeichel during France '98). Brought in to replace Louis van Gaal, who had departed to Barcelona, the Dane was not really expected to win silverware in his first season. Ajax had lost internationals Winston Bogarde and Patrick Kluivert to AC Milan, and champions PSV Eindhoven were still seen as the strongest contenders for the Dutch League. Yet Ajax thumped PSV 5-0 in the Dutch Cup final to complete their double. With both finalists qualifying for the European Cup in 1998-99, Holland will be represented in the Cup Winners Cup by one of the defeated semi-finalists in that competition – Heerenveen. A major factor

in Ajax's success – one that helped them to third place in the European rankings – was the form of Georgian Shota Arveladze. He scored 25 goals as Ajax averaged well over three goals per game during the 34-match League season to earn a reputation as one of the sport's most attack-minded sides. This is nothing new for Ajax fans. It was at Ajax that coach Rinus Michels invented the concept of 'total football' in the late 1960s.

The theory was simple – everyone could play anywhere, in any position, at any time. English fans first woke up to it when Liverpool were thrashed 5-1 in a European Cup tie in 1967, and Ajax eventually tuned their play to win that competition in the three consecutive years from 1971, while not conceding a goal in their three finals – against Panathinaikos, Inter Milan and Juventus. In 1998-99, the 10 new players that Olsen brought in during 1997-98, plus the team's more established stars such as Danny Blind and Dutch keeper Edwin van der Sar will be hoping to repeat their domestic success in Europe. Among the new talent recently brought to the club is 20-year-old South African striker Benni McCarthy – Player of the Year in the African Nations Cup and one of the most exciting prospects to have emerged from that continent.

AS Monaco Football Club
AS Monaco Football Club
AS Monaco Football Club
AS Monaco Football Club
AS Monaco Football Club
AS Monaco Football Club
AS Monaco Football Club
AS Monaco Football Club
AS Monaco Football Club
AS Monaco Football Club
AS Monaco Football Club
AS Monaco Football Club

AS Monaco *Football Club*

→ **Address** | Stade Louis II, 7 avenue des Castellans, 98000 Monaco

Tel: 00 377 92057473 | **Fax:** 00 377 92052454

Monaco attracted only four-figure crowds for the team's European Cup matches at home against Sporting Lisbon, Bayer Leverkusen and Lierse – and just 14,072 for the match with Manchester United in March 1998.

In 1997-98, AS Monaco made it to the semi-finals in their best ever performance in the European Cup but also lost 11 of their 34 games – and their title – in the French League.

→ **Ground:** Stade Louis II (15,000)   → **Manager:** Jean Tigana   → **Year formed:** 1924

The rich kids on the block became the nearly men of French football in 1997-98, as AS Monaco failed to win a single trophy. The club's international stars, backed by the coffers of Prince Rainier, were just not good enough to secure the silverware, despite reaching the semi-finals of the European Cup. Former French international star Jean Tigana continued to coach the same attacking, skill-based style he practised as a player, but it didn't prevent premature exits from the two domestic Cup competitions. Niort put Monaco out of the League Cup on a penalty shoot-out after a 1-1 draw and, after conquering Marseille 2-0 in the previous round, they fell to Paris St-Germain 1-0 in the quarter-final of the French Cup. In the League, Monaco kept up with the leaders for most of the season before falling away towards the finish and ending up in third place, nine points adrift of second-placed Metz. Temporary hope came in the European Cup. After a poor start in the Champions League – losing 3-0 away to Portugal's Sporting Lisbon – Monaco won four and drew one of their five remaining group games – thrashing Bayer Leverkusen 4-0 and Lierse SK 5-1 in the process – to finish at the head of their group. The first leg of the quarter-final against Manchester United at the Stade Louis II – a turgid affair in which the visitors sought and secured a goalless draw – showed no evidence of what would follow in the second leg. On 18 March 1998, 52,000 fans at Old Trafford were stunned after five minutes as David Trezeguet's brave, spectacular strike gave the French champions a shock lead. Despite the desperate efforts of United, notably a tireless David Beckham, Monaco held on to go through. But in the semi-finals, it was a different story, with Juventus beating the French champions 6-4 on aggregate. Former Celtic star John Collins and star striker Thierry Henry had an instrumental season on the left of midfield and up front, while the eccentric French national keeper Fabien Barthez looks set to entertain again in 1998-99. But with Lens now joining the established rivals such as Paris St-Germain things won't be easy for Monaco manager Tigana in 1998-99.

Barcelona *Football Club*

→ **Address** | FC Barcelona, Avenida Aristides Maillol, s/n 08028 Barcelona, Spain

Tel: 00 34 93 496 3600 | **Fax:** 00 34 93 411 2219

Barcelona supplied more players for France '98 than any other club in the world. Eight of them played for the Spanish team which failed to get past the first round.

Barcelona players celebrate winning the Spanish Cup after a dramatic final. Real Mallorca held on to the end of extra time, despite being down to nine men, but lost the penalty shoot-out 5-4.

→ **Web site:** http://www.fcbarcelona.es → **Ground:** Nou Camp (120,000) → **Manager:** Louis van Gaal → **Year formed:** 1899

Barcelona had a season of mixed blessings in 1997-98. The good news came at home, where they cruised to the League title after the New Year and retained the Spanish Cup – the 24th time they have secured the trophy, setting a new Spanish record. The bad news came in Europe, where they performed poorly in the Champions League and were forced to watch rivals Real Madrid take the top European trophy for the first time in 32 years. Beating Real twice in the League – 3-2 and 3-0 – offered some consolation. Even without Ronaldo, who had scored 34 of their 102 League goals in the 1996-97 season before his move to Inter Milan, Barcelona were not pressed for the 1997-98 title, especially as Real Madrid faltered mid-season to finish fourth. Even so, they lost 10 matches – which was not only more than the teams in second, third and fourth position, but also the team in 10th

position – and their season ended with three heavy defeats – 3-1 at home to Betis, 5-2 to Atletico Madrid away and 4-1 at home to Salamanca. But, only five of their 34 League matches ended in draws. The final of the Copa de Rey proved to be nail-biting stuff. Barcelona's opponents, lowly Real Mallorca, took a shock sixth minute lead and it wasn't until the 66th minute that Rivaldo was able to equalise. Then, six minutes from the end,

Mallorca had the first of two players sent off, the second coming three minutes into the first period of extra time. But Barca were unable to break down the nine men and the final went to penalties. Eventually, the double was decided by Barcelona goalkeeper Ruud Hesp. His knee saved the crucial spot-kick from Eskurza. Despite success at home, Barcelona's performance in the Champions League was embarrassing. They won only one game – thanks to a limp Newcastle display – three weeks after a 4-0 home defeat to Ukrainian side Dynamo Kiev. Much of the criticism of the team fell on the shoulders of Dutch manager Louis van Gaal whose insistence on giving all interviews in English proved highly unpopular with the Catalan fans. The fact that five Barcelona players plus Van Gaal and assistant coach Ronald Koeman were all Dutch fuelled the argument.

Bayern Munich *Football Club*

→ **Address** | Bayern Munich FC, Sabener Strasse 51, D-81547 Munich, Germany

Tel: 00 49 89 69 93 10 | **Fax:** 00 49 89 64 41 65

Bayern were pipped to the 1997-98 League Championship by Kaiserslautern, under the leadership of coach Otto Rehhagel. Two years before, Rehhagel had been sacked by Bayern.

The Bayern squad celebrate their 2-1 win over Duisburg in the German Cup – the only major piece of silverware in a relatively poor year. Thirty-seven year-old captain Lothar Matthaus (front, far right) went on to make history at France '98.

→ **Web site:** http://www.bayernmuenchen.de → **Ground:** Olympic Stadium (63,000) → **Manager:** Ottmar Hitzfeld → **Year formed:** 1900

Coming second in the Bundesliga by a point and winning the German Cup might satisfy most clubs – but not Bayern Munich. Not when your biggest rivals at home enjoy victory over you in Europe. With both Bayern and 1997 European Cup winners Borussia Dortmund in the running for the 1998 trophy – and both topping their groups in the Champions League – their quarter-final confrontation was a much-hyped occasion. Bayern had lacked consistency in the group games, shown by a 5-1 thrashing of Paris St-Germain and a 1-0 home defeat to Gothenburg. The quarter-final was settled by an extra-time goal from Dortmund's Stephane Chapuisat in the second leg and it was scant consolation to Bayern that the 1997 champions were later put in their place by Real Madrid in the semi-final. Wracked by internal conflicts, most publicly between club president Franz Beckenbauer

and veteran Italian coach Giovanni Trapattoni, it was somewhat impressive that Bayern should at least come close to doing the double at home. Bayern chased Kaiserslautern for the title – and a possible domestic double – from nine points adrift. It went down to the wire, with Bayern hoping that Kaiserslautern would slip up in their final game of the season while they won at home against Borussia Dortmund. They did indeed

exact revenge on the northerners, thrashing them 4-0, but Kaiserslautern held on 1-1 at bottom-of-the-table Bielefeld to snatch the most dramatic Championship for years. Criticised for his cautious approach, Trapattoni duly left – for Fiorentina – and wholesale changes of playing personnel were also expected by the start of the new season. The wealthiest club in Germany, Bayern can afford to splash out on several big-name players and during the summer welcomed the arrival of new manager Ottmar Hitzfeld. The club supplied six players for Berti Vogts' World Cup squad, the most notable being £2 million keeper Oliver Kahn, midfielder Dieter Hamann and skipper Lothar Matthaus, who was surprisingly recalled after a long period out of international football and went on to play more World Cup finals games than any other player in history.

Benfica *Football Club*

→ **Address** | Sport Lisboa e Benfica, Estadio da Luz, Avenida General Norton de Matos, 1500 Lisboa, Portugal

Tel: 00 351 1 726 6129 | **Fax:** 00 351 1 726 4761

Only four clubs have ever won the Portuguese Championship – Benfica (31 titles), FC Porto (18), Sporting Lisbon (16) and Belenenses (1). Porto are the only club not located in the capital.

Manager Graeme Souness trains with his Benfica players in the Stadium of Light. The former Liverpool and Scotland star took on Portugal's toughest job in 1997 and by the end of the season had ensured Benfica a place in the 1998-99 European Cup.

→ **Web site:** http://www.slbenfica.pt → **Ground:** Estadio da Luz (76,508) → **Manager:** Graeme Souness → **Year formed:** 1904

Benfica's famous Stadium of Light saw crowds rise to between 60,000 and 80,000 last season as Graeme Souness tried to bring back the glory days at the club. His last task, successfully accomplished, had been to save England's Southampton from relegation. In sunny Lisbon the brief was very different – win the Portuguese League. Benfica had last won the title in 1994 and since then FC Porto had taken it three consecutive times. The fans were seriously concerned. The acerbic Scot saw his side start poorly. He took over too late to prevent a weak exit from the Taca de Portugal (Portuguese Cup) at the hands of Sporting Braga, and the UEFA Cup run fizzled out in the first round with a 1-0 defeat by Bastia in Corsica. Only 20,000 witnessed the lame 0-0 draw in the second leg in Lisbon. Souness looked to the hardier climes of Europe to get some bite into his side. Striker

Brian Deane was bought from Sheffield United, defender Scott Minto arrived from Chelsea and midfielder Karel Poborsky came over from Manchester United. The side was stabilised and the Lions began to mount a serious challenge to Porto. Poborsky brought pace and width to the right of midfield, and went on to score five goals. He also supplied crosses for the striking pair of Deane and Nuno Gomes – second leading

goalscorer in the First Division in 1997-98, with 18 goals. The changes helped Benfica finish second (to Porto) – despite a thrilling finish, in which they beat Porto 3-0 in their last game of the season with goals from Deane, Poborsky and El Khalej. By securing the number two spot, Benfica also ensured a place in the expanded format European Cup for the 1998-99 season. In their Sixties heyday, Benfica twice won the European Cup, beating Barcelona 3-2 in 1961 and Real Madrid 5-3 the following year. The decade also saw three lost finals – to AC Milan in 1963, Inter in 1965 and Manchester United in 1968. The club also formed the backbone of the Portuguese team that reached the last four of the 1966 World Cup – including Pereira, Coluna, Germano, Simoes, Augusto, Torres and the incomparable Eusebio from Mozambique. Eusebio is now assistant coach at the club.

Borussia Dortmund Football Club
Borussia Dortmund Football Club
Borussia Dortmund Football Club
Borussia Dortmund Football Club
Borussia Dortmund Football Club
Borussia Dortmund Football Club
Borussia Dortmund Football Club
Borussia Dortmund Football Club
Borussia Dortmund Football Club
Borussia Dortmund Football Club
Borussia Dortmund Football Club

Borussia Dortmund *Football Club*

→ **Address** | BV Borussia Dortmund, Strobelallee 50, D-44139, Dortmund, Germany

Tel: 00 49 231 90200 | **Fax:** 00 49 231 9020105

In the 1993 UEFA Cup, a Juventus side that included Andreas Möller and Jurgen Kohler thrashed Dortmund 6-1 on aggregate. In 1997, the two players helped Borussia to European Cup glory – against Juventus.

Borussia's Stephane Chapuisat, Andreas Moller, Stefan Reuter and Paulo Sousa during their Champions League match against Sparta Prague in October 1997. The European Cup holders won five of their six matches but failed to repeat their success of 1996-97.

→ **Web site:** http://www.borussia-dortmund.de   → **Ground:** Westfalenstadion (69,000)   → **Manager:** Michael Skibbe   → **Year formed:** 1909

The 1997-98 season was one of anti-climax for Borussia Dortmund fans. After the German club's sensational win over favourites Juventus in the 1997 European Cup final, it looked like a successful run was on the cards in this season's bid for the European Cup. The club enjoyed an impressive Champions League – losing only one game (1-0 in Parma) and winning five of their group matches – before conquering fellow Germans Bayern Munich in the quarter-finals, with an extra-time goal from Stephane Chapuisat. Already languishing halfway down the League, Dortmund's hopes rested on the semi-final against Real Madrid, but the 2-0 lead established by the Spanish champions at home proved too much. There were several reasons for the decline in the club's fortunes, including injury, illness and tactical adjustment. But certain sales of players hadn't helped, including the loss of

midfield dynamo Paul Lambert to Celtic and Portuguese playmaker Paulo Sousa to Italy's Inter Milan. At the end of a season that left the club without a future in Europe, even coach Nevio Scala headed back to Italy. What Scala left behind was a squad that was on the brink of losing veteran defender Julio Cesar back to Brazil, and without Matthias Sammer, the inspirational German sweeper whose career could be finished by an

ongoing knee injury. Possibly Germany's best player in their Euro '96 triumph, Sammer couldn't make the German World Cup side in France, but it's a measure of Borussia's strength that despite finishing 10th in the Bundesliga they supplied five of the national squad. Best known to British fans was the influential midfielder Andreas Moller, but the others were no strangers either – defenders Jurgen Kohler and Stefan Reuter, along with midfielders Steffen Freund and Jorg Heinrich. Based in the traditional industrial heartland of the Ruhr Valley, Borussia first came to international prominence with a win over Liverpool in the 1966 Cup Winners Cup final at Hampden Park. Before their success against Italian club Juventus in 1997, their only other European final came in 1993 when they were thrashed 6-1 on aggregate in the UEFA Cup final – by Juventus.

Club Brugge Football Club
Club Brugge Football Club
Club Brugge Football Club
Club Brugge Football Club
Club Brugge Football Club
Club Brugge Football Club
Club Brugge Football Club
Club Brugge Football Club
Club Brugge Football Club
Club Brugge Football Club
Club Brugge Football Club
Club Brugge Football Club

320

Club Brugge *Football Club*

→ **Address** | Club Brugge KV, Olympialaan 74, 8200, Brugge 2, Belgium

Tel: 00 32 50 38 71 55 | **Fax:** 00 32 50 38 10 23

In the 1998-99 season, Brugge fans will be able to enjoy a new-look stadium, thanks to Euro 2000. The capacity has been increased from 18,000 to 30,000 in preparation for the tournament.

Club Brugge players celebrate their Championship triumph, with matches to spare. Brugge finished the season 18 points clear of the second placed team and scored at least twice as many goals as five of the other 17 teams in the league.

→ **Ground:** Olympia Stadium (30,000)   → **Manager:** Eric Gerets   → **Year formed:** 1891

The charming city of Bruges saw the Belgian League title return to its cobbled streets in 1998, as Club Brugge were crowned champions for the 11th time. For a time, it had also looked as though the double might be achieved for the second time in three years – Brugge did it in 1996 – but Genk had other ideas and won the Belgian Cup final with an emphatic 4-0 win, the biggest margin since Standard Liege beat Lokeren by the same score in 1981. Genk were the only club to give Brugge a run for their money. Formed in 1988 by the merger of Waterschei and Winterslag, the team from Hasselt nevertheless finished a massive 22 points adrift of the champions. Brugge had hinted of their comeback in Belgian football in 1997, when they had come close to winning the title but finished second to Lierse. Brugge owe their renaissance largely to the arrival of veteran Belgian international

Eric Gerets to the post of manager. Brugge remained unbeaten in their first 24 League games in 1997-98 – the best record in Europe – and dropped only six points in that period. While their domestic form was sensational, Brugge couldn't reproduce it in Europe. After disappointment in 1996-97, when they were beaten in the qualifying round of the European Cup by Steaua Bucharest, Brugge fell in the second round

of the UEFA Cup in 1997-98, going out 4-2 on aggregate to German club Bochum. Old heads in defence and midfield, plus a razor-sharp front-line, was Gerets' formula for League success. The backbone of the side was composed of veterans over 30 – keeper Dany Verlinden, defenders Vital Borkelmans and Lorenzo Staelens, and 37-year-old midfield general Franky van der Elst, the one-time West Ham whizzkid recalled to the Belgian national side in 1997. Gert Verheyen added class in midfield, while up front Edgar Jankauskas set the pace with five goals in eight starts and Belgian Gert Claessens scored 10 goals in the league before Christmas. It would be a brave man to bet against the 'Baauw-zwart" (blue and blacks) retaining their title in 1999 as Brugge reinforce their position as successors to Anderlecht as Belgium's most prominent club.

Dynamo Kiev Football Club
Dynamo Kiev Football Club
Dynamo Kiev Football Club
Dynamo Kiev Football Club
Dynamo Kiev Football Club
Dynamo Kiev Football Club
Dynamo Kiev Football Cl
Dynamo Kiev Football Cl
Dynamo Kiev Football Club
Dynamo Kiev Football Club
Dynamo Kiev Football Club
Dynamo Kiev Football Club

Dynamo Kiev *Football Club*

→ **Address** | Dynamo Kiev, Hrushevsky Str. 3, Kiev 252001, Ukraine

Tel: 00 380 44 22 83 270 | **Fax:** 00 380 44 22 83 297

The two top scorers in the 1997-98 Ukrainian League were both from Dynamo Kiev – Sergei Rebrov scored 22 goals and Andrei Shevchenko scored 19.

Dynamo Kiev players celebrate their impressive victory in the European Cup against Barcelona, winning at home 3-0. They also beat the Spanish side at the Nou Camp, 4-0.

→ **Web site:** None → **Ground:** Olimpiisky Stadium (100,169) → **Head coach:** Valeri Lobanovsky → **Year formed:** 1927

The most successful club in the history of Soviet football, Dynamo Kiev have predictably dominated the game in the Ukraine since the separate national league and cup competitions were established in 1992. In 1997-98, they won their sixth consecutive Championship, coming in five points ahead of the long-suffering Shakhtjor Donetsk and scoring 71 goals in 30 games. They also won the Ukrainian Cup 2-1 against CASC Kiev, on 31 May 1998, with two goals from striker Andrei Shevchenko. Meanwhile, Dynamo had much to prove in the European Cup in 1997-98 as in the previous year they had been ignominiously removed at the qualifying stage with a 6-2 aggregate loss to Rapid Vienna. But in 1997-98 it was a very different story. They began their challenge with a 3-1 away win over PSV Eindhoven. This sent them to the top of group C – on goal difference from Newcastle United – and

it was a position they were to remain in throughout the group matches. Newcastle earned a creditable 2-2 away draw to Dynamo which maintained the status quo at the top of the group, but in the next set of matches Dynamo pulled away by beating Barcelona 3-0 at home, and 4-0 at the Nou Camp, with Shevchenko grabbing all the goals. A 1-1 draw with PSV ensured qualification for both participants, despite

Dynamo losing 2-0 to Newcastle United through goals by John Barnes and Stuart Pearce. The Ukrainians looked serious contenders for the trophy but in the quarter-final their dodgy home form proved disastrous. After securing a priceless 1-1 draw with Juventus in Turin, they blew up in Kiev, allowing Fillipo Inzaghi to score a hat-trick in a 4-1 rout. As Dynamo were left to take the league and Cup title at home, several of their best players could reflect on a season of international disappointment, not only in the European Cup but in the World Cup qualifiers. In November 1997, the Ukrainian national team had been beaten by Croatia 3-1 on aggregate, ending their dreams of a place at France '98. Meanwhile, the club's officials are building for the future, having opened the first club store in the country and having invested in a new training facility in the suburb of Koncha-Zaspa.

Feyenoord Football Club
Feyenoord Football Club
Feyenoord Football Club
Feyenoord Football Club
Feyenoord Football Club
Feyenoord Football Club
Feyenoord Football Club
Feyenoord Football Club
Feyenoord Football Club
Feyenoord Football Club
Feyenoord Football Club
Feyenoord Football Club

322

Feyenoord *Football Club*

→ **Address** | FC Feyenoord, Van Zandvlietplein 1, 3077 AA, Rotterdam, Netherlands

Tel: 00 31 10 292 68 88 | **Fax:** 00 31 10 432 58 19

Ajax may be the most famous Dutch club, but it was Feyenoord who set the Dutch ball rolling in Europe with their 2-1 victory over Celtic in the 1970 European Cup final in Milan.

Feyenoord players acclaim their 2-0 victory over Juventus in the Champions League. It was a particularly sweet moment for Feyenoord's players as they had lost 5-1 to the same side two months before.

→ **Ground:** De Kuip Stadium (52,000)   → **Manager:** Leo Beenhakker   → **Year formed:** 1908

Feyenoord's 1997-98 season probably peaked as early as late August, when they qualified for the Champions League. Second in their domestic table the season before, they came through the qualifying round for the Champions League by beating Finnish side Jazz Pori 8-3 on aggregate, after setting up the victory with a 6-2 win in the home leg. This took them into the same group as Manchester United and Juventus. Their first match ended in a 5-1 defeat away from home by 10-man Juventus and they were perhaps lucky that the fixture list then brought them Kosice as their next opponents as the Slovakian side had lost their first game 3-0 at home to Manchester United and were to lose all of their games in the group, scoring only twice. Having restored their confidence by winning 2-0, Manchester United then did the double over them, winning 2-1 at home and 3-1 away.

Feyenoord gained a measure of revenge for Juventus' drubbing in the opening match when they defeated them 2-0 through two goals from the Brazilian Julio Ricardo Cruz. But none of this was enough to carry them through to the quarter-finals thanks to Manchester United losing their unbeaten record to Juventus in the final set of matches. There was no consolation for Feyenoord in the Eredivisie. They had lost

track of the leaders early on and never recovered to make much of a challenge to rivals Ajax. After a string of poor results, manager Arie Haan made way for former Ajax and Real Madrid coach Leo Beenhakker. The new manager was later quoted as saying it was his dream appointment to take charge of his hometown club. Feyenoord eventually clawed back enough games to finish fourth and earn a place in the 1998-99 UEFA Cup, but this was little consolation after Ajax won a record sixth League and Cup double. Ajax were one of only two teams to do the double over Feyenoord in the League, winning 1-0 away and 4-0 at home. In the Cup, Feyenoord were eliminated in the quarter-finals, crashing out 4-0 to PSV Eindhoven, with star player Cruz sent off in the 42nd minute. The club's record signing, Cruz ended the season as top scorer in the league with 20 goals.

Serie A

Inter Milan Football Club
Inter Milan Football Club
Inter Milan Football Club
Inter Milan Football Club
Inter Milan Football Club
Inter Milan Football Club
Inter Milan Football Club
Inter Milan Football Club
Inter Milan Football Club
Inter Milan Football Club
Inter Milan Football Club

323

Inter Milan *Football Club*

→ **Address** | Inter Milan FC, Stadio Giuseppe Meazza, Via Piccolomini 4, 20100 Milan, Italy

Tel: 00 39 2 771 51 | **Fax:** 00 39 2 781 514

Inter president Massimo Moratti is the son of Angelo Moratti, president during Inter's heyday in the 1960s, when they won the European Cup in successive seasons and reached three finals in four years.

Inter line up for their successful UEFA Cup quarter-final match against Schalke in March 1998. In the final, they beat Lazio 3-0, including a goal from Brazilian and World Cup star Ronaldo (front row, centre right).

→ **Web site:** http://www.inter.it   → **Ground:** Giuseppe Meazza (San Siro) (85,000)   → **Manager:** Gigi Simoni   → **Year formed:** 1908

Internazionale's president, Massimo Moratti, has invested a fortune in the club since taking over in February 1995 in an attempt to gain silverware. In 1997-98, his investment finally paid off. Until then, his club had continued to remain in AC Milan's shadow. They had reached the final of the UEFA Cup in 1997, which they were favourites to win, but lost to the German side, Schalke. But last season Inter fans were able to hold their heads up high in the streets of Milan. Not only did their side win the UEFA Cup but they also finished an amazing 25 points and eight places above their great city rivals, AC Milan, in Serie A. The UEFA Cup was secured in the final with a 3-0 victory over Roman side Lazio in the Parc des Princes in Paris. Along the way, Inter had secured victories over Swiss side Neuchatel Xamax, French sides Olympique Lyonnais and Strasbourg, plus Schalke and

Spartak Moscow. In the whole competition, they scored 20 goals. The star of Inter's team in 1997-98 was the Brazilian striker Ronaldo. While he finished the season with 34 goals from 47 outings, no one else in the team even made it into double figures, the second highest scorer being Frenchman Youri Djorkaeff, with eight strikes. Both stars were among the 11 players that Inter sent to the World Cup finals in France. The Inter

midfield of Djorkaeff and Argentinians Javier Zanetti and Diego Simeone combined power and style to supply Ronaldo and his Chilean partner Ivan Zamorano in the quest for honours. Ronaldo and Italian international goalkeeper Gianluca Pagliuca were the only two ever-present players in Inter's successful UEFA campaign. The keeper also never missed a game in the League, and with veteran captain Giuseppe Bergomi – who continued to be a rock at the heart of the defence and who was absent for only half a dozen League matches – they established the best defensive record in Serie A, conceding only 27 goals. In 1998-99, the team will be bolstered by the signing from Borussia Dortmund of Paulo Sousa, the Portuguese playmaker whose performance helped defeat Juventus in the 1997 European Cup final. Inter will be hoping he appears in the next final of the competition.

Juventus Football Club
Juventus Football Club
Juventus Football Club
Juventus Football Club
Juventus Football Club
Juventus Football Club
Juventus Football Club
Juventus Football Club
Juventus Football Club
Juventus Football Club
Juventus Football Club

Juventus *Football Club*

→ **Address** | Juventus FC, Piazza Crimea 7, 10131 Torino, Italy

Tel: 00 391165631 | **Fax:** 00 39116604134

Juve owe their famous black and white stripes to fashionable Notts County. A committee member was so impressed by County's strip on a trip to England in 1903 that he took a set back to Turin.

Alessandro Del Piero (centre) celebrates a goal against Monaco in the 1998 European Cup semi-final. Juventus beat the French champions 7-3 on aggregate but lost to Real Madrid 1-0 in the final.

→ **Web site:** http://www.juventus.it → **Ground:** Delle Alpi (71,000) → **Manager:** Marcello Lippi → **Year formed:** 1897

In 1997-98, Juventus proved once again that they are the greatest name in Italian football. Winners of the Italian League, runners-up in the Italian Cup and runners-up in the European Cup, they were unlucky not to make it a hat-trick of trophies. At the start of Juventus's European campaign, things were not looking good. They struggled to make the knock-out stage of the competition but once into the quarter-finals, they really motored, thrashing two group winners in Dynamo Kiev (5-2) and Monaco (6-4) to win through to the Amsterdam final. On paper, the side were unbeatable, despite being up against a strong Real Madrid team. Up front, Alessandro Del Piero had been joined by Filippo Inzaghi, and the French midfield pairing of Didier Deschamps and Zinedine Zidane, playing alongside Angelo di Livio (the 'Little Soldier'), was bolstered with the

ball-winning qualities of Dutchman Edgar Davids, dubbed the 'Pitbull' on his arrival from AC Milan for £3.4 million. But Real had waited 32 years for a win and secured it 1-0 – only Davids came close to scoring for Juventus. Meanwhile, Juventus were taking no prisoners in the Italian League. On the way to finishing top of the table with 74 points, five points clear of Inter, they had racked up a series of convincing wins

against Brescia (4-0), Bari (5-0), Udinese (4-1) and Empoli (5-2). In the Italian Cup, they made it to the semi-final against Lazio, where an own goal ended their run. Fuelled by the Agnelli family's Fiat wealth and passionate support, Juventus are a footballing icon. Despite the rise of AC Milan in the 1980s, Juventus still remain at the top. Quite apart from winning more Serie A titles (25) and more Italian Cups (9) than any other club, they have lifted the European Cup twice, the UEFA Cup three times and the Cup Winners Cup once. They have appeared in the last three European Cup finals, beating Ajax on penalties in 1996 and then, though favourites on both occasions, failing to capitalise on their class against Borussia in 1997 and Real Madrid in 1998. Even so, Juventus remain the team for Manchester United and Arsenal to fear in the European Cup in 1998-99.

Kaiserslautern Football Club
Kaiserslautern Football Club
Kaiserslautern Football Club
Kaiserslautern Football Club
Kaiserslautern Football Club
Kaiserslautern Football Club
Kaiserslautern Football Club
Kaiserslautern Football Club
Kaiserslautern Football Club
Kaiserslautern Football Club
Kaiserslautern Football Club
Kaiserslautern Football Club
Kaiserslautern Football Club

Kaiserslautern *Football Club*

→ **Address** | 1FC Kaiserslautern, Fritz-Walter Stadion, Stadionstrasse 11, 67653 Kaiserslautern, Germany

Tel: 00 49 631 31880 | **Fax:** 00 49 631 3188290

In 1998, Kaiserslautern Football Club (the name means Emperor's stream) became the first side since the Bundesliga began in 1963 to win the title the first season after promotion.

Ciriaco Sforza, Olaf Marschall, Axel Roos, Pavel Kuka, Harry Koch and Andreas Buck celebrate a goal against Borussia Moenchengladbach as newly promoted Kaiserslautern head towards the title.

→ **Web site:** http://www.fck.de   → **Ground:** Fritz-Walter Stadium (38,009)   → **Manager:** Otto Rehhagel   → **Year formed:** 1900

In 1996 Kaiserslautern, a relatively rural club by the big-city standards of the Bundesliga, won the German Cup by beating Karlsruher – and were also relegated from the Bundesliga after winning only six of their 34 matches. In 1998, just two years later, they astonished the whole of Europe by winning the League title and holding off powerful, wealthy Bayern Munich by a single point – gleaned on their last-day visit to Hamburg – to cause one of the biggest upsets since the Bundesliga began in 1963. But the story gets better. The brilliant coach responsible for this amazing revival is Otto Rehhagel, a man who twice won the German League and Cup with Werder Bremen – and who, in April 1996, was given the sack by impatient Bayern after less than a season in charge of the team. It must have given the 60-year-old miner's son from the Ruhr immense satisfaction that Kaiserslautern

beat Bayern twice in the League in 1997-98 before pipping them to the title. With the new UEFA ruling, both Kaiserslautern and Bayern Munich are representing Germany in the European Cup in 1998-99. But one player who may not figure is Andreas Brehme, capped 89 times for Germany and the man whose penalty won the World Cup in 1990. Now 37, and not always in the starting line-up in 1997-98, he has

nevertheless been a moving force at the club. But striker Olaf Marschall, whose 86th-minute penalty secured the vital point at Hamburg on 9 May 1998, is a crucial member of the team. Top scorer in the Bundesliga in 1997-98 with 20 goals – despite missing three months with a knee ligament injury – his form earned a recall to the German national team and a place in the World Cup squad – the only player from the 'Roten Teufel' (Red Devils) to be selected for France '98. In contrast to the politicking at Bayern, Kaiserslautern's success stems from solid teamwork and common goals. The current side contains the Danish international Michael Schjonberg-Christiansen, Czechs Miroslov Kadlee and Pavel Kuka, Marian Hristov of Bulgaria, Rodrigues Ratinho of Brazil and Ciriaco Sforza of Switzerland in midfield – plus a few emerging and experienced Germans.

Lazio Football Club
Lazio Football Club
Lazio Football Club
Lazio Football Club
Lazio Football Club
Lazio Football Club
Lazio Football Club
Lazio Football Club
Lazio Football Club
Lazio Football Club
Lazio Football Club
Lazio Football Club

Lazio *Football Club*

→ **Address** | Lazio SS, Via Novaro 32, 00195 Rome, Italy

Tel: 00 39 06 907 5711 | **Fax:** 00 39 06 904 00022

Vladimir Jugovic is mobbed by Lazio colleagues after his tie-winning goal against Atletico Madrid in the UEFA Cup semi-final in Spain in March 1998.

On 6 May 1998, Lazio were involved in their first ever European final and the first UEFA Cup final to be played over just one leg. They lost 3-0.

→ **Web site:** http://www.sslazio.it   → **Ground:** Olympic Stadium (81,903)   → **Manager:** Sven-Goran Eriksson   → **Year formed:** 1900

Lazio share the Olympic Stadium with their younger rivals Roma (founded in 1927) and at times it resembles a theatre of dreams more than a football arena. Surrounded by statues of Roman emperors and complemented by decorated floor mosaics, it saw its fair share of dramas during 1997-98. Last winners of Serie A back in 1974, Lazio made a brave attempt to acquire three trophies in 1997-98 – the League Championship, the Italian Cup and the UEFA Cup – but ended the season with just one. The League campaign didn't start well and by December Lazio were languishing in ninth place. The problems were up front, where an international trio so talented on paper – Roberto Mancini, Pierluigi Casiraghi and Croatian Alen Boksic – were not producing the goals. This was an extension of the previous season's failures, when the top scorer was midfielder Pavel Nedved with just

11 goals. Things were so bad that the Swedish coach Sven-Goran Eriksson, a man who had previously worked miracles with Sampdoria, had his car damaged by disgruntled supporters. But the turn of the year saw Lazio embark on a club record run of 24 games without defeat, putting them in contention with Juventus and Inter Milan for the Serie A title. In the UEFA Cup, having beaten Rotor Volgograd and Rapid Vienna

before Christmas, they saw off Auxerre 3-2 on aggregate in the quarter-final and Atletico Madrid in the semi-final, with the only goal of the tie coming in Spain from Yugoslavian anchor man Vladimir Jugovic. By the time they played the final, on 6 May 1998, their form had fallen away and they had slipped back to seventh place in Serie A. An exception to this run of poor form was on 29 April when they secured a European place for 1998-99 by coming from behind to beat AC Milan 3-2 on aggregate in the Italian Cup final – a result that cost AC coach Fabio Capello his job. It was just as well, for Inter, with Ronaldo rampant, beat Lazio 3-0 in the UEFA Cup final. With Lazio floating themselves on the stock market, club president Dino Zoff has shelled out an eight-figure sum for Chilean striker Marcelo Salas. With him up front, Lazio should be able to look forward to more success in 1998-99.

Lens Football Club
Lens Football Club
Lens Football Club
Lens Football Club
Lens Football Club
Lens Football Club
Lens Football Club
Lens Football Club
Lens Football Club
Lens Football Club
Lens Football Club
Lens Football Club
Lens Football Club
Lens Football Club

Ligue Nationale

327

Lens *Football Club*

→ **Address** | Racing Club de Lens, Stade Felix Bollaert, BP 236, F-62304, Lens, France

Tel: 00 33 321 69 28 99 | **Fax:** 00 33 321 69 28 96

Lens is owned by the city council, which has jurisdiction over 35,000 inhabitants of the town, although over 320,000 live in Lens as a whole.

Lens line up for the French Cup final against Paris St-Germain on 2 May 1998. They lost 2-1 – but seven days later won their first League championship.

→ **Ground:** Felix Bollaert Stadium (35,200)   → **Manager:** Daniel Leclercq   → **Year formed:** 1906

France warmed up for their World Cup extravaganza with the most exciting domestic title race for years, as two of the nations most unlikely contenders fought out the 1997-98 Championship to the bitter end. Lens and Metz, two clubs who had never won the Championship, both had a chance to make history on the final day of the season. Lens needed a draw at Auxerre to stave off their rivals, who had to beat Lyon at home. There was real pressure on the Lens players, as the weekend before they had frozen in front of 77,000 spectators at the Stade de France and lost the French Cup final 2-1 to a Paris St-Germain side who were apparently much more comfortable with their surroundings – and are certainly more used to success. The Lens players admitted afterwards that they had found the whole occasion incredibly daunting. Then, on the last day of the season, things began to look

very bleak when Auxerre took the lead. But this time, Lens fought off the nerves and came back in the second half, equalising through Yoann Lachor. The draw was secured and Lens were crowned Champions. It mattered little that the title was won on goal difference; it was won. Nearly 30,000 fans gathered in the Felix Bollaert Stadium to welcome their heroes when they arrived home in the early hours of the morning.

Chief among their stars was Daniel Leclercq, the 'Big Blond', a manager who has worked a small miracle with limited resources, and two of his Eastern European imports – Czech international Vladimir Smicer and Yugoslav striker Anton Drobnjak. Lens' story is nothing less than a football fairy tale. The modest club, struggling in an industrial area hampered by France's highest unemployment rate, owes much to the vision of Andre Delelis, the popular mayor who first brought European Championship games to the town and this year, following a £14.1 million improvement programme to the Felix Bollaert Stadium, secured a five-match World Cup package that included England's game against Colombia and Spain's 6-1 thrashing of Bulgaria. Whether the fairytale can continue with Lens being able to make a success of their Champions League campaign in 1998-99, only time will tell.

Paris St-Germain *Football Club*

Paris St-Germain Football Club
Paris St-Germain Football Club
Paris St-Germain Football Club
Paris St-Germain Football Club
Paris St-Germain Football Club
Paris St-Germain Football Club
Paris St-Germain Football Club
Paris St-Germain Football Club
Paris St-Germain Football Club
Paris St-Germain Football Club
Paris St-Germain Football Club

→ **Address** | Paris St-Germain, Parc des Princes, 24 Rue du Commandant-Guilbaud, 75016, Paris, France

Tel: 00 33 153 96 93 19 | **Fax:** 00 33 140 71 93 97

Paris St-Germain were not formed until 1970, when they rapidly became the fashionable side for Parisians to follow, winning the Cup for the first time in 1982 and their first League title four years later.

Following a poor season in the League, PSG's celebration of the 2-1 Cup final win over double-chasing Lens on 2 May was met with huge relief.

→ **Web site:** http://www.psg.tm.fr   → **Ground:** Parc des Princes (48,527)   → **Manager:** Alain Giresse   → **Year formed:** 1970

Runners-up to Monaco in 1997, Paris St-Germain had a poor season by their own recent high standards. In the League they started well, and by the halfway point had won nine of their 17 matches. But the club faded away during the second half of the season, winning only five more matches and losing eight. They ended the 1997-98 season in eighth place and were out of contention for a place in Europe for the following season. However, Paris St-Germain redeemed itself by winning both Cup competitions, ousting Bordeaux on penalties after a 2-2 draw in the League Cup and beating Lens 2-1 to lift the French Cup. At one point, it also looked like they might lift the European Cup but the Champions League proved a step too far for the Parisians. They won their first game at home to Gothenburg, 3-0, but then went down to two heavy away defeats – 3-1 to

Besiktas and 5-1 to Bayern Munich. They won their remaining three fixtures, including a face-saving 3-1 defeat of Bayern Munich at home, but finished second to the German club on goal difference. Both teams had 12 points, but Bayern had a goal difference of seven in their favour and Paris St-Germain had just one. The 5-1 hammering by Bayern cost Paris St-Germain dear – a lesser defeat and the French club would have been

through. As it was, Paris St-Germain failed to get through to the quarter-finals as one of the two best runners-up, again on goal difference. Juventus' 12 points and a goal difference of four edged them through with Bayer Leverkusen, who had 13 points. Still, there were encouraging signs for the flamboyant Paris St-Germain supporters. Frank Gava had an excellent season, while Marco Simone fitted in well after his move from AC Milan and scored 13 times in his first season in France, combining comfortably with Florian Maurice. The 1998-99 season will see the defence bolstered by Christian Worns, the German international signed from Bayer Leverkusen and he will play in front of the eccentric Bernard Lama, returning to Paris from West Ham. Up front, Patrice Loko will be under pressure to reclaim his place with the arrival of Parma's Brazilian Adailton.

Porto *Football Club*

→ Address | FC do Porto, Avenida Fernao de Magalhaes 1862-14, 4300 Porto, Portugal

Tel: 00 351 2 557 0400 | **Fax:** 00 351 2 557 0498

The highlight of Porto's history came in 1987, when they finally laid the European ghost of rivals Benfica to rest by winning the Champions Cup, beating Bayern Munich 2-1 in Vienna.

Porto's Brazilian striker Mario Jardel raises his arms after scoring against neighbours Boavista on 29 April 1998 to clinch the club's fourth consecutive League title.

→ Web site: http://www.fcporto.pt **→ Ground:** Estadio das Antas (76,000) **→ Manager:** Antonio Oliviera (to May 1998) **→ Year formed:** 1893

Portugal's oldest club became its second most successful in history in 1998, overtaking Sporting Lisbon with their 16th championship title. It was their fourth successive title and their 10th in 16 seasons. Even mighty Benfica, the country's most successful side, have found it hard to keep up in recent years. Porto won the championship by 13 points in 1996-1997 and by nine points last season. They scored 73 goals in 34 matches and won their final four games, including a 7-2 drubbing of Salgueiros in the penultimate game of the season. Five of those goals were scored by the Brazilian striker Mario Jardel, who topped the Portuguese list with 26 – 11 more than any other player. In a vintage season, Porto beat Sporting Braga 3-1 in the Cup final to record their first double for a decade. Jardel was ably supported by Sergio Conceicao, Paulinho Santos and

fellow Brazilian Artur, whose goals were vital in both games against Benfica. Yet Porto's domestic form was in startling contrast to their performances on the international stage. After a 1996-97 European Cup campaign of promise – when they won five of six games in the Champions League before being stuffed by a rampant Manchester United in the quarter-finals – Porto proved wanting last season. They

gleaned only three goals in six matches (all from Jardel) and finished ignominiously below Olympiakos of Greece and Rosenborg of Norway. They lost all of their away fixtures – 1-0 to Olympiakos, 2-0 to Rosenborg and 4-0 to Real Madrid. They also lost 2-0 at home to Real, although they held Rosenborg to a draw and beat Olympiakos 2-1. Changes were inevitable, and the coach Antonio Oliviera announced that he would be leaving the club at the end of the season – although there was a strong possibility that he would have been pushed had he remained. Oliviera had taken over from Bobby Robson and continued his success, bringing the club two championships. The requirements will be simple for the incoming coach – to keep Graeme Souness' revitalised Benfica at bay in the domestic league, and bring Porto their second European Cup triumph.

PSV Eindhoven *Football Club*

→ **Address** | PSV Eindhoven, Frederiklaan 10a, 5616 NH, Eindhoven, Netherlands

Tel: 00 31 40 250 5505 | **Fax:** 00 31 40 257 4782

Some 40,000 of Eindhoven's 200,000 urban population work directly or indirectly for Philips, Europe's largest electrical company and sponsors of PSV.

PSV players with the Johan Cruyff Shield after beating Roda JC 3-1 in the August 1997 curtain-raiser between Holland's League champions and Cup winners.

→ **Ground:** Philips Stadium (30,800)   → **Manager:** Bobby Robson   → **Year formed:** 1913

By their own exacting standards of recent years, PSV had a poor season in 1997-98. Having taken the Eredivisie title comfortably in 1997 from Feyenoord and Twente – with Ajax languishing 16 points adrift in fourth place – they suffered from a fierce Ajax revival in 1997-98 as the Amsterdammers cruelly turned the tables. PSV were hammered 5-0 by Ajax in the Cup final, with Jari Litmanen grabbing a hat-trick. This defeat was especially hurtful as it was the first time they had been beaten by Ajax in nearly three years. In the League, they were left trailing 17 points behind Ajax. However, they at least ensured themselves of a place in the 1998-99 Champions League by securing the runners-up position at home on the penultimate weekend of the League season by twice coming from behind to beat Groningen 6-2. Other highlights of their League season included their 4-3 defeat of

Ajax away and their 10-0 demolition of Volendam – with four of the goals coming in the final eight minutes. The European Cup was very different – a case of 'so near, yet so far'. PSV performed well away from Holland in the Champions League – drawing 2-2 in Barcelona and 1-1 in Kiev, and winning 2-0 at Newcastle – but their home form was poor and they never recovered from a 3-1 defeat at the hands of Dynamo Kiev in the

opening game. Their only victory at the Philips Stadium was a 1-0 win over a tame Newcastle. Success in the European Cup is important to a club which, in 1987-88, joined a very select band of clubs by winning the European Cup and their domestic League and Cup in the same season. Only Celtic (1967) and, ironically, Ajax (1972) had managed it before. By then, PSV had firmly established themselves alongside Feyenoord as a consistent force in Dutch football, a genuine co-challenger to the supremacy of Ajax. Yet like all Dutch clubs they are always having to sell their stars. In 1998, the key departures were to Britain – defenders Jaap Stam to Manchester United and Arthur Numan to Rangers, along with coach Dick Advocaat, who became Rangers' manager. PSV's 1998-99 season now lies in the hands of Bobby Robson – back for a second spell.

Real Madrid Football Club
Real Madrid Football Club
Real Madrid Football Club
Real Madrid Football Club
Real Madrid Football Club
Real Madrid Football Club
Real Madrid Football Club
Real Madrid Football Club
Real Madrid Football Club
Real Madrid Football Club
Real Madrid Football Club
Real Madrid Football Club

Real Madrid *Football Club*

→ **Address** | Real Madrid CF, Avenida Concha Espina, 1 28036 Madrid, Spain

Tel: 00 34 913 440052 | **Fax:** 00 34 913 440695

In 1997-98, Real captain Manuel Sanchis broke the Spanish League appearances record when he played his 462nd game for Real in his 15th season at the club.

Christian Karembeu's arrival from Sampdoria in mid-season was a much-needed boost to Real, helping the team beat Borussia Dortmund in the semi-final of the European Cup with a vital goal.

→ **Ground:** Santiago Bernabeu Stadium (104,290)   → **Manager:** Jupp Heynckes (to May 1998)   → **Year formed:** 1902

To British fans aching for meaningful success abroad, it may seem a little over the top for a club to sack its manager only days after winning the European Cup. Yet that was the fate that befell the hapless German coach Jupp Heynckes in his first season at Real Madrid, even though he bought the top prize back to the club after a gap of 32 years. For Real, the battle with Spanish rivals Barcelona is the only real yardstick for success. And while the Catalan club cantered to the Primera title, Real surrendered their crown to limp home fourth, an embarrassing 11 points adrift. Before their amazing triumph over Juventus in Amsterdam, Real's season looked to be nothing short of humiliating. Top of the table early on, their mid-season slump extended to an extraordinary run of six months without an away win. There were rumours of a $100 million (£62.5 million) debt as things

worsened with a first round Spanish Cup exit to Second Division Alaves. While Heynckes struggled to find the right blend for his star-studded but injury-hit team, their form in the Champions League remained remarkably buoyant. Real scored 13 goals in their three home games, dispatching the classiest side in their group, Porto, 4-0 in December. They finished top of the table in group D and went on to beat Bayer Leverkusen in the quarter-

finals and Borussia Dortmund in the semi-finals – by dint of a 2-0 home victory, followed by a goalless draw. This set up the final with Juventus and a sharply taken goal by Yugoslavia's star striker, Predrag Mijatovic, made sure it was a Real victory. Real's four players in Spain's surprisingly early-exiting World Cup squad featured a mean outfield trio – rugged defender Fernando Hierro and two talented youngsters up front, Fernando Morientes and Raul Gonzalez (the 'boy wonder' of Spanish football). With Argentinian Fernando Redondo, New Caledonian Frenchman Christian Karembeu, dreadlocked Dutchman Clarence Seedorf, Croatian ace Davor Suker and Mijatovic, Real could retain the European Cup in 1998-99, something a Spanish club hasn't managed since Real in 1960. But the fans will still expect to see Barcelona finish below them.

Spartak Moscow *Football Club*

→ **Address** | Spartak Moscow, Ist Koptelsky pereulok 18/2, 129 010 Moscow, Russia

Tel: 00 7 095 254 6619 | **Fax:** 00 7 095 254 6916

Spartak's 1997-98 UEFA Cup first round tie at home had to be replayed after it was discovered that one of the crossbars was 12cm too low.

Spartak Moscow upset the form book when they beat Ajax 3-1 in the first leg of the UEFA Cup quarter-final on 3 March 1998 in the Amsterdam Arena, setting up a semi-final date with Inter Milan.

→ **Web site:** http//www.spartak.com   → **Ground:** Luzhniki Stadium   → **Manager:** Oleg Ivanovich Romantsev   → **Year formed**: 1922

Of the five Moscow sides resident in the Russian First Division, Spartak are by far the most successful in recent years. They have won five of the six Russian Championships since the Soviet system gave way to separate national leagues. The Russian season runs from March to November and the 1997 season was a strange one for the faithful fans who trooped to Spartak's temporary home at the Lokomotiv stadium. Their true home, the old Lenin Stadium (now called the Luzhniki) is currently being rebuilt and is not expected to re-open until well into the 1998 season. In 1997, Spartak won the League with a record 73 points – five more than nearest rival Dinamo Moscow. But their success at home was tempered by their failure to get through the preliminary rounds of the European Cup, being beaten 2-1 on aggregate by Kosice of Slovakia. No Russian side has ever made the final of the European

Cup, although Spartak reached the semi-final in 1990-91. Russian teams are not helped by the fact that their season begins in March – there are obvious problems with players not having had enough match practice by the time the first rounds of European competition begin. But Spartak made the most of their consolation spot in the UEFA Cup, reaching the last four following wins over Sion, Real Valladolid, Karlsruher (beaten in extra time by

the only goal of the tie) and, in the quarter-finals, a shock victory over Dutch club Ajax – Spartak upset the formbook by winning 3-1 in Amsterdam and 1-0 in Moscow. In the semi-finals, a 2-1 defeat in Milan was equalised on aggregate in Russia when Andrei Tikhonov scored in the second leg, but on a surface resembling a muddy beach rather than a football pitch the irrepressible Ronaldo found the net twice to send the Italian club into the Paris final. One month later, Spartak did find some consolation at home when they beat Lokomotiv Moscow in the 1998 Cup final on 7 June – rescuing their place in Europe. Once again, it was Tikhonov who found the back of the net, in the 87th minute, and the striker looks like playing an important part in the 1998 season. He scored three goals in the first five league matches and helped the club towards the top of the table by the summer.

Stuttgart Football Club
Stuttgart Football Club
Stuttgart Football Club
Stuttgart Football Club
Stuttgart Football Club
Stuttgart Football Club
Stuttgart Football Club
Stuttgart Football Club
Stuttgart Football Club
Stuttgart Football Club
Stuttgart Football Club
Stuttgart Football Club

Stuttgart *Football Club*

→ **Address** | VfB Stuttgart, Mercedesstrasse 109, D-70372, Stuttgart, Germany

Tel: 00 49 711 55 00 70 | **Fax:** 00 49 711 55 00 733

Stuttgart have won the Bundesliga twice since it was set up in 1963 – in 1983-84 and 1991-92. They also twice won the former West German Championship – in 1949-50 and 1951-52.

Fredi Bobic is congratulated by Gerhard Poschner after scoring the winner for Stuttgart against Lokomotiv Moscow in the semi-final of the Cup Winners Cup.

→ **Ground:** Gottlieb-Daimler Stadium (53,218)   → **Manager:** Winfried Schaefer   → **Year formed:** 1893

Stuttgart coach Joachim Loew could count himself a little hard done by to be sacked by president Gerhard Mayer-Vorfelder at the end of the 1997-98 season. Not only had his side retained fourth place in the League – thus guaranteeing a UEFA Cup spot in 1998-99 – but they had also enjoyed a lucrative run to the Cup Winners Cup final against Chelsea in Stockholm. And it was Loew, after all, who had steered them to their German Cup victory in the first place, in May 1997. But football management today is tough, and there are always factors other than results. There were stories of criticism of the coach's leadership qualities and of in-fighting among players on the plane to Sweden. Certainly, Loew's team appeared to be missing the commitment and organisation usually displayed by German clubs when they took on Gianluca Vialli and Dennis Wise in the Cup Winners Cup final. Stuttgart's star

men were clearly off colour on 13 May. Bulgaria's playmaker Krassimir Balakov was largely innocuous and top scorer Fredi Bobic and his Nigerian partner Jonathan Akpoborie both lacked sharpness in front of goal. They could perhaps have done with the promptings of Elber, controversially sold to Bayern Munich earlier in the season. Earlier in the competition, Stuttgart had looked much more convincing. They had gained

victories in both legs of the semi-final, against Lokomotiv Moscow in April. And in their domestic campaign, Stuttgart had shown the fighting qualities which were lacking in the Cup Winners Cup final. Once as low as 10th place and hit by injuries, they fought back to fourth place, helped not only by Bobic's 13 goals but also by some inspired goalkeeping displays from the veteran Austrian international Franz Wohlfahrt. In midfield, the workrate of Marco Haber, Gerhard Poschner, Croatian Zvonimir Soldo and the Swiss Murat Yakin complemented the skills of Balakov. Stuttgart's new coach is Winfried Schaefer, who was sacked by Karlsruher after a 12-year stint, shortly before the club were relegated from the Bundesliga at the end of the 1997-98 season. No doubt Mayer-Vorfelder will be expecting Schaefer to reap the rewards that Loew so nearly achieved.

Time to sit back and take a break from the season to visit the highlights of the past. The following pages include a selection of past footballing masters, magical moments and history-making occasions. Included are 10 great players, two great teams, a mesmerising moment, a stunning goal and two decades of dominance.

SMOOTH OPERATOR

Pele

People are loose with labels in football. But you would have to be mad or biased not to recognise Pele's place as the greatest footballer of all time.

As a player, he possessed skills in abundance. He was simply the best-equipped exponent his sport has ever known. In fact, in purely footballing terms, Pele is

probably closest to being a god – he wasn't flawed with the sort of vulnerability or arrogance that so many other great players are, he was the complete footballer.

Pele was born Edson Arantes do Nascimento on 23 October 1940, in Brazil. A regular in the first team at Santos aged 16, he went on to win nine League Championship medals with the South American club. He was capped at just 17, scoring on his debut against

Argentina, and Europe first witnessed the might of Pele in the 1958 World Cup in Sweden. He missed the early games with injury but scored once against Wales, three times against France in the semi-final, and twice against the host nation in the final. And it was that first goal

against Sweden that made the world sit up and take notice of the young Brazilian. Standing in the crowded penalty area with his back to goal, Pele killed a long ball on his thigh, hooked it over his head, spun round his marker and smashed it home. A star was born.

"I can make goals out of nothing. This does not make me proud, it makes me humble. Because this is a talent that God gave me"

Magic touch: Pele was a maker as well as a taker of goals. Defenders were pulled to him like a magnet, releasing space for colleagues and creating opportunities that the visionary Pele ably exploited.

○ In his first season at Santos, Pele was the club's top scorer with an impressive 32 goals.

○ A World Cup winner in 1958 and 1970, Pele would have had a record three medals if a torn muscle had not meant his early exit from the 1962 Chile finals. In total, Pele scored 12 goals in 14 appearances in the finals, but he declined to play in the 1974 tournament in Germany, despite being only 33.

The 1966 England World Cup did not prove to be a happy experience for either Brazil or Pele. The favourites went out in the group stage and Pele vowed he would never play in another World Cup after some harsh tackling from the Bulgarians and Portuguese. Thankfully, he changed his mind, and four years later he was on his way to his fourth and final World Cup tournament in Mexico. At 29 Pele was at his peak, producing peerless performances that saw Brazil win the Jules Rimet trophy for an unheard of third time. In July 1971, Pele played his 111th and final international for Brazil and three years later he played his last game for Santos, ending a career which saw him score a record 1,281 goals in 1,363 senior appearances. Pele once said: "I can make goals out of nothing. This does not make me proud, it makes me humble. Because this is a talent that God gave me." In June 1975 he enjoyed a brief comeback when he signed a $4.5 million contract for the New York Cosmos, helping to popularise the game in the USA. The Brazilian finally hung up his professional boots in 1977, though he remains an excellent ambassador for the game.

Conquering hero: Pele's control and first touch were unsurpassed and he was renowned for his pace, as well as his languorous style. It was a combination of these talents that made him a hero, attracting the sort of adulation shown here at the 1970 World Cup.

Pele is the only player to have been with three World Cup-winning teams – in 1958, 1962 and 1970

BRAZILIAN BRILLIANCE

The 1958 World Cup

The Brazil of the 1958 World Cup was a side that eased its way to the country's much-awaited first victory in the competition, using a new, virtually unstoppable 4-2-4 formation. Manager Vicente Feola, aided by right-hand man Dr Hilary Gosling, was an intricate planner whose training sessions were famously joyous affairs which ensured that as well as being a group of extraordinarily talented individuals, including Pele and Garrincha, left, Brazil became truly a team.

For the first time in 1958, the world became aware of 17-year-old footballing genius Pele. But Pele was only one player in a team of stars which included Garrincha. The first two games Brazil played in the 1958 World Cup finals were played without Pele or Garrincha in the starting line-up. Brazil first beat Austria 3-0 and then registered a disappointing 0-0 draw against England. But for the next game, the manager dropped forward Mazzola and Flamengo's Joel. Pele and Garrincha were brought into the attack and one of the most-feared forward line-ups of all time was complete, with Vava and Mario Zagalo completing the quartet. The two midfielders were Didi (who had ensured Brazil's qualification with one of his trademark 'falling leaf' free kicks) and the strong-tackling Zito, with his pinpoint passing skills.

As well as being a group of extraordinarily talented individuals, Brazil became truly a team

Fair play: Brazil won many Swedish admirers at the 1958 World Cup finals and, as tribute to the losing opposition, did a lap of honour with the Swedish flag as well as the Brazilian flag.

○ The leading scorer in the Brazilian team of 1958 was Pele, who netted six times, despite missing the first two games.

○ Garrincha, known as the 'little bird', overcame incredible odds to become one of the most feared wingers the game has produced. He was born into poverty and contracted polio as a child, leaving him with a right leg so twisted that doctors feared he would never walk again. He was greatly mourned when he died – of alcoholic poisoning – in 1983.

The 1958 Brazilian squad was completed with the inclusion of the revolutionary four-man defence of Djalma Santos, Bellini, Orlando and Nilton Santos. Together with goalkeeper Gylmar, they did not concede a single goal until the semi-finals of the World Cup. "I could have lined up two different formations, they both would have done," said manager Vicente Feola of his squad. After winning their group by beating Russia 2-0 and disposing of Wales 1-0 in the quarter-final, the Brazilian team really came alive. In the semi-final against France they ran riot in the second half with Pele scoring a hat-trick in a 5-2 victory. Brazil were red-hot favourites

Team talent: the 1958 Brazilian side dazzled on their way to winning the Jules Rimet trophy for the first time. The nation went on to win the World Cup a further three times – in 1962, 1970 and 1994.

to beat the ponderous Swedish hosts in the final. Although Brazil went a goal down in the fourth minute, the game was clinched as early as the 56th, when Pele scored a goal of stunning quality to put Brazil 3-1 up. Receiving the ball on his thigh, he flicked it over his head, swivelled and volleyed it past the keeper. The youngster finished off the scoring with a majestic header to complete the 5-2 victory. Brazil's win was down to hard work as much as attacking flair and it was this combination that would ensure that within the next 12 years the World Cup final would be won a second and third time and the Jules Rimet trophy would be Brazil's for keeps.

Brazil are the only country to have appeared in the finals of every World Cup ever held

Maradona

To many, Diego Maradona is the second greatest footballer of all time – after Pele. But whereas Pele is universally loved, Maradona has been frequently vilified. To his detractors, any football ability has been heavily outweighed by the cheating, the drug-taking and the arrogance. But others are happy to forgive and prefer to concentrate on the goals, the accuracy of his left foot and the strength and balance which enabled Maradona to go past players so effortlessly.

Born in poverty in 1960 in Buenos Aires, Maradona made his league debut for Argentinos Juniors at 15 and his international debut at 16, the youngest player ever to play for his country. However, the teenager was devastated in 1978 when he was dropped from the Argentinian squad that won the World Cup, because manager Cesar Menotti feared for his development. In 1980, Maradona was sold to Boca Juniors for £1 million – one year later, he was sold to Barcelona for nearly five times as much. After a disappointing World Cup in Spain in 1982, in which he was sent off, Maradona was forced to wait another four years to truly work his magic. In the 1986 World Cup he led Argentina to victory, courting controversy (with his 'Hand of God' goal against England) and adulation (with spectacular goals).

To many, Maradona is the second greatest footballer. But whereas Pele is universally loved, Maradona has been frequently vilified

Argentinian handy work: Maradona punches the ball into the net in the 1986 World Cup quarter-final against England. He explained away the goal as being by "the hand of God".

○ Maradona played 90 games for Argentina, scoring 33 times.

○ In 1984, Maradona moved from Barcelona to Napoli. He helped the Italian side win their first Italian title in 1987, their second title in 1990 and their first European success – the UEFA Cup in 1988.

○ In January 1998, Maradona made an unsuccessful bid to buy and manage his old club, Napoli.

The World Cup in Mexico in 1986 saw Maradona at his peak – sadly, now the only way was down. During Italia '90, flashes of genius were punctuated by rule bending and a tendency to theatrics. An unattractive Argentina muddled their way through to the final, with Maradona – booed for much of the tournament – failing to find the net once. The following year he failed a test for cocaine and was banned from soccer for 15 months and in 1994 saw his World Cup ended abruptly when he again failed a drugs test. After a series of attempted comebacks, Maradona, now 38, continues to make the headlines but not in the way that he would hope.

Maradona the genius: in the 1982 World Cup, seen here taking on the Belgian defence, Maradona showed flashes of brilliance.

When Maradona moved to Napoli, in Italy, he set a world record transfer fee of £6.9 million

THE BEST OF TIMES...

George Best

George Best seemed to have it all – amazing balance, exquisite ball control, pace, impish invention, and an unerring eye for goal. But unlike other great players such as Matthews, Puskas, Pele, Charlton and Beckenbauer, Best failed to deliver in the second half of his career, becoming the victim of media pressure and personal problems. He may have been saved had he played for a successful national team but as a Northern Ireland international, the big stage always eluded him.

Born in Belfast on 22 May 1946 into a sporting family – his father was an amateur footballer and his mother a hockey player – Best played for his school and local youth club before arriving at Old Trafford in August 1961. The skinny teenager, initially overcome by homesickness, settled in and by the time he was 18 had secured a place in the United side and had won the first of his 37 Northern Ireland caps. In 1964-65, he missed only one League game and his 10 goals helped United to the League title – and into Europe. Best took full advantage, earning the nickname 'El Beatle' after a mesmerising display in United's 5-1 win over Benfica in Lisbon's Stadium of Light in 1966, although the team were to go out in the next round. The following season, Best again helped United to the Championship title.

After a mesmerising display in United's 5-1 win over Benfica in Lisbon's Stadium of Light in 1966, Best earned the nickname 'El Beatle'

Best women: the first football pop star, Best was often pictured at nightclubs with a bevy of beauties and dated four Miss Worlds.

○ A Northern Ireland International aged 17 – after only 15 League games – Best played only 37 times for his country, scoring nine goals.

○ Best scored 137 goals in 361 League matches for Manchester United and won two Championship medals and a European Cup medal with them.

In 1968, Best turned 22 and began to overtake Bobby Charlton and Denis Law as the crowd's idol at Old Trafford as he hit the pinnacle of his career. Leading League scorer with 28 goals, he was voted Footballer of the Year at home and helped United win the European Cup final at Wembley, coolly putting the second of United's four goals (in extra time) past his old foes, Benfica. Before the end of the year he had also been voted European Footballer of the Year. He had the world at his feet but barely two years later, the cracks were starting to show. Football's first pop star, Best lived a wild lifestyle fuelled by alcohol, adulation and a stream of beautiful women. Inevitably it was all fodder for the tabloids, who hounded him endlessly. In 1970, he made the news when he was suspended for four weeks after a run-in with a referee – and then returned to score six goals against Northampton in the FA Cup. But in the months that followed, Best was increasingly missing from training sessions both for Manchester United and Northern Ireland, as the papers were full of tales from nightclubs and glitzy restaurants. In 1972, he announced his retirement, two days short of his 26th birthday. After a short-lived comeback with United in 1973, he had short spells at a number of clubs including Los Angeles Aztecs in the NASL, Stockport County, Fulham, Hibernian, Cork Celtic and Bournemouth. He won his last cap for Ireland in 1977 and finally called it a day in 1983.

George Best always found defenders easier to beat than the bottle and he still continues to make headlines. His was a sad fall from grace, but those who saw him play will be forever grateful for those mouthwatering moments of magic that set this wayward, tragic genius apart. Best never denied his talent and once said: "I always felt I was better than anyone else. It was up to them to get the ball off me – and they couldn't."

Best moment: the European Cup Final was the biggest stage on which Best was able to parade his talents. In 1968, Manchester United became the first English club to bring home the European Cup, beating Benfica of Portugal 4-1, thanks in large part to the skilful mastery of Best.

In 1968, Best was Footballer of the Year, European Footballer of the Year and won a European Cup medal

FRENCH FLAIR

Michel Platini

An extraordinary talent emerged onto the world footballing scene in the early 1980s – a cool, good-looking midfield genius whose ability to score goals put most top strikers in the shade. The source was an unusual one, the industrial town of Nancy in north-eastern France. The player, Michel Platini, was to become the most inspirational captain his country had ever produced, leading his side to their first major Championship.

Born in Joeuf, France, on 21 June 1955, the grandson of an Italian immigrant, Platini began his career at Nancy, where his father Aldo was a coach. In seven seasons he scored 98 goals in 175 League games, in addition to the only goal of the 1978 French Cup final against Nice. Already a seasoned international, he moved to St Etienne in 1979 and helped them win the Championship the following year. After 58 goals in 107 League appearances (and an impressive 1982 World Cup), Platini headed for Turin after giants Juventus shelled out £1.2 million for the French maestro. In his first season, Platini was Serie A's leading scorer – from midfield – and became the first Frenchman since Raymond Kopa in 1958 to be voted European Footballer of the Year. In 1984 Juventus won the Serie A title and the Cup Winners Cup.

Platini's relaxed style of play perfectly suited his playboy image. Like all great players, he always seemed to have time and space

On the ball: Platini is best remembered as a taker rather than a maker of chances and had a marvellous ability to convert free-kicks from dangerous positions.

○ In all, Platini won a European Championship with France, the European Cup, Cup Winners Cup and two Serie A Championships with Juventus, as well as a clutch of personal trophies.

○ By the time Platini retired from the national game, he had 72 caps and 41 goals to his credit. He took over as manager of the French team and enjoyed limited success, before resigning after a poor performance in the 1992 European Championship finals. In 1998, he was at the helm of France '98 as co-chairman of the World Cup organising committee.

Head and shoulders above the rest:
Michel Platini holds aloft France's
European Championship trophy in 1984.

Platini's finest hour was to come in 1984, his vintage year. While he continued to excel at Juventus, he had also gradually begun to dominate the world scene.

Platini's career for France kicked off in March 1976, when he scored in the 2-2 draw with Czechoslovakia. In the 1978 World Cup in Argentina, France went out early but Platini's mission to restore pride in his national side was already well under way when he became captain in 1981.

In 1982 Platini took a strong squad, including Tigana, Six, Giresse and Rocheteau to the World Cup in Spain. Their progress was only stopped in the semi-final when Germany won on penalties.

By 1984, with the European Championship finals in France, there was genuine pressure on Platini's team. But he led by example, playing exquisitely and scoring a record nine goals, the last of them in the 2-0 final victory over Spain. His performance earned him World Footballer of the Year and European Footballer of the Year titles.

In 1985, Platini was again voted World Footballer of the Year, as well as European Footballer of the Year for a third time, when Juventus secured the European Cup – even though their 1-0 win over Liverpool (courtesy of Platini's penalty) was overshadowed by the 39 deaths at Brussels' Heysel Stadium. The following year, after the 1986 World Cup, Platini retired.

Platini's relaxed style of play perfectly suited his playboy image. Like all great players, he always seemed to have time and space. Shirt outside shorts, his touch and vision enabled him to turn defence into attack in one fluid movement, to make incisive passes, to open up the tightest of defences and to set up endless chances.

Platini is the only man to have been voted European Footballer of the Year three years in a row

MONTGOMERY MAGIC

1973 FA Cup final

Considered by many to be the greatest upset of them all, Sunderland's 1-0 win over Leeds United in 1973 made them the first Second Division side to win the FA Cup since the war. At the time, Don Revie's Leeds United were the best team in the country and their 12-man squad featured no fewer than 11 internationals. But the star at Wembley on 5 May 1973 belonged to Sunderland – goalkeeper Jim Montgomery, who made one of the greatest-ever saves.

Bob Stokoe, the Sunderland manager, had already been hailed as 'the Messiah of Roker Park' by the time Sunderland had beaten the odds to reach the FA Cup final after victories over Manchester City and Arsenal. Thirty thousand Rokerites travelled to Wembley to see their team rise to the occasion. The Leeds midfield of Billy Bremner and Johnny Giles was expected to run the show but instead they were matched by Sunderland's driving captain Bobby Kerr and the tenacious Micky Horswill. At the back, young Dave Watson, who would go on to play 65 times for England, was winning every header. Then, on 30 minutes, Sunderland scored from a corner on the left. The ball fell to Ian Porterfield, who controlled it on his thigh and slammed it into the net. You could hear the roar all the way to Wearside.

Montgomery sprang up and deflected the shot onto the bar. It was an incredible save

The hand of Jim: on the final whistle, Sunderland manager Bob Stokoe famously ran 50 yards across the pitch to embrace goalkeeping hero Jim Montgomery. "I suppose the whole thing was a miracle really," he said.

○ Leeds United lost the European Cup Winners Cup final to AC Milan, 11 days after losing the FA Cup final.

○ Despite their cup heroics, Sunderland were not promoted until 1976-77, only to be relegated the following year. In 1992, again in the Second Division, they got to the FA Cup final but lost 2-0 to Liverpool.

○ Sunderland were the first Division Two side to win the FA Cup and not get promoted in the same season.

One-nil down and 30 minutes into the FA Cup final, the Leeds players came forward in white droves, but the 11 men of Sunderland ran themselves into the famous Wembley turf, determined to protect their lead. In the 70th minute, it appeared that their rearguard action had failed... but that was just the cue for Jim Montgomery to take centre stage. Having already kept his side in the game with a string of fine saves, the former England youth and Under-23 player made a stunning save at the near post to push out a diving header from Trevor Cherry. But the ball dropped to Peter Lorimer and just six yards out, with Montgomery on the ground, Lorimer simply couldn't miss. Then, as the Scotland international and Leeds star hammered the ball goalwards, Montgomery sprang up and deflected the shot onto the bar. It was an incredible save. The ball was cleared and Sunderland won the Cup. No-one, least of all Montgomery, was underwhelmed by the moment. "When I die, I shall have my left hand embalmed," he said after the game.

Up for the cup: Jim Montgomery defies gravity to make his sensational save from Peter Lorimer (number seven), helping Sunderland to FA Cup victory in 1973.

In 1973, Sunderland became the only side since 1912 to have won the FA Cup without an international player

THE KAISER

Franz Beckenbauer

If a European footballer can claim to have 'won it all', that man is Franz Beckenbauer who seemed to stroll effortlessly to a phalanx of medals, honours and awards.

An advanced tactical thinker, he had an almost infallible knack of judging the right moment for the counter attack. Piercing through-balls, raking crossfield passes, swift interchanges, incisive runs, powerful shots – all were in the repertoire of a man whose imperious style earned him the nickname 'The Kaiser'.

Born in Munich, on 11 September 1945, Beckenbauer first played for 1860 Munich but at 13 joined rivals Bayern. In 1963, aged 18, he made his first-team debut as a left-winger – a position he later swapped for sweeper. When German coach Helmut Schoen saw Beckenbauer's talents, he awarded him his first cap in 1965, in a World Cup qualifier against Sweden. By the time he was 21, Beckenbauer had been voted Footballer of the Year at home and had played well in the five 1966 World Cup games before Germany lost 2-4 to England in the final. But then, in Mexico in 1970, when the Germans were 0-2 down to England in the quarter-final, The Kaiser's forceful play inspired a remarkable comeback to win 3-2. In the semi-final, Germany lost 3-4 to Italy, with Beckenbauer bravely playing on for half an hour with a dislocated shoulder.

An advanced tactical thinker, Beckenbauer had an almost infallible knack of judging the right moment for the counter attack

Winning ways: the peak of Beckenbauer's captaincy came in 1974, when he led the German side to World Cup victory. By the time he retired in 1977, he had earned 103 caps, including 50 as captain.

○ In 1990, Beckenbauer retired as manager of Germany after their World Cup victory. As captain, he had already won the 1972 European Championship and the 1974 World Cup. He also led Bayern Munich to four Bundesliga titles and four German Cup successes as well as three European Cups (1974, 1975 and 1976) and the Cup Winners Cup (1967). He was European Footballer of the Year in both 1972 and 1976.

○ Despite the inevitable tackling involved in his role as sweeper, Beckenbauer was never sent off in his 17-year career.

Always ahead of the game: an inspirational leader both on and off the field, Beckenbauer captained the German side from 1971-1977 and managed it from 1984 to 1990.

Beckenbauer was appointed captain of the German national side in 1971 and in 1972, after Bayern won the first of three Bundesliga titles, he led his country to European Championship success against the Soviet Union. He was crowned European Footballer of the Year for his efforts – an honour he earned again in 1976. But Beckenbauer's finest hour came in 1974. Having led Bayern to the first of three European Cup triumphs, he then masterminded the Germans' 2-1 victory in the World Cup final over Johan Cruyff's fancied Dutchmen, denying them the freedom and space they needed to pursue their 'total football'.

Beckenbauer played his 100th game for Germany in the 1976 European Championship and retired a year later. He continued his club career after Juventus first with America's New York Cosmos and later with SV Hamburg.

When Beckenbauer became national team manager in 1984, he set to work preparing the squad for the 1986 World Cup where the Germans narrowly lost to the Maradona-inspired Argentinians in the semi-final. But in 1990 he bowed out at the top, after securing the World Cup for his country. His career was best summed up by his 1966 World Cup team-mate Willi Schulz, who said: "He turned football into an art form."

In 1990, Franz Beckenbauer became the first man to have both captained and managed World Cup-winning sides

WE WANT MOORE

Bobby Moore

Only in rare circumstances does a player live for so long in the hearts and minds of football fans the length and breadth of the country. After leading England to World Cup glory in 1966 on home turf, Bobby Moore was instantly elevated to the status of national hero and recognised around the world as a footballing tour de force. His repertoire went beyond that of an ordinary defender – he was calm, skilful and had an expert understanding of the game.

Born in Barking, east London, in 1941, Bobby Moore did not have to travel far to join his first club, West Ham United. He signed for the Hammers in 1958 and made his League debut in the 1958-59, season against Manchester United at Upton Park. Moore captained West Ham to their first FA Cup win in 1964 and was instrumental in their successful bid to lift the European Cup Winners Cup the following season. The 1964 Player of the Year was a gifted central defender. Tall and immensely skilful, Moore was an expert reader of the game. His vision and ability to turn defence into attack, as well as his precision passing and strong tackling, marked him out as an exceptional player. His partnership with Geoff Hurst, both at club and at international level, remains one of the most effective the world has ever seen.

After leading England to World Cup glory in 1966 on home turf, Bobby Moore was elevated to the status of national hero

England's finest hour: Bobby Moore was made England captain in 1964 and reached the pinnacle of his career when he led the side that won the 1966 World Cup at Wembley.

○ Bobby Moore played 545 games for the Hammers in 16 years at the club. In 1974, he signed to Fulham for £20,000. In 1975, he played his old club in the 1975 FA Cup final at Wembley. Fulham lost.

○ Moore won 108 caps for England between 1962 and 1974. He was awarded an OBE in January 1967 for his services to football.

○ Bobby Moore and Billy Wright are the joint holders of the record for the number of England captaincies – each was captain 90 times.

In 1958, the 17-year-old Bobby Moore was capped by England at youth level for the first time. His first appearance for England seniors was against Peru in a pre-World Cup friendly four years later and he went on to play in the 1962 Chile finals, when the side progressed to the quarter-finals but lost 3-1 to Brazil. The next World Cup, in 1966, saw Moore's – and England's – finest hour. It was the West Ham defender who laid on the equaliser for club team-mate Geoff Hurst in the Wembley final, setting the team on the road to a 4-2 victory against West Germany. As England's youngest ever captain climbed the steps to collect the trophy for the first time, the host nation embraced a new national hero. Moore went on to play in the 1970 World Cup campaign, but England lost 3-2 to West Germany in the quarter-finals. He retired as a player in 1977 and later became manager at non-League Oxford City and Southend. In 1993, aged 51, Moore died of cancer just days after making his last appearance at Wembley, as a radio commentator.

Respect: Bobby Moore and Pele showed mutual respect for each other's talent after England played Brazil in the 1970 World Cup. Brazil went on to win the tournament, while England went out in the quarter-finals to West Germany.

Bobby Moore still holds the unbeaten record for appearances in the England Youth Team – 18 in total

MERSEYSIDE MAESTROS

Liverpool in the 1980s

Liverpool began the 1980s as masters of the English game. In the 1970s they had won four League championships, the FA Cup, the UEFA Cup twice and the European Cup two years running. Yet in the next 10 years, in an increasingly competitive environment, the club's record was even better.

At home, from 1980-81 to 1989-90, Liverpool won six League Championships and the FA Cup twice – including the double in 1986. They collected the League Cup four years in a row from 1981 and for the whole of the 1980s were never out of the top two in the final First Division table.

Liverpool's European success in the 1980s was breathtaking. They won the European Cup twice, adding to their two Seventies' successes, and perhaps would have succeeded again but for the Heysel stadium tragedy at the 1985 final. The secret of their success was the seamless morphing of one great team into another. As the big stars retired or moved on, fresh players were introduced with the heart and ability to continue the Liverpool tradition. When midfielder Ray Kennedy dropped out of contention, in came Ronnie Whelan; when keeper Ray Clemence left for Tottenham, Bruce Grobbelaar took over. When unknown striker Ian Rush signed from Chester in 1980, he became the ideal partner for Kenny Dalglish. Seven years and 207 goals later, he went to Juventus in Italy and John Aldridge took over…

As the big stars retired or moved on, fresh players were introduced with the heart and ability to continue the Liverpool tradition

Painting the town red: player-manager Kenny Dalglish and captain Alan Hansen share the spoils in 1986. Their FA Cup final victory over Everton gave Liverpool the double.

○ Liverpool beat arch-rivals Everton in three finals in the 1980s – the 1984 League Cup and the 1986 and 1989 FA Cups.

○ The Liverpool decade was tainted with tragedy as well as triumph – 39 Juventus fans died at the Heysel stadium in 1985, and 96 Liverpool fans died at Hillsborough in 1989.

○ Liverpool hold the record for the most number of points in a season, registering 90 in the old Division One in 1987-88.

Behind every great Liverpool team was an even greater boss. Back in 1974, when Bill Shankly retired, the club promoted his long-serving assistant Bob Paisley to manager. After a glorious nine-year reign, Paisley retired in 1983 and his successor, Joe Fagan, also came from the legendary 'Boot Room'. The low-profile Fagan kept up the winning tradition before giving way to the Kop's idol Kenny Dalglish, first as player-manager, then as manager.

Another factor in the Reds' success was the intense, intimidating atmosphere at Anfield. There was the famous Kop and there was Liverpool's awesome reputation on home ground. Few teams ever won there.

Most cupped manager: Bob Paisley is the most successful manager in English football. He won 13 trophies with his philosophy of "pass to the nearest red shirt" combined with constant movement and unstinting support play.

On the crest of a wave: 1984 was arguably the peak of the Liverpool era. Having won the League Cup for the fourth year running and completed a hat-trick of League titles, the team went on to beat AS Roma 4-2 on penalties to take the European Cup.

Liverpool have won 18 League titles – more than any other club in the English League

DUTCH MASTER

Johan Cruyff

The most exciting and advanced player in one of the game's golden eras, Johan Cruyff epitomised 'total football'. Cruyff was the attacking key in the Ajax and Dutch sides but he could appear anywhere, displaying his uncanny vision, sublime ball skills, marvellous balance, electrifying turn of speed and lethal finishing. And then there was the hallmark Cruyff turn – imitated, badly, by every park and playground wannabe in Europe.

Rinus Michels may have brought total football to the world without Johan Cruyff, but it would never have been as brilliant. We saw it at club level with Ajax's three successive European Cup wins from 1971 and we saw it at national level with the Dutch team that ripped the confused South Americans apart in the 1974 World Cup. First Holland beat Uruguay, then came Argentina and two goals from Cruyff, and finally Brazil, with yet another goal from Cruyff. Unfortunately, it was the well-organised Germans who won the day. By then Cruyff was a Barcelona player, bought by Michels for a world record £922,300 in the autumn of 1973, following Cruyff's orchestrated demolition of Juventus in the European Cup final. In his first season, he took Barcelona from mid-table to the title.

Cruyff was the attacking key in the Ajax and Dutch sides but he could appear anywhere, displaying his uncanny vision and ball skills

Nou man: As Barcelona's manager, Cruyff was the toast of the Nou Camp stadium, taking Barcelona to four successive championships and helping them to the European Cup in 1992.

○ Ajax can thank Mrs Cruyff for their 1970s success. A cleaner at the stadium offices in the 1950s, she persuaded the coaching staff to take the gangly 10-year-old Johan into one of their youth sections.

○ In the 1974 World Cup final, Berti Vogts marked Holland captain Cruyff out of the game and Holland failed to live up to the 'total football' tag. Their defeat has seen them ranked alongside the Hungarians of 1954 as the best team never to win the World Cup.

Total management: Cruyff guided
Ajax to three European Cup victories
as a player and one Cup Winners Cup
victory as technical director.

Born in Amsterdam on 25 April 1947, Cruyff made his first-team debut for Ajax in 1965, coming off the bench to score in the number 14 shirt. When he became a regular he asked if he could keep his 'lucky' number and made the 14 shirt his own for club – winning successive Dutch titles from 1966 to 1968 and scoring 33 goals to become leading scorer in the double season of 1966-67 – and country. He scored again on his Dutch debut – a 2-2 draw with Hungary – and went on to win 48 caps with his country, scoring 33 goals. Like his club career, his international career began to fade after 1974, and at only 30 he shocked his fans by not going to the 1978 World Cup in Argentina. He left Barcelona too, and played for the LA Aztecs and Washington Diplomats in the US for three years before returning to Ajax to win two more Championship medals. A spell at arch-rivals Feyenoord netted him his last medal in 1984. He switched back to Amsterdam to become technical director at Ajax and in 1987 moved to Barcelona as manager.

Cruyff was the first player to be voted European Footballer of the Year three times – in 1971, 1973 and 1974

HUNGARIAN HERO

Ferenc Puskas

Ferenc Puskas, one of the great players of all time, played for teams at their peak in the 1950s. His early days were at Honved, the Hungarian club that formed the backbone of the national side. The 'Magic Magyars', including Puskas, lost only one game – the 1954 World Cup final – in four years. Puskas also played for Real Madrid when they made history by winning the first five European Cup finals. As the player himself said: "Perhaps it is a little special to be Ferenc Puskas."

Ferenc Puskas was born in Budapest on 2 April 1927. He made his club debut at 16 and was capped for his country at 18. His exquisite ball control was the result of many hours of practice with the help of a tennis ball. His left foot was so lethal that he rarely resorted to using his right. His vision was incisive and his passing was inch-perfect. Yet Puskas, who later adopted Spanish nationality after the Hungarian uprising in 1956, was written off as too fat and too old to continue playing that year. The 'Galloping Major', as he was called, confounded his critics, however, by going on to play for another decade. His career was revived in Spain at Real Madrid, where he scored an impressive 35 goals in 39 European Cup matches and his partnership with the Argentinian Alfredo di Stefano was one that produced many memorable goals.

"His was a name fit for any sporting hall of fame, worthy of any and every superlative," Billy Wright, former England captain

Walking in a Puskas wonderland: Puskas puts Real Madrid's fifth goal into the back of the net during the team's 7-3 thrashing of Eintracht Frankfurt at Hampden Park in 1960.

○ Puskas scored 83 goals in 84 international games for Hungary. He was top scorer in the Hungarian and Spanish Leagues four times, and scored 35 goals in 39 European Cup matches for Real Madrid.

○ When the 1956 Hungarian uprising occurred, Honved were abroad, playing in a European Cup tie against Athletic Bilbao. Puskas and several team-mates decided to stay in the West. He settled in Vienna, but was denied a playing permit and was turned down by several Italian clubs, who thought he was too old. At 32, he signed to Real Madrid.

"His was a name fit for any sporting hall of fame, worthy of any and every superlative." So said Billy Wright, captain of the England side that was historically defeated at Wembley in November 1953 by the Magic Magyars. It was the first time that England had lost to a foreign team on home soil – and Puskas, who was captaining the Hungarians that afternoon, was credited as being the main inspiration, scoring two memorable goals in a resounding 6-3 victory.

The Wembley outing was no doubt one of Puskas's finest 90 minutes, yet it was hardly the exception to the rule. His was a career littered with glorious games and a prolific number of goals. One of his greatest games was for Real Madrid in the 1960 European Cup final at Hampden Park against Eintracht Frankfurt – a match watched by a record crowd of 135,000. Puskas's formidable partnership with Argentinian maestro Alfredo di Stefano hit perfection that balmy night in May. Puskas scored four glorious goals while Di Stefano bagged a hat-trick in Real's convincing 7-3 demolition of the German side. It was Real's fifth successive victory in a European Cup final – a record that remains unsurpassed. Puskas was adored by the Bernabeu fans, who christened him 'Canoncito' or the 'Little Cannon', and just as he had been the leading scorer in the Hungarian League with Honved for four seasons, he repeated the same feat at Real.

Puskas only appeared for his adopted country four times, including three disappointing performances in the 1962 World Cup finals in Chile. By the mid-Sixties, he himself was acknowledging that his career was now on the wane. He had helped Real to win five successive Championship titles between 1961 and 1965, and had appeared in three European Cup finals, scoring hat-tricks in two. In 1965, when Puskas was becoming noticeably portly, he still managed to put five goals past Dutch side Feyenoord.

In 1966, Puskas retired from the game. Even his outstanding skills and speed of thought could no longer compensate for ageing limbs and a burgeoning waistline. His early attempts at coaching, including a spell in Canada with Vancouver, were not promising. But in 1971, he took Greek side Panathinaikos to a European Cup final to face Johan Cruyff's mighty Ajax at Wembley. The Dutch side won 2-0.

The Galloping Major: Puskas possessed the most fearsome left-foot shot the game has ever seen, and a high proportion of his goals came from outside the area.

Ferenc Puskas is the only player to have scored two hat-tricks in European Cup finals – in 1960 and 1962

SO YOUNG

The Busby Babes

At 3.03am on Thursday, 6 February 1958, Flight 609 Zulu Uniform crashed trying to take off from Munich airport. The plane was carrying Matt Busby and his young Manchester United side back from a successful European Cup quarter-final against Red Star Belgrade. Twenty-three people died in all, including eight players. The final player to die, two weeks after the crash, was Duncan Edwards, pictured left, one of the finest young football talents England has ever produced.

The 40th anniversary of the Munich crash was commemorated in February 1998 with a ceremony at Old Trafford before the match with Bolton, and at a service at the cathedral. The event was made more poignant by the fact that the current team is, like Busby's 40 years before, largely made up of youngsters nurtured by the club. Busby had started to build his young side in the early 1950s. Although Manchester United had won the League in 1951-52, he knew that this particular team had peaked and set about introducing younger players. He began by wooing the best new talent in the country and building a team that won the Youth Cup five years running. In 1955-56 and 1956-57, the Busby Babes won the League comfortably. With an average age of 24 in 1958, they looked set to dominate domestic football for a decade.

With an average age of 24 in 1958, they looked set to dominate domestic football for a decade

Realising a dream: in 1968 Matt Busby managed the first English side to win the European Cup, 10 years after his Babes had won through to the European Cup semi-finals.

○ Duncan Edwards made his England debut at the age of 18 years and 183 days and held the record for the youngest player to debut for England this century until February 1998, when Michael Owen came on against Chile at the age of 18 years and 59 days. Edwards would have been 29 when England won the World Cup in 1966.

○ After recovering from his injuries, Matt Busby returned to the helm at Manchester United. It took him 10 years to achieve his goal of winning the European Cup with Manchester United.

The team for the final match the Busby Babes would play included Harry Gregg (25), recently signed from Doncaster, in goal and the three defenders Roger Byrne (28), Mark Jones (24) and Bill Foulkes (26). The midfield included Duncan Edwards (21), who had already been capped 18 times by England, and Eddie Colman (21), with Bobby Charlton (20) as a deep-lying centre forward. The wingers were Albert Scanlon (22) and Kenny Morgans (18), with Tommy Taylor (26) and Dennis Viollet (24) in the centre. They were an attacking side who were open to counter attacks on the break, which often meant high-scoring games. The Red Star game had finished 3-3 and the team's last match in England had been a 5-4 win over Arsenal. Byrne, Jones, Colman and Taylor died in the crash as did players Geoff Bent, David Pegg and Liam Whelan. Edwards died two weeks later in hospital. Others were too injured to play much of a part in the rest of the season and Busby himself had been given the last rites in hospital. The depleted United team gamely got to the FA Cup Final, which they lost 2-0 to Bolton Wanderers, but were knocked out of the European Cup by AC Milan and finished ninth in the League.

The last picture: five of the 11 team members who lined up before the Red Star Belgrade game in February 1958 were to die as a result of the Munich air disaster a few hours later.

In 1956, Busby's Babes became the youngest team to win the League – the average age of the players was 22

ENGLAND'S AMBASSADOR

Bobby Charlton

In a dramatic career spanning 18 years, Bobby Charlton became perhaps the most respected player in the game's history. He overcame the tragic death of his Manchester United colleagues in Munich in 1958 to rule the footballing world, and while today's players have pop-star status, Charlton was always the unassuming team man. Franz Beckenbauer once said: "He was a sportsman in the old-fashioned sense – a perfect gentleman, and a magnificent player."

Bobby Charlton was born in Ashington, Northumberland, on 11 October 1937. Nephew of Newcastle's Cup hero Jackie Milburn and younger brother of Leeds centre half Jack Charlton, he signed for United in 1955 at the age of 17. Along with manager Matt Busby's other young players, nicknamed the 'Busby Babes', Charlton played in three FA Youth Cup-winning sides. He made his first-team debut on 6 October 1956 against Charlton Athletic as a striker, scoring twice. United won the League that season, with the young Charlton scoring 10 times in only 14 appearances. But the following season tragedy struck the world of football. After a European Cup tie against Red Star Belgrade in February 1958, the plane carrying the United team, along with club officials and journalists, crashed on take-off at Munich.

"He was a sportsman in the old-fashioned sense – a perfect gentleman..." Franz Beckenbauer

Hot shot: for nearly two decades, defenders tried to stop Charlton unleashing his fearsome left foot. He began as a winger but soon became a striking inside forward and, by the mid-1960s, an attacking midfielder.

○ Charlton won two FA Cup runners-up medals, the first in 1957 when he was only 19, and the second a year later. He finally won a winner's medal in the Cup in 1963, when United beat Leicester City 3-1.

○ In April 1973, Charlton departed from Old Trafford after a record 754 senior games and 247 goals. He had a brief flirtation with management, becoming player-manager of Preston soon after leaving Manchester United – and taking his tally of League goals to 206.

Eight Busby Babes died in the Munich crash but Charlton was one of the few who survived. Overcoming his grief, he went on to win the first of his England caps against Scotland only weeks later, scoring in a 4-0 win. Despite two goals in his next game, Charlton was unimpressive against Yugoslavia and was omitted from the 1958 World Cup in Sweden. But he became an automatic choice for the 1966 World Cup in England and enjoyed an industrious, effective tournament, scoring with rifled long-distance shots against Mexico and, in the semi-final, against Portugal. Franz Beckenbauer man-marked Charlton in the final, resulting in them all but

United in victory: in 1968, at the age of 30 and as captain of Manchester United, Charlton made the crucial difference against Benfica at Wembley with two goals. Ten years after Munich, United became the first English club to win the European Cup.

cancelling each other out but Charlton's overall contribution was indisputable – earning him Footballer of the Year awards in both Britain and Europe. Charlton played his 106th and last game for England in the World Cup quarter-final against West Germany in 1970. Many people believe that it was Alf Ramsey's decision to substitute him – at 2-0 up with 20 minutes to go – that directly led to the 2-3 defeat. In 1984, Charlton joined the board of his beloved United, combining his work as a director with his soccer schools for children. His OBE, awarded in 1969, was followed by a CBE in 1974 and a knighthood in 1994.

Charlton set England records of 106 caps (later beaten by Bobby Moore and Peter Shilton) and 49 goals

WINNING WAYS

Arsenal in the 1930s

The Gunners have won a string of trophies and titles in the Nineties, under first George Graham and then Arsene Wenger – League champions in 1990-91, FA and League Cup winners in 1993, Cup Winners Cup victors in 1994, and League and FA Cup winners in 1998. Yet Arsenal's current run of form is still some way off recapturing the phenomenal domestic success enjoyed in the 1930s under the guidance of manager Herbert Chapman (1925-1934), pictured left.

The 1930s belonged to Arsenal. By the end of the decade, the club had won five League Championships (including a hat-trick in 1933, 1934 and 1935) and two FA Cups. The main architect of this glorious period was Herbert Chapman. His name was already synonymous with success – under the Yorkshireman's tutelage, Huddersfield had won a hat-trick of First Division Championships. When he arrived at Highbury in 1925, he went after the top players, including Sunderland's Charlie Buchan, and set about laying the foundations for success.

Sure enough, the club had its first taste of glory in 1930 when Arsenal won the FA Cup for the first time. But, tragically, Chapman died of pneumonia in January 1934 after taking the Gunners to two Championships and ensuring they were well on their way to a third.

The 1930s belonged to Arsenal. By the end of the decade, the club had won five League Championships and two FA Cups

Midfield maestro: Alex James, signed from Preston North End for £9,000 in June 1929, was a magical figure in Arsenal's midfield during the Thirties.

○ Arsenal's record of achievement in the 1930s included winning the FA Cup in 1930 and 1936 and the League Championship in 1931, 1933, 1934, 1935 and 1938.

○ When England beat world champions Italy 3-2 in November 1934, seven of the side were Arsenal players – Moss, Male, Hapgood, Copping, Bowden, Drake and Bastin.

○ Herbert Chapman was born in 1875 and died in 1934, aged 59.

Arsenal's wonder team was built around an astute tactical innovation. Traditionally, teams had played in a rigid 2-3-5 formation. Herbert Chapman and club captain Charlie Buchan plotted a new formation, pulling the centre half into defence to make a stronger, three-man back line. The so-called 'stopper' centre half had been proposed before, but Arsenal were the first to develop it. They also withdrew one of the inside forwards to link between defence and attack, creating the legendary 'W' formation – a system that England were later to adopt. Chapman introduced the formation as early as 1925 and over the course of the next few seasons, they perfected it. Herbie Roberts starred as the stopper centre half while Alex James ran riot in the midfield, linking defence and attack. James forged a devastating partnership with legendary winger Cliff Bastin, who went on to score 150 League goals, including 33 in the 1932-33 season. Arsenal won their first major trophy – the FA Cup – in 1930, Chapman's team beating his old club Huddersfield 2-0 in the Wembley final with goals from James and Lambert. The next season, 1930-31, Arsenal became the first southern club ever to take the First Division Championship, setting a record 66 points and scoring 127 goals in 42 matches.

Hitting new heights: Arsenal stamped their name on the 1930s. Their successes included a hat-trick of League Championships in 1932-33, 1933-34 and 1934-35, first under Herbert Chapman and then under George Allison.

Arsenal's Ted Drake still holds the club record for highest League scorer in a season – 42 (1934-35)

THE MAESTRO

Alfredo di Stefano

In the days before Pele, Alfredo di Stefano stood unchallenged as the greatest of South American footballers. Indeed there are those who claim he has been surpassed neither by Pele nor Maradona, because 'The Maestro' not only scored many spectacular goals – but also possessed a unique ability to dictate the way his teams played. Over a magical period with Real Madrid, he orchestrated five successive triumphs in the European Cup.

Grandson of an Italian immigrant, Alfredo Stefano di Stefano Lauhle was born in Barracas, a poor suburb of Buenos Aires, on 4 July 1926. Honing his ball-skills on the streets and later on a small farm – where he developed his legendary stamina – he made his league debut for River Plate at 17 as an outside right, but after two years on loan to Huracan he returned to become the spearhead of the River Plate forward line – known as 'La Maquina' (The Machine) for the merciless way they took defences apart. In 1947, he won the league title with his club and the South American Championship with his country. In 1949, following a players' strike in Argentina, he was tempted by the pirate league of Colombia – then outside FIFA's jurisdiction – and steered Millonarios to three successive league titles.

A Spanish court decided that Di Stefano should be shared by Real Madrid and Barcelona

Gimme five: Di Stefano poses with Real Madrid's first five European Cup trophies. He played in all five finals from 1956 to 1960.

○ Di Stefano was leading goalscorer in the Spanish league five times in the six seasons between 1954-1959.

○ In 1963, Di Stefano was kidnapped by guerrillas while Real Madrid were on tour in Venezuela. Released unharmed after three days, he played for FIFA's World XI against England at Wembley later that year.

○ Di Stefano scored in every one of Real Madrid's five European Cup finals, on his way to a record total of 49 goals in 58 games.

Di Stefano was still relatively unknown outside South America at the start of the 1950s, but all that was set to change. In 1953, Real Madrid and Barcelona were both courting his signature. Real agreed a fee with Millonarios, but Barcelona had a deal with River Plate, and a Spanish court came to the extraordinary decision that the clubs would share Di Stefano – he would play one season with Real and one with Barcelona. But after an unpromising start to the season the Catalans decided to sell their 50% share to Real. Four days after the purchase was completed, Di Stefano dramatically came to life with a hat-trick – in a 5-0 thrashing of Barcelona – and Real went on to take away their title. Even in his late thirties Di Stefano remained a bright star, helping the defence, directing midfield, setting up chances and scoring goals. In 1964 he left for a twilight season at Espanol before coaching in Spain and then Argentina, returning in 1970 to upset the formbook by taking Valencia to their first League Championship in 24 years.

Goal-getter: Di Stefano scores against Eintracht Frankfurt in the 1960 European Cup at Hampden Park. Di Stefano and Ferenc Puskas shared seven goals to climax five glorious seasons. Di Stefano later had two short spells managing the club, in 1982 and 1990.

Di Stefano played for three countries – Argentina (7 caps), Colombia (3) and Spain (31)

THE GEMMILL GOAL

Argentina 1978

The 1978 World Cup in Argentina was a bitter-sweet experience for Scottish fans – mostly bitter. After much talk, mainly by manager Ally MacLeod, that Scotland were going to win, the team started disastrously. They lost 3-1 to Peru, Willie Johnston was sent home after failing a dope test, and they drew with Iran 1-1. But then, against Holland, with three goals needed to qualify, Archie Gemmill scored to put Scotland two goals clear. The dream was back on.

Archie Gemmill was a hard-running midfielder, noted more for his tackling skills and ability to do little one-twos than his scoring skills. Born in Paisley, he started his career with St Mirren before moving to England to join Preston North End. At Derby he won two League Championships (1972-73 and 1974-75) before moving on to Nottingham Forest, where he rejoined manager Brian Clough and won a third Championship in the season leading up to the World Cup. Gemmill was not in the starting line-up against Peru, as Don Masson, Graeme Souness and Bruce Rioch were given the midfield positions. But he did come on as a substitute and was on from the start against Iran and Holland. He alone of the hapless Scotland squad was to return from Argentina with his reputation enhanced.

"It was an instinctive thing, there was nothing planned – I just kept going," Archie Gemmill

Part of Ally's army: Scottish fans witnessed an extraordinary piece of skill at the World Cup in 1978, when Archie Gemmill beat the Dutch defence.

○ Archie Gemmill won his 29th cap for Scotland in the game with Holland. He was to play 14 more times for his country.

○ His second goal against Holland was his fifth goal for Scotland. He was to score three more.

○ Archie Gemmill's son Scot Gemmill has followed in his father's footsteps, playing in the number 15 shirt for Scotland in France '98.

"Scotland are in dreamland": David Coleman's memorable commentary on BBC Television celebrated Gemmill's goal.

On 11 June 1978, Archie Gemmill and his Scottish team-mates stepped out into the San Martin Stadium in Mendoza, Argentina needing to beat Holland by three clear goals in order to qualify from Group 4. Within 34 minutes, Holland had scored through a Rob Rensenbrink penalty but a Kenny Dalglish equaliser and a penalty by Archie Gemmill set the scene for a thrilling finale. On 68 minutes, Gemmill picked up the ball on the right of midfield. "We were screaming to Archie to put the ball wide," recalled Ally MacLeod afterwards, "but he didn't." Instead, Gemmill went on an uncharacteristic slalom-style run that left first Ruud Krol, then Jan Poortvliet lunging at thin air and landing on their backsides. He jigged left and right, with the ball seemingly tied to his bootlaces. Then he put the ball coolly to the right of keeper Jan Jongbloed and into the back of the net. "It was an instinctive thing, there was nothing planned – I just kept going," explained Gemmill. "A brilliant individual goal by this hard little professional has put Scotland in dreamland," exclaimed BBC commentator David Coleman. But Scottish hopes were dashed just three minutes later when Johnny Rep scored with a 25-yard screamer. Holland went on to the final, where they lost to hosts Argentina, and the Tartan Army were left dreaming about what might have been. The Argentinian sports paper El Grafico voted Gemmill's goal the best of a tournament noted for its superb strikes, but even for Gemmill the memory is tainted by Scotland's lack of success in the tournament.

Archie and Scot Gemmill are the only father and son to have gone to a World Cup finals with Scotland

Statistics

Statistics

All the stats, figures and fixtures

This section includes the fixtures for the FA Carling Premiership and Nationwide Football League for 1998-99, plus all the stats and figures from the 1998 World Cup and the 1997-98 season. There are final tables for the English and Scottish leagues, as well as the final top tables for Belgium, France, Germany, Italy, the Netherlands, Portugal and Spain. For teams in the Premiership and Division One of the English League, as well as the top rung of the Scottish League, we provide a breakdown of their season, team-by-team. We also include the major Cup competitions in England, Scotland and Europe. Finally, the World Cup pages include the qualifying rounds and all the matches in the finals, as well as details of each country's performance.

Division One

League table

Teams	P
Nottingham Forest*	46
Middlesbrough*	46

Premiership 1997 | 98

	P	W	D	L	F	A	GD	Pts	Most yellow ca... / Player
	38	23	9	6	68	33	+35	78	Lucas Radebe
...ester United	38	23	8	7	73	26	+47	77	David Batty
...ool	38	18	11	9	68	42	+26	65	Jamie Fullarton
	38	20	3	15	71	43	+28	63	Paul Williams
...United	38	17	8	13	57	46	+11	59	Dennis Wise
...urn Rovers	38	16	10	12	57	52	+5	58	Lee Carsley
...Villa	38	17	6	15	49	48	+1	57	Paolo Di Canio
...am United	38	16	8	14	56	57	-1	56	Dejan Stefanovic
...County	38	16	7	15	52	49	+3	55	Steve Bould
...er City	38	13	14	11	51	41	+10	53	Patrick Vieira
...y City	38	12	16	10	46	44	+2	52	Jovo Bosancic
...mpton	38	14	6	18	50	55	-5	48	Adrian Moses
...stle	38	11	11	16	35	44	-9	44	Billy McKinlay
...am Hotspur	38	11	11	16	44	56	-12	44	Gudni Bergsson
...don	38	10	14	14	34	46	-12	44	Alan Thompson
...d Wednesday	38	11	8	18	52	67	-15	44	Mark Hughes
	38	9	13	16	41	56	-15	40	Frank Leboeuf

Cup

1997 | 98

Football Le...

Division One

League table

Oceania

First Round

Melanesian Group	P	W	D
Papua New Guinea	2	1	1
Solomon Islands	2	0	2
Vanuatu	2	0	1

Premiership 1997 | 98

Premiership
League table

Teams	P	W	D	L	F	A	GD	Pts	Most ye... / Player
Arsenal	38	23	9	6	68	33	+35	78	Lucas Ra...
Manchester United	38	23	8	7	73	26	+47	77	David Bat...
Liverpool	38	18	11	9	68	42	+26	65	Jamie Ful...
Chelsea	38	20	3	15	71	43	+28	63	Paul Willi...
Leeds United	38	17	8	13	57	46	+11	59	Dennis W...
Blackburn Rovers	38	16	10	12	57	52	+5	58	Lee Cars...
Aston Villa	38	17	6	15	49	48	+1	57	Paolo Di...
West Ham United	38	16	8	14	56	57	-1	56	Dejan Ste...
Derby County	38	16	7	15	52	49	+3	55	Steve Bo...
Leicester City	38	13	14	11	51	41	+10	53	Patrick Vie...
Coventry City	38	12	16	10	46	44	+2	52	Jovo Bos...
Southampton	38	14	6	18	50	55	-5	48	Adrian Mo...
Newcastle	38	11	11	16	35	44	-9	44	Billy McKi...
Tottenham Hotspur	38	11	11	16	44	56	-12	44	Gudni Ber...
Wimbledon	38	10	14	14	34	46	-12	44	Alan Thor...
Sheffield Wednesday	38	11	8	18	52	67	-15	44	Mark Hug...
Everton	38	9	13	16	41	56	-15	40	Frank Let...

Cup

1997 | 98

Oceania

First Round

Melanesian Group	P	W	D
Papua New Guinea	2	1	1
Solomon Islands	2	0	2
Vanuatu	2	0	1

97 | 98

Division One

League table

Teams

Premiership 1997 | 98

Premiership
League table

Teams	P	W	D	L	F	A	GD	Pts	Most yellow ca... / Player
Arsenal	38	23	9	6	68	33	+35	78	Lucas Radebe
Manchester United	38	23	8	7	73	26	+47	77	David Batty
Liverpool	38	18	11	9	68	42	+26	65	Jamie Fullarton
Chelsea	38	20	3	15	71	43	+28	63	Paul Williams
Leeds United	38	17	8	13	57	46	+11	59	Dennis Wise
Blackburn Rovers	38	16	10	12	57	52	+5	58	Lee Carsley
Aston Villa	38	17	6	15	49	48	+1	57	Paolo Di Canio
West Ham United	38	16	8	14	56	57	-1	56	Dejan Stefanovic
Derby County	38	16	7	15	52	49	+3	55	Steve Bould
Leicester City	38	13	14	11	51	41	+10	53	Patrick Vieira
Coventry City	38	12	16	10	46	44	+2	52	Jovo Bosancic
Southampton	38	14	6	18	50	55	-5	48	Adrian Moses
Newcastle	38	11	11	16	35	44	-9	44	Billy McKinlay
Tottenham Hotspur	38	11	11	16	44	56	-12	44	Gudni Bergsson
Wimbledon	38	10	14	14	34	46	-12	44	Alan Thompson
Sheffield Wednesday	38	11	8	18	52	67	-15	44	Mark Hughes

Cup

Oceania

First Round

Melanesian Group	P
Papua New Guinea	2
Solomon Islands	2

Premiership

League table

Teams	P	W	D	L	F	A	GD	Pts
Arsenal	38	23	9	6	68	33	+35	78
Manchester United	38	23	8	7	73	26	+47	77
Liverpool	38	18	11	9	68	42	+26	65
Chelsea	38	20	3	15	71	43	+28	63
Leeds United	38	17	8	13	57	46	+11	59
Blackburn Rovers	38	16	10	12	57	52	+5	58
Aston Villa	38	17	6	15	49	48	+1	57
West Ham United	38	16	8	14	56	57	-1	56
Derby County	38	16	7	15	52	49	+3	55
Leicester City	38	13	14	11	51	41	+10	53
Coventry City	38	12	16	10	46	44	+2	52
Southampton	38	14	6	18	50	55	-5	48
Newcastle	38	11	11	16	35	44	-9	44
Tottenham Hotspur	38	11	11	16	44	56	-12	44
Wimbledon	38	10	14	14	34	46	-12	44
Sheffield Wednesday	38	11	8	18	52	67	-15	44
Everton	38	9	13	16	41	56	-15	40
Bolton Wanderers*	38	9	13	16	41	61	-20	40
Barnsley*	38	10	5	23	37	82	-45	35
Crystal Palace*	38	8	9	21	37	71	-34	33

* relegated to Division One

Most yellow cards

Player	Club	Cards
Lucas Radebe	Leeds	12
David Batty	Newcastle	12
Jamie Fullarton	Crystal Palace	11
Paul Williams	Coventry	11
Dennis Wise	Chelsea	10
Lee Carsley	Derby	10
Paolo Di Canio	Sheffield Wednesday	10
Dejan Stefanovic	Sheffield Wednesday	10
Steve Bould	Arsenal	9
Patrick Vieira	Arsenal	9
Jovo Bosancic	Barnsley	9
Adrian Moses	Barnsley	9
Billy McKinlay	Blackburn	9
Gudni Bergsson	Bolton	9
Alan Thompson	Bolton	9
Mark Hughes	Chelsea	9
Frank Leboeuf	Chelsea	9
Paul Telfer	Coventry	9
Stefano Eranio	Derby	9
Peter Atherton	Sheffield Wednesday	9
Benito Carbone	Sheffield Wednesday	9
David Unsworth	West Ham	9
John Moncur	West Ham	9

Top scorers

Player	Team	Goals
Chris Sutton	Blackburn	18
Dion Dublin	Coventry	18
Michael Owen	Liverpool	18
Dennis Bergkamp	Arsenal	16
Kevin Gallacher	Blackburn	16
Jimmy Floyd Hasselbaink	Leeds	16
Andy Cole	Manchester	15
Jan Aage Fjortoft	Barnsley (Sheffield United 9)	15*
John Hartson	West Ham	15
Darren Huckerby	Coventry	14

* including goals at previous club

Most red cards

Player	Club	Cards
Slaven Bilic	Everton	3
David Batty	Newcastle	3
Jason Wilcox	Blackburn	2
Paul Williams	Coventry	2
Stefano Eranio	Derby	2
Francis Benali	Southampton	2
John Hartson	West Ham	2
Ben Thatcher	Wimbledon	2

Premiership
Team statistics

Arsenal

Highest attendance:	38,269 v Everton
Lowest attendance:	37,324 v Coventry
Average home attendance:	38,053
Heaviest defeat:	0-4 v Liverpool
Biggest win:	5-0 v Barnsley
	5-0 v Wimbledon
Longest winning sequence:	10
Longest unbeaten sequence:	18
Clean sheets:	19
Highest Saturday night position:	1st
Red cards:	3
Yellow cards:	72
Top scorer:	Dennis Bergkamp (16)

Barnsley

Highest attendance:	18,694 v Manchester United
Lowest attendance:	17,102 v Wimbledon
Average home attendance:	18,442
Heaviest defeat:	0-7 v Manchester United
Biggest win:	4-3 v Southampton
Longest winning sequence:	3
Longest unbeaten sequence:	3
Clean sheets:	6
Highest Saturday night position:	10th
Red cards:	5
Yellow cards:	70
Top scorer:	Neil Redfearn (10)

Aston Villa

Highest attendance:	39,372 v Arsenal
Lowest attendance:	29,343 v Southampton
Average home attendance:	36,136
Heaviest defeat:	0-5 v Blackburn
Biggest win:	4-1 v Everton
	4-1 v Tottenham
Longest winning sequence:	5
Longest unbeaten sequence:	5
Clean sheets:	9
Highest Saturday night position:	7th
Red cards:	2
Yellow cards:	45
Top scorer:	Dwight Yorke (12)

Blackburn Rovers

Highest attendance:	30,547 v Manchester United
Lowest attendance:	19,086 v Coventry
Average home attendance:	25,252
Heaviest defeat:	0-4 v Leeds
	0-4 v Manchester United
Biggest win:	7-2 v Sheffield Wednesday
Longest winning sequence:	3
Longest unbeaten sequence:	9
Clean sheets:	14
Highest Saturday night position:	1st
Red cards:	5
Yellow cards:	58
Top scorer:	Chris Sutton (18)

Premiership
Team statistics

Bolton Wanderers

Highest attendance:	25,000 v Arsenal
Lowest attendance:	22,706 v Wimbledon
Average home attendance:	24,352
Heaviest defeat:	0-5 v Sheffield Wednesday
Biggest win:	5-2 v Crystal Palace
Longest winning sequence:	2
Longest unbeaten sequence:	3
Clean sheets:	10
Highest Saturday night position:	8th
Red cards:	5
Yellow cards:	66
Top scorer:	Nathan Blake (12)

Coventry City

Highest attendance:	23,054 v Manchester United
Lowest attendance:	15,900 v Crystal Palace
Average home attendance:	19,722
Heaviest defeat:	0-3 v Manchester United
Biggest win:	5-1 v Bolton
Longest winning sequence:	5
Longest unbeaten sequence:	9
Clean sheets:	13
Highest Saturday night position:	8th
Red cards:	5
Yellow cards:	71
Top scorer:	Dion Dublin (18)

Chelsea

Highest attendance:	34,845 v Bolton
Lowest attendance:	29,075 v Sheffield Wednesday
Average home attendance:	33,387
Heaviest defeat:	2-4 v Liverpool
Biggest win:	6-0 v Barnsley
Longest winning sequence:	4
Longest unbeaten sequence:	6
Clean sheets:	14
Highest Saturday night position:	2nd
Red cards:	3
Yellow cards:	67
Top scorers:	Tore Andre Flo (11)
	Gianluca Vialli (11)

Crystal Palace

Highest attendance:	26,186 v Chelsea
Lowest attendance:	14,410 v Wimbledon
Average home attendance:	21,982
Heaviest defeat:	2-6 v Chelsea
Biggest win:	3-1 v Derby
	3-1 v Sheffield Wednesday
Longest winning sequence:	1
Longest unbeaten sequence:	4
Clean sheets:	6
Highest Saturday night position:	5th
Red cards:	3
Yellow cards:	73
Top scorer:	Neil Shipperley (7)

Derby County

Highest attendance:	30,492 v Liverpool
Lowest attendance:	25,625 v Southampton
Average home attendance:	29,104
Heaviest defeat:	0-5 v Leeds United
Biggest win:	5-2 v Sheffield Wednesday
Longest winning sequence:	3
Longest unbeaten sequence:	5
Clean sheets:	13
Highest Saturday night position:	6th
Red cards:	2
Yellow cards:	82
Top scorer:	Paulo Wanchope (13)

Leeds United

Highest attendance:	39,952 v Manchester United
Lowest attendance:	28,791 v Southampton
Average home attendance:	34,640
Heaviest defeat:	0-3 v Manchester United
	0-3 v West Ham
Biggest win:	5-0 v Derby
Longest winning sequence:	4
Longest unbeaten sequence:	7
Clean sheets:	11
Highest Saturday night position:	4th
Red cards:	5
Yellow cards:	79
Top scorer:	Jimmy Floyd Hasselbaink (16)

Everton

Highest attendance:	40,152 v Liverpool
Lowest attendance:	28,533 v Wimbledon
Average home attendance:	35,354
Heaviest defeat:	0-4 v Arsenal
Biggest win:	4-2 v Barnsley
Longest winning sequence:	3
Longest unbeaten sequence:	5
Clean sheets:	10
Highest Saturday night position:	12th
Red cards:	5
Yellow cards:	80
Top scorer:	Duncan Ferguson (11)

Leicester City

Highest attendance:	21,699 v Newcastle
Lowest attendance:	18,553 v Wimbledon
Average home attendance:	20,615
Heaviest defeat:	3-5 v Blackburn
Biggest win:	4-0 v Derby
Longest winning sequence:	2
Longest unbeaten sequence:	7
Clean sheets:	15
Highest Saturday night position:	3rd
Red cards:	2
Yellow cards:	46
Top scorer:	Emile Heskey (10)

Premiership
Team statistics

Liverpool

Highest attendance:	44,532 v Bolton
Lowest attendance:	34,705 v Sheffield Wednesday
Average home attendance:	40,628
Heaviest defeat:	1-4 v Chelsea
Biggest win:	5-0 v West Ham
Longest winning sequence:	5
Longest unbeaten sequence:	8
Clean sheets:	13
Highest Saturday night position:	2nd
Red cards:	2
Yellow cards:	54
Top scorer:	Michael Owen (18)

Newcastle United

Highest attendance:	36,783 v Aston Villa
Lowest attendance:	36,289 v Derby
Average home attendance:	36,670
Heaviest defeat:	1-4 v Leeds
Biggest win:	3-1 v Chelsea
Longest winning sequence:	2
Longest unbeaten sequence:	5
Clean sheets:	10
Highest Saturday night position:	6th
Red cards:	3
Yellow cards:	63
Top scorer:	John Barnes (6)

Manchester United

Highest attendance:	55,306 v Wimbledon
Lowest attendance:	55,008 v Southampton
Average home attendance:	55,164
Heaviest defeat:	2-3 v Arsenal
	2-3 v Coventry
Biggest win:	7-0 v Barnsley
Longest winning sequence:	6
Longest unbeaten sequence:	8
Clean sheets:	20
Highest Saturday night position:	1st
Red cards:	2
Yellow cards:	61
Top scorer:	Andy Cole (15)

Sheffield Wednesday

Highest attendance:	39,427 v Manchester United
Lowest attendance:	21,087 v Coventry
Average home attendance:	28,706
Heaviest defeat:	2-7 v Blackburn
Biggest win:	5-0 v Bolton
Longest winning sequence:	4
Longest unbeaten sequence:	5
Clean sheets:	8
Highest Saturday night position:	11th
Red cards:	4
Yellow cards:	72
Top scorer:	Paolo Di Canio (12)

Southampton

Highest attendance:	15,255 v Tottenham
Lowest attendance:	14,815 v Wimbledon
Average home attendance:	15,159
Heaviest defeat:	0-4 v Derby
Biggest win:	4-1 v Barnsley
Longest winning sequence:	3
Longest unbeaten sequence:	6
Clean sheets:	8
Highest Saturday night position:	10th
Red cards:	4
Yellow cards:	59
Top scorers:	Matt Le Tissier (11)
	Egil Ostenstad (11)

West Ham United

Highest attendance:	25,909 v Everton
Lowest attendance:	23,335 v Crystal Palace
Average home attendance:	25,075
Heaviest defeat:	0-5 v Liverpool
Biggest win:	6-0 v Barnsley
Longest winning sequence:	3
Longest unbeaten sequence:	7
Clean sheets:	8
Highest Saturday night position:	3rd
Red cards:	5
Yellow cards:	63
Top scorer:	John Hartson (15)

Tottenham Hotspur

Highest attendance:	35,995 v Southampton
Lowest attendance:	25,097 v Sheffield Wednesday
Average home attendance:	29,143
Heaviest defeat:	1-6 v Chelsea
Biggest win:	6-2 v Wimbledon
Longest winning sequence:	2
Longest unbeaten sequence:	5
Clean sheets:	10
Highest Saturday night position:	7th
Red cards:	2
Yellow cards:	58
Top scorer:	Jurgen Klinsmann (9)

Wimbledon

Highest attendance:	26,309 v Manchester United
Lowest attendance:	7,668 v Barnsley
Average home attendance:	16,665
Heaviest defeat:	2-6 v Tottenham
Biggest win:	4-1 v Barnsley
Longest winning sequence:	2
Longest unbeaten sequence:	4
Clean sheets:	13
Highest Saturday night position:	9th
Red cards:	2
Yellow cards:	49
Top scorers:	Efan Ekoku (4)
	Carl Cort (4)
	Carl Leaburn (4)
	Michael Hughes (4)
	Jason Euell (4)

Division One

League table

Teams	P	W	D	L	F	A	GD	Pts
Nottingham Forest*	46	28	10	8	82	42	+40	94
Middlesbrough*	46	27	10	9	77	41	+36	91
Sunderland	46	26	12	8	86	50	+36	90
Charlton Athletic**	46	26	10	10	80	49	+31	88
Ipswich Town	46	23	14	9	77	43	+34	83
Sheffield United	46	19	17	10	69	54	+15	74
Birmingham City	46	19	17	10	60	35	+25	74
Stockport County	46	19	8	19	71	69	+2	65
Wolverhampton Wanderers	46	18	11	17	57	53	+4	65
West Bromwich Albion	46	16	13	17	50	56	-6	61
Crewe Alexandra	46	18	5	23	58	65	-7	59
Oxford United	46	16	10	20	60	64	-4	58
Bradford City	46	14	15	17	46	59	-13	57
Tranmere Rovers	46	14	14	18	54	57	-3	56
Norwich City	46	14	13	19	52	69	-17	55
Huddersfield Town	46	14	11	21	50	72	-22	53
Bury	46	11	19	16	42	58	-16	52
Swindon Town	46	14	10	22	42	73	-31	52
Port Vale	46	13	10	23	56	66	-10	49
Portsmouth	46	13	10	23	51	63	-12	49
Queen's Park Rangers	46	10	19	17	51	63	-12	49
Manchester City†	46	12	12	22	56	57	-1	48
Stoke City†	46	11	13	22	44	74	-30	46
Reading†	46	11	9	26	39	78	-39	42

* automatically promoted to Premiership

** promoted to Premiership after play-offs

† relegated to Division Two

Most yellow cards

Player	Club	Cards
Stewart Talbot	Port Vale	11
Steve Jenkins	Huddersfield	10
Nigel Pepper	Bradford	9
Karl Ready	QPR	9
Darren Bullock	Swindon	9
Lee Hughes	West Brom	9
Peter Beagrie	Bradford	8
Jon Dyson	Huddersfield	8
Jason Cundy	Ipswich	8
Richard Edghill	Manchester City	8
Joey Beauchamp	Oxford	8
Phil Parkinson	Reading	8
Martin McIntosh	Stockport	8
Ally Pickering	Stoke	8
Graham Kavanagh	Stoke	8
Ty Gooden	Swindon	8

Most red cards

Player	Club	Cards
Nigel Pepper	Bradford	2
Gianluca Festa	Middlesbrough	2
Mike Milligan	Norwich	2
Andy Thomson	Portsmouth	2
Danny Maddix	QPR	2
Andy Bernal	Reading	2
Steve Sedgley	Wolves	2

Top scorers

Player	Team	Goals
Kevin Phillips	Sunderland	29
Pierre Van Hooijdonk	Nottingham Forest	29
David Johnson	Ipswich (Bury 5)	25*
Kevin Campbell	Nottingham Forest	23
Clive Mendonca	Charlton	23
Shaun Goater	Manchester City (Bristol City 17)	20*
Alun Armstrong	Middlesbrough (Stockport 12)	19*
Brett Angell	Stockport	18
Dele Adebola	Birmingham (Crewe 8)	15*
Marcus Stewart	Huddersfield	15
Paul Furlong	Birmingham	15

* including goals at previous club

Division One
Team statistics

Birmingham City

Highest attendance:	25,877 v Charlton
Lowest attendance:	14,552 v Bradford
Average home attendance:	18,751
Heaviest defeat:	1-3 v Bury
	1-3 v Middlesbrough
Biggest win:	7-0 v Stoke
Longest winning sequence:	3
Longest unbeaten sequence:	9
Clean sheets:	22
Highest Saturday night position:	2nd
Red cards:	4
Yellow cards:	57
Top scorer:	Paul Furlong (15)

Bury

Highest attendance:	11,216 v Manchester City
Lowest attendance:	4,602 v QPR
Average home attendance:	6,178
Heaviest defeat:	0-4 v Middlesbrough
Biggest win:	3-1 v Birmingham
Longest winning sequence:	2
Longest unbeaten sequence:	9
Clean sheets:	13
Highest Saturday night position:	7th
Red cards:	4
Yellow cards:	53
Top scorer:	Tony Ellis (7)

Bradford City

Highest attendance:	17,842 v Huddersfield
Lowest attendance:	13,021 v Reading
Average home attendance:	15,564
Heaviest defeat:	0-5 v Crewe
Biggest win:	4-1 v Reading
Longest winning sequence:	3
Longest unbeaten sequence:	7
Clean sheets:	12
Highest Saturday night position:	1st
Red cards:	8
Yellow cards:	63
Top scorers:	Edinho (10)
	Robert Steiner (10)

Charlton Athletic

Highest attendance:	15,815 v Nottingham Forest
Lowest attendance:	9,868 v Sheffield United
Average home attendance:	13,271
Heaviest defeat:	2-5 v Nottingham Forest
Biggest win:	5-0 v West Brom
Longest winning sequence:	8
Longest unbeaten sequence:	10
Clean sheets:	20
Highest Saturday night position:	3rd
Red cards:	1
Yellow cards:	69
Top scorers:	Clive Mendonca (23)

Division One
Team statistics

Crewe Alexandra

Highest attendance:	5,759 v Manchester City
Lowest attendance:	4,176 v Swindon
Average home attendance:	5,243
Heaviest defeat:	2-5 v Huddersfield
Biggest win:	5-0 v Bradford
Longest winning sequence:	4
Longest unbeaten sequence:	5
Clean sheets:	14
Highest Saturday night position:	11th
Red cards:	0
Yellow cards:	41
Top scorer:	Colin Little (13)

Ipswich Town

Highest attendance:	21,858 v Norwich
Lowest attendance:	8,938 v Stockport
Average home attendance:	14,893
Heaviest defeat:	0-3 v Charlton
Biggest win:	5-0 v Norwich
Longest winning sequence:	5
Longest unbeaten sequence:	16
Clean sheets:	17
Highest Saturday night position:	5th
Red cards:	3
Yellow cards:	49
Top scorer:	David Johnson (20)

Huddersfield Town

Highest attendance:	18,820 v Middlesbrough
Lowest attendance:	8,985 v Portsmouth
Average home attendance:	12,146
Heaviest defeat:	0-5 v Norwich
Biggest win:	5-1 v Oxford
Longest winning sequence:	3
Longest unbeaten sequence:	6
Clean sheets:	13
Highest Saturday night position:	13th
Red cards:	0
Yellow cards:	74
Top scorers:	Marcus Stewart (15)

Manchester City

Highest attendance:	32,040 v QPR
Lowest attendance:	24,058 v Charlton
Average home attendance:	28,197
Heaviest defeat:	0-3 v Reading
Biggest win:	6-0 v Swindon
Longest winning sequence:	2
Longest unbeaten sequence:	3
Clean sheets:	12
Highest Saturday night position:	16th
Red cards:	3
Yellow cards:	67
Top scorer:	Paul Dickov (9)

Middlesbrough

Highest attendance:	30,228 v Oxford
Lowest attendance:	29,414 v Charlton
Average home attendance:	29,997
Heaviest defeat:	0-5 v QPR
Biggest win:	6-0 v Swindon
Longest winning sequence:	4
Longest unbeaten sequence:	9
Clean sheets:	18
Highest Saturday night position:	1st
Red cards:	6
Yellow cards:	58
Top scorer:	Mikkel Beck (14)

Nottingham Forest

Highest attendance:	29,302 v Reading
Lowest attendance:	16,524 v Norwich
Average home attendance:	20,543
Heaviest defeat:	2-4 v Charlton
Biggest win:	5-2 v Charlton
Longest winning sequence:	4
Longest unbeaten sequence:	7
Clean sheets:	22
Highest Saturday night position:	1st
Red cards:	1
Yellow cards:	60
Top scorer:	Pierre Van Hooijdonk (29)

Norwich City

Highest attendance:	19,069 West Brom
Lowest attendance:	9,819 v Birmingham
Average home attendance:	14,444
Heaviest defeat:	0-5 v Ipswich
	0-5 v Wolves
Biggest win:	5-0 v Swindon
	5-0 v Huddersfield
Longest winning sequence:	2
Longest unbeaten sequence:	4
Clean sheets:	11
Highest Saturday night position:	12th
Red cards:	4
Yellow cards:	75
Top scorer:	Craig Bellamy (13)

Oxford United

Highest attendance:	9,486 v Nottingham Forest
Lowest attendance:	5,762 v Port Vale
Average home attendance:	7,487
Heaviest defeat:	1-5 v Huddersfield
Biggest win:	5-1 v Stoke
Longest winning sequence:	3
Longest unbeaten sequence:	5
Clean sheets:	16
Highest Saturday night position:	10th
Red cards:	2
Yellow cards:	65
Top scorer:	Joey Beauchamp (13)

Division One
Team statistics

Portsmouth

Highest attendance:	17,003 v Middlesbrough
Lowest attendance:	6,827 v Bradford
Average home attendance:	11,148
Heaviest defeat:	1-4 v Sunderland
Biggest win:	3-0 v West Brom
Longest winning sequence:	4
Longest unbeaten sequence:	7
Clean sheets:	9
Highest Saturday night position:	6th
Red cards:	4
Yellow cards:	58
Top scorer:	John Aloisi (12)

Queen's Park Rangers

Highest attendance:	17,614 v Ipswich
Lowest attendance:	8,853 v Bradford
Average home attendance:	13,082
Heaviest defeat:	0-4 v Nottingham Forest
Biggest win:	5-0 v Middlesbrough
Longest winning sequence:	4
Longest unbeaten sequence:	5
Clean sheets:	10
Highest Saturday night position:	2nd
Red cards:	4
Yellow cards:	69
Top scorer:	Mike Sheron (11)

Port Vale

Highest attendance:	13,853 v Stoke
Lowest attendance:	5,244 v Huddersfield
Average home attendance:	8,431
Heaviest defeat:	1-5 v Ipswich
Biggest win:	4-0 v Huddersfield
Longest winning sequence:	2
Longest unbeaten sequence:	3
Clean sheets:	10
Highest Saturday night position:	7th
Red cards:	0
Yellow cards:	67
Top scorer:	Lee Mills (14)

Reading

Highest attendance:	14,817 v Norwich
Lowest attendance:	6,685 v Crewe
Average home attendance:	9,675
Heaviest defeat:	0-6 v Tranmere Rovers
Biggest win:	4-0 v Sunderland
Longest winning sequence:	2
Longest unbeaten sequence:	7
Clean sheets:	12
Highest Saturday night position:	14th
Red cards:	5
Yellow cards:	71
Top scorer:	Carl Asaba (8)

Sheffield United

Highest attendance:	24,536 v Nottingham Forest
Lowest attendance:	14,120 v Ipswich
Average home attendance:	17,938
Heaviest defeat:	2-4 v West Brom
	2-4 v Sunderland
Biggest win:	5-1 v Stockport
Longest winning sequence:	2
Longest unbeaten sequence:	10
Clean sheets:	14
Highest Saturday night position:	3rd
Red cards:	2
Yellow cards:	60
Top scorers:	Brian Deane (10)
	Dean Saunders (10)
	Gareth Taylor (10)

Stoke City

Highest attendance:	26,664 v Manchester City
Lowest attendance:	8,423 v Oxford
Average home attendance:	14,944
Heaviest defeat:	0-7 v Birmingham
Biggest win:	3-0 v Wolves
Longest winning sequence:	2
Longest unbeaten sequence:	4
Clean sheets:	10
Highest Saturday night position:	7th
Red cards:	2
Yellow cards:	63
Top scorer:	Peter Thorne (12)

Stockport County

Highest attendance:	11,351 v Manchester City
Lowest attendance:	6,148 v Reading
Average home attendance:	8,322
Heaviest defeat:	1-5 v Sheffield United
Biggest win:	5-1 v Reading
Longest winning sequence:	4
Longest unbeaten sequence:	5
Clean sheets:	11
Highest Saturday night position:	7th
Red cards:	0
Yellow cards:	63
Top scorer:	Brett Angell (18)

Sunderland

Highest attendance:	41,214 v Stoke
Lowest attendance:	24,782 v Huddersfield
Average home attendance:	34,334
Heaviest defeat:	0-4 v Reading
Biggest win:	4-0 v Bradford
Longest winning sequence:	5
Longest unbeaten sequence:	16
Clean sheets:	14
Highest Saturday night position:	2nd
Red cards:	3
Yellow cards:	54
Top scorer:	Kevin Phillips (29)

Division One
Team statistics

Swindon Town

Highest attendance:	15,228 v Middlesbrough
Lowest attendance:	5,956 v Sheffield United
Average home attendance:	9,504
Heaviest defeat:	0-6 v Manchester City
	0-6 v Middlesbrough
Biggest win:	4-1 v Oxford
Longest winning sequence:	2
Longest unbeaten sequence:	4
Clean sheets:	12
Highest Saturday night position:	1st
Red cards:	4
Yellow cards:	82
Top scorer:	Chris Hay (14)

West Bromwich Albion

Highest attendance:	23,013 v Nottingham Forest
Lowest attendance:	12,403 v Ipswich
Average home attendance:	16,651
Heaviest defeat:	0-5 v Charlton
Biggest win:	4-2 v Sheffield United
Longest winning sequence:	4
Longest unbeaten sequence:	6
Clean sheets:	12
Highest Saturday night position:	1st
Red cards:	1
Yellow cards:	64
Top scorer:	Lee Hughes (14)

Tranmere Rovers

Highest attendance:	14,116 v Sunderland
Lowest attendance:	5,127 v Reading
Average home attendance:	8,000
Heaviest defeat:	0-3 v Birmingham
	0-3 v Crewe
	0-3 v Huddersfield
	0-3 v Middlesbrough
	0-3 v Sunderland
Biggest win:	6-0 v Reading
Longest winning sequence:	3
Longest unbeaten sequence:	5
Clean sheets:	16
Highest Saturday night position:	8th
Red cards:	2
Yellow cards:	60
Top scorer:	David Kelly (12)

Wolverhampton Wanderers

Highest attendance:	28,244 v West Brom
Lowest attendance:	19,785 v Reading
Average home attendance:	23,280
Heaviest defeat:	3-4 v Stockport
Biggest win:	5-0 v Norwich
Longest winning sequence:	3
Longest unbeaten sequence:	5
Clean sheets:	13
Highest Saturday night position:	6th
Red cards:	5
Yellow cards:	57
Top scorers:	Robbie Keane (11)

Division One play-offs
Semi-finals

10 May 1998	Ipswich Town	v	Charlton Athletic	0-1
13 May 1998	Charlton Athletic	v	Ipswich Town	1-0
10 May 1998	Sheffield United	v	Sunderland	2-1
13 May 1998	Sunderland	v	Sheffield United	2-0

Final

| 25 May 1998 | Charlton Athletic | v | Sunderland | 4-4 [7-6]* |

* Charlton Athletic promoted to the Premiership after penalty shoot-out

Division Two play-offs
Semi-finals

10 May 1998	Bristol Rovers	v	Northampton Town	3-1
13 May 1998	Northampton Town	v	Bristol Rovers	3-0
9 May 1998	Fulham	v	Grimsby Town	1-1
13 May 1998	Grimsby Town	v	Fulham	1-0

Final

| 24 May 1998 | Grimsby Town* | v | Northampton Town | 1-0 |

* Grimsby Town promoted to Division One

Division Three play-offs
Semi-finals

10 May 1998	Barnet	v	Colchester United	1-0
13 May 1998	Colchester United	v	Barnet	3-1
10 May 1998	Scarborough	v	Torquay United	1-3
13 May 1998	Torquay United	v	Scarborough	4-1

Final

| 22 May 1998 | Torquay United | v | Colchester United* | 0-1 |

* Colchester United promoted to Division Two

Division Two

League table

Teams	P	W	D	L	F	A	GD	Pts
Watford*	46	24	16	6	67	41	+26	88
Bristol City*	46	25	10	11	69	39	+30	85
Grimsby Town**	46	19	15	12	55	37	+18	72
Northampton Town	46	18	17	11	52	37	+15	71
Bristol Rovers	46	20	10	16	70	64	+6	70
Fulham	46	20	10	16	60	43	+17	70
Wrexham	46	18	16	12	55	51	+4	70
Gillingham	46	19	13	14	52	47	+5	70
Bournemouth	46	18	12	16	57	52	+5	66
Chesterfield	46	16	17	13	46	44	+2	65
Wigan Athletic	46	17	11	18	64	66	-2	62
Blackpool	46	17	11	18	59	67	-8	62
Oldham Athletic	46	15	16	15	62	54	+8	61
Wycombe Wanderers	46	14	18	14	51	53	-2	60
Preston North End	46	15	14	17	56	56	0	59
York City	46	14	17	15	52	58	-6	59
Luton Town	46	14	15	17	60	64	-4	57
Millwall	46	14	13	19	43	54	-11	55
Walsall	46	14	12	20	43	52	-9	54
Burnley	46	13	13	20	55	65	-10	52
Brentford†	46	11	17	18	50	71	-21	50
Plymouth Argyle†	46	12	13	21	55	70	-15	49
Carlisle United†	46	12	8	26	57	73	-16	44
Southend United†	46	11	10	25	47	79	-32	43

* automatically promoted to Division One
** promoted to Division One after play-offs
† relegated to Division Three

Top scorers

Player	Team	Goals
Barry Hayles	Bristol Rovers	23
Ade Akinbiyi	Gillingham	21
Shaun Goater	Bristol City	17
Ian Stevens	Carlisle	17
Mark Stallard	Wycombe	17
Andy Cooke	Burnley	16
Kevin Donovan	Grimsby	16
Carlo Corrazin	Plymouth	16
David Lowe	Wigan	16
Peter Beadle	Bristol Rovers	15
Paul Moody	Fulham	15

General statistics

Highest attendance:	Bristol City v Watford 19,141
Lowest attendance:	Wrexham v Southend 2,039
Highest win/defeat:	Bristol Rovers v Wigan 5-0
	Carlisle v Southend 5-0
	Fulham v Carlisle 5-0
Most yellow cards:	Brentford (78)
Most red cards:	Gillingham (8)

Division Three

League table

Teams	P	W	D	L	F	A	GD	Pts
Notts County*	46	29	12	5	82	43	+39	99
Macclesfield Town*	46	23	13	10	63	44	+19	82
Lincoln City*	46	20	15	11	60	51	+9	75
Colchester United**	46	21	11	14	72	60	+12	74
Torquay United	46	21	11	14	68	59	+9	74
Scarborough	46	19	15	12	67	58	+9	72
Barnet	46	19	13	14	61	51	+10	70
Scunthorpe United	46	19	12	15	56	52	+4	69
Rotherham United	46	16	19	11	67	61	+6	67
Peterborough United	46	18	13	15	63	51	+12	67
Leyton Orient	46	19	12	15	62	47	+15	66
Mansfield Town	46	16	17	13	64	55	+9	65
Shrewsbury Town	46	16	13	17	61	62	-1	61
Chester City	46	17	10	19	60	61	-1	61
Exeter City	46	15	15	16	68	63	+5	60
Cambridge United	46	14	18	14	63	57	+6	60
Hartlepool United	46	12	23	11	61	53	+8	59
Rochdale	46	17	7	22	56	55	+1	58
Darlington	46	14	12	20	56	72	-16	54
Swansea City	46	13	11	22	49	62	-13	50
Cardiff City	46	9	23	14	48	52	-4	50
Hull City	46	11	8	27	56	83	-27	41
Brighton & Hove Albion	46	6	17	23	38	66	-28	35
Doncaster Rovers†	46	4	8	34	30	113	-83	20

* automatically promoted to Division Two

** promoted to Division Two after play-offs

† relegated to Vauxhall Conference. Replaced by Halifax Town

Top scorers

Player	Team	Goals
Gary Jones	Notts County	28
Steve Whitehall	Mansfield	24
Darran Rowbotham	Exeter	21
Jimmy Quinn	Peterborough	20
Carl Griffiths	Leyton Orient	18
Lee Glover	Rotherham	17
Sean Devine	Barnet	16
Robbie Painter	Rochdale	16
Shaun Farrell	Notts County	15
Martin Carruthers	Peterborough	15
Gareth Williams	Scarborough	15

General statistics

Highest attendance:	Notts County v Rotherham 12,430
Lowest attendance:	Doncaster v Barnet 739
Biggest win/defeat:	Leyton Orient v Doncaster 8-0
Most yellow cards:	Leyton Orient (83)
Most red cards:	Swansea (8)

First Round

Date	Home		Away	Score	Attendance
14.11.97	Swansea City	v	Peterborough United	1-4	2,821
14.11.97	Bristol Rovers	v	Gillingham	2-2	4,825
15.11.97	Darlington	v	Solihull Borough	1-1	2,318
15.11.97	Chesterfield	v	Northwich Victoria	1-0	5,327
15.11.97	Hull City	v	Hednesford Town	0-2	6,091
15.11.97	Hartlepool United	v	Macclesfield Town	2-4	3,165
15.11.97	Chester City	v	Winsford United	2-1	3,885
15.11.97	Rochdale	v	Wrexham	0-2	3,956
15.11.97	Morecambe	v	Emley	1-1	1,496
15.11.97	Ilkeston Town	v	Boston United	2-1	2,504
15.11.97	Lincoln City	v	Gainsborough Trinity	1-1	6,013
15.11.97	Shrewsbury Town	v	Grimsby Town	1-1	3,193
15.11.97	Oldham Athletic	v	Mansfield Town	1-1	5,253
15.11.97	Rotherham United	v	Burnley	3-3	5,709
15.11.97	Southport	v	York City	0-4	3,952
15.11.97	Preston North End	v	Doncaster Rovers	3-2	7,953
15.11.97	Carlisle United	v	Wigan Athletic	0-1	5,182
15.11.97	Walsall	v	Lincoln United	2-0	3,279
15.11.97	Blackpool	v	Blyth Spartans	4-3	4,814
15.11.97	Scunthorpe United	v	Scarborough	2-1	3,039
15.11.97	Hereford United	v	Brighton & Hove Albion	2-1	5,787
15.11.97	Hayes	v	Borehamwood	0-1	1,343
15.11.97	Cheltenham Town	v	Tiverton Town	2-1	2,781
15.11.97	Billericay Town	v	Wisbech Town	2-3	1,947
15.11.97	Farnborough Town	v	Dagenham & Redbridge	0-1	1,236
15.11.97	Hendon	v	Leyton Orient	2-2	2,421
15.11.97	Brentford	v	Colchester United	2-2	2,899
15.11.97	Bournemouth	v	Heybridge Swifts	3-0	3,385
15.11.97	Wycombe Wanderers	v	Basingstoke Town	2-2	3,932
15.11.97	Woking	v	Southend United	0-2	5,000
15.11.97	Luton Town	v	Torquay United	0-1	3,446
15.11.97	Plymouth Argyle	v	Cambridge United	0-0	4,793
15.11.97	Exeter City	v	Northampton Town	1-1	4,605
15.11.97	Carshalton Athletic	v	Stevenage Borough	0-0	1,405
15.11.97	Slough Town	v	Cardiff City	1-1	2,262
15.11.97	King's Lynn	v	Bromsgrove Rovers	1-0	2,847
15.11.97	Barnet	v	Watford	1-2	4,040
15.11.97	Bristol City	v	Millwall	1-0	8,413
16.11.97	Notts County	v	Colwyn Bay	2-0	3,074
16.11.97	Margate	v	Fulham	1-2	5,100

First Round replays

Date	Home		Away	Score	Attendance
24.11.97	Stevenage Borough	v	Carshalton Athletic	5-0	2,377
25.11.97	Emley	v	Morecambe	3-3**[3-1]	2,439
25.11.97	Gainsborough Trinity	v	Lincoln City	2-3	5,723†
25.11.97	Grimsby Town	v	Shrewsbury Town	4-0	3,242

First Round replays (continued)

				Score	Attendance
25.11.97	Mansfield Town	v	Oldham Athletic	0-1	4,097
25.11.97	Burnley	v	Rotherham United	0-3	3,118
25.11.97	Leyton Orient	v	Hendon	0-1	3,355
25.11.97	Colchester United	v	Brentford	0-0**[4-2]	3,613
25.11.97	Basingstoke Town	v	Wycombe Wanderers	2-2**[5-4]	5,088
25.11.97	Cambridge United	v	Plymouth Argyle	3-2*	3,139
25.11.97	Northampton Town	v	Exeter City	2-1	5,259
25.11.97	Cardiff City	v	Slough Town	3-2*	2,343
25.11.97	Gillingham	v	Bristol Rovers	0-2	4,459
26.11.97	Solihull Borough	v	Darlington	3-3**[2-4]	2,000

Second Round

				Score	Attendance
05.12.97	Chester City	v	Wrexham	0-2	5,224
06.12.97	Scunthorpe United	v	Ilkeston Town	1-1	4,187
06.12.97	Lincoln City	v	Emley	2-2	3,729
06.12.97	Rotherham United	v	King's Lynn	6-0	5,883
06.12.97	Macclesfield Town	v	Walsall	0-7	3,556
06.12.97	Wigan Athletic	v	York City	2-1	4,021
06.12.97	Oldham Athletic	v	Blackpool	2-1	6,590
06.12.97	Grimsby Town	v	Chesterfield	2-2	4,762
06.12.97	Hednesford Town	v	Darlington	0-1	1,900
06.12.97	Preston North End	v	Notts County	2-2	7,583
06.12.97	Peterborough United	v	Dagenham & Redbridge	3-2	5,572
06.12.97	Cheltenham Town	v	Borehamwood	1-1	3,525
06.12.97	Cambridge United	v	Stevenage Borough	1-1	4,847
06.12.97	Torquay United	v	Watford	1-1	3,416
06.12.97	Cardiff City	v	Hendon	3-1	2,538
06.12.97	Fulham	v	Southend United	1-0	8,537
06.12.97	Colchester United	v	Hereford United	1-1	3,558
06.12.97	Northampton Town	v	Basingstoke Town	1-1	5,881
06.12.97	Wisbech Town	v	Bristol Rovers	0-2	3,593
07.12.97	Bournemouth	v	Bristol City	3-1	5,687

Second Round replays

				Score	Attendance
15.12.97	Stevenage Borough	v	Cambridge United	2-1	4,886
16.12.97	Chesterfield	v	Grimsby Town	0-2	4,553
16.12.97	Notts County	v	Preston North End	1-2*	3,052
16.12.97	Borehamwood	v	Cheltenham Town	0-2	1,615
16.12.97	Watford	v	Torquay United	2-1*	5,848
16.12.97	Hereford United	v	Colchester United	1-1**[5-4]	3,725
16.12.97	Basingstoke Town	v	Northampton Town	0-0**[3-4]	4,933
17.12.97	Ilkeston Town	v	Scunthorpe United	1-2	2,109
17.12.97	Emley	v	Lincoln City	3-3**[4-3]	4,891††

Third Round

				Score	Attendance
03.01.98	Portsmouth	v	Aston Villa	2-2	16,013
03.01.98	Arsenal	v	Port Vale	0-0	37,471
03.01.98	Leicester City	v	Northampton Town	4-0	20,608

* after extra time
** penalty shoot-out after extra time
† played at Lincoln
†† played at Huddersfield

Third Round (continued)

Date	Home		Away	Score	Attendance
03.01.98	Rotherham United	v	Sunderland	1-5	11,500
03.01.98	Leeds United	v	Oxford United	4-0	20,568
03.01.98	Sheffield United	v	Bury	1-1	14,009
03.01.98	Crewe Alexandra	v	Birmingham City	1-2	4,607
03.01.98	Liverpool	v	Coventry City	1-3	33,888
03.01.98	Grimsby Town	v	Norwich City	3-0	8,161
03.01.98	Queen's Park Rangers	v	Middlesbrough	2-2	13,379
03.01.98	Bristol Rovers	v	Ipswich Town	1-1	6,610
03.01.98	West Ham United	v	Emley	2-1	18,629
03.01.98	Manchester City	v	Bradford City	2-0	23,686
03.01.98	Swindon Town	v	Stevenage Borough	1-2	9,422
03.01.98	Derby County	v	Southampton	2-0	27,992
03.01.98	Crystal Palace	v	Scunthorpe United	2-0	11,624
03.01.98	Cardiff City	v	Oldham Athletic	1-0	6,635
03.01.98	Watford	v	Sheffield Wednesday	1-1	18,306
03.01.98	Preston North End	v	Stockport County	1-2	12,180
03.01.98	Blackburn Rovers	v	Wigan Athletic	4-2	22,402
03.01.98	Charlton Athletic	v	Nottingham Forest	4-1	13,827
03.01.98	Barnsley	v	Bolton Wanderers	1-0	15,042
04.01.98	Everton	v	Newcastle United	0-1	20,885
04.01.98	Chelsea	v	Manchester United	3-5	34,792
04.01.98	Wimbledon	v	Wrexham	0-0	6,348
05.01.98	Tottenham Hotspur	v	Fulham	3-0	27,909
13.01.98	West Bromwich Albion	v	Stoke City	3-1	17,598
13.01.98	Hereford United	v	Tranmere Rovers	0-3	7,473
13.01.98	Cheltenham Town	v	Reading	1-1	6,000
13.01.98	Bournemouth	v	Huddersfield Town	0-1	7,385
13.01.98	Peterborough United	v	Walsall	0-2	12,809
14.01.98	Darlington	v	Wolverhampton	0-4	5,018

Third Round replays

Date	Home		Away	Score	Attendance
13.01.98	Bury	v	Sheffield United	1-2	4,020
13.01.98	Middlesbrough	v	Queen's Park Rangers	2-0	21,817
13.01.98	Ipswich Town	v	Bristol Rovers	1-0	11,362
13.01.98	Wrexham	v	Wimbledon	2-3	9,539
14.01.98	Sheffield Wednesday	v	Watford	0-0**[5-3]	18,707
14.01.98	Aston Villa	v	Portsmouth	1-0	23,355
14.01.98	Port Vale	v	Arsenal	1-1**[3-4]	14,964
20.01.98	Reading	v	Cheltenham Town	2-1	9,686

Fourth Round

Date	Home		Away	Score	Attendance
24.01.98	Huddersfield Town	v	Wimbledon	0-1	14,533
24.01.98	Charlton Athletic	v	Wolverhampton	1-1	15,540
24.01.98	Tottenham Hotspur	v	Barnsley	1-1	28,722
24.01.98	Middlesbrough	v	Arsenal	1-2	28,264
24.01.98	Coventry City	v	Derby County	2-0	22,824
24.01.98	Leeds United	v	Grimsby Town	2-0	29,598

Fourth Round (continued)

Date	Home		Away	Score	Attendance
24.01.98	Crystal Palace	v	Leicester City	3-0	15,489
24.01.98	Birmingham City	v	Stockport County	2-1	15,662
24.01.98	Manchester United	v	Walsall	5-1	54,669
24.01.98	Ipswich Town	v	Sheffield United	1-1	14,654
24.01.98	Cardiff City	v	Reading	1-1	10,174
24.01.98	Aston Villa	v	West Bromwich Albion	4-0	39,372
24.01.98	Tranmere Rovers	v	Sunderland	1-0	14,055
25.01.98	Manchester City	v	West Ham United	1-2	26,495
25.01.98	Stevenage Borough	v	Newcastle United	1-1	8,040
26.01.98	Sheffield Wednesday	v	Blackburn Rovers	0-3	15,940

Fourth Round replays

Date	Home		Away	Score	Attendance
03.02.98	Wolverhampton	v	Charlton Athletic	3-0	20,429
03.02.98	Sheffield United	v	Ipswich Town	1-0	14,144
03.02.98	Reading	v	Cardiff City	1-1**[4-3]	11,808
04.02.98	Newcastle United	v	Stevenage Borough	2-1	36,705
04.02.98	Barnsley	v	Tottenham Hotspur	3-1	18,220

Fifth Round

Date	Home		Away	Score	Attendance
13.02.98	Sheffield United	v	Reading	1-0	17,845
14.02.98	Aston Villa	v	Coventry City	0-1	36,979
14.02.98	West Ham United	v	Blackburn Rovers	2-2	25,729
14.02.98	Leeds United	v	Birmingham City	3-2	35,463
14.02.98	Newcastle United	v	Tranmere Rovers	1-0	36,675
14.02.98	Wimbledon	v	Wolverhampton	1-1	15,603
15.02.98	Manchester United	v	Barnsley	1-1	54,700
15.02.98	Arsenal	v	Crystal Palace	0-0	37,164

Fifth Round replays

Date	Home		Away	Score	Attendance
25.02.98	Blackburn Rovers	v	West Ham United	1-1**[4-5]	21,972
25.02.98	Wolverhampton	v	Wimbledon	2-1	25,112
25.02.98	Barnsley	v	Manchester United	3-2	18,655
25.02.98	Crystal Palace	v	Arsenal	1-2	15,674

Sixth Round (Quarter-finals)

Date	Home		Away	Score	Attendance
08.03.98	Arsenal	v	West Ham United	1-1	38,077
07.03.98	Coventry City	v	Sheffield United	1-1	23,084
07.03.98	Leeds United	v	Wolverhampton	0-1	39,902
08.03.98	Newcastle United	v	Barnsley	3-1	36,695

Sixth Round (Quarter-finals) replays

Date	Home		Away	Score	Attendance
17.03.98	West Ham United	v	Arsenal	1-1**[3-4]	25,859
17.03.98	Sheffield United	v	Coventry City	1-1**[3-1]	29,034

Semi-finals

Date	Home		Away	Score	Attendance
05.04.98	Sheffield United	v	Newcastle United	0-1	53,452
05.04.98	Wolverhampton	v	Arsenal	0-1	39,372

Final

Date	Home		Away	Score	Attendance
16.05.98	Arsenal	v	Newcastle United	2-0	79,183†

** penalty shoot-out after extra time

† played at Wembley

Coca-Cola Cup 1997 | 98

First Round, first leg			Score
11.08.97	Doncaster Rovers	v Nottingham Forest	0-8
12.08.97	AFC Bournemouth	v Torquay United	0-1
12.08.97	Blackpool	v Manchester City	1-0
12.08.97	Brentford	v Shrewsbury Town	1-1
12.08.97	Bristol City	v Bristol Rovers	0-0
12.08.97	Cambridge United	v West Bromwich Albion	1-1
12.08.97	Cardiff City	v Southend United	1-1
12.08.97	Chester City	v Carlisle United	1-2
12.08.97	Colchester United	v Luton Town	0-1
12.08.97	Crewe Alexandra	v Bury	2-3
12.08.97	Darlington	v Notts County	1-1
12.08.97	Gillingham	v Birmingham City	0-1
12.08.97	Huddersfield Town	v Bradford City	2-1
12.08.97	Lincoln City	v Burnley	1-1
12.08.97	Macclesfield Town	v Hull City	0-0
12.08.97	Mansfield Town	v Stockport County	4-2
12.08.97	Northampton Town	v Millwall	2-1
12.08.97	Norwich City	v Barnet	2-1
12.08.97	Oldham Athletic	v Grimsby Town	1-0
12.08.97	Oxford United	v Plymouth Argyle	2-0
12.08.97	Peterborough United	v Portsmouth	2-2
12.08.97	Port Vale	v York City	1-2
12.08.97	Queen's Park Rangers	v Wolverhampton	0-2
12.08.97	Reading	v Swansea City	2-0
12.08.97	Rochdale	v Stoke City	1-3
12.08.97	Rotherham United	v Preston North End	1-3
12.08.97	Scarborough	v Scunthorpe United	0-2
12.08.97	Tranmere Rovers	v Hartlepool United	3-1
12.08.97	Walsall	v Exeter City	2-0
12.08.97	Wigan Athletic	v Chesterfield	1-2
12.08.97	Wrexham	v Sheffield United	1-1
12.08.97	Wycombe Wanderers	v Fulham	1-2
13.08.97	Brighton & Hove Albion	v Leyton Orient	1-1
13.08.97	Charlton Athletic	v Ipswich Town	0-1
13.08.97	Swindon Town	v Watford	0-2

First Round, second leg			Score
26.08.97	Barnet	v Norwich City	3-1
26.08.97	Birmingham City	v Gillingham	3-0
26.08.97	Bradford City	v Huddersfield Town	1-1
26.08.97	Bristol Rovers	v Bristol City	1-2*
26.08.97	Burnley	v Lincoln City	2-1
26.08.97	Bury	v Crewe Alexandra	3-3*
26.08.97	Carlisle United	v Chester City	3-0
26.08.97	Chesterfield	v Wigan Athletic	1-0

			Score
26.08.97	Exeter City	v Walsall	0-1
26.08.97	Fulham	v Wycombe Wanderers	4-4
26.08.97	Grimsby Town	v Oldham Athletic	5-0
26.08.97	Hartlepool United	v Tranmere Rovers	2-1
26.08.97	Hull City	v Macclesfield Town	2-1*
26.08.97	Ipswich Town	v Charlton Athletic	3-1
26.08.97	Leyton Orient	v Brighton & Hove Albion	3-1
26.08.97	Luton Town	v Colchester United	1-1
26.08.97	Manchester City	v Blackpool	1-0**[2-4]
26.08.97	Notts County	v Darlington	2-1*
26.08.97	Plymouth Argyle	v Oxford United	3-5
26.08.97	Portsmouth	v Peterborough United	1-2
26.08.97	Preston North End	v Rotherham United	2-0
26.08.97	Scunthorpe United	v Scarborough	2-1
26.08.97	Sheffield United	v Wrexham	3-1
26.08.97	Shrewsbury Town	v Brentford	3-5
26.08.97	Southend United	v Cardiff City	3-1
26.08.97	Stockport County	v Mansfield Town	6-3
26.08.97	Swansea City	v Reading	1-1
26.08.97	Torquay United	v AFC Bournemouth	1-1
26.08.97	Watford	v Swindon Town	1-1
26.08.97	York City	v Port Vale	1-1
27.08.97	Millwall	v Northampton Town	2-1**[2-0]
27.08.97	Nottingham Forest	v Doncaster Rovers	2-1
27.08.97	Stoke City	v Rochdale	1-1
27.08.97	West Bromwich Albion	v Cambridge United	2-1
27.08.97	Wolverhampton	v Queen's Park Rangers	1-2

Second Round, first leg			Score
16.09.97	Blackpool	v Coventry City	1-0
16.09.97	Burnley	v Stoke City	0-4
16.09.97	Chesterfield	v Barnsley	1-2
16.09.97	Fulham	v Wolverhampton	0-1
16.09.97	Huddersfield Town	v West Ham United	1-0
16.09.97	Hull City	v Crystal Palace	1-0
16.09.97	Ipswich Town	v Torquay United	1-1
16.09.97	Leyton Orient	v Bolton Wanderers	1-3
16.09.97	Luton Town	v West Bromwich Albion	1-1
16.09.97	Middlesbrough	v Barnet	1-0
16.09.97	Notts County	v Tranmere Rovers	0-2
16.09.97	Oxford United	v York City	4-1
16.09.97	Reading	v Peterborough United	0-0
16.09.97	Scunthorpe United	v Everton	0-1
16.09.97	Southend United	v Derby County	0-1
16.09.97	Sunderland	v Bury	2-1

Second Round, first leg (continued)

16.09.97	Watford	v	Sheffield United	1-1
16.09.97	Wimbledon	v	Millwall	5-1
16.09.97	Birmingham City	v	Stockport County	4-1
17.09.97	Blackburn Rovers	v	Preston North End	6-0
17.09.97	Grimsby Town	v	Sheffield Wednesday	2-0
17.09.97	Leeds United	v	Bristol City	3-1
17.09.97	Nottingham Forest	v	Walsall	0-1
17.09.97	Southampton	v	Brentford	3-1
17.09.97	Tottenham Hotspur	v	Carlisle United	3-2

Second Round, second leg

				Score
23.09.97	Barnet	v	Middlesbrough	0-2
23.09.97	Bury	v	Sunderland	1-2
23.09.97	Peterborough United	v	Reading	0-2
23.09.97	Sheffield United	v	Watford	4-0
23.09.97	Stockport County	v	Birmingham City	2-1
23.09.97	Torquay United	v	Ipswich Town	0-3
23.09.97	Tranmere Rovers	v	Notts County	0-1
23.09.97	West Bromwich Albion	v	Luton Town	4-2
23.09.97	York City	v	Oxford United	1-2
24.09.97	Stoke City	v	Burnley	2-0
24.09.97	Walsall	v	Nottingham Forest	2-2*
24.09.97	Wolverhampton	v	Fulham	1-0
29.09.97	West Ham United	v	Huddersfield Town	3-0
30.09.97	Barnsley	v	Chesterfield	4-1
30.09.97	Bolton Wanderers	v	Leyton Orient	4-4
30.09.97	Brentford	v	Southampton	0-2
30.09.97	Bristol City	v	Leeds United	2-1
30.09.97	Carlisle United	v	Tottenham Hotspur	0-2
30.09.97	Crystal Palace	v	Hull City	2-1*
30.09.97	Preston North End	v	Blackburn Rovers	1-0
01.10.97	Coventry City	v	Blackpool	3-1
01.10.97	Derby County	v	Southend United	5-0
01.10.97	Everton	v	Scunthorpe United	5-0
01.10.97	Millwall	v	Wimbledon	1-4
01.10.97	Sheffield Wednesday	v	Grimsby Town	3-2

Third Round

				Score
14.10.97	Arsenal	v	Birmingham City	4-1*
14.10.97	Barnsley	v	Southampton	1-2
14.10.97	Bolton Wanderers	v	Wimbledon	2-0*
14.10.97	Grimsby Town	v	Leicester City	3-1
14.10.97	Ipswich Town	v	Manchester United	2-0
14.10.97	Oxford United	v	Tranmere Rovers	1-1**[6-5]
14.10.97	Reading	v	Wolverhampton	4-2

14.10.97	Walsall	v	Sheffield United	2-1
15.10.97	Chelsea	v	Blackburn Rovers	1-1**[4-1]
15.10.97	Coventry City	v	Everton	4-1
15.10.97	Middlesbrough	v	Sunderland	2-0
15.10.97	Newcastle United	v	Hull City	2-0
15.10.97	Stoke City	v	Leeds United	1-3*
15.10.97	Tottenham Hotspur	v	Derby County	1-2
15.10.97	West Bromwich Albion	v	Liverpool	0-2
15.10.97	West Ham United	v	Aston Villa	3-0

Fourth Round

				Score
18.11.97	Arsenal	v	Coventry City	1-0*
18.11.97	Derby County	v	Newcastle United	0-1
18.11.97	Leeds United	v	Reading	2-3
18.11.97	Liverpool	v	Grimsby Town	3-0
18.11.97	Middlesbrough	v	Bolton Wanderers	2-1*
18.11.97	Oxford United	v	Ipswich Town	1-2*
19.11.97	Chelsea	v	Southampton	2-1*
19.11.97	West Ham United	v	Walsall	4-1

Quarter-finals

				Score
06.01.98	Reading	v	Middlesbrough	0-1
06.01.98	West Ham United	v	Arsenal	1-2
07.01.98	Ipswich Town	v	Chelsea	2-2**[1-4]
07.01.98	Newcastle United	v	Liverpool	0-2

Semi-finals, first leg

				Score
27.01.98	Liverpool	v	Middlesbrough	2-1
28.01.98	Arsenal	v	Chelsea	2-1

Semi-finals, second leg

				Score
18.02.98	Chelsea	v	Arsenal	3-1
18.02.98	Middlesbrough	v	Liverpool	2-0

Final

				Score
29.03.98	Chelsea	v	Middlesbrough	2-0*†

* after extra time

** penalty shoot-out after extra time

† played at Wembley

Scottish League 1997 / 1998

Premier Division

League table

Teams	P	W	D	L	F	A	GD	Pts
Celtic	36	22	8	6	64	24	+40	74
Rangers	36	21	9	6	76	38	+38	72
Heart of Midlothian	36	19	10	7	70	46	+24	67
Kilmarnock	36	13	11	12	40	52	-12	50
St Johnstone	36	13	9	14	38	42	-8	48
Aberdeen	36	9	12	15	39	53	-14	39
Dundee United	36	8	13	15	43	51	-8	37
Dunfermline	36	8	13	15	43	68	-25	37
Motherwell	36	9	7	20	46	64	-18	34
Hibernian*	36	6	12	18	38	59	-21	30

* relegated to Division One

Top scorers

Player	Team	Goals
Marco Negri	Rangers	32
Kjell Olofsson	Dundee United	18
Henrik Larsson	Celtic	16
Andy Smith	Dunfermline	16
Tommy Coyne	Motherwell	14
Jim Hamilton	Hearts	14
Owen Coyle	Motherwell	11
Jorg Albertz	Rangers	10
Craig Burley	Celtic	10
Billy Dodds	Aberdeen	10
Simon Donnelly	Celtic	10
Neil McCann	Hearts	10
George O'Boyle	St Johnstone	10
Paul Wright	Kilmarnock	10

Most yellow cards

Player	Club	Cards
Pat McGinlay	Hibernian	10
Andy Smith	Dunfermline	9
John McQuilan	St Johnstone	9
Gary Smith	Aberdeen	8
Tommy Boyd	Celtic	8
Barry Lavety	Hibernian	8
Raymond Montgomerie	Kilmarnock	8
Stephen McMillan	Motherwell	8
Alex Cleland	Rangers	8
Gordon Durie	Rangers	8
Gennaro Gattuso	Rangers	8

Most red cards

Player	Club	Cards
Ilian Kiriakov	Aberdeen	2
Dave Bowman	Dundee United	2
Gus MacPherson	Kilmarnock	2

Scottish League

Premier Division

Team statistics

Aberdeen

Highest attendance:	18,205 v Rangers
Lowest attendance:	8,661 v Dunfermline
Average home attendance:	13,250
Heaviest defeat:	0-5 v Dundee United
Biggest win:	3-0 v Motherwell
	3-0 v Hibernian
Longest winning sequence:	2
Longest unbeaten sequence:	3
Clean sheets:	10
Highest Saturday night position:	6th
Red cards:	4
Yellow cards:	49
Top scorer:	Billy Dodds (10)

Celtic

Highest attendance:	50,500 v St Johnstone
Lowest attendance:	46,206 v Dunfermline
Average home attendance:	48,838
Heaviest defeat:	0-2 v Motherwell
	0-2 v Rangers
Biggest win:	5-0 v Hibernian
Longest winning sequence:	8
Longest unbeaten sequence:	12
Clean sheets:	17
Highest Saturday night position:	1st
Red cards:	2
Yellow cards:	56
Top scorer:	Henrik Larsson (16)

Dundee United

Highest attendance:	14,200 v Rangers
Lowest attendance:	6,532 v Motherwell
Average home attendance:	9,077
Heaviest defeat:	1-5 v Rangers
Biggest win:	5-0 v Aberdeen
Longest winning sequence:	5
Longest unbeaten sequence:	6
Clean sheets:	6
Highest Saturday night position:	4th
Red cards:	4
Yellow cards:	51
Top scorer:	Kjell Olofsson (18)

Dunfermline Athletic

Highest attendance:	12,866 v Celtic
Lowest attendance:	4,811 v Motherwell
Average home attendance:	8,104
Heaviest defeat:	0-7 v Rangers
Biggest win:	3-1 v Motherwell
Longest winning sequence:	2
Longest unbeaten sequence:	5
Clean sheets:	4
Highest Saturday night position:	2nd
Red cards:	4
Yellow cards:	57
Top scorer:	Andy Smith (16)

Heart of Midlothian

Highest attendance:	17,657 v Celtic
Lowest attendance:	12,236 v Aberdeen
Average home attendance:	15,356
Heaviest defeat:	2-5 v Rangers
Biggest win:	5-3 v Kilmarnock
Longest winning sequence:	6
Longest unbeaten sequence:	13
Clean sheets:	9
Highest Saturday night position:	1st
Red cards:	1
Yellow cards:	52
Top scorer:	Jim Hamilton (14)

Hibernian

Highest attendance:	16,200 v Hearts
Lowest attendance:	9,126 v St Johnstone
Average home attendance:	12,072
Heaviest defeat:	2-6 v Motherwell
Biggest win:	5-2 v Dunfermline
Longest winning sequence:	1
Longest unbeaten sequence:	3
Clean sheets:	4
Highest Saturday night position:	1st
Red cards:	4
Yellow cards:	58
Top scorer:	Steve Crawford (9)

Premier Division
Team statistics

Motherwell

Highest attendance:	12,350 v Celtic
Lowest attendance:	4,517 v St Johnstone
Average home attendance:	7,306
Heaviest defeat:	0-4 v Dundee United
Biggest win:	6-2 v Hibernian
Longest winning sequence:	2
Longest unbeaten sequence:	3
Clean sheets:	5
Highest Saturday night position:	3rd
Red cards:	2
Yellow cards:	76
Top scorer:	Tommy Coyne (14)

Rangers

Highest attendance:	50,116 v Kilmarnock
Lowest attendance:	48,070 v Hibernian
Average home attendance:	49,359
Heaviest defeat:	0-2 v Celtic
	0-2 v St Johnstone
Biggest win:	7-0 v Dunfermline
Longest winning sequence:	4
Longest unbeaten sequence:	10
Clean sheets:	11
Highest Saturday night position:	1st
Red cards:	7
Yellow cards:	65
Top scorer:	Marco Negri (32)

Kilmarnock

Highest attendance:	18,070 v Celtic
Lowest attendance:	6,572 v St Johnstone
Average home attendance:	9,980
Heaviest defeat:	3-5 v Hearts
Biggest win:	4-1 v Motherwell
Longest winning sequence:	3
Longest unbeaten sequence:	8
Clean sheets:	10
Highest Saturday night position:	4th
Red cards:	4
Yellow cards:	49
Top scorer:	Paul Wright (10)

St Johnstone

Highest attendance:	10,455 v Celtic
Lowest attendance:	4,385 v Kilmarnock
Average home attendance:	6,704
Heaviest defeat:	2-3 v Rangers
	2-3 v Hearts
Biggest win:	4-3 v Motherwell
Longest winning sequence:	2
Longest unbeaten sequence:	6
Clean sheets:	12
Highest Saturday night position:	1st
Red cards:	2
Yellow cards:	64
Top scorer:	George O'Boyle (10)

Division One
League table

Teams	P	W	D	L	F	A	GD	Pts
Dundee*	36	20	10	6	52	24	+28	70
Falkirk	36	19	8	9	56	41	+15	65
Raith Rovers	36	17	9	10	51	33	+18	60
Airdrieonians	36	16	12	8	42	35	+7	60
Greenock Morton	36	12	10	14	47	48	-1	46
St Mirren	36	11	8	17	41	53	-12	41
Ayr United	36	10	10	16	40	56	-16	40
Hamilton Academical	36	9	11	16	43	56	-13	38
Partick Thistle**	36	8	12	16	45	55	-10	36
Stirling Albion**	36	8	10	18	40	56	-16	34

* promoted to Premier League

** relegated to Division Two

Division Two
League table

Teams	P	W	D	L	F	A	GD	Pts
Stranraer*	36	18	7	11	62	44	+18	61
Clydebank*	36	16	12	8	48	31	+17	60
Livingston	36	16	11	9	56	40	+16	59
Queen of the South	36	15	9	12	57	51	+6	54
Inverness Caledonian Thistle	36	13	10	13	65	51	+14	49
East Fife	36	14	6	16	51	59	-8	48
Forfar Athletic	36	12	10	14	51	61	-10	46
Clyde	36	10	12	14	40	53	-13	42
Stenhousemuir**	36	10	10	16	44	53	-9	40
Brechin City**	36	7	11	18	42	73	-31	32

* promoted to Division One

** relegated to Division Three

Division Three
League table

Teams	P	W	D	L	F	A	GD	Pts
Alloa Athletic*	36	24	4	8	78	39	+39	76
Arbroath*	36	20	8	8	67	39	+28	68
Ross County	36	19	10	7	71	36	+35	67
East Stirlingshire	36	17	6	13	50	48	+2	57
Albion Rovers	36	13	5	18	60	73	-13	44
Berwick Rangers	36	10	12	14	47	55	-8	42
Queen's Park	36	10	11	15	42	55	-13	41
Cowdenbeath	36	12	2	22	33	57	-24	38
Montrose	36	10	8	18	53	80	-27	38
Dumbarton	36	7	10	19	42	61	-19	31

* promoted to Division Two

Tennents Scottish Cup

First Round 06.12.97

			Score
Cowdenbeath	v	Montrose	0-0
Montrose	v	Cowdenbeath	2-1*
East Fife	v	Stranraer	2-3
Fraserburgh	v	Clyde	1-0
Inverness Caledonian Thistle	v	Whitehill Welfare	3-1

* replay held on 09.12.97

Second Round 03.01.98

			Score
Annan Athletic	v	Vale of Leithen	3-1
Arbroath	v	Queen of the South	1-1
Queen of the South	v	Arbroath	4-0*
Clydebank	v	Montrose	6-0
East Stirlingshire	v	Edinburgh City	1-1
Edinburgh City	v	East Stirlingshire	0-0 [4-3]†
Forfar Athletic	v	Albion Rovers	1-2
Inverness Caledonian Thistle	v	Queen's Park	2-0
Livingston	v	Berwick Rangers	2-1
Lossiemouth	v	Dumbarton	0-1
Peterhead	v	Alloa Athletic	0-2
Ross County	v	Brechin City	3-1
Stenhousemuir	v	Deveronvale	4-0
Stranraer	v	Fraserburgh	2-1

* replay held on 12.01.98

† replay held on 12.01.98 – decided by penalty shoot-out

Third Round 24.01.98

			Score
Airdrieonians	v	Ross County	2-2
Ross County	v	Airdrieonians	1-0*
Alloa Athletic	v	Ayr United	0-3
Celtic	v	Greenock Morton	2-0
Dumbarton	v	Motherwell	1-1
Motherwell	v	Dumbarton	1-0**
Dundee	v	St Mirren	4-2
Dundee United	v	Aberdeen	1-0
Dunfermline Athletic	v	Edinburgh City	7-2
Hamilton Academical	v	Rangers	1-2
Hearts	v	Clydebank	2-0
Hibernian	v	Raith Rovers	1-2

			Score
Inverness Caledonian Thistle	v	Annan Athletic	8-1
Livingston	v	Albion Rovers	3-3
Albion Rovers	v	Livingston	0-0 [6-5]†
Queen of the South	v	Stirling Albion	1-3
St Johnstone	v	Partick Thistle	1-0
Stenhousemuir	v	Falkirk	1-3
Stranraer	v	Kilmarnock	0-2

* replay held on 03.02.98

** replay held on 27.01.98

† replay held on 02.02.98 – decided by penalty shoot-out

Fourth Round 14.02.98

			Score
Ayr United	v	Kilmarnock	2-0
Dundee United	v	Inverness Caledonian Thistle	1-1
Inverness Caledonian Thistle	v	Dundee United	2-3**
Dunfermline Athletic	v	Celtic	1-2
Hearts	v	Albion Rovers	3-0
Motherwell	v	Rangers	2-2
Rangers	v	Motherwell	3-0*
Raith Rovers	v	Falkirk	1-3
Ross County	v	Dundee	1-1
Dundee	v	Ross County	3-0*
St Johnstone	v	Stirling Albion	3-1

* replay held on 17.02.98

** replay held on 18.02.98 – result after extra time

Fifth Round 07.03.98

			Score
Hearts	v	Ayr United	4-1
Falkirk	v	St Johnstone	3-0
Dundee United	v	Celtic	2-3
Rangers	v	Dundee	0-0
Dundee	v	Rangers	1-2*

* replay held on 18.03.98

Semi-finals 4.04.98

			Score
Falkirk	v	Hearts	1-2
Rangers	v	Celtic	2-1

Final 16.06.98

			Score
Hearts	v	Rangers	2-1

Coca-Cola Cup

First Round 02.08.97

			Score
Berwick Rangers	v	Brechin City	2-0
Arbroath	v	Queen of the South	0-4
Inverness Caledonian Thistle	v	Stenhousemuir	5-1
Forfar Athletic	v	Albion Rovers	1-0
Ross County	v	Montrose	2-1
Cowdenbeath	v	Alloa Athletic	0-2
Dumbarton	v	Queen's Park	1-1*[6-5]
East Stirlingshire	v	Stranraer	3-1

* penalty shoot-out after extra time

Second Round 09.08.97

			Score
Dundee	v	East Stirlingshire	1-0
East Fife	v	Kilmarnock	0-2
Hamilton Academical	v	Rangers	0-1
Hibernian	v	Alloa Athletic	3-1
Livingstone	v	Hearts	0-2
St Mirren	v	Clydebank	2-0
Raith Rovers	v	Forfar Athletic	5-0
Queen of the South	v	Dundee United	2-4
St Johnstone	v	Clyde	3-0
Berwick Rangers	v	Celtic	0-7**
Partick Thistle	v	Stirling Albion	2-3
Dumbarton	v	Aberdeen	1-5
Dunfermline Athletic	v	Ayr United	5-1
Ross County	v	Falkirk	0-3
Motherwell	v	Inverness Caledonian Thistle	2-2†[4-1]
Greenock Morton	v	Airdrieonians	4-1***

* played on 07.08.98 at Fir Park, Motherwell

** played at Tynecastle Stadium, Edinburgh

*** after extra time

† penalty shoot-out after extra time

Third Round 19.08.97

			Score
Rangers	v	Falkirk	4-1
St Johnstone	v	Celtic	0-1*
Raith Rovers	v	Hearts	1-2
Dundee	v	Aberdeen	0-3

20.08.97

			Score
Dundee United	v	Hibernian	2-1*
Stirling Albion	v	Kilmarnock	6-2
Dunfermline Athletic	v	St Mirren	2-0
Motherwell	v	Greenock Morton	3-0

* after extra time

Fourth Round 09.09.97

			Score
Dunfermline Athletic	v	Hearts	1-0*
Rangers	v	Dundee United	0-1*

* after extra time

Fourth Round 10.09.97

			Score
Celtic	v	Motherwell	1-0
Stirling Albion	v	Aberdeen	0-2

Semi-final 14.10.97

			Score
Dunfermline Athletic	v	Celtic	0-1*

* played at Ibrox Stadium, Glasgow

Semi-final 15.10.97

			Score
Aberdeen	v	Dundee United	1-3

* played at Tynecastle Stadium, Edinburgh

Final 30.11.97

			Score
Celtic	v	Dundee United	3-0*

* played at Celtic Park, Glasgow

Belgium

Division 1

Teams	P	W	D	L	F	A	GD	Pts
Club Brugge	34	26	6	2	78	29	+49	84
Genk	34	20	6	8	65	40	+25	66
Germinal Ekeren	34	17	7	10	60	48	+12	58
Anderlecht	34	16	9	9	53	37	+16	57
Harelbeke	34	15	10	9	50	31	+19	55
Lokeren	34	16	4	14	68	68	0	52
Lierse	34	14	8	12	54	45	+9	50
Ghent	34	11	14	9	50	44	+6	47
Standard Liege	34	11	10	13	53	50	+3	43
Excelsior Mouscron	34	11	8	15	39	45	-6	41
Lommelese	34	10	11	13	46	50	-4	41
Westerloo	34	9	14	11	52	56	-4	41
Charleroi	34	9	12	13	46	57	-11	39
St Truidense	34	8	13	13	32	45	-13	37
Aalst	34	9	9	16	51	66	-15	36
Beveren	34	7	11	16	30	48	-18	32
Molenbeek	34	8	7	19	39	74	-35	31
Royal Antwerp	34	6	7	21	38	71	-33	25

Germany

Bundesliga

Teams	P	W	D	L	F	A	GD	Pts
Kaiserslautern	34	19	11	4	63	39	+24	68
Bayern Munich	34	19	9	6	69	37	+32	66
Bayer Leverkusen	34	14	13	7	66	39	+27	55
VfB Stuttgart	34	14	10	10	55	49	+6	52
Schalke	34	13	13	8	38	32	+6	52
Hansa Rostock	34	14	9	11	54	46	+8	51
Werder Bremen	34	14	8	12	43	47	-4	50
Duisberg	34	11	11	12	43	44	-1	44
Hamburg	34	11	11	12	38	46	-8	44
Borussia Dortmund	34	11	10	13	57	55	+2	43
Hertha Berlin	34	12	7	15	41	53	-12	43
Bochum	34	11	8	15	41	49	-8	41
1860 Munich	34	11	8	15	43	54	-11	41
Wolfsburg	34	11	6	17	38	54	-16	39
Borussia Moenchengladbach	34	9	11	14	54	59	-5	38
Karlsruhe	34	9	11	14	48	60	-12	38
Cologne	34	10	6	18	49	64	-15	36
Arminia Bielefeld	34	8	8	18	43	56	-13	32

France

La Ligue Nationale

Teams	P	W	D	L	F	A	GD	Pts
Lens	34	21	5	8	55	30	+25	68
Metz	34	20	8	6	48	28	+20	68
Monaco	34	18	5	11	51	33	+18	59
Marseille	34	16	9	9	47	27	+20	57
Bordeaux	34	15	11	8	49	41	+8	56
Lyon	34	16	5	13	39	37	+2	53
Auxerre	34	14	9	11	55	45	+10	51
Paris St-Germain	34	14	8	12	43	35	+8	50
Bastia	34	13	11	10	36	31	+5	50
Le Havre	34	10	14	10	38	35	+3	44
Nantes	34	11	8	15	35	41	-6	41
Montpellier	34	10	11	13	32	42	-10	41
Strasbourg	34	9	10	15	39	43	-4	37
Rennes	34	9	9	16	36	48	-12	36
Toulouse	34	9	9	16	26	46	-20	36
Guingamp	34	9	8	17	30	42	-12	35
Chateauroux	34	8	7	19	31	59	-28	31
Cannes	34	7	7	20	32	59	-27	28

Italy

Serie A

Teams	P	W	D	L	F	A	GD	Pts
Juventus	34	21	11	2	67	28	+39	74
Inter Milan	34	21	6	7	62	27	+35	69
Udinese	34	19	7	8	62	40	+22	64
Roma	34	16	11	7	67	42	+25	59
Fiorentina	34	15	12	7	65	36	+29	57
Parma	34	15	12	7	55	39	+16	57
Lazio	34	16	8	10	53	30	+23	56
Bologna	34	12	12	10	55	46	+9	48
Sampdoria	34	13	9	12	52	55	-3	48
AC Milan	34	11	11	12	37	43	-6	44
Bari	34	10	8	16	30	45	-15	38
Empoli	34	10	7	17	50	58	-8	37
Piacenza	34	7	16	11	29	38	-9	37
Vicenza	34	9	9	16	36	61	-25	36
Brescia	34	9	8	17	45	63	-18	35
Atalanta	34	7	11	16	25	48	-23	32
Lecce	34	6	8	20	32	72	-40	26
Napoli	34	2	8	24	25	76	-51	14

Netherlands
Eredivisie

Teams	P	W	D	L	F	A	GD	Pts
Ajax	34	29	2	3	112	22	+90	89
PSV Eindhoven	34	21	9	4	95	44	+51	72
Vitesse	34	21	7	6	85	48	+37	70
Feyenoord	34	18	7	9	62	39	+23	61
Willem II	34	17	4	13	66	58	+8	55
Heerenveen	34	16	7	11	56	59	-3	55
Fortuna	34	14	6	14	51	53	-2	48
NEC	34	14	2	18	39	57	-18	44
Twente	34	11	10	13	41	42	-1	43
Utrecht	34	13	4	17	56	64	-8	43
De Graafschap	34	11	9	14	45	49	-4	42
NAC Breda	34	12	6	16	41	49	-8	42
Sparta	34	10	11	13	50	59	-9	41
Roda JC	34	10	8	16	44	45	-1	38
MUV	34	9	5	20	35	75	-40	32
RKC	34	8	7	19	48	71	-23	31
Groningen	34	7	10	17	42	65	-23	31
Volendam	34	5	6	23	33	102	-69	21

Spain
La Primera Liga

Teams	P	W	D	L	F	A	GD	Pts
Barcelona	38	23	5	10	78	56	+22	74
Athletic Bilbao	38	17	14	7	52	42	+10	65
Real Sociedad	38	16	15	7	60	37	+23	63
Real Madrid	38	17	12	9	63	45	+18	63
Mallorca	38	16	12	10	55	39	+16	60
Atletico Madrid	38	16	12	10	79	56	+23	60
Celta Vigo	38	17	9	12	54	47	+7	60
Real Betis	38	17	8	13	49	50	-1	59
Valencia	38	16	7	15	58	52	+6	55
Espanyol	38	12	17	9	44	31	+13	53
Valladolid	38	13	11	14	36	47	-11	50
Deportivo La Coruna	38	12	13	13	44	46	-2	49
Real Zaragoza	38	12	12	14	45	53	-8	48
Racing Santander	38	12	9	17	46	55	-9	45
Salamanca	38	12	9	17	46	46	0	45
Tenerife	38	11	12	15	44	57	-13	45
Compostela	38	11	11	16	56	66	-10	44
Oviedo	38	9	13	16	36	51	-15	40
Merida	38	9	12	17	33	53	-20	39
Sporting Gijon	38	2	7	29	31	80	-49	13

Portugal
1 Divisao

Teams	P	W	D	L	F	A	GD	Pts
Porto	34	24	5	5	75	38	+37	77
Benfica	34	20	8	6	62	29	+33	68
Vitoria Guimaraes	34	17	8	9	42	25	+17	59
Sporting Lisbon	34	15	11	8	45	31	+14	56
Maritimo	34	16	8	10	44	35	+9	56
Boavista	34	15	10	9	54	31	+23	55
Estrela Amadora	34	14	8	12	41	42	-1	50
Salgueiros	34	13	10	11	48	44	+4	49
Rio Ave	34	12	10	12	43	43	0	46
Braga	34	11	12	11	48	49	-1	45
Campomaiorense	34	11	7	16	53	58	-5	40
Leca	34	10	8	16	29	52	-23	38
Vitoria Setubal	34	10	7	17	38	43	-5	37
Farense	34	8	13	13	41	50	-9	37
Academica	34	8	12	14	27	41	-14	36
Chaves	34	10	5	19	31	55	-24	35
Varzim	34	6	11	17	26	51	-25	29
Belenenses	34	5	9	20	22	52	-30	24

UEFA Champions League

Group A

Date				Score	Attendance
17.09.97	Galatasaray	v	Borussia Dortmund	0-1	23,000
17.09.97	Sparta Prague	v	Parma	0-0	20,000
01.10.97	Borussia Dortmund	v	Sparta Prague	4-1	42,000
01.10.97	Parma	v	Galatasaray	2-0	5,922
22.10.97	Parma	v	Borussia Dortmund	1-0	13,000
22.10.97	Sparta Prague	v	Galatasaray	3-0	11,108
05.11.97	Borussia Dortmund	v	Parma	2-0	40,000
05.11.97	Galatasaray	v	Sparta Prague	2-0	15,000
27.11.97	Parma	v	Sparta Prague	2-2	16,200
27.11.97	Borussia Dortmund	v	Galatasaray	4-1	45,000
10.12.97	Sparta Prague	v	Borussia Dortmund	0-3	10,925
10.12.97	Galatasaray	v	Parma	1-1	14,000

Position	Team	P	W	D	L	F	A	Pts
1	Borussia Dortmund	6	5	0	1	14	3	15
2	Parma	6	2	3	1	6	5	9
3	Sparta Prague	6	1	2	3	6	11	5
4	Galatasaray	6	1	1	4	4	11	4

Group B

Date				Score	Attendance
17.09.97	Kosice	v	Manchester United	0-3	11,000
17.09.97	Juventus	v	Feyenoord	5-1	12,622
01.10.97	Manchester United	v	Juventus	3-2	53,428
01.10.97	Feyenoord	v	Kosice	2-0	31,500
22.10.97	Manchester United	v	Feyenoord	2-1	53,188
22.10.97	Kosice	v	Juventus	0-1	10,021
05.11.97	Feyenoord	v	Manchester United	1-3	42,500
05.11.97	Juventus	v	Kosice	3-2	3,505
26.11.97	Feyenoord	v	Juventus	2-0	35,000
27.11.97	Manchester United	v	Kosice	3-0	52,535
10.12.97	Kosice	v	Feyenoord	0-3	2,662
10.12.97	Juventus	v	Manchester United	1-0	47,000

Position	Team	P	W	D	L	F	A	Pts
1	Manchester United	6	5	0	1	14	5	15
2	Juventus	6	4	0	2	12	8	12
3	Feyenoord	6	3	0	3	8	10	9
4	Kosice	6	0	0	6	2	13	0

Group C

Date				Score	Attendance
17.09.97	Newcastle United	v	Barcelona	3-2	35,274
17.09.97	PSV Eindhoven	v	Dynamo Kiev	1-3	27,000
01.10.97	Barcelona	v	PSV Eindhoven	2-2	82,000
01.10.97	Dynamo Kiev	v	Newcastle United	2-2	100,000
22.10.97	PSV Eindhoven	v	Newcastle United	1-0	29,800
22.10.97	Dynamo Kiev	v	Barcelona	3-0	–
05.11.97	Newcastle United	v	PSV Eindhoven	0-2	35,517
05.11.97	Barcelona	v	Dynamo Kiev	0-4	52,000
26.11.97	Barcelona	v	Newcastle United	1-0	26,000
27.11.97	Dynamo Kiev	v	PSV Eindhoven	1-1	80,000
10.12.97	Newcastle United	v	Dynamo Kiev	2-0	33,509
10.12.97	PSV Eindhoven	v	Barcelona	2-2	29,400

Position	Team	P	W	D	L	F	A	Pts
1	Dynamo Kiev	6	3	2	1	13	6	11
2	PSV Eindhoven	6	2	3	1	9	8	9
3	Newcastle United	6	2	1	3	7	8	7
4	Barcelona	6	1	2	3	7	14	5

Group D

Date				Score	Attendance
17.09.97	Real Madrid	v	Rosenborg	4-1	85,000
17.09.97	Olympiakos Piraeus	v	Porto	1-0	60,006
01.10.97	Porto	v	Real Madrid	0-2	32,300
01.10.97	Rosenborg	v	Olympiakos Piraeus	5-1	16,038
22.10.97	Rosenborg	v	Porto	2-0	17,214
22.10.97	Real Madrid	v	Olympiakos Piraeus	5-1	48,000
05.11.97	Porto	v	Rosenborg	1-1	11,000
05.11.97	Olympiakos Piraeus	v	Real Madrid	0-0	55,000
27.11.97	Porto	v	Olympiakos Piraeus	2-1	7,000
27.11.97	Rosenborg	v	Real Madrid	2-0	19,900
10.12.97	Real Madrid	v	Porto	4-0	45,000
10.12.97	Olympiakos Piraeus	v	Rosenborg	2-2	21,000

Position	Team	P	W	D	L	F	A	Pts
1	Real Madrid	6	4	1	1	15	4	13
2	Rosenborg	6	3	2	1	13	8	11
3	Olympiakos Piraeus	6	1	2	3	6	14	5
4	Porto	6	1	1	4	3	11	4

UEFA Champions League (continued)

Group E

Date				Score	Attendance
17.09.97	Bayern Munich	v	Besiktas	2-0	38,000
17.09.97	Paris St-Germain	v	IFK Gothenburg	3-0	26,198
01.10.97	IFK Gothenburg	v	Bayern Munich	1-3	26,500
01.10.97	Besiktas	v	Paris St-Germain	3-1	20,000
22.10.97	Bayern Munich	v	Paris St-Germain	5-1	46,000
22.10.97	Besiktas	v	IFK Gothenburg	1-0	25,000
05.11.97	IFK Gothenburg	v	Besiktas	2-1	14,073
05.11.97	Paris St-Germain	v	Bayern Munich	3-1	32,274
26.11.97	IFK Gothenburg	v	Paris St-Germain	0-1	19,323
26.11.97	Besiktas	v	Bayern Munich	0-2	26,000
10.12.97	Bayern Munich	v	IFK Gothenburg	0-1	27,000
10.12.97	Paris St-Germain	v	Besiktas	2-1	34,038

Position	Team	P	W	D	L	F	A	Pts
1	Bayern Munich	6	4	0	2	13	6	12
2	Paris St-Germain	6	4	0	2	11	10	12
3	Besiktas	6	2	0	4	6	9	6
4	IFK Gothenburg	6	2	0	4	4	9	6

Group F

Date				Score	Attendance
17.09.97	Sporting Lisbon	v	AS Monaco	3-0	26,000
17.09.97	Bayer Leverkusen	v	Lierse SK	1-0	22,500
01.10.97	Lierse SK	v	Sporting Lisbon	1-1	7,100
01.10.97	AS Monaco	v	Bayer Leverkusen	4-0	6,500
22.10.97	Sporting Lisbon	v	Bayer Leverkusen	0-2	22,500
22.10.97	AS Monaco	v	Lierse SK	5-1	7,000
05.11.97	Lierse SK	v	AS Monaco	0-1	7,000
05.11.97	Bayer Leverkusen	v	Sporting Lisbon	4-1	22,500
26.11.97	AS Monaco	v	Sporting Lisbon	3-2	9,287
26.11.97	Lierse SK	v	Bayer Leverkusen	0-2	7,700
10.12.97	Sporting Lisbon	v	Lierse SK	2-1	10,000
10.12.97	Bayer Leverkusen	v	AS Monaco	2-2	22,500

Position	Team	P	W	D	L	F	A	Pts
1	AS Monaco	6	4	1	1	15	8	13
2	Bayer Leverkusen	6	4	1	1	11	7	13
3	Sporting Lisbon	6	2	1	3	9	11	7
4	Lierse SK	6	0	1	5	3	12	1

European Cup

Quarter-finals, first leg 04.03.98

			Score	Attendance
Bayer Leverkusen	v	Real Madrid	1-1	–
Juventus	v	Dynamo Kiev	1-1	40,723
Bayern Munich	v	Borussia Dortmund	0-0	60,000
AS Monaco	v	Manchester United	0-0	14,072

Quarter-finals, second leg 18.03.98

			Score	Attendance
Manchester United	v	AS Monaco	1-1**	52,000
Real Madrid	v	Bayer Leverkusen	3-0	59,000
Dynamo Kiev	v	Juventus	1-4	100,000
Borussia Dortmund	v	Bayern Munich	1-0*	48,500

Semi-finals, first leg 01.04.98

			Score	Attendance
Juventus	v	AS Monaco	4-1	56,000
Real Madrid	v	Borussia Dortmund	2-0	85,000

Semi-finals, second leg 15.04.98

			Score	Attendance
AS Monaco	v	Juventus	3-2	15,000
Borussia Dortmund	v	Real Madrid	0-0	48,500

Final 20.05.98

			Score	Attendance
Juventus	v	Real Madrid	0-1	45,700†

* after extra time

** AS Monaco went through on away goals

† played at the Amsterdam Arena, Amsterdam

First Round, first leg 16.09.97			Score	Attendance
Deportivo La Coruna	v	Auxerre	1-2	11,874
SV Austria Salzburg	v	Anderlecht	4-3	3,847
PAOK Salonika	v	Arsenal	1-0	40,000
Widzew Lodz	v	Udinese	1-0	5,343
Maribor Teatanic	v	Ajax	1-1	4,922
Olympique Lyonnais	v	Brondby	4-1	12,086
MPKC Mozyr	v	Dinamo Tbilisi	1-1	5,900
Real Valladolid	v	Skonto Riga	2-0	8,840
Vitoria Guimaraes	v	Lazio	0-4	5,500
Strasbourg	v	Rangers	2-1	12,450
MTK Budapest	v	Alania Vladikavkaz	3-0	–
Schalke 04	v	Hajduk Split	2-0	53,250
Bastia	v	Benfica	1-0	–
Sion	v	Spartak Moscow	0-1	5,000
Sampdoria	v	Athletic Bilbao	1-2	26,191
Girondins Bordeaux	v	Aston Villa	0-0	13,000
Steaua Bucharest	v	Fenerbahce	0-0	15,000
Rotor Volgograd	v	Orebro	2-0	15,000
FC Jazz Pori	v	TSV 1860 Munich	0-1	1,320
Trabzonspor	v	Bochum	2-1	7,835
Zagreb	v	Grasshoppers Zurich	4-4	20,148
Vitesse Arnhem	v	Braga	2-1	5,264
Rapid Vienna	v	Hapoel Petach-Tikva	1-0	20,000
Inter Milan	v	Neuchatel Xamax	2-0	15,225
Celtic	v	Liverpool	2-2	51,000
Mouscron	v	Metz	0-2	6,000
Twente Enschede	v	Lillestrom	0-1	7,514
Beitar Jerusalem	v	Club Brugge	2-1	8,000
Atletico Madrid	v	Leicester City	2-1	28,000
AGF Aarhus	v	Nantes	2-2	5,425
Karlsruher	v	Anorthosis Famagusta	2-1	11,000
OFI Crete	v	Ferencvaros	3-0	7,969

UEFA Cup

First Round, second leg 30.09.97			Score	Attendance
Auxerre	v	Deportivo La Coruna	0-0	10,047
Anderlecht	v	SV Austria Salzburg	4-2	13,902
Arsenal	v	PAOK Salonika	1-1	38,000
Udinese	v	Widzew Lodz	3-0	28,016
Ajax	v	Maribor Teatanic	9-1	41,500
Brondby	v	Olympique Lyonnais	2-3	8,138
Dinamo Tbilisi	v	MPKC Mozyr	1-0	–
Skonto Riga	v	Real Valladolid	1-0	2,000
Lazio	v	Vitoria Guimaraes	2-1	5,000
Rangers	v	Strasbourg	1-2	38,000
Alania Vladikavkaz	v	MTK Budapest	1-1	22,000
Hajduk Split	v	Schalke 04	2-3	1,600
Benfica	v	Bastia	0-0	20,000
**Spartak Moscow	v	Sion	2-2	8,350
***Spartak Moscow	v	Sion	5-1	24,500
Athletic Bilbao	v	Sampdoria	2-0	38,000
Aston Villa	v	Girondins Bordeaux	1-0*	33,100
Fenerbahce	v	Steaua Bucharest	1-2	25,210
Orebro	v	Rotor Volgograd	1-4	3,143
TSV 1860 Munich	v	FC Jazz Pori	6-1	7,500
Bochum	v	Trabzonspor	5-3	24,000
Grasshoppers Zurich	v	Zagreb	0-5	16,000
Braga	v	Vitesse Arnhem	2-0	11,000
Hapoel Petach-Tikva	v	Rapid Vienna	1-1	4,000
Neuchatel Xamax	v	Inter Milan	0-2	11,000
Liverpool	v	Celtic	0-0	38,000
Metz	v	Mouscron	4-1	7,457
Lillestrom	v	Twente Enschede	1-2	–
Club Brugge	v	Beitar Jerusalem	3-0	–
Leicester City	v	Atletico Madrid	0-2	20,776
Nantes	v	AGF Aarhus	0-1	15,368
Anorthosis Famagusta	v	Karlsruher	1-1	4,500
Ferencvaros	v	OFI Crete	2-1	7,697

* after extra time

** match declared void because crossbar was 12cm too low

*** played on 15.10.97

Second Round, first leg 21.10.97			Score	Attendance
Ajax	v	Udinese	1-0	44,000
Braga	v	Dinamo Tbilisi	4-0	5,000
Metz	v	Karlsruher	0-2	14,000
Strasbourg	v	Liverpool	3-0	18,813
Inter Milan	v	Olympique Lyonnais	1-2	16,085
Rapid Vienna	v	TSV 1860 Munich	3-0	26,500
MTK Budapest	v	Zagreb	1-0	18,000
Spartak Moscow	v	Real Valladolid	2-0	8,000
Schalke 04	v	Anderlecht	1-0	56,240
AGF Aarhus	v	Twente Enschede	1-9	–
Athletic Bilbao	v	Aston Villa	0-0	40,000
Auxerre	v	OFI Crete	3-1	–
Steaua Bucharest	v	Bastia	1-0	12,000
Rotor Volgograd	v	Lazio	0-0	18,000
Atletico Madrid	v	PAOK Salonika	5-2	35,000
Club Brugge	v	Bochum	1-0	–

Second Round, second leg 04.11.97			Score	Attendance
Udinese	v	Ajax	2-1	38,912
Dinamo Tbilisi	v	Braga	0-1	7,800
Karlsruher	v	Metz	1-1	20,000
Liverpool	v	Strasbourg	2-0	32,426
Olympique Lyonnais	v	Inter Milan	1-3	30,000
TSV 1860 Munich	v	Rapid Vienna	2-1	25,000
Zagreb	v	MTK Budapest	2-0	25,000
Real Valladolid	v	Spartak Moscow	1-2	16,700
Anderlecht	v	Schalke 04	1-2	–
Twente Enschede	v	AGF Aarhus	0-0	10,500
Aston Villa	v	Athletic Bilbao	2-1	35,915
OFI Crete	v	Auxerre	3-2	9,000
Bastia	v	Steaua Bucharest	3-2	10,000
Lazio	v	Rotor Volgograd	3-0	30,000
PAOK Salonika	v	Atletico Madrid	4-4	25,000
**Bochum	v	Club Brugge	4-1	24,000

Third Round, first leg 25.11.97			Score	Attendance
Rapid Vienna	v	Lazio	0-2	26,000
Braga	v	Schalke 04	0-0	18,000
Twente Enschede	v	Auxerre	0-1	9,600
Zagreb	v	Atletico Madrid	1-3	26,082
Strasbourg	v	Inter Milan	2-0	–
Steaua Bucharest	v	Aston Villa	2-1	19,500
Ajax	v	Bochum	4-2	50,000
Karlsruher	v	Spartak Moscow	0-0	12,000

Third Round, second leg 09.12.97			Score	Attendance
Lazio	v	Rapid Vienna	1-0	9,000
Schalke 04	v	Braga	2-0	56,863
Auxerre	v	Twente Enschede	2-0	11,756
Atletico Madrid	v	Zagreb	1-0	35,000
Inter Milan	v	Strasbourg	3-0	46,650
Aston Villa	v	Steaua Bucharest	2-0	35,102
***Bochum	v	Ajax	2-2	24,000
Spartak Moscow	v	Karlsruher	1-0*	30,000

Quarter-finals, first leg 03.03.98			Score	Attendance
Ajax	v	Spartak Moscow	1-3	–
Inter Milan	v	Schalke 04	1.0	44,889
Lazio	v	Auxerre	1-0	35,000
Atletico Madrid	v	Aston Villa	1-0	–

Quarter-finals, second leg 17.03.98			Score	Attendance
Spartak Moscow	v	Ajax	1-0	36,000
Schalke 04	v	Inter Milan	1-1*	–
Auxerre	v	Lazio	2-2	20,000
Aston Villa	v	Atletico Madrid	2-1	38,500

Semi-finals, first leg 31.03.98			Score	Attendance
Atletico Madrid	v	Lazio	0-1	45,000
Inter Milan	v	Spartak Moscow	2-1	57,803

Semi-finals, second leg 31.03.98			Score	Attendance
Lazio	v	Atletico Madrid	0-0	50,000
Spartak Moscow	v	Inter Milan	1-2	35,000

Final 06.05.98			Score	Attendance
Lazio	v	Inter Milan	0-3	45,000†

* after extra time

** played on 06.11.97

*** played on 11.12.97

† played at Parc des Princes, Paris

Cup Winners Cup 1997 | 98

First Round, first leg 18.09.97

			Score	Attendance
Kocaelispor	v	National Bucuresti	2-0	5,794
APOEL Nicosia	v	Sturm Graz	0-1	3,700
IBV Vestmannaeyjar	v	VfB Stuttgart	1-3	3,148
Boavista	v	Shakhtyor Donetsk	2-3	–
Germinal Ekeren	v	Crvena Zvezda	3-2	3,700
AIK Solna	v	Primorje	0-1	4,100
AEK Athens	v	Dinaburga	5-0	–
Slavia Prague	v	Lucerne	4-2	5,614
Hapoel Beer-Sheva	v	Roda JC	1-4	3,240
Zagreb	v	Tromso	3-2	569
FC Copenhagen	v	Ararat Yerevan	3-0	–
Belshina Bobruisk	v	Lokomotiv Moscow	1-2	3,594
Chelsea	v	Slovan Bratislava	2-0	23,000
Nice	v	Kilmarnock	3-1	10,000
Real Betis	v	Budapest VSC	2-0	5,300
Vicenza	v	Legia Warsaw	2-0	10,081

First Round, second leg 02.10.97

			Score	Attendance
National Bucuresti	v	Kocaelispor	0-1	5,000
Sturm Graz	v	APOEL Nicosia	3-0	10,000
VfB Stuttgart	v	IBV Vestmannaeyjar	2-1	12,483
Shakhtyor Donetsk	v	Boavista	1-1	25,000
Crvena Zvezda	v	Germinal Ekeren	1-1	48,000
Primorje	v	AIK Solna	1-1*	1,132
Dinaburga	v	AEK Athens	2-4	500
Lucerne	v	Slavia Prague	0-2	5,614
Roda JC	v	Hapoel Beer-Sheva	10-0	5,010
Tromso	v	Zagreb	4-2*	3,893
Ararat Yerevan	v	FC Copenhagen	0-2	200
Lokomotiv Moscow	v	Belshina Bobruisk	3-0	1,500
Slovan Bratislava	v	Chelsea	0-2	11,003
Kilmarnock	v	Nice	1-1	8,403
Budapest VSC	v	Real Betis	0-2	1,200
Legia Warsaw	v	Vicenza	1-1	4,022

Second Round, first leg 23.10.97

			Score	Attendance
Tromso	v	Chelsea	3-2	6,432
Germinal Ekeren	v	VfB Stuttgart	0-4	2,704
Lokomotiv Moscow	v	Kocaelispor	2-1	3,500
Shakhtyor Donetsk	v	Vicenza	1-3	15,286
Real Betis	v	FC Copenhagen	2-0	7,800
AEK Athens	v	Sturm Graz	2-0	13,000

Cup Winners Cup

Second Round, first leg 23.10.97 (continued)

			Score	Attendance
Nice	v	Slavia Prague	2-2	14,200
Primorje	v	Roda JC	0-2	984

Second Round, second leg 06.11.97

			Score	Attendance
Chelsea	v	Tromso	7-1	29,000
VfB Stuttgart	v	Germinal Ekeren	2-4	10,000
Kocaelispor	v	Lokomotiv Moscow	0-0	10,000
Vicenza	v	Shakhtyor Donetsk	2-1	–
FC Copenhagen	v	Real Betis	1-1	10,140
Sturm Graz	v	AEK Athens	1-1	15,000
Slavia Prague	v	Nice	1-1	7,312
Roda JC	v	Primorje	4-0	8,000

Quarter-finals, first leg 05.03.98

			Score	Attendance
Roda JC	v	Vicenza	1-4	14,000
Slavia Prague	v	VfB Stuttgart	1-1	8,712
AEK Athens	v	Lokomotiv Moscow	0-0	30,000
Real Betis	v	Chelsea	1-2	19,300

Quarter-finals, second leg 19.03.98

			Score	Attendance
Vicenza	v	Roda JC	5-0	–
VfB Stuttgart	v	Slavia Prague	2-0	18,921
Lokomotiv Moscow	v	AEK Athens	2-1	–
Chelsea	v	Real Betis	3-1	–

Semi-finals, first leg 02.04.98

			Score	Attendance
Vicenza	v	Chelsea	1-0	–
VfB Stuttgart	v	Lokomotiv Moscow	2-1	14,416

Semi-finals, second leg 16.04.98

			Score	Attendance
Chelsea	v	Vicenza	3-1	33,810
Lokomotiv Moscow	v	VfB Stuttgart	0-1	22,000

Final 13.05.98

			Score	Attendance
Chelsea	v	VfB Stuttgart	1-0	30,216†

* after extra time

† played at Rasunda Stadium, Stockholm

Africa (CAF)

First Round, first leg

Date				Score
31.05.96	Mauritania	v	Burkina Faso	0-0
1.06.96	Namibia	v	Mozambique	2-0
1.06.96	Malawi	v	South Africa	0-1
1.06.96	Uganda	v	Angola	0-2
1.06.96	Guinea-Bissau	v	Guinea	3-2
1.06.96	Gambia	v	Liberia	2-1
1.06.96	Sudan	v	Zambia	2-0
2.06.96	Swaziland	v	Gabon	0-1
2.06.96	Burundi	v	Sierra Leone	1-0
2.06.96	Madagascar	v	Zimbabwe	1-2
2.06.96	Congo	v	Ivory Coast	2-0
2.06.96	Mauritius	v	Congo DR (Zaire)	1-5
2.06.96	Rwanda	v	Tunisia	1-3
2.06.96	Kenya	v	Algeria	3-1
2.06.96	Togo	v	Senegal	2-1
8.06.96	Tanzania	v	Ghana	0-0

First Round, second leg

Date				Score
14.06.96	Algeria	v	Kenya	1-0
15.06.96	Senegal	v	Togo	1-1
15.06.96	South Africa	v	Malawi	3-0
16.06.96	Burkina Faso	v	Mauritania	2-0
16.06.96	Mozambique	v	Namibia	1-1
16.06.96	Angola	v	Uganda	3-1
16.06.96	Guinea	v	Guinea-Bissau	3-1
16.06.96	Gabon	v	Swaziland	2-0
16.06.96	Sierra Leone	v	Burundi	0-1
16.06.96	Zimbabwe	v	Madagascar	2-2
16.06.96	Ivory Coast	v	Congo	1-1
16.06.96	Congo DR (Zaire)	v	Mauritius	2-0
16.06.96	Tunisia	v	Rwanda	2-0
16.06.96	Zambia	v	Sudan	3-0
17.06.96	Ghana	v	Tanzania	2-1
23.06.96	Liberia	v	Gambia	4-0

Second Round

Group 1

	P	W	D	L	F	A	Pts
Nigeria*	6	4	1	1	10	4	13
Guinea	6	4	0	2	10	5	12
Kenya	6	3	1	2	11	12	10
Burkina Faso	6	0	0	6	7	17	0

Group 2

	P	W	D	L	F	A	Pts
Tunisia*	6	5	1	0	10	1	16
Egypt	6	3	1	2	15	5	10
Liberia	6	1	1	4	2	10	4
Namibia	6	1	1	4	6	17	4

Group 3

	P	W	D	L	F	A	Pts
South Africa*	6	4	1	1	7	3	13
Congo	6	3	1	2	5	5	10
Zambia	6	2	2	2	7	6	8
Congo DR (Zaire)	6	0	2	4	4	9	2

Group 4

	P	W	D	L	F	A	Pts
Cameroon*	6	4	2	0	10	4	14
Angola	6	2	4	0	7	4	10
Zimbabwe	6	1	1	4	6	7	4
Togo	6	1	1	4	6	14	4

Group 5

	P	W	D	L	F	A	Pts
Morocco*	6	5	1	0	14	2	16
Sierra Leone†	5	2	1	2	4	6	7
Ghana	6	1	3	2	7	7	6
Gabon	5	0	1	4	1	11	1

* Nigeria, Tunisia, South Africa, Cameroon and Morocco qualified
† Sierra Leone replaced Burundi in the Second Round after Burundi withdrew due to political reasons

Asia (AFC)

First Round

Group 1	P	W	D	L	F	A	Pts
Saudi Arabia	6	5	1	0	18	1	16
Malaysia	6	3	2	1	5	3	11
Chinese Taipei	6	1	1	4	4	13	4
Bangladesh	6	1	0	5	4	14	3

Group 2	P	W	D	L	F	A	Pts
Iran	6	5	1	0	39	3	16
Kyrgyzstan	5	3	0	2	12	11	9
Syria	5	2	1	2	27	5	7
Maldives	6	0	0	6	0	59	0

Group 3	P	W	D	L	F	A	Pts
United Arab Emirates	4	3	1	0	7	1	10
Jordan	4	1	1	2	4	4	4
Bahrain	4	1	0	3	3	9	3

Group 4	P	W	D	L	F	A	Pts
Japan	6	5	1	0	31	1	16
Oman	6	4	1	1	14	2	13
Macao	6	1	1	4	3	28	4
Nepal	6	0	1	5	2	19	1

Group 5	P	W	D	L	F	A	Pts
Uzbekistan	6	5	1	0	20	3	16
Yemen	6	2	2	2	10	7	8
Indonesia	6	1	4	1	11	6	7
Cambodia	6	0	1	5	2	27	1

Group 6	P	W	D	L	F	A	Pts
South Korea	4	3	1	0	9	1	10
Thailand	4	1	1	2	5	6	4
Hong Kong	4	1	0	3	3	10	3

Group 7	P	W	D	L	F	A	Pts
Kuwait	4	4	0	0	10	1	12
Lebanon	4	1	1	2	4	7	4
Singapore	4	0	1	3	2	8	1

Group 8	P	W	D	L	F	A	Pts
China	6	5	1	0	13	2	16
Tajikistan	6	4	1	1	15	2	13
Turkmenistan	6	2	0	4	8	13	6
Vietnam	6	0	0	6	2	21	0

Group 9	P	W	D	L	F	A	Pts
Kazakhstan	4	4	0	0	15	2	12
Iraq	4	2	0	2	14	8	6
Pakistan	4	0	0	4	3	22	0

Group 10	P	W	D	L	F	A	Pts
Qatar	3	3	0	0	14	0	9
Sri Lanka	3	1	1	1	4	4	4
India	3	1	1	1	3	7	4
Philippines	3	0	0	3	0	10	0

Second Round

Group A	P	W	D	L	F	A	Pts
Saudi Arabia*	8	4	2	2	8	6	14
Iran	8	3	3	2	13	8	12
China	8	3	2	3	11	14	11
Qatar	8	3	1	4	7	10	10
Kuwait	8	2	2	4	7	8	8

Group B	P	W	D	L	F	A	Pts
South Korea*	8	6	1	1	19	7	19
Japan	8	3	4	1	17	9	13
United Arab Emirates	8	2	3	3	9	12	9
Uzbekistan	8	1	3	4	13	18	6
Kazakhstan	8	1	3	4	7	19	6

Play-off

Date				Score
16.11.97	Japan**	v	Iran***	3-2

* South Korea and Saudi Arabia qualified

** Japan qualified after winning by golden goal

*** Iran qualified for Asia-Oceania play-off

Oceania

First Round

Melanesian Group	P	W	D	L	F	A	Pts
Papua New Guinea	2	1	1	0	3	2	4
Solomon Islands	2	0	2	0	2	2	2
Vanuatu	2	0	1	1	2	3	1

Polynesian Group	P	W	D	L	F	A	Pts
Tonga	2	2	0	0	3	0	6
Western Samoa	2	1	0	1	2	2	3
Cook Islands	2	0	0	2	1	4	0

First Round play-off

Date				Score
15.02.97	Tonga	v	Soloman Islands	0-4
01.3.97	Soloman Islands	v	Tonga	9-0

Second Round

Group 1	P	W	D	L	F	A	Pts
Australia	4	4	0	0	26	2	12
Solomon Islands	4	1	1	2	7	21	4
Tahiti	4	0	1	3	2	12	1
Group 2	P	W	D	L	F	A	Pts
New Zealand	4	3	0	1	13	1	9
Fiji	4	2	0	2	4	7	6
Papua New Guinea	4	1	0	3	2	11	3

Third Round

Date				Score
28.06.97	New Zealand	v	Australia	0-3
05.07.97	Australia	v	New Zealand	2-0

Asia/Oceania

Play-off

Date				Score
22.11.97	Iran	v	Australia	1-1
29.11.97	Australia	v	Iran*	2-2

* Iran qualified on away goals

South America (CONMEBOL)

	P	W	D	L	F	A	Pts
Argentina*	16	8	6	2	23	13	30
Paraguay*	16	9	2	5	21	14	29
Colombia*	16	8	4	4	23	15	28
Chile*	16	7	4	5	32	18	25
Peru	16	7	4	5	19	20	25
Ecuador	16	6	3	7	22	21	21
Uruguay	16	6	3	7	18	21	21
Bolivia	16	4	5	7	18	21	17
Venezuela	16	0	3	13	8	41	3

* Argentina, Paraguay, Colombia and Chile qualified

Caribbean and Central America (CONCACAF)

Caribbean First Round†

Series A

	P	W	D	L	F	A	Pts
Dominican Republic	2	2	0	0	6	3	6
Aruba	2	0	0	2	3	6	0

Series B

	P	W	D	L	F	A	Pts
Grenada	2	2	0	0	8	1	6
Guyana	2	0	0	2	1	8	0

Series D

	P	W	D	L	F	A	Pts
Dominica	2	1	1	0	6	4	4
Antigua and Barbuda	2	0	1	1	4	6	1

Caribbean Second Round

Series 2

	P	W	D	L	F	A	Pts
Dominican Republic	2	1	1	0	2	1	4
Netherlands Antilles	2	0	1	1	1	2	1

Series 4

	P	W	D	L	F	A	Pts
Haiti	2	2	0	0	7	1	6
Grenada	2	0	0	2	1	7	0

Series 5

	P	W	D	L	F	A	Pts
Cuba	2	2	0	0	6	0	6
Cayman Islands	2	0	0	2	0	6	0

Series 7

	P	W	D	L	F	A	Pts
St Kitts & Nevis	2	2	0	0	6	1	6
Saint Lucia	2	0	0	2	1	6	0

Series 8

	P	W	D	L	F	A	Pts
St Vincent/Grenadine	2	2	0	0	9	1	6
Puerto Rico	2	0	0	2	1	9	0

Series 10

	P	W	D	L	F	A	Pts
Barbados	2	2	0	0	2	0	6
Dominica	2	0	0	2	0	2	0

Series 11

	P	W	D	L	F	A	Pts
Jamaica	2	2	0	0	2	0	6
Surinam	2	0	0	2	0	2	0

Caribbean Third Round

Series A

	P	W	D	L	F	A	Pts
Cuba	2	1	1	0	7	2	4
Haiti	2	0	1	1	2	7	1

† Series C not played because Bahamas withdrew

Series B

	P	W	D	L	F	A	Pts
St Vincent/Grenadine	2	0	2	0	2	2	2
St Kitts & Nevis	2	0	2	0	2	2	2

Series C

	P	W	D	L	F	A	Pts
Jamaica	2	2	0	0	3	0	6
Barbados	2	0	0	2	0	3	0

Series D

	P	W	D	L	F	A	Pts
Trinidad and Tobago	2	2	0	0	12	1	6
Dominican Republic	2	0	0	2	1	12	0

Central America Third Round

Series E

	P	W	D	L	F	A	Pts
Guatemala	2	2	0	0	3	1	6
Nicaragua	2	0	0	2	1	3	0

Series F

	P	W	D	L	F	A	Pts
Panama	2	2	0	0	6	2	6
Belize	2	0	0	2	2	6	0

Semi-final Round

Group 1

	P	W	D	L	F	A	Pts
United States	6	4	1	1	10	5	13
Costa Rica	6	4	0	2	9	5	12
Guatemala	6	2	2	2	6	9	8
Trinidad and Tobago	6	0	1	5	3	9	1

Group 2

	P	W	D	L	F	A	Pts
Canada	6	5	1	0	10	1	16
El Salvador	6	3	1	2	12	6	10
Panama	6	1	2	3	8	11	5
Cuba	6	1	0	5	4	16	3

Group 3

	P	W	D	L	F	A	Pts
Jamaica	6	4	1	1	12	3	13
Mexico	6	4	0	2	14	6	12
Honduras	6	3	1	2	18	11	10
St Vincent/Grenadine	6	0	0	6	6	30	0

Final Round

	P	W	D	L	F	A	Pts
Mexico*	10	4	6	0	23	7	18
United States*	10	4	5	1	17	9	17
Jamaica*	10	3	5	2	7	12	14
Costa Rica	10	3	3	4	13	12	12
El Salvador	10	2	4	4	11	16	10
Canada	10	1	3	6	5	20	6

* Mexico, United States and Jamaica qualified

Europe (UEFA)

Group 1

Date				Score
24.04.96	Greece	v	Slovenia	2-0
01.09.96	Greece	v	Bosnia-Herzegovina	3-0
01.09.96	Slovenia	v	Denmark	0-2
08.10.96	Bosnia-Herzegovina	v	Croatia	1-4
09.10.96	Denmark	v	Greece	2-1
10.11.96	Slovenia	v	Bosnia-Herzegovina	1-2
10.11.96	Croatia	v	Greece	1-1
29.03.97	Croatia	v	Denmark	1-1
02.04.97	Bosnia-Herzegovina	v	Greece	0-1
02.04.97	Croatia	v	Slovenia	3-3
30.04.97	Denmark	v	Slovenia	4-0
30.04.97	Greece	v	Croatia	0-1
08.06.97	Denmark	v	Bosnia-Herzegovina	2-0
20.08.97	Bosnia-Herzegovina	v	Denmark	3-0
06.09.97	Croatia	v	Bosnia-Herzegovina	3-2
06.09.97	Slovenia	v	Greece	0-3
10.09.97	Denmark	v	Croatia	3-1
10.09.97	Bosnia-Herzegovina	v	Slovenia	1-0
11.10.97	Slovenia	v	Croatia	1-3
11.10.97	Greece	v	Denmark	0-0

	P	W	D	L	F	A	Pts
Denmark*	8	5	2	1	14	6	17
Croatia	8	4	3	1	17	12	15
Greece	8	4	2	2	11	4	14
Bosnia-Herzegovina	8	3	0	5	9	14	9
Slovenia	8	0	1	7	5	20	1

Group 2

Date				Score
01.09.96	Moldova	v	England	0-3
05.10.96	Moldova	v	Italy	1-3
09.10.96	Italy	v	Georgia	1-0
09.10.96	England	v	Poland	2-1
09.11.96	Georgia	v	England	0-2
10.11.96	Poland	v	Moldova	2-1
12.02.97	England	v	Italy	0-1
29.03.97	Italy	v	Moldova	3-0
02.04.97	Poland	v	Italy	0-0
30.04.97	England	v	Georgia	2-0
30.04.97	Italy	v	Poland	3-0
31.05.97	Poland	v	England	0-2
07.06.97	Georgia	v	Moldova	2-0
14.06.97	Poland	v	Georgia	4-1
10.09.97	England	v	Moldova	4-0
10.09.97	Georgia	v	Italy	0-0
24.09.97	Moldova	v	Georgia	0-1
07.10.97	Moldova	v	Poland	0-3
11.10.97	Georgia	v	Poland	3-0
11.10.97	Italy	v	England	0-0

	P	W	D	L	F	A	Pts
England*	8	6	1	1	15	2	19
Italy	8	5	3	0	11	1	18
Poland	8	3	1	4	10	12	10
Georgia	8	3	1	4	7	9	10
Moldova	8	0	0	8	2	21	0

Group 3

Date				Score
02.06.96	Norway	v	Azerbaijan	5-0
31.08.96	Azerbaijan	v	Switzerland	1-0
01.09.96	Hungary	v	Finland	1-0
06.10.96	Finland	v	Switzerland	2-3
09.10.96	Norway	v	Hungary	3-0
10.11.96	Switzerland	v	Norway	0-1
10.11.96	Azerbaijan	v	Hungary	0-3
02.04.97	Azerbaijan	v	Finland	1-2
30.04.97	Norway	v	Finland	1-1
30.04.97	Switzerland	v	Hungary	1-0
08.06.97	Finland	v	Azerbaijan	3-0
08.06.97	Hungary	v	Norway	1-1
20.08.97	Hungary	v	Switzerland	1-1
20.08.97	Finland	v	Norway	0-4
06.09.97	Azerbaijan	v	Norway	0-1
06.09.97	Switzerland	v	Finland	1-2
10.09.97	Hungary	v	Azerbaijan	3-1
10.09.97	Norway	v	Switzerland	5-0
11.10.97	Finland	v	Hungary	1-1
11.10.97	Switzerland	v	Azerbaijan	5-0

	P	W	D	L	F	A	Pts
Norway*	8	6	2	0	21	2	20
Hungary	8	3	3	2	10	8	12
Finland	8	3	2	3	11	12	11
Switzerland	8	3	1	4	11	12	10
Azerbaijan	8	1	0	7	3	22	3

Group 4

Date				Score
01.06.96	Sweden	v	Belarus	5-1
31.08.96	Belarus	v	Estonia	1-0
31.08.96	Austria	v	Scotland	0-0
01.09.96	Latvia	v	Sweden	1-2
05.10.96	Estonia	v	Belarus	1-0
05.10.96	Latvia	v	Scotland	0-2
09.10.96	Belarus	v	Latvia	1-1
09.10.96	Sweden	v	Austria	0-1
09.11.96	Austria	v	Latvia	2-1
10.11.96	Scotland	v	Sweden	1-0
11.02.97	Estonia	v	Scotland	0-0
29.03.97	Scotland	v	Estonia	2-0
02.04.97	Scotland	v	Austria	2-0
30.04.97	Latvia	v	Belarus	2-0
30.04.97	Sweden	v	Scotland	2-1
30.04.97	Austria	v	Estonia	2-0
18.05.97	Estonia	v	Latvia	1-3
08.06.97	Belarus	v	Scotland	0-1
08.06.97	Latvia	v	Austria	1-3
08.06.97	Estonia	v	Sweden	2-3
20.08.97	Estonia	v	Austria	0-3
20.08.97	Belarus	v	Sweden	1-2
06.09.97	Latvia	v	Estonia	1-0
06.09.97	Austria	v	Sweden	1-0
07.09.97	Scotland	v	Belarus	4-1
10.09.97	Sweden	v	Latvia	1-0
10.09.97	Belarus	v	Austria	0-1
11.10.97	Scotland	v	Latvia	2-0
11.10.97	Austria	v	Belarus	4-0
11.10.97	Sweden	v	Estonia	1-0

	P	W	D	L	F	A	Pts
Austria*	10	8	1	1	17	4	25
Scotland**	10	7	2	1	15	3	23
Sweden	10	7	0	3	16	9	21
Latvia	10	3	1	6	10	14	10
Estonia	10	1	1	8	4	16	4
Belarus	10	1	1	8	5	21	4

Group 5

Date				Score
01.09.96	Israel	v	Bulgaria	2-1
01.09.96	Russia	v	Cyprus	4-0
08.10.96	Luxembourg	v	Bulgaria	1-2
09.10.96	Israel	v	Russia	1-1
10.11.96	Luxembourg	v	Russia	0-4
10.11.96	Cyprus	v	Israel	2-0
14.12.96	Cyprus	v	Bulgaria	1-3
15.12.96	Israel	v	Luxembourg	1-0
29.03.97	Cyprus	v	Russia	1-1
31.03.97	Luxembourg	v	Israel	0-3
02.04.97	Bulgaria	v	Cyprus	4-1
30.04.97	Israel	v	Cyprus	2-0
30.04.97	Russia	v	Luxembourg	3-0
08.06.97	Bulgaria	v	Luxembourg	4-0
08.06.97	Russia	v	Israel	2-0
20.08.97	Bulgaria	v	Israel	1-0
07.09.97	Luxembourg	v	Cyprus	1-3
10.09.97	Bulgaria	v	Russia	1-0
11.10.97	Cyprus	v	Luxembourg	2-0
11.10.97	Russia	v	Bulgaria	4-2

	P	W	D	L	F	A	Pts
Bulgaria*	8	6	0	2	18	9	18
Russia	8	5	2	1	19	5	17
Israel	8	4	1	3	9	7	13
Cyprus	8	3	1	4	10	15	10
Luxembourg	8	0	0	8	2	22	0

* Denmark, England, Norway, Austria and Bulgaria qualified

** Scotland qualified as highest runner-up

World Cup qualifying rounds 1997 | 98

Group 6

Date				Score
24.04.96	Yugoslavia	v	Faroe Islands	3-1
02.06.96	Yugoslavia	v	Malta	6-0
31.08.96	Faroe Islands	v	Slovakia	1-2
04.09.96	Faroe Islands	v	Spain	2-6
18.09.96	Czech Republic	v	Malta	6-0
22.09.96	Slovakia	v	Malta	6-0
06.10.96	Faroe Islands	v	Yugoslavia	1-8
09.10.96	Czech Republic	v	Spain	0-0
23.10.96	Slovakia	v	Faroe Islands	3-0
10.11.96	Yugoslavia	v	Czech Republic	1-0
13.11.96	Spain	v	Slovakia	4-1
14.12.96	Spain	v	Yugoslavia	2-0
18.12.96	Malta	v	Spain	0-3
12.02.97	Spain	v	Malta	4-0
31.03.97	Malta	v	Slovakia	0-2
02.04.97	Czech Republic	v	Yugoslavia	1-2
30.04.97	Malta	v	Faroe Islands	1-2
30.04.97	Yugoslavia	v	Spain	1-1
08.06.97	Faroe Islands	v	Malta	2-1
08.06.97	Yugoslavia	v	Slovakia	2-0
08.06.97	Spain	v	Czech Republic	1-0
20.08.97	Czech Republic	v	Faroe Islands	2-0
24.08.97	Slovakia	v	Czech Republic	2-1
06.09.97	Faroe Islands	v	Czech Republic	0-2
10.09.97	Slovakia	v	Yugoslavia	1-1
24.09.97	Malta	v	Czech Republic	0-1
24.09.97	Slovakia	v	Spain	1-2
11.10.97	Malta	v	Yugoslavia	0-5
11.10.97	Spain	v	Faroe Islands	3-1
11.10.97	Czech Republic	v	Slovakia	3-0

	P	W	D	L	F	A	Pts
Spain*	10	8	2	0	26	6	26
Yugoslavia	10	7	2	1	29	7	23
Czech Republic	10	5	1	4	16	6	16
Slovakia	10	5	1	4	18	14	16
Faroe Islands	10	2	0	8	10	31	6
Malta	10	0	0	10	2	37	0

Group 7

Date				Score
02.06.96	San Marino	v	Wales	0-5
31.08.96	Wales	v	San Marino	6-0
31.08.96	Belgium	v	Turkey	2-1
05.10.96	Wales	v	Netherlands	1-3
09.10.96	San Marino	v	Belgium	0-3
09.11.96	Netherlands	v	Wales	7-1
10.11.96	Turkey	v	San Marino	7-0
14.12.96	Wales	v	Turkey	0-0
14.12.96	Belgium	v	Netherlands	0-3
29.03.97	Wales	v	Belgium	1-2
29.03.97	Netherlands	v	San Marino	4-0
02.04.97	Turkey	v	Netherlands	1-0
30.04.97	Turkey	v	Belgium	1-3
30.04.97	San Marino	v	Netherlands	0-6
07.06.97	Belgium	v	San Marino	6-0
20.08.97	Turkey	v	Wales	6-4
06.09.97	Netherlands	v	Belgium	3-1
10.09.97	San Marino	v	Turkey	0-5
11.10.97	Belgium	v	Wales	3-2
11.10.97	Netherlands	v	Turkey	0-0

	P	W	D	L	F	A	Pts
Netherlands*	8	6	1	1	26	4	19
Belgium	8	6	0	2	20	11	18
Turkey	8	4	2	2	21	9	14
Wales	8	2	1	5	20	21	7
San Marino	8	0	0	8	0	42	0

World Cup

Group 8

Date				Score
24.04.96	Macedonia	v	Liechtenstein	3-0
01.06.96	Iceland	v	Macedonia	1-1
31.08.96	Liechtenstein	v	Republic of Ireland	0-5
31.08.96	Romania	v	Lithuania	3-0
05.10.96	Lithuania	v	Iceland	2-0
09.10.96	Lithuania	v	Liechtenstein	2-1
09.10.96	Iceland	v	Romania	0-4
09.10.96	Republic of Ireland	v	Macedonia	3-0
09.11.96	Liechtenstein	v	Macedonia	1-11
10.11.96	Republic of Ireland	v	Iceland	0-0
14.12.96	Macedonia	v	Romania	0-3
29.03.97	Romania	v	Liechtenstein	8-0
02.04.97	Macedonia	v	Republic of Ireland	3-2
02.04.97	Lithuania	v	Romania	0-1
30.04.97	Liechtenstein	v	Lithuania	0-2
30.04.97	Romania	v	Republic of Ireland	1-0
21.05.97	Republic of Ireland	v	Liechtenstein	5-0
07.06.97	Macedonia	v	Iceland	1-0
11.06.97	Iceland	v	Lithuania	0-0
20.08.97	Liechtenstein	v	Iceland	0-4
20.08.97	Republic of Ireland	v	Lithuania	0-0
20.08.97	Romania	v	Macedonia	4-2
06.09.97	Iceland	v	Republic of Ireland	2-4
06.09.97	Liechtenstein	v	Romania	1-8
06.09.97	Lithuania	v	Macedonia	2-0
10.09.97	Romania	v	Iceland	4-0
10.09.97	Lithuania	v	Republic of Ireland	1-2
11.10.97	Iceland	v	Liechtenstein	4-0
11.10.97	Republic of Ireland	v	Romania	1-1
11.10.97	Macedonia	v	Lithuania	1-2

	P	W	D	L	F	A	Pts
Romania*	10	9	1	0	37	4	28
Republic of Ireland	10	5	3	2	22	8	18
Lithuania	10	5	2	3	11	8	17
Macedonia	10	4	1	5	22	18	13
Iceland	10	2	3	5	11	16	9
Liechtenstein	10	0	0	10	3	52	0

Group 9

Date				Score
31.08.96	Northern Ireland	v	Ukraine	0-1
31.08.96	Armenia	v	Portugal	0-0
05.10.96	Northern Ireland	v	Armenia	1-1
05.10.96	Ukraine	v	Portugal	2-1
09.10.96	Albania	v	Portugal	0-3
09.10.96	Armenia	v	Germany	1-5
09.11.96	Albania	v	Armenia	1-1
09.11.96	Germany	v	Northern Ireland	1-1
09.11.96	Portugal	v	Ukraine	1-0
14.12.96	Northern Ireland	v	Albania	2-0
14.12.96	Portugal	v	Germany	0-0
29.03.97	Northern Ireland	v	Portugal	0-0
29.03.97	Albania	v	Ukraine	0-1
02.04.97	Ukraine	v	Northern Ireland	2-1
02.04.97	Albania	v	Germany	2-3
30.04.97	Armenia	v	Northern Ireland	0-0
30.04.97	Germany	v	Ukraine	2-0
07.05.97	Ukraine	v	Armenia	1-1
07.06.97	Ukraine	v	Germany	0-0
07.06.97	Portugal	v	Albania	2-0
20.08.97	Ukraine	v	Albania	1-0
20.08.97	Northern Ireland	v	Germany	1-3
20.08.97	Portugal	v	Armenia	3-1
06.09.97	Armenia	v	Albania	3-0
06.09.97	Germany	v	Portugal	1-1
10.09.97	Albania	v	Northern Ireland	1-0
10.09.97	Germany	v	Armenia	4-0
11.10.97	Portugal	v	Northern Ireland	1-0
11.10.97	Germany	v	Albania	4-3
11.10.97	Armenia	v	Ukraine	0-2

	P	W	D	L	F	A	Pts
Germany*	10	6	4	0	23	9	22
Ukraine	10	6	2	2	10	6	20
Portugal	10	5	4	1	12	4	19
Armenia	10	1	5	4	8	17	8
Northern Ireland	10	1	4	5	6	10	7
Albania	10	1	1	8	7	20	4

Play-offs

Date				Score
29.10.97	Croatia	v	Ukraine	2-0
29.10.97	Republic of Ireland	v	Belgium	1-1
29.10.97	Hungary	v	Yugoslavia	1-7
29.10.97	Russia	v	Italy	1-1

Date				Score
15.11.97	Yugoslavia*	v	Hungary	5-0
15.11.97	Ukraine	v	Croatia*	1-1
15.11.97	Belgium*	v	Republic of Ireland	2-1
15.11.97	Italy*	v	Russia	1-0

* Spain, Netherlands, Romania, Germany, Yugoslavia, Croatia, Belgium, Italy, qualified

World Cup finals 1998

Group stage

Group A

Date				Score	Attendance
10.06.98	Brazil	v	Scotland	2-1	80,000
10.06.98	Morocco	v	Norway	2-2	29,750
16.06.98	Scotland	v	Norway	1-1	30,236
16.06.98	Brazil	v	Morocco	3-0	33,266
23.06.98	Brazil	v	Norway	1-2	55,500
23.06.98	Scotland	v	Morocco	0-3	35,000

Position	Team	P	W	D	L	F	A	GD	Pts
1	Brazil	3	2	0	1	6	3	+3	6
2	Norway	3	1	2	0	5	4	+1	5
3	Morocco	3	1	1	1	5	5	0	4
4	Scotland	3	0	1	2	2	6	-4	1

Group B

Date				Score	Attendance
11.06.98	Italy	v	Chile	2-2	31,800
11.06.98	Cameroon	v	Austria	1-1	37,500
17.06.98	Chile	v	Austria	1-1	36,000
17.06.98	Italy	v	Cameroon	3-0	35,000
23.06.98	Italy	v	Austria	2-1	75,000
23.06.98	Chile	v	Cameroon	1-1	39,000

Position	Team	P	W	D	L	F	A	GD	Pts
1	Italy	3	2	1	0	7	3	+4	7
2	Chile	3	0	3	0	4	4	0	3
3	Austria	3	0	2	1	3	4	-1	2
4	Cameroon	3	0	2	1	2	5	-3	2

Group C

Date				Score	Attendance
12.06.98	Saudi Arabia	v	Denmark	0-1	38,140
12.06.98	France	v	South Africa	3-0	55,077
18.06.98	South Africa	v	Denmark	1-1	36,500
18.06.98	France	v	Saudi Arabia	4-0	75,000
24.06.98	France	v	Denmark	2-1	43,500
24.06.98	South Africa	v	Saudi Arabia	2-2	36,500

Position	Team	P	W	D	L	F	A	GD	Pts
1	France	3	3	0	0	9	1	+8	9
2	Denmark	3	1	1	1	3	3	0	4
3	South Africa	3	0	2	1	3	6	-3	2
4	Saudi Arabia	3	0	1	2	2	7	-5	1

Group D

Date				Score	Attendance
12.06.98	Paraguay	v	Bulgaria	0-0	27,650
13.06.98	Spain	v	Nigeria	2-3	33,257
19.06.98	Nigeria	v	Bulgaria	1-0	48,500
19.06.98	Spain	v	Paraguay	0-0	35,300
24.06.98	Spain	v	Bulgaria	6-1	40,500
24.06.98	Nigeria	v	Paraguay	1-3	36,500

Position	Team	P	W	D	L	F	A	GD	Pts
1	Nigeria	3	2	0	1	5	5	0	6
2	Paraguay	3	1	2	0	3	1	+2	5
3	Spain	3	1	1	1	8	4	+4	4
4	Bulgaria	3	0	1	2	1	7	-6	1

World Cup finals 1998

Group stage

Group E

Date				Score	Attendance
13.06.98	South Korea	v	Mexico	1-3	37,588
13.06.98	Netherlands	v	Belgium	0-0	75,000
20.06.98	Belgium	v	Mexico	2-2	34,750
20.06.98	Netherlands	v	South Korea	5-0	60,000
25.06.98	Netherlands	v	Mexico	2-2	35,500
25.06.98	Belgium	v	South Korea	1-1	48,500

Position	Team	P	W	D	L	F	A	GD	Pts
1	Netherlands	3	1	2	0	7	2	+5	5
2	Mexico	3	1	2	0	7	5	+2	5
3	Belgium	3	0	3	0	3	3	0	3
4	South Korea	3	0	1	2	2	9	-7	1

Group F

Date				Score	Attendance
14.06.98	Yugoslavia	v	Iran	1-0	30,392
15.06.98	Germany	v	USA	2-0	43,875
21.06.98	Germany	v	Yugoslavia	2-2	40,775
21.06.98	USA	v	Iran	1-2	44,000
25.06.98	Germany	v	Iran	2-0	35,000
25.06.98	USA	v	Yugoslavia	0-1	39,000

Position	Team	P	W	D	L	F	A	GD	Pts
1	Germany	3	2	1	0	6	2	+4	7
2	Yugoslavia	3	2	1	0	4	2	+2	7
3	Iran	3	1	0	2	2	4	-2	3
4	USA	3	0	0	3	1	5	-4	0

Group G

Date				Score	Attendance
15.06.98	England	v	Tunisia	2-0	54,587
15.06.98	Romahia	v	Colombia	1-0	37,572
22.06.98	Colombia	v	Tunisia	1-0	35,000
22.06.98	Romania	v	England	2-1	37,500
26.06.98	Romania	v	Tunisia	1-1	80,000
26.06.98	Colombia	v	England	0-2	41,275

Position	Team	P	W	D	L	F	A	GD	Pts
1	Romania	3	2	1	0	4	2	+2	7
2	England	3	2	0	1	5	2	+3	6
3	Colombia	3	1	0	2	1	3	-2	3
4	Tunisia	3	0	1	2	1	4	-3	1

Group H

Date				Score	Attendance
14.06.98	Argentina	v	Japan	1-0	33,400
14.06.98	Jamaica	v	Croatia	1-3	38,058
20.06.98	Japan	v	Croatia	0-1	39,000
21.06.98	Argentina	v	Jamaica	5-0	48,500
26.06.98	Argentina	v	Croatia	1-0	35,000
26.06.98	Japan	v	Jamaica	1-2	43,500

Position	Team	P	W	D	L	F	A	GD	Pts
1	Argentina	3	3	0	0	7	0	+7	9
2	Croatia	3	2	0	1	4	2	+2	6
3	Jamaica	3	1	0	2	3	9	-6	3
4	Japan	3	0	0	3	1	4	-3	0

World Cup 1998

Round 2

Date				Score	Attendance
27.06.98	Italy Christian Vieri	v	Norway	1-0	55,000
27.06.98	Brazil Cesar Sampaio (2) Ronaldo (2)	v	Chile Marcelo Salas	4-1	45,500
28.06.98	France Laurent Blanc	v	Paraguay	1-0*	38,100
28.06.98	Nigeria Tijani Babangida	v	Denmark Peter Moller, Brian Laudrup, Ebbe Sand, Thomas Helveg	1-4	77,000
29.06.98	Germany Jurgen Klinsmann Oliver Bierhoff	v	Mexico Luis Hernandez	2-1	29,800
29.06.98	Netherlands Dennis Bergkamp Edgar Davids	v	Yugoslavia Slobodan Komljenovic	2-1	33,500
30.06.98	Romania	v	Croatia Davor Suker	0-1	31,800
30.06.98	Argentina Gabriel Batistuta Javier Zanetti	v	England Alan Shearer Michael Owen	2-2**[4-3]	30,600

Quarter-finals

Date				Score	Attendance
03.07.98	Italy	v	France	0-0**[3-4]	77,000
03.07.98	Brazil Bebeto Rivaldo (2)	v	Denmark Martin Jorgensen Brian Laudrup	3-2	35,500
04.07.98	Netherlands Patrick Kluivert Dennis Bergkamp	v	Argentina Claudio Lopez	2-1	55,000
04.07.98	Germany	v	Croatia Robert Jarni Goran Vlaovic Davor Suker	0-3	39,100

Semi-finals

Date				Score	Attendance
07.07.98	Brazil Ronaldo	v	Netherlands Patrick Kluivert	1-1**[4-2]	55,000
08.07.98	France Lilian Thuram (2)	v	Croatia Davor Suker	2-1	76,000

Third place play-off

Date				Score	Attendance
11.07.98	Netherlands Boudewijn Zenden	v	Croatia Robert Prosinecki Davor Suker	1-2	45,500

Final

Date				Score	Attendance
12.07.98	Brazil	v	France Zinedine Zidane (2) Emmanuel Petit	0-3	74,000

Brazil: Claudio Taffarel; Cafu; Aldair; Junior Baiano; Cesar Sampaio (Edmundo 75); Roberto Carlos; Dunga; Ronaldo; Rivaldo; Leonardo (Denilson 45); Bebeto

France: Fabien Barthez; Bixente Lizarazu; Marcel Desailly; Lilian Thuram; Frank Leboeuf; Emmanuel Petit; Didier Deschamps; Christian Karembeu (Alain Boghossian 58); Zinedine Zidane; Youri Djorkaeff; (Patrick Vieira 76); Stephane Guivarc'h (Christophe Dugarry 66)

* golden goal in extra time

** penalty shoot-out after extra time

World Cup finals 1998

Team statistics

Argentina

Games played:	5
Games won:	3
Games lost:	1
Games drawn:	1*
Goals conceded:	4
Top scorer:	Gabriel Batistuta (5)
Highest attendance:	55,000 v Netherlands
Lowest attendance:	30,600 v England
Heaviest defeat:	1-2 v Netherlands
Biggest win:	5-0 v Japan
Final placing:	Quarter-final loser
Red cards:	1
Yellow cards:	11

Belgium

Games played:	3
Games won:	0
Games lost:	0
Games drawn:	3
Goals conceded:	3
Top scorer:	Marc Wilmots (2)
Highest attendance:	75,000 v Netherlands
Lowest attendance:	34,750 v Mexico
Heaviest defeat:	None
Biggest win:	None
Final placing:	Third in Group E
Red cards:	1
Yellow cards:	4

Austria

Games played:	3
Games won:	0
Games lost:	1
Games drawn:	2
Goals conceded:	4
Top scorers:	Anton Polster (1)
	Ivica Vastic (1)
	Andreas Herzog (1)
Highest attendance:	75,000 v Italy
Lowest attendance:	36,000 v Chile
Heaviest defeat:	1-2 v Italy
Biggest win:	None
Final placing:	Third in Group B
Red cards:	0
Yellow cards:	5

Brazil

Games played:	7
Games won:	4
Games lost:	2
Games drawn:	1
Goals conceded:	10
Top scorer:	Ronaldo (4)
Highest attendance:	80,000 v Scotland
Lowest attendance:	33,266 v Morocco
Heaviest defeat:	0-3 v France
Biggest win:	4-1 v Chile
Final placing:	Runners-up
Red cards:	0
Yellow cards:	12

Bulgaria

Games played:	3
Games won:	0
Games lost:	2
Games drawn:	1
Goals conceded:	7
Top scorer:	Emil Kostadinov (1)
Highest attendance:	48,500 v Nigeria
Lowest attendance:	27,650 v Paraguay
Heaviest defeat:	1-6 v Spain
Biggest win:	None
Final placing:	Fourth in Group D
Red cards:	1
Yellow cards:	7

Chile

Games played:	4
Games won:	0
Games lost:	1
Games drawn:	3
Goals conceded:	8
Top scorer:	Marcelo Salas (4)
Highest attendance:	45,500 v Brazil
Lowest attendance:	36,000 v Austria
Heaviest defeat:	1-4 v Brazil
Biggest win:	None
Final placing:	Second round loser
Red cards:	0
Yellow cards:	11

Cameroon

Games played:	3
Games won:	0
Games lost:	1
Games drawn:	2
Goals conceded:	5
Top scorers:	Pierre Njanka (1)
	Patrick Mboma (1)
Highest attendance:	39,000 v Chile
Lowest attendance:	35,000 v Italy
Heaviest defeat:	0-3 v Italy
Biggest win:	None
Final placing:	Fourth in Group B
Red cards:	3
Yellow cards:	6

Colombia

Games played:	3
Games won:	1
Games lost:	2
Games drawn:	0
Goals conceded:	3
Top scorer:	Leider Preciado (1)
Highest attendance:	41,275 v England
Lowest attendance:	35,000 v Tunisia
Heaviest defeat:	0-2 v England
Biggest win:	1-0 v Tunisia
Final placing:	Third in Group G
Red cards:	0
Yellow cards:	5

* games decided by penalty shoot-outs are classed as draws

Team statistics (continued)

Croatia

Games played:	7
Games won:	5
Games lost:	2
Games drawn:	0
Goals conceded:	5
Top scorer:	Davor Suker (6)
Highest attendance:	76,000 v France
Lowest attendance:	31,800 v Romania
Heaviest defeat:	1-2 v France
Biggest win:	3-0 v Germany
Final placing:	Third
Red cards:	0
Yellow cards:	18

England

Games played:	4
Games won:	2
Games lost:	1
Games drawn:	1*
Goals conceded:	4
Top scorers:	Michael Owen (2)
	Alan Shearer (2)
Highest attendance:	54,587 v Tunisia
Lowest attendance:	30,600 v Argentina
Heaviest defeat:	1-2 v Romania
Biggest wins:	2-0 v Tunisia
	2-0 v Colombia
Final placing:	Second round loser
Red cards:	1
Yellow cards:	5

Denmark

Games played:	5
Games won:	2
Games lost:	2
Games drawn:	1*
Goals conceded:	7
Top scorer:	Brian Laudrup (2)
Highest attendance:	77,000 v Nigeria
Lowest attendance:	36,500 v South Africa
Heaviest defeat:	2-3 v Brazil
Biggest win:	4-1 v Nigeria
Final placing:	Quater-final loser
Red cards:	2
Yellow cards:	12

France

Games played:	7
Games won:	6
Games lost:	0
Games drawn:	1*
Goals conceded:	2
Top scorer:	Thierry Henry (3)
Highest attendance:	77,000 v Italy
Lowest attendance:	38,100 v Paraguay
Heaviest defeat:	None
Biggest win:	4-0 v Saudi Arabia
Final placing:	Winners
Red cards:	3
Yellow cards:	12

Germany

Games played:	5
Games won:	3
Games lost:	1
Games drawn:	1*
Goals conceded:	6
Top scorers:	Oliver Bierhoff (3)
	Jurgen Klinsmann (3)
Highest attendance:	43,875 v USA
Lowest attendance:	29,800 v Mexico
Heaviest defeat:	0-3 v Croatia
Biggest wins:	2-0 v Iran
	2-0 v USA
Final placing:	Quarter-final losers
Red cards:	1
Yellow cards:	10

Italy

Games played:	5
Games won:	3
Games lost:	0*
Games drawn:	2
Goals conceded:	3
Top scorer:	Christian Vieri (5)
Highest attendance:	77,000 v France
Lowest attendance:	31,800 v Chile
Heaviest defeat:	None
Biggest win:	3-0 v Cameroon
Final placing:	Quarter-final losers
Red cards:	0
Yellow cards:	11

Iran

Games played:	3
Games won:	1
Games lost:	2
Games drawn:	0
Goals conceded:	4
Top scorers:	Hamid-Reza Estili (1)
	Mehdi Mahdavikia (1)
Highest attendance:	44,000 v USA
Lowest attendance:	30,392 v Yugoslavia
Heaviest defeat:	0-2 v Germany
Biggest win:	2-1 v USA
Final placing:	Third in Group F
Red cards:	0
Yellow cards:	3

Jamaica

Games played:	3
Games won:	1
Games lost:	2
Games drawn:	0
Goals conceded:	9
Top scorer:	Theodore Whitmore (1)
Highest attendance:	48,500 v Argentina
Lowest attendance:	38,058 v Croatia
Heaviest defeat:	0-5 v Argentina
Biggest win:	2-1 v Japan
Final placing:	Third in Group H
Red cards:	1
Yellow cards:	5

* games decided by penalty shoot-outs are classed as draws

Team statistics (continued)

Japan

Games played:	3
Games won:	0
Games lost:	3
Games drawn:	0
Goals conceded:	4
Top scorer:	Masashi Nakayama (1)
Highest attendance:	43,500 v Jamaica
Lowest attendance:	33,400 v Argentina
Heaviest defeat:	1-2 v Jamaica
Biggest win:	None
Final placing:	Fourth in Group H
Red cards:	0
Yellow cards:	7

Morocco

Games played:	3
Games won:	1
Games lost:	1
Games drawn:	1
Goals conceded:	5
Top scorers:	Abdeljilil Hadda (2)
	Salaheddine Bassir (2)
Highest attendance:	35,000 v Scotland
Lowest attendance:	29,750 v Norway
Heaviest defeat:	0-3 v Brazil
Biggest win:	3-0 v Scotland
Final placing:	Third in Group A
Red cards:	0
Yellow cards:	4

Mexico

Games played:	4
Games won:	1
Games lost:	1
Games drawn:	2
Goals conceded:	7
Top scorer:	Luis Hernandez (4)
Highest attendance:	37,588 v South Korea
Lowest attendance:	29,800 v Germany
Heaviest defeat:	1-2 v Germany
Biggest win:	3-1 v South Korea
Final placing:	Second round loser
Red cards:	2
Yellow cards:	7

Netherlands

Games played:	7
Games won:	3
Games lost:	1
Games drawn:	3*
Goals conceded:	7
Top scorer:	Dennis Bergkamp (3)
Highest attendance:	75,000 v Belgium
Lowest attendance:	33,500 v Yugoslavia
Heaviest defeat:	1-2 v Croatia
Biggest win:	5-0 v South Korea
Final placing:	Fourth
Red cards:	2
Yellow cards:	9

Nigeria

Games played:	4
Games won:	2
Games lost:	2
Games drawn:	0
Goals conceded:	9
Top scorers:	Garba Lawal (1)
	Mutiu Adepoju (1)
	Victor Ikpeba (1)
	Sunday Oliseh (1)
	Wilson Oruma (1)
	Tijani Babangida (1)
Highest attendance:	77,000 v Denmark
Lowest attendance:	33,257 v Spain
Heaviest defeat:	1-4 v Denmark
Biggest win:	3-2 v Spain
Final placing:	Second round loser
Red cards:	0
Yellow cards:	8

Paraguay

Games played:	4
Games won:	1
Games lost:	1
Games drawn:	2
Goals conceded:	2
Top scorers:	Celso Ayala (1)
	Miguel Benitez (1)
	Jose Cardoso (1)
Highest attendance:	38,100 v France
Lowest attendance:	27,650 Bulgaria
Heaviest defeat:	0-1 v France
Biggest win:	3-1 v Nigeria
Final placing:	Second round loser
Red cards:	0
Yellow cards:	8

Norway

Games played:	4
Games won:	1
Games lost:	1
Games drawn:	2
Goals conceded:	5
Top scorers†:	Dan Eggen (1)
	Harvard Flo (1)
	Tore Andre Flo (1)
	Kjetil Rekdal (1)
Highest attendance:	55,500 v Brazil
Lowest attendance:	29,750 v Morocco
Heaviest defeat:	0-1 v Italy
Biggest win:	2-1 v Brazil
Final placing:	Second round loser
Red cards:	0
Yellow cards:	7

Romania

Games played:	4
Games won:	2
Games lost:	1
Games drawn:	1
Goals conceded:	3
Top scorer:	Viorel Moldovan (2)
Highest attendance:	80,000 v Tunisia
Lowest attendance:	31,800 v Croatia
Heaviest defeat:	0-1 v Croatia
Biggest win:	2-1 v England
Final placing:	Second round loser
Red cards:	0
Yellow cards:	10

† plus one own goal scored by Youssef Chippo (Morocco)

* games decided by penalty shoot-outs are classed as draws

World Cup finals 1998

Team statistics (continued)

Saudi Arabia

Games played:	3
Games won:	0
Games lost:	2
Games drawn:	1
Goals conceded:	7
Top scorers:	Sami Al-Jaber (1)
	Youssef Al-Thyniyan (1)
Highest attendance:	75,000 v France
Lowest attendance:	36,500 v South Africa
Heaviest defeat:	0-4 v France
Biggest win:	None
Final placing:	Fourth in Group C
Red cards:	1
Yellow cards:	3

South Africa

Games played:	3
Games won:	0
Games lost:	1
Games drawn:	2
Goals conceded:	6
Top scorer:	Shaun Bartlett (2)
Highest attendance:	55,077 v France
Lowest attendance:	36,500 v Saudi Arabia
Heaviest defeat:	0-3 v France
Biggest win:	None
Final placing:	Third in Group C
Red cards:	1
Yellow cards:	7

Scotland

Games played:	3
Games won:	0
Games lost:	2
Games drawn:	1
Goals conceded:	6
Top scorers:	John Collins (1)
	Craig Burley (1)
Highest attendance:	80,000 v Brazil
Lowest attendance:	30,236 v Norway
Heaviest defeat:	0-3 v Morocco
Biggest win:	None
Final placing:	Fourth in Group A
Red cards:	1
Yellow cards:	4

South Korea

Games played:	3
Games won:	0
Games lost:	2
Games drawn:	1
Goals conceded:	9
Top scorers:	Ha Seok-Ju (1)
	Yoo Sang-Chui (1)
Highest attendance:	60,000 v Netherlands
Lowest attendance:	37,588 v Mexico
Heaviest defeat:	0-5 v Netherlands
Biggest win:	None
Final placing:	Fourth in Group E
Red cards:	1
Yellow cards:	7

Spain

Games played:	3
Games won:	1
Games lost:	1
Games drawn:	1
Goals conceded:	4
Top scorers:	Fernando Hierro (2)
	Kiko Narvaez (2)
	Fernando Morientes (2)
Highest attendance:	40,500 v Bulgaria
Lowest attendance:	33,257 v Nigeria
Heaviest defeat:	2-3 V Nigeria
Biggest win:	6-1 v Bulgaria
Final placing:	Third in Group D
Red cards:	0
Yellow cards:	7

USA

Games played:	3
Games won:	0
Games lost:	3
Games drawn:	0
Goals conceded:	5
Top scorer:	Brian McBride (1)
Highest attendance:	44,000 v Iran
Lowest attendance:	39,000 v Yugoslavia
Heaviest defeat:	0-2 v Germany
Biggest win:	None
Final placing:	Fourth in Group F
Red cards:	0
Yellow cards:	4

Tunisia

Games played:	3
Games won:	0
Games lost:	2
Games drawn:	1
Goals conceded:	4
Top scorer:	Skander Souayah (1)
Highest attendance:	54,587 v England
Lowest attendance:	35,000 v Colombia
Heaviest defeat:	0-2 v England
Biggest win:	None
Final placing:	Fourth in Group G
Red cards:	0
Yellow cards:	7

Yugoslavia

Games played:	4
Games won:	2
Games lost:	1
Games drawn:	1
Goals conceded:	4
Top scorer:	Slobodan Komljenovic (2)
Highest attendance:	40,775 v Germany
Lowest attendance:	30,392 v Iran
Heaviest defeat:	1-2 v Netherlands
Biggest wins:	1-0 v USA
	1-0 v Iran
Final placing:	Second round loser
Red cards:	0
Yellow cards:	7

08/08/98
Nationwide Football
League Division 1
Barnsley v West Brom
Bradford v Stockport
Bristol City v Oxford Utd
Bury v Huddersfield
Crystal Palace v Bolton
Norwich v Crewe
Port Vale v Birmingham
Portsmouth v Watford
Sheff Utd v Swindon
Sunderland v QPR
Wolverhampton v Tranmere
Nationwide Football
League Division 2
Bournemouth v Lincoln City
Burnley v Bristol Rovers
Colchester v Chesterfield
Gillingham v Walsall
Macclesfield v Fulham
Man City v Blackpool
Northampton v Stoke
Oldham v Notts County
Preston v York
Wigan v Millwall
Wrexham v Reading
Wycombe v Luton
Nationwide Football
League Division 3
Brentford v Mansfield
Carlisle v Brighton
Chester v Leyton Orient
Darlington v Barnet
Hartlepool v Cardiff
Peterborough v Halifax
Plymouth v Rochdale
Rotherham v Hull
Scarborough v Southend
Shrewsbury v Scunthorpe
Swansea v Exeter
Torquay v Cambridge Utd

09/08/98
Nationwide Football
League Division 1
Grimsby v Ipswich

14/08/98
Nationwide Football
League Division 2
Fulham v Man City

15/08/98
FA Carling Premiership
Blackburn v Derby
Coventry v Chelsea
Everton v Aston Villa
Man Utd v Leicester
Middlesbrough v Leeds
Newcastle v Charlton
Sheff Wed v West Ham
Wimbledon v Tottenham
Nationwide Football
League Division 1
Bolton v Grimsby
Crewe v Barnsley
Huddersfield v Port Vale
Ipswich v Bury
Oxford Utd v
Wolverhampton
QPR v Bristol City
Stockport v Norwich
Swindon v Sunderland
Tranmere v Portsmouth
Watford v Bradford

West Brom v Sheff Utd
Nationwide Football
League Division 2
Blackpool v Oldham
Bristol Rovers v Reading
Chesterfield v Burnley
Lincoln City v Wigan
Luton v Preston
Millwall v Wycombe
Notts Co v Bournemouth
Stoke v Macclesfield
Walsall v Northampton
Wrexham v Colchester
York v Gillingham
Nationwide Football
League Division 3
Barnet v Hartlepool
Brighton v Chester
Cambridge Utd v Swansea
Cardiff v Peterborough
Exeter v Scarborough
Halifax v Brentford
Hull v Darlington
Leyton Orient v Rotherham
Mansfield v Plymouth
Rochdale v Torquay
Scunthorpe v Carlisle
Southend v Shrewsbury

16/08/98
FA Carling Premiership
Southampton v Liverpool
Nationwide Football
League Division 1
Birmingham v C Palace

17/08/98
FA Carling Premiership
Arsenal v Nottm Forest

21/08/98
Nationwide Football
League Division 1
Barnsley v Stockport
Nationwide Football
League Division 3
Shrewsbury v Cardiff

22/08/98
FA Carling Premiership
Charlton v Southampton
Chelsea v Newcastle
Derby v Wimbledon
Leicester v Everton
Liverpool v Arsenal
Nottm Forest v Coventry
Tottenham v Sheff Wed
West Ham v Man Utd
Nationwide Football
League Division 1
Bristol City v Watford
Bury v Crewe
Crystal Palace v Oxford
Grimsby v Huddersfield
Norwich v QPR
Port Vale v West Brom
Portsmouth v Ipswich
Sheff Utd v Birmingham
Sunderland v Tranmere
Wolverhampton v Swindon
Nationwide Football
League Division 2
Bournemouth v Millwall
Burnley v York
Colchester v Fulham
Gillingham v Bristol Rovers

Macclesfield v Lincoln City
Man City v Wrexham
Northampton v Notts Co
Oldham v Chesterfield
Preston v Stoke
Reading v Luton
Wigan v Blackpool
Wycombe v Walsall
Nationwide Football
League Division 3
Brentford v Brighton
Carlisle v Rochdale
Darlington v Halifax
Hartlepool v Scunthorpe
Peterborough v Southend
Plymouth v Cambridge
Rotherham v Cambridge
Scarborough v Mansfield
Swansea v Leyton Orient
Torquay v Exeter

23/08/98
FA Carling Premiership
Aston Villa v
Middlesbrough
Nationwide Football
League Division 1
Bradford v Bolton
Nationwide Football
League Division 3
Chester v Hull

24/08/98
FA Carling Premiership
Leeds v Blackburn

28/08/98
Nationwide Football
League Division 1
Crewe v Bradford
Watford v Wolverhampton
Nationwide Football
League Division 3
Halifax v Shrewsbury

29/08/98
FA Carling Premiership
Arsenal v Charlton
Blackburn v Leicester
Coventry v West Ham
Everton v Tottenham
Middlesbrough v Derby
Sheff Wed v Aston Villa
Southampton v Forest
Wimbledon v Leeds
Nationwide Football
League Division 1
Birmingham v Barnsley
Bolton v Sheff Utd
Huddersfield v Portsmouth
Ipswich v Sunderland
Oxford Utd v Grimsby
QPR v Bury
Stockport v Crystal Palace
Swindon v Port Vale
Tranmere v Bristol City
West Brom v Norwich
Nationwide Football
League Division 2
Blackpool v Gillingham
Bristol Rovers v Wigan
Chesterfield v Reading
Fulham v Bournemouth
Lincoln City v Preston
Luton v Colchester
Millwall v Macclesfield
Notts County v Man City
Stoke v Oldham
Walsall v Burnley
Wrexham v Northampton
York v Wycombe

Macclesfield v Lincoln City
Man City v Wrexham
Northampton v Notts Co
Oldham v Chesterfield
Preston v Stoke
Reading v Luton
Wigan v Blackpool
Wycombe v Walsall
Nationwide Football
League Division 3
Barnet v Brentford
Brighton v Torquay
Cambridge v Hartlepool
Cardiff v Rotherham
Exeter v Carlisle
Hull v Peterborough
Orient v Scarborough
Mansfield v Swansea
Rochdale v Darlington
Scunthorpe v Plymouth
Southend v Chester

30/08/98
FA Carling Premiership
Newcastle v Liverpool

31/08/98
Nationwide Football
League Division 1
Barnsley v Oxford Utd
Bradford v Birmingham
Bristol City v Huddersfield
Bury v Swindon
Crystal Palace v Tranmere
Grimsby v West Brom
Port Vale v Ipswich
Portsmouth v QPR
Sheff Utd v Crewe
Sunderland v Watford
Wolves v Stockport
Nationwide Football
League Division 2
Colchester v Stoke
Macclesfield v Notts Co
Northampton v Lincoln City
Preston v Chesterfield
Wigan v Luton
Wycombe v Bristol Rovers
Nationwide Football
League Division 3
Brentford v Rochdale
Darlington v Cardiff
Hartlepool v Hull
Peterborough v Exeter
Plymouth v Halifax
Rotherham v Mansfield
Scarborough v Brighton
Shrewsbury v Barnet
Swansea v Scunthorpe

01/09/98
Nationwide Football
League Division 1
Norwich v Bolton
Nationwide Football
League Division 2
Bournemouth v Blackpool
Burnley v Millwall
Gillingham v Wrexham
Oldham v Fulham
Nationwide Football
League Division 3
Carlisle v Southend
Chester v Cambridge Utd
Torquay v Leyton Orient

02/09/98
Nationwide Football
League Division 2
Man City v Walsall
Reading v York

04/09/98
Nationwide Football
League Division 1
Tranmere v Bradford
Nationwide Football
League Division 3
Halifax v Hartlepool

05/09/98
Nationwide Football
League Division 1
Birmingham v Bury
Bolton v Port Vale
Crewe v Sunderland
Huddersfield v Sheff Utd
Ipswich v Wolverhampton
QPR v Barnsley
Stockport v Grimsby
Swindon v Bristol City
Watford v Norwich
West Brom v C Palace
Nationwide Football
League Division 2
Blackpool v Northampton
Bristol Rovers v Preston
Chesterfield v Gillingham
Fulham v Wycombe
Lincoln City v Oldham
Luton v Burnley
Millwall v Man City
Notts County v Wigan
Stoke v Bournemouth
Walsall v Reading
Wrexham v Macclesfield
York v Colchester
Nationwide Football
League Division 3
Barnet v Peterborough
Brighton v Swansea
Cambridge v Scarborough
Cardiff v Plymouth
Exeter v Chester
Leyton Orient v Carlisle
Mansfield v Darlington
Rochdale v Shrewsbury
Scunthorpe v Torquay
Southend v Rotherham

06/09/98
Nationwide Football
League Division 1
Oxford Utd v Portsmouth

08/09/98
FA Carling Premiership
Leeds v Southampton
Nottm Forest v Everton
Nationwide Football
League Division 1
Barnsley v Norwich
Birmingham v Stockport
Bury v Portsmouth
Crewe v Crystal Palace
Huddersfield v Watford
Ipswich v Bradford
QPR v Tranmere
Sheff Utd v Grimsby
Sunderland v Bristol City
West Brom v Bolton
Nationwide Football
League Division 2
Blackpool v Notts County
Bristol R v Chesterfield
Fulham v Stoke
Gillingham v Northampton
Man City v Bournemouth
Oldham v Macclesfield
Walsall v York
Wigan v Colchester
Wrexham v Luton
Wycombe v Preston
Nationwide Football
League Division 3
Cardiff v Barnet
Carlisle v Swansea
Darlington v Hartlepool
Exeter v Brighton

Hull v Rochdale
Leyton Orient v Mansfield
Peterborough v Chester
Rotherham v Plymouth
Scunthorpe v Cambridge
Southend v Halifax
Torquay v Brentford

09/09/98
FA Carling Premiership
Aston Villa v Newcastle
Chelsea v Arsenal
Derby v Sheff Wed
Leicester v Middlesbrough
Liverpool v Coventry
Man Utd v Charlton
Tottenham v Blackburn
West Ham v Wimbledon
Nationwide Football
League Division 1
Swindon v Oxford Utd
Nationwide Football
League Division 2
Millwall v Lincoln City
Reading v Burnley
Nationwide Football
League Division 3
Scarborough v Shrewsbury

11/09/98
Nationwide Football
League Division 1
Tranmere v Huddersfield
Nationwide Football
League Division 3
Halifax v Cardiff

12/09/98
FA Carling Premiership
Aston Villa v Wimbledon
Charlton v Derby
Chelsea v Nottm Forest
Everton v Leeds
Leicester v Arsenal
Man Utd v Coventry
Newcastle v Southampton
Sheff Wed v Blackburn
West Ham v Liverpool
Nationwide Football
League Division 1
Bolton v Birmingham
Bradford v Sheff Utd
Bristol City v West Brom
Crystal Palace v Port Vale
Grimsby v Barnsley
Oxford Utd v Ipswich
Portsmouth v Swindon
Stockport v Crewe
Watford v QPR
Wolves v Sunderland
Nationwide Football
League Division 2
Bournemouth v Wigan
Burnley v Wycombe
Chesterfield v Walsall
Colchester v Gillingham
Lincoln City v Blackpool
Luton v Bristol Rovers
Macclesfield v Man City
Northampton v Oldham
Notts County v Fulham
Preston v Reading
Stoke v Millwall
York v Wrexham
Nationwide Football
League Division 3
Barnet v Hull
Brentford v Rotherham
Brighton v Southend
Cambridge v Orient
Chester v Torquay

Fixtures

Hartlepool v Exeter
Mansfield v Carlisle
Plymouth v Darlington
Rochdale v Scunthorpe
Shrewsbury v
Peterborough
Swansea v Scarborough

13/09/98
FA Carling Premiership
Tottenham v
Middlesbrough
Nationwide Football
League Division 1
Norwich v Bury

18/09/98
Nationwide Football
League Division 2
Walsall v Notts County

19/09/98
FA Carling Premiership
Coventry v Newcastle
Derby v Leicester
Leeds v Aston Villa
Liverpool v Charlton
Middlesbrough v Everton
Nottm Forest v West Ham
Southampton v Tottenham
Wimbledon v Sheff Wed
Nationwide Football
League Division 1
Barnsley v Crystal Palace
Birmingham v Grimsby
Bury v Tranmere
Crewe v Bolton
Huddersfield v
Wolverhampton
Ipswich v Bristol City
Port Vale v Portsmouth
QPR v Stockport
Sheff Utd v Norwich
Sunderland v Oxford Utd
Swindon v Watford
Nationwide Football
League Division 2
Blackpool v Luton
Bristol Rovers v
Lincoln City
Fulham v York
Gillingham v Burnley
Man City v Chesterfield
Millwall v Northampton
Oldham v Preston
Reading v Colchester
Wigan v Macclesfield
Wrexham v Stoke
Wycombe Wanderers v
Bournemouth
Nationwide Football
League Division 3
Cardiff v Rochdale
Carlisle v Chester
Darlington v Shrewsbury
Exeter v Barnet
Hull v Halifax
Leyton Orient v Brighton
Peterborough v Plymouth
Rotherham v Hartlepool
Scarborough v Brentford
Scunthorpe v Mansfield
Southend v Cambridge Utd
Torquay v Swansea

20/09/98
FA Carling Premiership
Arsenal v Man Utd
Nationwide Football
League Division 1
West Brom v Bradford

21/09/98
FA Carling Premiership
Blackburn v Chelsea

25/09/98
Nationwide Football
League Division 1
Tranmere v Swindon

26/09/98
FA Carling Premiership
Aston Villa v Derby
Charlton v Coventry
Chelsea v Middlesbrough
Everton v Blackburn
Man Utd v Liverpool
Newcastle v Nottm Forest
Sheff Wed v Arsenal
Tottenham v Leeds
Nationwide Football
League Division 1
Bolton v Huddersfield
Bradford v Barnsley
Bristol City v Crewe
Grimsby v Tranmere
Norwich v Birmingham
Oxford Utd v QPR
Portsmouth v Sunderland
Stockport v West Brom
Watford v Ipswich
Wolverhampton v Bury
Nationwide Football
League Division 2
Bournemouth v Oldham
Burnley v Wigan
Chesterfield v Wrexham
Colchester v Wycombe
Lincoln City v Fulham
Luton v Walsall
Macclesfield v Reading
Northampton v Man City
Notts County v Millwall
Preston v Gillingham
Stoke v Blackpool
York v Bristol Rovers
Nationwide Football
League Division 3
Barnet v Rotherham
Brentford v Darlington
Brighton v Scunthorpe
Cambridge v Exeter
Chester v Cardiff
Halifax v Torquay
Hartlepool v Peterborough
Mansfield v Hull
Plymouth v Scarborough
Rochdale v Leyton Orient
Shrewsbury v Carlisle
Swansea v Southend

27/09/98
FA Carling Premiership
Leicester v Wimbledon
Nationwide Football
League Division 1
Crystal Palace v Sheff Utd

28/09/98
FA Carling Premiership
West Ham v Southampton

29/09/98
Nationwide Football
League Division 1
Bolton v Swindon
Bradford v Port Vale
Bristol City v Barnsley
Grimsby v Crewe
Norwich v Sunderland
Oxford Utd v West Brom
Portsmouth v Birmingham

Stockport v Huddersfield
Tranmere v Ipswich
Watford v Sheff Utd
Wolverhampton v Queens
Park Rangers

30/09/98
Nationwide Football
League Division 1
Crystal Palace v Bury

03/10/98
FA Carling Premiership
Blackburn v West Ham
Coventry v Aston Villa
Derby v Tottenham
Leeds v Leicester
Middlesbrough v Sheff Wed
Nottm Forest v Charlton
Southampton v Man Utd
Wimbledon v Everton
Nationwide Football
League Division 1
Barnsley v Bolton
Birmingham v Tranmere
Bury v Bristol City
Crewe v Wolverhampton
Huddersfield v Oxford Utd
Ipswich v Crystal Palace
Port Vale v Norwich
QPR v Grimsby
Sheff Utd v Portsmouth
Sunderland v Bradford
Swindon v Stockport
Nationwide Football
League Division 2
Blackpool v York
Bristol R v Bournemouth
Fulham v Luton
Gillingham v Macclesfield
Man City v Burnley
Millwall v Chesterfield
Oldham v Colchester
Reading v Stoke
Walsall v Preston
Wigan v Northampton
Wrexham v Lincoln City
Wycombe v Notts County
Nationwide Football
League Division 3
Cardiff v Brighton & Hove
Albion
Carlisle v Barnet
Darlington v Swansea
Exeter v Mansfield
Hull v Cambridge Utd
Leyton Orient v Hartlepool
Peterborough v Brentford
Rotherham v Shrewsbury
Scarborough v Chester
Scunthorpe v Halifax
Southend United v
Rochdale
Torquay v Plymouth

04/10/98
FA Carling Premiership
Arsenal v Newcastle
Liverpool v Chelsea
Nationwide Football
League Division 1
West Bromwich Albion v
Watford

09/10/98
Nationwide Football
League Division 2
Colchester v Burnley
Nationwide Football
League Division 3
Mansfield v Torquay

10/10/98
Nationwide Football
League Division 1
Bradford v Bury
Bristol City v Portsmouth
Crewe v West Brom
Norwich v Grimsby
Oxford Utd v Tranmere
QPR v Ipswich
Stockport v Bolton
Sunderland v C Palace
Swindon v Huddersfield
Watford v Birmingham
Wolverhampton v Sheff Utd
Nationwide Football
League Division 2
Blackpool v Millwall
Fulham v Reading
Gillingham v Wycombe
Macclesfield v
Bournemouth
Man City v Preston
Northampton v Bristol R
Notts County v Lincoln City
Oldham v Wigan
Wrexham v Walsall
York v Luton
Nationwide Football
League Division 3
Barnet v Chester
Cambridge Utd v Brighton
Carlisle v Scarborough
Darlington v Peterborough
Hartlepool v Shrewsbury
Hull v Cardiff
Leyton Orient v Exeter
Plymouth v Mansfield
Rochdale v Halifax
Scunthorpe v Southend
Swansea v Rotherham

11/10/98
Nationwide Football
League Division 1
Barnsley v Port Vale

12/10/98
Nationwide Football
League Division 2
Stoke v Chesterfield

16/10/98
Nationwide Football
League Division 3
Halifax v Barnet

17/10/98
FA Carling Premiership
Arsenal v Southampton
Chelsea v Charlton
Everton v Liverpool
Man Utd v Wimbledon
Middlesbrough v Blackburn
Newcastle v Derby
Nottm Forest v Leeds
West Ham v Aston Villa
Nationwide Football
League Division 1
Birmingham City v Crewe
Alexandra
Bolton v Oxford Utd
Bury v Stockport
Crystal Palace v Norwich
Grimsby v Bradford
Huddersfield v QPR
Ipswich v Swindon
Port Vale v Bristol City
Portsmouth v
Wolverhampton Wanderers
Sheff Utd v Barnsley
Tranmere v Watford

Nationwide Football
League Division 2
Bournemouth v
Northampton
Bristol Rovers v Wrexham
Burnley v Notts County
Chesterfield v York
Lincoln City v Stoke
Luton v Oldham
Millwall v Fulham
Preston v Colchester
Reading v Gillingham
Walsall v Blackpool
Wigan v Man City
Wycombe v Macclesfield
Nationwide Football
League Division 3
Brentford v Hartlepool
Brighton v Mansfield
Cardiff v Cambridge Utd
Chester v Swansea
Exeter v Scunthorpe
Peterborough v Rochdale
Rotherham v Darlington
Scarborough v Hull
Shrewsbury v Plymouth
Southend v Leyton Orient
Torquay v Carlisle

18/10/98
FA Carling Premiership
Coventry v Sheff Wed
Nationwide Football
League Division 1
West Brom v Sunderland

19/10/98
FA Carling Premiership
Leicester v Tottenham

20/10/98
Nationwide Football
League Division 1
Birmingham v Swindon
Bolton v Watford
Bury v Oxford Utd
C Palace v Wolves
Grimsby v Bristol City
Ipswich v Norwich
Port Vale v Crewe
Portsmouth v Bradford
Sheff Utd v Stockport
County
Tranmere v Barnsley
Nationwide Football
League Division 2
Bournemouth v Gillingham
Bristol Rovers v Stoke
Burnley v Oldham
Chesterfield v Notts Co
Lincoln City v Man City
Luton v Northampton
Preston v Macclesfield
Walsall v Colchester
Wigan v Fulham
Wycombe Wanderers v
Wrexham
Nationwide Football
League Division 3
Brentford v Scunthorpe
Brighton & Hove Albion v
Plymouth
Cardiff v Leyton Orient
Chester v Hartlepool
Exeter v Hull
Halifax v Cambridge Utd
Peterborough v Carlisle
Rotherham v Rochdale
Shrewsbury v Swansea
Southend v Mansfield
Torquay v Darlington

21/10/98
Nationwide Football
League Division 1
Huddersfield v Sunderland
West Brom v QPR
Nationwide Football
League Division 2
Millwall v York
Reading v Blackpool
Nationwide Football
League Division 3
Scarborough v Barnet

23/10/98
Nationwide Football
League Division 1
Bristol City v Bolton

24/10/98
FA Carling Premiership
Aston Villa v Leicester
Charlton v West Ham
Derby v Man Utd
Liverpool v Nottm Forest
Sheff Wed v Everton
Southampton v Coventry
Tottenham v Newcastle
Wimbledon v
Middlesbrough
Nationwide Football
League Division 1
Barnsley v Portsmouth
Bradford v Crystal Palace
Crewe v Tranmere
Norwich v Huddersfield
Oxford Utd v Sheff Utd
Stockport v Ipswich
Sunderland v Bury
Swindon v West Brom
Watford v Port Vale
Wolverhampton v Grimsby
Nationwide Football
League Division 2
Blackpool v Chesterfield
Colchester v Bournemouth
Fulham v Walsall
Gillingham v Luton
Macclesfield v Burnley
Man City v Reading
Northampton v Preston
Notts County v Bristol R
Oldham v Wycombe
Stoke v Wigan
Wrexham v Millwall
York v Lincoln City
Nationwide Football
League Division 3
Barnet v Brighton
Cambridge v Shrewsbury
Carlisle v Cardiff
Darlington v Exeter
Hartlepool v Torquay
Hull v Rochdale
Leyton Orient v Halifax
Mansfield v Peterborough
Plymouth v Chester
Rochdale v Scarborough
Scunthorpe v Rotherham
Swansea v Brentford

25/10/98
FA Carling Premiership
Blackburn v Arsenal
Leeds v Chelsea
Nationwide Football
League Division 1
QPR v Birmingham

31/10/98
FA Carling Premiership
Chelsea v Aston Villa

Coventry v Arsenal
Derby v Leeds
Everton v Man Utd
Leicester v Liverpool
Newcastle v West Ham
Sheff Wed v Southampton
Wimbledon v Blackburn
Nationwide Football League Division 1
Birmingham v Huddersfield
Bradford v Bristol City
Bury v Watford
Grimsby v Crystal Palace
Ipswich v West Brom
Oxford Utd v Crewe
Port Vale v Sheff Utd
Portsmouth v Norwich
Swindon v QPR
Tranmere v Stockport
Wolverhampton v Barnsley
Nationwide Football League Division 2
Blackpool v Fulham
Bournemouth v Preston
Bristol Rovers v Walsall
Burnley v Wrexham
Lincoln City v Gillingham
Luton v Chesterfield
Macclesfield v Northampton
Man City v Colchester
Millwall v Oldham
Notts County v Stoke
Wigan v York
Wycombe v Reading
Nationwide Football League Division 3
Barnet v Rochdale
Brentford v Carlisle
Brighton v Hartlepool
Cardiff v Exeter
Chester v Shrewsbury
Halifax v Swansea
Leyton Orient v Scunthorpe
Mansfield v Cambridge Utd
Peterborough v Rotherham
Plymouth v Hull
Scarborough v Torquay
Southend v Darlington

01/11/98
FA Carling Premiership
Middlesbrough v Forest
Nationwide Football League Division 1
Bolton v Sunderland

02/11/98
FA Carling Premiership
Tottenham v Charlton

06/11/98
Nationwide Football League Division 2
Colchester v Macclesfield

07/11/98
FA Carling Premiership
Arsenal v Everton
Aston Villa v Tottenham
Blackburn v Coventry
Charlton v Leicester
Liverpool v Derby
Nottm Forest v Wimbledon
Southampton v
Middlesbrough
Nationwide Football League Division 1
Barnsley v Bury
Bristol City v Wolves
Crewe v Swindon

C Palace v Portsmouth
Huddersfield v Ipswich
Norwich v Bradford
QPR v Bolton
Sheff Utd v Tranmere
Sunderland v Grimsby
Watford v Oxford Utd
West Brom v Birmingham
Nationwide Football League Division 2
Chesterfield v Lincoln City
Fulham v Bristol Rovers
Gillingham v Wigan
Northampton v Wycombe Wanderers
Oldham v Man City
Preston v Burnley
Reading v Bournemouth
Stoke v Luton
Walsall v Millwall
Wrexham v Blackpool
York v Notts County
Nationwide Football League Division 3
Cambridge Utd v Barnet
Carlisle v Halifax
Darlington v Brighton
Exeter v Southend
Hartlepool v Plymouth
Hull v Leyton Orient
Rochdale v Mansfield
Rotherham v Scarborough
Scunthorpe v Chester
Shrewsbury v Brentford
Swansea v Peterborough
Torquay v Cardiff

08/11/98
FA Carling Premiership
Leeds v Sheff Wed
Man Utd v Newcastle
West Ham v Chelsea
Nationwide Football League Division 1
Stockport v Port Vale

10/11/98
Nationwide Football League Division 2
Bristol Rovers v Blackpool
Burnley v Stoke
Chesterfield v
Bournemouth
Colchester v Northampton
Gillingham v Oldham
Luton v Notts County
Preston v Millwall
Walsall v Lincoln City
Wrexham v Fulham
Wycombe Wanderers v
Man City
York v Macclesfield
Nationwide Football League Division 3
Barnet v Scunthorpe
Brentford v Southend
Cardiff v Scarborough
Darlington v Carlisle
Halifax v Chester
Hartlepool v Mansfield
Hull v Brighton
Peterborough v Cambridge
Plymouth v Swansea
Rochdale v Exeter
Rotherham v Torquay
Shrewsbury v Orient

11/11/98
Nationwide Football League Division 2
Reading v Wigan

14/11/98
FA Carling Premiership
Arsenal v Tottenham
Charlton v Middlesbrough
Chelsea v Wimbledon
Liverpool v Leeds
Man Utd v Blackburn
Newcastle v Sheff Wed
Southampton v Aston Villa
West Ham v Leicester
Nationwide Football League Division 1
Barnsley v Ipswich
Birmingham v Oxford Utd
Bolton v Tranmere
Bradford v Swindon
Crewe v QPR
C Palace v Bristol City
Grimsby v Portsmouth
Norwich v Wolverhampton
Port Vale v Sunderland
Sheff Utd v Bury
Stockport v Watford
West Brom v Huddersfield

15/11/98
FA Carling Premiership
Coventry v Everton

16/11/98
FA Carling Premiership
Nottm Forest v Derby

20/11/98
Nationwide Football League Division 3
Mansfield v Barnet

21/11/98
FA Carling Premiership
Aston Villa v Liverpool
Blackburn v Southampton
Leeds v Charlton
Leicester v Chelsea
Middlesbrough v Coventry
Sheff Wed v Man Utd
Tottenham v Nottm Forest
Wimbledon v Arsenal
Nationwide Football League Division 1
Bristol City v Stockport
Bury v Grimsby
Huddersfield v Bradford
Ipswich v Bolton
Oxford Utd v Port Vale
Portsmouth v West Brom
QPR v Sheff Utd
Sunderland v Barnsley
Swindon v Crystal Palace
Tranmere v Norwich
Watford v Crewe
Nationwide Football League Division 2
Blackpool v Preston
Bournemouth v Burnley
Fulham v Chesterfield
Lincoln City v Luton
Macclesfield v Walsall
Man City v Gillingham
Millwall v Bristol Rovers
Northampton v Reading
Notts County v Colchester
Oldham v Wrexham
Stoke v York
Wigan v Wycombe
Nationwide Football League Division 3
Brighton v Halifax
Cambridge v Darlington
Carlisle v Rotherham
Chester v Rochdale

Exeter v Shrewsbury
Leyton Orient v Brentford
Scarborough v Hartlepool
Scunthorpe v Hull
Southend v Plymouth
Torquay v Peterborough

22/11/98
FA Carling Premiership
Derby v West Ham
Nationwide Football League Division 1
Wolves v Birmingham
Nationwide Football League Division 3
Swansea v Cardiff

23/11/98
FA Carling Premiership
Everton v Newcastle

27/11/98
Nationwide Football League Division 1
Barnsley v Huddersfield
Nationwide Football League Division 3
Halifax v Mansfield

28/11/98
FA Carling Premiership
Charlton v Everton
Chelsea v Sheff Wed
Coventry v Leicester
Man Utd v Leeds
Newcastle v Wimbledon
Nottingham Forest v Aston Villa
Southampton v Derby
West Ham United v Tottenham
Nationwide Football League Division 1
Birmingham v Bristol City
Bolton v Bury
Bradford v QPR
Crewe v Ipswich
Crystal Palace v Watford
Grimsby v Swindon
Port Vale v Tranmere
Sheff Utd v Sunderland
Stockport v Portsmouth
Nationwide Football League Division 2
Bristol Rovers v Oldham
Burnley v Blackpool
Chesterfield v Macclesfield
Colchester v Millwall
Gillingham v Fulham
Luton v Man City
Preston v Wigan
Reading v Lincoln City
Walsall v Bournemouth
Wrexham v Notts County
Wycombe Wanderers v Stoke
York v Northampton
Nationwide Football League Division 3
Barnet v Torquay
Brentford v Chester
Cardiff v Southend
Darlington v Scarborough
Hartlepool v Swansea
Hull v Carlisle
Peterborough v Scunthorpe
Plymouth v Leyton Orient
Rochdale v Cambridge Utd
Rotherham v Exeter
Shrewsbury v Brighton

29/11/98
FA Carling Premiership
Arsenal v Middlesbrough
Liverpool v Blackburn
Nationwide Football League Division 1
Norwich v Oxford Utd
West Brom v Wolves

05/12/98
FA Carling Premiership
Aston Villa v Man Utd
Blackburn v Charlton
Derby v Arsenal
Everton v Chelsea
Leeds v West Ham
Leicester v Southampton
Tottenham v Liverpool
Wimbledon v Coventry
Nationwide Football League Division 1
Bristol City v Sheff Utd
Bury v West Brom
Huddersfield v C Palace
Ipswich v Birmingham
Oxford Utd v Bradford
Portsmouth v Crewe
QPR v Port Vale
Sunderland v Stockport
Swindon v Norwich
Tranmere v Grimsby
Watford v Barnsley
Wolverhampton v Bolton

06/12/98
FA Carling Premiership
Middlesbrough v
Newcastle

07/12/98
FA Carling Premiership
Sheff Wed v Nottm Forest

11/12/98
Nationwide Football League Division 1
Bury v Sheff Utd
Nationwide Football League Division 3
Brighton v Rotherham
Mansfield v Shrewsbury

12/12/98
FA Carling Premiership
Aston Villa v Arsenal
Blackburn v Newcastle
Derby v Chelsea
Everton v Southampton
Leicester v Nottm Forest
Middlesbrough v West Ham
Sheff Wed v Charlton
Tottenham v Man Utd
Nationwide Football League Division 1
Bristol City v C Palace
Huddersfield v West Brom
Ipswich v Barnsley
Oxford Utd v Birmingham
QPR v Crewe
Sunderland v Port Vale
Swindon v Bradford
Tranmere v Bolton
Watford v Stockport
Wolverhampton v Norwich
Nationwide Football League Division 2
Blackpool v Wycombe
Bournemouth v York
Fulham v Burnley
Lincoln City v Colchester
Macclesfield v Luton

Man City v Bristol Rovers
Millwall v Reading
Northampton v Chesterfield
Notts County v Preston
Oldham v Walsall
Stoke v Gillingham
Wigan v Wrexham
Nationwide Football League Division 3
Cambridge Utd v Plymouth
Carlisle v Hartlepool
Chester v Darlington
Exeter v Brentford
Orient v Peterborough
Scarborough v Halifax
Scunthorpe v Cardiff
Southend v Barnet
Swansea v Rochdale
Torquay v Hull

13/12/98
FA Carling Premiership
Wimbledon v Liverpool
Nationwide Football League Division 1
Portsmouth v Grimsby

14/12/98
FA Carling Premiership
Leeds v Coventry

16/12/98
FA Carling Premiership
Man Utd v Chelsea

18/12/98
Nationwide Football League Division 2
Bristol Rovers v Macclesfield
Colchester v Blackpool
Nationwide Football League Division 3
Rotherham v Chester
Shrewsbury v Torquay

19/12/98
FA Carling Premiership
Chelsea v Tottenham
Coventry v Derby
Liverpool v Sheff Wed
Man Utd v Middlesbrough
Newcastle v Leicester
Nottm Forest v Blackburn
Southampton v Wimbledon
West Ham v Everton
Nationwide Football League Division 1
Barnsley v Swindon
Birmingham v Sunderland
Bolton v Portsmouth
Bradford v Wolverhampton
Crewe v Huddersfield
Crystal Palace v QPR
Grimsby v Watford
Norwich v Bristol City
Port Vale v Bury
Stockport v Oxford Utd
West Brom v Tranmere
Nationwide Football League Division 2
Burnley v Northampton
Chesterfield v Wigan
Gillingham v Notts County
Luton v Millwall
Preston v Fulham
Reading v Oldham
Walsall v Stoke
Wrexham v Bournemouth
Wycombe v Lincoln City

Fixtures

York v Man City
Nationwide Football
League Division 3
Barnet v Leyton Orient
Brentford v Cambridge Utd
Cardiff v Mansfield
Darlington v Scunthorpe
Halifax v Exeter
Hartlepool v Southend
Hull v Swansea
Peterborough v
Scarborough
Plymouth v Carlisle
Rochdale v Brighton

20/12/98
FA Carling Premiership
Arsenal v Leeds
Nationwide Football
League Division 1
Sheff Utd v Ipswich

21/12/98
FA Carling Premiership
Charlton v Aston Villa

26/12/98
FA Carling Premiership
Arsenal v West Ham
Blackburn v Aston Villa
Coventry v Tottenham
Everton v Derby
Man Utd v Nottm Forest
Middlesbrough v Liverpool
Newcastle v Leeds
Sheff Wed v Leicester
Southampton v Chelsea
Wimbledon v Charlton
Nationwide Football
League Division 1
Birmingham v Sheff Utd
Bolton v Bradford
Crewe v Bury
Huddersfield v Grimsby
Ipswich v Portsmouth
Oxford Utd v C Palace
QPR v Norwich
Stockport v Barnsley
Swindon v Wolverhampton
Tranmere v Sunderland
Watford v Bristol City
West Brom v Port Vale
Nationwide Football
League Division 2
Blackpool v Wigan
Bristol Rovers v Gillingham
Chesterfield v Oldham
Fulham v Colchester
Lincoln City v Macclesfield
Luton v Reading
Millwall v Bournemouth
Notts Co v Northampton
Stoke v Preston
Walsall v Wycombe
Wrexham v Man City
York v Burnley
Nationwide Football
League Division 3
Barnet v Plymouth
Brighton v Brentford
Cambridge v Rotherham
Cardiff v Shrewsbury
Exeter v Torquay
Halifax v Darlington
Hull v Chester
Leyton Orient v Swansea
Mansfield v Scarborough
Rochdale v Carlisle
Scunthorpe v Hartlepool
Southend United v
Peterborough

28/12/98
FA Carling Premiership
Aston Villa v Sheff Wed
Charlton v Arsenal
Derby v Middlesbrough
Leicester v Blackburn
Liverpool v Newcastle
Forest v Southampton
Tottenham v Everton
West Ham v Coventry
Nationwide Football
League Division 1
Barnsley v QPR
Bradford v Tranmere
Bristol City v Swindon
Bury v Birmingham
C Palace v West Brom
Grimsby v Stockport
Port Vale v Bolton
Portsmouth v Oxford Utd
Sheff Utd v Huddersfield
Sunderland v Crewe
Wolverhampton v Ipswich
Nationwide Football
League Division 2
Bournemouth v Luton
Burnley v Lincoln City
Colchester v Bristol Rovers
Macclesfield v Blackpool
Man City v Stoke
Northampton v Fulham
Oldham v York
Preston v Wrexham
Reading v Notts County
Wigan v Walsall
Wycombe v Chesterfield
Nationwide Football
League Division 3
Brentford v Cardiff
Carlisle v Cambridge Utd
Chester v Mansfield
Darlington v Leyton Orient
Hartlepool v Rochdale
Peterborough v Brighton
Plymouth v Exeter
Rotherham v Halifax
Scarborough v Scunthorpe
Shrewsbury v Hull
Swansea v Barnet
Torquay v Southend

29/12/98
FA Carling Premiership
Chelsea v Man Utd
Leeds v Wimbledon
Nationwide Football
League Division 1
Norwich v Watford
Nationwide Football
League Division 2
Gillingham v Millwall

02/01/99
Nationwide Football
League Division 2
Bournemouth v Fulham
Burnley v Walsall
Colchester v Luton
Gillingham v Blackpool
Macclesfield v Millwall
Man City v Notts County
Northampton v Wrexham
Oldham v Stoke
Preston v Lincoln City
Reading v Chesterfield
Wigan v Bristol Rovers
Wycombe v York
Nationwide Football
League Division 3
Brentford v Barnet
Carlisle v Exeter

Chester v Southend
Darlington v Rochdale
Hartlepool v Cambridge
Peterborough v Hull
Plymouth v Scunthorpe
Rotherham v Cardiff
Scarborough v Orient
Shrewsbury v Halifax
Swansea v Mansfield
Torquay v Brighton

09/01/99
FA Carling Premiership
Arsenal v Liverpool
Blackburn v Leeds
Coventry v Nottm Forest
Everton v Leicester
Man Utd v West Ham
Middlesbrough v Aston
Villa
Newcastle v Chelsea
Sheff Wed v Tottenham
Southampton v Charlton
Wimbledon v Derby
Nationwide Football
League Division 1
Birmingham v Port Vale
Bolton v Crystal Palace
Crewe v Norwich
Huddersfield v Bury
Ipswich v Grimsby
Oxford Utd v Bristol City
QPR v Sunderland
Stockport v Bradford
Swindon v Sheff Utd
Tranmere v Wolverhampton
Watford v Portsmouth
West Brom v Barnsley
Nationwide Football
League Division 2
Blackpool v Man City
Bristol Rovers v Burnley
Chesterfield v Colchester
Fulham v Macclesfield
Lincoln City v Bournemouth
Luton v Wycombe
Millwall v Wigan
Notts County v Oldham
Reading v Wrexham
Stoke v Northampton
Walsall v Gillingham
York v Preston
Nationwide Football
League Division 3
Barnet v Darlington
Brighton v Carlisle
Cambridge Utd v Torquay
Cardiff v Hartlepool
Exeter v Swansea
Halifax v Peterborough
Hull v Rotherham
Leyton Orient v Chester
Mansfield v Brentford
Rochdale v Plymouth
Scunthorpe v Shrewsbury
Southend v Scarborough

15/01/99
Nationwide Football
League Division 2
Colchester v Wrexham

16/01/99
FA Carling Premiership
Aston Villa v Everton
Charlton v Newcastle
Chelsea v Wimbledon
Derby v Blackburn
Leeds v Middlesbrough
Leicester v Man Utd
Liverpool v Southampton

Nottm Forest v Arsenal
Tottenham v Wimbledon
West Ham v Sheff Wed
Nationwide Football
League Division 1
Barnsley v Birmingham
Bradford v Crewe
Bristol City v Tranmere
Bury v QPR
Crystal Palace v Stockport
Grimsby v Oxford Utd
Norwich v West Brom
Port Vale v Swindon
Portsmouth v Huddersfield
Sheff Utd v Bolton
Sunderland v Ipswich
Wolverhampton v Watford
Nationwide Football
League Division 2
Bournemouth v Notts Co
Burnley v Chesterfield
Gillingham v York
Macclesfield v Stoke
Man City v Fulham
Northampton v Walsall
Oldham v Blackpool
Preston v Luton
Reading v Bristol Rovers
Wigan v Lincoln City
Wycombe v Millwall
Nationwide Football
League Division 3
Brentford v Halifax
Carlisle v Scunthorpe
Chester v Brighton
Darlington v Hull
Hartlepool v Barnet
Peterborough v Cardiff
Plymouth v Mansfield
Rotherham v Leyton Orient
Scarborough v Exeter
Shrewsbury v Southend
Swansea v Cambridge Utd
Torquay v Rochdale

23/01/99
Nationwide Football
League Division 2
Blackpool v Bournemouth
Bristol Rovers v Wycombe
Chesterfield v Preston
Fulham v Oldham
Lincoln City v Northampton
Luton v Wigan
Millwall v Burnley
Notts Co v Macclesfield
Stoke v Colchester
Walsall v Man City
Wrexham v Gillingham
York v Reading
Nationwide Football
League Division 3
Barnet v Shrewsbury
Brighton v Scarborough
Cambridge Utd v Chester
Cardiff v Darlington
Exeter v Peterborough
Halifax v Plymouth
Hull v Hartlepool
Leyton Orient v Torquay
Mansfield v Rotherham
Rochdale v Brentford
Scunthorpe v Swansea
Southend v Carlisle

30/01/99
FA Carling Premiership
Arsenal v Chelsea
Blackburn v Tottenham
Charlton v Man Utd
Coventry v Liverpool

Everton v Nottm Forest
Middlesbrough v Leicester
Newcastle v Aston Villa
Sheff Wed v Derby
Southampton v Leeds
Wimbledon v West Ham
Nationwide Football
League Division 1
Birmingham v Bradford
Bolton v Norwich
Crewe v Sheff Utd
Huddersfield v Bristol City
Ipswich v Port Vale
Oxford Utd v Barnsley
QPR v Portsmouth
Stockport v Wolves
Swindon v Bury
Tranmere v Crystal Palace
Watford v Sunderland
West Brom v Grimsby
Nationwide Football
League Division 2
Blackpool v Macclesfield
Bristol Rovers v Colchester
Chesterfield v Wycombe
Fulham v Northampton
Lincoln City v Burnley
Luton v Bournemouth
Millwall v Gillingham
Notts County v Reading
Stoke v Man City
Walsall v Wigan
Wrexham v Preston
York v Oldham
Nationwide Football
League Division 3
Barnet v Swansea
Brighton v Peterborough
Cambridge Utd v Carlisle
Cardiff v Brentford
Exeter v Plymouth
Halifax v Rotherham
Hull v Shrewsbury
Leyton Orient v Darlington
Mansfield v Chester
Rochdale v Hartlepool
Scunthorpe v Scarborough
Southend v Torquay

05/02/99
Nationwide Football
League Division 2
Colchester v York
Nationwide Football
League Division 3
Swansea v Brighton

06/02/99
FA Carling Premiership
Aston Villa v Blackburn
Charlton v Wimbledon
Chelsea v Southampton
Derby v Everton
Leeds v Newcastle
Leicester v Sheff Wed
Liverpool v Middlesbrough
Nottm Forest v Man Utd
Tottenham v Coventry
West Ham v Arsenal
Nationwide Football
League Division 1
Barnsley v Crewe
Bradford v Watford
Bristol City v QPR
Bury v Ipswich
C Palace v Birmingham
Grimsby v Bolton
Norwich v Stockport
Port Vale v Huddersfield
Portsmouth v Tranmere
Sheff Utd v West Brom

Sunderland v Swindon
Wolverhampton v Oxford
Nationwide Football
League Division 2
Bournemouth v Stoke
Burnley v Luton
Gillingham v Chesterfield
Macclesfield v Wrexham
Man City v Millwall
Northampton v Blackpool
Oldham v Lincoln City
Preston v Bristol Rovers
Reading v Walsall
Wigan v Notts County
Wycombe v Fulham
Nationwide Football
League Division 3
Brentford v Hull
Carlisle v Leyton Orient
Chester v Exeter
Darlington v Mansfield
Hartlepool v Halifax
Peterborough v Barnet
Plymouth v Cardiff
Rotherham v Southend
Scarborough v Cambridge
Utd
Shrewsbury v Rochdale
Torquay v Scunthorpe

12/02/99
Nationwide Football
League Division 2
Colchester v Wigan

13/02/99
FA Carling Premiership
Aston Villa v Leeds
Charlton v Liverpool
Chelsea v Blackburn
Everton v Middlesbrough
Leicester v Derby
Man Utd v Arsenal
Newcastle v Coventry
Sheff Wed v Wimbledon
Tottenham v Southampton
West Ham v Nottm Forest
Nationwide Football
League Division 1
Bolton v West Brom
Bradford v Ipswich
Bristol City v Sunderland
Crystal Palace v Crewe
Grimsby v Sheff Utd
Norwich v Barnsley
Oxford Utd v Swindon
Portsmouth v Bury
Stockport v Birmingham
Tranmere v QPR
Watford v Huddersfield
Wolverhampton v Port Vale
Nationwide Football
League Division 2
Bournemouth v Man City
Burnley v Reading
Chesterfield v Bristol R
Lincoln City v Millwall
Luton v Wrexham
Macclesfield v Oldham
Northampton v Gillingham
Notts County v Blackpool
Preston v Wycombe
Stoke v Fulham
York v Walsall
Nationwide Football
League Division 3
Barnet v Cardiff
Brentford v Torquay
Brighton v Exeter
Cambridge v Scunthorpe
Chester v Peterborough

Fixtures 1998 | 99

Halifax v Southend
Hartlepool v Darlington
Mansfield v Leyton Orient
Plymouth v Rotherham
Rochdale v Hull
Shrewsbury v Scarborough
Swansea v Carlisle

20/02/99
FA Carling Premiership
Arsenal v Leicester
Blackburn v Sheff Wed
Coventry v Man Utd
Derby v Charlton
Leeds v Everton
Liverpool v West Ham
Middlesbrough v
Tottenham
Nottm Forest v Chelsea
Southampton v Newcastle
Wimbledon v Aston Villa
**Nationwide Football
League Division 1**
Barnsley v Grimsby
Birmingham v Bolton
Bury v Norwich
Crewe v Stockport
Huddersfield v Tranmere
Ipswich v Oxford Utd
Port Vale v Crystal Palace
QPR v Watford
Sheff Utd v Bradford
Sunderland v Wolves
Swindon v Portsmouth
West Brom v Bristol City
**Nationwide Football
League Division 2**
Blackpool v Lincoln City
Bristol Rovers v Luton
Fulham v Notts County
Gillingham v Colchester
Man City v Macclesfield
Millwall v Stoke
Oldham v Northampton
Reading v Preston
Walsall v Chesterfield
Wigan v Bournemouth
Wrexham v York
Wycombe v Burnley
**Nationwide Football
League Division 3**
Cardiff v Halifax
Carlisle v Mansfield
Darlington v Plymouth
Exeter v Hartlepool
Hull v Barnet
Leyton Orient v Cambridge
Peterborough v
Shrewsbury
Rotherham v Brentford
Scarborough v Swansea
Scunthorpe v Rochdale
Southend v Brighton
Torquay v Chester

27/02/99
FA Carling Premiership
Aston Villa v Coventry
Charlton v Nottm Forest
Chelsea v Liverpool
Everton v Wimbledon
Leicester v Leeds
Man Utd v Southampton
Newcastle v Arsenal
Sheff Wed v Middlesbrough
Tottenham v Derby
West Ham v Blackburn
**Nationwide Football
League Division 1**
Bolton v Crewe
Bradford v West Brom

Bristol City v Ipswich
Crystal Palace v Barnsley
Grimsby v Birmingham
Norwich v Sheff Utd
Oxford Utd v Sunderland
Portsmouth v Port Vale
Stockport v QPR
Tranmere v Bury
Watford v Swindon
Wolves v Huddersfield
**Nationwide Football
League Division 2**
Bournemouth v Wycombe
Burnley v Gillingham
Chesterfield v Man City
Colchester v Reading
Lincoln City v Bristol R
Luton v Blackpool
Macclesfield v Wigan
Northampton v Millwall
Notts County v Walsall
Preston v Oldham
Stoke v Wrexham
York v Fulham
**Nationwide Football
League Division 3**
Barnet v Exeter
Brentford v Scarborough
Brighton v Leyton Orient
Cambridge Utd v Southend
Chester v Carlisle
Halifax v Hull
Hartlepool v Rotherham
Mansfield v Scunthorpe
Plymouth v Peterborough
Rochdale v Cardiff
Shrewsbury v Darlington
Swansea v Torquay

02/03/99
**Nationwide Football
League Division 1**
Barnsley v Bradford
Birmingham v Norwich
Bury v Wolverhampton
Crewe v Bristol City
Huddersfield v Bolton
Ipswich v Watford
Port Vale v Grimsby
Sheff Utd v Crystal Palace
Sunderland v Portsmouth
West Brom v Stockport

03/03/99
**Nationwide Football
League Division 1**
QPR v Oxford Utd
Swindon v Tranmere

06/03/99
FA Carling Premiership
Arsenal v Sheff Wed
Blackburn v Everton
Coventry v Charlton
Derby v Aston Villa
Leeds v Tottenham
Liverpool v Man Utd
Middlesbrough v Chelsea
Nottm Forest v Newcastle
Southampton v West Ham
Wimbledon v Leicester
**Nationwide Football
League Division 1**
Barnsley v Bristol City
Birmingham v Portsmouth
Bury v Crystal Palace
Crewe v Grimsby
Huddersfield v Stockport
Ipswich v Tranmere
Port Vale v Bradford
QPR v Wolverhampton

Sheff Utd v Watford
Sunderland v Norwich
Swindon v Bolton
West Brom v Oxford Utd
**Nationwide Football
League Division 2**
Blackpool v Stoke
Bristol Rovers v Barnsley
Fulham v Lincoln City
Gillingham v Preston
Man City v Wycombe
Millwall v Notts County
Oldham v Bournemouth
Reading v Macclesfield
Walsall v Luton
Wigan v Burnley
Wrexham v Chesterfield
Wycombe v Colchester
**Nationwide Football
League Division 3**
Cardiff v Chester
Carlisle v Shrewsbury
Darlington v Brentford
Exeter v Cambridge Utd
Hull v Mansfield
Leyton Orient v Rochdale
Peterborough v Hartlepool
Rotherham v Barnet
Scarborough v Plymouth
Scunthorpe v Brighton
Southend v Swansea
Torquay v Halifax

09/03/99
**Nationwide Football
League Division 1**
Bolton v Barnsley
Bradford v Sunderland
Bristol City v Bury
Crystal Palace v Ipswich
Grimsby v QPR
Norwich v Port Vale
Oxford Utd v Huddersfield
Portsmouth v Sheff Utd
Stockport v Swindon
Tranmere v Birmingham
Watford v West Brom
Wolverhampton Wanderers
v Crewe
**Nationwide Football
League Division 2**
Bournemouth v Bristol R
Burnley v Man City
Chesterfield v Millwall
Colchester v Oldham
Lincoln City v Wrexham
Luton v Fulham
Macclesfield v Gillingham
Northampton v Wigan
Notts County v Wycombe
Wanderers
Preston v Walsall
York v Blackpool
**Nationwide Football
League Division 3**
Barnet v Carlisle
Brentford v Peterborough
Cambridge Utd v Hull
Chester v Scarborough
Halifax v Scunthorpe
Hartlepool v Leyton Orient
Mansfield v Exeter
Plymouth v Torquay
Rochdale v Southend
Shrewsbury v Rotherham
Swansea v Darlington

10/03/99
**Nationwide Football
League Division 2**
Stoke v Reading

**Nationwide Football
League Division 3**
Brighton v Cardiff

12/03/99
**Nationwide Football
League Division 2**
Bristol Rovers v Fulham

13/03/99
FA Carling Premiership
Chelsea v West Ham
Coventry v Blackburn
Derby v Liverpool
Everton v Arsenal
Leicester v Charlton
Middlesbrough v
Southampton
Newcastle v Man Utd
Sheff Wed v Leeds
Tottenham v Aston Villa
Wimbledon v Nottm Forest
**Nationwide Football
League Division 1**
Birmingham v West Brom
Bolton v QPR
Bradford v Norwich
Bury v Barnsley
Grimsby v Sunderland
Ipswich v Huddersfield
Oxford Utd v Watford
Port Vale v Stockport
Portsmouth v C Palace
Swindon v Crewe
Tranmere v Sheff Utd
Wolves v Bristol City
**Nationwide Football
League Division 2**
Blackpool v Wrexham
Bournemouth v Reading
Burnley v Preston
Lincoln City v Chesterfield
Luton v Stoke
Macclesfield v Colchester
Man City v Oldham
Millwall v Walsall
Notts County v York
Wigan v Gillingham
Wycombe v Northampton
**Nationwide Football
League Division 3**
Barnet v Cambridge Utd
Brentford v Shrewsbury
Brighton v Darlington
Cardiff v Torquay
Chester v Scunthorpe
Halifax v Carlisle
Leyton Orient v Hull
Mansfield v Rochdale
Peterborough v Swansea
Plymouth v Hartlepool
Scarborough v Rotherham
Southend v Exeter

20/03/99
FA Carling Premiership
Arsenal v Coventry
Aston Villa v Chelsea
Blackburn v Wimbledon
Charlton v Tottenham
Leeds v Derby
Liverpool v Leicester
Man Utd v Everton
Forest v Middlesbrough
Southampton v Sheff Wed
West Ham v Newcastle
**Nationwide Football
League Division 3**
Barnsley v Wolverhampton
Bristol City v Bradford
Crewe v Oxford Utd

Crystal Palace v Grimsby
Huddersfield v Birmingham
Norwich v Portsmouth
QPR v Swindon
Sheff Utd v Port Vale
Stockport v Tranmere
Sunderland v Bolton
Watford v Bury
West Brom v Ipswich
**Nationwide Football
League Division 2**
Chesterfield v Luton
Colchester v Man City
Fulham v Blackpool
Gillingham v Lincoln City
Northampton v
Macclesfield
Oldham v Millwall
Preston v Bournemouth
Reading v Wycombe
Stoke v Notts County
Walsall v Bristol Rovers
Wrexham v Burnley
York v Wigan
**Nationwide Football
League Division 3**
Cambridge Utd v Mansfield
Carlisle v Brentford
Darlington v Southend
Exeter v Cardiff
Hartlepool v Brighton
Hull v Plymouth
Rochdale v Barnet
Rotherham v Peterborough
Scunthorpe v Leyton Orient
Shrewsbury v Chester
Swansea v Halifax
Torquay v Scarborough

26/03/99
**Nationwide Football
League Division 3**
Halifax v Leyton Orient

27/03/99
**Nationwide Football
League Division 1**
Birmingham v QPR
Bolton v Bristol City
Bury v Sunderland
Crystal Palace v Bradford
Grimsby v Wolverhampton
Huddersfield v Norwich
Ipswich v Stockport
Port Vale v Watford
Portsmouth v Barnsley
Sheff Utd v Oxford Utd
Tranmere v Crewe
West Brom v Swindon
**Nationwide Football
League Division 2**
Bournemouth v Colchester
Bristol Rovers v Notts Co
Burnley v Macclesfield
Chesterfield v Blackpool
Lincoln City v York
Luton v Gillingham
Millwall v Wrexham
Preston v Northampton
Reading v Man City
Walsall v Fulham
Wigan v Stoke
Wycombe v Oldham
**Nationwide Football
League Division 3**
Brentford v Swansea
Brighton v Barnet
Cardiff v Carlisle
Chester v Plymouth
Exeter v Darlington
Peterborough v Mansfield

Rotherham v Scunthorpe
Scarborough v Rochdale
Shrewsbury v Cambridge
Southend v Hull
Torquay v Hartlepool

02/04/99
**Nationwide Football
League Division 2**
Colchester v Preston
Northampton v
Bournemouth
Oldham v Luton

03/04/99
FA Carling Premiership
Aston Villa v West Ham
Blackburn v Middlesbrough
Charlton v Chelsea
Derby v Newcastle
Leeds v Nottm Forest
Liverpool v Everton
Sheff Wed v Coventry
Southampton v Arsenal
Tottenham v Leicester
Wimbledon v Man Utd
**Nationwide Football
League Division 1**
Barnsley v Sheff Utd
Bradford v Grimsby
Bristol City v Port Vale
Crewe v Birmingham
Norwich v Crystal Palace
Oxford Utd v Bolton
QPR v Huddersfield
Stockport v Bury
Sunderland v West Brom
Swindon v Ipswich
Watford v Tranmere
Wolves v Portsmouth
**Nationwide Football
League Division 2**
Blackpool v Walsall
Fulham v Millwall
Gillingham v Reading
Macclesfield v Wycombe
Man City v Wigan
Notts County v Burnley
Stoke v Lincoln City
Wrexham v Bristol Rovers
York v Chesterfield
**Nationwide Football
League Division 3**
Barnet v Halifax
Cambridge Utd v Cardiff
Carlisle v Torquay
Darlington v Rotherham
Hartlepool v Brentford
Hull v Scarborough
Leyton Orient v Southend
Mansfield v Brighton
Plymouth v Shrewsbury
Rochdale v Peterborough
Scunthorpe v Exeter
Swansea v Chester

05/04/99
FA Carling Premiership
Chelsea v Leeds
Coventry v Southampton
Everton v Sheff Wed
Man Utd v Derby
Middlesbrough v
Wimbledon
Newcastle v Tottenham
Nottm Forest v Liverpool
West Ham v Charlton
**Nationwide Football
League Division 1**
Birmingham v Watford
Bolton v Stockport

Bury v Bradford
C Palace v Sunderland
Grimsby v Norwich
Huddersfield v Swindon
Ipswich v QPR
Port Vale v Barnsley
Portsmouth v Bristol City
Sheff Utd v Wolverhampton
Tranmere v Oxford Utd
West Brom v Crewe

**Nationwide Football
League Division 2**
Bristol R v Northampton
Burnley v Colchester
Chesterfield v Stoke
Lincoln City v Notts County
Millwall v Blackpool
Preston v Man City
Reading v Fulham
Wigan v Oldham
Wycombe Wanderers v Gillingham

**Nationwide Football
League Division 3**
Brentford v Plymouth
Cardiff v Hull
Chester v Barnet
Exeter v Leyton Orient
Halifax v Rochdale
Peterborough v Darlington
Rotherham v Swansea
Scarborough v Carlisle
Shrewsbury v Hartlepool
Southend v Scunthorpe
Torquay v Mansfield

06/04/99
FA Carling Premiership
Arsenal v Blackburn
Leicester v Aston Villa
**Nationwide Football
League Division 2**
Bournemouth v Macclesfield
Luton v York
Walsall v Wrexham
**Nationwide Football
League Division 3**
Brighton v Cambridge Utd

09/04/99
**Nationwide Football
League Division 3**
Swansea v Shrewsbury

10/04/99
FA Carling Premiership
Aston Villa v Southampton
Blackburn v Man Utd
Derby v Nottm Forest
Leeds v Liverpool
Leicester v West Ham
Middlesbrough v Charlton
Sheff Wed v Newcastle
Tottenham v Arsenal
Wimbledon v Chelsea
**Nationwide Football
League Division 1**
Barnsley v Tranmere
Bradford v Portsmouth
Bristol City v Grimsby
Crewe v Port Vale
Norwich v Ipswich
Oxford Utd v Bury
QPR v West Brom
Stockport v Sheff Utd
Sunderland v Huddersfield
Swindon v Birmingham
Watford v Bolton
Wolverhampton Wanderers v Crystal Palace

**Nationwide Football
League Division 2**
Blackpool v Reading
Colchester v Walsall
Fulham v Wigan
Gillingham v Bournemouth
Macclesfield v Preston
Man City v Lincoln City
Northampton v Luton
Notts Co v Chesterfield
Oldham v Burnley
Stoke v Bristol Rovers
Wrexham v Wycombe
York v Millwall
**Nationwide Football
League Division 3**
Barnet v Scarborough
Cambridge Utd v Halifax
Carlisle v Peterborough
Darlington v Torquay
Hartlepool v Chester
Hull v Exeter
Leyton Orient v Cardiff
Mansfield v Southend
Plymouth v Brighton
Rochdale v Rotherham
Scunthorpe v Brentford

11/04/99
FA Carling Premiership
Everton v Coventry

13/04/99
**Nationwide Football
League Division 2**
Blackpool v Burnley
Bournemouth v Walsall
Fulham v Gillingham
Lincoln City v Reading
Macclesfield v Chesterfield
Northampton v York
Notts County v Wrexham
Oldham v Bristol Rovers
Wigan v Preston
**Nationwide Football
League Division 3**
Brighton v Shrewsbury
Cambridge Utd v Rochdale
Carlisle v Hull
Chester v Brentford
Exeter v Rotherham
Leyton Orient v Plymouth
Mansfield v Halifax
Scunthorpe v Peterborough
Southend v Cardiff
Swansea v Hartlepool
Torquay v Barnet

14/04/99
**Nationwide Football
League Division 2**
Man City v Luton
Millwall v Colchester
Stoke v Wycombe
**Nationwide Football
League Division 3**
Scarborough v Darlington

16/04/99
**Nationwide Football
League Division 2**
Colchester v Notts County

17/04/99
FA Carling Premiership
Arsenal v Wimbledon
Charlton v Leeds
Chelsea v Leicester
Coventry v Middlesbrough
Liverpool v Aston Villa

Man Utd v Sheff Wed
Newcastle v Everton
Nottm Forest v Tottenham
Southampton v Blackburn
West Ham v Derby
**Nationwide Football
League Division 1**
Barnsley v Sunderland
Birmingham v Wolves
Bolton v Ipswich
Bradford v Huddersfield
Crewe v Watford
Crystal Palace v Swindon
Grimsby v Bury
Norwich v Tranmere
Port Vale v Oxford Utd
Sheff Utd v QPR
Stockport v Bristol City
West Brom v Portsmouth
**Nationwide Football
League Division 2**
Bristol Rovers v Millwall
Burnley v Bournemouth
Chesterfield v Fulham
Gillingham v Man City
Luton v Lincoln City
Preston v Blackpool
Reading v Northampton
Walsall v Macclesfield
Wrexham v Oldham
Wycombe v Wigan
York v Stoke
**Nationwide Football
League Division 3**
Barnet v Mansfield
Brentford v Leyton Orient
Darlington v Cambridge
Halifax v Brighton
Hartlepool v Scarborough
Hull v Scunthorpe
Peterborough v Torquay
Plymouth v Southend
Rochdale v Chester
Rotherham v Carlisle
Shrewsbury v Exeter

18/04/99
**Nationwide Football
League Division 3**
Cardiff v Swansea

24/04/99
FA Carling Premiership
Aston Villa v Nottm Forest
Blackburn v Liverpool
Derby v Southampton
Everton v Charlton
Leeds v Man Utd
Leicester v Coventry
Middlesbrough v Arsenal
Sheff Wed v Chelsea
Tottenham v West Ham
Wimbledon v Newcastle
**Nationwide Football
League Division 1**
Bristol City v Birmingham
Bury v Bolton
Huddersfield v Barnsley
Ipswich v Crewe
Oxford Utd v Norwich
Portsmouth v Stockport
QPR v Bradford
Sunderland v Sheff Utd
Swindon v Grimsby
Tranmere v Port Vale
Watford v Crystal Palace
**Nationwide Football
League Division 2**
Blackpool v Bristol Rovers
Bournemouth v Chesterfield

Fulham v Wrexham
Lincoln City v Walsall
Macclesfield v York
Man City v Wycombe
Millwall v Preston
Northampton v Colchester
Notts County v Luton
Oldham v Gillingham
Stoke v Burnley
Wigan v Reading
**Nationwide Football
League Division 3**
Brighton v Hull
Cambridge v Peterborough
Carlisle v Darlington
Chester v Halifax
Exeter v Rochdale
Orient v Shrewsbury
Mansfield v Hartlepool
Scarborough v Cardiff
Scunthorpe v Barnet
Southend v Brentford
Swansea v Plymouth
Torquay v Rotherham

25/04/99
**Nationwide Football
League Division 1**
Wolves v West Brom

01/05/99
FA Carling Premiership
Arsenal v Derby
Charlton v Blackburn
Chelsea v Everton
Coventry v Wimbledon
Liverpool v Tottenham
Man Utd v Aston Villa
Newcastle v Middlesbrough
Nottm Forest v Sheff Wed
Southampton v Leicester
West Ham v Leeds
**Nationwide Football
League Division 1**
Barnsley v Watford
Birmingham v Ipswich
Bolton v Wolverhampton
Bradford v Oxford Utd
Crewe v Portsmouth
C Palace v Huddersfield
Grimsby v Tranmere
Norwich v Swindon
Port Vale v QPR
Sheff Utd v Bristol City
Stockport v Sunderland
West Brom v Bury
**Nationwide Football
League Division 2**
Bristol Rovers v Man City
Burnley v Fulham
Chesterfield v Northampton
Colchester v Lincoln City
Gillingham v Stoke
Luton v Macclesfield
Preston v Notts County
Reading v Millwall
Walsall v Oldham
Wrexham v Wigan
Wycombe v Blackpool
York v Bournemouth
**Nationwide Football
League Division 3**
Barnet v Southend
Brentford v Exeter
Cardiff v Scunthorpe
Darlington v Chester
Halifax v Scarborough
Hartlepool v Carlisle
Hull v Torquay

Peterborough v Orient
Plymouth v Cambridge Utd
Rochdale v Swansea
Rotherham v Brighton
Shrewsbury v Mansfield

08/05/99
FA Carling Premiership
Aston Villa v Charlton
Blackburn v Nottm Forest
Derby v Coventry
Everton v West Ham
Leeds v Arsenal
Leicester v Newcastle
Middlesbrough v Man Utd
Sheff Wed v Liverpool
Tottenham v Chelsea
Wimbledon v Southampton
**Nationwide Football
League Division 2**
Blackpool v Colchester
Bournemouth v Wrexham
Fulham v Preston
Lincoln City v Wycombe
Macclesfield v Bristol R
Man City v York
Millwall v Luton
Northampton v Burnley
Notts County v Gillingham
Oldham v Reading
Stoke v Walsall
Wigan v Chesterfield
**Nationwide Football
League Division 3**
Brighton v Rochdale
Cambridge Utd v Brentford
Carlisle v Plymouth
Chester v Rotherham
Exeter v Halifax
Leyton Orient v Barnet
Mansfield v Cardiff
Scarborough v Peterborough
Scunthorpe v Darlington
Southend v Hartlepool
Swansea v Hull
Torquay v Shrewsbury

09/05/99
**Nationwide Football
League Division 1**
Bristol City v Norwich
Bury v Port Vale
Huddersfield v Crewe
Ipswich v Sheff Utd
Oxford Utd v Stockport
Portsmouth v Bolton
QPR v Crystal Palace
Sunderland v Birmingham
Swindon v Barnsley
Tranmere v West Brom
Watford v Grimsby
Wolverhampton v Bradford

16/05/99
FA Carling Premiership
Arsenal v Aston Villa
Charlton v Sheff Wed
Chelsea v Derby
Coventry v Leeds
Liverpool v Wimbledon
Man Utd v Tottenham
Newcastle v Blackburn
Nottm Forest v Leicester
Southampton v Everton
West Ham v Middlesbrough

Index

Index

Index

Acknowledgements

Pictures

Placement Key: t=top; b=bottom; tl=top left; tc=top centre; tr=top right; cal=centre above left; cac= centre above centre; car= centre above right; cl= centre left; c = centre; cr= centre right; centre below left = cbl; cbc=centre below centre; cbr=centre below right; bl= bottom left; bc= bottom centre; br= bottom right.

The publishers would like to thank the following individuals, companies, and picture libraries for their kind permission to reproduce their photographs. Special thanks to Colin Pantor at Empics, George Impey and Claire Sullivan at Action Images and Lorna Machray at PA News.

Abbott, Mead & Vickers: Snickers 115; **Aberdeen FC:** 294; **Action Images:** 9tc/tr/cl/c/cbr/bl, 10t/b, 11b, 15t, 18t, 19t , 20t/b, 21t, 22t, 23t/b, 27t, 44t, 46b, 60t/b,61,71, 76t, 81, 84t, 87, 90t, 94b, 96t, 109, 112t/b, 113, 114t/b, 116b, 124b, 127, 130b, 141, 162, 165t, 182, 183t/c, 184, 187t,191t/c, 196, 197t/c, 202, 203c, 209t/c/b, 211c/b, 217t, 219c, 219b, 221t/c, 223t/c/b, 225t/c/b, 227t, 228, 229t/c, 231t/c/b, 233t/c, 235t, 237t, 239t, 244, 245t/c; Chris Barry 186; Lee Beskeen 191b; Andy Couldridge 159b; Stuart Franklin 42b, 323; Brandon Malone 35b, 58t, 84b, 95; Tony Marshall 66; Alex Morton 94t, 155tr/c/bl, 326, 331; Nick Potts 58b; John Sibley 4br, 26t , 31cac/cbl/br, 55, 103, 150t, 152t, 164, 239c; Darren Walsh 5bl, 9tl/car/cbc, 14t, 25b, 31cal/cr/bc, 152b, 153; Aubrey Washington 185t; **Adidas/Hill & Knowlton:** 102b; **Allsport:** 3bc, 77, 161c, 176, 335cac/cbl/bc, 345, 348b, 349, 366b; Ben Arnold 171t; Shaun Botterill 13b, 50t, 137t, 169b, 177t, 181t/c; Clive Brunskill: 25t, 121, 129, 137b , 169c, 355; Simon Bruty 80t, 96b; David Cannon 5bl, 126b, 335t/ car/ cbc, 352, 353b; Chris Cole 78t, 120t; Phil Cole 163t/c, 171b, 189t, 195c, 213b, 227b; Stu Forester 42t,89,159t/c, 161t 169t, 171c, 185b 203b; John Gichigi 151,218; Laurence Griffiths 33, 80b; Mike Hewitt 171t, 195b; Hulton Deutsch 335tr/c/cal/cr/bc/bl, 336t/b, 344t, 350t, 351, 357, 358b, 360b, 361; Brian Kidd 136b; Ross Kinnaird 35t, 40t, 45, 50b; Michael King 344t; David Leah 340t; Alex Livesey 3br,155tl/car/cbc, 158, 193t; David Mannon 344b; MSI 343, 367; Steve Powell 341; Craig Prentis 183b; Gary M Prior 9cal/cbl/ br,12b, 67, 171b, 179t/b, 180,195t; Tony Quinn 140b; Ben Radford 49, 167t, 185c, 190,193b, 197b; Dave Rogers 197c; Mark Thompson 174,175t/b/c, 181b, 199c, 203t; Aubrey Washington 140t; **AP Photo:** 133, 321; Adil Bradlow 133, 146t; Jacques Brinon 328; Luca Bruno 9cr/cal/bc, 13t; Jacques Collet 70; Mohamed El-Dakhakny 125; Diether Endlicher 68; Luisa Ferreira 318; Armando Franca 329; David Guttendelder 147; Gerrit de Heus 330; Misha Japaridze 65; Shizuo Kambayashi 144t; Thomas Kienzle 333; Carlos Lares 143; Michael Lipchitz 324; Francois Mori 43b, Max Nash 19b; Srdjan Petrovic 119; Laurent Rebours 16b, 44b, 88b; Mohammad Sayyad 15b, 149t; Jason South 148b/149b; Tomas Turek/CTK 74; Yonhap 31tl/car/cbc, 122b, 145; Vincent Yu 144b; Dusan Vranic 332; Carlo Wrede 142t; **BSkyB:** 104-5; Sam Teare 7, 104t; **Barnet FC:** 270; **Barnsley FC:** 198; **Raymond Besant:** 295t, 307t/c; **Birmingham City FC:** Roy Smiljanic: 196; **Blackpool FC:** Phil Heywood 246; **Bournemouth FC:** Sporting Media/Mike Cunningham:247; **Brentford FC:** 271; **Brighton & Hove Albion FC:** 272; **Bristol City FC:** 206; **Bristol Rovers FC:** 248; **Burnley FC:** 249; **Bury FC:** 208; **Cambridge United FC:** 273; **Cardiff City FC:** 274; **Carlisle United FC:** 275; **Celtic FC:** 4bc, 155tc/cl/cbr, 296; **Chester City FC:** 276; **Chesterfield FC:** 250; **Colchester United FC:** 251; **Corbis:** Pablo Corral 100b, 142b; Hulton-Deutsch Collection 54t; PeterJohnson 146b; Niall Macleod 24t, 132t; Rafael Roa 354b; Kim Sayer 118t; UPI /Bettmann 338b, 339, 350b; Michael S. Yamshita 134b; **Crewe Alexandra FC:** 210; **Crystal Palace FC:** 212; **Darlington FC:** 277; **Doncaster Rovers FC:** Paul Gilligan 56b; **Dundee FC:** FotoPress 298; **Dundee United FC:** FotoPress 300; **Dunfermline FC:** Ian Malcom 302; **Empics:** 4bl, 22b, 31tr/c/bl, 75, 85, 86t/b,88t, 91, 92t, 93, 205b, 217b, 221b, 241t/c/b, 305t; Matthew Ashton 17b, 41b, 57,62, 82b, 116t, 167c, 121b, 128b, 177c, 211t, 229b, 235c, 237b, 243c/b, 245b, 295c/b, 305b, 309b, 315, 316, 327; Paul Baker 14b, 205t; Don Balon 364b; Barnaby's Picture 360t; Barry Bland 16t, 90b, 165b; Steve Cambell 187c; Peter Clarke 21b; Chris Cole 166, 179c; Barry Coombs 160, 173c/b, 213t, 215c,

243t; Mike Egerton 17t, 26b, 100t, 139, 197t, 237c, 311c, Steve Etherington 161b; Laurence Griffiths 108b, 217c; David Hewitson 130t; Tom Honan 29t; Paul Marriott 168, 197t, 213c; John Marsh 194; Tony Marshall 34t, 46t ,66, 131, 167b, 215b, 219t, 233b, 297t; Matthew McGinlay 205c; Steve Mitchell 27b, 101, 128b, 170; Presse Sport 364t; Peter Robinson 38b; Neal Simpson 48t, 92b, 108t , 120b, 132b, 138t, 139, 163b, 173t , 177b,187b, 189b, 193c, 197b,199t/b, 213c, 227c, 235b, 239b, 311t, 314; Michael Steele 11t, 28b, 39, 41t, 43t, 47, 59, 72, 178, 188, 189c, 215t, 322; Chris Turvey 12t, 48b, 83, 136t, 192 Nico Vereecken; 320; Leo Vogelzang 24b Peter Wilcock 138b, 172; Witters German Soccer 34b, 40b,317, 319, 325, 348t **Exeter City FC:** 278; **The Football Association:** 124t; **Football Trust:** 56t; **Fullham FC:** Allsport 252; **Getty Images:** 356t, 358t; Hulton Getty/Evening Standard 135; **Gillingham FC:** 253; **Glasgow Rangers FC:** 310; **Matt Gore:** 207t/c/b; **Grimsby FC:** 214; **Halifax Town FC:** 5bc, 155cac/bl/br, 279; **Hartlepool United FC:** 280; **Heart of Midlothian FC:** 304; **Huddersfield Town FC:** 216; **Hull City FC:** 281; **Kilmarnock FC:** Tom Brown 306; **Leyton Orient FC:** 282; **Lincoln City FC:** 254; **Luton Town FC:** 255; **Macclesfield Town FC:** 256; **Manchester City FC:** Proffional Sport International: 257; **Mansfield Town FC:** 283; **Millwall FC:** 256; **Motherwell FC:** 308; **Mirror Syndication International:** 78b, 79, 99, 123, 346b, 347; **News International Syndication:** 122t; **North East Press Ltd/Sunderland Echo:** 118b; **Northampton Town FC:** 257; **Norwich City FC:** 220; **Notts County FC:** 260; **Oldham Athletic FC:** 261; **Oxford United FC:** 222; **PA News:** 28t, 29b, 31tc/cl/cbr, 32b, 38t, 54b, 97, 98t/b, 126t, 134t, 335tc/cl/cbr, 342b, 346t, 356b, 362t/b, 363, 365, 366t; Adam Butler 64; EPA Photo/AFP/Jack Guez 32t; Fiona Hanson110b; Stefan Rousseau 110t, 117; John Stillwell 18b,150b; Paul Treacy 82t; **Perthshire Advertiser:** 313t/b; **Peterborough United FC:** 284; **Plymouth Argyle FC:** Dave Rowntre 285; **Popperfoto:** 76b, 148t, 337, 338t, 340b, 342t, 353t, 359; Reuters/Mikhail Chernickin 332, Thomas/BTS 51t, 102t; **Port Vale FC:** 226; **Portsmouth FC:** 224; **Preston North End FC:** 262; **Reading FC:** 263; **Retna:** Bruce Fredericks 107; Soulla Petrou 106b; Michael Putland 106t; **Rochdale FC:** Alpha Photgraphy 286; **Rotherham United FC:** 287; **Saatchi and Saatchi:** Frank Fennell: 111; **Scarborough FC:** 288; **Scottish News and Sport:** 52t, 53, 297b/c, 299t/c/b,301t/c/b, 303t/c/b, 305c, 307b, 309t/c, 311b,313c; Alan Harvey 52b; **Scunthorpe United FC:** 289; **Sheffield United FC:** 230; **Shrewsbury Town FC:** 290; **Southend United FC:** 291; **St Johnstone FC:** Louis Flood Photographers 312; **Stockport County FC:** 232; **Stoke City FC:** 264; **Sunderland FC:** 234; **Swansea City FC:** 292; **Swindon Town FC:** 236; **Telegraph and Argus, Bradford:** 204; **Torquay United FC:** 293; **Tranmere Rovers:** 238; **Walsall FC:** 265; **Watford FC:** 3bl, 155cal/cr/bc, 240; **West Bromwich Albion:** Paper Palin 242; **Wigan Athletic FC:** 264; **Wrexham FC:** 265; **Wycombe Wanderers FC:**266; **York City FC:** 267.

Front Jacket:Action Images/Brandon Malone

Words

Judith Addleson, Geoff Almond, Nicola Bailey, Gianni Benato, Steven Booth, Les Bradd, James Brewer, Dougie & Eddie Brimson, Tim Carder, Clive Carpenter, Darren Cohen, Ian Cook, Kevin Davies, Deloitte & Touche, Jim Drewett, Les Duckworth, Mick Everett, Paula Field, Anthony Forrester, Jim Foulerton, Terry Frost, Aubrey Ganguly, Brian Glanville, Alexis Goodman, Roger Harrison, Diane Hehir, Steve Henderson, Ron Hockings, Martin Horsfield, Keith Howard, Kevin Hughes, Andi Jenkins, Dave Jennings, Chris Kershaw, Sarah Kovandzich, Alex Leith, Russell Lewin, John Ley, Keith McAllister, Graham McGilliard, Derek McGregor, Jim McSherry, John Mack, John Maddocks, Ridge Mahoney, Andee Maisner, Chris Mason, Tony Matthews, Ian Mills, John Mitchell, Stewart Newport, Richard Owen, Charles Phillips, S J Rendell, Jack Retter, Lee Rich, David Roberts, Anne Sandford, Richard Shepherd, Duncan Sibbald, Sir Norman Chester Centre for Football Research, Jim Slater, Hugh Sleight, Ray Spiller, Chas Sumner, Paul Third, Ian Thomas, Roger Triggs, Frank Tweddle, Tim Unwin, Jonathan Wall, Roger Wash, Scot Weston, Brian Wheeler, Mike Wilson